INTERMEDIARY LIABILITY AND FREEDOM OF EXPRESSION IN THE EU:
FROM CONCEPTS TO SAFEGUARDS

INTERMEDIARY LIABILITY AND FREEDOM OF EXPRESSION IN THE EU: FROM CONCEPTS TO SAFEGUARDS

Aleksandra Kuczerawy

intersentia
Cambridge – Antwerp – Chicago

KU LEUVEN CITIP
CENTRE FOR IT & IP LAW

Intersentia Ltd
Sheraton House | Castle Park
Cambridge | CB3 0AX | United Kingdom
Tel.: +44 1223 370 170 | Fax: +44 1223 370 169
Email: mail@intersentia.co.uk
www.intersentia.com | www.intersentia.co.uk

Distribution for the UK and Ireland:
NBN International
Airport Business Centre, 10 Thornbury Road
Plymouth, PL6 7 PP
United Kingdom
Tel.: +44 1752 202 301 | Fax: +44 1752 202 331
Email: orders@nbninternational.com

Distribution for Europe and all other countries:
Intersentia Publishing nv
Groenstraat 31
2640 Mortsel
Belgium
Tel.: +32 3 680 15 50 | Fax: +32 3 658 71 21
Email: mail@intersentia.be

Distribution for the USA and Canada:
Independent Publishers Group
Order Department
814 North Franklin Street
Chicago, IL60610
USA
Tel.: +1 800 888 4741 (toll free) | Fax: +1312 337 5985
Email: orders@ipgbook.com

Intermediary Liability and Freedom of Expression in the EU: From Concepts to Safeguards

Cover image: Maria Papaefstathiou aka It's Just Me (www.itsjustme.net)

ISBN 978-1-78068-714-8
ISBN 978-1-78068-715-5 (pdf)
D/2019/7849/5
NUR 827

GPRC
Guaranteed
Peer Reviewed
Content

British Library Cataloguing in Publication Data. A catalogue record for this book is available from the British Library.

FOREWORD

It is my pleasure to respond to the request of Aleksandra Kuczerawy and her supervisor to write a foreword to the book.

I was a member of Aleksandra's PhD examination committee. I was able to see how she progressed in her research, undertaken under the able supervision of Peggy Valcke and co-supervision of Eva Lievens. From the very beginning Aleksandra wanted to bring Article 10 of the European Convention on Human Rights, which guarantees the right to freedom of expression, into the discussion about the role of internet hosting services with respect to content created by their users. What place Article 10 would receive, was not clear from the outset. Aleksandra's ideas developed as she went deeper into the analysis of the various aspects of the conduct expected from hosting services.

In front of the reader is an original study, in which the author applies elements taken from the case law of the European Court of Human Rights (on Article 10 of the European Convention) and the European Court of Justice (on the corresponding Article 11 of the Charter of Fundamental Rights) to a context that is not the "natural" context for the application of Article 10 of the Convention or Article 11 of the Charter.

Indeed, both Articles guarantee a right of individuals vis-à-vis the State (and, in the case of the Charter, vis-à-vis the European Union). Aleksandra recalls that there are three principles with which any interference by the State with freedom of expression must comply (legal certainty, legitimacy and proportionality). On the basis of the case law of the two European courts she then develops five criteria, which she argues should be taken into account by anyone who sets up a mechanism for the removal, by a hosting service, of content placed on the internet by a third party. The five criteria are: quality of the law, protection of the democratic society, tailored response, procedural fairness and effective remedy.

A removal measure is a specific form of interference with the right to freedom of expression, in this case the right of the third party which placed the content on the internet. It is an interference by a private person, the hosting service, not by a State body. The criteria drawn from the case law on freedom of expression are thus receiving a new meaning, as it is obvious that they cannot be applied to actions of private parties in exactly the same way as they are applied to actions of public bodies.

The five criteria are first used as assessment criteria for the evaluation of a number of existing mechanisms of response, by a hosting service, to notice given to it of allegedly illegal or infringing online content. After having critically examined the existing systems, Aleksandra comes up with a list of safeguards, grouped around the five assessment criteria, which she recommends to include in the EU intermediary liability regime, in order to make that regime compliant with fundamental rights, in particular the right to freedom of expression of the affected third party.

The result is a set of very concrete recommendations for the attention, in particular, of the European Union. The latter has a positive obligation to protect freedom of expression while regulating the relationship between host services – entrusted with the task of controlling online content – and their users. Aleksandra's recommendations can assist the Union bodies in fulfilling that obligation.

I read this book with great interest. It is a fine example of application of known concepts to new areas, resulting in novel and well-argued findings. The fact that these findings are moreover formulated in such a way that they can be of practical significance, gives an important added value to the book.

At a moment when the contours of freedom of expression and the limits of restrictions of that freedom are subject of sometimes heated debate, it is refreshing to see how a researcher like Aleksandra comes up with solutions that are based on a solid understanding of what freedom of expression implies in an online context. She is guided by the principle that restrictions of that freedom are permissible only to the extent that there is a fair balance between the fundamental right of the person who expresses his or her opinion and the competing interests which the restrictions are intended to protect. As far as I can see, the safeguards which she proposes are realistic, and at the same time capable of contributing to the setting-up of mechanisms that do strike the required faire balance.

One may hope that the competent authorities take due notice of Aleksandra's recommendations. In the meantime her findings can be used to assess the compatibility with the European Convention and the Charter of any measure taken under a "notice and action" mechanism. Aleksandra's book is not only an addition to the existing state of the art with respect to the removal of online content, but also a practical instrument for practitioners and policy makers. What more can be said about the merits of a fruit of academic research?

Paul Lemmens
Professor, Catholic University of Leuven
Judge, European Court of Human Rights

ACKNOWLEDGMENTS

When I started working at CiTiP (then ICRI), I thought I would never write a PhD. It almost turned out to be true. There are quite a few people I want to thank for proving me wrong. I thank Prof. Peggy Valcke for her support, guidance and patience and for giving me the space to develop my own ideas. I thank Prof. Eva Lievens, on whose good advice I could always count. I am also grateful to my advisory committee, that is, Prof. Paul Lemmens – who always found time to meet me and explain the intricacies of human rights law, and Dr. Tarlach McGonagle – who offered great advice in moments when I felt completely lost. I also owe a lot to Prof. Marie-Christine Janssens – whose support and encouragement always gave me energy. I am thankful to Em. Prof. Dr. Jacques Herbots for chairing my examination committee. Finally, special thanks also go to Prof. Geertrui Van Overwalle, who never allowed me to doubt myself and, at the same time, offered great tips on methodology.

CiTiP is a great place to conduct research and I have been lucky to work in such a stimulating environment. I am grateful to my wonderful colleagues, who taught me a lot, in particular Eleni, Eva, Katleen, Katrien, Fanny, Griet, PJ, Yung Shin, Niels, Amandine, Valerie, Ingrid and Pierre. Of course, I cannot forget my office-buddy Jef, with whom I shared an intellectual safe harbour for exchanging ideas (and also a plant). I would also like to acknowledge people whose work inspired me and who never got (visibly) tired of my questions, especially, Christina Angelopoulos, Martin Husovec, Daphne Keller, Joe McNamee, K.S. Park, Sophie Stalla-Bourdillon, Jennifer Urban, Joris van Hoboken, and Dirk Voorhoof.

Furthermore, I must thank my family and friends. My mom, who taught me that education is a girl's best friend; my brother, whose composure in stressful moments is unparalleled; Dziadek Heniek, who is my biggest fan; and the Makowiecki family who took me into their home and suffered through my teenage-rebel-year-abroad. I express my gratitude to Willem and Paula, who hosted me in Zandvliet, fed me world-famous soup, entertained me, and took care of me. And extra cheers to Willem, who actually read my whole manuscript. I could not have asked for a better place to finish my "boekske". I also need to thank all my friends for not giving up on me when I disappeared for months into my writing den. Special thanks go to Joanna and Aleksandra, for the weekly teleconferences; Irini and Laura for reminding me to exercise regularly; and

Asia, Ilona and Magda for the regular check-ups. Yung Shin, whose constant push was a great accelerator of my finishing process; Ewa, who tested on me various remedies for stress-relief; and Laura, who read my text and taught me where to put "also" in a sentence.

Finally, I want to thank Brendan for his endless love, support, patience and revisions. I would not have made it without you.

Aleksandra Kuczerawy
Zandvliet, 11.05.2018

CONTENTS

INTRODUCTION

1. CONTEXT OF THE RESEARCH

NEW METHODS OF COMMUNICATION – The development of the Internet has brought with it new methods of communication. By lowering the threshold for content production and distribution, the Internet made publishing one's thoughts and opinions easier than ever before. This shift has had a great empowering and democratizing effect, giving a voice to the silent and less powerful members of society. For example, social networking sites enable individuals to keep up with an international network of friends and allow organizations to engage with audiences with specific interests. The new methods of communication can also play a role in political interactions. For example, they allow people to express their support for a particular cause, or facilitate the organization of protests against unpopular governmental policies.

ILLEGAL OR INFRINGING CONTENT – The new methods of communication, however, also provide a channel for less positive occurrences, such as the distribution of illegal or infringing content. In the context of the presented research, illegal content is understood as any material violating the existing (objective) rules of law (e.g. incitement to violence or hate speech), whereas infringing content refers to material violating subjective rights of individuals (e.g. privacy, intellectual property or good name).[1]

LIMITED EDITORIAL CONTROL – Before the advent of the Internet, distribution of content on a large scale was dependent on traditional publishing and broadcasting mechanisms. Under these mechanisms, material to be published

---

1 Literature on the topic also distinguishes a category of "harmful content" understood as content that is not prohibited by law but may be inappropriate for some audiences therefore its distribution may be restricted. This thesis focuses on illegal and infringing content, understood as content that is prohibited by law and/ or the publication or dissemination of which interferes with the rights and freedoms of others. On many occasions illegal or infringing content may also be considered "harmful", but the harmful category is broader. According to Akdeniz, '*the difference between illegal and harmful content is that the former is criminalized by national laws, while the latter is considered offensive, objectionable, unwanted, or disgusting by some people but is generally not criminalized by national laws*'. See Y. Akdeniz, "Who watches the watchmen? The role of filtering software in Internet content regulation", in C. Möller, A. Amouroux, (eds), *The media freedom Internet cookbook*, Vienna, OSCE, 2004, p. 104, https://www.osce.org/fom/13836?download=true.

goes through a process of editorial control, which implies that such material is subject to scrutiny before being made available to the public at large. For many online applications, such as blogs, discussion groups or social networking sites, however, there is no functional equivalent. The absence of any selectivity in this context can result in illegal or infringing content becoming readily available online. Since there is no selection process, responsibility seems to rest entirely with the author, who might be impossible to identify. This situation sparked concerns among policymakers, who sought remedying measures. However, rather than introducing centralized oversight and enforcement, policymakers decided to look for private actors who could be enlisted in the realization of the public policy objectives, and who could play the role of "gatekeepers".

THE RISE OF GATEKEEPERS – The concept of a "gatekeeper" was used by Reinier H. Kraakman in 1986[2] to describe '*private parties who are able to disrupt misconduct by withholding their cooperation from wrongdoers*'.[3] Through the concept of vicarious liability, these gatekeepers can be incentivized to prevent misconducts by withholding their support, in the form of a specific good, service or certification that is crucial for the wrongdoer to succeed.[4] By putting private actors in a position where they face a risk of liability for failure to disrupt misconduct, policymakers can effectively make them responsible for the advancement of public policy objectives. Such an arrangement allows for a relatively effortless solution (for the policymakers) to the problem of illegal content online.[5]

INTERNET INTERMEDIARIES – In the online environment a type of entity exists, which seems perfect for this role. Internet intermediaries, who are placed between parties to intermediate, include Internet service providers (ISPs), hosting providers, search engines, e-commerce intermediaries, Internet payment systems and participative Web platforms.[6] The role of Internet intermediaries is to '*provide access to, host, transmit and index content originated by third parties on the Internet; facilitate interactions or transactions between third parties on the Internet; or provide other Internet-based services to third parties*'.[7] Since they are actually enablers of Internet communications, they are often considered to be a point of control for online content.[8] It is very tempting, therefore, to assign

2 H.R. Kraakman, "Gatekeepers: The Anatomy of a Third-Party Enforcement Strategy", *Journal of Law, Economics, and Organization*, Vol. 2, No. 1, 1986, pp. 53–105.

3 *Ibid.*, p. 53.

4 *Ibid.*

5 See J. Zittrain, "A History of Online Gatekeeping", *Harvard Journal of Law and Technology*, Vol. 19, No. 2, 2006, p. 258.

6 OECD, The Economic and Social Role of Internet Intermediaries, April 2010, pp. 9–14.

7 *Ibid.*

8 J. Zittrain, "A History of Online Gatekeeping", *o.c.*, p.258. C. Wong, J.X. Dempsey, "Mapping Digital Media: The Media and Liability for Content on the Internet", *Open Society Foundation, Reference Series*, No.12, 2011, p.14.

them a responsibility similar to that of the publishers. However, the role they play in providing access to online content is, by and large, merely technical in nature. Many intermediaries are relatively passive conduits. As such, they are more akin to distributors, who are not required to exercise any form of content control.[9] Nevertheless, Internet intermediaries do possess means to eliminate access to objectionable material and, at the same time, are often able to facilitate identification of wrongdoers.[10] With such power at their hands, they seem to be natural candidates for the role of gatekeepers.

REGULATORY RESPONSE – Since the emergence of the Internet industry, the liability of the Internet intermediaries for third parties' content was seen as a problematic issue. To address the problem, and to provide some level of legal certainty, a limited liability regime for Internet intermediaries was introduced as a compromise. The compromise consisted of three basic principles: (1) lack of responsibility of intermediaries for third-party content distributed on the Internet and for transactions taking place on their platform if they do not modify the content and are not aware of its illegal character; (2) no general obligation to monitor content; and (3) an obligation to act expeditiously to remove illegal content upon notification.[11] This approach was the result of strong lobbying by the emerging Internet industry who perceived liability for third parties' content as a major risk to their operations.[12] The immunity that was introduced intended to stimulate growth and innovation of the newly born technology and provide positive incentives for further development. The regime then gradually made its way into regulatory instruments at both regional and national level. In the US, the first act that addressed the issue of liability of Internet intermediaries for illegal or infringing content was Section 230 of the Communications Decency Act (CDA) 1996. Intellectual property violations were addressed separately in the Digital Millennium Copyright Act (DMCA) 1998. The second instrument created a safe harbour scheme for several groups of Internet intermediaries, namely: mere conduits, hosts, and linking tools such as search engines and hyper-links.[13] In the European Union, the issue of intermediary liability was addressed in the E-Commerce Directive 2000/31.[14] The Directive takes a

---

9 J. Zittrain, "A History of Online Gatekeeping", *o.c.*; CompuServe, 776 F. Supp.; Prodigy, 1995 WL 323710.

10 J. Zittrain, "A History of Online Gatekeeping", *o.c.*, p. 254.

11 OECD, Directorate for Science, Technology and Industry, Committee for Information, Computer and Communication Policy, *The Role of Internet Intermediaries In Advancing Public Policy Objectives, Forging partnerships for advancing public policy objectives for the Internet economy*, Part II, 22 June 2011, p.6.

12 *Ibid.*, p.11.

13 OECD, *The Role of Internet Intermediaries In Advancing Public Policy Objectives, Forging partnerships for advancing public policy objectives for the Internet economy*, p. 14.

14 Directive 2000/31/EC of 8 June 2000 on certain legal aspects of information society services, in particular electronic commerce, in the Internal Market (Directive on electronic commerce), *O.J.* L 178, 17 July 2000.

horizontal approach, which means that it applies to various domains and any kind of illegal or infringing content.[15] It provides liability exemptions for three groups of Internet intermediaries depending on the type of service they provide: mere conduit, caching, or hosting.

HOSTING SERVICES – Hosting services, which are the focal point of this book, consist of the storage of information provided by a recipient of the service, at his request. Such storage may be provided for a prolonged period of time, and may also be the primary object of the service.[16] A distinction can be made between several types of hosting services, depending on their proximity to the content providers.[17] For example, one category of hosting providers delivers applications such as Facebook, Twitter or Blogger, which store content created by their users (hosting at the application level). Providers of such platforms are directly connected to the content providers who sign up for their services. Another category of hosting providers delivers the technical infrastructure upon which applications are hosted. They store the whole platforms such as Facebook, Twitter or Blogger on their servers (hosting at the network level).[18] Since content providers do not select the hosting providers at the network level, their connection is indirect. This book focuses primarily on hosting providers at the application level and the content removal mechanisms that are targeted towards them.

REMOVAL OF CONTENT – Under Article 14 of the E-Commerce Directive, hosting providers can benefit from a liability exemption provided they act expeditiously to remove or disable access to information upon obtaining knowledge about its illegal character. Disabling (or blocking) access to information means that information remains online, but is not accessible under predefined conditions, e.g. from certain locations or to certain groups of users. Removal, on the other hand, erases the information from its hosting location and, unless previously copied, eliminates it completely from the Internet. The first type of response is requested mainly from hosting providers at the network level. Since they host whole platforms on their servers they usually have no means to remove a single piece of content. This, however, can be done by hosting

---

15 N. Helberger, et al., "Legal Aspects of User Created Content" in IDATE, TNO, IViR, User-Created Content: Supporting a Participative Information Society, Study for the European Commission (DG INFSO), December 2008, available at: www.ivir.nl/publications/helberger/User_created_content.pdf.

16 I. Walden, Y. Cool, E. Montero, "Directive 2000/31/EC –Directive on electronic commerce" in A. Bullesbach, Y. Poullet, C. Prins (eds), *Concise European IT Law*, Kluwer Law International Alphen aan den Rijn, 2005, p. 243, 253.

17 Content provider is understood broadly, as everyone uploading content (text, audio, video, pictures) for dissemination to an unlimited or specified audience.

18 See more on Internet intermediaries as layered services in J. Riordan, *The Liability of Internet Intermediaries*, Oxford University Press, 2016, p. 37.

providers at the application level. As indicated above, this book focuses on hosting providers at application level and therefore on the removal of specific items of illegal or infringing content.

NOTICE AND ACTION – The provider of a hosting service can obtain knowledge about the illicit character of hosted content in a number of ways. He could identify such content through his own activities or he could be notified by a third party. Third party notifications can stem either from public authorities or from private entities. In the latter case, public authorities are not involved in the content removal process. Instead, the hosting provider is called upon directly by a private individual to take down the content in question (notice and takedown). As a result, it becomes the provider's task to assess whether the complaint is credible and to make a decision about its illegal or infringing character. The provider can either leave the content as it is and risk liability for it, or relieve himself of the problem altogether by simply removing the content. There are, however, also other possibilities. For example, the hosting provider could first contact the content provider to help determine whether or not the complaint is well founded. "Notice and action" is the term used to refer to the various procedures followed by Internet intermediaries for the purpose of removing illegal content upon receipt of notification. The intermediary may, for example, take down illegal content, block it, or request that it be voluntarily taken down by the persons who posted it online.[19]

2. PROBLEM STATEMENT

PRIVATE ENFORCEMENT – Burdening Internet intermediaries with the task of assessing the legitimacy of complaints has frequently been called unfair.[20] As private companies, Internet intermediaries do not have the competences and sufficient legal knowledge to make the necessary balancing of the rights in question. This is particularly the case if the content is not manifestly illegal, which may occur where subjective rights of individuals (rather than objective rules of law) are at stake.[21] Furthermore, enlisting private companies to decide

[19] European Commission, Communication to the European Parliament, The Council, The Economic and Social Committee and The Committee of Regions, A coherent framework for building trust in the Digital Single Market for e-commerce and online services {SEC(2011) 1640 final}, p. 13, ft. 49, http://eur-lex.europa.eu/LexUriServ/LexUriServ.do?uri=COM:2011:0942:FIN:EN:PDF.

[20] E. Lievens, *Protecting Children in the Digital Era – the Use of Alternative Regulatory Instruments*, Martinus Nijhoff Publishers, International Studies in Human Rights, Leiden, 2010, p. 360, referencing E. Montero, "La responsibilite des prestataires intermediaries sur les reseaux", in E. Montero (ed.), *Le commerce electronique europeen sur les rails?*, Cahiers du CRID, Brussel, Bruylant, 2001, 289–290.

[21] R. J. Barceló and K. Koelman, "Intermediary Liability In The E-Commerce Directive: So Far So Good, But It's Not Enough", *Computer Law & Security Report* 2000, vol. 4, pp. 231–239.

upon such delicate issues can have many undesirable effects.[22] For example, Google was once pressured to remove an offensive anti-Muslim movie from its platform YouTube. Google refused to comply with a request of the US government to remove the video from the Internet, arguing that no policies were violated. At the same time it decided arbitrarily to block access to the video from certain countries. As a result, Google was accused of paternalism and moral policing of free expression.[23]

The nature of notice and action mechanisms implies that intermediaries shall, as a rule, experience a conflict of interests. In order to exonerate themselves from possible liability, they must decide swiftly about removing or blocking content. In such circumstances, the most cautionary approach is to act upon any indication of illegality, without engaging in any (possibly burdensome and lengthy) balancing of the rights at stake. As a result, there is often no real investigation into the illicit character of the content.[24] This may lead to preventive over-blocking of entirely legitimate content. In fact, the notice and action mechanism creates '*an incentive to systematically take down material, without hearing from the party whose material is removed, thus preventing such a party from its right to evidence its lawful use of the material*'.[25] This could easily lead to private censorship. It also opens a way to potential abuse by fictitious victims, for example by business competitors or political adversaries.[26] The CoE Human Rights Guidelines for Internet Service Providers also highlights these issues.[27] The Guidelines state that ISPs providing access services, hosting, applications or content should not be '*expected to advise on what content or behaviours are*

See also R. J. Barceló, On-line intermediary liability issues: comparing EU and US legal frameworks, E.I.P.R. 2000, p. 111. The Organization for Security and Co-Operation in Europe and Reporters Sans Frontiers, Joint declaration on guaranteeing media freedom on the Internet, 18 June 2005, available at: www.osce.org/fom/15657.

22 Council of Europe (Council of Ministers), Declaration on freedom of communications on the Internet, 28 May 2003, available at: www.coe.int/t/informationsociety/documents/Freedom%20of%20communication%20on%20the%20Internet_en.pdf.

23 YouTube under new pressure over anti-Muslim film, BBC News, 19.09.2012, at: www.bbc.com/news/technology-19648808.

24 Discussion in C. Ahlert, C. Marsden and C. Yung, "How Liberty Disappeared from Cyberspace: the Mystery Shopper Tests Internet Content Self-Regulation" http://pcmlp.socleg.ox.ac.uk/wp-content/uploads/2014/12/liberty.pdf.

25 R. J. Barceló and K. Koelman, "Intermediary Liability In The E-Commerce Directive: So Far So Good, But It's Not Enough", *o.c.*, p. 231.

26 T. Verbiest, Study on the liability of Internet Intermediaries, Markt/2006/09/E, 12 November 2007, p.15; OECD, The Economic and Social Role of Internet Intermediaries, *o.c.*, p.20; J. Urban and L. Quilter, "Efficient Process or 'Chilling Effects'? Take-down Notices Under Section 512 of the Digital Millennium Copyright Act: Summary Report", http://mylaw.usc.edu/documents/512Rep-ExecSum_out.pdf.

27 Council of Europe, Human rights guidelines for Internet Service Providers – Developed by the Council of Europe in co-operation with the European Internet Service Providers Association (EuroISPA), July 2008, available at: www.coe.int/t/dghl/standardsetting/media/Doc/H-Inf(2008)009_en.pdf, paras 16 and 24.

illegal and/or harmful'.[28] Likewise, the 2018 CoE Recommendation on the Roles and Responsibilities of Internet Intermediaries states that intermediaries should respect the human rights of their users and affected parties in all their actions.[29]

POTENTIAL INTERFERENCE – A process whereby a private party arbitrarily decides whether content should be removed or blocked can lead to interference with the right to freedom of expression, as delineated in Article 10 ECHR[30] and Article 11 CFEU.[31] A number of organizations, including the Council of Europe, have expressed concerns about the possible "chilling effect" on freedom of expression.[32] Current notice and action mechanisms also appear to be at odds with the principles of proportionality and due process.[33]

NO IMPLEMENTATION GUIDELINES – At EU level, there are no established guidelines with regard to the implementation of notice and action. The Directive left the subject matter to the discretion of the Member States.[34] Article 16 and Recital 40 of the Directive merely encourage self-regulation in this field. The majority of the Member States opted for a verbatim transposition of the Directive and included the same encouragement for self-regulatory approach.[35] This however proved to be inefficient – most of the countries never introduced any self-regulatory measures. The result is a lack of any firm safeguards in most of the EU countries.[36] The question should therefore be asked whether the existing European legal framework on intermediary liability should be amended to ensure safeguards to effectively protect the right to freedom of expression.

---

28 *Ibid.*, in para. 21.

29 Council of Europe, Recommendation CM/Rec(2018)2 of the Committee of Ministers to member States on the roles and responsibilities of internet intermediaries, 7 March 2018, https://rm.coe.int/1680790e14, p. 3.

30 Council of Europe, Convention for the Protection of Human Rights and Fundamental Freedoms, CETS No. 005, 04 November 1950, Rome, http://conventions.coe.int/Treaty/en/Treaties/Html/005.htm;

31 Charter of Fundamental Rights of the European Union, 2000/C 364/1, 18 December 2000, www.europarl.europa.eu/charter/pdf/text_en.pdf.

32 For example, Council of Europe, Declaration on freedom of communications on the Internet, *o.c.*; Council of Europe, Human rights guidelines for Internet Service Providers, *o.c.*, paras 16, 21 and 24; See also: C. Wong, J.X. Dempsey, Mapping Digital Media: The Media and Liability for Content on the Internet, *o.c., p. 16;* Electronic Frontier Foundation, "Takedown Hall of Shame," www.eff.org/takedowns; and Lumen Database (formerly Chilling Effects Clearinghouse), https://lumendatabase.org/topics/14.

33 See M. Horten, *The Copyright Enforcement Enigma – Internet Politics and the 'Telecoms Package'*, Palgrave Macmillan, 2011, p. 48–50.

34 Recital 46 E-Commerce Directive.

35 T. Verbiest, Study on the liability of Internet Intermediaries, *o.c.*, p. 14–16.

36 European Commission, Online Services, Including E-commerce in Single Market, Commission Staff Working Paper, Accompanying the document: Communication from the Commission to the European Parliament, the Council The European Economic and Social Committee and the Committee of the Regions, A Coherent framework to boost confidence in the Digital Single Market of e-commerce and other online services, COM(2011) 942.

3. RESEARCH HYPOTHESIS AND QUESTIONS

RESEARCH HYPOTHESIS – Internet intermediaries are increasingly enlisted to assist in the realization of public policy objectives. The research hypothesis of this thesis is that, when States assign such a role to Internet intermediaries, they have a positive obligation to ensure that appropriate safeguards are in place. Specifically, they must provide for adequate safeguards to effectively protect the human rights enshrined in the European Convention of Human Rights, and the Charter of Fundamental Rights of the European Union and particularly freedom of expression. In this thesis the term "State" refers to the legislature, both at national and EU level.

RESEARCH OBJECTIVES – The overall objective of this thesis is to identify which safeguards should be in place to ensure that the right to freedom of expression is respected by hosting providers when implementing notice and action mechanisms. A clear delineation of uniform safeguards will help ensure that fundamental rights are more effectively protected. Moreover, it will be argued that a matter of such importance should not be left to self-regulation and that the proposed uniform safeguards should be codified in a formal legal framework.

More specifically, the envisaged output includes:

1. A comprehensive overview of Internet intermediary liability regimes;
2. An articulation of issues that arise when applying the existing notice and action mechanisms in practice;
3. An articulation of assessment criteria based on the functional analysis of the case law surrounding the relevant human rights law instruments; and
4. Recommendations and guidance as to whether (and how) the current regulatory approach towards notice and action should be modified, specifically in terms of safeguards for freedom of expression.

INNOVATIVE CHARACTER – A number of studies have already been undertaken to describe the general issues surrounding the liability of Internet intermediaries.[37] Other studies were targeted at specific issues restricted to the

37 P. Van Eecke, M. Truyens, EU study on the New rules for a new age? Legal analysis of a Single Market, a study commissioned by the European Commission's Information Society and Media Directorate-General, November 2009; First Report on the Application of Directive 2000/31/EC of the European Parliament and of the Council of 8 June 2000 on the Directive on Electronic Commerce, COM(2003) 702 final, Brussels, 21 November 2003; N. Helberger, et al., "Legal Aspects of User Created Content", *o.c.*; C. Kastberg Nielsen *et al.*, Study on The Economic Impact of the Electronic Commerce Directive, Final Report, Part II, DG Internal Market and Services, European Commission, September 2007; F. Le Borgne-Bachschmidt, et al., User-Created-Content: Supporting a participative Information Society Final Report, Understanding the Digital World, SMART 2007/2008; T. Verbiest, Study on the liability of Internet Intermediaries, *o.c.*; OECD, The Role of Internet Intermediaries In Advancing

context in which they arose (e.g. copyright, protection of minors, position of search engines).[38] In recent years, the topic has gained more traction, which has resulted in several new studies.[39] However, there has been no extensive study analysing the possibility of introducing procedural safeguards in notice and action mechanisms to effectively protect the right to freedom of expression. The current research involves a comprehensive analysis of issues identified by leading scholars, practitioners and regulatory authorities. It goes beyond a descriptive overview of relevant developments in legislation, jurisprudence and doctrine by contextualizing the issue of enlisting private entities to realize public policy objectives. Specifically, the research frames the issue in terms of current policy discussions involving concepts such as "gatekeeping", "responsibilization", and "decentred regulation".[40]

RELEVANCE – This book aims to identify safeguards to promote compliance of the EU intermediary liability regime with fundamental rights, in particular the right to freedom of expression. The final output contributes to academic discourse, ongoing policy debates and the doctrinal state of the art in the area of intermediary liability and human rights protection. It also contributes to

---

Public Policy Objectives, Forging partnerships for advancing public policy objectives for the Internet economy, *o.c.*

38 L. Edwards, Report to World Intellectual Property Organisation (WIPO) on The Role and Responsibilities of Online Intermediaries in the Field of Copyright and Related Works, Geneva, June 2011; See M. Horten, *The Copyright Enforcement Enigma – Internet Politics and the 'Telecoms Package'*, *o.c.*; E. Lievens, *Protecting Children in the Digital Era – the Use of Alternative Regulatory Instruments*, *o.c.;* C. Angelopoulos, *European intermediary liability in copyright: A tort-based analysis*, Doctoral thesis, University of Amsterdam, 2016; F. Kreiken, *Large-scale copyright enforcement and human rights safeguards in online markets*, Doctoral thesis, TU Delft, 2017; J. van Hoboken, *Search Engine Freedom: On the Implications of the Right to Freedom of Expression for the Legal Governance of Web Search Engines*, Kluwer Law International, 2012.

39 J. Riordan, *The Liability of Internet Intermediaries*, *o.c.* The Manila Principles on Intermediary Liability Background Paper, Version 1.0, 30 May 2015, https://www.eff.org/files/2015/07/08/manila_principles_background_paper.pdf. Swiss Institute of Comparative Law, Comparative Study on Filtering, blocking and take-down of illegal content on the Internet, Report commissioned by the Council of Europe, 20 December 2015, www.coe.int/en/web/freedom-expression/study-filtering-blocking-and-take-down-of-illegal-content-on-the-internet. Council of Europe, Recommendation CM/Rec(2018)2 of the Committee of Ministers to member States on the roles and responsibilities of internet intermediaries, *o.c.* United Nations, Report of the Special Rapporteur David Kaye on the promotion and protection of the right to freedom of opinion and expression, A/HRC/38/35, 6 April 2018, https://documents-dds-ny.un.org/doc/UNDOC/GEN/G18/096/72/PDF/G1809672.pdf?OpenElement.

40 See, respectively, H.R. Kraakman, "Gatekeepers: The Anatomy of a Third-Party Enforcement Strategy", *Journal of Law, Economics, and Organization*, Vol. 2, No. 1, 1986, pp. 53–105; A. Wakefield, J. Fleming, *SAGE Dictionary of Policing*, SAGE Publications Ltd., 2009; J. Black, "Decentring Regulation: Understanding the Role of Regulation and Self-Regulation in a 'Post-Regulatory' World", *Current Legal Problems*, Vol. 54, Issue 1, January 2001, pp. 103–146.

academic discussions regarding the growing reliance on private enforcement mechanisms and the potential of procedural safeguards to accommodate this new paradigm. The output benefits scholars and policymakers, as well as the society and the industry. Moreover, it informs them on the strengths and vulnerabilities of the current approach. The research subject thus has an innovative character and is of use in both the European and international context.

RESEARCH QUESTIONS – The book starts from the observation that the EU intermediary liability regime incentivizes Internet intermediaries to remove content from their platforms without the proper balancing of rights at stake.

The research aims to provide an answer to the following (normative) question:

> Which safeguards should be implemented to ensure compliance of the notice and action mechanism implied in Article 14 of the E-commerce Directive with the right to freedom of expression?

In developing an answer to this question, the following (descriptive) research questions guide the analysis:

- Is the notice and action mechanism under EU law compatible with the right to freedom of expression, as recognized by Article 10 ECHR, and Article 11 EU Charter (in other words, is it compatible with the negative obligation of States)?
- Is there a positive obligation derived from the relevant human rights law instruments (in particular Article 10 ECHR, and Article 11 EU Charter) for States to establish a formal legal framework for notice and action procedures?
- If yes, what are the minimum safeguards (substantive and procedural) necessary to ensure effective protection of human rights in the context of notice and action procedures?

4. METHODOLOGY

GUIDING PRINCIPLES – Safeguards for freedom of expression in the context of notice and action should advance the principles of (1) legal certainty, (2) legitimacy, and (3) proportionality. They constitute three guiding principles for the book. The guiding principles were developed in light of the problem statement of this book, which identified several issues surrounding the liability of Internet intermediaries.

Figure 1 – Interdependencies between the identified issues and the guiding principles

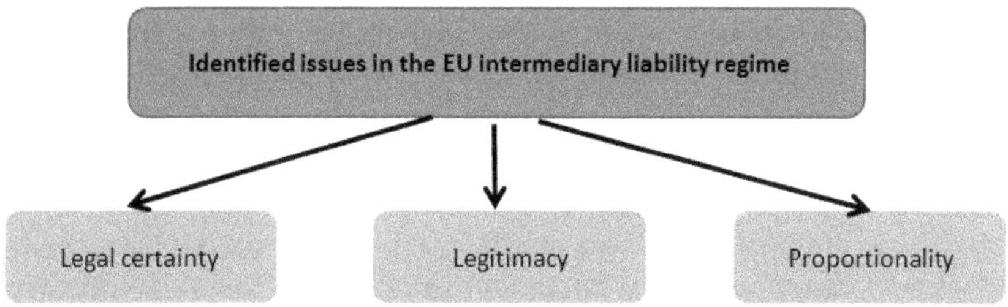

The meaning of the guiding principles is derived from the conditions for a lawful interference specified by the ECHR and CFEU. The principle of legal certainty entails that *'all law must be sufficiently precise to allow the person-if need be, with appropriate advice-to foresee, to a degree that is reasonable in the circumstances, the consequences which a given action may entail'*.[41] This means that the laws applicable to a particular behaviour or situation must be known and their outcome can be foreseen. In that sense, the principle of legal certainty also encompasses the principle of transparency. The principle of legitimacy refers to the rights and interest that need to be protected. Those are the aims that a State may legitimately pursue, and that may justify restrictions to the rights and freedoms to the extent that such restrictions are necessary and proportionate.[42] The principle of proportionality means that a public authority may not impose measures unless they are strictly necessary in the public interest to achieve the purpose of the measure. Thus, any measure that affects a fundamental right should be necessary, appropriate, and reasonable in order to achieve the objective. In cases where the exercise of a Convention right is interfered with in realization of the public policy objectives, the proportionality test and balancing of rights should apply.

ASSESSMENT CRITERIA – To provide an answer to the main research question of the book and determine which safeguards are necessary for notice and action mechanisms, it is essential to establish assessment criteria. The specific criteria are developed through a functional analysis[43] of case law of the ECtHR and CJEU, in particular regarding Article 10 and Article 11 of the

---

41 J. R. Maxeiner, "Legal Certainty: A European Alternative to American Legal Indeterminacy?" *Tulane Journal of International & Comparative Law*, Vol. 15, No. 2, 2007, p. 541; ECtHR, *Korchuganova v. Russia*, No. 75039/01, 8 June 8 2006.

42 See O. De Schutter, F. Tulkens, "The European Court of Human Rights as a Pragmatic Institution", in E. Brems (ed.), *Conflicts Between Fundamental Rights*, Intersentia, Antwerp-Oxford- Portland, 2008, pp. 169–216, p. 177.

43 G. Wilson, "Comparative Legal Scholarship" in M. McConville and W.H. Chui, (eds.), *Research Methods of Law*, Edinburgh, Edinburgh University Press, 2007, p. 87–103.

respective instruments. Guidance, moreover, is obtained by reviewing the procedural provisions of these human rights instruments, specifically Articles 6 (right to a fair trial) and 13 (right to effective remedy) of the ECHR, as well as Article 47 (right to an effective remedy and to a fair trial) of the CFEU. The procedural provisions of both instruments are used as a source of inspiration for safeguards in notice and action mechanisms where certain decisions about fundamental rights are delegated to private entities. The selected criteria are not organized according to the guiding principles as they, in many instances, overlap and advance more than one of the guiding principles. The selected criteria are applied as a positive assessment framework, against which existing response mechanisms to infringing online content is measured. The role of the exercise is to inform the selection of safeguards that promote compliance of the EU intermediary liability regime with fundamental rights, in particular, the right to freedom of expression.

Figure 2 – Interdependencies between the guiding principles, the assessment criteria and safeguards

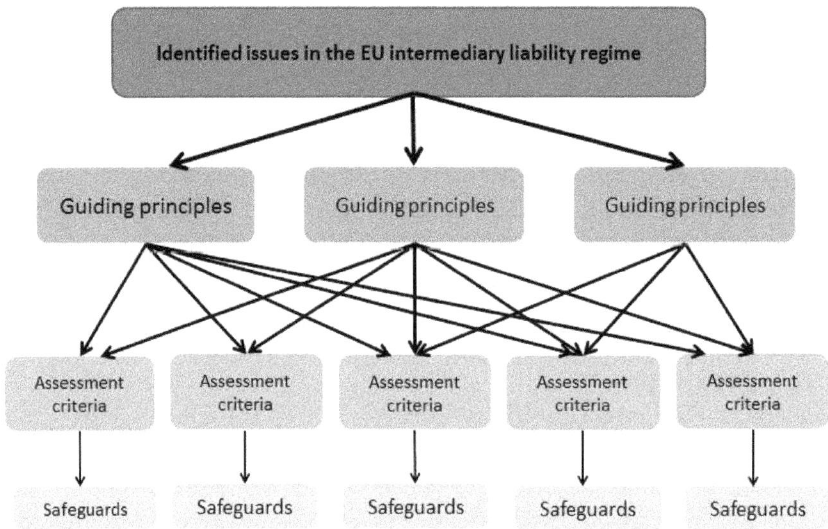

5. STRUCTURE

STATE OF THE ART – Part I starts by analysing the context of the research and the main concepts that underlie the intermediary liability regime. It describes the tendency of States to increasingly co-opt private entities in the realization of public policy objectives. Specifically, it presents the concept of gatekeeping and shows how it was gradually introduced into the media, and later new media, environment. Next, the origin and development of intermediary liability regimes is presented. The objective of this research phase is to gain a better understanding of the gatekeeping role of Internet intermediaries. Part I also presents different approaches to intermediary liability by comparing the EU E-Commerce Directive with the US approach in Section 230 CDA and the DMCA. It also describes the legal status of the right to freedom of expression under both regimes.

Part I, moreover, describes the initiatives of the European Commission within the review of the E-Commerce Directive, including its transition to the broader notion of notice and action. This phase of the research analyses the developments and conducts a critical assessment of the EU intermediary liability regime.

NORMATIVE FRAMEWORK – Part II provides an analysis of the core concepts and principles of human rights law, such as the principles of proportionality, due process or the right to effective remedy. It also includes a functional analysis of the relevant case law of the European Court of Human Rights and the European Court of Justice. The analysis makes it possible to determine whether States have a positive obligation to introduce procedural safeguards for freedom of expression when delegating the realization of public policy objectives to the Internet intermediaries. This examination allows, moreover, to define the criteria required to select the necessary safeguards to ensure effective protection to the right to freedom of expression.

EVALUATION OF EXISTING NOTICE AND ACTION MECHANISMS – Part III consists of an analysis of various legal responses to illegal content online. It presents different national approaches to tackling illegal content online. In addition to the notice and take down mechanism, Part III analyses other forms of notice and action, such as notice and stay down, notice and notice (including graduated response), and full immunity of intermediaries. The analysis is based on a review of legislation, jurisprudence and legal doctrine. The presented notice and action mechanisms are critically evaluated according to the assessment criteria. The main objective of this research component is to study and conceptualize the types of legal responses that have been developed to determine if and how they safeguard the right to freedom of expression when addressing the problem of illegal content online. The findings of this exercise further serve to propose procedural safeguards in the final phase of the research.

RECOMMENDATIONS – The final phase of this book provides an answer to the main research question in the form of normative recommendations. In this part, the lessons learnt from the preceding phases are used as a basis to identify safeguards for the right to freedom of expression in notice and action mechanisms. The safeguards aim to promote compliance of the EU intermediary liability regime with basic human rights principles, i.e. legal certainty, legitimacy, and proportionality. Considering that notice and action mechanisms are used to tackle a variety of illegal and infringing content and activities, the proposed safeguards also point out a variety of forms they could take and provide an analysis of their potential advantages and disadvantages.

PART I

STATE OF THE ART

CHAPTER 1
THE CONCEPT OF 'GATEKEEPING'

1. THEORIES OF GATEKEEPING

THE ORIGINS – The concept of "gatekeeping" is not a new one. It was first introduced by Kurt Lewin in 1947, in a study entitled '*Theories of channels and gate keepers*'.[44] The study dealt with the question of how to raise homeland consumption of secondary cuts of beef during wartime.[45] Lewin used the concept to describe the role of wives and mothers who decide what foods to place on the dinner table to illustrate how one can change the eating habits of a population.[46] According to his theory, it is the gatekeeper who decides what to reject or allow through the gate to enter the channel, effectively controlling movement within the channel.

GATEKEEPER LIABILITY – The basis of the concept of "gatekeeping" can be traced back further, however, to the tort doctrine of vicarious liability and the concept of "collateral" liability.[47] Vicarious liability is a liability that a supervisory part (e.g. employer) bears for the actionable conduct of a subordinate (e.g. employee) based on the relationship between the two parties.[48] Collateral liability refers to '*efforts to deter primary wrongdoers directly by enlisting their associates and market contacts as de facto "cops on the beat"*'.[49]

In the most influential work on gatekeeping, R.H. Kraakman applied Lewin's concept of gatekeeping to the liability of accountants and lawyers for their clients, and employers for their employees, which he described as gatekeeper liability.[50]

44 K. Lewin, "Frontiers in group dynamics. II. Channels of group life; social planning and action research". *Human Relations*, Vol. 1, Nr 2, 1947, pp. 143–153.

45 C. Roberts, "Gatekeeping theory: An evolution", Presented at Communication Theory and Methodology Division Association for Education in Journalism and Mass Communication, San Antonio, Texas, August 2005, www.reelaccurate.com/about/gatekeeping.pdf, p. 3.

46 E. B. Laidlaw, *Internet Gatekeepers, Human Rights and Corporate Social Responsibilities*, Doctoral thesis, London School of Economics and Political Science, 2012, p. 45.

47 J. Zittrain, "A History of Online Gatekeeping", *o.c.*, p. 256.

48 B. A. Garner (ed.), *Black's Law Dictionary*, Third Pocket Edition, 2001, p. 247.

49 R. H. Kraakman, "Gatekeepers: The Anatomy of a Third-Party Enforcement Strategy", *o.c.*, p.53, and ft.1. Kraakman attributes the metaphor to Jeremy Bentham and the doctrine of *respondeat superior*.

50 *Ibid.*, p. 53.

Kraakman defined the concept as '*liability imposed on private parties who are able to disrupt misconduct by withholding their cooperation from wrongdoers*'.[51]

In this type of liability, intermediaries who provide some form of support to wrongdoing are asked to withhold it, and are penalized if they do not.[52] The support usually consists of a specialized good, service, or certification that is essential for the wrongdoing to succeed.[53] It is, therefore, the "gate" that the gatekeeper keeps. Kraakman proposed four criteria for evaluating gatekeeping regimes. According to this author, successful gatekeeping requires:

> '(1) serious misconduct that practicable penalties cannot deter; (2) missing or inadequate private gatekeeping incentives; (3) gatekeepers who can and will prevent misconduct reliably, regardless of the preferences and market alternatives of wrongdoers; and (4) gatekeepers whom legal rules can induce to detect misconduct at reasonable cost'.[54]

Kraakman's definition of gatekeepers and gatekeeping liability is a basis for the research presented in this book. It should be mentioned, however, that theories of gatekeeping have evolved further, both in offline and online contexts.

NON-STATE ACTORS – From the broader perspective of regulatory studies, gatekeepers are non-state actors who have '*the capacity to alter the behaviour of others in circumstances where the state has limited capacity to do same*'.[55] By putting them in a position where they face a risk of liability for failure to disrupt misconduct, these non-state actors can effectively be made responsible for the advancement of public policy objectives. The concept of 'responsibilization' refers to a process '*whereby subjects are rendered individually responsible for a task which previously would have been the duty of another – usually a state agency – or would not have been recognized as a responsibility at all*'.[56]

According to Black, when there is a shift 'in the locus of the activity of 'regulating' from the state to other, multiple, locations, and the adoption on the part of the state of particular strategies of regulation', it is a situation of "decentred regulation".[57] Non-state agents are expected to serve the public interest; however, they are not subject to the professional norms in public service

51 *Ibid.*, p. 53.
52 J. Zittrain, "A History of Online Gatekeeping", *o.c.*, p. 256.
53 R. H. Kraakman, "Gatekeepers: The Anatomy of a Third-Party Enforcement Strategy", *o.c.*, p. 54.
54 *Ibid.*, p. 54.
55 E. B. Laidlaw, "A framework for identifying Internet information gatekeepers", *International Review of Law, Computers & Technology*, Vol. 24, Issue 3, pp. 263–276, p. 264.
56 A. Wakefield, J. Fleming, *SAGE Dictionary of Policing*, SAGE Publications Ltd., 2009.
57 J. Black, "Decentring Regulation: Understanding the Role of Regulation and Self-Regulation in a 'Post-Regulatory' World", *Current Legal Problems*, Vol. 54, Issue 1, January 2001, pp. 103–146, p. 110–2.

normally imposed on such institutions.[58] This is why, when non-state actors take on roles traditionally reserved for public actors, the situation raises public law concerns as it can produce an accountability gap concerning fundamental rights.[59] According to Freeman,

> '[t]o the extent that private actors increasingly perform traditionally public functions unfettered by the scrutiny that normally accompanies the exercise of public power, private participation may indeed raise accountability concerns that dwarf the problem of unchecked agency discretion. In this view, private actors do not raise a new democracy problem; they simply make the traditional one even worse because they are considerably more unaccountable than agencies'.[60]

Moreover, she observes that private actors may also threaten other public law values, such as openness, fairness, participation, consistency, rationality and impartiality of decision-making.[61]

2. GATEKEEPING IN MEDIA

GATEKEEPERS IN MASS-MEDIA – When Lewin was working on his theory, he realized that the gatekeeping model goes far beyond food choices. As he wrote, the theory of gates '*holds not only for food channels but also for the traveling of a news item through certain communication channels in a group*'.[62] In accordance with his prediction, the concept of gatekeeping has developed the most in the area of mass media (but also in the financial services industry).[63]

In the context of mass media, gatekeeping has become a metaphor for the way the media make decisions about which stories to run or discard as well as when and how much attention to give to them.[64] It describes the work of editors who choose certain items for publication which they consider more important or more interesting than others, from the enormous amount of news produced

---

58 J. Freeman, "Private Parties, Public Functions and the New Administrative Law", in D. Dyzenhaus (ed.), *Recrafting the Rule of Law*, Oxford: Hart Publishing, 1999, pp. 331–335.

59 E. B. Laidlaw, "A framework for identifying Internet information gatekeepers", *o.c.*, p. 264.

60 J. Freeman, "Private Parties, Public Functions and the New Administrative Law", *o.c.*, p. 335.

61 *Ibid.*, p. 335.

62 K. Lewin, "Frontiers in group dynamics. II. Channels of group life; social planning and action research". *o.c.*, p. 145.

63 E. B. Laidlaw, "A framework for identifying Internet information gatekeepers", *o.c.*, p. 264.

64 E. B. Laidlaw, *Internet Gatekeepers, Human Rights and Corporate Social Responsibilities*, *o.c.*, p. 48. See also C. Roberts, "Gatekeeping theory: An evolution", *o.c.*; W. Breed, "Social control in the newsroom: A functional analysis", *Social Forces* Vol.33, Issue 4, May 1955, pp. 326–335; S. D. Reese, and J. Ballinger, "The roots of a sociology of news: Remembering Mr. Gates and social control in the newsroom", *Journalism and Mass Communication Quarterly*, Vol. 78, Issue 4, December 2000, pp. 641–658.

every day.[65] The remainder of the news is condemned '*to oblivion and the wastebasket*'.[66] Shoemaker defined such gatekeeping as '*the process of culling and crafting countless bits of information into the limited number of messages that reach people every day*'.[67]

EDITORIAL CONTROL IN TRADITIONAL MEDIA – The ability to give voice to some information and discard the other gave mass media great gatekeeping powers. The freedom to decide about the broadcasted message provides substantial editorial independence. But with great powers comes great responsibility, in this case, "editorial responsibility". Editorial responsibility can be explained in terms of oversight reflected in the applied routines and in moderating and editing content, especially when it comes from external content creators.[68] It is, therefore, an act of putting editorial policy into effect and assuming responsibility for the published content.[69]

Editorial responsibility of publishers in traditional media ensures that editorial control is retained over programming and content. Due to this editorial control, in many forms of traditional media, both the author of content and the publisher (for example, the newspaper or television station) can be held liable for the broadcasted content.[70]

Information law burdens traditional media providers with extensive duties of care for own and third party content.[71] In the common law tradition, a person who publishes a defamatory statement of another in principle bears the same liability for the statement as if they had created it.[72] Publisher liability stems from the theory that a publisher has the knowledge, opportunity, and ability to exercise editorial control over the content of his publications.[73] It is distinguished from distributor liability, as it would be impossible for newsstands, bookshops or libraries to control every publication before distributing it.[74] A similar publisher

---

65 R. E. Park, *The Immigrant Press and Its Control*, Harper & Brothers, New York, 1922, p. 328.

66 *Ibid.*, p. 328.

67 P. Shoemaker, T. Vos, *Gatekeeping Theory*, Routledge, 2009, p. 1; and see P. Shoemaker, et al., "Individual and Routine Forces in Gatekeeping", *Journalism and Mass Communication Quarterly*, Vol. 78, Issue 2, June 2001, pp. 233–246.

68 See K. Jakubowicz, "Do we know a medium when we see one? New media ecology", in M. E. Price, S. G. Verhulst, L. Morgan (eds.), *Routledge Handbook of Media Law*, Routledge, 2013, p. 454.

69 *Ibid.*, p. 454.

70 C. Wong, J.X. Dempsey, "Mapping Digital Media: The Media and Liability for Content on the Internet", *o.c.*, p. 13. See also P.J. Ombelet, A. Kuczerawy, P. Valcke, "Supervising Automated Journalists in the Newsroom: Liability for Algorithmically Produced News Stories", *Revue du droit des technologies de l'information*, Vol. 61 2016, pp. 5–19.

71 N. Helberger et al., *o.c.*, p. 229.

72 Digital Media Law Project, Immunity for Online Publishers Under the Communications Decency Act: Background on Publisher and Distributor Liability, www.dmlp.org/legal-guide/immunity-online-publishers-under-communications-decency-act.

73 *Ibid.*

74 *Ibid.*

liability model functions in the continental law tradition. The publisher-model of responsibility covers both print media and broadcasting media. Under this model, full liability for the disseminated content is laid on the publisher, independent of whether the content is his own or third party content.[75] The underlying rationale is to protect the public's interest in the quality and lawfulness of media content.[76] Specific rules defining the limits of the publisher model, for example in the context of printed press and TV broadcasting, have historically been regulated by national policies, hence the rules are generally not harmonized in the EU.[77]

Broad democratization brought by new media reduced the traditional role of publishers and editors in the information circulation process. The known publishing model is difficult to apply in an ecosystem when anyone with access can publish content without first being scrutinized by a publisher. It does not mean, however, that the new media environment is free from gatekeepers.

FAILED DISINTERMEDIATION – The Internet, with its empowering and democratizing effect, brought a change to the process of selecting and crafting stories to be published for a broad audience. Some authors argue that in a modern information society the power of gatekeepers seems to diminish.[78] This is because '*the Internet defies the whole notion of a "gate" and challenges the idea that journalists (or anyone else) can or should limit what passes through it*'.[79] It was predicted that the Internet would give individuals the ability to communicate directly with each other, resulting in "disintermediation" of communication.[80]

Others, however, point out that this has not been the case.[81] Instead, we have simply exchanged one set of intermediaries (e.g., newspaper publishers

---

75 N. Helberger et al., User-Created-Content: Supporting a participative Information Society, Understanding the Digital World, Study for the European Commission conducted by IDATE, TNO and IViR, Final Report 2008, p. 265.

76 N. Helberger et al., *o.c.*, p. 265.

77 P.J. Ombelet, A. Kuczerawy, P. Valcke, Legal / regulatory requirements analysis – Media law and Freedom of expression, Deliverable D1.2c, REVEAL project, 30 April 2016, p. 9. But see E. Brogi, P. L. Parcu, "The Evolving Regulation of the Media in Europe as an Instrument for Freedom and Pluralism", *EUI Working Paper RSCAS* 2014/09, 2014, for the evolution of the EU regulation of the audiovisual media services and media pluralism. See also P. Valcke, D. Stevens, E. Werkers, and E. Lievens, "Audiovisual Media Services in the EU: Next Generation Approach or Old Wine in New Barrels?" *Communications & Strategies*, No. 71, 3rd Quarter 2008, p. 103.

78 J.B. Singer, "Stepping back from the gate: Online newspaper editors and the co-production of content in Campaign 2004", *Journalism and Mass Communication Quarterly*, Vol. 83, Issue 2, 2006, pp. 265–280, p. 265.

79 *Ibid.*

80 See for example R. Gellman, "Disintermediation and the Internet", *Government Information Quarterly*, Vol. 13, Issue 1, 1996, pp. 1–8, p.2; and A. L. Shapiro, *The Control Revolution: How the Internet is Putting Individuals in Charge and Changing the World We Know*, PublicAffairs, 2000.

81 D. Ardia, "Free Speech Savior or Shield for Scoundrels: an Empirical Study of Intermediary Immunity Under Section 230 of the Communications Decency Act", *Loyola of Los Angeles Law Review*, Vol. 43, No. 2, 2010, pp. 373 – 506, p. 383.

and broadcast stations) for another set of intermediaries (e.g., Internet service providers, content hosts, and search providers).[82] The concept of gatekeeping, therefore, remains valid, although some argue that it must be adjusted to the new environment.

NETWORK GATEKEEPER THEORY – According to Laidlaw, traditional definitions, such as Kraakman's, tend to focus on gatekeepers' capacity to prevent third party misbehaviour.[83] Moreover, the problem with the traditional gatekeeping theories is that they treat the "gated" individuals in a static way, which fails to capture the fluid, dynamic, and unstable environment of the Internet, and gives little attention to their rights.[84] The term "gated" was introduced by Barzilai-Nahon to refer to those on whom the gatekeeping is exercised.[85] The same author proposed Network Gatekeeper Theory (NGT), developed with the Internet in mind, to bring in a more flexible construct of information control.[86] Laidlaw supplements this theory by adding a human rights dimension and proposing a concept of Internet information gatekeepers (IGG).[87]

Despite the enormous value of these theories, they are not developed further here. The focus of this book is precisely on the threat of liability imposed on gatekeepers to prevent third-party misconduct. For this reason, it is based on the original definition established by Kraakman. The rights of the users – the gated – are of crucial importance, but this book argues that the obligation to protect the rights belongs primarily to the State, which cannot absolve itself from this responsibility, even when designating gatekeepers.

---

82 J. M. Balkin, "Media Access: A Question of Design", *George Washington Law Review*, Vol. 76, No. 4, 2008, pp. 101–118, p. 114–116.

83 E. B. Laidlaw, "A framework for identifying Internet information gatekeepers", *o.c.*, p. 265.

84 *Ibid.*

85 *Ibid.*

86 K. Barzilai-Nahon, "Toward a Theory of Network Gatekeeping: A Framework for Exploring Information Control", *Journal of the American Society for Information Science and Technology*, Vol. 59, Issue 9, 2008, pp.1493–1512.

87 E. B. Laidlaw, *Internet Gatekeepers, Human Rights and Corporate Social Responsibilities*, *o.c.*, p. 53.

CHAPTER 2
GATEKEEPING IN ONLINE MEDIA

1. NEW MEDIA, NEW CHALLENGES?

NEW DEVELOPMENTS – The media environment is constantly changing. From wall paintings through story tellers, to newspapers, newer and better methods of communication are constantly developing. Currently, the term "old media" is used for traditional communication delivery systems, such as newspapers, magazines, radio and television. These systems are described as '*independent, static, historical*'.[88] The crucial question, however, is what exactly constitutes "new media"?

There is no single definition of new media. Some authors described it as 'fluid, individualized connectivity', 'a medium to distribute control and freedom', and a 'form of distribution as independent as the information it relayed'.[89] Voithofer, for example, contrasts the new media with the old media by reference to changes in production due to convergence of technology and media, including storage (digitization and indexing), presentation (on some form of monitor display), and distribution over (wired or wireless) telecommunication networks.[90] Others refer to new media technologies simply as Web 2.0, which 'encompass a wide variety of web-related communication technologies, such as blogs, wikis, online social networking, virtual worlds and other social media forms'.[91] Web 2.0 as a term is focused on participative environment.[92] According to Stephen Fry,

> 'Web 2.0 is an idea in people's heads rather than a reality. It's actually an idea that the reciprocity between the user and the provider is what is emphasised. In other

---

88 L. W. Friedman, H. H. Friedman, "The New Media Technologies: Overview and Research Framework", April 2008, https://ssrn.com/abstract=1116771, p. 2.

89 W. Hui Kyong Chun, "Did Somebody Say New Media?" in W. Hui Kyong Chun and T. Keenan (eds.), *New Media, Old Media: A History and Theory Reader*, Routledge Taylor & Francis Group, 2006.

90 R. Voithofer, "Designing new media education research: the materiality of data, representation and dissemination", *Educational Researcher*, Vol. 34, Issue 9, 2005, pp. 3–14, p. 4.

91 L. W. Friedman, H. H. Friedman, "The New Media Technologies: Overview and Research Framework", *o.c.*, p. 1.

92 See the discussion by Tim O'Reilly about the coining of the term: 'What is Web 2.0' (30 September 2005), at www.oreillynet.com/pub/a/oreilly/tim/news/2005/09/30/what-is-web-20.html.

words, genuine interactivity, if you like, simply because people can upload as well as download'.[93]

Arguably, some of the new media technologies are not exactly new anymore.[94] Yet, the term is still commonly used. The category is extremely broad but there are several aspects that unite the various technologies and define their unique character. Friedman and Friedman summarize them as the 5 C's: communication, collaboration, community, creativity, and convergence.[95] New media technologies are focused on communication, which can be unidirectional, collaborative, or networked.[96] They enable collaboration over the Internet, for example through wikis or social media networks. They foster a sense of community among like-minded groups and individuals who might be otherwise disconnected. Finally, they incentivize creativity by facilitating editing of content, which keeps receiving new life fuelled by people's ideas.

The arrival of "new media" was initially feared to bring about the end of old media.[97] Some compared old media to the telegraph, which was virtually replaced by the telephone – and more recently by email.[98] This has not happened. The old media evolved and adapted under the pressure of the new developments, often merging with them.[99] Today, old media still exists and often provides an equivalent in a form of new media. For example, newspapers and magazines have their online versions, and television networks produce online content. Rather than replacing old media, therefore, new media became a supplement, often working together with the old media to further the same goals.[100]

MEDIA CONVERGENCE – Widespread digitization and the Internet contributed to convergence of technology on an unprecedented scale. The European Commission defined media convergence as '*the ability of different network platforms to carry essentially similar kinds of services, or the coming*

93 Video interview with Stephen Fry, as referenced by E. B. Laidlaw, *Internet Gatekeepers, Human Rights and Corporate Social Responsibilities*, *o.c.*, p. 15.

94 See J. Macnamara, *The 21st Century Media (r)evolution: Emergent Communication Practices*, Peter Lang Publishing, 2010, p. 19–22.

95 L. W. Friedman, H. H. Friedman, "The New Media Technologies: Overview and Research Framework", *o.c.*, p. 9.

96 See *Ibid.*, p. 10.

97 See for example P. Meyer, *The Vanishing Newspaper*, Columbia: University of Missouri Press, 2004.

98 See J. Balkin, "Media Access: A Question of Design", *o.c.*, p. 105.

99 See K. Jakubowicz, A Notion of new Media, Keynote speech prepared for delivery during the 1st Council of Europe Conference of Ministers Responsible for Media and New Communication Services, Reykjavik, May 28–29, 2009. See also R. Kleis Nielsen, S. A. Ganter, "Dealing with digital intermediaries: A case study of the relations between publishers and platforms", *New Media & Society*, 17 April 2017, pp. 1–18.

100 See L. W. Friedman, H. H. Friedman, "The New Media Technologies: Overview and Research Framework", *o.c.*, p. 2.

together of consumer devices such as the telephone, television and personal computer'.[101] In 2013 the same institution described it as the '*progressive merger of traditional broadcast services and the internet'*.[102] It leads to a blurring of the lines between the familiar twentieth-century consumption patterns and the new services delivered to computers.[103] Citizens gain access to an unparalleled amount of information and content beyond national offerings but tailored to their interests, which can improve participation in opinion making.[104]

In the new media, a broad variety of convergence can be distinguished, for example convergence of technology (e.g. computer technology and entertainment technology), convergence of media (e.g. newspapers with online presence), convergence of consumption (e.g. technologies allowing "multimedia multitasking" – combining several media, such as telephone, camera and music, in one), and convergence of roles (between different actors).[105] Convergent media challenges the traditional division between actors who are involved in the media production chain. The blurred lines often make it difficult to clearly distinguish between the author, editor and publisher of the content.[106] This is especially visible in the phenomenon of user-generated content, where content – once put online – starts living its own life being constantly edited, mashed up, added-to and republished by other users.[107]

REGULATORY CONVERGENCE – The converging media landscape triggered a new regulatory approach, leading to "regulatory convergence". Traditionally, various sectors of the media have been regulated separately. In response to the convergence of media, some countries (e.g., United Kingdom, Italy and Bosnia and Herzegovina), have merged previously separate regulatory authorities for broadcasting and telecommunications into single "converged" bodies.[108] In the United Kingdom, five regulators were merged into one converged regulator, OFCOM, which unites both spectrum and content regulation. A similar

---

101 European Commission, Green Paper on the convergence of the telecommunications, media and information technology sectors, and the implications for regulation, COM (1997) 623 final, 03 December 1997, p. 1.

102 European Commission, Green Paper, Preparing for a Fully Converged Audiovisual World: Growth, Creation and Values, COM (2013) 231 final, Brussels, 24 April 2013.

103 *Ibid.*

104 *Ibid.*

105 See L. W. Friedman, H. H. Friedman, "The New Media Technologies: Overview and Research Framework", *o.c.*, p. 11–15.

106 P.J. Ombelet, A. Kuczerawy, P. Valcke, "Supervising Automated Journalists in the Newsroom: Liability for Algorithmically Produced News Stories", *o.c.* See more in N. Helberger *et al.*, User-Created-Content: Supporting a participative Information Society, *o.c.*, p. 173.

107 See more in P. Valcke, M. Lenaerts and A. Kuczerawy, "Who's Author, Editor and Publisher in User-Generated Content?" in P. Lambert (ed.), *User Generated Content, in Social Networking: Law, Rights and Policy*, 2014, pp. 83–99.

108 See more in Council of Europe, Directorate General of Human Rights and Legal Affairs, Converging media – convergent regulators? The future of broadcasting regulatory authorities in South-Eastern Europe, Conference organised by the Council of Europe and the OSCE Mission to Skopje, 1–2 October 2007, Skopje, https://rm.coe.int/1680483b31.

approach was taken in Bosnia and Herzegovina, where the Communications Regulatory Agency was created. In Italy, where no regulatory authority existed before, a converged regulator AGCOM was established. In other countries, however, the approach has not yet changed with separate regulators remaining in charge of their respective areas.[109]

NEW NOTION OF MEDIA – Developments in the media environment revealed that some of the traditional concepts and definitions require a re-evaluation. In 2009, Karol Jakubowicz observed that in the 21st century, the communication mode is no longer one-to-many, but many-to-many.[110] He identified, moreover, three new notions of media: digital, convergent media into which all existing media may one day evolve; media created by new actors, including social, citizen and user-generated media; and media-like activities performed by non-traditional media actors.[111]

The change was also observed by policy-makers. The Council of Europe pointed out that such a '*fluid and multi-dimensional reality*' must be embraced and reflected in media-related policy.[112] In the Recommendation on the new notion of media, the CoE stated that,

> '[a]ll actors – whether new or traditional – who operate within the media ecosystem should be offered a policy framework which guarantees an appropriate level of protection and provides a clear indication of their duties and responsibilities in line with Council of Europe standards'.[113]

The CoE recommended that Member States adopt a new, broad notion of media, which encompasses all actors involved in the production and dissemination of content as well as applications that are designed to facilitate interactive mass communication or other content-based large-scale interactive experiences.[114] Within this broad category, the CoE distinguished media actors and providers of intermediary or auxiliary services. One qualifier that the CoE specified for all these types of services is that they retain editorial control or oversight of their content.[115] Providers of intermediary or auxiliary services may contribute to the functioning of a media but generally they do not exercise editorial control and have no (or limited) editorial responsibility.[116] For this reason they should

---

109 See J. E. Fell, in Converging media – convergent regulators? The future of broadcasting regulatory authorities in South-Eastern Europe, *o.c.*, p. 9.

110 K. Jakubowicz, "A Notion of new Media", *o.c.*

111 *Ibid.*

112 Council of Europe, Recommendation CM/Rec(2011)7 of the Committee of Ministers to member states on a new notion of media, 21 September 2011.

113 *Ibid.*

114 *Ibid.*

115 *Ibid.*

116 *Ibid.*

not be considered as media. The Recommendation provided a set of criteria and indicators to 1) facilitate categorisation of particular activities, services or actors as media; and 2) inspire appropriate form (differentiated) and level (graduated) of response (see more *infra*).

To qualify an actor as media, the CoE provides six criteria: 1) intent to act as media; 2) purpose and underlying objectives; 3) editorial control; 4) professional standards; 5) outreach and dissemination; and 6) public expectation. Each criterion has several indicators, but the approach is flexible, meaning that not all indicators need to be met to fulfil a particular criterion. Moreover, not all the criteria carry equal weight. Not meeting criteria such as intent (criterion 1) or public expectation (criterion 6) should not automatically disqualify a service from being considered as media. On the other hand, the absence of criteria such as purpose (criterion 2), editorial control (criterion 3) or outreach and dissemination (criterion 5) would most likely disqualify a service from being regarded as media. Actors that do not meet the core criteria (but meet the remaining criteria) may qualify as intermediaries or auxiliaries.

GRADUATED AND DIFFERENTIATED APPROACH – The CoE observed that the new media policies should reflect the evolving ecosystem, and in particular the roles and specific functions played by the actors involved. Media policies should offer a response that would be of appropriate form (differentiated) and level (graduated), according to the part that media services play in content production and dissemination processes.[117] This means that the role they play in the communication process, either as media or as intermediaries – according to the provided criteria, should be reflected in the policy framework.

To facilitate adequate determination of the protections, rights, and responsibilities appropriate for the different actors and services the CoE Recommendation provided a set of standards applied to media in the new ecosystem. The offered guidance, however, is much broader than the criteria for identifying the media actors (see *Supra*). The application of standards is set to evolve in line with developments as regards media actors, services and activities. The CoE provides standards in the areas of 1) rights, privileges and prerogatives; 2) media pluralism and diversity of content; 3) media responsibilities; and 4) reference instruments.[118]

MEDIA AND DEMOCRACY – Media in general, as a means of mass communication, enables people to exercise their right to seek and receive information. By providing a space for public debate, it has become the most important tool for freedom of expression, which is indispensable for genuine democracy and democratic processes.[119] In a democratic society, as described by

117 *Ibid.*
118 *Ibid.*
119 *Ibid.*

the Council of Europe, '*people must be able to contribute to and participate in the decision-making processes which concern them*'.[120] The new information and communication technologies, in particular, provide opportunities to strengthen the participation, initiative and involvement of citizens in national, regional and local public life and in decision-making processes.[121] Through these means they can contribute to more dynamic, inclusive and direct forms of democracy, genuine public debate, better legislation and active scrutiny of the decision-making processes.[122]

Despite rapid developments in the ecosystem, the role of the media in a democratic society has not changed.[123] As pointed out by Laidlaw, '*[e]very communication technology from the printing press to the radio has at one time been celebrated as having a democratising force*'.[124] After all, they can all be considered conduits for speech.[125] The new media technologies, however, offer unique opportunities by levelling the playing field for all individuals, whether professional or not.[126] Technology has become the great equalizer and has significantly lowered threshold for content production.[127] As stated by Jakubowicz, the '*floodgates to universal expression are wide open*'.[128] Considerably lower costs, reduced technical and professional requirements, and decentralised architecture allow for new ways of disseminating content as well as an unprecedented level of interaction and engagement by users.[129] Increased participation in the creation process and in the dissemination of information and content provides new opportunities for democratic citizenship and strengthens the democratising force of the new media.[130]

---

120 *Ibid.*

121 See Council of Europe, Recommendation CM/Rec(2007)16 of the Committee of Ministers to member states on measures to promote the public service value of the Internet, 7 November 2007.

122 *Ibid.*

123 Council of Europe, Recommendation CM/Rec(2011)7 of the Committee of Ministers to member states on a new notion of media, *o.c.*

124 E. B. Laidlaw, *Internet Gatekeepers, Human Rights and Corporate Social Responsibilities*, *o.c.*, p. 16.

125 See J. Balkin, "Media Access: A Question of Design", *o.c.*, p. 104–107.

126 See M. J. Johnson, P. W. Wilcox, "The World of Connected Things", *The Journal of Government Financial Management*, Vol. 56, Issue 4, Winter 2007, pp. 48 – 53.

127 L. W. Friedman, H. H. Friedman, "The New Media Technologies: Overview and Research Framework", *o.c.*, p. 12. See also E. Lievens, *Protecting Children in the Digital Era – the Use of Alternative Regulatory Instruments*, *o.c.*, p. 23.

128 K. Jakubowicz, A Notion of new Media, *o.c.*

129 Council of Europe, Recommendation CM/Rec(2011)7 of the Committee of Ministers to member states on a new notion of media, *o.c.* See also Y. Benkler, *The Wealth of Networks: How Social Production Transforms Markets and Freedom*, Yale University Press, 2006, p. 271.

130 See Council of Europe, Recommendation CM/Rec(2011)7 of the Committee of Ministers to member states on a new notion of media, *o.c.*

RISKS IN NEW MEDIA – The arrival of new media brought great expectations about their democratising power. The Internet was viewed as a vast library that anyone can access, and a platform where anyone *'can become a town crier with a voice that resonates farther than it could from any soapbox'*.[131] With time, however, it became clear that the great potential of the Internet also has its downsides. Difficult problems that have emerged include digital divide, concentration of the market, and quality control.[132] Jakubowicz pointed out the problem of fragmentation and "ego-casting", explained as *'the ability to screen out content we are not comfortable or do not agree with'*.[133] The phenomenon leads to the creation of information "echo chambers", which insulate the user from the opinion of others making the experience personalized but segregated and sound proofed.[134] Recently the trend has even received the catchier name of "filter bubbles" when performed by algorithms.[135] These aspects can potentially undermine social cohesion and national unity, perhaps leading to the disintegration of the democratic polity.[136] After observing the US presidential elections in 2016, the unavoidable conclusion is that Jakubowicz was right and his predictions turned out to be more than just grim forecasts.[137] This, however, is not the only problem.

With new media technologies, innovative techniques have supplemented traditional modes of control over speech and surveillance.[138] These new techniques are provided by the very same forces that have democratized and decentralized the production and transmission of information in the digital

---

131 *ACLU* v. *Reno*, (1997) 521 U.S. 844, Justice Stevens delivering the opinion of the Court, pp. 852–3, 896–7.

132 E. B. Laidlaw, *Internet Gatekeepers, Human Rights and Corporate Social Responsibilities*, *o.c.*, p. 17.

133 See K. Jakubowicz, A Notion of new Media, *o.c.*

134 See more in S. Flaxman, S. Goel, J.M. Rao, "Filter Bubbles, Echo Chambers, ad Online News Consumption", *Public Opinion Quarterly*, Vol. 80, Special Issue, 2016, pp. 298–320, where the authors argue that the magnitude of the effects is relatively modest. See also J. Zittrain, Facebook Could Decide an Election Without Anyone Ever Finding Out, where he called it "digital gerrymandering", 2 June 2014, https://newrepublic.com/article/117878/information-fiduciary-solution-facebook-digital-gerrymandering.

135 See more in E. Pariser, *The Filter Bubble: How the New Personalized Web Is Changing What We Read and How We Think*, Penguin Books, 2012. See also I. Lambrecht, The Filter Bubble: to burst or to blow over?, 29 November 2016, https://www.law.kuleuven.be/citip/blog/the-filter-bubble-to-burst-or-to-blow-over/. See also C. Morgan, Why 'Popping' the Social Media Filter Bubble Misses the Point, 16 November 2016, https://motherboard.vice.com/en_us/article/pgkxng/why-popping-the-social-media-filter-bubble-misses-the-point.

136 K. Jakubowicz, A Notion of new Media, *o.c.*

137 See more in M. M. El-Barmawy, Your Filter Bubble is Destroying Democracy, 18 November 2016, https://www.wired.com/2016/11/filter-bubble-destroying-democracy/; and W. Rinehart, The Election of 2016 and the Filter Bubble Thesis in 2017, 15 September 2016, https://medium.com/@willrinehart/the-election-of-2016-and-the-filter-bubble-thesis-in-2017-51cd7520ed7.

138 J. Balkin, "Old School/New School Speech Regulation", *Harvard Law Review*, Vol 127, 20 June 2014, p. 2297.

era.[139] The secret lies in controlling the infrastructure, which became the "gate", and as put by Balkin, '*the central battleground over free speech in the digital era*'.[140] Providers of the infrastructure possess an immense power to control access to media. What is crucial for this book, the infrastructure is largely held in private hands. Nevertheless, it is often merged and incorporated by governments to regulate speech in the new environment. After the experiences of the last two years, it has become clear that for the Internet to ensure the sought freedoms it cannot simply be left alone by governments. The idea cannot be seriously sustained.[141] Treating the Internet as a separate place that will flourish if untouched by regulation, albeit very idealistic as a notion, ignores the indirect ways that governments regulate and impact cyber-space with the help of private gatekeepers.[142]

2. INTERNET INTERMEDIARIES AS POINTS OF CONTROL

DEFINITION – In the online environment, one category of private entities that control the infrastructure are Internet intermediaries. Intermediaries, in general, are placed between parties to intermediate. They could be '*any entity that enables the communication of information from one party to another*'.[143] Inserting intermediaries between interacting parties in the online environment is necessitated by the ways the Internet works. Despite the initial claims of "disintermediation", it is rarely possible for two parties to be directly connected to each other.[144] In most of the cases, we all need some type of "middleman" to make the interaction possible. The category of Internet intermediaries is broad and covers any type of activity effectively facilitating online interactions. According to the OECD, Internet intermediaries '*bring together or facilitate transactions between third parties on the Internet*'.[145]

The scope of the term is usually delineated in practical terms by enumeration of the currently existing types of intermediaries. The category includes Internet service providers (ISPs), hosting providers, search engines, e-commerce

---

139 *Ibid.*

140 See *Ibid.*, p. 2296.

141 B. Frydman, I. Rorive, "Regulating Internet Content through Intermediaries in Europe and the USA", *Zeitschrift für Rechtssoziologie*, Vol. 23, No. 1, pp. 41–59, 2002, p. 58.

142 See E. B. Laidlaw, *Internet Gatekeepers, Human Rights and Corporate Social Responsibilities*, *o.c.*, p. 13.

143 T.F. Cotter, "Some Observations on the Law and Economics of Intermediaries", *Michigan State Law Review*, Vol. 67, 2006, pp. 68–71.

144 See R. J. Mann, S. R. Belzley, "The Promise of Internet Intermediary Liability", *William & Mary Law Review*, Vol.47, Issue 1, 2005, p. 254.

145 OECD, The Economic and Social Role of Internet Intermediaries, *o.c., p.* 9.

intermediaries, Internet payment systems and participative Web platforms.[146] Some sources also list caching providers, auction platforms, and hyperlinks, as well as blogs, forums and social networks, content aggregators, video sharing websites, domain name providers, cloud computing platforms, registration authorities, admin-C and gambling services.[147]

Internet intermediaries come in all shapes and sizes. They vary widely in scope and market share.[148] Several intermediaries operate across multiple sectors (e.g. search engines and advertising platforms). Some function both in off-line and on-line environments (e.g. payment services), while others exist solely online (e.g. domain registrars).[149] Large intermediaries that own global platforms, significant market share and sophisticated enforcement capabilities may be described as "macrointermediaries".[150] The term is based on the concept of "macrogatekeepers" used by Barzilai-Nahon to describe companies that facilitate the flow of information on the Internet.[151]

FUNCTION AND ROLES – Communication on the Internet is only possible through a series of intermediaries.[152] Typically, Internet intermediaries are for-profit entities that provide commercial and technical services that enable the Internet to function.[153] They provide the infrastructure and the software through which information is processed and on which online communities are built.[154] This book adopts the broad definition of the OECD, which describes the role of Internet intermediaries as to

> 'provide access to, host, transmit and index content originated by third parties on the Internet; facilitate interactions or transactions between third parties on the Internet; or provide other Internet-based services to third parties'.[155]

INTERNET INTERMEDIARIES AS GATEKEEPERS – Internet Intermediaries, who are the actual enablers of Internet communications, are often seen as natural

---

146 *Ibid.*, pp. 9–14.

147 See T. Verbiest, G. Spindler *et al.*, "Study on the Liability of Internet Intermediaries", *o.c.*, p. 7; and P. Van Eecke, M. Truyens, "Legal analysis of a Single Market for the Information Society, New rules for a new age?" *o.c.* Executive Summary, p. 6.

148 N. Tusikov, *Chokepoints - Global Private Regulation on the Internet*, University of California Press, November 2016, p. 6.

149 *Ibid.*, p. 6.

150 *Ibid.*, p. 6.

151 K. Barzilai-Nahon, "Toward a Theory of Network Gatekeeping: A Framework for Exploring Information Control", *o.c.*, pp.1493–1512.

152 See Manila Principles on Intermediary Liability Background Paper, *o.c.*, p. 3.

153 N. Tusikov, *Chokepoints - Global Private Regulation on the Internet*, *o.c.*,, p. 6.

154 P. Van Eecke, M. Truyens, "Legal analysis of a Single Market for the Information Society, New rules for a new age?" *o.c.*, p. 6.

155 OECD, The Economic and Social Role of Internet Intermediaries, *o.c.*, pp. 9–14.

points of control for online content.[156] This is because they have a capacity to restrain multiple wrongdoings by focusing on a single choke point.[157] Due to this ability, they are in a powerful position to shape the provision of essential Internet services. In particular, they can eliminate access to service, objectionable material and, quite often, identify wrongdoers.[158] They are, therefore, capable of affecting directly and indirectly the behaviour of their users.[159] With such power at their hands, they seem to be natural candidates for the role of gatekeepers. As private parties who are able to disrupt misconduct by withholding their cooperation from wrongdoers, they certainly fit the definition of Kraakman. States, therefore, have '*increasingly delegated traditional regulatory and police functions to the intermediaries that design and organise digital environments*' because of the real control they possess.[160] Such a delegated private enforcement constitutes an effective way of fulfilling public policy objectives.[161]

INTERMEDIARIES AS PROXY CENSORS – Arguably, Internet intermediaries fit perfectly in the role of "Internet police" and are able to fill the void left by removing editorial control of the publishers from the communication process. They can act where States, who do not own the infrastructure of free expression, have no effective control. Within the chain, they are considered as the weak link that States could enlist as "proxy censors" to control the flow of information.[162] The only way for the States to maintain control of the online expression is to coerce or co-opt such private entities to assist in speech regulation and surveillance.[163] This approach is an example of "collateral censorship", where the State regulates party A in order to control speaker B.[164] Co-opting private entities to regulate speech of their users allows States to achieve regulatory goals in a discreet manner. The method is less visible and less obvious than classic

156 J. Zittrain, "A History of Online Gatekeeping", *o.c.*, p.254; C. Wong, J.X. Dempsey, "Mapping Digital Media: The Media and Liability for Content on the Internet", *o.c.*, p. 14.

157 See G. B. Dinwoodie, "A Comparative Analysis of the Secondary Liability of Online Service Providers", in G. B. Dinwoodie, *Secondary Liability of Internet Service Providers*, Ius Comparatum – Global Studies in Comparative Law, Springer, 2018, p. 12.

158 E. Montero and Q. Van Enis, "Enabling freedom of expression in light of filtering measures imposed on Internet intermediaries: Squaring the circle", *Computer Law & Security Review*, Vol. 27, 2011, pp. 21–35.

159 See S. Stalla-Bourdillon, "Chilling ISPs… when private regulators act without adequate public framework", *Computer Law & Security Review*, Vol. 26, 2010, pp. 290–297, p. 291.

160 L. Belli and C. Sappa, "The Intermediary Conundrum: Cyber-Regulators, Cyber-Police or Both?", *JIPITEC* Vol. 8, 2017, p. 183 para 9.

161 C. Angelopoulos et al., "Study of fundamental rights limitations for online enforcement through self-regulation", Institute for Information Law (IViR), 2016, p. 1.

162 S. F. Kreimer, "Censorship by Proxy: The First Amendment, Internet Intermediaries, and the Problem of the Weakest Link", *Faculty Scholarship*, Paper 127, 2006, p. 14.

163 J. Balkin, "Old School/New School Speech Regulation", *o.c.*, p. 2298.

164 *Ibid.*

State intervention.[165] Measures employed by the intermediaries often work automatically and in the background and therefore they can stay under the radar and avoid being labelled as State interference. According to Balkin, '*low salience and use of private parties can help governments preserve legitimacy even as their policies block, limit, or spy on expression*'.[166] This approach allows them to effectively sidestep certain safeguards otherwise applicable to direct State interference.[167] As a result, speech could be suppressed without the protections that the legal system normally grants when the limitation originates from the State.[168] The implemented measures, as a result, may enforce rules in a way that interferes with fundamental rights of the users.[169]

INCENTIVIZING INTERMEDIARIES – Despite their technical abilities to shape the behaviour of the user, Internet intermediaries are not "natural" gatekeepers.[170] They have had little if any interest in adopting private law enforcement roles, which they take up in response to considerable pressure from States and industry groups or as a reaction to legal uncertainty of their situation.[171] They do not choose that role, but rather fall into it because of technology they provide or social behaviour that they enable.[172] The availability of a variety of infringing and illegal content online has obviously raised concerns among policymakers. To address the problem, they appointed private actors to achieve or preserve public policy objectives. In most cases, the role of gatekeepers was not assigned to the Internet intermediaries directly, but rather through a (more or less) subtle provision of incentives, or as described by Balkin, '*a combination of carrots and sticks*'.[173] Such incentives can take the form of

165 See D. E. Bambauer, "Orwell's Armchair", *University of Chicago Law Review*, Vol. 79, 2012, p. 863. See also S. F. Kreimer, "Censorship by Proxy: The First Amendment, Internet Intermediaries, and the Problem of the Weakest Link", *o.c.*, p. 28.

166 J. Balkin, "Old School/New School Speech Regulation", *o.c.*, p. 2298.

167 See C. Angelopoulos et al., "Study of fundamental rights limitations for online enforcement through self-regulation", *o.c.*, p. 61.

168 D. Tambini, D. Leonardi, and C. Marsden, "The privatisation of censorship: self regulation and freedom of expression", in D. Tambini, D. Leonardi, and C. Marsden, *Codifying cyberspace: communications self-regulation in the age of internet convergence*, Routledge / UCL Press, Abingdon, UK, 2008, p. 411.

169 See C. Angelopoulos et al., "Study of fundamental rights limitations for online enforcement through self-regulation", *o.c.*

170 See J. McNamee, "The slide from "self-regulation" to corporate censorship", European Digital Rights Initiative, 2011, https://www.edri.org/files/EDRI_selfreg_final_20110124.pdf, p. 4; and N. Tusikov, *Chokepoints – Global Private Regulation on the Internet*, *o.c.*, p. 30.

171 N. Tusikov, *Chokepoints – Global Private Regulation on the Internet*, *o.c.*, p. 30.

172 See E. B. Laidlaw, *Internet Gatekeepers, Human Rights and Corporate Social Responsibilities*, *o.c.*, p. 51.

173 J. Balkin, "Old School/New School Speech Regulation", *o.c*, p. 2299. See also S. Stalla-Bourdillon, "Chilling ISPs... when private regulators act without adequate public framework", *o.c.*, p. 290.

government pressure, both formal and informal.[174] An example of the former could be the activities of police referral units such as the UK's Counter-Terrorism Internet Referral Unit (CTIRU), which monitor social media and flag supposedly terroristic content to the intermediary to determine whether it constitutes a breach of the Terms of Service.[175] The latter usually occur through government criticism, sometimes even expressed off-the record and in a private setting.[176] Such methods of achieving regulatory goals are referred to as "regulation by raised eyebrow"[177] or "soft censorship".[178]

Another form of incentive, which is the topic of this book, is a provision of legal immunity in return for assisting the State's efforts at speech control.[179] Intermediaries are offered liability exemptions for third party content, but only under specifically designed conditions.[180] To avoid potential liability, intermediaries must react to a notification and take down (or block access to) illegal content that they are hosting. In theory, under this approach intermediaries do not have any obligation to act. However, when they risk being held liable for their users' activities, it is not surprising that they introduce and implement a variety of speech restricting measures.[181] It is also not surprising that they might be too quick to take down content that puts them in danger.[182] As put by Zittrain, intermediaries may tend to '*overblock content in an attempt to avoid any possible suggestion of liability*'.[183] Effectively, the regime places intermediaries in a position to decide which content can remain online and

174 See C. Angelopoulos et al., "Study of fundamental rights limitations for online enforcement through self-regulation", o.c, p. 57-62

175 See Council of the European Union, EU Counter-terrorism Coordinator input for the preparation of the informal meeting of Justice and Home Affairs Ministers in Riga on 29 January 2015, DS 1035/15, 17 January 2015, see: www.statewatch.org/news/2015/jan/eu-council-ct-ds-1035-15.pdf. See more in C. Angelopoulos et al., Study of fundamental rights limitations for online enforcement through self-regulation, *o.c.*, p. 59.

176 See H. Siddique, "Facebook Removes Mexican Beheading Video", *The Guardian*, 23 October 2013, www.theguardian.com/technology/2013/oct/23/facebook-removes-beheading-video; and P. Donahue, "Merkel Confronts Facebook's Zuckerberg Over Policing Hate Posts", *Bloomberg*, 26 September 2015, www.bloomberg.com/news/articles/2015-09-26/merkel-confronts-facebook-s-zuckerberg-over-policing-hate-posts. See more in C. Angelopoulos et al., "Study of fundamental rights limitations for online enforcement through self-regulation", *o.c.*, p. 57–61.

177 Y. Benkler, "A Free Irresponsible Press: Wikileaks and the Battle over the Soul of the Networked Fourth Estate", *Harvard Civil Rights-Civil Liberties Law Review*, Vol. 46, 2011, p. 311.

178 See D. E. Bambauer, "Orwell's Armchair", *o.c.*

179 See J. Balkin, "Old School/New School Speech Regulation", *o.c*, p. 2299.

180 See S. F. Kreimer, "Censorship by Proxy: The First Amendment, Internet Intermediaries, and the Problem of the Weakest Link", *o.c*, p. 23.

181 L. Belli and C. Sappa, "The Intermediary Conundrum: Cyber-Regulators, Cyber-Police or Both?", *o.c.*, para 1.

182 D. Tambini, D. Leonardi, and C. Marsden, "The privatisation of censorship: self regulation and freedom of expression", *o.c.*, p. 424.

183 J. Zittrain, "A History of Online Gatekeeping", *o.c.*, p. 262.

which should be removed. The conditional liability for third party content is, therefore, an example of indirect public ordering.[184]

(IN)VOLUNTARY COOPERATION – Threatening intermediaries with regulation or legal action leads them to entering different types of "voluntary" agreements. Birnhack and Elkin-Koren labelled them '*the Invisible Handshake: this is a regulatory framework that facilitates an alliance between nodes of control of the private sector and the State*'.[185] Such agreements are usually non-binding and informal, and often described as "industry-led" or "private".[186] As pointed out by Tusikov, such agreements are at their core intended to push intermediaries to go beyond what they are required to do by law, in the protection of rights.[187] She gives an example of the failed SOPA and PIPA bills in the US, that were effectively implemented through '*a series of informal, non-legally binding handshake agreements*' with Internet companies and online payment providers that incorporated SOPA's toughest and most controversial provisions.[188] Advocates of this position refer to it as a "beyond-compliance" regulatory strategy, which applies State pressure to encourage and compel intermediaries to exceed their legal responsibilities.[189] Such agreements are a direct result of State pressure therefore they can hardly be called voluntary or private.

SELF-REGULATION – Another form of agreements exists when private entities across one sector enter into collaboration with one another in an attempt to self-organise for self-regulatory purposes.[190] Self-regulation is a way that '*complements, or obviates the need for, formal legislation*'.[191] The term self-regulation might suggest that it consists of a regulatory process undertaken by all regulatees, which interact together to organize their relationships themselves.[192] However, in these circumstances intermediaries are not regulating themselves, but '*they are regulating their consumers for the expected benefit of third parties*'.[193]

184 D. Tambini, D. Leonardi, and C. Marsden, "The privatisation of censorship: self regulation and freedom of expression", *o.c.*, p. 424.

185 M. D. Birnhack, N. Elkin-Koren, "The invisible handshake: the re-emergence of the state in the digital environment", *Virginia Journal of Law and Technology, Vol. 8, Summer* 2003, p. 11.

186 N. Tusikov, *Chokepoints – Global Private Regulation on the Internet*, *o.c.*, p. 4.

187 *Ibid.*

188 See more *Ibid.*, p. 3.

189 See *Ibid.*, p. 4–5. For an example see European Commission, Report from the Commission to the European Parliament and the Council on the functioning of the Memorandum of Understanding on the Sale of Counterfeit Goods via the Internet, COM/2013/0209 final, http://eur-lex.europa.eu/legal-content/EN/TXT/?uri=CELEX%3A52013DC0209, p. 5–6.

190 C. Angelopoulos et al., "Study of fundamental rights limitations for online enforcement through self-regulation", *o.c*, p. 1.

191 *Ibid.*, p. 5.

192 S. Stalla-Bourdillon, "Chilling ISPs… when private regulators act without adequate public framework", *o.c.*, p. 291.

193 J. McNamee, "The slide from 'self-regulation' to corporate censorship", *o.c.*

Moreover, in "pure" self-regulation the State has no role to play.[194] Yet, the European Commission has advocated the use of self-regulation as the most appropriate form of regulating the Internet and mobile technologies.[195] The main reason is that self-regulation offers the flexibility necessary in areas where technological developments occur constantly.[196] For example, this approach can be found in the Audiovisual Media Services Directive (Article 4(7)) and in the E-Commerce Directive (Article 16).[197] The latter specifically invites Member States and the Commission to encourage the drawing up of codes of conduct at Community level, by trade, professional and consumer associations or organisations, designed to contribute to the proper implementation of Articles 5 to 15.

Some authors argue, however, that many of the so-called self-regulatory mechanisms, similar to the "voluntary agreements", are not self-driven at all. Rather, they should be called "devolved law enforcement", adopted in response to State pressure and unclear legal protections.[198] As a result, private entities are put in a position of '*the police, judge, jury and executioner with regard to alleged infringements of either the law or of their own terms and conditions which may be stricter than law*'.[199]

REGULATING SPEECH THROUGH TERMS AND CONDITIONS – On the Internet, accessibility of content is to a large extent dependent on the technical service providers – the Internet intermediaries. The content policing activities of the service providers result from two, closely related, phenomena: 1) the policing role is indirectly bestowed upon them by the States through the introduction of liability exemptions; 2) certain limitations are introduced by service providers according to their business models (e.g., topical groups or content appropriate to certain age groups – for example 'no nudity'). It is, after all, reasonable that a service provider creates an environment that he deems appropriate for its service and specifies the rules to be followed by the users. The regulation of speech through terms and conditions is not, however, without any risk. Specifically, the risk is that the internal rules on speech will become the main point of reference for enforcing the limitations and will slowly become a generally applied standard.

---

194 Hans-Bredow Institut, Regulated Self-Regulation as a Form of Modern Government: Study commissioned by the German Federal Commissioner for Cultural and Media Affairs (Interim Report, October 2001), p. 3. See also Mandelkern Group on Better Regulation Final Report, 13 November 2001, p. 83, where self-regulation is defined as 'control of activities by the private parties concerned without the direct involvement of public authorities'.

195 C. Angelopoulos et al., Study of fundamental rights limitations for online enforcement through self-regulation, *o.c.*, p. 1.

196 *Ibid.*

197 Directive 2010/13/EU of the European Parliament and of the Council of 10 March 2010 on the coordination of certain provisions laid down by law, regulation or administrative action in Member States concerning the provision of audiovisual media services (Audiovisual Media Services Directive), OJ L 95/1 2010.

198 See J. McNamee, "The slide from 'self-regulation' to corporate censorship", *o.c.*

199 *Ibid.*, p. 4.

Although the question of limitations of freedom of expression through terms and conditions of private service providers is undeniably linked with the research topic of this book, it will not be addressed further in detail. Similarly, privatized law enforcement mechanisms, such as voluntary agreements (whether truly voluntary or not), and self-regulatory collaborative mechanisms (pure or not) provide effective means of control of online communication and expression. As such, they are occasionally mentioned in this book. They are not, however, the primary topic of this book. The focus of this book concerns the interference with online freedom of expression that can be attributed to the State's indirect responsibilization of service providers through liability exemption regimes and State-provided notice and action mechanisms. Specifically, it seeks to determine whether the situation in which the State encourages interference with freedom of expression by private entities, is compatible with the relevant human rights law instruments.

3. REGULATORY RESPONSE

EARLY COMPROMISE – Since the emergence of the Internet industry, the liability of Internet intermediaries has been considered a problematic issue. Providers of intermediary services, such as access providers and hosts, quickly became aware of the potentially high risks in content liability cases.[200] Their main areas of concern included a) the potential negative consequences of liability on growth and innovation; b) their lack of effective legal or actual control over the content; as well as c) the inequity of imposing liability upon a mere intermediary.[201] In the light of the emerging case law and a lack of harmonisation, the young Internet industry launched a plea for immunity for third party's content.[202] In response, policy makers around the world developed limited liability regimes. These regimes generally consisted of two basic principles: a) lack of liability of intermediaries for third-party content provided they do not modify that content and are not aware of its illegal character; and b) no general obligation to monitor content.[203] Such immunity was meant to stimulate growth and innovation of the newly born technology and provide positive incentives for further development.[204]

This regime then gradually made its way into regulatory instruments at both the national and regional level. This regime could first be spotted in the US in the Section 230 CDA and soon after in the DMCA, addressing violations of intellectual property rights. The latter instrument introduced an additional

200 OECD, The Role of Internet Intermediaries In Advancing Public Policy Objectives, Forging partnerships for advancing public policy objectives for the Internet economy, *o.c.*, p. 11.
201 *Ibid.*, p. 6.
202 *Ibid.*, p. 11.
203 *Ibid.*, p. 6.
204 *Ibid.*, p. 11.

immunity condition, which requires intermediaries to act expeditiously to remove illegal content upon notification ("notice and take down"). In the European Union, the regime was incorporated in the E-Commerce Directive 2000/31, which was later implemented in all EU Member States. The Directive, however, did not explicitly provide a notice and take down mechanism but merely implied it through the conditions for liability exemption.

NOTICE AND ACTION – Despite considerable differences in the details, almost all schemes for the removal of undesirable content from the Internet are described as a notice and take down (NTD) regime.[205] A more appropriate term is 'notice and action' (N&A), which covers a variety of mechanisms designed to eliminate illegal or infringing content from the Internet upon request of the rights holder. Notice and action is a broad term that comprises several mechanisms with different types of responses to illegal content. They are all, however, initiated by a notice (from the rights holder, third party, organization, etc.). According to the European Commission,

> 'The notice and action procedures are those followed by the intermediary internet providers for the purpose of combating illegal content upon receipt of notification. The intermediary may, for example, take down illegal content, block it, or request that it be voluntarily taken down by the persons who posted it online'.[206]

A broader range of actions against content can be taken providing a possibility for a variety of responses such as the notice and take down (NTD), notice and stay down (NSD), or notice and notice (NN).

NOTICE AND ACTION AND THE RIGHT TO FREEDOM OF EXPRESSION – Notice and action provides rights holders with an opportunity to call upon an intermediary directly to remedy a wrongdoing they believe they have been subject to. Remedying action can take the form of removal or blocking of access to the content in question, although specific steps of procedures may vary.[207] Notice and action is based on a relatively simple idea of a complaint mechanism that would equip anyone who feels that their rights have been infringed with a tool that does not require investing significant resources or effort. As such, it does provide certain advantages. It takes a practical approach allowing for swift relief, far quicker than the relief typically provided by the judiciary. In the context of online expression, where information spreads in a flash, the benefits

---

205 See T. Moore and R. Clayton, "The Impact of Incentives on Notice and Takedown", Proc. of Seventh Workshop on the Economics of Information Security (WEIS 2008). 22 June 2008, www.cl.cam.ac.uk/~rncl/takedown.pdf.

206 Commission Communication, A coherent framework for building trust in the Digital Single Market for e-commerce and online services, *o.c.*, p. 13, ft. 49.

207 See more in Part III Chapter 2.

of a swift reaction are clear. By creating such a possibility, States provided an efficient, direct and accessible form of redress mechanism.[208] For the reasons of practicality and efficiency, involvement of intermediaries in content regulation seems inevitable. As pointed out by Thompson, involving intermediaries in making autonomous decisions as to '*whether or not to take content down is, in fact, something that cannot practicably be forestalled, on pain of completely undermining the way the Internet operates*'.[209]

Notice and action mechanisms, however, put intermediaries in a position where they have to decide on issues that do not fall within their competences. First, they have to assess whether the complaint is credible and then, make a decision about the infringing character of the content. Decisions regarding specific complaints have a direct effect on the right to freedom of expression and the right to effective remedy as they lead either to removal of content from the Internet (or alternatively a reduction of its visibility) or maintenance of the content online, which denies the rights holder's claim. The mechanism, therefore, creates a situation where intermediaries are essentially required to decide about fundamental human rights. This is obviously problematic because, as private companies, intermediaries are not qualified to replace courts of law in such a relevant task. This approach has been described as an '*inappropriate transfer of juridical authority to the private sector*'.[210]

RISK OF OVER-COMPLIANCE – Moreover, it does not help that refusal to take down content puts the intermediaries at actual risk of being held liable for the third party content. Obviously, the most cautionary approach is to act upon any indication of illegality, without engaging in any sophisticated balancing of rights in conflict. It is not surprising, therefore, that in many cases, investigations of the illicit character of the content and balancing of the rights at stake is minimal (at best) or non-existent.[211] This often leads to preventive over-blocking of entirely legitimate content, or in other words, to "over-compliance" with takedown requests. Conditional liability exemptions for intermediaries with notice and action mechanisms create an incentive to take down material that is not in any way unlawful.

---

208 See also J. Riordan, *The Liability of Internet Intermediaries*, *o.c.*, p. 64.

209 M. Thompson, "Beyond Gatekeeping: The Normative Responsibility of Internet Intermediaries", *Vanderbilt Journal of Entertainment & Technology Law*, Vol. 18, No. 4, 2016, University of Hong Kong Faculty of Law Research Paper No. 2015/045, p. 793.

210 European Commission, Summary of the results of the Public Consultation on the future of electronic commerce in the Internal Market and the implementation of the Directive on electronic commerce (2000/31/EC) http://ec.europa.eu/internal_market/consultations/docs/2010/ecommerce/summary_report_en.pdf, p. 12.

211 See discussion in C. Ahlert, C. Marsden and C. Yung, How Liberty Disappeared from Cyberspace: the Mystery Shopper Tests Internet Content Self-Regulation, *o.c.*

4. GATEKEEPING AS INDIRECT INTERFERENCE

NEW CHALLENGES – Before the advent of the Internet, distribution of content on a large scale was dependent on traditional publishing and broadcasting mechanisms. Under these mechanisms, material to be published goes through a process of editorial control, which implies that such material is subject to scrutiny before being made available to the public. Such mechanisms were missing in the online environment, which raised concerns about the unrestricted availability of harmful, infringing or illegal content. To address the problem, States co-opted Internet intermediaries to discreetly regulate the behaviour of their users through a variety of technical measures. In order to enlist the intermediaries to police the Internet, States came up with a particularly convincing argument in the form of conditional liability exemptions for the content of their users. The method is subtle as it formally does not require the intermediaries to do anything, but offers a benefit of immunity if they follow. Such indirect responsibilization of the intermediaries allowed States to maintain some level of control without attracting too much attention and having to confront claims of States' interference with the online flow of information.

INCREASING RESPONSIBILIZATION – The trend is constantly on the rise.[212] States continue to delegate investigative, monitoring, policing, judging and sanctioning powers to the intermediaries.[213] It can be traced in numerous attempts in the EU to responsibilize online platforms for regulating content. For example, it is apparent in the Code of Conduct on Countering Illegal Hate Speech Online announced by the Commission in May 2016.[214] The initiative, launched in cooperation with a select number of IT companies, urges the intermediaries to '*take the lead*' on countering the spread of illegal hate speech online.[215] The delegation of enforcement activities from State to private companies seems even bolder than the limited liability regime foreseen in the E-Commerce Directive. Similar concerns can be formulated in relation to the Commission's proposals for

212 See P. Van Eecke, B. Ooms, "ISP liability and the e-commerce directive: a growing trend toward greater responsibility for ISPs", *Journal of Internet Law*, Vol. 11, Issue 3, 2007.

213 J. McNamee, "The slide from "self-regulation" to corporate censorship", *o.c.*, p. 7.

214 The Code of Conduct on Countering Illegal Hate Speech Online, http://ec.europa.eu/justice/fundamental-rights/files/hate_speech_code_of_conduct_en.pdf.

215 See more in EDRi, Guide to the Code of Conduct on Hate Speech, 3 June 2016, https://edri.org/guide-code-conduct-hate-speech/; Article 19, EU: European Commission's Code of conduct for Countering Illegal Hate Speech Online and the Framework Decision – legal analysis, June 2016, https://www.article19.org/data/files/medialibrary/38430/EU-Code-of-conduct-analysis-FINAL.pdf; A. Kuczerawy, The Code of Conduct on Online Hate Speech: an example of state interference by proxy? 20 July 2016, https://www.law.kuleuven.be/citip/blog/the-code-of-conduct-on-online-hate-speech-an-example-of-state-interference-by-proxy/.

a new directive on copyright in the Digital Single Market[216] and an amendment to the AVMS Directive.[217] The former requires the service providers to monitor their platforms for copyright-infringing content[218], while the latter requires video-sharing and possibly social media platforms to restrict access to harmful – but not necessarily illegal – content (to protect minors) as well as to content that incites violence or hatred (to protect all citizens).[219] None of these initiatives, however, contain clear safeguards to ensure effective protection to the right to freedom of expression.[220] McNamee calls this trend of abdicating responsibility by States for the achievement of public policy objectives as taking the "easy option".[221] It may be indeed seen as passing the hot potato instead of approaching it responsibly in a way that conforms to the principles of the rule of law.

RISKS TO FUNDAMENTAL RIGHTS – The involvement of intermediaries in curtailing the free flow of information among Internet users leads to numerous concerns, in particular in relation to the right to freedom of expression. Potential risks include undue restrictions to speech through a form of private or corporate censorship[222], possibly creating a "chilling effect" on the right to freedom of expression.[223] Intermediaries are simply more cautious when they act on any indication of illegality, whether true or not. This is because they are placed under such a strong fear of liability claims that they impose upon themselves measures

216 Proposal for a Directive of the European Parliament and of the Council on copyright in the Digital Single Market, Brussels, 14 September 2016, COM(2016) 593 final – 2016/0280 (COD), http://eur-lex.europa.eu/legalcontent/EN/TXT/?uri=CELEX:52016PC0593.

217 Proposal for a Directive amending Directive 2010/13/EU on the coordination of certain provisions laid down by law, regulation or administrative action in Member States concerning the provision of audiovisual media services in view of changing market realities, Brussels, 25 May 2016, COM/2016/0287 final – 2016/0151 (COD), http://eur-lex.europa.eu/legal-content/EN/TXT/?qid=1464618463840&uri=COM:2016:287:FIN.

218 See more in S. Stalla-Bourdillon et al., Open Letter to the European Commission – On the Importance of Preserving the Consistency and Integrity of the EU Acquis Relating to Content Monitoring within the Information Society, 19 October 2016, https://papers.ssrn.com/sol3/papers.cfm?abstract_id=2850483; and S. Stalla-Bourdillon et al., A Brief Exegesis of the Proposed Copyright Directive, 30 November 2016, https://papers.ssrn.com/sol3/papers.cfm?abstract_id=2875296.

219 See more in M. Fernández Pérez, VMSD: European Parliament set to vote whether it's allowed to vote, 17 May 2017, https://edri.org/avmsd-european-parliament-set-to-vote-whether-its-allowed-to-vote/.

220 See M. Schaake et al., Open letter sent to Commissioner Ansip – MEPs want notice and action directive, 10 May 2107, https://marietjeschaake.eu/en/meps-want-notice-and-action-directive.

221 J. McNamee, "The slide from 'self-regulation' to corporate censorship", *o.c.*, p. 6.

222 R. J. Barceló, "On-line intermediary liability issues: comparing EU and US legal frameworks", *o.c.*, p. 111; OSCE and Reporters Sans Frontiers, Joint declaration on guaranteeing media freedom on the Internet, *o.c.*

223 See for examples of concerns expressed in: Council of Europe, Declaration on freedom of communications on the Internet, *o.c.*; Council of Europe, Human rights guidelines for Internet Service Providers, *o.c.*, paras 16 and 24; see also T. Verbiest, Spindler G., et al., Study on the liability of Internet Intermediaries, *o.c.*, p.15; OECD, The Economic and Social Role of Internet Intermediaries, *o.c.*, p. 9–14.

'appropriate for making them immune to any subsequent accusation but is of a kind that threatens the freedom of expression of Internet users'.[224] The actions of private companies result in legal content being effectively banned, which is a dangerous situation for democracy.[225] The democratising potential of the Internet, therefore, is being *'constrained by measures imposed in an attempt to control the perceived dangers posed by the medium'.*[226]

INDIRECT INTERFERENCE – Delegation of enforcement measures to private entities can give rise to various legal issues that affect the fundamental rights of Internet users. The indirect responsibilization of intermediaries creates a situation where legislation provides an incentive and allows private entities to interfere with the freedom of expression of the Internet users. Delegating powers to private entities to make decisions regarding fundamental human rights, such as freedom of expression, may be accepted as a method to provide a quick, effective and accessible redress mechanism for online infringements. It should come equipped, however, with certain protective measures in the form of substantive and procedural safeguards developed by States. As observed by Frydman and Rorive already in 2002, '*it is not enough to get the ISPs to do the job of the police, it is also necessary to give them guidelines defining the limits of the right to free speech and offering procedural guarantees against censorship*'.[227] Such safeguards are currently missing in the EU.[228] The legislature therefore is indirectly contributing to the interference by private individuals – a type of "State interference by proxy".[229] This problem was spotted earlier. In 2014, for example, a report by Douwe Korff commissioned by the CoE Commissioner for Human Rights stated that:

> 'Member states should stop relying on private companies that control the Internet and the wider digital environment to impose restrictions that are in violation of the state's human rights obligations'.[230]

---

224 E. Montero and Q. Van Enis, "Enabling freedom of expression in light of filtering measures imposed on Internet intermediaries: Squaring the circle", *o.c.*, p. 34.

225 J. McNamee, "The slide from 'self-regulation' to corporate censorship", *o.c.*, p. 33. See also S. F. Kreimer, "Censorship by Proxy: The First Amendment, Internet Intermediaries, and the Problem of the Weakest Link", *o.c.*, p. 23.

226 L. Cooke, "Controlling the Net: European approaches to content and access regulation", *Journal of Information Science*, Vol. 33 Issue 3, 2007, pp. 360–376, Abstract.

227 B. Frydman, I. Rorive, "Regulating Internet Content through Intermediaries in Europe and the USA", *o.c.*, p. 59.

228 See also C. Angelopoulos et al., Study of fundamental rights limitations for online enforcement through self-regulation, *o.c.*, p. 2.

229 A. Kuczerawy, "The Power of Positive Thinking: Intermediary Liability and the Effective Enjoyment of the Right to Freedom of Expression", *JIPITEC* Vol. 8 2017, p. 226, para. 7.

230 D. Korff, The rule of law on the Internet and in the wider digital world, Issue paper published by the Commissioner for Human Rights, Strasbourg, 2014, Recommendation 14, p. 23.

Nevertheless, attempts to enlist private intermediaries to regulate online speech continue. In late 2017, a group of MEP's wrote a letter to the European Commission expressing concerns about the path the EC chose in an attempt to address the problem of illegal content online. In the letter, the MEP's reminded the Commissioners that:

> 'a clear focus on preserving fundamental rights, enhancing transparency, and limiting the privatization of content removal decisions, is essential to create a legal framework that does not lend itself to abuse'.[231]

According to human rights instruments, such as the European Convention on the protection of Human Rights and Fundamental Freedoms (ECHR)[232] and the Charter of Fundamental Rights of the EU (CFEU)[233], States should not interfere with the exercise of protected rights (unless specific requirements are met). The States, however, should also protect fundamental human rights from interferences by others, perhaps even more so if such interference is encouraged by the States themselves.

231 M. Schaake, et al., Letter to the commission on notice and action procedures, 5 December 2017, https://www.politico.eu/wp-content/uploads/2017/12/Notice-and-action-letter-MEPs-05122017.pdf.

232 Council of Europe, Convention for the Protection of Human Rights and Fundamental Freedoms (ECHR), *o.c.*

233 Charter of Fundamental Rights of the European Union (CFEU), *o.c.*

CHAPTER 3

FREEDOM OF EXPRESSION IN THE EU AND THE US

A FUNDAMENTAL HUMAN RIGHT – Freedom of expression is a fundamental human right and '*one of the basic conditions for its progress and for the development of every man*'.[234] The right is expressed in a number of international, regional and national legislative texts. This book focuses on the compatibility of the notice and action mechanisms with European fundamental rights instruments. For this reason, this chapter discusses the two most relevant documents, namely, the European Convention of Human Rights (ECHR) and the Charter of Fundamental Rights of the EU (CFEU). Additionally, the chapter presents the perspective from the US as a country with a different approach to the right to freedom of expression – enshrined in the First Amendment to the Constitution of the USA – and the most established intermediary liability regime.

1. THE EUROPEAN CONVENTION ON HUMAN RIGHTS

HEART OF THE FUNDAMENTAL RIGHTS PROTECTION – The ECHR constitutes the heart of the protection of human rights in Europe.[235] The Convention is an instrument of the Council of Europe. It was adopted in 1950 and ratified by 47 countries, including all the members of the European Union. The ECHR has been incorporated into most of these countries national legislations and is binding as part of their legal systems.[236] Enforcement of the Convention is overseen by the European Court of Human Rights (ECtHR). The Convention provides everyone with the possibility to complain about an infringement of their rights by their State and receive a binding judgement. When the ECtHR delivers a judgment finding a violation, the file is transmitted

---

234 ECtHR, *Perna v. Italy*, 06 May 2003, para. 39.

235 J. van Hoboken, *Search Engine Freedom: On the Implications of the Right to Freedom of Expression for the Legal Governance of Web Search Engines*, *o.c.*, p. 60.

236 M. Macovei, *Freedom of expression – A guide to the implementation of Article 10 of the European Convention of Human Rights*, Human rights handbooks, No. 2, Strasbourg, Council of Europe, 2004, p. 5.

to the Committee of Ministers of the Council of Europe, which confers with the country concerned to decide how the judgment should be executed.[237]

SCOPE OF APPLICATION – The ECHR requires States to secure the rights and freedoms of '*everyone within their jurisdiction*'.[238] This includes the right to freedom of expression, which is provided in Article 10 ECHR. According to the provision,

> Everyone has the right to freedom of expression. This right shall include freedom to hold opinions and to receive and impart information and ideas without interference by public authority and regardless of frontiers. This article shall not prevent States from requiring the licensing of broadcasting, television or cinema enterprises.[239]

The right to freedom of expression under the ECHR has a broad scope of application. It applies to the rights of everyone, which means it is not limited to citizens, or natural persons only. Companies have benefited from Article 10 the same way as people have.[240] The right extends to any expression regardless of its content, its form (any word, picture, image or action to express an idea, etc.)[241], its speaker, or the type of medium used.[242] Information of a commercial nature is also protected although the Court has granted governments a wider margin of appreciation to restrict commercial speech as opposed to other forms of expression (see more *infra*). The right protects not only information and ideas that are favourably received or deemed inoffensive, but also those that offend, shock or disturb the State or any sector of the population.[243] As pointed out by the Court, '*such are the demands of that pluralism, tolerance and broadmindedness without which there is no democratic society*'.[244]

However, there exists one significant exception to this rule designed to prevent misuse or abuse of the Convention by those whose intentions are contrary to the letter and spirit of the instrument.[245] The exception applies,

---

237 European Court of Human Rights: The ECHR in 50 questions, 2014, https://www.echr.coe.int/Documents/50Questions_ENG.pdf, Question 40, p. 10. See more on the execution of judgments of the ECtHR in: Supervision of execution of judgments of the European Court of Human Rights, https://www.coe.int/en/web/cm/execution-judgments.

238 Article 1 ECHR.

239 Article 10 ECHR.

240 See ECtHR, *Autronic AG v. Switzerland*, 22 May 1990. L. Woods, "Freedom of expression in the European Union", *European Public Law*, Vol. 12, Issue 3, September 2006, p. 378.

241 M. Macovei, *Freedom of expression – A guide to the implementation of Article 10 of the European Convention of Human Rights, o.c.*, p. 15.

242 *Ibid.*, p. 7.

243 ECtHR, *Handyside v. the United Kingdom*, 7 December 1976, para. 49; see also ECtHR, *Perna v. Italy, o.c.*, para. 39.

244 ECtHR, *Handyside v. the United Kingdom, o.c.*, para. 49.

245 T. McGonagle, "The Council of Europe against online hate speech: Conundrums and challenges, Expert paper", doc.no. MCM 2013(005), the Council of Europe Conference of Ministers responsible for Media and Information Society, 'Freedom of Expression

for example, to hate speech, including xenophobic or anti-Semitic speech, or dissemination of racism and Nazi ideology.[246] The justification for this exception is provided in Article 17 ECHR, which states that

> 'Nothing in this Convention may be interpreted as implying for any State, group or person any right to engage in any activity or perform any act aimed at the destruction of any of the rights and freedoms set forth herein or at their limitation to a greater extent than is provided for in the Convention'.

The rationale for the provision is the 'theory of the paradox of tolerance': 'an absolute tolerance may lead to the tolerance of the ideas promoting intolerance, and the latter could then destroy the tolerance'.[247]

INTERFERENCE WITH THE RIGHT – The Convention is addressed to the States signatories to the Convention. This means that the States cannot interfere with the exercise of the right to freedom of expression of anyone. Apart from the prohibition to interfere (negative dimension), the Convention possesses a positive dimension, meaning that the States should also protect the right from interference by others.[248]

Moreover, the right to freedom of expression is not absolute. Restrictions could take the form of '*formalities, conditions, restrictions or penalties*' (Article 10 para. 2 ECHR), and may be allowed if they comply with three conditions.[249] Specifically, they must be (1) prescribed by law, (2) introduced for protection of one of the listed legitimate aims[250], and (3) necessary in a democratic society.[251]

---

and Democracy in the Digital Age: Opportunities, Rights, Responsibilities', Belgrade, 7–8 November 2013, p. 9.

246 ECtHR, *Garaudy v. France*, 24 June 2003: '*Accordingly, the Court considers that, in accordance with Article 17 of the Convention, the applicant cannot rely on the provisions of Article 10 of the Convention regarding his conviction for denying crimes against humanity*"; ECtHR, *Gündüz v. Turkey*, 04 December 2003: '*That being so, as a matter of principle it may be considered necessary in certain democratic societies to sanction or even prevent all forms of expression which spread, incite, promote or justify hatred based on intolerance (including religious intolerance), provided that any 'formalities', 'conditions', 'restrictions' or 'penalties' imposed are proportionate to the legitimate aim pursued*; European Commission of Human Rights, *Kühnen v. Germany*, 12 May 1988. See also ECtHR, *Perinçek v. Switzerland*, 15 October 2015. See M. Macovei, *Freedom of expression – A guide to the implementation of Article 10 of the European Convention of Human Rights*, *o.c.*, p. 7. See more in T. McGonagle, The Council of Europe against online hate speech: Conundrums and challenges, *o.c.*, p. 9.

247 M. Macovei, *Freedom of expression – A guide to the implementation of Article 10 of the European Convention of Human Rights*, *o.c.*, p. 7.

248 See ECtHR, *Özgür Gündem v. Turkey*, 16 March 2000, para. 42–43. See more in Part II Chapter 3.

249 M. Macovei, *Freedom of expression – A guide to the implementation of Article 10 of the European Convention of Human Rights*, *o.c.*,, p. 25.

250 Article 10 para. 2 ECHR: such as national security, territorial integrity or public safety, for the prevention of disorder or crime, for the protection of health or morals, for the protection of the reputation or the rights of others, for preventing the disclosure of information received in confidence, or maintaining the authority and impartiality of the judiciary.

251 See more in Part II Chapter 2.

RIGHT TO FREEDOM OF EXPRESSION AND THE INTERNET – Article 10 covers all means of dissemination of information, as any restriction imposed on the means inevitably interferes with the right to receive and impart information.[252] Consequently, the Internet and any other existing and future communication technology fall within the scope of Article 10 ECHR.[253] The Council of Europe has underlined out on multiple occasions the utmost importance of respecting freedom of expression (and all other rights enshrined in the ECHR) in the information age, regardless of new technological developments.[254] Governments have been called upon to ensure that '*freedom of expression and information is fully respected with regard to Internet content with any restrictions not going beyond what is necessary in a democratic society*'.[255]

THE EU AND THE COE – In theory, the legal orders of the two international organizations – the Council of Europe and the European Union – are completely distinct from one another. All Member States of the European Union, however, are also signatories to the ECHR. To be eligible for membership of the EU, candidates must be members of the Council of Europe and ratify the Convention.[256] This means that all Member States of the EU are bound by the Convention. The EU itself is not (yet) a party to the ECHR.[257] The ECHR and its judicial mechanism, therefore, do not formally apply to EU acts. This divergence shall be rectified when the EU, as an organization, will become a party to the Convention, as foreseen in Article 6.2 TEU: *the Union shall accede to the European Convention for the Protection of Human Rights and Fundamental*

252 ECtHR, *Autronic AG v. Switzerland*, 22 May 1990, para. 47; ECtHR, *Murphy v. Ireland*, 10 July 2003, para. 61.

253 E. Lievens, *Protecting Children in the Digital Era – the Use of Alternative Regulatory Instruments*, *o.c.* p. 310. See more in E. Barendt, *Freedom of speech*, Oxford University Press, 2005, 451–474.

254 Council of Europe, Democracy, human rights and the rule of law in the Information Society, Contribution by the Council of Europe to the 2nd Preparatory Committee for the World Summit on the Information Society, 07 December 2002, www.coe.int/t/e/integrated_projects/democracy/02_activities/04_w.s.i.s/90IP1(2002)27.asp; Council of Europe, Declaration on freedom of communication on the Internet, *o.c.*; Council of Europe (Standing Committee on Transfrontier TV), Statement (2002)1 on human dignity and the fundamental rights of others, 12–13 September 2002, www.coe.int/t/dghl/standardsetting/media/T-TT/T-TT(2006)012rev_en.asp#TopOfPage; Council of Europe (Committee of Ministers), Recommendation CM/Rec(2007)11 on promoting freedom of expression and information in the new information and communications environment, 26 October 2007.

255 Council of Europe, Democracy, human rights and the rule of law in the Information Society, *o.c.*

256 J. van Hoboken, *Search Engine Freedom: On the Implications of the Right to Freedom of Expression for the Legal Governance of Web Search Engines*, *o.c.*, p. 61.

257 See more in G.-B. Spirchez, "Current Aspects of the European Union Accession to the European Convention of Human Rights", *Euromentor*, Vol. 6 Issue 2, Jun 2015, p. 123–129.

Freedoms.[258] The accession is taking longer than anticipated and is currently uncertain.[259]

2. THE CHARTER OF FUNDAMENTAL RIGHTS OF THE EUROPEAN UNION

A FUNDAMENTAL VALUE IN THE EU – In the EU, the right to freedom of expression, information and press is protected by Article 11 of the Charter of Fundamental Rights of the European Union (CFEU).[260] The article also covers media pluralism (Article 11.2 CFEU). Freedom of expression and information, as well as the freedom of the press, are considered essential for democracy, which is a fundamental value at the core of the European Union (Article 2 Treaty on European Union (TEU)).[261] According to Article 11 CFEU,

> 'Everyone has the right to freedom of expression. This right shall include freedom to hold opinions and to receive and impart information and ideas without interference by public authority and regardless of frontiers'.[262]

SCOPE OF APPLICATION – Article 11 CFEU addresses freedom of expression generally without specifying particular forms or categories of expression. Similarly as with the ECHR, freedom of expression applies to the traditional printed press and electronic media (radio and television), as well as the new media (e.g. publishing on Internet).

As clarified by Article 52.3 of the Charter, the meaning and scope of the right to freedom of expression is the same as those guaranteed by the ECHR. This means that the Charter should be interpreted in accordance with the Convention

---

258 Treaty on European Union, Consolidated Version, Official Journal of the European Union C 326/15, 26 October 2012, http://eur-lex.europa.eu/legal-content/EN/TXT/PDF/?uri=CELEX:12012M/TXT&from=en

259 In 2014 the CJEU delivered an opinion in which it rejected the draft agreement on the accession of the European Union to the ECHR due the incompatibility with EU law. CJEU, Opinion 2/13, 18 December 2014. See also G. Gotev, Court of Justice rejects draft agreement of EU accession to ECHR, 14 January 2015, https://www.euractiv.com/section/justice-home-affairs/news/court-of-justice-rejects-draft-agreement-of-eu-accession-to-echr/; S. Peers, The CJEU and the EU's accession to the ECHR: a clear and present danger to human rights protection, 18 December 2014, http://eulawanalysis.blogspot.be/2014/12/the-cjeu-and-eus-accession-to-echr.html; J. Odermatt, "A Giant Step Backwards? Opinion 2/13 on the EU's Accession to the European Convention on Human Rights", Leuven Centre for Global Governance Studies, Working Paper No. 150 – February 2015.

260 Charter of Fundamental Rights of the European Union (CFEU), *o.c.*

261 European Parliament, Press Freedom in the EU: Legal Framework and Challenges, Briefing, April 2015, www.europarl.europa.eu/EPRS/EPRS-Briefing-554214-Press-freedom-in-the-EU-FINAL.pdf.

262 Article 11 CFEU.

and jurisprudence of the ECtHR.[263] The provision, however, does not prevent Union law from providing more extensive protection.[264] The Convention is considered '*a lowest common denominator as to the substance of fundamental rights and that there is nothing to preclude the European Union, like the parties to the Convention, from providing itself with a higher level of Protection*'.[265] Moreover, Article 53 aims to maintain the level of protection currently afforded by Union law, national law and international law, with a clear emphasis on the level of protection granted in the ECHR.[266]

LIMITATIONS TO THE RIGHT – Under the Charter, limitations on the right to freedom of expression are possible if they comply with specific conditions provided in Article 52.1 CFEU. To be allowed, any limitation must be (1) provided by law, (2) subject to the principle of proportionality and (3) necessary and genuinely meet objectives of general interest recognised by the Union (see more *infra*).[267] Following the provision of Article 52.3 levelling the protection in the CFEU with that in the ECHR, the limitations which may be imposed may not exceed those provided by Article 10(2) of the Convention, without prejudice to any restrictions which Community competition law may impose on Member States' rights to introduce the licensing arrangements referred to in Article 10(1) of the ECHR.[268]

3. THE FIRST AMENDMENT TO THE US CONSTITUTION

BILL OF RIGHTS – The US Constitution attributes high value to expressive liberties.[269] The most important freedom of expression provision in the United States is provided in the First Amendment of the United States Bill of Rights.[270] The provision states that,

> 'Congress shall make no law [...] abridging the freedom of speech, or of the press; or the right of the people peaceably to assemble, and to petition the government for a redress of grievances'.

---

263 See L. Woods, "Freedom of expression in the European Union", *o.c.*, p. 373 and further.
264 Article 52.3 CFEU.
265 CJEU, Case C-340/00P *Commission* v. *Cwic*, Opinion of the Advocate-General, para. 29.
266 Praesidium of the Convention, Explanations relating to the Charter of Fundamental Rights, (2007/C 303/02) 14 December 2007. Explanation on Article 53.
267 Article 52.1 CFEU.
268 EU Network of Independent Experts on Fundamental Rights, Commentary of the Charter of Fundamental Rights of the European Union, June 2006, p. 122.
269 See in general F. Schauer, "The Exceptional First Amendment", KSG Working Paper No. RWP05-021, February 2005.
270 United States Constitution, Bill of Rights, Adopted 1791.

The Bill of Rights is a part of the United States Constitution and is therefore, subject to judicial review by the United States Supreme Court. First Amendment case law is famous for its complexity and inconsistencies.[271] A detailed discussion of the US constitutional law and constitutional review of state and federal laws is beyond the scope of this book. It is important, however, to provide a background to enable further discussion of the US intermediary liability legislation, which is significant to properly address the research question of this book.

LIMITATIONS AND LEVEL OF SCRUTINY – The First Amendment not only protects the freedom of speech or of the press, but also the freedom to receive and distribute information and ideas, similar to Article 10 ECHR.[272] The First Amendment, however, lacks a provision legitimizing interferences such as the one found in Article 10 of the Convention.[273] This has made the First Amendment a powerful tool for speech protection but resulted in intricate judicial review.[274] The Supreme Court has developed a complex set of criteria determining the scope of the right to free speech and conditions under which different types of government interference can be accepted as legitimate.[275] Most notably, the Court distinguished, through its case law, between protected and unprotected speech as well as between content-based and content-neutral (time place and manner) restrictions on speech.[276]

The distinction between protected and unprotected speech, referred to as two-level theory of speech, was adopted by the Supreme Court in *Chaplinsky*.[277] In this judgment, involving the constitutionality of a prosecution of offensive language against a police officer, the Supreme Court clarified that some categories of expression and information are not protected and can be the legitimate subject of government interference.[278] Specifically, the Court stated that,

---

271 J. van Hoboken, *Search Engine Freedom: On the Implications of the Right to Freedom of Expression for the Legal Governance of Web Search Engines*, *o.c.*, p. 65.

272 *Griswold v. Connecticut*, 381 U.S. 479 (1965).

273 See F. Schauer, "Freedom of Expression Adjudication in Europe and America: A Case Study in Comparative Constitutional Architecture", KSG Working Paper No. RWP05-019, February 2005, p. 4–5.

274 J. van Hoboken, *Search Engine Freedom: On the Implications of the Right to Freedom of Expression for the Legal Governance of Web Search Engines*, *o.c.*, p. 65.

275 See more in E. Chemerinsky, "The First Amendment: When the Government Must Make Content-Based Choices", *Cleveland State Law Review*, Vol. 42 1994, pp. 199–214, p. 201–207.

276 See J. E. Nowak, R. D. Rotunda, *Principles of Constitutional Law*, 4th Edition, Concise Hornbooks, 2010, p. 613–624. See also R. G. Wright, "Content-Neutral and Content-Based Regulations of Speech: A Distinction That is No Longer Worth the Fuss", *Florida Law Review*, Vol. 67, 2016, p. 2081, arguing that the binary distinction between content-neutral and content-based speech regulations has become less clear and practical.

277 *Chaplinsky v. New Hampshire*, 315 U.S. 568, 571 (1942).

278 See J. E. Nowak, R. D. Rotunda, Principles of Constitutional Law, *o.c.*, p. 712.

> 'There are certain well-defined and narrowly limited classes of speech, the prevention and punishment of which has never been thought to raise any Constitutional problem. These include the lewd and obscene, the profane, the libelous, and the insulting or 'fighting' words – those which by their very utterance inflict injury or tend to incite an immediate breach of the peace. It has been well observed that such utterances are no essential part of any exposition of ideas, and are of such slight social value as a step to truth that any benefit that may be derived from them is clearly outweighed by the social interest in order and morality'.[279]

The distribution of unprotected material, such as obscenity, is by itself not protected by the First Amendment.[280] Regulations targeting unprotected speech, however, are still scrutinized for their effects on constitutionally protected communications.[281]

Content-neutral restrictions limit communication without regard to the message conveyed, while content-based restrictions limit communication specifically because of the message conveyed.[282] The differentiation between content-neutral (or time place or manner) and content-based restrictions is relevant to establish the level of scrutiny by the Court.[283] Content-based restrictions are subject to strict scrutiny.[284] Specific examples of strict scrutiny include the doctrines relating to overbreadth and vagueness, and the Court's case law relating to prior restraints.[285] A content-based restriction of protected speech can only be legitimate if it is narrowly targeted and if it furthers a compelling state interest that could not be achieved through less restrictive means.[286] Application of this strict standard usually leads to the invalidation of a law.[287] Content-neutral restrictions are submitted to a lower standard of constitutional review (i.e. intermediate scrutiny) than content-based restriction.[288] A content-neutral restriction must further an important governmental interest, unrelated

279 *Chaplinsky v. New Hampshire*, 315 U.S. 568, 571 (1942).

280 *United States v. Reidel*, 402 U.S. 351 (1971).

281 See e.g. *New York Times Co. v. Sullivan, 376 U.S. 254 (1964)*; *Smith v. California*, 361 U.S. 147 (1959).

282 See G. R. Stone, "Content Regulation and the First Amendment", *William & Mary Law Review*, Vol. 25, p. 190.

283 See L. Gielow Jacobs, "Clarifying the Content-Based/Content Neutral and Content/Viewpoint Determinations", *McGeorge Law Review*, Vol. 34, 2003, p. 596.

284 See *Ibid.*, p. 598.

285 J. van Hoboken, *Search Engine Freedom: On the Implications of the Right to Freedom of Expression for the Legal Governance of Web Search Engines, o.c.*, p. 65. See also, G. R. Stone et al., *Constitutional Law*, 5th Edition, Aspen Publishers, 2005, p. 1143.

286 See E. Kagan, "Private Speech, Public Purpose: The Role of Governmental Motive in First Amendment Doctrine", *University of Chicago Law Review*, vol. 63, 1996, p. 444.

287 *Ibid.*.

288 See *Turner Broad. Sys., Inc. v. FCC*, 512 U.S. 622, 642 (1994) ('[R]egulations that are unrelated to the content of speech are subject to an intermediate level of scrutiny ... because in most cases they pose a less substantial risk of excising certain ideas or viewpoints from the public dialogue.').

to the suppression of speech and whose incidental restriction of protected speech is not greater than is necessary to further that interest.[289] This means that any content-based effects should still constitute an important part of the intermediate scrutiny applied to content neutral government action.[290] The review of content-neutral restrictions, therefore, involves a mode of balancing, while the scrutiny of content-based restrictions of protected speech involves a presumption that restrictions are not legitimate.[291]

In the context of intermediary liability, it should be noted that the application of the First Amendment differs for copyright infringement and other unlawful activity.[292] Free speech concerns are considered to be internalized into copyright law itself and copyright law is content neutral, therefore, US courts usually refuse to admit a separate freedom of expression defence in copyright cases.[293] In cases of liability for other illegal content, the Courts need to balance restrictions on free speech and distributor liability with the requirements of the First Amendment.[294]

4. INTERIM CONCLUSION

SIMILARITIES AND DIFFERENCES – The three instruments described in this Chapter provide the fundamental rights framework that constitutes the point of reference for this book. Even though Article 10 ECHR and Article 11 CFEU are contained in international instruments, whereas the First Amendment is part of a national constitution, their role is similar. There are, however, significant differences between their approach to the protection of freedom of expression.

Both in the ECHR and the CFEU the right to freedom of expression is not absolute. Restrictions may be allowed if they comply with the specified conditions. Moreover, in both instruments there is no hierarchy of rights, which means balancing exercise is required in case of a conflict between various protected rights. The First Amendment does not contain a provision legitimizing interferences. This has made the First Amendment a powerful tool for speech protection which often takes precedence over other rights. A set of criteria and conditions for legitimate interference exists, but has been developed by the Supreme Court. Another difference is that the ECHR possesses a negative

---

289 See J. E. Nowak, R. D. Rotunda, *Principles of Constitutional Law*, *o.c.*, p. 616–620.

290 See L. Gielow Jacobs, "Clarifying the Content-Based/Content Neutral and Content/Viewpoint Determinations", *o.c.*, p. 626.

291 See J. E. Nowak, R. D. Rotunda, *Principles of Constitutional Law*, *o.c.*, p. 616–620.

292 K.J. Koelman, "Online Intermediary Liability", in P.B. Hugenholtz (ed.), *Copyright and Electronic Commerce. Legal Aspects of Electronic Copyright Management*, Information Law Series -8, Kluwer Law International, 2000, pp. 7–58, pp. 42–44.

293 See *Eldred v. Ashcroft*, 537 U.S. 186 (2003).

294 J. van Hoboken, *Search Engine Freedom: On the Implications of the Right to Freedom of Expression for the Legal Governance of Web Search Engines*, *o.c.*, p. 131.

dimension (prohibition to interfere or obligation to respect), and a positive dimension (obligation to protect).[295] A similar distinction can be made under the CFEU, although here the positive dimension is less obvious.[296] The First Amendment does not have a positive dimension. Restriction of speech imposed by private entities is not considered a violation of the First Amendment rights. These differences have practical implications for the regulation of online content.

295 See more in Part II Chapter 2 and 3.
296 *Ibid.*

CHAPTER 4

INTERNET INTERMEDIARY LIABILITY IN THE EU AND THE US

SHIFT IN FOCUS – The arrival of new technologies made traditional content regulation problematic, unfeasible, and unpractical in the context of the Internet.[297] Removal of technical and geographical boundaries democratized the flow of information but proved challenging for regulators, litigants and the creative industries.[298] Yet the first to decide on issues of intermediary liability were judges, not the legislature.[299] From the late 1990s, when the Internet became popular among the general public, courts across the EU held service providers liable for their users' information.[300] The first wave of lawsuits ran counter to efforts to popularize and facilitate e-commerce and endangered the development of the Internet and the Web generally.[301] Legislators, however, found it inappropriate to apply the traditional liability criteria to intermediaries' activities considering the volumes of information that they process.[302] The ensuing legal uncertainty led legislatures in the U.S. and Europe to enact specific rules about the legal responsibility of Internet intermediaries.[303]

1. DIRECTIVE 2000/31/EC

ORIGIN AND DEVELOPMENT – In the European Union, Directive 2000/31 regulates the liability of online intermediaries on certain legal aspects of

297 *Ibid.*, p. 127.

298 See Part I Chapter 2.

299 S. Stalla-Bourdillon, "Internet intermediaries as responsible actors? Why it is time to rethink the e-Commerce Directive as well…" in L. Floridi and M. Taddeo, *The Responsibilities of Online Service Providers*, Springer, 2016.

300 P. Van Eecke, "Online Service Providers and Liability: a Plea for a Balanced Approach", *Common Market Law Review*, Vol. 48, Issue 5, 2011, pp. 1455–1502, p. 1455.

301 E.g. in Germany, Felix Somm, the general manager of CompuServe Germany, was prosecuted for facilitating access to violent and child sexual abuse material stored in newsgroups accessible by CompuServe's customers; in Belgium, the Commercial Court of Brussels issued an injunction against hosting provider Skynet for storing illegal MP3 files; in the UK, internet access provider Demon was held liable for defamatory statements uploaded by one of its users. P. Van Eecke, "Online Service Providers and Liability: a Plea for a Balanced Approach', *o.c.*, p. 1455, ft. 1.

302 *Ibid.*, p. 1456.

303 J. van Hoboken, *Search Engine Freedom: On the Implications of the Right to Freedom of Expression for the Legal Governance of Web Search Engines*, *o.c.*, p. 128.

information society services, in particular electronic commerce in the Internal Market (E-Commerce Directive, ECD).[304] The E-Commerce Directive was proposed by the European Commission in 1998, and signed by the European Parliament and the Council of the EU in June 2000. Member States had until January 2002 to implement the Directive into their national legal orders.[305]

As observed in the preamble to the Directive, the development of the information society services within the Community was hindered by a number of legal obstacles that made the exercise of the freedom of establishment and the freedom to provide services less attractive.[306] Moreover, '*these obstacles arise from divergences in legislation and from the legal uncertainty as to which national rules apply to such services*'.[307] The goal of the Directive, therefore, was to create a legal framework to ensure the free movement of information society services between Member States. The Directive aimed to achieve this by realizing two main objectives. In the first instance, it sought to remove certain legal obstacles hampering the development of electronic commerce within the internal market. At the same time, it also aimed at providing legal certainty and ensuring consumer confidence towards electronic commerce. The development of electronic commerce was considered a crucial factor that would stimulate economic growth and investment in innovation by European companies, and which could also enhance the competitiveness of European industry.[308] So far, the Directive succeeded in achieving its objectives only partially.[309] Although steady growth of cross-border activity has been observed in the last few years, more needs to be done in order to achieve the Directive's full potential.[310] According to

304 Directive 2000/31 *o.c.*

305 See more in: First Report on the Application of Directive 2000/31/EC of the European Parliament and of the Council of 8 June 2000 on the Directive on Electronic Commerce, COM(2003) 702 final, Brussels, 21.11.2003.

306 Freedom of establishment (Articles 49 to 55 TFEU) and freedom to provide services (56 to 62 TFEU) are intended to guarantee the mobility of businesses and professionals within the EU. See more at: www.europarl.europa.eu/aboutparliament/en/displayFtu.html?ftuId=FTU_3.1.4.html.

307 Recital (5) to the E-Commerce Directive.

308 Recital (2) to the E-Commerce Directive.

309 Since the introduction of the Directive, e-commerce in the EU has generally grown. However, it is still less advanced than in the United States and the Asia-Pacific region. See more in Commission Communication, A coherent framework for building trust in the Digital Single Market for e-commerce and online services, *o.c.*, p. 6. For the analysis of the remaining obstacles to the development of the e-commerce in the EU see also Commission Staff Working Document Online services, including e-commerce, in the Single Market, Brussels, 11 January 2012 SEC(2011) 1641 final http://ec.europa.eu/internal_market/e-commerce/docs/communication2012/SEC2011_1641_en.pdf; and Summary of the results of the Public Consultation on the future of electronic commerce in the Internal Market and the implementation of the Directive on electronic commerce (2000/31/EC), available at: http://ec.europa.eu/internal_market/consultations/docs/2010/e-commerce/summary_report_en.pdf. See also European Commission, Consumer Conditions Scoreboard, Consumers at home in the single market http://ec.europa.eu/consumers/consumer_evidence/consumer_scoreboards/index_en.htm.

310 Commission Communication, A coherent framework for building trust in the Digital Single Market for e-commerce and online services, *o.c.*, p. 6.

Stalla-Bourdillon, apart from stimulating the growth of the digital single market, two additional rationales can be extracted from the text of the Directive: securing freedom of expression, and encouraging content regulation at the initiative of Internet intermediaries.[311] Understanding the precise implications of each rationale and determining the balance between them is considered one of several difficulties in interpreting and applying the EU legal framework on intermediary liability.[312] The issue is discussed further in Part I Chapter 6 of this book.

SCOPE – The E-Commerce Directive applies to "information society services." Such services are defined as '...any service normally provided for remuneration, at a distance, by electronic means and at the individual request of a recipient of services' (Article 2.a E-Commerce Directive following the definition by Article 1(2) of Directive 98/34/EC as amended by Directive 98/48/EC). The notion of "information society services" covers a wide range of services. Many of the economic activities that take place online fall under the scope of the E-Commerce Directive. Examples of services falling under this broad definition can be found in Recital (18) to the Directive. They may include (in so far as they represent an economic activity): online contracting, services providing transmission of information via communication networks, services providing access to a communication network, hosting of information, as well as services that do not give rise to online contracting, e.g. those that offer online information or commercial communications or those that provide tools allowing for search, access and retrieval of data.[313]

The key elements to determine whether or not a particular service can be qualified as an information society service are the following:

- Remuneration[314];
- Distance;
- Electronic means;
- Individual request of a recipient.[315]

---

311 S. Stalla-Bourdillon, "Sometimes one is not enough! Securing freedom of expression, encouraging private regulation, or subsidizing Internet intermediaries or all three at the same time: the dilemma of Internet intermediaries' liability", *Journal of International Commercial Law and Technology* Vol. 7, Issue 2, 2012, p. 156.

312 See *Ibid.*, p. 156.

313 See Recital (18) to the E-Commerce Directive for more examples.

314 The element of remuneration does not necessarily refer to the specific way in which the service is financed. Rather, it refers to the existence of an economic activity or an activity for which an economic consideration is given in return. Information society services therefore extend to services which are not remunerated by those who receive them. This means that a service financed through advertising, for example social networking site or a search engine, would be classified as an information society service.

315 The element of "individual request of a recipient of services" covers an activity of visiting a website. The transmission of data is initiated on demand, by an individual 'requesting' the

The E-Commerce Directive also excludes a number of services and legal issues from its scope such as questions covered by the Data Protection Directive, issues related to taxation; questions relating to agreements or practices governed by cartel law and the activities of notaries or equivalent professions to the extent that they involve a direct and specific connection with the exercise of public authority.[316]

LIABILITY EXEMPTIONS FOR INTERMEDIARIES – Section 4 of the E-Commerce Directive regulates the liability of intermediary service providers. This part of the Directive contains provisions introducing liability exemptions for certain types of intermediary services. Only three types of services are covered, namely "mere conduit" (Article 12), "caching", (Article 13) and "hosting" (Article 14). In order to benefit from these exemptions, providers of such services must comply with the conditions of each article.

The liability provisions of the E-Commerce Directive reconciled the two main arguments of the debate taking place between the Internet industry and EU policy makers at the time. On the one hand, there was the concern that if intermediaries were to be held liable for third party content on similar grounds as 'publishers,' this could restrain service providers from entering the market.[317] On the other hand, the European Commission recognized the role that online intermediaries could play in limiting illegal online content and, through that, improve public trust and confidence in the Internet as a safe space for economic activity.[318] The balance that was reached was meant to stimulate growth and innovation of the newly born technology and provide positive incentives for further development, which would effectively contribute to reaching the goals delineated in the E-Commerce Directive.[319]

The scope of the liability exemptions in the E-Commerce Directive is horizontal. This means that the liability exemptions cover various types of illegal content and activities (infringements on copyright, defamation, content harmful to minors, unfair commercial practices, etc.) and different kinds of liability (criminal, civil, direct, indirect).[320] The protection of the Directive is situated at the service level, and not at the company level. Therefore, a single company '*can at the same time act as a mere conduit, caching and/or hosting provider*'.[321]

URL or following a link.

316 See Article 5.1 E-Commerce Directive.

317 OECD, The Role of Internet Intermediaries In Advancing Public Policy Objectives, Forging partnerships for advancing public policy objectives for the Internet economy, *o.c.*, p. 12.

318 *Ibid.*, p. 12.

319 See Recitals 1–6 of the E-Commerce Directive.

320 N. Helberger, et al., Legal Aspects of User Created Content, *o.c.*, p. 220.

321 P. Van Eecke, "Online Service Providers and Liability: a Plea for a Balanced Approach", *o.c.*, p. 1462.

Questions concerning liability or injunctions[322] must be assessed by taking into account the specific service in question.[323]

If the conditions for being exempt from liability are not met, this does not mean that the intermediary is automatically liable. The effect is that the intermediary can no longer rely on the immunity provided by the Directive. The question of liability is then determined under the applicable material law specific to the type of infringing content in each Member State.[324]

MERE CONDUIT – Article 12 targets traditional Internet access providers and infrastructure operators. The liability exemption provided in this provision refers to providers of "mere conduit" services, which are described as:

- Services which consist of the transmission in a communication network of information provided by a recipient of the service ('transmission services'); and
- Services which consist of the provision of access to a communication network ('access services').

Recital (42) further stipulates that the exemptions provided by the Directive apply only to cases 'where the activity of the information society service provider is limited to the technical process of operating and giving access to a communication network (...)'.[325] It further elaborates that such activities are of a mere technical, automatic, and passive nature, which implies that the information society service provider has neither knowledge of nor control over the information it transmits or stores. While Recital (42) purports to address all of the exemptions of the Directive, one might argue that the scope of this part of the recital should be limited to the transmission and access services identified in Articles 12 and 13, which address access and transmission services (see more *infra* Part II Chapter 6).[326] The services described in Article 12 are sometimes compared to postal services, which are similarly not held liable for the illegal content of a letter.

---

322 Martin Husovec defines "an injunction" as a court order by which an individual is required to perform, or is restrained from performing a particular act (for instance provide information, implement technical features, refrain from providing service to somebody). See M. Husovec, *Injunctions Against Intermediaries in the European Union – Accountable But Not Liable?*, Cambridge University Press 2017, p. 12.

323 *Ibid.*

324 P. Van Eecke, M. Truyens, Legal analysis of a Single Market for the Information Society, New rules for a new age? *o.c.*

325 Recital (42) to the E-Commerce Directive.

326 See P. Van Eecke, "Online Service Providers and Liability: a Plea for a Balanced Approach",*o.c.*; E. Montéro, "Les responsabilités liées au web 2.0", *Revue du Droit des Technologies de l'Information* n° 32, 2008, p. 367.

The mere conduit exemption of liability only applies on the condition that the service provider:

(a) Does not initiate the transfer of data;
(b) Does not select the recipient of the data; and
(c) Does not select or modify the transmitted data.

The liability exemption for mere conduits also extends to the automatic, intermediate, and transient storage of the information transmitted. This is the case if the storage takes place for the sole purpose of carrying out the transmission in the communication network. Moreover, the information cannot be stored for any period longer than is reasonably necessary for the transmission (Article 12.2). Despite the lack of liability of the service provider (when the conditions are met), national courts and administrative authorities may direct prohibitory injunctions towards a provider of a mere conduit service. Such injunctions must be in accordance with the law of the Member State where the case is adjudicated (Article 12.3).[327]

CACHING – Caching is defined as 'the automatic, intermediate and temporary storage of that information, performed for the sole purpose of making more efficient the information's onward transmission to other recipients of the service upon their request'.[328]

The provision is targeted at providers of so called "proxy-servers", which store local copies of websites to speed up the subsequent consultation of these websites by other customers.[329] The exemption covers only information society services which consist of the transmission in a communication network of information provided by a recipient of the service ("transmission services") (Article 13.1).[330] Just as mere conduits, providers of this type of service can only be exempted from liability if they are in no way involved with the information transmitted (Recital (43)). In addition, the following five conditions must be met in order for a service provider to benefit from the caching exemption (Article 13.1):

327 See CJEU, *UPC Telekabel Wien*, Case C 314/12, 27 March 2014 addressing an injunction towards an Internet service provider to block access of its customers to a website making available to the public copyright infringing materials.

328 Article 13.1 to the E-Commerce Directive.

329 P. Van Eecke, "Online Service Providers and Liability: a Plea for a Balanced Approach", *o.c.*, p. 1462.

330 When comparing the caching exemption with the exemption for transient storage under the 'mere conduit' rule of Article 12.2, the wording appears to be very similar. The key difference between the caching exemption for transient storage and the exemption for transient storage under the mere conduit provision therefore is the purpose for which the storage is taking place. See A. Lodder, "Directive 2000/31 on certain legal aspects of information society services, in particular electronic commerce, in the Internal Market", in A. Lodder A. and Kasspersen (eds.*), eDirectives: Guide to European Union Law on E-commerce – Article by Article Comments*, Kluwer Law international, 2002, p. 88.

- The (service) provider may not modify the information as it would deprive him of the position of the intermediary;
- The provider has to comply with conditions on access to the information;
- The provider must update the information regularly in accordance with the generally recognized rules and practices in this area;
- The provider may not interfere with the lawful use of technology that is used to measure the use of information;
- The provider must remove the cached information immediately upon obtaining actual knowledge that the initial source of the information is removed, access to it has been disabled, or that a court administrative authority has ordered such removal or disablement.

The liability exemption for caching does not affect the power of courts or administrative authorities to issue prohibitory injunctions in accordance with the national legal system (Article 13.2). As pointed out by Van Eecke, Article 13 is rarely the subject of litigation.[331]

HOSTING – Article 14 of the E-Commerce Directive provides a liability exemption for hosting service providers, that is, information society services consisting of the storage of information provided by a recipient of the service at his request. Typically, it concerns webhosting services that provide web space to their users, where users can upload content to be published on a website (e.g. YouTube).[332] However, numerous other services also fall within the scope of Article 14 and the precise extent of its scope is a subject of intense discussion.[333]

The storage by "hosting" service providers differs from the storage carried out in the context of mere conduit or caching mainly in terms of the purposes for which the storage takes place. In contrast to mere conduit or caching services, hosting storage is not merely 'incidental' to the provision of the transmission or access services.[334] Storage may be provided for a prolonged period of time, and may also be the primary object of the service.[335] The Court of Justice of the EU specified that in order to enjoy the benefit of the liability exemption, a

---

331 P. Van Eecke, "Online Service Providers and Liability: a Plea for a Balanced Approach", *o.c.*, p. 1463.

332 Van Eecke P., Truyens M., Legal analysis of a Single Market for the Information Society, New rules for a new age? *o.c.*, Chapter 6: Liability of Online Intermediaries, p. 9.

333 P. Van Eecke, "Online Service Providers and Liability: a Plea for a Balanced Approach", *o.c.*, p. 1463. See more in Part I Chapter 6.

334 I. Walden, Y. Cool, E. Montero, "Directive 2000/31/EC –Directive on electronic commerce", *o.c.*, p. 253.

335 This exemption was originally aimed at ISP's providing space on their Internet servers for third parties' websites, or bulletin boards or chat room services provided by the ISP itself – where the ISP only provides technical means for the users' communication without interfering with the content being communicated between the user, see S.S. Jakobsen, "Mobile Commerce and ISP Liability in the EU", *International Journal of Law and Information Technology*, Vol. 19, no. 1, 2010, p. 44.

service provider's conduct must be neutral. The Court further defined neutrality as a conduct that is '*technical, automatic and passive, pointing to a lack of knowledge or control of the data which it stores*'.[336] The exemptions provided by the E-Commerce Directive are defined in functional terms (i.e. in terms of the activity being performed), not in terms of the qualification of the actor. While the European legislator arguably only envisioned providers whose services consisted mainly, if not exclusively, of the performance of operations of a strictly technical nature, the scope of the exemption may also be applied to other entities – provided that the conditions set forth by Article 14 are met. As a result, the exemption may in principle benefit any type of service provider who stores content at the request of the recipient; including so-called 'web 2.0' service providers.[337]

A hosting service provider shall not be liable for the information stored, on the condition that:

- The provider is not aware of the facts or circumstances from which the illegal activity or information is apparent – with regard to civil claims for damages, and he does not have actual knowledge of the illegal activity or information – with regard to other claims (Article 14.1.a); or
- The provider, upon obtaining such knowledge or awareness, acts expeditiously to remove or to disable access to the information (Article 14.1.b).

The Directive introduces different levels of knowledge with regard to criminal and civil liability. For the former, "actual knowledge" is required, while for the latter it is enough to establish "constructive knowledge" of the service provider. It is not entirely clear, however, what the boundary is between these types of knowledge. For example, the interpretations of "actual knowledge" range among the EU countries from knowledge obtained through a court order, to informal notice by a user, which, however, should be sufficiently substantiated.[338] Divergent case law across the EU shows that there is a lack of consistency in the interpretation of these terms and the following requirements for a valid notice.[339]

The exemption of Article 14 does not apply when the recipient of the service is acting under the authority or the control of the provider (Article 14.2). For example, if the service provider is acting as an employer or supervisor of the

[336] CJEU, *Google France and Google v. Louis Vuitton Malletier a.o.*, Joined Cases C-236/08 to C-238/08, 23 March 2010, paras. 113–114. The European Court of Justice addressed the issue of neutrality of hosting service providers also in the L'Oréal eBay case. CJEU, *L'Oréal v. eBay*, Case C-324/09, 12 July 2011, paras. 112 – 116.

[337] See E. Montéro, "Les responsabilités liées au web 2.0", *o.c.*

[338] CJEU, *L'Oréal v. eBay*, Case C-324/09, 12 July 2011. See more in Part I Chapter 6.

[339] See for example: BGH, 23/09/2003, VI ZR 335/02; Dutch Supreme Court 25 November 2005, LJN Number AU4019, case number C04/234HR; M. Turner(ed.) & J. Llevat, "The Spanish Supreme Court clarifies the concept of actual knowledge in connection with ISP's liability", *Computer Law & Security Review*, Volume 26, Issue 4, 2010, pp. 440–441.

service recipient, it will not qualify for the exemption if the content was introduced pursuant to its instructions. Similarly, as in the case of the mere-conduit and caching services, the liability exemption does not affect the possibility of a court or administrative authority, in accordance with Member States' regulations, requiring the service provider to terminate or prevent an infringement (Article 14.3).

Article 14.3, additionally, creates the possibility for Member States to establish specific procedures governing the removal or disabling of access to information. The Directive does not clarify any details for taking down or blocking access to content. As a result, there are no guidelines on how such processes should be handled by service providers, nor safeguards to ensure proportionality or due process. Procedural aspects were left entirely to the discretion of the Member States. Such a delegation can be seen also in Recital 46, which stipulates that the removal or disabling of access should be undertaken in observance of the right to freedom of expression and of procedures established for this purpose at national level. Some EU countries have provided a more detailed regulation for the hosting exemption by introducing formal notification procedures (notice and take down). Many, however, opted for a verbatim transposition of the Directive, leaving, therefore, this matter unattended (see more *infra*).[340]

NO GENERAL OBLIGATION TO MONITOR – Member States may not impose on providers of services covered by Articles 12, 13, and 14 (i.e. mere conduit, caching or hosting) a general obligation to monitor information they transmit or store (Article 15). The same provision states that they cannot introduce a general obligation to actively look for facts or circumstances indicating illegal activity. An obligation to conduct general monitoring of content, if permitted, would counteract the limited liability paradigm.[341] This is because intermediary service providers actively seeking illegal activities would no longer be neutral and passive in nature. Moreover, a general monitoring obligation could lead to censorship and consequently have a negative impact on freedom of expression.[342]

The prohibition towards monitoring obligations refers solely to monitoring of a general nature. It does not concern monitoring obligations in a specific case, nor does it affect orders by national authorities in line with national legislation (Recital (47)).[343] The Directive also allows Member States to require hosting providers to apply duties of care, which can reasonably be expected from them

---

340 First Report on the Application of Directive 2000/31/EC, *o.c.* See more in Part I Chapter 5 and 6.

341 OECD, The Role of Internet Intermediaries in Advancing Public Policy Objectives, Forging partnerships for advancing public policy objectives for the Internet economy, *o.c.*, p. 15.

342 *Ibid.* p. 36. See also Council of Europe, Human rights guidelines for Internet Service Providers, *o.c.*, p. 3.

343 Application of Article 15 differs across the EU in case of injunctions. For example, in Germany a host may still be required to actively monitor his platform for further infringing activity. See more in T. Verbiest, Spindler G, et al., Study on the liability of Internet Intermediaries – General trends in Europe, *o.c.*, p. 85 and Part III Chapter 2 of this thesis.

(Recital (48)). Such duties of care, however, should only be introduced to detect and prevent certain types of illegal activities, foreseen by national law.[344] To the confusion of many, the Directive does not specify what exactly such duties of care entail. As a result, the boundary between such duties and general monitoring is not clear.[345] Some authors consider Recital (48) as contradictory to Article 15.[346]

The prohibition of Article 15 is addressed to the Member States' legislators. They are not allowed to introduce regulations that would require providers of the specified services to monitor the information they store or transmit. This does not mean that service providers cannot take up such activities on their own. The prohibition should not be read as a prohibition against service providers monitoring information. Most of the service providers in the EU do perform certain monitoring activities to maintain a "civilized" environment on their service. Voluntary monitoring, however, can prove detrimental. Exercising too much control could compromise the neutral status of the intermediary and, in consequence, deprive them of the safe harbour protection.[347] The EU intermediary regime does not contain a provision which protects intermediaries from liability should their voluntary monitoring prove imperfect (such as the one offered by the Section 230(c)(2) CDA in the US). As a result, service providers are careful not to shoot themselves in the foot through their own overzealous activities.[348] The European Commission is currently deliberating whether to introduce such a change in the EU intermediary liability regime.[349]

Article 15 (2) defines two additional obligations that Member States may impose upon information society service providers. The first provides Member States with the possibility to require service providers to inform authorities about any alleged illegal activities of their users. Such notification would need to be given as soon as the provider becomes aware of the illegal activity. Secondly, Member States may also establish obligations on providers to disclose the identity of users with whom they have storage agreements. Establishing these obligations is not a requirement and is left to the discretion of the Member States.[350]

---

344 Prohibition of the general monitoring obligation was addressed by the Court of Justice of the European Union in two cases, CJEU, *Scarlet v. SABAM*, C-70/10, 24 November 2011, and CJEU, *SABAM v. Netlog*, C-360/10, 16 February 2012.

345 See more in P. Valcke, A. Kuczerawy, P.J. Ombelet, "Did the Romans Get it Right? What Delfi, Google, eBay, and UPC TeleKabel Wien Have in Common", in L. Floridi and M. Taddeo (eds.), *The Responsibilities of Online Service Providers*, Springer, 2016.

346 R. J. Barceló and K. Koelman, "Intermediary Liability In The E-Commerce Directive: So Far So Good, But It's Not Enough", *o.c.*, p. 232.

347 See OECD, The Role of Internet Intermediaries In Advancing Public Policy Objectives, Forging partnerships for advancing public policy objectives for the Internet economy, *o.c.*, p. 15–16.

348 See P. Valcke, A. Kuczerawy, P.J. Ombelet, "Did the Romans Get it Right? What Delfi, Google, eBay, and UPC TeleKabel Wien Have in Common", *o.c.*, p. 114.

349 See more in Part I Chapters 5 and 6.

350 The possibility of introducing an obligation to disclose the identity of recipients was questioned in the Promusicae case, CJEU, *Promusicae v. Telefonica de Espana*, C 275/06,

The regime laid out by the E-Commerce Directive has been in place for almost two decades now, without any update or amendment. During this time, a number of issues have been identified with regard to its functioning.[351] The issues relevant to the topic of this book are described further in Part I Chapter 6.

2. DIGITAL MILLENNIUM COPYRIGHT ACT

ORIGIN AND DEVELOPMENT – Section 202 of the Digital Millennium Copyright Act (DMCA) 1998 (codified at 17 U.S.C. §512) regulates intermediary liability for copyright infringements by third parties.[352]

Under US law, secondary copyright liability comes in two forms, resulting either from "contributory infringement" or from "vicarious infringement".[353] Contributory infringement requires actual or constructive knowledge of the direct infringement and, additionally, a material contribution to the direct infringement.[354] The question of material contribution was addressed, for example, in *Perfect 10 v. Visa International*, where the Court found that the role of credit card companies in processing payments for infringing material cannot be considered as material.[355]

Vicarious infringement requires financial benefit from the direct infringement as well as both the right and the ability to supervise the direct infringer.[356] For the service provider to financially benefit from an infringement there must be a '*causal relationship between the infringing activity and any financial benefit [the] defendant reaps*'. This could happen, for example if a service provider displays advertisements, for which he receives payments, next to third party content, which proves to be copyright infringing.[357] The ability to supervise the direct infringer is a fact-specific question, which is focused on the relationship

---

29 January 2008. See more: F. Coudert, E. Werkers, "In The Aftermath of the Promusicae Case: How to Strike the Balance?", *International Journal of Law and Information Technology*, Vol. 18, Issue 1, 2010, pp. 50–71.

351 See Commission Communication, A coherent framework for building trust in the Digital Single Market for e-commerce and online *o.c.*, p. 41.

352 Section 202 of the Digital Millennium Copyright Act (codified at 17 U.S.C. §512), available: https://www.law.cornell.edu/uscode/text/17/512.

353 See e.g., *Metro-Goldwyn-Mayer Studios, Inc. v. Grokster, Ltd.*, 545 U.S. 913 (2005), 930 (2005). A. Holland et al., "Online Intermediaries Case Studies Series: Intermediary Liability in the United States", The Global Network of Internet & Society Research Centers, 2015, p. 8.

354 See e.g. *Metro-Goldwyn-Mayer Studios, Inc. v. Grokster, Ltd.*, 545 U.S. 913 (2005). See also *Sony Corp. of America v. Universal City Studios, Inc.* 464 U.S. 417, 442 (1984); and *Viacom International, Inc. v. YouTube, Inc.*, No. 07 Civ. 2103 (settled).

355 See *Perfect 10 v. Visa International*, 494 F.3d 788 (9th Cir. 2007).

356 A. Holland et al., "Online Intermediaries Case Studies Series: Intermediary Liability in the United States", *o.c.*, p. 10.

357 See *Columbia Pictures Indus. v. Gary Fung*, 710 F.3d 1020.

between the direct infringer and the alleged secondary infringer.[358] In *Grokster*, the US Supreme Court described the service provider's failure to undertake '*filtering tools or other mechanisms to diminish the infringing activity using their software*' as additional evidence of unlawful objectives and '*underscore[ing] Grokster's and StreamCast's intentional facilitation of their users' Infringement*'.[359]

SCOPE – The DMCA regulates the responsibility of online intermediaries with regard to third party copyright infringements. The most relevant aspect of the law is that it provides safe harbours for a selection of service providers as well as an elaborate procedure for removal of copyright infringing information in the form of a notice and takedown mechanism. Section 512 creates several categories of protection for the online service providers. The law covers the providers of services such as transitory digital network communications, system caching, information residing on systems or networks at direction of users, and information location tools. Section 512(c) DMCA describes the conditions for liability exemption for "information residing on systems or networks at direction of users", which can benefit the providers of hosting services. According to this provision, the hosting provider is exonerated from any direct, contributory or vicarious liability for copyright infringements it is hosting under three cumulative conditions.[360] Specifically:

- the host must not have actual knowledge that the hosted content is infringing or must not be aware of facts or circumstances from which infringing activity is apparent;
- if the host has the right and ability to control the infringing activity, it must not receive a financial benefit directly attributable to the infringing activity;
- upon receiving proper notification of an alleged infringement, the host must '*act expeditiously to remove or disable access to the material*'.[361]

NOTICE AND TAKE DOWN PROCEDURE – The crucial element of the DMCA is that it allows and expects Internet intermediaries to disable access to material or activity claimed to be infringing as long as they act in good faith in response to a claim or based on facts of circumstances that the material or activity is infringing (Section 512(g)(1)). The notice and takedown procedure specifies what information has to be included in a notice to be considered valid. Upon receipt of

---

358 See *A&M Records, Inc. v. Napster, Inc.*, 239 F.3d 1004 (9th Cir. 2001), at 1023. See also A. Holland et al., "Online Intermediaries Case Studies Series: Intermediary Liability in the United States", *o.c.*, p. 10.

359 *Metro-Goldwyn-Mayer Studios Inc. v. Grokster, Ltd.*, 545 U.S. 913, 939, 125 S. Ct. 2764, 2781, 162 L. Ed. 2d 781 (2005).

360 See R. Julia-Barcelo, "On-line intermediary liability issues: comparing E.U. and U.S. legal frameworks", *o.c.*, pp. 105–119.

361 Section 512 (c) DMCA.

a statutorily compliant notice, the on-line intermediary will be regarded as having the required level of knowledge.[362] Moreover, the procedure contains procedural guarantees, which can be seen as informed by freedom of expression concerns.[363] For example, a hosting provider has to notify its customers if it decides to remove or disable access to material (Section 512(g)(2)). Additionally, the DMCA contains a disincentive to issue fraudulent notifications of infringement (Section 512(f)) and a procedure to put the removed content back online (Section 512(g)(B)). The latter procedure, however, is rarely used.[364] Moreover, to be eligible for the liability limitations of DMCA, service providers have to implement a policy that provides for the termination of access of repeat infringers and to accommodate and not interfere with standard technical measures to prevent infringements from taking place (Section 512(i)). Details of the DMCA notice and take down procedure are analysed further in Part III Chapter 2 of this book.

3. SECTION 230 OF THE COMMUNICATIONS DECENCY ACT

ORIGIN AND DEVELOPMENT – The first online defamation cases in the US in the 1990s were resolved in the absence of specific rules for the liability of different kinds of Internet intermediaries.[365] In *Cubby, Inc. v. CompuServe Inc.* a New York district court ruled that the provider of the bulletin board service CompuServe should be considered '*the functional equivalent of a more traditional news vendor*'.[366] According to the Court, CompuServe had '*no more editorial control over such a publication than [...] a public library, book store, or newsstand, and it would be no more feasible for CompuServe to examine every publication it carries for potentially defamatory statements than it would be for any other distributor to do so*'.[367] As a result of this assessment, the Court established the distributor standard for an Internet intermediary, meaning that it would only be liable if it '*knew or had reason to know of the allegedly defamatory [...] statements*'.[368] After this promising start, however, the New York Supreme Court reversed the distributor liability approach in *Stratton Oakmont, Inc. v.*

362 See J. Urban, L. Quilter, "Efficient Process or 'Chilling Effects'?" *o.c.*, p. 5; see also R. Julia-Barcelo, "On-line intermediary liability issues: comparing E.U. and U.S. legal frameworks", *o.c.*, pp. 105–119.

363 J. van Hoboken, *Search Engine Freedom: On the Implications of the Right to Freedom of Expression for the Legal Governance of Web Search Engines*, *o.c.*, p. 132.

364 See J. Urban, L. Quilter, "Efficient Process or 'Chilling Effects'?" *o.c.*, p. 5. See more in Part III Chapter 2.1.

365 J. van Hoboken, *Search Engine Freedom: On the Implications of the Right to Freedom of Expression for the Legal Governance of Web Search Engines*, *o.c.*, p. 133.

366 *Cubby, Inc. v. CompuServe Inc.*, 776 F. Supp. 135 (S.D.N.Y. 1991).

367 *Ibid.*

368 *Ibid.*

Prodigy Services Co.[369] The Court ruled that an online bulletin board operator is liable if it exercises control over the selection of content, for example by actively removing messages it deemed offensive using technical filtering products and content screening guidelines for its moderators.[370]

As a response to *Prodigy*, the US Congress introduced Section 230(c) of the Communications Decency Act (CDA)[371] in 1996, as part of a greater law to address the transmission of offensive and obscene content to minors.[372] The bulk of the law was struck down by the Supreme Court, which held parts of the CDA unconstitutional for its overbroad limitations on protected speech.[373] The only part that survived scrutiny addresses the liability of intermediaries for content other than copyright infringements.

Congress passed the CDA with two main goals in mind: (1) promoting online innovation, and (2) encouraging online intermediaries to voluntarily police content provided by their users.[374] Specifically, the goal was to '*encourage telecommunications and information service providers to deploy new technologies and policies*' to block or filter offensive material.[375] It was, therefore, initially not meant to protect free expression but rather, to allow private entities to censor sexually explicit content disseminated through various media. Interestingly, the attempt to allow censorship by private entities was the reason why most parts of the CDA were struck down by the Supreme Court, which considered them as an overbroad and vague form of content-based speech suppression and therefore violating the First Amendment.[376] Section 230 is the only part of the CDA that survived the review by the US courts.

SCOPE – According to Section 230, '[n]o provider or user of an interactive computer service shall be treated as the publisher or speaker of any information provided by another information content provider'.[377] To apply Section 230 protection, a defendant must demonstrate that (1) it is a provider or user of an interactive computer service; (2) it is being treated as the publisher of content; and (3) that the

369 *Stratton Oakmont v. Prodigy Servs. Co.*, 1995 WL 323710 (N.Y. Sup. Ct. May 24, 1995).

370 See more in Part III Chapter 4.

371 47 U.S. Code §230 – Protection for private blocking and screening of offensive material.

372 P. Ehrlich, "Communications Decency Act 230", *Berkeley Technology Law Journal*, Vol. 17 Issue 1, 2002, p. 401.

373 See *Reno v. ACLU*, 521 U.S. 844 (1997). P. Ehrlich, "Communications Decency Act 230", *o.c.*, p. 401.

374 See 47 U.S.C §230(b).

375 S. REP. NO. 104–23, at 59 (1995), as referenced by D. Keats Citron and B. Wittes, "The Internet Will Not Break: Denying Bad Samaritans Section 230 Immunity", University of Maryland Francis King Carey School of Law, Legal Studies Research Paper No. 2017–22, p. 4.

376 In *Reno v. ACLU*, 521 U.S. 844 (1997) the Supreme Court struck down provisions of the CDA that criminalized the "knowing" transmission of obscene or indecent messages to underage recipients. 521 U.S. at 849 and at 858–60, 874–76.

377 47 U.S.C. §230(c)(1).

content is provided by another content provider.[378] Section 230 does not protect statements published by the interactive computer provider directly. This means that the operator of a website may be liable when it is alleged that 'the defendants themselves create, develop, and post original, defamatory information'.[379]

An "interactive computer service" is defined as 'any information service, system, or access software provider that provides or enables computer access by multiple users to a computer server…'.[380] The definition covers different types of online intermediaries, including Internet service providers, social media websites, blogging platforms, and search engines.[381] Moreover, Section 230 covers a wide variety of actions that can be taken by interactive computer services over third party content, as evidenced in the extensive case-law. For example, Section 230 applies to basic editorial functions, such as deciding whether to publish, remove, or edit content[382]; soliciting users to submit legal content[383] but also other content[384]; for example, paying a third party to create or submit content[385] or allowing users to respond to forms or drop-downs to submit content.[386, 387] Most notably, Section 230 applies when intermediaries keep content online even after being notified that the material is unlawful.[388] Such was the finding in Zeran v. AOL, which is considered the most important ruling on Section 230 to date.[389] The case concerned a cyber-harassment attack on AOL's message boards against businessman Zeran. The Court ruled that the CDA protection for third party content is not eliminated even if the plaintiff had issued a demand letter or a takedown notice. Moreover, the Court clarified that Section 230 protects websites' decisions regarding publishing, editing or removing third party content, unlike traditional publishers, who would become liable for undertaking such activities.[390] The ruling came not long after the enactment of Section 230 when its reading was not entirely clear yet. It ensured Section 230's status as a supplement to the First Amendment's protection for free

---

378 A. Holland et al., "Online Intermediaries Case Studies Series: Intermediary Liability in the United States", *o.c.*, p. 6.

379 *MCW, Inc. v. Badbusinessbureau.com*, LLC, 2004 WL 833595, No. 3:02-CV-2727-G at *9 (N.D. Tex. April 19, 2004).

380 47 U.S.C §230(f)(2).

381 See D. Ardia, "Free Speech Savior or Shield for Scoundrels: an Empirical Study of Intermediary Immunity Under Section 230 of the Communications Decency Act", *o.c.*, p. 387–89.

382 *Donato v. Moldow*, 865 A.2d 711 (N.J. Super. Ct. 2005).

383 *Corbis Corporation v. Amazon.com, Inc.*, 351 F.Supp.2d 1090 (W.D. Wash. 2004).

384 *Global Royalties, Ltd. v. Xcentric Ventures*, LLC, 544 F. Supp. 2d 929, 933 (D. Ariz. 2008).

385 *Blumenthal v. Drudge*, 992 F. Supp. 44 (D.D.C. 1998).

386 *Carafano v. Metrosplash.com*, 339 F.3d 1119 (9th Cir. 2003).

387 A. Holland et al., "Online Intermediaries Case Studies Series: Intermediary Liability in the United States", *o.c.*, p. 7.

388 *Zeran v. America Online, Inc.*, 129 F.3d 327 (4th Cir. 1997).

389 E. Goldman, "The Ten Most Important Section 230 Rulings", *Tulane Journal of Technology & Intellectual Property*, Vol. 20, 2017.

390 See *Ibid.*, p. 2.

expression.[391] Moreover, the expansive interpretation of the scope of Section 230 set the tone for the case-law to follow.[392]

Not all activities by interactive computer services are protected by CDA. As shown in other cases, courts are unlikely to grant immunity when an interactive computer service edits the content of a third party thus materially altering its meaning to make it actionable; requires users to submit unlawful content[393]; or if the service promises to remove material and then fails to do so.[394, 395] In case such actions are taken by an intermediary, it is deemed to have "developed" the content by '*materially contributing to the alleged illegality of the conduct*'.[396]

GOOD SAMARITAN CLAUSE – The main goals of the CDA are especially visible in Section 230(c)(2), which reflects Congress's desire to encourage moderation of user content.[397] The provision states that online service providers shall not be held liable based on:

> 'any action voluntarily taken in good faith to restrict access to or availability of material that the provider or user considers to be obscene, lewd, lascivious, filthy, excessively violent, harassing, or otherwise objectionable, whether or not such material is constitutionally protected [... or ...] any action taken to enable or make available to information content providers or others the technical means to restrict access to [such material]'.[398]

The provision aims to ensure protection of the "computer Good Samaritans", that is, online service providers, who take '*steps to screen indecency and offensive material for their customers*'.[399] The need to protect such online service providers became the ambition of the lawmakers after *Stratton-Oakmont v. Prodigy Services*.[400] In this pre-CDA case, an online service provider, Prodigy, was found liable as a publisher for defamatory content by third parties, because it had tried to detect and remove objectionable content through the use of filtering software but had failed to do so perfectly. Members of Congress agreed that holding Good Samaritans liable is not the way to go by stating that,

---

391 See *Ibid.*

392 See *Ibid.*

393 *Fair Housing Council v. Roommates.com*, LLC, 521 F.3d 1157, 1175 (9th Cir. 2008) (en banc).

394 *Barnes v. Yahoo!, Inc*, 570 F.3d 1096 (9th Cir. 2009).

395 A. Holland et al., "Online Intermediaries Case Studies Series: Intermediary Liability in the United States", *o.c.*, p. 7.

396 *Jones v. Dirty World Entertainment Recordings*, LLC, 2014 WL 2694184 (6th Cir. 2014).

397 J. Kosseff, "Twenty Year of Intermediary Immunity: the US Experience", *Scripted*, Vol. 14, Issue 1, June 2017, p. 12.

398 47 U.S.C. §230(c)(2).

399 As described by Representative Cox, in 141 CONG. REC. H8469 (daily ed. Aug. 4, 1995), as referenced by D. Keats Citron and B. Wittes, The Internet Will Not Break: Denying Bad Samaritans Section 230 Immunity, *o.c.*, ft. 17.

400 *Stratton Oakmont v. Prodigy Servs. Co.*, 1995 WL 323710 (N.Y. Sup. Ct. May 24, 1995).

> 'One of the specific purposes of this section is to overrule Stratton-Oakmont v. Prodigy and any other similar decisions which have treated such providers and users as publishers or speakers of content that is not their own because they have restricted access to objectionable material. The conferees believe that such decisions create serious obstacles to the important federal policy of empowering parents to determine the content of communications their children receive through interactive computer services.'[401]

The risk was that the *Prodigy* decision would prevent online service providers from taking up any monitoring and censoring activities for fear of becoming liable for third party content.[402] Instead of improved screening, this would lead to no screening at all, as it would be safer for the providers to maintain the position of purely passive conduits.[403] Those concerns led to the introduction of the immunity for online service providers '*protecting from liability those providers and users seeking to clean up the Internet*'.[404] According to van Hoboken, the clause legally permits Internet intermediaries to restrict, in good faith, access to or the availability of material that they consider '*otherwise objectionable, whether or not such material is constitutionally protected*', effectively legitimizing interferences with lawful content.[405] US courts have interpreted Section 230 broadly. Starting with *Zeran*, courts began applying the protection regardless of whether an online service provider actually took any steps towards regulating its website content.[406] This means that the "Good Samaritan" protection applies even if the online service providers are not acting at all like the Good Samaritans they were expected to be.

RARE EXCEPTIONS – On rare occasions the broad immunity provided by Section 230 proves insufficient. *Roommates.com* concerned a roommate-

---

401 House of Representatives Report 104–458 (1996), at p. 194, https://www.congress.gov/104/crpt/hrpt458/CRPT-104hrpt458.pdf.

402 As described by Representative Bob Goodlatte, 'Currently, however, there is a tremendous disincentive for online service providers to create family friendly services by detecting and removing objectionable content. These providers face the risk of increased liability where they take reasonable steps to police their systems. A New York judge recently sent the online services the message to stop policing by ruling that Prodigy was subject to a $200 million libel suit simply because it did exercise some control over profanity and indecent material'. 141 CONG. REC. H8471 (daily ed. Aug. 4, 1995)., as referenced by D. Keats Citron and B. Wittes, "The Internet Will Not Break: Denying Bad Samaritans Section 230 Immunity", *o.c.*, ft. 21.

403 See D. Keats Citron and B. Wittes, "The Internet Will Not Break: Denying Bad Samaritans Section 230 Immunity", *o.c.*, p. 4.

404 H.R. REP. NO. 104–223, at 3 (1995), as referenced by D. Keats Citron and B. Wittes, "The Internet Will Not Break: Denying Bad Samaritans Section 230 Immunity", *o.c.*, p. 5.

405 J. van Hoboken, *Search Engine Freedom: On the Implications of the Right to Freedom of Expression for the Legal Governance of Web Search Engines*, *o.c.*, p. 136.

406 A. M. Sevanian, "Section 230 of the Communications Decency Act: A 'Good Samaritan' Law Without the Requirement of Acting as a 'Good Samaritan'", *UCLA Entertainment Law Review*, Vol. 21, Issue 1, 2014, p. 122–146, p. 126.

matching service that allowed users to post and search for roommate listings. Users had to fill out a questionnaire that specified, among other details, their sexual orientation, gender, and whether they had children. The questionnaire also had an "Additional Comments" section that allowed users to describe other characteristics that they were, or were not, looking for in a roommate. In that section users specified that they are looking, for example, for a roommate of a specific gender or marital status or that they categorically did not want a roommate of a specific religion or ethnicity.[407] Those practices got the website in trouble with the Fair Housing Council of San Fernando Valley, which alleged that Roommates.com violated state and federal housing laws prohibiting discrimination based on sex, sexual orientation, and familial status. Roommates.com argued that if any discrimination occurred, it was a result of the user-provided content, therefore, Section 230 applied. Interestingly, the Court of Appeals for the Ninth Circuit agreed with that argument but only partially. The majority of the *en banc* panel ruled that the website was not immune for content that was posted on the website as a response to the questionnaire created by Roommates.com. Chief Judge Kozinski reasoned that Roommates.com created the questions about gender, sexual orientation, and familial status therefore, as the information content provider, Roommates.com '*can claim no immunity for posting them on its website, or for forcing subscribers to answer them as a condition of using its services*'.[408] At the same time, the Chief Judge concluded that Roommates.com was entitled to Section 230 immunity for any allegedly discriminatory statements that users voluntarily submitted in the "Additional Comments" section.[409] The 2008 *Roommates.com* opinion is the most frequently cited exception to *Zeran*'s defence-favourable ruling.[410] The case, however, provides an interesting twist. In 2012 the case came back to court, which ruled this time that the website was never covered by the housing anti-discrimination laws.[411] As a result, the same Court as before concluded that Roommates.com never had any illegal content at all, making the previous ruling effectively pointless.[412]

In 2009 – therefore before the reversal of Roommates.com – the Tenth Circuit Court of Appeals embraced, and even extended, the original *Roommates.com* exception.[413] In *FTC v. Accusearch*, the Court held that '*a service provider is "responsible" for the development of offensive content only if it in some way*

407 *Fair Housing Council of San Fernando Valley v Roommates.com*, [2008] 521 F.3d 1157 (9th Cir.) (en banc).

408 *Ibid.*

409 *Ibid.*

410 E. Goldman, "The Ten Most Important Section 230 Rulings", *o.c.*, p. 2.

411 *Fair Housing Council of San Fernando Valley v. Roommate.com*, [2012] WL 310849 (9th Cir.).

412 E. Goldman, "The Ten Most Important Section 230 Rulings, Tulane Journal of Technology & Intellectual Property, Vol. 20, 2017, p. 3.

413 *Ibid.*, p. 4.

specifically encourages development of what is offensive about the content'.[414] The *Accusearch* ruling now sometimes contributes to the loss of defence, rather than the problematic *Roommates.com*.[415] There are more examples of failed immunity defences under Section 230 CDA, but they do not occur very often. Section 230 CDA is further analysed in Part III Chapter 2.4.

4. INTERIM CONCLUSION

INTERACTION BETWEEN THE ACTS – The EU and US intermediary liability regimes emerged in the 1990s. The backbone of the regimes is based on the same principles, but they differ in the approach they have taken. Section 230 CDA came first in 1996, with a goal to promote private enforcement to counter obscene content. The law received an expansive interpretation in *Zeran*, which led to almost absolute immunity for third party content other than copyright infringements. Next, in 1998, came the DMCA, which allowed for a quick and easy way for victims of copyright infringement to short-circuit the distribution of copyrighted material online.[416] The method chosen, in the form of notice and takedown mechanism, ensured a relatively inexpensive tool that is not overly burdensome on intermediaries.[417] The E-Commerce Directive is the European response to the adoption by the US federal legislator of the DMCA. The Directive builds upon the German Multimedia Act of 1997 but it is strongly influenced by the US instrument.[418]

SIMILARITIES AND DIFFERENCES – All three acts provide that Internet intermediaries have no obligations to monitor content of their users. Moreover, they cannot be held liable for third party content when they have no knowledge of the illegality. Under Section 230 CDA, however, intermediaries cannot be held liable even if they do have such knowledge. The EU opted for a horizontal application, while the US took a vertical approach, separating the regimes for copyright infringements and any other infringements. This means that the notice and take down mechanism in the US applies solely to copyright infringements while in the EU it can be used for any type of infringing or illegal content. The EU E-Commerce Directive, however, merely implies the existence of take down mechanisms without specifying the applicable procedures. The details were left to the discretion of the EU Member States. The US notice and

---

414 *Fed. Trade Comm'n v. Accusearch Inc.*, 570 F.3d 1187 (10th Cir. 2009).

415 See E. Goldman, "The Ten Most Important Section 230 Rulings", *o.c.*, p. 4.

416 J. Urban, L. Quilter, "Efficient Process or 'Chilling Effects'"? *o.c.*, p. 4.

417 See *Ibid.*

418 S. Stalla-Bourdillon, "Sometimes one is not enough!" *o.c.*, p. 157. For comments on the German Multimedia Act see R. Julia-Barcelo, "Liability for on-line intermediaries: a European perspective", *European Intellectual Property Review*, Vol. 20, 1998, p. 456.

take down is provided explicitly and described in detail in the DMCA itself, leaving little doubt about its implementation in practice. The EU Directive also did not opt for a Good Samaritan-type clause, such as provided in Section 230 CDA.[419] This means that intermediaries in the EU must be careful when they undertake monitoring and filtering activities of the content on their platforms. The Directive, unlike the US acts, did not address the position and obligations of search engines. Consequences of those differences influence the issues that can be identified in each regime. They are also reflected in the detailed analysis of the US acts and national implementations of the Directive. The problematic aspects of the EU E-Commerce Directive are discussed further in Part I Chapter 6 of this book. A detailed analysis of the different regimes is conducted in Part III Chapter 2 of this book.

COMPATIBILITY WITH HUMAN RIGHTS – Notice and action mechanisms, sometimes simply called notice and takedown mechanisms, are the core focus of this book. They allow the intermediaries to enforce the law (and their own policies) and make decisions about content online without the involvement of public authorities. Through such mechanisms, together with the promise of liability exemption, States enlist the intermediaries to police the Internet. Delegation of enforcement measures to the private entities affects the fundamental rights of Internet users. In particular, the indirect responsibilization of the intermediaries allows for interference with the freedom of expression of the Internet users by private entities. This observation led to one of the research questions of this book:

> **Is the notice and action mechanism under EU law compatible with the right to freedom of expression, as recognized by Article 10 ECHR, and Article 11 EU Charter?**

419 P. Valcke, A. Kuczerawy, P.J. Ombelet, "Did the Romans Get it Right? What Delfi, Google, eBay, and UPC TeleKabel Wien Have in Common", *o.c.*, p. 114.

CHAPTER 5
TOWARDS PLATFORM RESPONSIBILITY

1. REVIEW OF THE E-COMMERCE DIRECTIVE

THE FUTURE OF ELECTRONIC COMMERCE – Ten years after the adoption of the E-Commerce Directive, in 2010, the European Commission launched a public consultation on this instrument as part of its periodic review process.[420] Stakeholders were generous in their responses, thereby providing considerable insight into the various perspectives. Responses were submitted by businesses and business associations (which included different types of intermediaries, as well as copyright industry), civil society, public authorities, lawyers, and individual citizens.[421] The consultation revealed that the majority of respondents generally did not see a need for a revision of the Directive at that stage. Some of them, however, expressed concern about the limited protection for freedom of expression offered by the Directive.[422] Many respondents identified the need to clarify certain aspects of the Directive, particularly with regard to intermediary liability for third-party content. The most "thorny" issue was the functioning of the notice and take down procedures. The public consultation revealed that a number of problems with regard to such procedures still persisted. Most of the stakeholders mentioned legal uncertainty as an issue, highlighting that several key terms remain subject to divergent interpretations – not only across Europe but also among different stakeholders. Right holders generally complained about the time during which illegal content stays online, while civil society pointed out that often legal content is taken down without good reason. Many stakeholders felt that the current approach incentivises unnecessary and undesirable restrictions on the freedom of expression.[423] The European Commission concluded that procedures aimed at

---

420 Public consultation on the future of electronic commerce in the internal market and the implementation of the Directive on electronic commerce (2000/31/EC), http://ec.europa.eu/internal_market/consultations/2010/e-commerce_en.htm.

421 Summary of the results of the Public Consultation on the future of electronic commerce in the Internal Market and the implementation of the Directive on electronic commerce (2000/31/EC), *o.c.*

422 See Art. 19 Response to the Consultation, November 2010, www.article19.org/data/files/pdfs/submissions/responseto-eu-consultation.pdf, p. 9: 'Any revisions to the Ecommerce Directive need to fully take into account the freedom of expression requirements of the European Convention on Human Rights and other international obligations'.

423 Art. 19 Response to the Consultation, *o.c.*, p. 9.

eliminating illegal online content should lead to a quicker takedown, but at the same time should better respect fundamental rights – in particular the freedom of expression – and should increase legal certainty for online intermediaries.[424] Based on these findings, the Commission decided in 2011 to focus its efforts on developing a new European framework for notice and action.[425]

NOTICE AND ACTION INITIATIVE – In January 2012, the European Commission announced a new initiative on notice and action procedures.[426] The goal of this initiative is to set up a horizontal European framework for notice and action procedures, to combat illegality on the Internet and to ensure the transparency, effectiveness, and proportionality of notice and action mechanisms, as well as compliance with fundamental rights. The Commission considered such a framework to be necessary for several reasons.[427] First of all, it observed that intermediary service providers continue to struggle with legal uncertainty. Such uncertainty is attributable, at least in part, to the fragmentation of the rules and practices for eliminating illegal online content which are applicable within the EU.[428] In the EC's opinion, such fragmentation hinders the development of online business.

Secondly, according to the EC, the existing mechanisms for the elimination of illegal content from the online environment are often ineffective and inefficient.[429] As expressed in the 2011 Communication, the Commission felt that it is still too rare and takes too long to remove even obviously criminal content such as child sexual abuse material, much to the frustration of citizens. This was considered detrimental to the confidence of citizens and businesses on the Internet.[430] At the same time, it is not uncommon that legal content is taken down, due to incorrect or disproportionate measures. Such measures, moreover, deny content providers their right to be heard and to defend their rightful publication of content. According to the EC, citizens complain about these aspects, as well as a lack of transparency of the employed mechanisms. Therefore,

---

424 European Commission on Notice and Action Procedures, http://ec.europa.eu/internal_market/e-commerce/notice-andaction/index_en.htm.

425 Commission Communication, A coherent framework for building trust in the Digital Single Market for e-commerce and online services, *o.c.*, p. 12–15.

426 *Ibid.*

427 Roadmap – Initiative on a clean and open Internet: procedures for notifying and acting on illegal content hosted by online intermediaries, http://ec.europa.eu/governance/impact/planned_ia/docs/2012_markt_007_notice_and_takedown_procedures_en.pdf.

428 Commission Communication, A coherent framework for building trust in the Digital Single Market for e-commerce and online services, *o.c.*, p. 6.

429 The term 'efficiency' is understood mainly as the speed with which content is taken down. Speed is only one parameter by which one can assess the effectiveness of takedown procedures. From a normative perspective, it is equally important that the takedown process sufficiently balances all the rights at stake. For purposes of conceptual clarity, however, this thesis uses the term 'efficiency' to refer to the response time of take down requests.

430 Commission Communication, A coherent framework for building trust in the Digital Single Market for e-commerce and online services, *o.c.*, p. 14.

the European Commission expressed its intention to improve the existing mechanisms to eliminate illegal online content. The revised framework for these procedures should be more efficient, guarantee legal certainty to all parties involved, as well as proportionality of the rules governing businesses. Moreover, respect for fundamental rights, within these procedures, should be ensured. This last objective is, however, phrased in a rather vague manner, without particular focus given to freedom of expression. Unfortunately, the Communication does not contain any further details on how such effect should be achieved.

NOTICE AND ACTION CONSULTATION – A more thorough analysis of the existing problems related to the elimination of illegal content was conducted in the Commission Staff Working Document on Online services, which accompanied the 2012 Communication.[431] The Working Document identified a range of issues regarding the regulation of intermediary liability in the E-Commerce Directive. The bulk of the analysis focuses on issues of fragmentation and legal uncertainty. Additionally, it discusses some specific problems of the notice and action mechanisms. All of these factors can have a negative impact on the freedom of expression of content providers, as well as content receivers.[432]

Following the publication of the Staff Working Document, in 2012, the EC decided to launch a new public consultation. This time the consultation was dedicated entirely to notice and action mechanisms for notifying and acting on illegal content hosted by online intermediaries. It consisted of a number of questions concerning the most pressing issues, such as:

- What is the scope of the term 'hosting' and which types of new services should it cover?
- Should there be rules to avoid abusive notices and what should they entail?
- Should hosting service providers consult the providers of alleged illegal content before taking action?
- How should the hosting service provider act with regard to illegal content and whether there should be an established sequence of actions?
- How can unjustified action against legal content be best prevented?
- Should hosting service providers be protected against liability that could result from taking pro-active measures?

Similar to the previous consultation, the EC received a large number of responses from a wide range of stakeholders. Unfortunately, the Commission has never released all responses but some of them were published by their authors nevertheless.[433]

431 European Commission, Online Services, Including e-commerce in Single Market, Commission Staff Working Paper, *o.c.*

432 See more *infra* Part I Chapter 6.

433 For the analysis of the available responses see A. Kuczerawy, "Intermediary Liability & Freedom of Expression: Recent Developments in the EU Notice & Action Initiative",

NOTICE AND ACTION DIRECTIVE? – In 2013 Brussels insiders revealed that the EC was working not only on a feedback to the consultation, but was actually preparing a proposal for a new Notice and Action Directive. Such a Directive would address the problem of Internet intermediaries' uncertainty without the need of amending the whole E-Commerce Directive. The plan for the Notice and Action Directive was to harmonize the procedures for obtaining knowledge, for processing and evaluating notices and acting upon them.[434] The proposal, however, has never been officially released. Several commentators suggested that the proposal was withdrawn due to heavy industry lobbying and a general sensitivity of the issue, especially in the light of the 2014 European elections.[435] Some feared that the planned initiative might be downgraded to a mere recommendation. This brought about disappointment from some Members of the European Parliament. In an open letter to the Internal Market and Services Commissioner Michael Barnier, they expressed their concerns that '*the political process will not gain legitimacy if publically elected representatives are not allowed to scrutinize and debate proposals of concern in a transparent and democratic manner*'.[436] This would be a risk if the draft directive did not reach the Parliament as a result of being converted into a recommendation. When speaking to the European Parliament in 2014, Commissioner Barnier indicated, however, that work on the Notice and Action initiative shall continue.[437]

2. DIGITAL SINGLE MARKET STRATEGY

NO REVISION OF THE DIRECTIVE? – After a break for the elections, the EU legislature returned to the topic of notice and action. In May 2015, the Commission announced a plan to assess the role of online platforms in the Communication on a Digital Single Market Strategy for Europe (DSM).[438] The document announced that platforms are increasingly taking centre stage with

---

Computer Law and Security Review, Vol. 31. Issue 1 2015, pages 46–56.

434 M. Husovec, *Injunctions Against Intermediaries in the European Union – Accountable But Not Liable?, o.c.*, p. 53.

435 M. Horten, Notice and action directive to be blocked as EU backs down, 28 July 2013, www.iptegrity.com/index.php/ipred/893-notice-and-action-directive-to-be-blocked-as-eu-backs-down.

436 Open Letter to Commissioner Barnier, https://ameliaandersdotter.eu/sites/default/files/letter_commissioner_barnier_notice_and_takedown.pdf.

437 M. Horten, Notice of Action! Barnier to resurrect take-down directive, 6 February 2014, www.iptegrity.com/index.php/ipred/945-notice-of-action-eu-commission-to-revive-take-down-directive.

438 European Commission, Commission Communication to the European Parliament, The Council, The Economic and Social Committee and The Committee of Regions, Online Platforms and the Digital Single Market Opportunities and Challenges for Europe, Brussels, 25 May 2016 COM(2016) 288 final, http://eurlex.europa.eu/legalcontent/EN/TXT/HTML/?uri=CELEX:52016DC0288&from=EN. The Communication was originally published in May

respect to access to information and content for many parts of society. According to the Commission, this role, '*necessarily, brings with it a wider responsibility*'. After holding another consultation[439], the Commission concluded in 2016 that it would maintain the existing intermediary liability regime while implementing a sectorial, problem-driven approach.[440] This means that the Commission plans to tackle the identified problems without re-opening the discussions on the E-Commerce Directive.[441] A similar approach was expressed in the 2018 analysis conducted for the European Parliament.[442] The author of the document, Jan Bernd Nordemann, argues that there '*seems to be no pressing need for a reform*' of the regime.[443] According to the author, the provisions seem to be sufficiently flexible to adapt to new business models, making them in general future proof. The fact that certain legal questions arising with regard to Articles 12 to 15 E-Commerce Directive remain unclear is because they have not been yet addressed by the CJEU. This situation, however, does '*not justify a reform, as it can be expected that the case law will answer the questions adequately respecting the different rights and interest at stake.*[444]

THE ROLE OF ONLINE PLATFORMS – The current policy discourse is steadily shifting from intermediary liability to intermediary responsibility.[445] In this book the former is understood as a negligence-based (*ex post*) approach while the latter emphasizes the need for proactive measures (*ex ante*). The shift is visible in several initiatives of the Commission that clearly steer in the direction of responsibilizing online platforms for regulating content by requiring them to take certain proactive measures. The Commission has started implementing this approach by introducing amendments or new legislation in different regulatory areas. In 2016, it took the form of a proposal for a Directive amending

---

2015, however, the website of the European Commission contains a slightly updated version of the document dated from May 2016.

439 See European Commission, Full report on the results of the public consultation on the Regulatory environment for Platforms, Online Intermediaries and the Collaborative Economy: Online Platforms Public Consultation Synopsis Report, 25 May 2016, https://ec.europa.eu/digital-single-market/en/news/full-report-results-public-consultation-regulatory-environment-platforms-online-intermediaries.

440 Commission Communication, Online Platforms and the Digital Single Market Opportunities and Challenges for Europe, *o.c.*

441 See more in S. Stalla-Bourdillon, "Internet intermediaries as responsible actors? Why it is time to rethink the e-Commerce Directive as well…", *o.c.*

442 J. B. Nordemann, Liability of Online Service Providers for Copyrighted Content – Regulatory Action Needed? In-depth analysis for Policy Department A upon request of the European Parliament's Committee on the Internal Market and Consumer Protection, IP/A/IMCO/2017-08 PE 614.207, January 2018, p. 4 and following.

443 *Ibid.*

444 *Ibid.*

445 See G. F. Frosio, "Why Keep a Dog and Bark Yourself? From Intermediary Liability to Responsibility", *International Journal of Law and Information Technology*, Vol. 26, Issue 1, 1 March 2018, Pages 1–33, p. 8.

the Audiovisual Media Services Directive and a proposal for a Directive on copyright in the Digital Single Market.[446] Moreover, the Commission introduced soft law initiatives, such as the EU Internet Forum against Terrorism and the Code of Conduct on Countering Illegal Hate Speech Online.[447] Recently, the Commission confirmed its stance regarding the Code of Conduct by urging IT companies to act faster to tackle online hate speech or face laws forcing them to do so.[448] It seems, therefore, that the Commission's solution to the problem of illegal and harmful online content is to place even greater responsibilities on private actors to take action.

GUIDELINES ON TACKLING ILLEGAL CONTENT ONLINE – A new confirmation of the tendency for greater responsibilization came in 2017, in the form of a new EC Communication, under the apt title "Towards an enhanced responsibility of online platforms".[449] The title gives away the main intention of the document, which is to lay down a set of guidelines and principles for online platforms to step up the fight against illegal content online in cooperation with national authorities, Member States and other relevant stakeholders.[450] It also aims to facilitate and intensify the implementation of good practices for preventing, detecting, removing and disabling access to illegal content with a goal to ensure the effective removal of illegal content, increased transparency and the protection of fundamental rights online.[451] Moreover, the 2017 Communication aims to provide clarifications to platforms on their liability when they take proactive steps to detect, remove or disable access to illegal content (the so-called "Good Samaritan" actions).[452] However, the guidelines and principles provided in the Communication not only target the detection and removal of illegal content, but they also seek to address concerns in

---

446 See Proposal for a Directive amending AVMS Directive 2010/13/EU, *o.c.*; Proposal for a Directive on copyright in the Digital Single Market, *o.c.*

447 See the EU Internet Forum against Terrorism: Bringing together governments, Europol and technology companies to counter terrorist content and hate speech online, Brussels, 3 December 2015, http://europa.eu/rapid/press-release_IP-15-6243_en.htm; Code of Conduct on Countering Illegal Hate Speech Online, *o.c.*

448 See European Commission, Fighting illegal online hate speech: first assessment of the new code of conduct, 6 December 2016, http://ec.europa.eu/newsroom/just/item-detail.cfm?item_id=50840. See also, F. Yun Che, EU urges U.S. tech giants to act faster against hate speech, 4 December 2016, www.reuters.com/article/us-eu-hate-speech-idUSKBN13T0XI.

449 European Commission, Commission Communication to the European Parliament, The Council, The Economic and Social Committee and The Committee of Regions, Tackling Illegal Content Online – Towards an enhanced responsibility of online platforms, Brussels, 28 September 2017, COM(2017) 555 final, https://ec.europa.eu/digital-single-market/en/news/communication-tackling-illegal-content-online-towards-enhanced-responsibility-online-platforms.

450 *Ibid.*, p. 3.

451 *Ibid.*

452 *Ibid.*

relation to over-removal of legal content.[453] The Communication is a response to the European Council's statements that it '*expects industry to … develop new technology and tools to improve the automatic detection and removal of content that incites to terrorist acts*' and the European Parliament's calls '*to strengthen measures to tackle illegal and harmful content*'.[454]

The Communication presents several safeguards for free expression, for example it proposes the introduction of a counter-notice mechanism, and promotes redress mechanisms, transparency and accountability. These positive elements are unfortunately over-shadowed by the negative ones, such as a strong emphasis on speed and volume of takedowns, promotion of automatic filtering tools, or opening the possibility for notice and stay down mechanisms.[455] What is the most striking, however, is the strong focus on the role of online platforms in enforcing the rule of law online. The Communication highlights that conviction repetitively, for example by stating that,

> 'online platforms which mediate access to content for most internet users carry a significant societal responsibility in terms of protecting users and society at large and preventing criminals and other persons involved in infringing activities online from exploiting their services'.[456]

Moreover, these 'online platforms should decisively step up their actions to address this problem, as part of the responsibility which flows from their central role in society'.[457] The Communication proposes that criteria to ensure a high quality of notices and faster removal of illegal content should be agreed by the industry at EU level. Such criteria should be based notably on respect for fundamental rights and of democratic values.[458] The Communication continuously emphasizes that the suggested measures and safeguards should be taken "voluntarily".

---

453 *Ibid.*, p. 6.

454 *Ibid.*, p. 2; European Parliament resolution 15 June 2017 on online platforms (2016/2274(INI)).

455 For criticism of the Communication see EDRi, Commission's position on tackling illegal content online is contradictory and dangerous for free speech, 28 September, 2017, https://edri.org/commissions-position-tackling-illegal-content-online-contradictory-dangerous-free-speech/; CDT, Tackling 'Illegal' Content Online: The EC Continues Push for Privatised Law Enforcement, 3 October 2017, https://cdt.org/blog/tackling-illegal-content-online-the-ec-continues-push-for-privatised-law-enforcement/; S. Stalla-Bourdillon, The EU approach to content regulation online: tackling (il)legal content online with upload and re-upload filters! 11 October 2017, https://peepbeep.wordpress.com/2017/10/11/the-eu-approach-to-content-regulation-online-tackling-illegal-content-online-with-upload-and-re-upload-filters/; G. Smith, Towards a filtered internet: the European Commission's automated prior restraint machine, 25 October 2017, www.cyberleagle.com/2017/10/towards-filtered-internet-european.html.

456 European Commission, Tackling Illegal Content Online – Towards an enhanced responsibility of online platforms, *o.c.*, p. 2.

457 *Ibid.*

458 *Ibid.*, p. 6.

RECOMMENDATION TO EFFECTIVELY TACKLE ILLEGAL CONTENT – In March 2018 the Commission issued yet another document addressing the problem of tackling illegal content online. The Recommendation on Measures to Effectively Tackle Illegal Content Online is a follow-up to the Communication from September 2017. The non-binding instrument sets out certain main principles that should guide the activities of the Member States and of the service providers concerned in effective tackling illegal content online. Another goal of the instrument is to safeguard the balanced approach that the E-Commerce Directive seeks to ensure.[459] The Recommendation highlights, again, that intermediaries have particular societal responsibilities to help tackle illegal content disseminated through the use of their services. Those responsibilities imply that the intermediaries should be able to make swift decisions regarding possible actions with respect to illegal content online, and that they should put in place effective and appropriate safeguards. Overall, however, the Recommendation appears to take a more nuanced approach than the Communication. The recommendations provided are directed to both Member States and the intermediaries. The instrument provides two types of recommendations: general recommendations applicable to all types of illegal content and specific recommendations relating to terrorist content.[460]

ANOTHER CONSULTATION – Despite having recently published two documents on the topic of illegal content online, in April 2018 the Commission announced another public consultation on measures to further improve the effectiveness of the fight against illegal content online.[461] Through the consultation the Commission intends to collect evidence on the effectiveness of measures and the scale of the problem of illegal content online. By the end of 2018, the Commission plans to explore further measures to improve the effectiveness of combating illegal content online.

3. INTERIM CONCLUSION

TOWARDS ENHANCED RESPONSIBILITY – Policy initiatives on combatting illegal content online started in 2010 with the review of the E-Commerce Directive and now continue under the umbrella of the Digital Single Market initiatives. Numerous initiatives that took place in this period suggest that the European Commission does not see the tackling of illegal content and activities

---

459 European Commission, Recommendation on Measures to Effectively Tackle Illegal Content Online, Brussels, 1 March 2018, C(2018) 1177 final, p. 3.

460 See more on the provided recommendations in Part III Chapter 3.

461 European Commission, Public consultation on measures to further improve the effectiveness of the fight against illegal content online, April 2018, https://ec.europa.eu/eusurvey/runner/illegal_content_onlin e.

online as its own role and responsibility. Moreover, they also suggest that the Commission attempts to assign the task of developing human rights complaint criteria or appropriate safeguards to private entities. The Communication acknowledges that a '*harmonised and coherent approach to removing illegal content does not exist at present in the EU*'.[462] This is true, yet it is somewhat surprising that instead of developing the missing rules to be followed by private companies, the EC requests that these companies develop the rules themselves. It would appear that the role foreseen for the State is merely subsidiary, as it is not taking a leading role but '*should be offered the possibility to participate*' in the reporting mechanisms, where relevant.[463] It is questionable whether it is acceptable for States to encourage or coerce Internet intermediaries to take "voluntary" measures that would not be permitted by international law or national constitutions, if they were provided for by law.[464] The Commission delegates tasks to the online platforms, partially due to their possession of technical means to identify and remove such content and partially because of the restrictions imposed by Article 15 of the E-Commerce Directive. However, such blatant off-loading of the basic State's obligation to regulate poses a question crucial to this book:

> **Is there a positive obligation derived from the relevant human rights law instruments (in particular Article 10 ECHR, and Article 11 EU Charter) for States to establish a formal legal framework for notice and action procedures?**

In this book the term "State" is used to mean legislature, both at national and EU level. The question is important to answer the main research question of this book. It is dealt with in Part II.

---

462 European Commission, Tackling Illegal Content Online – Towards an enhanced responsibility of online platforms, *o.c.*, p. 5.

463 *Ibid.*, p. 9.

464 EDRi, A letter to the Digital Economy Commissioner Mariya Gabriel, 20 October 2017, https://edri.org/files/letter_coherent_rightsbasedapproach_illegalcontent_20171020.pdf, p. 2.

CHAPTER 6
MAIN CRITICISMS

INTRODUCTION – The intermediary liability regime in the EU has been criticized from the beginning of its existence. This chapter provides an overview of the problematic issues identified in the regime, such as policy incoherence in general and specific aspects of the notice and take down mechanism in particular. The identified issues shall be used to develop the positive assessment framework in Part II Chapter 4 of this book.

1. POLICY INCOHERENCE

ADVERSE EFFECT – Policy incoherence can adversely affect the compatibility of the EU intermediary liability regime with human rights obligations. "Vertical incoherence" occurs in situations where States take on human rights commitments with no regard to implementation.[465] "Horizontal incoherence", on the other hand, describes a situation where different departments of the government (e.g. in charge of trade or development) work at cross purposes with the State's human rights obligation and the agencies responsible for implementing them.[466]

Both types of incoherence can be found under the current EU intermediary liability regime. The EU, acting as a legislator, is bound by the EU Charter of Fundamental Rights. Moreover, the EU is actively working on joining the European Convention on Human Rights, as foreseen in Article 6.2 TEU.[467] The EU's commitment to human rights protection seems to be clear.[468] That being said, the EU intermediary liability regime does not actively safeguard the right to freedom of expression – other than vaguely mentioning it in the preamble to the E-Commerce Directive.[469] As has been hitherto argued in this book, the right to freedom of expression is insufficiently protected in this context. This

---

465 Human Rights Council, Guiding Principles on Business and Human Rights: Implementing the United Nations 'Protect, Respect and Remedy' Framework, 16 June 2011, www.ohchr.org/Documents/Publications/GuidingPrinciplesBusinessHR_EN.pdf, p. 10.

466 *Ibid.*

467 Article 6.2 TEU: '*the Union shall accede to the European Convention for the Protection of Human Rights and Fundamental Freedoms* ', Treaty on European Union, *o.c.*

468 See more in Part II Chapters 2 and 3.

469 Recitals (9) and (46) to the E-Commerce Directive.

constitutes a situation of "vertical incoherence" since not enough regard is given to the implementation of the right to freedom of expression.

At the same time, there also seems to be a degree of "horizontal incoherence" among EU bodies in this area. Numerous EU institutions and departments work on different aspects of e-commerce and online communication. As put by Husovec, the '*E-Commerce Directive is going through a hard time. Numerous policy initiatives and judgements of the Court are exposing its provisions to a real stress test.*'[470] The goal of the E-Commerce Directive is to improve the internal market and strengthen the position of EU based online businesses.[471] Such attempts may require limiting liability of online intermediaries for third party content.[472] At the same time, several EU institutions also work on initiatives that promote swift removal of online content which contains racist and hate speech or which infringes rights of the copyright holders.[473] Providing immunity for user-generated content on the one hand, and, on the other hand, inviting service providers to police content in the current regime, may easily lead to contradictory results. For example, the Communication on online platforms indicated that '*a number of online platforms in the public consultation raised the concern that the introduction of voluntary measures would mean they would no longer benefit from the exemption from intermediary liability under the e-Commerce Directive*'.[474] Moreover, all of these goals (strengthening the position of EU based online businesses and fighting hate speech or copyright infringements online), have so far, given little consideration to the freedom of expression aspects.[475]

---

470 M. Husovec, "Holey Cap! CJEU Drills (Yet) Another Hole in the E-Commerce Directive's Safe Harbors", *Journal of Intellectual Property Law & Practice*, Vol. 12, Issue 2, 1 February 2017, pp. 115–125, p. 115.

471 Recital (2) to the E-Commerce Directive. See also A. Kuczerawy, J. Ausloos, "NoC Online Intermediaries Case Studies Series: European Union and Google Spain", 2015, http://papers.ssrn.com/sol3/papers.cfm?abstract_id=2567183, p. 5.

472 Recitals 1–6 of the E-Commerce Directive. See also A. Kuczerawy, J. Ausloos, "NoC Online Intermediaries Case Studies Series", *o.c.*, p. 7.

473 For example, the Code of Conduct on illegal online hate speech announced by the European Commission and IT Companies, European Commission – Press release, Brussels, 31 May 2016, http://europa.eu/rapid/press-release_IP-16-1937_en.htm; European Parliament speaks out against online homo- and transphobic hate speech, 29 April 2016, www.lgbt-ep.eu/press-releases/european-parliament-speaks-out-against-online-homo-and-transphobic-hate-speech/; European Parliament, Directorate-General for Internal Policies, Policy Department C: Citizens' Rights And Constitutional Affairs, The European legal framework on hate speech, blasphemy and its interaction with freedom of expression, LIBE, 2015, www.europarl.europa.eu/thinktank/en/document.html?reference=IPOL_STU(2015)536460. In the context of copyright, see: Modernisation of the EU copyright rules, 14 September 2016, https://ec.europa.eu/digital-single-market/en/modernisation-eu-copyright-rules; and also: BREAKING: Commission unveils new copyright package, The IPKat, 14 September 2016, http://ipkitten.blogspot.be/2016/09/breaking-commission-unveils-new.html.

474 Commission Communication, Online Platforms and the Digital Single Market Opportunities and Challenges for Europe, *o.c.*, p. 9.

475 See for example A. Kuczerawy, "Intermediary Liability & Freedom of Expression: Recent Developments in the EU Notice & Action Initiative", *o.c.*; A. Kuczerawy, The Code of Conduct on Online Hate Speech: an example of state interference by proxy?, *o.c.*

CHILD EXPLOITATION DIRECTIVE – Measures against certain types of illegal content online are included in Directive 2011/92/EU on combating the sexual abuse and sexual exploitation of children and child pornography.[476] Article 25 provides that

> 'Member States shall take the necessary measures to ensure the prompt removal of web pages containing or disseminating child pornography hosted in their territory and to endeavour to obtain the removal of such pages hosted outside of their territory'.[477]

Further, the provision also allows Member States to take measures to block access to web pages containing or disseminating child pornography on the Internet within their territory.[478] These measures must be set, however, by transparent procedures and provide adequate safeguards, in particular ensuring that the restriction is limited to what is necessary and proportionate, and that users are informed of the reason for the restriction. Those safeguards shall also include the possibility of judicial redress.[479] According to Recital (47) of the Directive, the necessary measures for removal or blocking access could be achieved through voluntary actions.[480] Already in 2012 civil society raised the issue of possible interference with the right to freedom of expression when the measures would be taken by private entities.[481] At that time however, the concern was disregarded.[482]

In 2016 the Commission published two implementation reports on the Directive, a general one and a specific one addressing the implementation of Article 25 of the Directive.[483] The latter report, despite being delayed for a year,

---

476 Directive 2011/92/EU of the European Parliament and of the Council of 13 December 2011 on combating the sexual abuse and sexual exploitation of children and child pornography, and replacing Council Framework Decision 2004/68/JHA, OJ L 335, 17 December 2011.

477 Article 25.1 of Directive 2011/92/EU.

478 Article 25.2 of Directive 2011/92/EU.

479 *Ibid.*

480 Recital (47) of Directive 2011/92/EU.

481 EDRi's letter to the Commission on the blocking aspect of the Child Exploitation Directive, 2 November 2012, https://edri.org/files/blocking_20121102.pdf.

482 European Commission's response to EDRi's letter on the blocking aspect of the Child Exploitation Directive, 26 November 2012, https://edri.org/files/priebe_response.pdf.

483 See European Commission, Report from the Commission to the European Parliament and the Council assessing the extent to which the Member States have taken the necessary measures in order to comply with Directive 2011/93/EU of 13 December 2011 on combating the sexual abuse and sexual exploitation of children and child pornography, Brussels, 16.12.2016 COM(2016) 871 final, http://eur-lex.europa.eu/legal-content/EN/TXT/PDF/?uri=CELEX:52016DC0871&from=EN; and European Commission, Report from the Commission to the European Parliament and the Council assessing the implementation of the measures referred to in Article 25 of Directive 2011/93/EU of 13 December 2011 on combating the sexual abuse and sexual exploitation of children and child pornography, Brussels, 16.12.2016 COM(2016) 872 final, http://eur-lex.europa.eu/legal-content/EN/TXT/PDF/?uri=CELEX:52016DC0872&from=EN.

fails to provide almost any meaningful data on the implementation of Article 25. For example, the report does not indicate how frequently law enforcement authorities take action after content is reported, nor the numbers of takedowns, the speed of processing reports of possibly illegal material, the delays in takedowns due to ongoing investigations, the number of websites appearing in blocking lists, the technologies used for blocking, the length of time sites stay on the blocking lists, or the location of sites on the blocking lists.[484] Moreover, the report fails to assess whether Member States implemented any of the safeguards listed in Article 25.2. The report received a sombre response from the European Parliament in 2017, in the form of a Resolution, criticizing the European Commission for failing to take the issue seriously.[485] Specifically, the Parliament

> '[d]eplores that the Commission was not able to present its implementation reports within the deadline set out in Article 28 of Directive 2011/93/EU and that the two evaluation reports presented by the Commission merely documented transposition into national law by Member States and did not fully assess their compliance with the Directive; requests the Member States to cooperate and forward to the Commission all of the relevant information on the implementation of the Directive, including statistics'.[486]

The implementation report provides an instance of policy incoherence at the EU level. The described situation is an example of when States take on commitments with no regard to implementation. Moreover, the subsequent Resolution of the Parliament points out the problem of formulating policy that is not based on evidence and empirical data. Such an approach creates a risky situation of law-making that is more of a display of showmanship rather than a comprehensive solution to a serious concern. As will be argued in Parts II and III, laws allowing for interference with the right to freedom of expression must ensure a certain degree of quality, which in this context means that they should be based on evidence.

PROPOSAL FOR A DIRECTIVE ON COPYRIGHT IN DSM – The problem of horizontal incoherence continues to trouble EU policy makers. It can be observed in the most recent documents released in realization of the Digital Single Market strategy. Specifically, the inconsistence can be spotted in the 2016 proposal for a

484 M. Fernández Pérez, Commission Report on child protection online lacks facts and evidence, 12 July 2017, https://edri.org/commission-report-on-child-protection-online-lacks-facts-and-evidence/.

485 European Parliament resolution of 14 December 2017 on the implementation of Directive 2011/93/EU of the European Parliament and of the Council of 13 December 2011 on combating the sexual abuse and sexual exploitation of children and child pornography (2015/2129(INI)), 14 December 2017.

486 *Ibid.*, point 3.

Directive on Copyright in the Digital Single Market.[487] Until the proposal was released, EU copyright law already comprised of more than 10 Directives.[488] The question of making copyrighted works available on the Internet is addressed in the Copyright Directive 2001/29/EC.[489] Article 8.3 of the Copyright Directive harmonises injunctions claims against Internet intermediaries[490] by providing that:

> 'Member States shall ensure that rightholders are in a position to apply for an injunction against intermediaries whose services are used by a third party to infringe a copyright or related right'.[491]

For other IP rights, Article 11 3rd sentence of the Enforcement Directive provides for the same remedy.[492] Essential parts of the EU copyright framework date back to 2001 and are not always adapted to the digital landscape.[493] The proposal for a

---

487 European Commission, Proposal for a Directive on copyright in the Digital Single Market, *o.c.*

488 Specifically, Directive on the coordination of certain rules concerning copyright and rights related to copyright applicable to satellite broadcasting and cable retransmission ("Satellite and Cable Directive"), 27 September 1993; Directive on the legal protection of databases ("Database Directive"), 11 March 1996; Directive on the harmonisation of certain aspects of copyright and related rights in the information society ("InfoSoc Directive"), 22 May 2001; Directive on the resale right for the benefit of the author of an original work of art ("Resale Right Directive"), 27 September 2001; Directive on the enforcement of intellectual property right ("IPRED"), 29 April 2004; Directive on rental right and lending right and on certain rights related to copyright in the field of intellectual property ("Rental and Lending Directive"), 12 December 2006; Directive on the legal protection of computer programs ("Software Directive"), 23 April 2009; Directive on the term of protection of copyright and certain related rights amending the previous 2006 Directive ("Term Directive"), 27 September 2011; Directive on certain permitted uses of orphan works ("Orphan Works Directive"), 25 October 2012; Directive on collective management of copyright and related rights and multi-territorial licensing of rights in musical works for online use in the internal market ("CRM Directive"), 26 February 2014; Directive on certain permitted uses of certain works and other subject matter protected by copyright and related rights for the benefit of persons who are blind, visually impaired or otherwise print-disabled (Directive implementing the Marrakech Treaty in the EU), 13 September 2017.

489 Directive 2001/29/EC of the European Parliament and of the Council of 22 May 2001 on the harmonisation of certain aspects of copyright and related rights in the information society, OJ L 167, 22 June 2001.

490 See more on injunctions against intermediaries and the interactions between the Copyright Directive and the E-Commerce Directive in M. Husovec, *Injunctions Against Intermediaries in the European Union – Accountable But Not Liable?, o.c.*

491 Article 8.3 Copyright Directive 2001/29/EC.

492 Corrigendum to Directive 2004/48/EC of the European Parliament and of the Council of 29 April 2004 on the enforcement of intellectual property rights, OJ L 157, 30 April 2004. See also European Commission, Communication from the Commission to the European Parliament, the Council, the European Economic and Social Committee, Guidance on certain aspects of Directive 2004/48/EC of the European Parliament and of the Council on the enforcement of intellectual property rights {SWD(2017) 431 final} – {SWD(2017) 432 final}, Brussels, 29.11.2017, COM(2017) 708 final.

493 See European Commission, State of the Union 2016: Questions and answers on the modernisation of EU copyright rules for the digital age, Strasbourg, 14 September 2016,

Directive on Copyright in DSM, released in September 2016, aims to modernise EU copyright rules.[494]

Article 13 of the proposed Copyright Directive in DSM addresses the 'Use of protected content by information society service providers storing and giving access to large amounts of works and other subject-matter uploaded by their users'. Specifically, this provision requires such service providers to use effective content recognition technologies to ensure the functioning of agreements concluded with right holders for the use of their works or to prevent the availability on their services of works identified by right holders.[495] It would seem, therefore, that Article 13 of the proposal envisages a general monitoring obligation that is incumbent upon a great number of intermediary service providers. Since it would require systematic monitoring of the entirety of their user and users' content basis to prevent any future infringement of intellectual property rights, it can hardly be considered a specific monitoring obligation.[496] As it stands, Article 13 contradicts Article 15 of the E-Commerce Directive. It also goes against the CJEU's reasoning in Scarlet v. Sabam and Sabam v. Netlog.[497]

The provision in Article 13 is further explained in Recital (38), where the issue becomes confusing. Recital (38) declares that when a provider stores and provides access to the public to copyright-protected works or other subject-matter uploaded by its users, unless it is eligible for the hosting safe harbour of the E-Commerce Directive, it is performing an act of communication to the public. It is therefore infringing and is liable for that infringement.[498] As stated by Angelopoulos, '*for a nonchalant statement hidden in a recital, this is quite the dramatic development of EU copyright law*'.[499] In the E-Commerce Directive, web hosting is a passive activity and in Recital (38) of the Copyright Directive the same activity is redefined as an active communication to the public, accompanied by a claim that the E-Commerce Directive remains in force.[500] The Recital further states that:

http://europa.eu/rapid/press-release_MEMO-16-3011_en.htm.

494 European Commission, Modernisation of the EU copyright rules, *o.c.*

495 See Article 13 of the Proposal for a Directive on copyright in the Digital Single Market.

496 See S. Stalla-Bourdillon et al., "A brief exegesis of the proposed Copyright Directive", *o.c.*

497 CJEU, *Scarlet Extended SA v. Société belge des auteurs, compositeurs et éditeurs SCRL (SABAM)*, C 70/10, 24 November 2011 and CJEU, *Belgische Vereniging van Auteurs, Componisten en Uitgevers CVBA (SABAM) v. Netlog NV*, Case C 360/10, 16 February 2012.

498 C. Angelopoulos, EU Copyright Reform: Outside the Safe Harbours, Intermediary Liability Capsizes into Incoherence, 6 October 2016, http://kluwercopyrightblog.com/2016/10/06/eu-copyright-reform-outside-safe-harbours-intermediary-liability-capsizes-incoherence/.

499 C. Angelopoulos, EU Copyright Reform: Outside the Safe Harbours, Intermediary Liability Capsizes into Incoherence, *o.c.*

500 EDRi, Deconstructing the Article 13 of the Copyright proposal of the European Commission, Revision 2, https://edri.org/files/copyright/copyright_proposal_article13.pdf.

> 'In respect of Article 14, it is necessary to verify whether the service provider plays an active role, including by optimising the presentation of the uploaded works or subject matter or promoting them, irrespective of the nature of the means used therefor'.[501]

This wording seeks to transpose the very specific logic used by the CJEU in a counterfeiting case.[502] Recital (38) seems to assert that "active role" includes '*optimising [...] irrespective of the nature of the means used therefor*', which contradicts the provisions of the E-Commerce Directive (Recital (43)) providing that active involvement does '*not cover manipulations of a technical nature which take place in the course of the transmission as they do not alter the integrity of the information contained in the transmission*'.[503] This means, that under the proposed Directive, all hosting services that optimise content in any way are understood to be "active" and therefore presumed to be aware of illegal activities.[504]

MORE CONFUSION – The 2017 Communication on Tackling Illegal Content Online is adding to the confusion. The Communication explains that, according to the Commission:

> 'taking such voluntary, proactive measures does not automatically lead to the online platform losing the benefit of the liability exemption provided for in Article 14 of the E-Commerce Directive'.[505]

Under the Communication, therefore, Internet providers are understood not to have knowledge of illegal content, even if they are actively searching for it. The Communication attempts to explain why these two positions are not inconsistent. The reason, according to the Commission, is a very specific interpretation of the *L'Oréal v. eBay* ruling, which states that the mere fact that an online platform takes certain measures relating to the provision of its services in a general manner does not necessarily mean that it plays an active role in respect of the individual content items it stores.[506] In the view of the Commission, such measures can, and should, also include proactive measures to detect and remove illegal content online.[507] It is doubtful, however, whether any court would agree

501 Recital (38) of the Proposal for a Directive on copyright in the Digital Single Market.
502 CJEU, *L'Oreal SA v. eBay*, Case C324/09, 12 July 2011.
503 Recital (43) of the E-Commerce Directive. See EDRi, Deconstructing the Article 13 of the Copyright proposal of the European Commission, *o.c.*
504 J. McNamee, Commission's position on tackling illegal content online is contradictory and dangerous for free speech, 28 September 2017, https://edri.org/commissions-position-tackling-illegal-content-online-contradictory-dangerous-free-speech/.
505 European Commission, Tackling Illegal Content Online – Towards an enhanced responsibility of online platforms, *o.c.*, p. 10.
506 *Ibid.*, p. 11.
507 *Ibid.*

that taking pro-active measures to monitor content of users does not lead to obtaining (at least constructive) knowledge of illegalities on the platform.

FURTHER WORKS ON THE COPYRIGHT DIRECTIVE – The European Commission launched its proposal in September 2016. It was then sent to the European Parliament and the Council of the European Union. On 21 February 2018, the rapporteur of the European Parliament's Committee on Legal Affairs (JURI) Axel Voss issued suggestions for a compromise on the proposal text.[508] The proposal maintains Article 13 of the Directive, however, it adds a rule that platforms which allow users to upload content are not obliged to install any pre-filtering technology if they obtained a licensing agreement with rights holders. This "compromise" has been criticized for potentially reinforcing the dominant positions of platforms like Facebook or YouTube, who are already concluding such licence agreements.[509] At the same time, non-profit platforms such as Wikipedia would be forced to employ upload filters. In June 2018, the Legal Affairs Committee narrowly approved the text (with minor changes) to negotiate directly with the Council in the so-called "trilogue" process.[510]

In the meanwhile, the problem of non-profit platforms was being addressed at the Council level. The Bulgarian Presidency issued a compromise version of the proposal on 23 March 2018.[511] The text of recital 37a in the Presidency text intends to clarify which services will not be covered. This recital takes out internet access providers, cloud services such as cyberlockers, online marketplaces, online encyclopaedias, scientific or educational repositories, or open source software developing platforms which do not store and give access to content for profit making purposes. Further, the Council version contains an additional subsection to Recital (38), expanding it all the way to (38e). For example, Recital (38C), states that

> 'When online content sharing service providers communicate to the public, they should not benefit from the limited liability provided for in Article 14 of Directive 2000/31/EC for the purposes of copyright relevant acts. This should not affect

508 See Proposal for a Directive on Copyright in the Digital Single Market, Draft compromise amendments on Article 13 and corresponding recitals, Version 1, 21 February 2018, https://juliareda.eu/wp-content/uploads/2018/02/20180221-Draft-CA-on-Article-13_v1.pdf.

509 M. Schmid, Final Copyright "compromise": Upload filters for everyone but Google & Co, 23 February 2018, https://edri.org/final-copyright-compromise-upload-filters-everyone-google-co/.

510 J. Vincent, EU takes first step in passing controversial copyright law that could 'censor the internet', 20 June 2018, https://www.theverge.com/2018/6/20/17482554/eu-european-union-copyright-filter-article-11-13-passes-juri-vote.

511 See Proposal for a Directive of the European Parliament and of the Council on copyright in the Digital Single Market – Consolidated Presidency Compromise Proposal. Interinstitutional File: 2016/0280 (COD), Brussels, 23 March 2018. http://data.consilium.europa.eu/doc/document/ST-7450–2018-INIT/en/pdf.

> the possibility for the same online content sharing providers to benefit from such exemption of liability for other purposes than copyright when they are providing their services and host content at the request of their users in accordance with Article 14 of Directive 2000/31/EC'.[512]

Such a formulation suggests that the Council would like to take copyright infringement online out of the scope of the E-Commerce Directive, going against its horizontal character. It is clear that it becomes increasingly difficult to maintain coherence between the E-Commerce Directive in its current form, and the variety of policy goals on the EU's agenda. It is beyond the scope of this book to conduct a detailed analysis of the multiple versions of the proposed Directive on Copyright in DSM. The process will not be finalized before the end of 2018. It should be mentioned, however, that in a surprise move the Parliament rejected the Committee's position, opening it up for further debate. In July 2018' vote, 318 MEPs voted against the draft law, and 278 in favour.[513] In the next step, the entire Parliament will vote on changes to the Committee position on September 12, 2018.

PROPOSAL FOR AMENDING THE AVMS DIRECTIVE – Another example of incoherence can be found in the proposed amendment to the 2010 Audiovisual Media Services Directive (the "AVMS Directive").[514] The European Commission introduced the idea for the reform in May 2016. The current AVMS Directive regulates traditional TV broadcasters and on-demand services in the EU.[515] The Directive contains, among other measures, rules on audiovisual advertising, jurisdiction over providers, promotion of European works, and on providers' obligations with regards to commercial communications, protection of minors from potentially harmful content, and fight against incitement to hatred. The reason for the change is explained by the document, stating that the current AVMSD does not apply to user-generated content on video-sharing platforms since the providers of such platforms often do not have editorial responsibility for the content stored on their platforms.[516] Moreover, in many cases these services are subject to the e-Commerce Directive, as they constitute information society services. The new proposal, therefore, aims to broaden the scope of the AVMS Directive to cover the regulation of video-sharing platforms and possibly also other social media companies.[517] The crucial provision of

---

512 *Ibid.* Recital (38c), p. 32.

513 J. Vincent, EU sends controversial internet copyright reforms back to the drawing board, 5 July 2018, https://www.theverge.com/2018/7/5/17535874/eu-copyright-law-article-11-13-rejected-first-vote.

514 European Commission, Proposal for a Directive amending AVMS Directive 2010/13/EU, *o.c.*

515 AVMS Directive 2010/13/EU *o.c.*, p. 1–24.

516 European Commission, Proposal for a Directive amending AVMS Directive 2010/13/EU, *o.c.*

517 The proposal aims to target social media platforms if they provide a service that falls under the definition of a video-sharing platform. See Recital (3) of the Proposal for a Directive

the amendment is contained in Article 28a, which requires Members States to ensure that video-sharing platform providers take appropriate measures to: '*a) protect minors from content which may impair their physical, mental or moral development*'; and '*b) protect all citizens from content containing incitement to violence or hatred directed against a group of persons or a member of such a group defined by reference to sex, race, colour, religion, descent or national or ethnic origin*'. Article 28a is, supposedly, without prejudice to Articles 14 and 15 of Directive 2000/31/EC. The proposal lists a number of measures to achieve this result, for example, establishing mechanisms for users of video-sharing platforms to report or flag content or establishing and operating age verification systems. Another measure consists of defining in the terms and conditions of the video-sharing platforms the concepts of incitement to violence or hatred and of content which may impair the physical, mental or moral development of minors (Article 28a 2a). This means that the proposal would require Internet platforms to regulate legal content based on their terms of service, not the law.[518] This could lead to deleting anything potentially problematic. Moreover, the proposal constitutes yet another attempt to enlist Internet service providers to police content.

CODE OF CONDUCT ON COUNTERING ILLEGAL HATE SPEECH – In May 2016 the European Commission announced yet another initiative to tackle illegal content online. This time the initiative focused on hate speech online. The Code of Conduct on Countering Illegal Hate Speech Online[519] was launched in cooperation with a select number of IT companies, such as Facebook, YouTube (Google), Twitter and Microsoft, united under the banner of the "EU Internet Forum".[520] The Code is a soft law initiative by which the involved IT companies guide their own activities, at the incentive of the Commission. In the Code of Conduct, IT companies commit themselves to "take the lead" on countering the spread of illegal hate speech online. Moreover, they agreed with the Commission to:

amending AVMS Directive 2010/13/EU. See also M. Fernández Pérez, Audiovisual Media Services Directive reform: Document pool, 15 May 2017, https://edri.org/avmsd-reform-document-pool/.

518 *Ibid.*

519 European Commission, Countering illegal hate speech online #NoPlace4Hate, 16 March 2018, http://ec.europa.eu/newsroom/just/item-detail.cfm?item_id=54300.

520 Not much information is publically available on the EU Internet Forum. It consists of Internet industry (mainly from the US), Commission officials and Member state representatives, civil society was initially not included and later on joined the discussions (but not negotiations) soon to withdrew from the initiative completely. See more in K. Fiedler, Launch of the EU Internet Forum – behind closed doors and without civil society, 5 August 2015, https://edri.org/launch-of-the-eu-internet-forum-behind-closed-doors-and-without-civil-society/; and EDRi on IT-Forum, 16 December 2015, https://edri.org/files/IT-Forum_EDRi_Position.pdf; and EDRi and Access Now withdraw from the EU Commission IT Forum discussions, 31 May 2016, https://edri.org/edri-access-now-withdraw-eu-commission-forum-discussions/.

- have in place clear and effective processes to review notifications regarding illegal hate speech on their services so that they can remove or disable access to such content;
- provide Rules or Community Guidelines clarifying that they prohibit the promotion of incitement to violence and hateful conduct;
- review such requests against their rules and community guidelines and, where necessary, national laws upon receipt of a valid removal notification;
- review the majority of valid notifications for removal of illegal hate speech in less than 24 hours and remove or disable access to such content, if necessary.

The Code was criticized from the beginning by civil society organizations and academics.[521] The main points of criticism focused on the overly broad definition of "hate speech", the risk of excessive interference with the right to freedom of expression, and a lack compliance with the principles of legality, proportionality, and due process. Strictly speaking, any interference with freedom of expression resulting from the implementation of the Code cannot be attributed directly to the Commission, as the restrictions would be administered by the IT companies. Nevertheless, it is clear that the Commission's role is not merely as a facilitator, but as an initiator of the interference with the fundamental right by private entities. Similarly, as in the proposed Copyright Directive in DSM and the amendments to the AVMS Directive, the Code is based on the delegation of enforcement activities from States to private companies by encouraging them to undertake "voluntary" actions and the elevation of terms and conditions above the law.

Since the adoption of the Code, the Commission conducts yearly evaluations through a monitoring exercise.[522] The evaluation is performed in collaboration with civil society organisations from different EU countries. Using a commonly agreed methodology, these organisations test how the IT companies apply the Code of Conduct in practice. So far, three evaluations have taken place, indicating clearly that the focus is placed mainly on the rate and speed of removals, which are steadily growing. At the same time, the second evaluation report pointed out that work should continue on providing '*minimum procedural requirements for the notice and action procedures of online intermediaries*'.[523]

---

521 See for example, J. McNamee, Guide to the Code of Conduct on Hate Speech, *o.c.*; Article 19, European Commission's Code of Conduct for Countering Illegal Hate Speech Online and the Framework Decisions, *o.c.*; CDT, Letter to European Commission on Code of Conduct for "Illegal" Hate Speech Online, *o.c.*

522 See European Commission, Code of Conduct on countering online hate speech – results of evaluation show important progress, 1 June 2017, http://ec.europa.eu/newsroom/just/item-detail.cfm?item_id=71674; and European Commission, Results of Commission's last round of monitoring of the Code of Conduct against online hate speech, 19 January 2018, http://ec.europa.eu/newsroom/just/item-detail.cfm?item_id=612086.

523 See European Commission, Code of Conduct on countering illegal hate speech online: One year after – Fact Sheet, June 2017, http://ec.europa.eu/newsroom/just/item-detail.cfm?item_

Specifically, such requirements should include quality criteria for notices, counter-notice procedures, reporting obligations, third-party consultation mechanisms and dispute resolution systems.[524]

2. NOTICE AND ACTION PROCEDURES

INTRODUCTION – The intermediary liability regime of the E-Commerce Directive has been scrutinized ever since its enactment. An inventory of the critical remarks was provided in the Commission Staff Working Document on Online Services in 2012.[525] The bulk of the analysis focuses on issues of fragmentation and legal uncertainty. Additionally, it discusses some specific problems of the notice and action mechanisms. All of these factors can have a negative impact on the freedom of expression of content providers, as well as content receivers. The following section summarizes the most relevant criticism contained in the Staff Working Document and is further expanded with relevant case law and doctrine.

LEGAL FRAGMENTATION – The main issue is a lack of uniform rules for notice and action mechanisms across the EU. This is considered to be one of the major obstacles for intermediary service providers as well as for victims of illegal content seeking to exercise their rights.[526] It could also lead to a race to the bottom, in a way that intermediaries would adopt the interpretation followed by the countries with the most restrictive rules on content. This would allow them to keep their response consistent across different countries and, at the same time, ensure the highest chance of protection against possible liability. Such an approach, however, could be highly detrimental for freedom of expression.

LEGAL UNCERTAINTY – Legal uncertainty is the most common complaint of stakeholders with regard to the notice and action regime. Legal uncertainty is problematic because vague rules can push intermediaries to adopt overly cautious behaviour. When not sure about their legal situation, they may prefer to err on the side of caution, which means that they eliminate disputed content, even if it is actually legitimate. The most common criticism by stakeholders refers to the unclear scope of the definitions of intermediaries. Particularly in the case of "new" services (e.g. video-sharing sites or social networking sites), it can be difficult to establish whether they can benefit from the safe harbours

id=71674.

524 *Ibid.*

525 European Commission, Online Services, Including e-commerce in Single Market, Commission Staff Working Paper, *o.c.*

526 *Ibid.*, p. 24–26.

offered by the Directive. Further, they complain about the unclear conditions for exoneration.

ACTIVE AND PASSIVE HOSTING – Another major issue concerns the distinction between active and passive hosting providers. The requirement that an intermediary's activities are of a mere technical, automatic, and passive nature is based on Recital (42) of the E-Commerce Directive. These properties of the service imply that the intermediary has neither knowledge of nor control over the information it transmits or stores. The wording of the recital, however, is problematic. While it purports to address all of the exemptions of the Directive, some argue that the scope of this recital should be limited to the transmission and access services identified in Articles 12 (mere conduit) and 13 (caching). As is further clarified in Recital (43), not being involved in any way with the transmitted information is actually a condition for liability exemption for mere conduit and caching services. The exemption for hosting in Article 14 of the Directive is not limited in scope to either transmission or access services. According to Van Eecke, Article 14 in fact does not require a passive role of the hosting provider in order for the protection regime to apply.[527] A hosting provider can still be protected even if it is not completely passive – as long as it does not have knowledge or control over the data which is being stored. This approach is referred to as '*storage but no knowledge*' test.[528] Following this line of reasoning, active intermediaries could still benefit from the safe harbour offered by the E-Commerce Directive, provided that they do not have knowledge or control over the data which is being stored.

The restrictive interpretation of Recital (42) is not commonly agreed on. In *Google Adwords*, the CJEU considered that Recital (42) also applies to hosting services.[529] The CJEU held that, in order to establish whether the liability of a referencing service provider may be limited under Article 14 of Directive 2000/31, it is necessary to examine whether the role played by that service provider is neutral, in the sense that its conduct is merely technical, automatic and passive. If this is the case, the referencing service provider cannot be held liable for the data stored at the request of an advertiser and any trademark infringements resulting thereof, unless, after having obtained knowledge of the unlawful nature of those data or of that advertiser's activities, it fails to act expeditiously to remove or to disable access to the data concerned. The CJEU clarified that the mere fact that a referencing service is subject to payment, that the provider sets the payment terms or that it provides general information to its clients cannot have the effect of depriving that provider of the exemptions from

527 P. Van Eecke, "Online Service Providers and Liability: a Plea for a Balanced Approach", *o.c.*, p. 1463.

528 *Ibid.*, p. 1472–1474.

529 CJEU, *Google France Inc.* v. *LouisVuitton Malletier e.a.*, Joined Cases C-236, 237 & 238/08, 23 March 2010, paras. 113–114.

liability provided for in the E-Commerce Directive. In the same vein, the Court pointed out that concordance between the keyword selected and the search term entered by an internet user is not sufficient in itself to justify the view that Google has knowledge of, or control over, the data entered into its system by advertisers and stored in memory on its server. By contrast, if the provider takes up a more active role in the drafting of the commercial message which accompanies the advertising link or in the establishment or selection of keywords, this may trigger liability. The CJEU left it to the national court to assess the actual role played by Google.

In *L'Oréal v. eBay*, however, the CJEU seemingly reduced the standard by replacing the "neutrality" requirement with "lack of knowledge".[530] The CJEU ruled that Article 14 of the Directive applies to hosting providers if they do not play an active role that would allow them to have knowledge or control of the stored data (paragraphs 112–116). The main factor is how the service is designed or operated. The fact that the operator of a website sets the terms of its service, is remunerated for that service and provides general information to its customers cannot have the effect of denying it the exemptions from liability provided for by Directive 2000/31 (paragraph 115). These types of activities would not lead, in the CJEU's opinion, to the knowledge or control of the stored information. Such an effect could be achieved, however, if the service provider assisted customers in optimising the presentation of certain information, or promoted certain information (paragraph 116).

KNOWLEDGE – Article 14 of the E-Commerce Directive provides for a liability exemption for third party content on the condition that the service provider has not had "actual knowledge of illegal activity or information" and, as regards claims for damages, has not been "aware of facts or circumstances from which the illegal activity or information is apparent" (i.e. constructive knowledge).[531] Upon obtaining such knowledge or awareness, the service provider has to act expeditiously to remove, or disable access to, the information. Apparent illegality occurs, according to CJEU in *L'Oréal v. eBay*, when '*any diligent economic operator should have identified the illegality in question*' (para. 120).[532] Such "constructive knowledge" covers every situation in which the provider concerned becomes aware, in one way or another, of such facts or circumstances (para. 121). In particular, it covers both the situation where the operator of an

530 CJEU, *L'Oréal v. eBay*, Case C-324/09, 12 July 2011, paras. 112 – 116.

531 H. Kaspersen and A. Lodder (eds.), *E-directive: guide to European Union law on e-commerce: commentary on the directives on distance selling, electronics signatures, electronic commerce, copyright in the information society, and data protection*, Den Haag, Kluwer, 2002, p. 88–89. This distinction, however, has not been transposed into all national legislations. See more in: P. Van Eecke, M. Truyens, Legal analysis of a Single Market for the Information Society, New rules for a new age? *o.c.*, p.19, ft. 97.

532 CJEU, *L'Oréal v. eBay*, Case C-324/09, 12 July 2011.

online marketplace uncovers an illegal activity or illegal information as the result of an investigation undertaken on its own initiative, and the situation where the operator is notified by a third party. Such notification represents, as a general rule, a factor indicating "awareness", although it could turn out to be insufficiently precise or inadequately substantiated (para. 122). Requirements for valid notification, as well as interpretations of actual and constructive knowledge, differ across EU countries. Divergent case law across the EU shows that there is lack of consistency in the interpretation of these terms and the associated requirements for liability exemptions.[533]

NO PROCEDURE –The E-Commerce Directive implies a notice and take down mechanism but does not explicitly provide for one. The problems resulting from this approach start as early as defining the requirements for valid notice. On the one hand, the notice should be sufficiently detailed for service providers to locate and assess the illegality of the content, but on the other hand, it cannot place too heavy a burden on notice providers.[534] At EU level, however, no guidelines were put forth concerning the implementation of notice and action. The introduction of the actual procedures was left entirely to the discretion of the Member States. Recital (46) of the E-Commerce Directive explicitly confirms that the removal or disabling of access should be undertaken in observance of the right to freedom of expression and procedures should be established for this purpose at national level. In its Article 16 and Recital (40), the Directive encourages self-regulation in this field. Since the majority of the Member States chose for a verbatim transposition of the Directive, the matter was mostly left to self-regulation.[535] However, this self-regulatory approach proved to be insufficient. The result is a lack of any firm safeguards for freedom of expression in the process of online content removal in many jurisdictions.[536]

RESPONSE TIME – Once a notice has been issued, the hosting provider is expected to react. The timeframe for this action, however, is not specified and opinions differ as to when this timeframe starts running. The term "expeditiously" is likewise understood differently by various stakeholders. There is also disagreement as to whether the EU should specify what constitutes an

533 See for example: BGH, 23/09/2003, VI ZR 335/02; Dutch Supreme Court 25 November 2005, LJN Number AU4019, case number C04/234HR; M. Turner(ed.) & J. Llevat, "The Spanish Supreme Court clarifies the concept of actual knowledge in connection with ISP's liability", *o.c.*

534 European Commission, Online Services, Including e-commerce in Single Market, Commission Staff Working Paper, *o.c.*, p. 43.

535 T. Verbiest et al., Study on the Liability of Internet Intermediaries, commissioned by the European Commission, *o.c.*

536 European Commission, Online Services, Including e-commerce in Single Market, Commission Staff Working Paper, *o.c.*, p. 43–47.

"expeditious" reaction.[537] The right holders claim that the term should be clearly defined and that the given time period should be short. Intermediaries, on the other hand often argue that leaving the meaning of this term open would provide them with some flexibility in applying it. The term is also very likely to be context dependent. From the perspective of freedom of expression, reaction time matters in the sense that it either encourages a swift take down (short response time) or it allows for a more thorough assessment of the content (longer, more flexible period). An almost-immediate response does not leave much room for deliberations. The flexible approach, on the other hand, allows for a more balanced response and could more readily promote fair consideration of the content provider's interests. It should be clear, however, that in this discussion the nature of the infringement should also be taken into account. The same response time will not work in every context. For example, a 12 hours period might seem short in some instances (e.g. defamatory statements) but might be too long in case of live streaming of copyrighted material.

ABUSIVE NOTICE – Wrongful notices perhaps present the greatest risk to freedom of expression in the current legal framework. Wrongful notices might be issued in good or bad faith but in both cases they can lead to removal of legitimate content. Certain stakeholders argue that penalization of such wrongful notices would help decrease their number.[538] In their opinion, the issuers of a take down notice currently have nothing to lose so they just go ahead and try.[539] This, in combination with the absence of any incentive to conduct a thorough assessment, together with a risk of being held liable, results in a situation where the contested information is often removed or blocked by service providers without giving it a second thought. This leads to situations when legitimate content, for example criticism in academic discussion or research, political speech, parody or tribute, suffers from such risk-averse behaviour by intermediaries.[540] The question is also asked of who is to be held liable in such situations (the notice provider or the service provider).[541] Most of the commentators argue that the ISPs should not be blamed in this type of case,

---

537 *Ibid.*, p. 37–39.

538 European Commission, Summary of the results of the Public Consultation on the future of electronic commerce in the Internal Market and the implementation of the Directive on electronic commerce, *o.c.*, p. 12.

539 Electronic Frontier Foundation, Takedown Hall of Shame, www.eff.org/takedowns – documenting abuses of US trademark and copyright law to silence critics or political opponents. In the global context see Onlinecensorship.org, https://onlinecensorship.org/.

540 T. Verbiest et al., Study on the liability of Internet Intermediaries, *o.c.*, p.15; OECD, The Economic and Social Role of Internet Intermediaries, *o.c.*, ft. 83; CDT, Shielding the Messengers: Protecting Platforms for Expression and Innovation, Version 2, updated December 2012, https://cdt.org/insight/shielding-the-messengers-protecting-platforms-for-expression-and-innovation/.

541 European Commission, Online Services, Including e-commerce in Single Market, Commission Staff Working Paper, *o.c.*, p. 46.

providing that they followed the applicable NTD procedure.[542] Currently, this issue is addressed only by some national legislations while others do not attend to this issue at all.[543]

COUNTER-NOTIFICATION – In its Staff Working Document, the European Commission also contemplates the use of 'counter-notices' to help protect freedom of expression.[544] Counter-notices can be found in the DMCA, which contains liability exemptions similar to those of the ECD. Several EU countries have also introduced such a measure in their national notice and takedown procedures, but it has not become a standard part of the procedure across Europe.[545] The objective of these counter-notice mechanisms is to give the providers of allegedly illegal content an opportunity to answer to the allegations of illegality. Proponents argue that such a right to respond would introduce an important element of the due process. It would secure a right to defence for content providers and would result in a better assessment of the content.[546] Such a mechanism could be one way of limiting excessive take downs. Critics argue, however, that a counter-notice mechanism would make the whole process more burdensome, slow and ineffective, and that it would not be appropriate in case of manifestly illegal content (e.g. child sexual abuse material). Most of this criticism comes, unsurprisingly, from the copyright industry. This group of stakeholders systematically emphasize the importance of efficiency in the take down process. However, American scholars also point out the weaknesses of this safeguard. Some research shows that, at least in the context of the DMCA, counter-notice is rarely used in practice.[547] This is because it is considered an added cost, which individuals are not willing to accept when exercising their right to free speech.[548] Moreover, individuals are often intimidated by the penalties for perjury in case of misrepresentation.[549]

---

542 *Ibid.*

543 See more in First Report on the Application of Directive 2000/31/EC, *o.c.*

544 European Commission, Online Services, Including e-commerce in Single Market, Commission Staff Working Paper, *o.c.*, p. 45.

545 In particular Finland, Hungary, Lithuania, and Spain. See more in First Report on the Application of Directive 2000/31/EC *o.c*; and Part III Chapter 3 of this thesis.

546 GNI, Comments on the Public Consultation on Procedures for Notifying and Acting on Illegal Content Hosted by Online Intermediaries, 5 September 2012, http://globalnetworkinitiative.org/sites/default/files/GNI%20Comments%20on%20EC%20Notice%20and%20Action%20consult.pdf.

547 J. Urban, J. Karaganis, and B. L. Schofield, "Notice and Takedown in Everyday Practice", UC Berkeley Public Law Research Paper No. 2755628, p.42; J. Urban and L. Quilter, Efficient Processes or Chilling Effects?, *o.c.*, p. 679.

548 See more in W. Seltzer, "The Politics of Internet Control and Delegated Censorship", *The American Society of International Law*, April 10, 2008; W. Seltzer, "Free Speech Unmoored in Copyright's Safe Harbor: Chilling Effects of the DMCA on the First Amendment", *Harvard Journal of Law & Technology*, Vol. 24, Number 1 Fall 2010.

549 See A. Bridy, D. Keller, U.S. Copyright Office Section 512 Study: Comments in Response to Notice of Inquiry, 31 March 2016, p. 29. See more in Part III Chapter 2.1.

LACK OF REDRESS MECHANISMS – The E-Commerce Directive provides a possibility of remedy for online infringements of rights, such as intellectual property rights. Already in the 2010 consultation stakeholders noticed, however, that the Directive does not provide the users whose content had been removed with a possibility to object such a decision.[550] Takedown of certain online content may have a negative impact on the exercise of the rights to freedom of expression and information.[551] It may impact, moreover, the right to effective remedy if no redress mechanism for wrongful takedown is available. To prevent such an effect, an appeal mechanism should be provided to contest arbitrary takedown decisions by intermediaries. Such mechanisms should allow restoration of the content online as well as the possibility to appeal to a higher authority.[552] One step towards providing such a mechanism is through the introduction of a counter-notice.[553] Moreover, to satisfy the right to effective remedy a possibility of judicial redress should always be available. Currently, the E-Commerce Directive does not provide such safeguards.[554] In theory, the fact that the Directive does not mention such a possibility does not prevent content providers from attempting to exercise their rights in courts. The lack of such a safeguard, however, may create an effective obstacle in exercising this right.

---

550 See Summary of the results of the Public Consultation on the future of electronic commerce in the Internal Market and the implementation of the Directive on electronic commerce *o.c.*, p. 12.

551 European Commission, Online Services, Including e-commerce in Single Market, Commission Staff Working Paper, *o.c.*, p. 44.

552 J. Panday et al., Comparative Study Of Intermediary Liability Regimes Chile, Canada, India, South Korea, UK and USA in support of the Manila Principles On Intermediary Liability, 1 July 2015, p. 54.

553 European Commission, Online Services, Including e-commerce in Single Market, Commission Staff Working Paper, *o.c.*, p. 44.

554 Respect for the right to effective remedy is mentioned explicitly in the Communication from the Commission to the European Parliament, the Council, the European Economic and Social Committee and the Committee of the Regions, A Single Market for Intellectual Property RightsBoosting creativity and innovation to provide economic growth, high quality jobs and first class products and services in Europe, COM(2011) 287 24 May 2011, http://ec.europa.eu/internal_market/copyright/docs/ipr_strategy/COM_2011_287_en.pdf. The Communication announces a review of the Enforcement Directive that should in particular find ways to combat infringements of IPR via the Internet more effectively by '*tackling the infringements at their source and, to that end, foster cooperation of intermediaries, such as internet service providers while respecting all fundamental rights recognised by the EU Charter of Fundamental Rights, in particular also the rights to private life, protection of personal data, freedom of expression and information and to an effective remedy*'.

CHAPTER 7
CONCLUSION

FREEDOM OF EXPRESSION ON THE INTERNET – Freedom of expression is a core democratic value. It is an *'essential foundation'* of any democratic society and *'one of the basic conditions for its progress and for the development of every man'*.[555] Access to diverse and pluralistic information on the Internet is fundamental for democracy and cultural diversity.[556] In this regard, the Internet acts as a tool for citizens to actively participate in building and strengthening democratic societies.[557] As pointed out by the ECtHR, in *Yildrim*, *'Internet has now become one of the principal means by which individuals exercise their right to freedom of expression and information, providing as it does essential tools for participation in activities and discussions concerning political issues and issues of general interest'*.[558]

Moreover, the Committee of Ministers observed that

> 'the exercise and enjoyment of the right to freedom of expression by individuals, including the right to receive and impart information and ideas, as well as their participation in democratic life, are increasingly reliant upon the accessibility and quality of an Internet connection'.[559]

CO-OPTING INTERNET INTERMEDIARIES – The EU intermediary liability regime places Internet intermediaries in the role of gatekeepers. By providing the incentive of a liability exemption, States ensure cooperation of intermediaries in policing content on the Internet. To minimize the risk of potential liability, Internet intermediaries are eager to remove impugned content. This mechanism results in a situation where private entities are co-opted by the States to decide about matters which affect the fundamental human right to freedom of expression. Effectively, the intermediaries are given power to decide whether content should stay accessible or be removed.

---

555 ECtHR, *Handyside v. the United Kingdom*, 7 December 1976, par. 49.

556 Council of Europe, Recommendation CM/Rec(2016)1 of the Committee of Ministers to member States on protecting and promoting the right to freedom of expression and the right to private life with regard to network neutrality, 13 January 2016.

557 Council of Europe, Recommendation CM/Rec(2014)6 of the Committee of Ministers to member States on a Guide to human rights for Internet users, 16 April 2014.

558 ECtHR, *Ahmet Yıldırım v. Turkey*, 18 March 2013, para. 54.

559 Council of Europe, Recommendation CM/Rec(2016)1, *o.c.*

PRAGMATIC APPROACH – Enlisting private entities to decide on the availability of online content has both advantages and disadvantages. The advantages are situated mainly in the area of efficiency and effectiveness. In the context of online expression, where information spreads in a flash, the benefits of a swift reaction are clear. Infringing or illegal content which remains online for an extended period of time can cause serious harm – some of it irreparable (e.g. reputational). Providing a rapid response mechanism such as notice and action as a readily available remedy, before the somewhat lingering judiciary reacts, is not unreasonable. The question is, however, whether such a mechanism should have built-in safeguards to ensure respect for fundamental human rights and prevent over-compliance.[560]

FROM ISSUES TO SAFEGUARDS – There are multiple issues with the EU intermediary liability regime and the notice and takedown mechanism. Policy incoherence at EU level, both vertical and horizontal, can have an adverse effect on freedom of expression. The current intermediary liability regime, moreover, enhances the risk of over-compliance and therefore lack of proportionality of response mechanisms. Lack of legal certainty taints the regime as a whole, as well as specific aspects of the notice and action mechanisms. Specific issues with the latter can be grouped into different categories, including quality of law (uncertainty and fragmentation), procedural fairness (lack of due process, e.g. counter notifications), and effective remedy. The issues place the EU intermediary liability regime at odds with its fundamental human rights framework. In particular, they increase the risk of undue interference with the right to freedom of expression, as they directly affect availability to express and receive information freely in the online environment.

560 See e.g. Recommendation CM/Rec(2014)6 and Explanatory Memorandum, *o.c.*

PART II

NORMATIVE FRAMEWORK

CHAPTER 1
INTRODUCTION

RESEARCH OBJECTIVE – The aim of Part II is to develop a normative framework for the evaluation of the notice and action mechanisms. This exercise will allow the formulation of an opinion about the compatibility of notice and action with the right to freedom of expression, as protected by the European Convention on Human Rights and the Charter of Fundamental Rights of the European Union. Specifically, Part II will establish assessment criteria that will be applied in Part III to evaluate existing notice and action mechanisms.

METHOD – In order to evaluate the compatibility of notice and action with the right to freedom of expression, a set of criteria is necessary. The criteria will be developed through a functional analysis of case law of the ECtHR and CJEU, in particular regarding Article 10 and Article 11. Guidance, moreover, will be obtained by reviewing the procedural provisions of these human rights instruments, specifically Articles 6 (right to a fair trial) and 13 (right to effective remedy) of the ECHR, as well as Article 47 (right to an effective remedy and to a fair trial) of the CFEU. The procedural provisions of both instruments will be used as a source of inspiration for safeguards in notice and action mechanisms where certain decisions about fundamental rights are delegated to private entities. The assessment criteria will be used as a positive assessment framework against which existing response mechanisms to illegal online content – currently used around the world – shall be measured in Part III.

OUTLINE – This Part of the book provides

(1) an analysis of whether the notice-and-take down mechanism resulting from the intermediary liability of the E-Commerce Directive is compatible with the relevant human rights law instruments (in particular art. 10 ECHR, art. 11 EU Charter) (Chapter 1);
(2) an analysis of whether there exists a positive obligation derived from the relevant human rights law instruments for a State to introduce safeguards (procedural and substantive) for freedom of expression in the notice-and-take down mechanism (Chapter 2);
(3) an inventory of criteria that should be taken into account when designing a removal mechanism that respects the right to freedom of expression in the online environment (Chapter 3).

CHAPTER 2

INTERFERENCE WITH FREEDOM OF EXPRESSION (OBLIGATION TO RESPECT)

1. THE EUROPEAN CONVENTION ON HUMAN RIGHTS

NOT AN ABSOLUTE RIGHT – The fundamental human right to freedom of expression, under the European Convention of Human Rights is not absolute. Article 10.2 of the Convention provides that

> 'The exercise of these freedoms, since it carries with it duties and responsibilities, may be subject to such formalities, conditions, restrictions or penalties as are prescribed by law and are necessary in a democratic society, in the interests of national security, territorial integrity or public safety, for the prevention of disorder or crime, for the protection of health or morals, for the protection of the reputation or rights of others, for preventing the disclosure of information received in confidence or for maintaining the authority and impartiality of the judiciary'.

FORMS OF INTERFERENCE – Interference with freedom of expression can take a variety of forms (formalities, conditions, restrictions or penalties). For example, an interference could take the form of a criminal conviction[561] (fine or imprisonment), a court order to pay civil damages[562], the prohibition of publication[563], the confiscation of publications[564], an order to reveal journalists' sources and/or imposing sanctions for failure to do so.[565] The European Court of Human Rights analyses each case to determine whether a measure introduced by the national authorities constitutes an interference with freedom of expression.

---

561 ECtHR, *Barfod v. Germany*, 1989.

562 ECtHR, *Muller v. Switzerland*, 1988.

563 ECtHR, *Sunday Times (2) v. the United Kingdom*, 1991; *Observer and Guardian v. the United Kingdom*, 1991.

564 ECtHR, *Handyside v. the United Kingdom*, 7 December 1976; *Muller v. Switzerland*, 1988.

565 ECtHR, *Goodwin v. the United Kingdom*, 1996.

NO OBLIGATION TO INTERFERE – National authorities are not obliged to interfere with freedom of expression every time one of the grounds listed in paragraph 2 is at stake. Rather, it is considered that the public authorities have the possibility, not the obligation, to restrict the exercise of the right to freedom of expression.[566] As pointed out in *Handyside v. the UK*,

> 'in no case does Article 10 para. 2 (art. 10-2) compel [the Contracting States] to impose "restrictions" or "penalties" in the field of freedom of expression'.[567]

NO HIERARCHY OF RIGHTS – There is no hierarchy between the rights and freedoms protected by the Convention. If such a hierarchy existed, it would imply that the other rights could take precedence over the right to freedom of expression, which is not the case.[568] As stated by Sottiaux, *there is no place in modern human rights law for such a hierarchy*.[569]

REQUIREMENTS FOR INTERFERENCE – Any restrictions to the exercise of the right to freedom of expression must meet the (cumulative) requirements specified in Article 10.2 ECHR. In essence, the interference must be '*prescribed by law*', have a '*legitimate aim*' corresponding to one or more of the grounds for interference (exhaustively) enumerated in Article 10.2, and be '*necessary in a democratic society*'. The Court analyses each requirement consecutively. If one of the requirements is not complied with the whole exercise comes to an end. The ECtHR applies a strict interpretation of the established conditions, which means that

> '... no other criteria than those mentioned in the exception clause itself may be at the basis of any restrictions, and these criteria, in turn, must be understood in such a way that the language is not extended beyond its ordinary meaning'.[570]

1.1. PRESCRIBED BY LAW

BASIS IN LAW – Any interference with freedom of expression by States must have a basis in national law.[571] It can be a written and public law adopted by the Parliament but in a few cases the ECtHR has accepted other forms of "law",

---

566 See M. Macovei, *Freedom of expression – A guide to the implementation of Article 10 of the European Convention of Human Rights*, *o.c.*, p. 17.

567 ECtHR, *Handyside v. the United Kingdom*, 7 December 1976, par. 54.

568 See M. Macovei, *Freedom of expression – A guide to the implementation of Article 10 of the European Convention of Human Rights*, *o.c.*, p. 17.

569 S. Sottiaux, *Terrorism and the Limitations of Rights. The European Convention on Human Rights and the United States Constitution*, Hart Publ., Oxford – Portland, Oregon, 2007. Some authors argue in favour of a hierarchization of human rights. O. De Schutter, F. Tulkens, "The European Court of Human Rights as a Pragmatic Institution", *o.c.*, ft. 22.

570 ECtHR, *Sunday Times v. the United Kingdom*, Report of the Commission, B. 28, paras. 194–195.

571 Article 10.2 ECHR.

such as common law rules or principles of international law as a legal basis for interference with freedom of expression.[572]

The ECtHR accepts, in some cases, the 'law-like' status of the decisions made by non-state bodies to whom the 'rule-making power' was delegated.[573] In *Barthold v. Germany*, the European Court of Human Rights specified that the Rules of Professional Conduct of the Veterinary Surgeons' Council were '*to be regarded as a 'law' within the meaning of Article 10§2 of the Convention. The competence of the Veterinary Surgeons' Council in the sphere of professional conduct derives from the independent rule-making power that the veterinary profession – in company with other liberal professions – traditionally enjoys, by parliamentary delegation (...)*'.[574] The competence of the Veterinary Surgeons' Council, however, is exercised '*under the control of the State, which in particular satisfies itself as to observance of national legislation, and the Council is obliged to submit its rules of professional conduct to the Land Government for approval (...).*'[575]

CO- AND SELF-REGULATORY MEASURES – The ECtHR places the burden to develop a legal framework clarifying issues such as responsibility and liability on States' authorities.[576] The ECtHR has stated that self- and co-regulatory mechanisms may suffice, on the condition that they include effective guarantees of rights and effective remedies for violations of rights.[577] For co-regulatory measures, the Court demands a considerable degree of government involvement, for example the approval of the rules. It is not entirely clear to what extent an equivalent self-regulatory framework would suffice.[578] Self-regulatory measures generally have no or a very limited degree of government involvement.[579] An

572 ECtHR, *Sunday Times v. the United Kingdom*, 26 April 1979, para. 47; ECtHR, *Groppera Radio AG and others v. Switzerland*, 28 March 1990, para. 68. See also: M. Macovei, *Freedom of expression – A guide to the implementation of Article 10 of the European Convention of Human Rights, o.c.*, p. 25. Macovei explains further: "*[f]reedom of expression is such an important value that its restriction should always receive the democratic legitimacy which is only given by the parliamentary debates and vote*" (p. 25).

573 See ECtHR, *Barthold v. Germany*, 25 March 1985. See also Hans-Bredow-Institut for Media Research, University of Hamburg, Study on Co-Regulation Measures in the Media Sector, Final Report, Study for the European Commission, Directorate Information Society and Media, 2006.

574 ECtHR, *Barthold v. Germany*, 25 March 1985, para. 46.

575 ECtHR, *Barthold v. Germany*, 25 March 1985, para. 46.

576 Angelopoulos C. et al., Study of fundamental rights limitations for online enforcement through self-regulation, *o.c.*, p. 18.

577 See ECtHR, *Peck v. the United Kingdom*, no. 44647/98, ECHR 2003-I, paras. 108 and 109. See also Angelopoulos C. et al., Study of fundamental rights limitations for online enforcement through self-regulation, *o.c.*, p. 18; and Hans-Bredow-Institut for Media Research, Study on Co-Regulation Measures in the Media Sector, *o.c.*, pp. 147–152.

578 Angelopoulos C. et al., Study of fundamental rights limitations for online enforcement through self-regulation, *o.c.*, p. 18.

579 See also: E. Lievens, *Protecting Children in the Digital Era – the Use of Alternative Regulatory Instruments, o.c.*, p. 391.

example could be the recently announced Code of Conduct on Countering Illegal Hate Speech Online.[580] The Code was launched as a cooperation initiative between a number of IT companies.[581] The rules of the Code were specified by the companies involved who declared that they will review complaints with regard to their online content on the basis of their own terms and conditions. The EC supports the initiative, and even pushes for its "voluntary" adoption[582], but does not influence the specific provision of the terms and conditions. It is doubtful, whether the Code, which relies mainly on the companies' own terms and conditions, as a basis for interference with freedom of expression, would pass the foreseeability test.

Internet hosting providers often justify content removals by reference to their general terms and conditions. Terms and conditions are not approved by the State. Rather, they are considered the "house rules" which the users can either respect or leave. In fact, they constitute a contract between the service provider and its users. Regulating speech through terms and conditions creates a number of problematic issues. As was specified earlier, this is not the subject of this book.

ACCESSIBILITY AND FORESEEABILITY – Additional guidance on the 'prescribed by law' requirement can be found in the ECtHR case law. A regulation allowing for interference must be adequately accessible and foreseeable.[583] In other words, the regulation must be phrased with sufficient precision so that individuals are able to anticipate the consequences of their actions. The ECtHR clarified in the *Sunday Times v. the United Kingdom*:

> 'Firstly, the law must be adequately accessible: the citizen must be able to have an indication that is adequate in the circumstances of the legal rules applicable to a given case. Secondly, a norm cannot be regarded as a 'law' unless it is formulated with sufficient precision to enable the citizen to regulate his conduct: he must be able – if need be with appropriate advice – to foresee, to a degree that is reasonable in the circumstances, the consequences which a given action may entail'.[584]

Moreover,

> 'Those consequences need not be foreseeable with absolute certainty: experience shows this to be unattainable. Again, whilst certainty is highly desirable, it may bring in its train excessive rigidity and the law must be able to keep pace with changing circumstances. Accordingly, many laws are inevitably couched in terms which, to

---

580 Code of Conduct on Countering Illegal Hate Speech Online, *o.c.*

581 A. Kuczerawy, The Code of Conduct on Online Hate Speech: an example of State interference by proxy, *o.c.*

582 See B. Stur, Brussels calls for faster removal of illegal content online, 9 January 2018, https://www.neweurope.eu/article/brussels-calls-faster-removal-illegal-content-online/.

583 ECtHR, *Sunday Times v. the United Kingdom*, 26 April 1979, para. 49.

584 ECtHR, *Sunday Times v. the United Kingdom*, 26 April 1979, para. 49.

a greater or lesser extent, are vague and whose interpretation and application are questions of practice'.[585]

QUALITY OF LAW – In the 2013 case *Ahmet Yildrim v. Turkey*, which concerned wholesale blocking of access to the Internet as a preventive measure, the ECtHR also addressed the requirement of "prescribed by law".[586] This means that, the interference must have a basis in domestic law, but also that the legal basis must meet certain requirements of "quality".[587] Specifically, the Court highlighted that the law must be foreseeable and accessible, and that it should be compatible with the rule of law.[588] The Court found that while the interfering measure had a basis in domestic law, it was not sufficient to satisfy the requirement of being prescribed by law.

According to the ECtHR, it would be contrary to the rule of law, 'for a legal discretion granted to the executive to be expressed in terms of an unfettered power'.[589] The ECtHR has clarified that there must be 'a measure of legal protection in domestic law against arbitrary interferences by public authorities with the rights guaranteed by the Convention'.[590] For this reason, 'the law must indicate with sufficient clarity the scope of any such discretion and the manner of its exercise'.[591] In the Yildrim case, that would amount to ensuring a tight control over the scope of bans and effective judicial review to prevent any abuse of power.[592] The analysed legislation lacked such elements, therefore the ECtHR declared it did not satisfy the foreseeability requirement and did not afford the applicant the degree of protection to which he was entitled by the rule of law in a democratic society.[593]

On other occasions the ECtHR also pointed to a variety of procedural safeguards that the measures taken to interfere with the right to freedom of expression should adhere to, in order to avoid arbitrariness.[594] For example,

---

585 *Ibid.*

586 ECtHR, *Ahmet Yıldırım v. Turkey*, 18 March 2013.

587 *Ibid.*, para. 57.

588 *Ibid.*

589 *Ibid.*, para. 59.

590 *Ibid.* ECtHR, *Malone v. the United Kingdom, 1984.*

591 ECtHR, *Ahmet Yıldırım v. Turkey*, 18 March 2013, para. 59. Also ECtHR, *Sunday Times v. the United Kingdom*, 26 April 1979, para. 49, and ECtHR, *Maestri v. Italy* [GC], para. 30, ECHR 2004-I.

592 ECtHR, *Ahmet Yıldırım v. Turkey*, 18 March 2013, para. 64. See also ECtHR, *Association Ekin v. France*, para. 58, ECHR 2001-VIII, and, *mutatis mutandis*, ECtHR, *Editorial Board of Pravoye Delo and Shtekel v. Ukraine*, para. 55, ECHR 2011.

593 ECtHR, *Ahmet Yıldırım v. Turkey*, 18 March 2013, para. 67.

594 The European Court of Human Rights addressed the importance of certain 'procedural guarantees' also under the condition of 'necessity in a democratic society'. Cf. ECtHR, *Steur v. the Netherlands*, 28 October 2003; ECtHR, *Veraart v. the Netherlands*, 30 November 2006. For more on procedural guarantees see Part II Chapter 3.1.4.

decisions of regulatory bodies need to be duly reasoned and open to judicial review and procedures need to be open and transparent.[595] As explained by the ECtHR in *Malone v. the United Kingdom*, *'[e]specially where a power of the executive is exercised in secret, the risks of arbitrariness are evident'*.[596]

In the concurring opinion of the *Yildrim* case, judge Pinto De Albuquerque articulated further guidelines addressing the quality of law. Specifically, he identified a set of minimum criteria for legislation on Internet blocking measures. The minimum criteria included clear definition of elements such as (1) categories of subjects to which the blocking order applies; (2) categories of blocking orders; as well as (3) time limitations and (4) territorial scope (among others).[597] The proposed minimum criteria illustrate how the condition of 'prescribed by law', and especially the requirement of quality of law, can be operationalized in the context of rules allowing for blocking measure on the Internet. Several of the proposed criteria also appear in the positive assessment framework of this book.

1.2. LEGITIMATE AIM

EXHAUSTIVE LIST OF GROUNDS – Interference with freedom of expression must be based on one of the grounds enumerated in Article 10.2 ECHR. The list consists of:

> 'National security, territorial integrity or public safety, for the prevention of disorder or crime, for the protection of health or morals, for the protection of the reputation or rights of others, for preventing the disclosure of information received in confidence, or for maintaining the authority and impartiality of the judiciary'.[598]

The list of grounds is exhaustive and corresponds to the values or interests protected by the Convention. It is possible that a restriction is based on more than one of the available legitimate aims. Different combinations of the available legitimate aims are possible. The following paragraphs shall provide, by way of illustration, examples of instances where the ECtHR assessed the legitimacy of measures involving content regulation and the accessibility of information on the Internet.

PREVENTION OF DISORDER OF CRIME – *K.U. v. Finland* concerned a grave infringement of a minor's right to privacy (through a publication of his personal data on a dating website by another person) and the State's obligation

595 ECtHR, *Glas Nadezhda and Elenkov v. Bulgaria*, 11 October 2007, paras 50–51; ECtHR, *Meltex Ltd and Mesrop Movsesyan v. Armenia*, 17 June 2008, para. 81.

596 ECtHR, *Malone v. the United Kingdom*, 1984.

597 ECtHR, *Ahmet Yıldırım v. Turkey*, 18 March 2013, concurring opinion.

598 Article 10. 2 ECHR.

to protect it.[599] With regard to balancing the right to privacy with the freedom of expression interests, the ECtHR explicitly stated that,

> 'Although freedom of expression and confidentiality of communications are primary considerations (...), such guarantee cannot be absolute and must yield on occasion to other legitimate imperatives, such as the prevention of disorder or crime or the protection of the rights and freedoms of others'.[600]

PROTECTION OF HEALTH OR MORALS – *Mouvement Raëlien Suisse v. Switzerland* concerned a denial of authorisation to display posters on a public highway by an international association whose members believe life on earth was created by extra-terrestrials.[601] Although the poster itself was not objectionable, it contained a reference to the website of the association, which promoted ideas of cloning and "geniocracy" (i.e. government by those with a higher intelligence). The ECtHR observed that those websites were accessible to everyone, including minors, which meant that the impact of the posters on the general public would have been multiplied.[602] Moreover, some of the members of the association had been accused of sexual offences against minors. The Court recognized the arguments of the national authorities that the restriction prohibiting the poster pursued the legitimate aims of the prevention of crime, the protection of health or morals and the protection of the rights of others.[603] The multiplying effect of the Internet made the State's interest in prohibiting the poster advertising campaign all the greater.[604]

PROTECTION OF RIGHTS OF OTHERS – *Editions Plon v. France* concerned a prohibition of a distribution of a book describing the health issues of a former French president, written by his doctor.[605] The book had been disseminated through the traditional methods and also on the Internet. The injunction had been requested by the late president's widow and children, who complained of a breach of medical confidentiality, an invasion of the president's privacy and injury to his relatives' feelings. The ECtHR recognized that the interference was intended to prevent the disclosure of information received in confidence (information covered under the national legislation by the rules of medical confidentiality) and protecting the rights of others (honour, reputation and privacy of the President, and of his widow and children, to whom they were transferred on his death).[606] Nevertheless, the ECtHR observed that by the

599 ECtHR, *K.U. v. Finland*, 02 December 2008.
600 *Ibid.*, para. 49.
601 ECtHR, *Mouvement Raëlien Suisse v. Switzerland*, 13 January 2011.
602 *Ibid.*, para. 54.
603 *Ibid.*, paras. 46, 56 and 57.
604 *Ibid.*, para. 54.
605 ECtHR, *Editions Plon v. France*, ECHR 2004-IV.
606 *Ibid.*, par. 34.

time the ban was issued the information in the book was to a large extent no longer confidential in practice. Consequently, the preservation of medical confidentiality no longer constituted an overriding requirement.[607] The ECtHR concluded that there was no longer a "pressing social need" justifying the continued ban on distribution of the book.[608]

RESTRICTIVE INTERPRETATION – The reason for interference must correspond with (at least) one of the legitimate aims listed in Article 10.2. The interest to be protected must, moreover, be real, and not a mere and uncertain possibility.[609] The ECtHR interprets possible grounds for interference restrictively. According to Rzeplinski, the ECtHR established a legal standard that in any borderline case, the freedom of the individual must be favourably balanced against the State's claim of overriding interest.[610] Narrowing down possible restrictions and interferences, while broadening the scope of application of the right to freedom of expression and information is aimed to guarantee and upgrade freedom of expression in Europe's democracies.[611]

1.3. NECESSARY IN A DEMOCRATIC SOCIETY

NECESSITY – For the interference with Article 10 ECHR to be accepted by the ECtHR, it must be "necessary in a democratic society".[612] The notion of necessity was explained in *Handyside v. the UK*, which concerned sanctions imposed on the publisher (i.e., criminal conviction, the seizure, forfeiture and destruction of the matrix and of copies of the book).[613] The ECtHR acknowledged that the notion of necessity can have different meanings. The adjective "necessary", within the meaning of Article 10.2 ECHR, is not synonymous with "indispensable"[614], or the words "absolutely necessary" and "strictly necessary"[615] and the phrase "to

607 *Ibid.*, par.53.

608 *Ibid.*, par. 55.

609 M. Macovei, *Freedom of expression – A guide to the implementation of Article 10 of the European Convention of Human Rights, o.c.*, p. 28.

610 A. Rzeplinski, Restrictions on the expression of opinions or disclosure of information on domestic or foreign policy of the State, Document prepared by the Secretary General's monitoring unit, Compliance with commitments entered into by Member States: Information concerning the Committee of Ministers' monitoring procedure, Freedom of expression and restrictions included in the penal code and other legal texts: seminars held in Budapest and in Strasbourg, Monitor/Inf (97) 3, Council of Europe.

611 D. Voorhoof, "Freedom of Expression under the European Human Rights System. From Sunday Times (n° 1) v. U.K. (1979) to Hachette Filipacchi Associés ("Ici Paris") v. France (2009)", *Inter-American and European Human Rights Journal*, Vol. 2 Issue 1–2, 2010, pp. 3–49, p. 20.

612 Article 10.2 ECHR.

613 ECtHR, *Handyside v. the United Kingdom*, 7 December 1976.

614 Article 2.2 ECHR.

615 Article 6. 1 ECHR.

the extent strictly required by the exigencies of the situation".[616, 617] Neither has it the flexibility of such expressions as "admissible", "ordinary"[618], or "useful"[619], "reasonable"[620] and "desirable"'.[621]

PRESSING SOCIAL NEED – To be considered "necessary in democratic society" interference with freedom of expression must be justified by the existence of a "pressing social need".[622] As the Court explained in *Handyside*, '*it is for the national authorities to make the initial assessment of the reality of the pressing social need implied by the notion of "necessity"*' in a specific case.[623] Even though a certain margin of appreciation is left to the Member States, the supervisory role of the ECtHR empowers it to give a final ruling on whether a "restriction" is reconcilable with freedom of expression as protected by Article 10.[624] To answer that question the Court must essentially establish whether the reasons for the interference were "relevant and sufficient" and whether the administered measure was "proportionate to the legitimate aims pursued".[625]

MARGIN OF APPRECIATION – In cases where the States are granted a margin of appreciation, national authorities are required to give due consideration to the particular interests protected by the Convention. National authorities '*must in principle be left a choice between different ways and means of meeting this obligation*'.[626] The ECtHR performs the assessment in the light of the specific circumstances of the case. Depending on the circumstances and the legitimate aim, the Court might assess the necessity of interference differently. The supervisory role of the ECtHR is '*limited to reviewing whether or not the particular solution adopted can be regarded as striking a fair balance*'.[627]

In the area of political speech the margin of appreciation is narrower and there is little scope under Article 10 of the Convention for restrictions on

616 Article 15.1 ECHR.
617 ECtHR, *Handyside v. the United Kingdom*, 7 December 1976, para. 48.
618 Article 4.3 ECHR.
619 The French text of the first paragraph of Article 1 of Protocol No. 1 ECHR.
620 Articles 5.3 and 6. 1 ECHR.
621 ECtHR, *Handyside v. the United Kingdom*, 7 December 1976, para. 48.
622 ECtHR, *Observer and Guardian v. the United Kingdom*, 26 November 1991, para. 57. See also: Council of Europe, *Freedom of expression in Europe: case-law concerning article 10 of the European Convention on Human Rights*, Strasbourg, Council of Europe Publishing, 2007, p. 9.
623 ECtHR, *Handyside v. the United Kingdom*, 7 December 1976, para. 48.
624 See D. Voorhoof, "Freedom of Expression under the European Human Rights System. From Sunday Times (n° 1) v. U.K. (1979) to Hachette Filipacchi Associés ("Ici Paris") v. France (2009)", *o.c.*, p. 18. See also Council of Europe, *Freedom of expression in Europe: case-law concerning article 10 of the European Convention on Human Rights*, *o.c.*, p. 9.
625 See for example ECtHR, *Stoll* v. *Switzerland*, [GC], 10 December 2007; ECtHR, *Féret* v. *Belgium*, 16 July 2009. P. van Dijk, F. van Hoof, A. van Rijn, L. Zwaak (eds), *Theory and practice of the European Convention on Human Rights*, Antwerpen, Intersentia, 2006, 775.
626 ECtHR, *Hatton and Others v. the United Kingdom*, [GC] 8 July 2003, para. 123.
627 *Ibid.*

freedom of expression.[628] In cases concerning religious freedom the ECtHR generally leaves national authorities a wider margin of appreciation.[629] The same applies to cases concerning conflicts between "morals" and freedom of expression.[630] This approach is explained by a different understanding of "morals" in the Member States.[631] In *Handyside v. the UK*, the original edition of the book and its numerous translations circulated freely in the majority of the Member States.[632] The Court explained that each country fashioned their approach in the light of the situation in their territories. Specifically, they have had regard *to 'the different views prevailing there about the demands of the protection of morals in a democratic society'*.[633] As further stated by the Court,

> 'it is not possible to find in the domestic law of the various Contracting States a uniform European conception of morals. The view taken by their respective laws of the requirements of morals varies from time to time and from place to place, especially in our era which is characterised by a rapid and far-reaching evolution of opinions on the subject'.[634]

LIMITED DISCRETION – Even though the margin of appreciation is wider with respect to "morals", it is not unlimited.[635] As the ECtHR described in the *Open Door* case, the discretion is not "unfettered and unreviewable".[636] The case concerned a permanent prohibition against the Dublin Well Woman and Open Door to provide information and advice to pregnant women on abortion outside Ireland. The Court examined whether the interference was justified by a "pressing social need" and whether it was proportionate with the legitimate aim pursued. The Court was struck by the absolute nature of the injunction which imposed a "perpetual" restraint on the provision of information *'regardless of age or state of health or their reason of seeking counselling on the termination of pregnancy'*.[637] The sweeping nature of the restraint led the Court to declaring it overly broad and disproportionate.

---

628 ECtHR, *Wingrove v. the United Kingdom*, 25 November 1996, para. 58; ECtHR, *Ceylan v. Turkey* [GC], 8 July 1999, para. 34. See also D. Voorhoof, "Freedom of Expression under the European Human Rights System. From Sunday Times (n° 1) v. U.K. (1979) to Hachette Filipacchi Associés ("Ici Paris") v. France (2009)", *o.c.*, p. 23.

629 For example ECtHR, *Leyla Şahin v. Turkey*, 10 November 2005.

630 For example ECtHR, *Handyside v. the United Kingdom*, 7 December 1976; ECtHR, *Open Door and Dublin Well Woman v. Ireland*, 29 October 1992; ECtHR, *Mouvement Raëlien Suisse v. Switzerland*, 13 January 2011.

631 See M. Macovei, *Freedom of expression – A guide to the implementation of Article 10 of the European Convention of Human Rights*, *o.c.*, p. 43.

632 ECtHR, *Handyside v. the United Kingdom*, 7 December 1976, para. 43.

633 *Ibid.*, para. 57.

634 *Ibid.*, para. 48.

635 ECtHR, *Open Door and Dublin Well Woman v. Ireland*, 29 October 1992, para. 68.

636 *Ibid.*

637 *Ibid.*, para. 73.

PROPORTIONALITY – According to the ECtHR there should be a 'reasonable relationship of proportionality between the means employed and the aim sought to be achieved'.[638]

As described by John Joseph Cremona, the principle of proportionality 'though nowhere in the European Convention on Human Rights mentioned in express terms, permeates the whole of its fabric (...). Essentially this is but another facet of the concept of balance, and balance is very much at the centre of the whole subject of the protection of human rights, there begins a sort of inbuilt balancing mechanism in the whole structure of the Convention'.[639]

Proportionality of a measure can be assessed by analysing the following three elements:

1) *Effectiveness* – was the measure reasonably likely to achieve its objective ("suitability" test)?
2) *Least intrusive means* – were there other less restrictive means capable of producing the desired result ("necessity" test)?
3) *Balance of interests* – what are the consequences on fundamental rights when assessed against the objectives pursued by the weighing of interests at stake (proportionality test "*stricto sensu*")?[640]

The first two elements concern the relationship between the aims of a measure and the means chosen to achieve these aims.[641] It is, therefore, a test of means and ends.[642] The third element concerns the relationship between the interests at stake.[643] Not all three elements are always analysed in each case.[644] In particular, the necessity test is sometimes left out.[645] The ECtHR is focused mainly on the

638 ECtHR, *Ashingdane v. the United Kingdom*, 28 May 1985, para. 57, Series A, no. 93.

639 J.J. Cremona, "The Proportionality Principle in the Jurisprudence of the European Court of Human Rights", in Beyerlin, Bothe, Hofmann and Petersmann (eds.), *Recht zwischen Umbrauch und Bewahrung – Festschrijft fur Rudolf Bernhardt*, 1995, p.323, as referred by J. Christoffersen, *Fair Balance: Proportionality, Subsidiarity and Primarity in the European Convention on Human Rights*, 2009, p. 2.

640 T. Tridimas, *The General Principles of EU Law*, 2nd ed., Oxford EC Law Library, 2007, p.139. See also F.G. Jacobs, "Recent developments in the principle of Proportionality in European Community Law", in E. Ellis (ed.), *The Principle of Proportionality in the Laws of Europe*, Hart Publishing, Oxford, 1999, p. 1–22.

641 J. Christoffersen, *Fair Balance: Proportionality, Subsidiarity and Primarity in the European Convention on Human Rights*, 2009, p. 164.

642 J. Gerards, "How to improve the necessity test of the European Court of Human Rights", *International Journal of Constitutional Law*, Vol. 11, No. 2, 2013, pp. 466–490, p. 469.

643 *Ibid.*

644 S. van Drooghenbroeck, *La proportionnalité dans le droit de la Convention européenne des droits de l'homme: prendre l'idée simple au sérieux*, [Proportionality in the Law of the European Convention on Human Rights], Publications Fac St Louis 2001, p. 83, as referred by J. Gerards, How to improve the necessity test of the European Court of Human Rights, *o.c.*, p. 468, footnote 9.

645 J. Gerards, "How to improve the necessity test of the European Court of Human Rights", *o.c.*, p. 468.

assessment of the overall balance of interests that has been struck by the national authorities, as '*the search for a fair balance is inherent to the Convention*'.[646, 647]

EFFECTIVENESS – The effectiveness test allows for review of particular elements of reasonableness of a measure i.e. its suitability to achieve the aim pursued.[648] The outcome of the test depends on how one articulates the "legitimate" aim that is being pursued. If, like in *Open Door*, the restricted information could still have been obtained through other sources (e.g. magazines, telephone books, or leaflets), the measure was not effective in preventing women from accessing this type of information.[649] In another example prohibition of the publication of a book in order to maintain confidentiality of medical information was not considered reasonable where the information was already published on the Internet.[650]

The goal of the effectiveness test is to assess the causal relationship between means and ends.[651] In some cases the use of common sense is enough to assess that a certain measure cannot be effective to achieve the aim.[652] In most cases, however, many different factors exist that can impact the effectiveness of a measure. It can be extremely difficult to assess the complex relationship between the effect of a measure and the effects caused by other factors.[653] Moreover, it should be highlighted that full effectiveness is rarely achievable, as '*almost no means will be perfectly suited to achieving its ends*'.[654]

LEAST RESTRICTIVE MEANS – Ideally, if interference with a fundamental right is necessary, it should take the form of a measure that causes the least possible prejudice to the rights in question.[655]

---

646 For example ECtHR, *Soering v. UK*, 07 July 1989, para. 89.

647 S. van Drooghenbroeck, La proportionnalité dans le droit de la Convention européenne des droits de l'homme: prendre l'idée simple au sérieux, *o.c.*, p. 85 (2001), as referred by J. Gerards, "How to improve the necessity test of the European Court of Human Rights", *o.c.*, p. 468, footnote 11.

648 For example in ECtHR, *Soltsyak v. Russia*, 10 February 2011, para. 52–53.

649 ECtHR, *Open Door and Dublin Well Woman v. Ireland*, 29 October 1992. In addition, the measure was of a general nature, which led the Court to declaring the interference disproportionate and not answering a pressing social need.

650 ECtHR, *Editions Plon v. France*, ECHR 2004-IV, para. 53.

651 J. Gerards, "How to improve the necessity test of the European Court of Human Rights", *o.c.*, p. 474.

652 *Ibid.*, p. 473, in reference to ECtHR, Soltsyak v. Russia, 10 February 2011.

653 J. Gerards, How to improve the necessity test of the European Court of Human Rights, *o.c.*, p. 474.

654 *Ibid.*

655 See ECtHR, *Ürper and Others v. Turkey*, 20 October 2009; and ECtHR, *Mouvement Raëlien Suisse v. Switzerland*, 13 January 2011. See also D. Voorhoof D. et al and T. McGonagle (Ed. Sup.), *Freedom of Expression, the Media and Journalists: Case-law of the European Court of Human Rights*, IRIS Themes, Vol. III, 4th edition, European Audiovisual Observatory, Strasbourg, 2017, p. 285.

In *Ürper*, the ECtHR found a complete ban on newspapers publishing articles supporting PKK not acceptable. The Court considered that, 'less draconian measures could have been envisaged, such as the confiscation of particular issues of the newspapers or restrictions on the publication of specific articles'.[656] The Court based the decision, therefore, on the concrete and demonstrable existence of alternatives, 'which would have been less onerous yet equally effective'.[657]

The issue was addressed also in *Mouvement Raëlien Suisse v. Switzerland*.[658] The ECtHR considered that the authorities had sufficient reasons to deny, for the protection of health and morals and for the prevention of crime, the authorisation to display posters on the public highway by the association.[659] The original problem was not so much with the poster but the '*more general context surrounding it, especially the ideas expressed in the books and the content of the websites of the association*'.[660] The association, however, remained free to express its beliefs through numerous other means of communication at its disposal. In the Court's opinion, such limitation of the scope of the interference to one channel of information proved that it was not disproportionate. As observed by Voorhoof, '*to limit the scope of the impugned restriction to the display of posters in public places was a way of ensuring the minimum impairment of the applicant association's rights*'.[661]

The ECtHR, however, rarely applies this test.[662] Already in the *Belgian Linguistic case*, the Court declared that the purpose of the measure was "plausible in itself" and it was '*not for the Court to determine whether it is possible to realise it in another way*'.[663] In *James and Others v. the UK* the Court rejected strict necessity as a decisive element to establish whether a violation occurred.[664] The level of intrusiveness constitutes '*only one factor, along with others, relevant for determining whether the means chosen could be regarded as reasonable and suited to achieving the legitimate aim being pursued, having regard to the need to strike a "fair balance"*'.[665] The availability of a better solution, therefore, is not a decisive

---

656 ECtHR, *Ürper and Others v. Turkey*, 20 October 2009, para. 43.

657 J. Gerards, "How to improve the necessity test of the European Court of Human Rights", *o.c.*, p. 483.

658 ECtHR, *Mouvement Raëlien Suisse v. Switzerland*, no. 16354/06, 13 January 2011.

659 *Ibid.*, paras. 56 and 57.

660 *Ibid.*, para. 54.

661 D. Voorhoof et al and T. McGonagle (Ed. Sup.), *Freedom of Expression, the Media and Journalists: Case-law of the European Court of Human Rights*, *o.c.*, p. 285.

662 J. Gerards, "How to improve the necessity test of the European Court of Human Rights", *o.c.*, p. 483. See for more examples in S. van Drooghenbroeck, *La proportionnalité dans le droit de la Convention européenne des droits de l'homme: prendre l'idée simple au sérieux*, *o.c.*, p. 197, as referred by J. Gerards, "How to improve the necessity test of the European Court of Human Rights", *o.c.*, p. 483, footnote 100.

663 ECtHR, *Belgian Linguistic case*, 23 July 1968, para. 13 (question 2).

664 ECtHR, *James and Others v. the UK*, 21 February 1986, para. 51.

665 *Ibid.*

factor.[666] It is not the Court's task to say whether the measure taken represented the best solution for dealing with the problem.[667] Moreover, the availability of alternative solutions does not in itself render the interference unjustified.[668] The availability of a less intrusive measure, even though not decisive, can still constitute part of the proportionality assessment conducted by the Court.

BALANCE OF INTERESTS – The Convention 'implies a just balance between the protection of the general interest of the Community and the respect due to fundamental human rights while attaching particular importance to the latter'.[669] The ECtHR pointed out that 'an interference must achieve a "fair balance" between the demands of the general interest of the community and the requirements of the protection of the individual's fundamental rights'.[670]

The fundamental right to freedom of expression may be restricted to protect the legitimate interests listed in Article 10.2 ECHR. This includes restrictions for the sake of other fundamental rights protected by the Convention. There is, however, no formal hierarchy among the Convention rights. In case of a conflict between the protected rights '*regard must be had to the fair balance that has to be struck between the relevant competing interests*'.[671]

As stated by the Court in *Chassagnou and Others v. France,* in situations where

> '(...) "rights and freedoms" are themselves among those guaranteed by the Convention or its Protocols, it must be accepted that the need to protect them may lead States to restrict other rights or freedoms likewise set forth in the Convention. It is precisely this constant search for a balance between the fundamental rights of each individual which constitutes the foundation of a "democratic society"'.[672]

Balancing of interests, in general, is a classical technique used by courts, including the European Court of Human Rights, to solve situations of conflicts between rights.[673] The ECtHR, in its subsidiary role, '*is limited to reviewing whether or not the particular solution adopted can be regarded as striking a fair balance*'.[674]

---

666 J. Christoffersen, *Fair Balance: Proportionality, Subsidiarity and Primarity in the European Convention on Human Rights*, *o.c.*, p. 132–135.

667 *Mutatis mutandis*, ECtHR, *James and Others v. the UK*, 21 February 1986, para. 51.

668 *Ibid.*

669 ECtHR, *Belgian Linguistic case*, 23 July 1968, part I. A, para. 5.

670 ECtHR, *Chassagnou and Others v. France*, [GC], 29 April 1999, para. 75.

671 ECtHR, *Von Hannover v. Germany* (no. 2), 7 February 2012, para. 99; and ECtHR, *White v. Sweden*, 19 September 2006, para. 20.

672 ECtHR, *Chassagnou and Others v. France*, [GC], 29 April 1999, para. 113.

673 O. De Schutter, F. Tulkens, "The European Court of Human Rights as a Pragmatic Institution", *o.c.*, p. 188.

674 ECtHR, *Hatton and Others v. the United Kingdom*, 8 July 2003, para. 123.

According to Barak, balancing is 'an analytical process that places the proper purpose of the limiting law on one side of the scales and the limited constitutional right on the other, while balancing the benefit gained by the proper purpose with the harm it causes to the right'.[675] According to De Schutter and Tulkens, balancing of rights 'consists in weighing the rights in conflict against one another, and affording a priority to the right which is considered to be of greater "value"'.[676] Balancing of rights is often criticized as a method of resolving conflicts between the Convention rights.[677] For example, the method is accused of creating a problem of "incommensurability".[678] Despite the criticism, the method is used by the ECtHR, which considers that the search for fair balance is inherent to the Convention.[679]

CASE-BY-CASE ASSESSMENT – The role of the ECtHR is to find a balance between the rights and interests, or between several Convention rights, that come into conflict with each other. In such instances, the Court will consider all aspects "in light of the case as a whole". This means that the balancing exercise must be performed on a case-by-case basis, taking into account the specific circumstances of each case.

Striking the balance between conflicting rights (or rights and interests) requires answering multiple questions, depending on which rights and/ or interests are at stake. For example, in the context of the protection of morals, the elements that should be taken into account in the balancing exercise include: the target group of the expression; the measures to limit access to the respective form of expression (as proving attempts to reduce the "immoral" impact); and a real damage to "morals".[680] In conflicts between Articles 10 and 8 ECHR the Court has established a list of criteria which is used in the balancing exercise

---

675 A. Barak, *Proportionality. Constitutional Rights and their Limitations*, Cambridge University Press, 2012, p. 343.

676 O. De Schutter, F. Tulkens, "The European Court of Human Rights as a Pragmatic Institution", *o.c.*, p. 191.

677 A detailed critical analysis of the fair balance method, however, falls outside the scope of this thesis. For more see: P. A. Van Malleghem, *Proportionality and the Erosion of Formalism*, Doctroal thesis, KU Leuven, 2016, p. 85–117; S. Smet, *Resolving Conflicts between Human Rights: a legal theoretical analysis in the context of the ECHR*, Ghent University, 2013–2014, p. 133 – 182; and O. De Schutter, F. Tulkens, "The European Court of Human Rights as a Pragmatic Institution", *o.c.*

678 As described by Justice Antonin Scalia, the balancing test refers to the scale analogy, which '*is not really appropriate, since the interests on both sides are incommensurate. It is more like judging whether a particular line is longer than a particular rock is heavy*'. Concurring opinion of Justice Antonin Scalia in United States Supreme Court, *Bendix Autolite v. Midwesco Enterprises*, 17 June 1988.

679 For example ECtHR, *Soering v. UK*, 07 July 1989, para. 89; ECtHR, *Verein gegen Tierfabriken Schweiz (VgT) v. Switzerland* (No. 2), 30 June 2009, para. 81.

680 See M. Macovei, *Freedom of expression – A guide to the implementation of Article 10 of the European Convention of Human Rights*, *o.c.*, p. 45.

(see more *infra*).[681] The criteria are applied to specific circumstances of a case.[682] It is inevitable, however, that '*the tension between the principle of freedom of expression in a democracy and the need for public or private interests to restrict this freedom results in a permanent struggle to find a fair balance between the competing interests and values concerned*'.[683]

PUBLIC INTEREST – The first element, to which the ECtHR pays particular attention when balancing the competing interests and values, is whether the restricted speech contributed to a debate on matters of public interest.[684] The public interest factor is assessed by the ECtHR especially in the context of disclosure of information in the course of media or journalistic activities.[685] The role of the press is to impart information and ideas on all matters of public interest. Press freedom and debate on matters of public interest are '*inherent characteristics and necessary conditions for a democratic society*'.[686] In *Sunday Times* the Court recognised '*the right of the public to be properly informed*' about matters of interest for society and established a higher level of protection for journalistic reporting on matters of public interest.[687] In *Guja* v. *Moldova* the Court specified, that

> 'In a democratic system the acts or omissions of government must be subject to the close scrutiny not only of the legislative and judicial authorities but also of the media and public opinion. The interest which the public may have in particular information can sometimes be so strong as to override even a legally imposed duty of confidence.'[688]

BALANCING FREEDOM OF EXPRESSION AND RIGHT TO PRIVACY – The complexity of the balancing exercise, with a variety of factors to be taken

---

681 See ECtHR, *Axel Springer AG v. Germany*, 7 February 2012; ECtHR, *Von Hannover v. Germany* (no. 2), 7 February 2012.

682 Specifically, the Court examines: who is invoking the right to freedom of expression, what was published, broadcasted or imparted, who was eventually criticized or insulted, what medium was used, who could receive the information, where and under which circumstances something was made public, etc. See D. Voorhoof, "Freedom of Expression under the European Human Rights System. From Sunday Times (n° 1) v. U.K. (1979) to Hachette Filipacchi Associés ("Ici Paris") v. France (2009)", *o.c.* p. 19.

683 D. Voorhoof, "Freedom of Expression under the European Human Rights System. From Sunday Times (n° 1) v. U.K. (1979) to Hachette Filipacchi Associés ("Ici Paris") v. France (2009)", *o.c.*, p. 65.

684 For example ECtHR, *Radio Twist a.s. v. Slovakia*, 19 December 2006; ECtHR, *Guja* v. *Moldova* 12 February 2008.

685 For example ECtHR, *Sunday Times v. the United Kingdom*, 26 April 1979; ECtHR, *Bladet Tromsø and Stensaas v. Norway*, 20 May 1999.

686 See D. Voorhoof, "Freedom of Expression under the European Human Rights System. From Sunday Times (n° 1) v. U.K. (1979) to Hachette Filipacchi Associés ("Ici Paris") v. France (2009)", *o.c.*, p. 11.

687 *Ibid.*, p. 10.

688 ECtHR, *Guja* v. *Moldova* 12 February 2008, para. 74.

into account, is particularly visible in conflicts between the right to freedom of expression and the right to privacy (Article 8 ECHR).[689] This is one of the most common conflicts appearing before the Court in cases involving online content restrictions. The Court has recognized on numerous occasions that the right to privacy may be a legitimate reason for restricting freedom of expression.[690] It has even stated that such restrictions may concern information that has already entered the public domain.[691] For example, in *Aleksey Ovchinnikov* the Court held that:

> 'in certain circumstances a restriction on reproducing information that has already entered the public domain may be justified, for example to prevent further airing of the details of an individual's private life which do not come within the scope of any political or public debate on a matter of general importance'.[692]

The ECtHR, through its case law, established a list of criteria to take into account when balancing the right to freedom of expression with the right to private life. The list contains the following factors:

- Contribution to a debate of general interest;
- How well known is the person concerned and what is the subject of the report?
- Prior conduct of the person concerned;
- Method of obtaining the information and its veracity;
- Content, form and consequences of the publication;
- Severity of the sanction imposed.[693]

The ECtHR applies the list to a presented case and analyses the listed factors in the light of the specific circumstances of the case.

In *ORF v Austria*, which concerned a restriction on publication of information about a release on parole of a well-known member of the neo-Nazi scene in Austria, the Court went on to specify that:

> 'a number of elements are to be taken into account when weighing the individual's interest not to have his physical appearance disclosed against the public's interest in the publication of his picture. Elements that will be relevant are the degree of notoriety of the person concerned, the lapse of time since the conviction and the release, the nature of the crime, the connection between the contents of the report

689 For example ECtHR, *Aleksey Ovchinnikov v Russia*, 16 March 2011; ECtHR, *Österreichischer Rundfunk v. Austria*,7 December 2006; ECtHR, *Hachette Filipacchi Associés ("Ici Paris") v. France*, 23 July 2009.
690 For example ECtHR, *Aleksey Ovchinnikov v Russia*, 16 March 2011.
691 *Ibid.*
692 *Ibid.*, para. 50.
693 For example ECtHR, *Axel Springer AG v. Germany*, 7 February 2012; ECtHR, *Von Hannover v. Germany* (no. 2), 7 February 2012.

> and the picture shown and the completeness and correctness of the accompanying text'.[694]

In *Hachette Filipacchi Associés ("Ici Paris") v. France*[695] the Court decided that, even though the article in question did not contribute to a debate of public interest, the privacy interests of the plaintiff did not prevail as (a) the photographs published with the article had been derived from advertising material and had not been obtained through contentious or undercover methods that interfered with the privacy of the persons concerned; (b) the relevant information about the plaintiff's lifestyle had been previously disclosed by the plaintiff himself in his autobiography.

NO IDLE GOSSIP – The existence of a mere public interest in information is not enough to justify restrictions on other fundamental rights.[696] Freedom of the press does not '*extend to idle gossip about intimate or extra-marital relations merely serving to satisfy the curiosity of a certain readership and not contributing to any public debate in which the press has to fulfil its role of "public watchdog"*.'[697] The Court adopted a similar position in *Von Hannover v. Germany.*[698] In this case the Court clarified that the publication of photos and articles,

> 'the sole purpose of which was to satisfy the curiosity of a particular readership regarding the details of the applicant's private life, cannot be deemed to contribute to any debate of general interest to society despite the applicant being known to the public.'[699]

CHILLING EFFECT – When assessing an interference, the ECtHR looks beyond the case at hand and considers possible future implications as well. For example, the ECtHR checks whether the interference could potentially lead to a "chilling effect".[700] The ECtHR takes into account whether the interference, e.g. the stringency of the measures or severity of penalties could lead to "self-

694 ECtHR, *Österreichischer Rundfunk v. Austria*,7 December 2006.

695 ECtHR, *Hachette Filipacchi Associés ("Ici Paris") v. France*, 23 July 2009.

696 See also ECtHR, *Standard Verlags GmbH (n° 2) v. Austria*, 4 June 2009.

697 See D. Voorhoof, "Freedom of Expression under the European Human Rights System. From Sunday Times (n° 1) v. U.K. (1979) to Hachette Filipacchi Associés ("Ici Paris") v. France (2009)", *o.c.*, p. 29.

698 ECtHR, *Von Hannover v. Germany*, 26 April 2004; See also ECtHR, *Von Hannover v. Germany* (no. 2), 7 February 2012.

699 ECtHR, *Von Hannover v. Germany*, 26 April 2004, para. 65.

700 For example ECtHR, *Mosley v the United Kingdom*, 10 May 2011. See B. A. Garner (ed.), *Black's Law Dictionary*, *o.c.* See also R. Ó. Fathaigh, "Article 10 and the chilling effect principle", *European Human Rights Law Review*, Issue 3, 2013, pp. 304–313. For more on the US origins of this concept, see F. Schauer, "Fear, risk and the First Amendment: Unravelling the chilling effect", *Boston University Law Review* 1978, Vol. 58, Issue 5, 685–732.

censorship", and as a result, may have a detrimental effect towards freedom of expression in the future.[701] Restrictions are analysed in the light of the deterrent effect they could have on other individuals wanting to exercise their right to freedom of expression at a later date.[702] The ECtHR generally tries to avoid discouragement from exercising one's rights.[703] The chilling effect factor can be often found in cases related to journalistic activities, such as *Mosley v. the United Kingdom*.[704] This case concerned the call for a specific measure – a legally binding pre-notification rule – designed to ensure the effective protection of the right to respect for private life stemming from Article 8 ECHR. The application followed a newspaper publication of details of Mr. Mosley's sexual activities. The applicant advocated for a pre-notification duty on the side of the press, which would be triggered where any aspect of private life was engaged. The Court considered that installing punitive fines or criminal sanctions to encourage compliance with any pre-notification requirement might operate as a form of censorship prior to publication. Such measures '*would create a chilling effect which would be felt in the spheres of political reporting and investigative journalism, both of which attract a high level of protection under the Convention*'.[705]

CONCLUDING REMARKS – Freedom of expression, protected under Article 10 of the Convention, is not an absolute right. Restrictions may be permitted, if they comply with the conditions specified in Article 10 §2 ECHR, that is where they are "prescribed by law", for protection of one of the "legitimate aims" and "necessary in democratic society". This means that mechanisms that allow for the removal of illegal or infringing content from the Internet can be in line with the Convention, as long as they respect the conditions. The fact that certain types of content are restricted through the Notice-and-Takedown mechanism does not, as such, amount to a violation of the Convention. The next question is whether the same conclusion could be reached with regard to the right to freedom of expression under the European Charter of Fundamental Rights (CFEU).

---

701 See T. McGonagle, *Freedom of expression and defamation: A study of the case law of the European Court of Human Rights*, Council of Europe Publishing, 2016, p. 24.

702 B. A. Garner (ed.), *Black's Law Dictionary*, *o.c.*

703 J. Van Hoboken, *o.c.*, p. 66. See also ECtHR, *Mosley v the United Kingdom*, 10 May 2011, para. 125–132 (rejecting the notion of requiring prior notice for privacy-interfering publications with reference to the chilling effect of such a requirement). See also ECtHR, *Goodwin v. United Kingdom*, 27 March 1996, para. 39 (addressing the deterrent effect of a legal obligation for journalists to reveal the source of their information).

704 ECtHR, *Mosley v the United Kingdom*, 10 May 2011.

705 *Ibid.*, para. 129.

2. THE CHARTER OF FUNDAMENTAL RIGHTS OF THE EUROPEAN UNION

FUNDAMENTAL VALUE – At the EU level, the right to freedom of expression, as well as press freedom, is protected by Article 11 of the Charter of Fundamental Rights of the European Union (CFEU) (see more *Supra*).[706]

RESTRICTIONS – Restrictions to the right to freedom of expression are allowed providing that certain conditions are met. These conditions are not specified in Article 11 CFEU but in Article 52, which refers generally to all the rights and freedoms protected by the Charter. According to Article 52.1:

> 'Any limitation on the exercise of the rights and freedoms recognised by this Charter must be provided for by law and respect the essence of those rights and freedoms. Subject to the principle of proportionality, limitations may be made only if they are necessary and genuinely meet objectives of general interest recognised by the Union or the need to protect the rights and freedoms of others.'

The wording of the article is similar to that of Article 10.2 of the Convention. The 'general interest' grounds are an open class of overriding interest. Areas in which the EU regulation restricts speech, however, must fall under the public interest grounds of Article 10.2 ECHR.[707] Furthermore, as specified in Article 52.3 of the Charter:

> 'In so far as this Charter contains rights which correspond to rights guaranteed by the Convention for the Protection of Human Rights and Fundamental Freedoms, the meaning and scope of those rights shall be the same as those laid down by the said Convention. This provision shall not prevent Union law providing more extensive protection.'

The combination of these two provisions leads to the conclusion that the allowed limitations on the right to freedom of expression cannot exceed those provided by Article 10.2 ECHR.[708]

Considering that the Charter should be interpreted in accordance with the Convention and jurisprudence of the ECtHR, the following sections point out only the relevant aspects of the rights limitation, in light of the CJEU cases relevant for this book.

---

706 Charter of Fundamental Rights of the European Union (CFEU), *o.c.*

707 L. Woods, "Article 11", in S. Peers et al. (eds.), *The EU Charter of Fundamental Rights – A Commentary*, Hart Publishing, Oxford and Portland, Oregon, 2014, p. 327.

708 EU Network of Independent Experts on Fundamental Rights, *o.c.*, p. 116.

PROPORTIONALITY – The evaluation of proportionality is given a central position in the CJEU cases. It has been addressed, for example, in *L'Oreal SA v. eBay* and *Telekabel Wien*.

In *L'Oreal SA v. eBay*, the CJEU stated that in case of copyright infringements by the users of online marketplaces, national courts can order operators of these marketplaces to take measures not only to bring the infringements to an end, but also to prevent further infringements of the same type.[709] The measures, however, must be effective and proportionate.[710]

The *Telekabel Wien* case concerned a court injunction prohibiting an internet service provider (intermediary) from allowing its customers access to a website that disseminated copyrighted content without the agreement of the right holders, when the injunction did not specify the measures to be taken. The CJEU ruled that such injunction is not precluded by the fundamental rights recognised by the EU but the measures taken must be proportional.[711] For example, they should not unnecessarily deprive internet users of the possibility of lawfully accessing the information available.[712]

BALANCING OF RIGHTS – Like the ECHR, the CFEU does not provide for a hierarchy of rights and therefore, a balancing exercise may be necessary. In *Satamedia*[713], the balancing exercise concerned three fundamental rights protected by the Charter: freedom of expression and the right to privacy and data protection. The case concerned the further dissemination of personal tax information, which had previously been made public by the tax authorities, by means of a text messaging service. This service, which was offered by a private company (Satamedia), allowed mobile telephone users to receive information on individual taxpayers at a charge. According to the CJEU, in order to reconcile the two fundamental rights, the Member States are required to provide for a number of derogations or limitations in relation to the protection of data and, therefore, the fundamental right to privacy.[714] Those derogations in the data protection law must be made solely for journalistic purposes or the purpose of artistic or literary expression, which fall within the scope of the fundamental right to freedom of expression, in so far as they are necessary to reconcile the right to privacy with the rules governing freedom of expression.[715] It is therefore

---

709 CJEU, *L'Oreal SA v. eBay*, Case C324/09, 12 July 2011, p. 144.

710 *Ibid.*, p. 139, 141, 144.

711 CJEU, *UPC Telekabel Wien GmbH v. Constantin Film Verleih GmbH, Wega Filmproduktionsgesellschaft mbH*, C 314/12, 27 March 2014, p. 46.

712 *Ibid.*, p. 64.

713 CJEU, *Tietosuojavaltuutettu v. Satakunnan Markkinapörssi Oy and Satamedia Oy*, C73/07, 16 December 2008. N.B., this case eventually led to a GC judgment of the ECtHR (Satakunnan Markkinapörssi Oy and Satamedia Oy v. Finland, 27 June 2017).

714 CJEU, *Tietosuojavaltuutettu v. Satakunnan Markkinapörssi Oy and Satamedia Oy*, C73/07, 16 December 2008, p. 55.

715 *Ibid.*

not possible to give an automatic priority to freedom of expression over data protection and privacy.[716] As stated by Woods, '*even fundamental rights do not have automatic priority over other societal interests.*'[717]

In *Promusicae,* the CJEU was called upon to reconcile the requirements of the protection of the right to respect for private life, the rights to protection of property and to an effective remedy.[718] Specifically, the CJEU was asked whether Member States are obliged to lay down an obligation for ISPs to communicate personal data in order to ensure effective protection of copyright (in the context of civil proceedings). The answer was negative. The CJEU, however, pointed out that Member States, when transposing directives into their legal regime, must '*rely on an interpretation of the directives which allows a fair balance to be struck between the various fundamental rights protected by the Community legal order*'.[719] Moreover, Member States

> 'must not only interpret their national law in a manner consistent with those directives but also make sure that they do not rely on an interpretation of them which would be in conflict with those fundamental rights or with the other general principles of Community law, such as the principle of proportionality'.[720]

Two cases involving *Sabam* concerned requests by the Belgian rights' management company to install filtering mechanisms to prevent copyright infringements.[721] In the first case, *Scarlett Extended,* the request was directed to an ISP provider and in the second case, *Sabam v. Netlog,* to a hosting service provider – a social networking site. The requested mechanism was intended to apply to all information, by all users, as a preventive measure, for an unlimited period of time and exclusively at the expense of the service providers. In both cases the CJEU ruled the requested mechanisms as '*not respecting the requirement that a fair balance be struck between the right to intellectual property, on the one hand, and the freedom to conduct business, the right to protection of personal data and the freedom to receive or impart information, on the other*'.[722]

Filtering of content is also a subject of the recent referral to the CJEU. In January 2018 the supreme court of Austria ('*Oberste Gerichtshof*') referred a question to the Court of Justice on the scope of Article 15 of the E-Commerce

716 L. Woods, "Article 11", *o.c.*, p. 330.
717 *Ibid.*
718 CJEU, *Productores de Música de España (Promusicae) v.Telefónica de España SAU,* Case C 275/06, 29 January 2008, p. 65.
719 *Ibid.*, p. 68.
720 *Ibid.*
721 CJEU, *Scarlet Extended SA v. Société belge des auteurs, compositeurs et éditeurs SCRL (SABAM),* C 70/10, 24 November 2011 and CJEU, *Belgische Vereniging van Auteurs, Componisten en Uitgevers CVBA (SABAM) v. Netlog NV,* Case C 360/10, 16 February 2012.
722 CJEU, *Scarlet Extended,* p. 53; and CJEU, *Sabam v. Netlog,* p. 51.

Directive and the host provider privilege.[723] This time, however, the case concerned hate speech and defamatory content. Specifically, the Austrian court requested clarification on a possibility of an injunction to remove specific information but also other information that is a) identical in wording, and b) not identical in wording but similar in meaning.[724] The case requires balancing between the rights to privacy (due to the personal data processing that the automatic filtering would require), freedom of expression, and freedom to conduct a business on the one hand, and combating hate speech on the other. The ruling should also provide guidance regarding whether requiring pro-active measures to identify future infringing posts could result in a general obligation to monitor. For this reason, the ruling is eagerly awaited.

NO ABSOLUTE RIGHTS – The rights protected by the Charter, like the rights in the Convention, are not absolute. Article 52.1 CFEU allows for limitations of the rights provided that certain conditions are met. The Court of Justice of the EU has held that

> 'it is settled case-law that fundamental rights do not constitute unfettered prerogatives and may be restricted, provided that the restrictions in fact correspond to objectives of general interest pursued by the measure in question and that they do not involve, with regard to the objectives pursued, a disproportionate and intolerable interference which infringes upon the very substance of the rights guaranteed'.[725]

In the context of protection of (intellectual) property the CJEU explicitly stated that there is 'nothing whatsoever in the wording of that provision or in the Court's case-law to suggest that that right is inviolable and must for that reason be absolutely protected'.[726] The same applies to the right to freedom of expression.

3. INTERIM CONCLUSION

REQUIREMENTS FOR INTERFERENCE – Freedom of expression is not an absolute right, neither under the Convention, nor under the Charter. This means

723 OGH, case number 6Ob116/17b, see https://www.ris.bka.gv.at/Dokumente/Justiz/JJT_20171025_OGH0002_0060OB00116_17B0000_000/JJT_20171025_OGH0002_0060OB00116_17B0000_000.pdf.

724 M. Brüß, Austria refers Facebook 'Hate-Speech' case to the CJEU, 30 January 2018, http://ipkitten.blogspot.fr/2018/01/austria-refers-facebook-hate-speech.html.

725 CJEU, *Alassini and Others*, Joined Cases C-317/08, C-318/08, C-319/08 and C-320/08, 18 March 2010, para. 63, with reference to case CJEU, C-28/05 *Doktor and Others* [2006] ECR I-5431, para. 75 and the case-law cited, and the judgment of the ECtHR, *Fogarty v United Kingdom*, para. 33, ECHR 2001-XI (extracts).

726 CJEU, *Scarlet Extended*, C-70/10, 24 November 2011, para 43–45.

that notice and action mechanisms, *per se*, are not incompatible with the human rights instruments. Interference may be allowed, when it satisfies the conditions specified by each instrument. To be permitted, interference must be prescribed by law, for a legitimate aim, and necessary in a democratic society. The conditions put forward by both the Convention and the Charter can be linked to three fundamental human rights principles, namely the principle of a) legal certainty, b) legitimacy, c) and proportionality. The three principles shall be the guiding principles for the research conducted in this book. They will facilitate the search for the most adequate solutions to the proposed research question regarding the necessary procedural safeguards for the freedom of expression in the notice and action mechanisms.[727]

[727] See more in Part II Chapter 4.2.

CHAPTER 3

POSITIVE OBLIGATIONS FOR FREEDOM OF EXPRESSION (OBLIGATION TO PROTECT)

1. POSITIVE OBLIGATIONS – THE EUROPEAN CONVENTION ON HUMAN RIGHTS

1.1. POSITIVE OBLIGATIONS UNDER THE ECHR – GENERAL

TWO DIMENSIONS OF THE RIGHT – The Convention protects the rights and freedoms of everyone from unjustified interference by States. The negative obligations of the Convention strictly define the limits of interference that States cannot cross. Defined as a "duty to abstain", it provides '*a qualified prohibition for the State and public authorities to interfere*'.[728] Apart from the negative dimension, which was discussed in the previous Chapter, the Convention also contains a positive one. The positive dimension requires the States to ensure the *effective enjoyment* of the rights and freedoms guaranteed by the Convention. As observed by Merrils,

> '... the Convention is mainly concerned not with what a State must do, but with what it must not do; that is, with its obligation to refrain from interfering with the individual's rights. Nevertheless, utilising the principle of effectiveness, the Court has held that even in respect of provisions which do not expressly create a positive obligation, there may sometimes be a duty to act in a particular way.'[729]

The concept of positive obligations is based on Article 1 of the Convention, which requires that '[t]he High Contracting Parties shall secure to everyone within their jurisdiction the rights and freedoms defined in Section I of this Convention.'[730]

---

728 D. Voorhoof, *Critical perspectives on the scope and interpretation of Article 10 of the European Convention on Human Rights* (Mass media files No. 10), Strasbourg, Council of Europe Press, 1995, p. 54.

729 J.G. Merrills, *The Development of International Law by the European Court of Human Rights*, Manchester, MUP, 1993, p. 103.

730 Article 1 ECHR.

BELGIAN LINGUISTIC CASE – The concept of positive obligations appeared in the Court's reasoning in the late 1960's, under the impact of the *Belgian Linguistic case*.[731] In this case, the Belgian government argued that the Convention (and the Protocol) are inspired '*by the "classic conception of freedoms"*', in contrast to the rights:

> '[t]he individual freedoms place purely negative duties on the governmental authorities (...). The commitments undertaken by the States by virtue of the Convention and the Protocol possess therefore an essentially negative character.'[732]

The Court disagreed, however, with the Belgian government's argument and considered that:

> '[n]o distinctions should be made in this respect according to the nature of these rights and freedoms and of their correlative obligations, and for instance as to whether the respect due to the right concerned implies positive action or mere abstention.'[733]

The Court observed, moreover, that such an approach can be concluded from the very general nature of the terms used in Article 14 of the Convention, which states that '*the enjoyment of the rights and freedoms set forth in this Convention shall be secured (...)*'.[734]

JUDICIAL CONSTRUCT – Certain positive obligations are explicitly imposed by the wording of the Convention, for example Article 6 (obligation to provide a fair trial).[735] In other cases the ECtHR has implied a more extensive and less clearly defined set of positive obligations.[736] According to Feldman, this is a result of '*... the dynamic interpretation of the Convention in the light of changing social and moral assumptions*' which lead to the development of '*... more extensive obligations on states than are immediately obvious from a superficial perusal of the text.*'[737] This is referred to as '*the general evolution and "socialising" of the Convention rights and freedoms*'.[738] Since the Belgian linguistic case, the ECtHR has constantly broadened this category of obligations by adding new elements, until almost all the standard-setting provisions of the Convention now

731 ECtHR, *Belgian Linguistic case*, 23 July 1968.
732 *Ibid.*, I.A para1.
733 *Ibid.*, I.B para9.
734 *Ibid.*
735 D. Feldman, *Civil Liberties and Human Rights in England and Wales*, 2nd edition, Oxford, OUP, 2002, p. 53.
736 *Ibid.*
737 *Ibid.*, p. 55.
738 D. Voorhoof, *Critical perspectives on the scope and interpretation of Article 10 of the European Convention on Human Rights*, o.c., p. 54.

have a dual aspect in terms of their requirements.[739] Seen as a 'decisive weapon', the concept serves the purpose of giving effect to the Convention rights.[740]

OBLIGATION TO PROTECT – The purpose of the doctrine of positive obligations is to guarantee individuals the *effective enjoyment* of their fundamental rights.[741] The Court has not provided an authoritative definition of positive obligations.[742] In the dissenting opinion in *Gul v Switzerland,* Judge Martens defined the concept as '*requiring member states to... take action.*'[743] This 'obligation to do something' is sometimes also described as an 'obligation to protect' or 'obligation to implement'.[744] According to Voorhoof, '*the modern State within the Convention's sphere has a kind of "promotional obligation" or an "ecological liability" in the human rights field which obliges it to go beyond mere abstention and to take positive action*'.[745] In practice, positive obligations require national authorities to take the necessary measures to safeguard the right.[746] The offered protection of the rights should be practical and effective and not merely theoretical. It is therefore not enough for States to simply 'not interfere'. Rather, they may also be required to take pro-active steps, through various policy measures, to prevent interferences, including by private parties.[747] Moreover, the positive obligation remains valid even if the state 'outsources' regulation, for example to alternative regulatory bodies.[748] As the Court held in *Costello-Roberts v. the UK*, '*the State cannot absolve itself from responsibility by delegating its obligations to private bodies or individuals*'.[749]

---

739 J.-F. Akandji-Kombe, *Human rights handbooks, No. 7. Positive Obligations under the European Convention on Human Rights. A guide to the implementation of the European Convention of Human Rights*, Council of Europe, 2007, p. 6.

740 *Ibid.*, p.6 referring to the term used by Professor J.-P. Marguénaud in *La Cour europeenne des Droits de l'Homme*, Dalloz, Paris, coll. Connaissance du droit, 2nd edition, p. 36.

741 *Ibid.*, p. 6.

742 A.R. Mowbray, *The Development of Positive Obligations under the European Convention on Human Rights by the European Court of Human Rights*, Hart Publishing, Oxford – Portland Oregon, 2004, p. 2.

743 Dissenting Opinion of Judge Martens in ECtHR, *Gul v Switzerland* 1996-I 165.

744 J.-F. Akandji-Kombe, *Human rights handbooks, No. 7. o.c.*, p. 5.

745 D. Voorhoof, *Critical perspectives on the scope and interpretation of Article 10 of the European Convention on Human Rights, o.c.*, p. 55.

746 For example, ECtHR, *Hokkanen v. Finland*, 24 August 1994.

747 D. Voorhoof, *Critical perspectives on the scope and interpretation of Article 10 of the European Convention on Human Rights, o.c., p.*59–60; D. Voorhoof, Co-regulation and European basic rights, Presentation at the Expert Conference on Media Policy *More trust in content – The potential of self- and co-regulation in digital media*, Leipzig, 9–11 May 2007, as referred to by E. Lievens, *Protecting Children in the Digital Era – the Use of Alternative Regulatory Instruments, o.c.*, p. 388, ft. 38; A. Clapham,"The 'Drittwirkung' of the Convention", in R.S.J. Macdonald, F. Matscher and H. Petzold, *The European system for the protection of human rights*, Dordrecht, Martinus Nijhoff Publishers, 1993, p. 163.

748 D. Voorhoof, Co-regulation and European basic rights, *o.c.*

749 ECtHR, *Costello-Roberts v. the United Kingdom*, 25 March 1993, Series A no. 247-C, para. 27; see also, ECtHR, *Van der Mussele v. Belgium*, 23 November 1983, Series A no. 70, paras. 29–30.

VIOLATIONS BY PRIVATE PARTIES – States are answerable for any violation of the protected rights and freedoms of anyone within their jurisdiction – or competence – at the time of the violation.[750] In a number of cases, the ECtHR has acknowledged that States have a positive obligation to protect their citizens against violations of the fundamental rights by other citizens. In the context of Article 8 (Right to respect for private and family life), the Court held in *X. and Y. v Netherlands* that the Convention creates obligations for States which may require the adoption of measures '*even in the sphere of the relations of individuals between themselves*'.[751] In the context of Article 11 (Freedom of assembly and association), the Convention may require '*positive measures to be taken, even in the sphere of relations between individuals, if need be*'.[752] According to Clapham, '*[t]he obligation extends to taking preventive action*'; and it '*may mean actual expenditure and the deployment of resources to ensure that the right can be freely exercised without interference from private individuals*'.[753] States can be held responsible for the lack of such protective measures.[754] In *Appleby and others v. the United Kingdom*, the Court addressed the question of positive obligations with regard to Article 10 of the Convention. Specifically, the Court analysed whether there exists a positive obligation of the State to protect the right to freedom of expression from violations by other private individuals. The case concerned applicants who had been stopped from setting up a stand and distributing leaflets in a shopping centre owned by a private company (Postel).

> 'The Court does not find that the authorities bear any direct responsibility for this restriction on the applicants' freedom of expression. It is not persuaded that any element of State responsibility can be derived from the fact that a public development corporation transferred the property to Postel or that this was done with ministerial permission. The issue to be determined is whether the respondent State has failed in any positive obligation to protect the exercise of the applicants' Article 10 rights from interference by others – in this case, the owner of the Galleries'.[755]

HORIZONTAL EFFECT – One way for the State to fulfil its duty to protect those under its jurisdiction is by guaranteeing observance of the Convention in relations between individuals. Extending the scope of the Convention to private relationships between individuals is called the "horizontal effect".

---

750 ECtHR, *Assanidzé v. Georgia*, 8 April 2004.
751 ECtHR, *X. and Y. v Netherlands*, 26 March 1985, para. 23.
752 ECtHR, *Plattform "Arzte fur das Leben" v Austria*, 21 June 1988, para. 32.
753 A. Clapham, *Human Rights in the Private Sphere*, Oxford, Clarendon Press, 1993, p. 345.
754 For instance: ECtHR, *Fuentes Bobo v. Spain*, 29 February 2000, para. 38; ECtHR, *Özgür Gündem v. Turkey*, 16 March 2000, paras 42–43; ECtHR, *VGT Verein v. Tierfabriken*, 28 June 2001, para. 45. See also: P. Van Dijk, F. Van Hoof, A. Van Rijn, L. Zwaak (eds), *Theory and practice of the European Convention on Human Rights*, o.c., p. 30.
755 ECtHR, *Appleby and others v. the United Kingdom*, 06 May 2003, para. 41 (emphasis added).

The horizontal effect is considered 'in its entirety, a consequence of the theory of positive obligations'.[756] It has developed, despite the Court's declaration in *Vgt Verein Gegen Tierfabriken v. Switzerland that,*

> 'The Court does not consider it desirable, let alone necessary, to elaborate a general theory concerning the extent to which the Convention guarantees should be extended to relations between private individuals inter se.'[757]

The horizontal effect is linked to the German *Drittwirkung* theory. As Clapham explains:

> 'The word Drittwirkung originates from a doctrinal debate in Germany and means 'third-party effect'. It refers to the possible application of the German Basic Law in cases where both parties are private parties. The 'third party' refers to the party outside the classic individual / State relationship who is affected by the constitutional norms'.[758]

There are, however, conceptual difficulties with describing horizontal application of the Convention as *Drittwirkung.*[759]

INDIRECT DRITTWIRKUNG – There are two interpretations of the notion of "horizontal effect". According to the first view, human rights provisions apply to relations between private individuals and a State, but also to legal relations between private parties. If the Convention rights are recognised in a State's national law as having direct effect, individuals can invoke these rights before national courts in conflicts between themselves.[760] Since the scope *ratione personae* of the Convention extends only to signatory States, no complaint can be lodged against individuals before the European Court of Human Rights. If a national court's decision is in conflict with the Convention, however, a complaint against the State can be lodged before the European Court of Human Rights.[761] According to the second view, the horizontal effect is indirect, meaning that individuals can enforce human rights provisions against other individuals only indirectly by relying on the positive obligations of the State to protect their

---

756 F. Akandji-Kombe, *Human rights handbook, No. 7. o.c.*, p. 15.

757 ECtHR, *Vgt Verein Gegen Tierfabriken v. Switzerland,* 28 June 2001, para. 46.

758 A. Clapham, "The 'Drittwirkung' of the Convention", *o.c.*, p. 165 (original emphasis).

759 C. Angelopoulos et al., Study of fundamental rights limitations for online enforcement through self-regulation, *o.c.*, p. 33; See also D.J. Harris, M. O'Boyle, E.P. Bates & C. Buckley, *Law of the European Convention on Human Rights,* 3rd ed., Oxford, Oxford University Press, 2014, p. 23.

760 P. Van Dijk, F. Van Hoof, A. Van Rijn, L. Zwaak (eds), *Theory and practice of the European Convention on Human Rights*, *o.c.*, p. 30.

761 A. Clapham, "The 'Drittwirkung' of the Convention", *o.c.*, p. 198.

rights.[762] According to this interpretation, interference with the Convention rights by an individual is not directly attributed to the State. It might be linked, however, to a failing of the State to prevent the interference by not implementing effective protection. It is therefore the inability of the State to legally or materially prevent the violation that could lead to the Court holding it responsible.[763] The approach was evident, for example, in *Appleby and others v. the UK* (cited above). As has been explained in the CoE Handbook on positive obligations,

> 'The state becomes responsible for violations committed between individuals because there has been a failure in the legal order, amounting sometimes to an absence of legal intervention pure and simple, sometimes to inadequate intervention, and sometimes to a lack of measures designed to change a legal situation contrary to the Convention.'[764]

POSITIVE OBLIGATION OR NEGATIVE OBLIGATION – It should also be highlighted that it is not always evident whether the interference with a right results from non-compliance with the positive or negative obligation by the State.[765] In other words, it might be difficult to distinguish whether interference is a result of direct actions of a State or its inactivity to ensure effective protection from interference by private parties. For example, in the context of environmental cases the right to private life (Article 8 ECHR) may apply '*whether the pollution is directly caused by the State or whether State responsibility arises from the failure to regulate private industry properly*'.[766]

The Court has explained on several occasions already that the 'boundaries between the State's positive and negative obligations under the Convention do not lend themselves to precise definition'.[767] For this reason, as stated in Hatton, the Court is not required to decide whether the case falls into the one category or the other.[768]

Most importantly, however, the Court made it clear that

> '[w]hether the case is analysed in terms of a positive duty on the State or in terms of interference by a public authority which needs to be justified, the criteria to be applied do not differ in substance'.[769]

---

762 P. Van Dijk, F. Van Hoof, A. Van Rijn, L. Zwaak (eds), *Theory and practice of the European Convention on Human Rights*, *o.c.*, p. 29.

763 J.-F. Akandji-Kombe, *Human rights handbooks, No. 7. o.c.*, p. 14.

764 *Ibid.*, p. 15.

765 For example ECtHR, *Hatton and Others v. the United Kingdom*, 8 July 2003, para. 98.

766 *Ibid.* See also other environmental cases, for example ECtHR, *Powell and Rayner*, 21 February 1990, para. 41; ECtHR, *López Ostra*, 09 December 1994, para. 51.

767 ECtHR, *Verein gegen Tierfabriken Schweiz v. Switzerland (no. 2) [GC]*, 30 June 2009, para. 82. See also ECtHR, *Von Hannover v. Germany (no. 2)* [GC], 7 February 2012, para. 99.

768 ECtHR, *Hatton and Others v. the United Kingdom*, 8 July 2003, para. 119.

769 ECtHR, *Verein gegen Tierfabriken Schweiz v. Switzerland (no. 2) [GC]*, 30 June 2009, para. 82. See also ECtHR, *Von Hannover v. Germany (no. 2)* [GC], 7 February 2012, para. 99; ECtHR,

The Court emphasized, moreover, that regardless of the classification as a positive or negative obligation case, in '*both contexts regard must be had to the fair balance to be struck between the competing interests at stake*'.[770]

1.2. POSITIVE OBLIGATIONS AND FREEDOM OF EXPRESSION

POSITIVE DIMENSION OF FREEDOM OF EXPRESSION – The right to freedom of expression constrains governments' ability to interfere in the circulation of information and ideas. In this sense, it is first and foremost a 'negative' right. But the right to freedom of expression also contains a 'positive' dimension. According to the Court, '*in addition to the primarily negative undertaking of a State to abstain from interference in Convention guarantees, 'there may be positive obligations inherent' in such guarantees*'.[771]

EFFECTIVE EXERCISE OF THE RIGHT – The obligation to take necessary measures to protect freedom of expression is drawn from Article 10 in conjunction with Article 1.[772] The duty to protect the right to freedom of expression involves an obligation for governments to promote this right and to provide for an environment where it can be effectively exercised without being unduly curtailed. The Declaration of Freedom of Expression and Information of the Committee of Ministers recognised that '*States have the duty to guard against infringements of the freedom of expression and information and should adopt policies designed to foster as much as possible a variety of media and a plurality of information sources, thereby allowing a plurality of ideas and opinions*'.[773]

The 'positive action' approach was also reflected in the final report of the Sevilla Colloquium of 1985 on the European Convention of Human Rights, which declared that,

> '[g]iven the socio-economic conditions of our society, which do not favour equality and in which organised groups hold important portions of power, it is the State's responsibility to ensure the effectiveness of the implementation of freedom of expression and information in practice'.[774]

Hatton and Others v. the United Kingdom, 8 July 2003, para. 98; ECtHR, *Powell and Rayner*, 21 February 1990, para. 41; ECtHR, *López Ostra*, 09 December 1994, para. 51.

770 ECtHR, *Verein gegen Tierfabriken Schweiz v. Switzerland (no. 2) [GC]*, 30 June 2009, para. 82. See also ECtHR, *Von Hannover v. Germany (no. 2)* [GC], 7 February 2012, para. 99

771 ECtHR, *Verein gegen Tierfabriken Schweiz (VgT) v. Switzerland*, 28 June 2001, para. 45.

772 J.-F. Akandji-Kombe, *Human rights handbook, No. 7. o.c.*, p. 8.

773 Committee of Ministers, The Declaration of Freedom of Expression and Information Adopted by the Committee of Ministers on 29 April 1982 at its 70th Session, www.right2info.org/resources/publications/instruments-and-standards/coe_decl-on-foe-and-foi_1982; as referred by D. Voorhoof, *Critical perspectives on the scope and interpretation of Article 10 of the European Convention on Human Rights*, *o.c.*, p. 57.

774 D. Voorhoof, *Critical perspectives on the scope and interpretation of Article 10 of the European Convention on Human Rights*, *o.c.*, p. 57.

INFRINGEMENTS BY PRIVATE INDIVIDUALS – The European Court of Human Rights accepts that Article 10 ECHR can be invoked not only in vertical relations but also in horizontal relations.[775] This could happen, for example, in situations '*where a State had taken or failed to take certain measures*'.[776] In *Fuentes Bobo v. Spain* the Court held that Article 10 applies in relations between an employer and an employee as they are governed by public law, but also to relations which are governed by private law.[777] Specifically, the Court acknowledged that '*a positive obligation can rest with the authorities to protect the freedom of expression against infringements, even by private persons*'.[778]

PROTECTIVE MEASURES – Providing for an environment where the right can be effectively exercised can take the form of protective measures, for example protecting journalists against unlawful violent attacks. The Court recognized such an obligation in the *Özgür Gündem v. Turkey* case:

> 'Genuine, effective exercise of [the right to freedom of expression] does not depend merely on the State's duty not to interfere, but may require positive measures of protection, even in the sphere of relations between individuals [...].'[779]

The Court's reasoning was similar to the reasoning found in other cases concerning the existence of positive obligations (e.g., cases involving Article 8 ECHR).[780] The Court went on to hold Turkey responsible for failing to comply with its positive obligation to ensure effective respect for the rights guaranteed in the Convention.[781]

LACK OF LEGAL FRAMEWORK – The question of positive obligations to secure exercise of freedom of expression was addressed in *Verein gegen Tierfabriken Schweiz (VgT) v. Switzerland*.[782] The case concerned the Swiss commercial television company's refusal to broadcast the applicant association's commercial advocating for protection of farming animals. The applicants argued

---

775 For example ECtHR, *Fuentes Bobo v. Spain*, 29 February 2000.

776 P. Van Dijk, F. Van Hoof, A. Van Rijn, L. Zwaak (eds), *Theory and practice of the European Convention on Human Rights*, *o.c.*, p. 784.

777 P. Van Dijk, F. Van Hoof, A. Van Rijn, L. Zwaak (eds), *Theory and practice of the European Convention on Human Rights*, *o.c.*, p. 785. See also P. Leerssen, "Cut Out By The Middle Man The Free Speech Implications Of Social Network Blocking and Banning In The EU", JIPITEC Vol. 6, 2015, p. 103.

778 ECtHR, *Fuentes Bobo v. Spain*, 29 February 2000. See also: P. Van Dijk, F. Van Hoof, A. Van Rijn, L. Zwaak (eds), *Theory and practice of the European Convention on Human Rights*, *o.c.*, p. 784–785.

779 ECtHR, *Özgür Gündem v. Turkey*, 16 March 2000, para. 43 (emphasis added).

780 A.R. Mowbray, *The Development of Positive Obligations under the European Convention on Human Rights by the European Court of Human Rights*, *o.c.*, p. 195.

781 ECtHR, *Özgür Gündem v. Turkey*, 16 March 2000, §46.

782 ECtHR, *Verein gegen Tierfabriken Schweiz (VgT) v. Switzerland*, 28 June 2001.

that the State '*is not permitted to delegate functions to private persons in such a way that fundamental rights are undermined by the resulting "privatisation"*'.[783] According to the Swiss government, the refusal to broadcast did not render them liable because the government exercised no supervision over the commercial television company. In response, the Court declared that '*[t]he responsibility of a State may then be engaged as a result of not observing its obligation to enact domestic legislation*' and considered the refusal to broadcast as an interference with the applicants' right to freedom of expression by public authority.[784]

STATE'S INTERFERENCE OF FAILURE TO ACT – The question of lack of domestic legislation was raised also in the *Editorial Board of Pravoye Delo and Shtekel v. Ukraine* case where the Court revisited the question of protection of journalists.[785] The case concerned a lack of an appropriate regulatory framework to ensure effective protection of journalists. The infringement in this case, however, was not committed by private individuals but by the State, through the court's ruling which imposed an obligation on a journalist to apologise in a defamation case. The Court considered that '*the absence of a sufficient legal framework at the domestic level allowing journalists to use information obtained from the Internet without fear of incurring sanctions seriously hinders the exercise of the vital function of the press as a "public watchdog"*'.[786] A lack of adequate safeguards in the domestic law, in this case, was not a matter of positive obligations to protect from interference by private parties, but rather the State's own direct infringement of the right, because the interference was not prescribed by law. The key take-away is that lack of an appropriate legal framework may lead to holding the State responsible either for its own interference (negative dimension) or for its failure to act (positive dimension) if the interference was by a private party. The applied principles are nevertheless similar, as the ECtHR has explained on several occasions.[787]

MARGIN OF APPRECIATION TO SPECIFY THE MEANS – When deciding about the existence of a positive obligation, the ECtHR must strike a fair balance between the general interests of the community and the interest of the individual.[788] States enjoy a large margin of appreciation in determining which

783 *Ibid.*, para. 38.

784 ECtHR, *Verein gegen Tierfabriken Schweiz (VgT) v. Switzerland*, 28 June 2001, para. 45 and 48.

785 ECtHR, *Editorial Board of Pravoye Delo and Shtekel v. Ukraine*, 5 May 2011.

786 *Ibid.*, par. 64.

787 See for example ECtHR, *Hatton and Others v. the United Kingdom*, 8 July 2003, para. 98. In the context of Art. 10 ECHR see ECtHR, *Verein gegen Tierfabriken Schweiz v. Switzerland (no. 2) [GC], 30 June 2009*, para. 82. See also ECtHR, *Von Hannover v. Germany (no. 2)* [GC], 7 February 2012, para. 99.

788 ECtHR, *Özgür Gündem v. Turkey*, 16 March 2000, para. 43; ECtHR, *Appleby and others v. the United Kingdom*, 06 May 2003, para. 40.

steps are necessary to secure effective enjoyment of a right. In selecting the most appropriate measures they should take into account the needs and resources of individuals as well as society more broadly.[789] In *Özgür Gündem v. Turkey* the Court specified that,

> '[t]he scope of this obligation will inevitably vary, having regard to the diversity of situations obtaining in Contracting States, the difficulties involved in policing modern societies and the choices which must be made in terms of priorities and resources.'[790]

Moreover, 'the scope of the positive obligation must be interpreted in a way which does not impose an impossible or disproportionate burden on the authorities.'[791]

NO FREEDOM OF FORUM – In *Appleby and others v. the United Kingdom*, the applicants had lodged a complaint against the UK after they were stopped from setting up a stand and distributing leaflets in a privately owned shopping centre. The Court did not find that the authorities bore any direct responsibility for the restriction on the applicants' freedom of expression.[792] The question at stake, however, was whether the UK had failed in any positive obligation to protect the exercise of the applicants' right to freedom of expression from interference by others – in this case, the owners of the shopping centre.[793] The Court pointed out that freedom of expression was not the only right at stake in the case, and acknowledged a conflict with the property rights of the owner of the shopping centre under Article 1 of Protocol No. 1.[794] Despite its relevance, Article 10 does not bestow any "freedom of forum" for the exercise of the right to freedom of expression.[795] The Court clarified that where

> 'the bar on access to property has the effect of preventing any effective exercise of freedom of expression or it can be said that the essence of the right has been destroyed, the Court would not exclude that a positive obligation could arise for the State to protect the enjoyment of the Convention rights by regulating property rights'.[796]

---

789 ECtHR, *Węgrzynowski and Smolczewski v. Poland*, Strasbourg, 16 July 2013.
790 ECtHR, *Özgür Gündem v. Turkey*, 16 March 2000, para. 43
791 ECtHR, *Keenan v United Kingdom*, 3 April 2001, para. 90. ECtHR, *Özgür Gündem v. Turkey*, 16 March 2000, para. 43.
792 ECtHR, *Appleby and others v. the United Kingdom*, 06 May 2003, para. 41.
793 *Ibid.*
794 *Ibid.*, para. 43.
795 T. McGonagle, "The State and beyond: activating (non-)media voices", in H. Sousa et al. (ed.), *Media Policy and Regulation: Activating Voices, Illuminating Silences*, Conference contribution, Braga: University of Minho – Communication and Society Research Centre (CECS), 2013, pp. 187–198, p. 190.
796 ECtHR, *Appleby and others v. the United Kingdom*, 06 May 2003, para. 47.

In *Appleby*, the applicants were able to exercise their right through several alternative means, therefore the Court did not find that the UK failed in its positive obligation to protect the applicants' freedom of expression.[797] As pointed out by Leerssen, the test of "viable alternatives" from *Appleby* speaks to a very real concern regarding the position of online intermediaries.[798]

ALTERNATIVE EXPRESSIVE OPPORTUNITIES – The Court addressed the question of alternative expressive opportunities in *Khurshid Mustafa & Tarzibachi*.[799] The case concerned the termination of a tenancy agreement by a landlord because of the tenants' refusal to dismantle a satellite dish. The dish was installed to receive television programmes from the tenants' native country. The Court observed that different media are not necessarily interchangeable – they have different purposes and are used in different ways by different individuals and groups.[800] The Court rejected, therefore, the idea that different media are functionally equivalent.[801] This is also the reason why different media are regulated differently.[802] The Court also acknowledged that it is not its role to settle disputes of a purely private nature. Nevertheless, it cannot remain passive where a national court's interpretation of a legal act, including a private contract, appears unreasonable, arbitrary, discriminatory or, more broadly, inconsistent with the principles underlying the Convention.[803] The Court found, in result, that the State failed in their positive obligation to protect that right to freedom of expression.[804] This means that in order to comply with the obligation to protect the right to freedom of expression, the State might be required to set certain limits for rules that private owners establish on their property.

---

797 *Ibid.*, para. 49. See more in T. McGonagle, "The State and beyond: activating (non-)media voices", *o.c.*, p. 190.

798 P. Leerssen, "Cut Out By The Middle Man The Free Speech Implications Of Social Network Blocking and Banning In The EU", *o.c.*, p. 104.

799 ECtHR, *Khurshid Mustafa & Tarzibachi v. Sweden*, 16 December 2008, para. 45.

800 T. McGonagle, "Positive obligations concerning freedom of expression: mere potential or real power?" in O. Andreotti (ed.), *Journalism at risk: Threats, challenges and perspective*, Council of Europe, 2015, pp. 9–37, p. 24; see also T. McGonagle, "The Council of Europe's standards on access to the media for minorities: A tale of near misses and staggered successes", in M. Amos, J. Harrison, & L. Woods, (eds.), *Freedom of Expression and the Media*, Leiden/Boston, Martinus Nijhoff Publishers, 2012, pp. 111–140, at 118–124.

801 T. McGonagle, "Positive obligations concerning freedom of expression: mere potential or real power?" *o.c.*, p. 24.

802 See also ECtHR, *Węgrzynowski and Smolczewski v. Poland*, 16 July 2013. T. McGonagle, "Positive obligations concerning freedom of expression: mere potential or real power?", *o.c.*, p. 24.

803 ECtHR, *Khurshid Mustafa & Tarzibachi v. Sweden*, 16 December 2008, para. 33.

804 *Ibid.*, para. 50.

RIGHT TO REPLY – In *Melnychuk v. Ukraine*, the Court addressed a particular form of access – the right to reply.[805] The Court noted that 'as a general principle, newspapers and other privately-owned media must be free to exercise editorial discretion in deciding whether to publish articles, comments and letters submitted by private individuals'.[806] Nevertheless, "exceptional circumstances" may arise 'in which a newspaper may legitimately be required to publish, for example, a retraction, an apology or a judgment in a defamation case'.[807] This particular case concerned a right to reply, which the Court considered an important element of freedom of expression. This follows from the need to be able to contest untruthful information, but also to ensure a plurality of opinions, especially in matters of general interest such as literary and political debate.[808] According to the Court, such situations may create a positive obligation 'for the State to ensure an individual's freedom of expression in such media'.

Recently, in *Eker v. Turkey*[809], the Court derived the right of reply from both Article 10 and Article 8 ECHR.[810] Specifically, the Court held that a right of reply is intended to ensure a plurality of opinions, particularly in areas of general interest.[811] The Court added, with regard to Article 8, that a right to reply is also meant to afford all persons the possibility of protecting themselves against certain statements or opinions disseminated by the mass media that are likely to be injurious to their private life, honour and dignity, as well as reputation.[812] Basing a right to reply on Article 8 goes back to the ECtHR's initial approach in *Ediciones Tiempo SA v Spain*.[813] The new case law suggests that a right of reply '*requires more than merely the retraction of incorrect facts and offers an opportunity to vindicate reputational rights*'.[814]

---

805 ECtHR, *Melnychuk v. Ukraine,* Decision of inadmissibility of the European Court of Human Rights (Second Section) of 5 July 2005. See also ECtHR, *Kaperzyński v. Poland*, 3 April 2012; and ECtHR, *Marunic v. Croatia*, 28 March 2017. See also C. Angelopoulos et al., Study of fundamental rights limitations for online enforcement through self-regulation, *o.c.*, p. 33; See also D.J. Harris, M. O'Boyle, E.P. Bates & C. Buckley, *Law of the European Convention on Human Rights, o.c.*, p. 36.

806 ECtHR, *Melnychuk v. Ukraine,* Decision of inadmissibility of the European Court of Human Rights (Second Section) of 5 July 2005.

807 *Ibid.*

808 *Ibid.*

809 ECtHR, *Eker v. Turkey App*, 24 October 2017.

810 See more in F. Hempel, "The right of reply under the European Convention on Human Rights: an analysis of Eker v Turkey App no 24016/05 (ECtHR, 24 October 2017)", *Journal of Media Law*, 4 April 2018, p.1–20.

811 *Ibid.*, para. 43 and 48.

812 *Ibid.*, para. 47 and 50.

813 ECtHR, *Ediciones Tiempo SA v. Spain*, 12 July 1989.

814 F. Hempel, "The right of reply under the European Convention on Human Rights: an analysis of Eker v Turkey App no 24016/05 (ECtHR, 24 October 2017)", *o.c.*, p. 8. The reliance upon both Article 8 and Article 10 ECHR to derive a right of reply is sometimes referred to as the 'two-pillar theory' (*Ibid.*).

FAVOURABLE ENVIRONMENT – The Court pronounced perhaps the most far-reaching positive obligation in relation to freedom of expression in a broad sense in *Dink v. Turkey*.[815] In this case, the Court explained that States are required to create a favourable environment for participation in public debate for everyone and to enable the expression of ideas and opinions without fear.[816] This finding contains great potential for further development.[817] According to McGonagle, it could constitute '*the beginning of a new phase in the development of the positive obligations doctrine, at least in respect of the right to freedom of expression*'.[818]

1.3. INTERPLAY BETWEEN SUBSTANTIVE AND PROCEDURAL OBLIGATIONS

"SUBSTANTIVE" AND "PROCEDURAL" OBLIGATIONS – States' positive obligations, for example under Articles 2 (right to life), 3 (prohibition of torture) and 5 (right to liberty and security), also have a procedural dimension. The Court articulated a distinction between "procedural" and "substantive" obligations in *Öneryıldız v. Turkey*, which concerned interference with Article 2 (right to life) ECHR.[819] Substantive obligations require States to take the basic measures needed to ensure full enjoyment of the rights guaranteed by the Convention, for example by giving legal recognition to the status of transsexuals.[820] Procedural obligations, on the other hand, require states to organise domestic procedures to ensure better protection of persons, for example by providing sufficient remedies in case of rights violations.[821] This may include the requirement that parents participate in proceedings involving their children[822] or the right to an effective investigation.[823] The ECtHR has provided guidance on what criteria must be met for an investigation to be considered effective.[824]

---

815 ECtHR, *Dink v. Turkey*, 14 September 2010. See C. Angelopoulos et al., Study of fundamental rights limitations for online enforcement through self-regulation, *o.c.*, p. 38.

816 C. Angelopoulos et al., Study of fundamental rights limitations for online enforcement through self-regulation, *o.c.*, p. 38, referring to ECtHR, *Dink v. Turkey*, 14 September 2010, para. 137.

817 C. Angelopoulos et al., Study of fundamental rights limitations for online enforcement through self-regulation, *o.c.*, p. 38.

818 T. McGonagle, "Positive obligations concerning freedom of expression: mere potential or real power?" *o.c.*, p. 11.

819 ECtHR, *Öneryıldız v. Turkey*, 30 November 2004, para. 99.

820 For example, ECtHR, *Rees v. the United Kingdom*, 17 October 1986. J.-F. Akandji-Kombe, *Human rights handbooks, No. 7. o.c.*, p.16.

821 J.-F. Akandji-Kombe, *Human rights handbooks, No. 7. o.c.*, p. 16.

822 For example ECtHR, *B v. the United Kingdom*, 26 May 1987; ECtHR, *Ignoccolo-Zenide v. Romania*, 25 January 2000.

823 J.-F. Akandji-Kombe, *Human rights handbooks, No. 7. o.c.*, p. 16.

824 In ECtHR, *Enukidze and Girgvliani v. Georgia*, 26 April 2011, para. 242. See more in T. McGonagle, "Positive obligations concerning freedom of expression: mere potential or real power?", *o.c.*, p. 17.

INTERPLAY – The concept of "positive obligations" allows the ECtHR to strengthen, and sometimes even to extend, the substantive requirements of the Convention and to '*link them to procedural obligations which are independent of Articles 6 and 13 and additional to those covered by those articles*'.[825] Different combinations of substantive and procedural obligations have allowed the ECtHR to broaden its range of scrutiny.[826] If the complaint is formulated appropriately, the Court can analyse a variety of interactions between substantive and procedural obligations. This may lead to a somewhat complex situation, whereby rights which are traditionally seen as substantive (e.g. Article 2 and Article 3) may be analysed from the perspectives of both substantive and procedural obligations (e.g. Article 6 and Article 13).[827] At the same time, the requirements of Article 6 and Article 13 may also enter the frame of the Convention's substantive provisions.[828] This means that the same complaint can be examined from several perspectives, and a violation can be found in some or in all of them.[829]

PROCEDURAL FAIRNESS – The interplay between rights and obligations played a part in the Court's decision in *Steel and Morris v. the United Kingdom*.[830] An advocacy group released a leaflet accusing McDonald's restaurants of a number of wrongdoings (e.g. abusive and immoral farming and employment practices, deforestation, and exploitation of children through aggressive advertising). In response McDonald's lodged a defamation case against the group. The case concerned an interference with the applicants' right to freedom of expression, as well as an interference with the applicants' right to fair trial by not providing them with legal aid in the defamation case. The Court held that the State enjoys a margin of appreciation when choosing the means which enable a company to challenge allegations that put its reputation at risk.[831] In such a case, however, a measure of procedural fairness and equality of arms should be provided for, in order to safeguard the countervailing interests in free expression and open debate.[832] The fact that the applicants had no access to legal aid, which constituted a violation of Article 6.1, contributed to the Court's finding that there was no correct balance between the need to protect the applicants' rights to freedom of expression and the need to protect McDonald's rights and reputation.[833] This finding, together with a lack of procedural fairness

825 J.-F. Akandji-Kombe, *Human rights handbooks, No. 7. o.c.*, p.6.

826 *Ibid.*, p. 16.

827 For example ECtHR, *Kurt v. Turkey,* 25 May 1998; ECtHR, *Tanis and others v. Turkey,* 2 August 2005.

828 For example ECtHR, *Tanis and others v. Turkey,* 2 August 2005. J.-F. Akandji-Kombe, *Human rights handbooks, No. 7. o.c.*, p. 17.

829 *Ibid.*

830 ECtHR, *Steel and Morris v. the United Kingdom*, 15 February 2005.

831 *Ibid.*, para. 94.

832 *Ibid.*, para. 95.

833 *Ibid.*

and equality of arms gave rise to a breach of Article 10.[834] The interference in *Steel and Morris v. the United Kingdom* was one of the State, and not of a private individual. The case shows that in certain circumstances states' failure to act (here by not ensuring procedural fairness) might be considered by the ECtHR as a factor when assessing proportionality of the interference. It also shows that there may be a thin line sometimes between substantial and procedural rights, as well as negative and positive obligations – which depends on who commits the original violation.

1.4. POSITIVE OBLIGATIONS AND PROCEDURAL SAFEGUARDS

OUTLINE – The doctrine of "positive obligations" puts a strong focus on procedural factors. Apart from the procedural positive obligations (in the context of the substantive provisions), the Convention also contains traditional procedural rights, which generally require States to take action.[835] Combining the two types of obligations can help to give maximum effect to Convention rights.[836] In the context of this book, the most relevant procedural rights are Article 6 – providing a right to fair trial, and Article 13 – providing a right to effective remedy. The two rights are directed to States, which are responsible for ensuring their effective enjoyment. Even though their horizontal application is sometimes mentioned, in this book they will mainly serve as a source of inspiration for procedures which could contribute to strengthening the protection of freedom of expression in the content removal mechanisms.

RIGHT TO FAIR TRIAL – Article 6 of the Convention guarantees that

> '[i]n the determination of his civil rights and obligations or of any criminal charge against him, everyone is entitled to a fair and public hearing within a reasonable time by an independent and impartial tribunal established by law.(...)'

Moreover, the pronouncement of the judgement has to be public (with few exceptions, e.g. in the interests of minors). The second paragraph guarantees a presumption of innocence and the third paragraph contains a non-exhaustive list of rights, which – in criminal cases – are linked to the notion of 'fair trial'.[837] Article 6 ECHR is applicable in criminal cases and in non-criminal

---

834 *Ibid.*

835 For example Article 6 ECHR – a right to a fair trail, and Article 13 ECHR – a right to effective remedy.

836 J.-F. Akandji-Kombe, *Human rights handbook, No. 7. o.c.*, p. 59.

837 E. Lievens, *Protecting Children in the Digital Era – the Use of Alternative Regulatory Instruments, o.c.* p. 324, referring to B. De Smet, J. Lathouwers, et al., "Artikel 6: recht op

cases where civil rights and obligations are at stake. The ECtHR has developed an autonomous interpretation of the notion "civil rights and obligations".[838] Article 6 comes into play when there is a real and serious dispute related to an actual right, such as the right to freedom of expression in Article 10 ECHR. The dispute may be between individuals or between an individual and the State.[839]

Article 6 embodies a number of elements, not all of which are relevant for this book. The different aspects of Article 6 are used in the development of the positive assessment framework of the book. It is already worth pointing out, however, that the most crucial elements are the requirements of a "fair and public hearing" and an "independent and impartial tribunal established by law".

POSITIVE OBLIGATIONS AND ARTICLE 6 – Article 6 provides an extensive array of positive obligations[840], and it is the duty of the State to ensure their practical and effective realization.[841] They include an obligation to determine cases within a reasonable time and the duty of criminal justice authorities to inform charged persons of the detailed nature of the accusations against them. The Court has also found several implied positive obligations under Article 6.[842] In *Airey v Ireland*, for example, the Court stated that

> 'fulfilment of a duty under the Convention on occasion necessitates some positive action on the part of the State; in such circumstances, the State cannot simply remain passive and 'there is... no room to distinguish between acts and omissions. The obligation to secure an effective right of access to the courts falls into this category of duty.'[843]

The ECtHR has been steadily extending the scope of positive obligations under Article 6. This tendency is interpreted as *'an acknowledgement of the significance of positive obligations under this crucial Article'*.[844]

---

eerlijk proces" [*"Article 6: right to fair trial"*], in: J. Vande Lanotte, Y. Haeck, *Handboek EVRM: Deel II: Artikelsgewijze commentaar (Volume I)* [*ECHR: Part II: Commentary on the articles*], Antwerpen, Intersentia, 2004, p. 386 [in Dutch].

838 See, A.R. Mowbray, *Cases & Materials on the European Convention on Human Rights*, London, Butterworths, 2001, pp. 235–58.

839 E. Lievens, *Protecting Children in the Digital Era – the Use of Alternative Regulatory Instruments*, *o.c.*, p. 324, referring to B. De Smet, J. Lathouwers, et al., "Artikel 6: recht op eerlijk proces", *o.c.*, p. 388 [in Dutch].

840 A.R. Mowbray, *The Development of Positive Obligations under the European Convention on Human Rights by the European Court of Human Rights*, *o.c.*, p. 124.

841 N. Mole and C. Harby, *The right to a fair trial: a guide to the implementation of Article 6 of the European Convention on Human Rights (Human rights handbooks, No. 3)*, Strasbourg, Council of Europe, 2006, p. 6.

842 For example ECtHR, *Airey v Ireland*, 9 October, 1979. A.R. Mowbray, *The Development of Positive Obligations under the European Convention on Human Rights by the European Court of Human Rights*, *o.c.*, p. 125.

843 ECtHR, *Airey v Ireland*, 9 October, 1979, par. *25*.

844 A.R. Mowbray, *The Development of Positive Obligations under the European Convention on Human Rights by the European Court of Human Rights, Hart Publishing*, *o.c.*, p. 125.

RIGHT TO EFFECTIVE REMEDY – Article 13 guarantees that

> '[e]veryone whose rights and freedoms as set forth in this Convention are violated shall have an effective remedy before a national authority notwithstanding that the violation has been committed by persons acting in an official capacity.'

Article 13 ECHR specifies (together with Article 5 paras. 4 and 5 and Article 6 para. 1) the obligation for Contracting States to secure everyone within their jurisdiction with the rights and freedoms of the Convention. The States are responsible for the establishment and remedying of violations of Convention rights. The right to effective remedy is invoked when another fundamental right of the Convention, for example freedom of expression, is allegedly violated. It is, nevertheless, an autonomous right.[845] In case of a violation, the remedy should be capable of stopping the violation, or allowing the obtainment of an adequate redress, including compensation.[846] The remedy should, moreover, be effective in practice and in law.[847] The purpose of the provision is to '*enable the domestic system to play its part to the full by obliging states to make provision for the necessary remedies to redress situations at variance with the Convention.*'[848] As the Court stated in *Kaya v. Turkey,* Article 13

> 'guarantees the availability at the national level of a remedy to enforce the substance of the Convention rights and freedoms in whatever form they might happen to be secured in the domestic legal order. The effect of Article 13 is thus to require the provision of a domestic remedy to deal with the substance of the relevant Convention complaint and to grant appropriate relief.'[849]

POSITIVE OBLIGATIONS AND ARTICLE 13 – Similar to Article 6, Article 13 contains procedural guarantees which States must effectively ensure. The major principles governing these positive obligations were explained in *Silver and Others v United Kingdom.*[850] Here, the Court ruled that

> 'where an individual has an arguable claim to be the victim of a violation of the rights set forth in the Convention, he should have a remedy before a national authority in order both to have his claim decided and, if appropriate, to obtain redress'.[851]

---

845 E. Lievens, *Protecting Children in the Digital Era – the Use of Alternative Regulatory Instruments, o.c.,* p. 418.

846 For example ECtHR, *Kaya v. Turkey*, 19 February 1998.

847 E. Lievens, *Protecting Children in the Digital Era – the Use of Alternative Regulatory Instruments, o.c.,* p. 418.

848 J.-F. Akandji-Kombe, *Human rights handbook, No. 7. o.c.*, p. 59.

849 ECtHR, *Kaya v. Turkey*, 19 February 1998, para. 106.

850 A.R. Mowbray, *The Development of Positive Obligations under the European Convention on Human Rights by the European Court of Human Rights, Hart Publishing, o.c.*, p. 205.

851 ECtHR, *Silver and Others v United Kingdom*, 25 March 1983, p. 113.

The claimant must be able to make an 'arguable claim' that he or she has been the victim of a violation of one of the rights guaranteed by the Convention.[852] The ECtHR has not defined the notion of arguability and instead, makes an assessment in the light of the circumstances of each case.[853] According to Mowbray, '*[i]n practical terms applicants need to ensure that they have at least a prima facie case of a violation of Convention rights*'.[854]

The application of Article 13 depends on the manner in which the State concerned has chosen to discharge its obligation under Article 1 directly, to secure the rights and freedom set out in the Convention to anyone within its jurisdiction.[855] In *Silver*, the Court clarified that

> 'neither Article 13 nor the Convention in general lays down for the Contracting States any given manner for ensuring within their internal law the effective implementation of any of the provisions of the Convention – for example, by incorporating the Convention into domestic law'.[856]

The Court, however, addressed the question of providing effective domestic remedies through the availability of suitable non-judicial agencies. In a number of cases, the Court has analysed the powers, procedures and independence of such non-judicial bodies strictly.[857] In light of *Silver*, it seems very unlikely that the Court would recognize non-judicial bodies which only possess advisory powers as providing an effective remedy.[858] In *Chahal v United Kingdom*, the Court went on to clarify that the advisory panel (which failed to allow Chahal legal representation and only provided him with an outline of the grounds for his deportation) did not constitute an effective remedy because it offered insufficient procedural safeguards to the applicants.[859]

---

852 A.R. Mowbray, *The Development of Positive Obligations under the European Convention on Human Rights by the European Court of Human Rights, Hart Publishing, o.c.*, p. 206.

853 A.R. Mowbray, *The Development of Positive Obligations under the European Convention on Human Rights by the European Court of Human Rights, Hart Publishing, o.c.*, p. 206, in reference to ECtHR, *Boyle and Rice v United Kingdom*, 24 March 1988, para. 55.

854 A.R. Mowbray, *The Development of Positive Obligations under the European Convention on Human Rights by the European Court of Human Rights, Hart Publishing, o.c.*, p. 206, in reference to ECtHR, *Boyle and Rice v United Kingdom*, 24 March 1988, para. 54.

855 ECtHR, *Silver and Others v United Kingdom*, 25 March 1983, p. 113.

856 *Ibid.*

857 For example, ECtHR, *Silver and Others v United Kingdom*, 25 March 1983; and ECtHR, *Chahal v United Kingdom*, 15 November 1996.

858 A.R. Mowbray, *The Development of Positive Obligations under the European Convention on Human Rights by the European Court of Human Rights, o.c.*, p. 207. More on the Parliamentary Ombudsman see, S. Bailey, B. Jones and A.R. Mowbray, *Cases and Materials on Administrative Law*, 3rd edn., London, Sweet & Maxwell, 1997, ch. 4.

859 ECtHR, *Chahal v United Kingdom*, 15 November 1996, p. 154. See also A.R. Mowbray, *The Development of Positive Obligations under the European Convention on Human Rights by the European Court of Human Rights, o.c.*, p. 207.

Article 13 is considered an *important source of institutional positive obligations.*[860] Similarly to Article 6, Article 13 has undergone a significant expansion in the range of positive obligations recognised by the Court under this provision.[861] One example is the obligation of states to provide an effective domestic remedy to handle complaints of alleged unreasonable delays in civil and criminal proceedings.[862]

HORIZONTAL EFFECT OF ARTICLE 13 – Article 13 provides that the right to effective remedy is guaranteed '*notwithstanding that the violation has been committed by persons acting in an official capacity*'. This provision is generally directed at laws that provide public officials with immunity from human rights infringements.[863] It has also been suggested, however, that the provision might imply that '*an effective legal remedy within the meaning of Article 13 must also [...] be furnished when the violation has been committed by a private individual, raising the possibility of indirect Drittwirkung of the Convention rights between citizens*'.[864] Others have similarly argued that the wording of Article 13 shows that '*the scope of the Convention is not limited to persons exercising public authority*'.[865] Such an interpretation is usually limited to cases where a positive obligation exists to protect individuals' rights in relation to Article 2 (right to life) or Article 3 (protection from torture and other inhuman or degrading treatment or punishment) against serious violations committed by other individuals.[866] The Court has recognized, however, the applicability of Article 13 in relation to Article 11, which '*sometimes requires positive measures to be taken, even in the sphere of relations between individuals, if need be*'.[867] According to Lievens, it is conceivable to consider the applicability of Article 13 to relations between individuals possible also in the context of Article 10 ECHR.[868]

CONCLUDING REMARKS – The European Court of Human Rights has recognized that States have certain positive obligations in relation to Article 10.

---

860 A.R. Mowbray, *The Development of Positive Obligations under the European Convention on Human Rights by the European Court of Human Rights*, *o.c.*, p. 220.

861 *Ibid.*

862 For example ECtHR, *Kudla v Poland*, 26 October 2000.

863 E. Lievens, *Protecting Children in the Digital Era – the Use of Alternative Regulatory Instruments*, *o.c.*, p. 421.

864 P. Van Dijk, F. Van Hoof, A. Van Rijn, L. Zwaak (eds), *Theory and practice of the European Convention on Human Rights*, *o.c.*, p. 1024.

865 C. Ovey, R. White, Jacobs and White, *The European Convention on Human Rights*, Oxford, Oxford University Press, 2006, p. 470.

866 P. Van Dijk, F. Van Hoof, A. Van Rijn, L. Zwaak (eds), *Theory and practice of the European Convention on Human Rights*, *o.c.*, p. 1024. See also E. Lievens, *Protecting Children in the Digital Era – the Use of Alternative Regulatory Instruments*, *o.c.*, p. 422.

867 ECtHR, *Plattform Ärtze für das Leben v. Austria*, 21 June 1988, para. 32.

868 E. Lievens, *Protecting Children in the Digital Era – the Use of Alternative Regulatory Instruments*, *o.c.*, p. 422.

The Court's recognition of positive obligations in relation to Article 10 is '*nascent and piecemeal, but steady*'.[869] Especially in *Dink*, the essential obligation for States to ensure a favourable environment for public debate '*gives a new sense of coherence to a disparate set of positive obligations*' as identified by the Court.[870] As far as procedural safeguards are concerned, reference should also be made to Articles 6 and 13 ECHR (which may overlap with each other in certain instances).[871] The two Articles, however, are directed to States. The focus of this book is on notice and action mechanisms where decisions about removal of content are made by Internet hosts, i.e. private parties. Strict compliance with the requirements of Articles 6 and 13 by private parties cannot be expected. Elements of the two provisions can be used, however, as inspiration for the development of assessment criteria.[872]

2. POSITIVE OBLIGATIONS – THE CHARTER OF FUNDAMENTAL RIGHTS

2.1. POSITIVE OBLIGATIONS UNDER THE CHARTER – GENERAL

INTRODUCTION – Like the rights guaranteed by the Convention, the rights guaranteed in the Charter can be interfered with both by States (vertical interference) and by private individuals (horizontal interference).

The question relevant for this book is whether the Charter creates a positive obligation, in the same way as the Convention, for the States, but also for the EU acting as a legislator, to protect the Charter rights and to create an environment in which these rights can be effectively enjoyed. To find the answer, the scope of application of the Charter must be analysed.

SCOPE OF APPLICATION OF THE CHARTER – Article 51.1 of the Charter defines the scope of application of the Charter:

---

869 C. Angelopoulos et al., Study of fundamental rights limitations for online enforcement through self-regulation, *o.c.*, p. 38. The authors consider that this statement applies not only to Article 10 but also to other "communication rights". "Communication rights" are '*a term of convenience that covers a cluster of rights that are indispensable for the effective exercise of communicative freedoms. These rights typically include the right to freedom of expression, freedom of assembly and association, privacy, etc. They also include the right to an effective remedy whenever the aforementioned rights have been violated, as well as various process rights that serve to guarantee procedural fairness and justice*'.

870 T. McGonagle, "Positive obligations concerning freedom of expression: mere potential or real power?" *o.c.*, p. 30.

871 E. Lievens, *Protecting Children in the Digital Era – the Use of Alternative Regulatory Instruments*, *o.c.*, p. 422.

872 See Part II Chapter 4.

> 'The provisions of this Charter are addressed to the institutions, bodies, offices and agencies of the Union with due regard for the principle of subsidiarity and to the Member States only when they are implementing Union law. They shall therefore respect the rights, observe the principles and promote the application thereof in accordance with their respective powers (...)'.[873]

Article 51 should be read in conjunction with Article 52, which specifies the conditions for limitation of rights. The scope of the Charter should also be assessed in the context of the subsidiarity and proportionality principles stated in Articles 51.1 and 52.1. Additionally, Article 52.3 refers explicitly to the level of protection awarded in the ECHR,

> 'In so far as this Charter contains rights which correspond to rights guaranteed by the Convention for the Protection of Human Rights and Fundamental Freedoms, the meaning and scope of those rights shall be the same as those laid down by the said Convention. This provision shall not prevent Union law providing more extensive protection'.[874]

Finally, Article 53 of the Charter lays down a minimum common denominator for the level of protection of the rights. This provision, according to the Explanations document, is intended '*to maintain the level of protection currently afforded within their respective scope by Union law, national law and international law*'[875], with a clear emphasis on the level of protection granted in the ECHR.

HORIZONTAL APPLICATION OF THE CHARTER – According to Article 51.1 CFEU, the Charter applies to the '*EU institutions and to the Member States*' when they are implementing EU law, but does not address applicability to private parties.[876] For this reason, some commentators argue that the Charter cannot create horizontal effects.[877] The argument is that a horizontal application would involve the CJEU acting beyond the reach of its jurisdiction and as a consequence, extending the scope of EU law via the Charter, contrary to the language of Article 51.2 CFEU.[878] Others argue that Article 51 does not

---

873 Article 51.1 CFEU, emphasis added.

874 Article 52.3 CFEU.

875 Praesidium of the Convention, Explanations relating to the Charter of Fundamental Rights, *o.c.* Explanation on Article 53.

876 E. Frantziou, "The Horizontal Effect of the Charter of Fundamental Rights of the EU: Rediscovering the Reasons for Horizontality", *European Law Journal*, Vol. 21, No. 5, September 2015, pp. 657–679.

877 See K. Lenaerts, "Exploring the Limits of the EU Charter of Fundamental Rights", *European Constitutional Law Review*, Vol. 8, 2012, p. 377, ft. 11.

878 E. Frantziou, "The Horizontal Effect of the Charter of Fundamental Rights of the EU: Rediscovering the Reasons for Horizontality", *o.c.*, ft. 10 referring to Opinion of Advocate General Trstenjak, delivered on 8 September 2011 in Case C-282/10, *Dominguez v. Centre Informatique Du Centre Ouest Atlantique*, judgment of 24 January 2012. Article 51(2) EUCFR

specifically exclude horizontal effect.[879] In the EU legal order, rights derived from primary law can in principle be applied horizontally. The Charter has the status of primary EU law, and bears '*the same legal value as the Treaties*'.[880] It must be capable, therefore, of being invoked horizontally, where a particular provision fulfils the conditions for direct effect.[881] This means that the provision in question should be clear, unconditional, sufficiently precise and not requiring further implementing measures.[882] The rule on horizontal application of primary EU law has been recognized since *Defrenne v. Sabena*.[883] In this case, the CJEU preferred to focus on the spirit of the right, rather than the precise wording of the provision. The CJEU held that,

> 'The fact that certain provisions (...) are formally addressed to the Member States does not prevent rights from being conferred at the same time on any individual who has an interest in the performance of the duties thus laid down.(...)'.[884]

INDIRECT HORIZONTAL EFFECT – The question of direct horizontal applicability of the Charter is a topic of ongoing debate.[885] Indirect horizontal application appears to be less contentious. This takes place, for example, when national courts interpret the implementation of the EU law in accordance with the Charter when resolving conflicts between individuals.[886] But what happens in situations where the interference on the horizontal level is caused by the States' failure to protect a right? After all, it could be argued that private actors can only exercise power which is conferred on them by laws; therefore the '*government is always somehow implicated in private decisions*'.[887]

---

provides: 'This Charter does not extend the field of application of Union law beyond the powers of the Union or establish any new power or task for the Union, or modify powers and tasks as defined in the Treaties'.

879 E. Frantziou, "The Horizontal Effect of the Charter of Fundamental Rights of the EU: Rediscovering the Reasons for Horizontality", *o.c.*, p. 659.

880 Article 6(1) TEU.

881 E. Frantziou, "The Horizontal Effect of the Charter of Fundamental Rights of the EU: Rediscovering the Reasons for Horizontality", *o.c.*

882 E. Frantziou, "The Horizontal Effect of the Charter of Fundamental Rights of the EU: Rediscovering the Reasons for Horizontality", *o.c.*, ft. 9 referring to CJEU Case 26/62, *Van Gend en Loos v. Nederlandse Administratie der Belastingen* [1963] ECR 1.

883 CJEU, Case 43/75, *Defrenne v. Sabena* (No 2) [1976] ECR 455.

884 *Ibid.*, paras 31–39; see also CJEU, Case C-438/05, *The international Transport Workers' Federation & The Finnish Seamen's Union v. Viking Line. ABP & Oü Viking Line Eesti* [2007] ECR I-10779, paras 58–59.

885 For example in E. Frantziou, "The Horizontal Effect of the Charter of Fundamental Rights of the EU: Rediscovering the Reasons for Horizontality", *o.c*; and D. Leczykiewicz, "Horizontal application of the Charter of Fundamental Rights", *European Law Review*, Vol. 38, 2013, p. 479.

886 See J. Blackstock, "The EU Charter of Fundamental Rights: scope and competence", *Justice Journal*, 2012, pp. 19–31, p. 22.

887 M. Tushnet, "The issue of state action/horizontal effect in comparative constitutional law", *International Journal of Constitutional Law*, Vol. 1, Number 1, 2003, pp. 79–98, p. 79.

OBLIGATION TO "PROMOTE" – According to Articles 51, 52 and 53, rights in the Charter must be respected and principles merely observed, but both have to be "promoted". Moreover, the meaning and the scope of the rights protected by both the ECHR and CFEU should be the same. This includes the meaning given through the jurisprudence of the Court of Human Rights, which explicitly recognizes the existence of positive obligations.[888] The EU can provide greater protection of the same right, but certainly not less.[889] In the Explanations to the Charter, the Praesidium of the Convention (which drafted the Charter) further clarified the distinction between the rights and principles.[890] According to the Explanations, the principles do not '*give rise to direct claims for positive action by the Union's institutions or Member States authorities*'.[891] *A contrario*, it could be concluded that such claims are possible with regard to the rights in the Charter.

The three articles together provide valuable information. The negative obligation (to respect) is clearly articulated. The existence of the positive obligation (to protect) is less obvious. The provided wording such as "promotion of application of the rights" and "protection of the rights", suggests that the scope of application encompasses both the negative and positive obligations. This conclusion is additionally strengthened by the *a contrario* reading of the Explanations. According to Blackstock, '*even the most conservative interpretation could not deter an individual bringing an action against the State for failing to prevent the violating act of a private individual (in the exercise of a positive obligation)*'.[892]

2.2. EFFECTIVE PROTECTION OF CHARTER RIGHTS

TREATY ON EUROPEAN UNION – Article 4(3) [TEU] requires Member States to take all measures necessary to guarantee the application and effectiveness of Community law.[893] Moreover, according to Article 19(1) [TEU], Member States shall provide remedies sufficient to ensure effective legal protection in the fields covered by Union law.[894]

CJEU GUIDANCE – The role of positive obligations under the Charter is less developed than under the ECHR. When interpreting the EU secondary law (or

[888] J. Blackstock, "The EU Charter of Fundamental Rights: scope and competence", *o.c.*, p. 28.

[889] *Ibid.*

[890] See also L. Bojarski, D. Schindlauer, K. Wladasch, The European Charter of Fundamental Rights as a Living Instrument – Manual, publication produced within the project "Making the CFREU a Living Instrument" (JUST/2012/FRAC/AG/2705), co-funded by the European Commission, 2014, p. 95.

[891] Praesidium of the Convention, Explanations relating to the Charter of Fundamental Rights, *o.c.* Explanation on Article 52.

[892] J. Blackstock, "The EU Charter of Fundamental Rights: scope and competence", *o.c.*, p. 22.

[893] Article 4(3) TEU. See also CJEU, *Nunes et de Matos*, C-186/98, 8 July 1999, para. 9.

[894] Article 19(1) TEU, second subparagraph.

implementation thereof) in light of the fundamental rights, the CJEU provides, however, some useful guidance. In a number of cases the CJEU specifically addressed the issue of effective protection of the Charter rights.[895]

The argument of effective protection was used, for example in *Promusicae*.[896] The case was one of the first in which the CJEU '*relied on fundamental rights as a device of moderation*'.[897] The CJEU found that the analysed disclosure of personal data *may* be justified as it may fall within the derogation for '*the protection of the rights and freedoms of others*'.[898] The CJEU clarified, however, that if Member States were to introduce such a measure to promote the effective protection of copyright, they must ensure that the measure allows for a fair balance to be struck between the various fundamental rights.[899] As observed by Husovec, '*Union law does not mandate such a disclosure mechanism, but conditionally permits it, if the proportionality between fundamental rights is respected*'.[900]

A similar issue was at stake in *Coty Germany*[901], which concerned a demand for information from a bank following an instance of trademark infringement. The CJEU referred to its *Promusicae* reasoning but highlighted a major difference. In *Coty Germany*, the provision of the German law at issue allowed for an unlimited and unconditional refusal to disclose the information.[902] The provision therefore prevented the effective exercise of the right to property. As a result, the ruling went further than in *Promusicae*. Instituting a remedy of disclosing personal data is no longer an optional choice for Member States, as its unavailability can infringe the fundamental right to an effective remedy and the fundamental right to (intellectual) property.[903] The CJEU stated that

---

895 For example, the CJEU pointed out the need for effective protection of intellectual property also in L'Oreal v. E-Bay case C-324/09, para 131 ("effective protection of intellectual property"). CJEU C-479/04 [2006] *Laserdisken* ECR I-0808, para 62, 64; Case C-482/09 [2011] *Budějovický Budvar* I-08701, Opinion of AG, footnote 29 ("The right to property, under which the right to intellectual property falls, is according to the Court's case-law a fundamental right which is protected in the Community legal order as a general principle of Community law").

896 The ruling was issued before the Charter became binding. Today, it would be resolved with an explicit reference to Article 51.1 of the Charter.

897 M. Husovec, "Intellectual Property Rights and Integration by Conflict: The Past, Present and Future", *Cambridge Yearbook of European Legal Studies*, Vol. 18, 2016, pp. 239–269, p. 248.

898 As a result of a joint reading reading of Article 15(1) of the Directive 2002/58/EC and Article 13(1)(g) of the Directive 95/46/EC. See M. Husovec, "Intellectual Property Rights and Integration by Conflict: The Past, Present and Future", *o.c.*, ft. 52.

899 CJEU, *Productores de Música de España (Promusicae) v Telefónica de España SAU*, C-275/06, 29 January 2008, para. 68.

900 M. Husovec, "Intellectual Property Rights and Integration by Conflict: The Past, Present and Future", *o.c.*, p. 249.

901 CJEU, *Coty Germany GmbH v Stadtsparkasse Magdeburg*, C-580/13, 16 July 2015. At the time, however, the EU Charter was already legally binding.

902 *Ibid.*, para. 37.

903 M. Husovec, "Intellectual Property Rights and Integration by Conflict: The Past, Present and Future", *o.c.*, p. 257.

'[t]he right to information which is intended to benefit the applicant in the context of proceedings concerning an infringement of his right to property thus seeks, in the field concerned, to apply and implement the fundamental right to an effective remedy guaranteed in Article 47 of the Charter, and thereby to ensure the effective exercise of the fundamental right to property, which includes the intellectual property right protected in Article 17(2) of the Charter.'[904]

The CJEU went from recognizing the need for effective protection in *Promusicae*, to requiring that effective exercise of a fundamental right is ensured in *Coty Germany*. According to Husovec, the ruling effectively recognized a positive obligation to introduce a protective remedy.[905]

In *Telekabel Wien*, the CJEU added an interesting twist to the effective protection theory. According to the Court, the measures which are taken by the addressee of an injunction when implementing that injunction must be sufficiently effective to ensure genuine protection of the fundamental right at issue, that is, the right to intellectual property.[906] At the same time, however, the CJEU reminded that the right to intellectual property is not inviolable and that nothing in the wording of Article 17.2 CFEU suggests that it must be absolutely protected.[907] For this reason,

'when the addressee of an injunction such as that at issue in the main proceedings chooses the measures to be adopted in order to comply with that injunction, he must ensure compliance with the fundamental right of internet users to freedom of information'.[908]

Effectively, the CJEU imposed the duty to balance the fundamental rights at stake directly on intermediaries, instead of the States.[909] The CJEU continued to specify that the adopted measures must serve to bring an end to a third party's infringement of copyright or of a related right but without affecting Internet users who are using the provider's services to lawfully access information.[910] If such a result was not achieved, '*the provider's interference in the freedom of*

904 CJEU, *Coty Germany GmbH v Stadtsparkasse Magdeburg*, C-580/13, 16 July 2015, para. 29, emphasis added.

905 M. Husovec, "Intellectual Property Rights and Integration by Conflict: The Past, Present and Future", *o.c.*, p. 257. See also M. Husovec, *Injunctions Against Intermediaries in the European Union - Accountable But Not Liable?, o.c.*, pp. 122 – 137.

906 CJEU, *UPC Telekabel Wien GmbH v. Constantin Film Verleih GmbH, Wega Filmproduktionsgesellschaft mbH*, C 314/12, 27 March 2014, para. 62.

907 *Ibid.*, para. 61.

908 *Ibid.*, para. 55.

909 C. Angelopoulos, S. Smet, "Notice-and-fair-balance: how to reach a compromise between fundamental rights in European intermediary liability", *Journal of Media Law*, Vol. 8, Issue 2, 2016, pp. 266–301, p. 281.

910 CJEU, *UPC Telekabel Wien GmbH v. Constantin Film Verleih GmbH, Wega Filmproduktionsgesellschaft mbH*, C 314/12, 27 March 2014, para. 56.

information of those users would be unjustified in the light of the objective pursued'.[911]

STRIKING A FAIR BALANCE – The need to ensure that the protected rights can be exercised without undue limitation is expressed in terms of respecting the requirement of striking a fair balance between different rights in conflict. In *Coty Germany*, the CJEU noted that

> 'Article 52(1) of the Charter states, inter alia, that any limitation on the exercise of the rights and freedoms recognised must respect the essence of those rights and freedoms and that it is apparent from the case-law of the Court that a measure which results in serious infringement of a right protected by the Charter is to be regarded as not respecting the requirement that such a fair balance be struck between the fundamental rights which must be reconciled'.[912]

In *Telekabel Wien*, the CJEU clarified that the chosen measures are not incompatible with the requirement of a fair balance between all applicable fundamental rights, provided that (i) they do not unnecessarily deprive internet users of the possibility of lawfully accessing the information available and (ii) that they have the effect of preventing unauthorised access to protected material or, at least, of making it difficult to achieve and of seriously discouraging internet users from accessing the protected material (even if the chosen measures are not capable of stopping the infringement completely).[913]

ASSESSMENT OF COMPATIBILITY WITH THE CHARTER – As the CJEU observed in Schmidberger, 'measures which are incompatible with observance of the human rights thus recognised are not acceptable in the Community'.[914] Moreover, in Kadi I, 'all Community acts must respect fundamental rights, that respect constituting a condition of their lawfulness which it is for the Court to review'.[915]

Both EU secondary law and national law falling within the scope of EU law must be interpreted in light of the Charter.[916] Moreover, any possible conflicts with fundamental rights can be tested against the Charter, which provides grounds for judicial review.[917] The CJEU can declare a national provision

911 *Ibid.*, para. 56.
912 CJEU, *Coty Germany GmbH v Stadtsparkasse Magdeburg*, C-580/13, 16 July 2015, para. 35.
913 CJEU, *UPC Telekabel Wien GmbH v. Constantin Film Verleih GmbH, Wega Filmproduktionsgesellschaft mbH*, C 314/12, 27 March 2014, para. 63.
914 CJEU, *Eugen Schmidberger, Internationale Transporte und Planzüge v Republik Österreich*, C-112/00, 12 June 2003, para. 73.
915 CJEU, *Yassin Abdullah Kadi and Al Barakaat International Foundation v Council of the European Union and Commission of the European Communities (Kadi I)*, Joined cases C-402/05 P and C-415/05 P, 3 September 2008, para. 285.
916 K. Lenaerts, "Exploring the Limits of the EU Charter of Fundamental Rights", *o.c.*, p. 376.
917 *Ibid.*, p. 376.

implementing EU law incompatible under Art. 51.1 CFEU.[918] Upon a request based on Art. 267 TFEU, the CJEU can also directly invalidate a provision or a whole act of secondary Union law, such as a directive.[919]

DIGITAL RIGHTS IRELAND – In *Digital Rights Ireland*, the CJEU was called upon to assess the validity of the Data Retention Directive (2006/24/EC).[920] In a request for a preliminary ruling, the High Courts of Ireland and Austria posed several questions about compatibility of Directive 2006/24/EC with the Charter (specifically with its Articles 7, 8, and 11 of the Charter).[921] First, the CJEU established that the Directive constitutes an interference with the right to privacy and data protection.[922] Next, the CJEU examined whether the interference satisfied the conditions of Article 52.1 CFEU, specifically, whether it is (1) provided for by law, (2) respects the essence of the rights and freedoms, (3) is subject to the principle of proportionality, and (4) whether the limitations are necessary and genuinely meet objectives of general interest recognised by the Union or the need to protect the rights and freedoms of others.[923] When performing the analysis, the CJEU also made reference to the related case law of the Strasbourg Court. The CJEU found that the interference was prescribed by the Directive and therefore "prescribed by law". Moreover, the CJEU declared that it did not adversely affect the essence of the rights to privacy and data protection.[924] The fight against international terrorism in order to maintain international peace and security, which was the purpose of the Directive, constitutes an objective of general interest.[925] The crucial point of the analysis, therefore, was the question of proportionality of the administered measures. The CJEU pointed out that derogations and limitations to the protection of personal data must apply only so far as is strictly necessary.[926] The CJEU found that the Directive defined no limits of the scope, and failed to lay down any objective criterion to determine the limits of the access to the retained data.[927] Furthermore, the Directive did not contain sufficient substantive and procedural conditions relating to the access and reuse of the retained data but '*merely provides that each Member State is to define the procedures to be followed and the conditions to be fulfilled in order to gain access to the retained data in accordance with necessity and proportionality requirements*'.[928] For these reasons, the CJEU decided that

---

918 See CJEU, *Hernández and Others*, Case C-198/13, 10 July 2014, para. 33–36.
919 Article 267 TFEU, *o.c.*, p. 47–390.
920 CJEU, *Digital Rights Ireland Ltd and Seitlinger and others*, Joined Cases C 293/12 and C 594/12, 8 April 2014.
921 *Ibid.*, para. 17 - 21.
922 *Ibid.*, para. 34 - 37.
923 *Ibid.*, para. 38.
924 *Ibid.*, paras. 39 and 40.
925 *Ibid.*, paras. 42 - 44.
926 *Ibid.*, para. 52.
927 *Ibid.*, para. 60.
928 *Ibid.*, para. 61.

> 'Directive 2006/24 does not provide for sufficient safeguards, as required by Article 8 of the Charter, to ensure effective protection of the data retained against the risk of abuse and against any unlawful access and use of that data'.[929]

As a result of the analysis, the CJEU ruled that 'the EU legislature has exceeded the limits imposed by compliance with the principle of proportionality in the light of Articles 7, 8 and 52(1) of the Charter'[930] and declared the Directive invalid.[931] As regards Article 11 of the Charter, the CJEU acknowledged that data retention may have a chilling effect on individual freedom of expression.[932] Unfortunately, the CJEU did not see a need to examine the validity of the Directive in the light of Article 11 of the Charter.[933]

The CJEU did not refer explicitly to positive obligations but pointed out the lack of effective protection, which should have been ensured by providing sufficient safeguards. It is therefore clearly an example of a legislator's failure to act. The result of the failure was a disproportionate interference which led the CJEU to declaring the Directive non-compliant with the Charter and invalidating it entirely.

MAX SCHREMS V. DATA PROTECTION COMMISSIONER – Similar arguments were used by the CJEU in 2015 to invalidate the EC Decision 2000/520/EC on the adequacy of the protection provided by the safe harbour privacy principles.[934] *Schrems* concerned the ability of national supervisory authorities to examine a person's claim concerning the protection of his rights and freedoms in regard to the processing of his personal data, which had been transferred from a Member State to a third country, when that person contends that the law and practices in force in the third country do not ensure an adequate level of protection.[935] When answering that question the CJEU observed that Decision 2000/520/EC enables interference, founded on national security and public interest requirements or on domestic legislation of the US, with the fundamental rights of the individuals whose personal data is transferred from the EU to the US.[936] Moreover, Decision 2000/520 does not contain any finding regarding the existence of rules adopted by the US intended to limit such interference[937], nor does it refer to the existence of effective legal protection against interference of that kind.[938]

Referring amply to the *Digital Rights Ireland*, the CJEU repeated that EU legislation involving interference with fundamental rights (guaranteed in

929 *Ibid.*, para. 66.
930 *Ibid.*, para. 69.
931 *Ibid.*, para. 71.
932 *Ibid.*, para. 28.
933 *Ibid.*, para. 70.
934 CJEU, *Maximillian Schrems v. Data Protection Commissioner*, C-362/14, 6 October 2015.
935 *Ibid.*, para. 37.
936 *Ibid.*, para. 87.
937 *Ibid.*, para. 88.
938 *Ibid.*, para. 89.

Articles 7 and 8 CFEU) must lay down clear and precise rules governing the scope and application of a measure and imposing minimum safeguards, so that the persons concerned have sufficient guarantees enabling their data to be effectively protected against the risk of abuse and against any unlawful access and use.[939] Likewise, the CJEU observed that legislation that does not provide for any possibility for an individual to pursue legal remedies to have access to his personal data, or to obtain the rectification or erasure of such data, does not respect the essence of the fundamental right to effective judicial protection, as provided in Article 47 CFEU.[940]

In light of these findings, the CJEU pointed out that the EC did not state, in Decision 2000/520, that the US "ensures" an adequate level of protection by reason of its domestic law or its international commitments and declared the decision invalid.[941]

CONCLUDING REMARKS – Based on the analysis above, this book argues that there exists a positive obligation to ensure effective exercise of the fundamental rights under the Charter. The obligation applies not only to Member States when they implement the EU law, but also to the EU acting as a legislator. It would be unreasonable to think that the EU could demand compliance with the Charter rights from Member States when they implement EU law, but would not be itself obliged to comply. This conclusion finds support also in the CJEU's observations in *Schmidberger* and *Kadi I*. Even without an explicit reference to the doctrine of positive obligations, the CJEU is able to achieve a similar result using the principle of proportionality and the requirements of fair balancing and effective protection.

RELEVANCE FOR THE RESEARCH QUESTION – EU secondary law can be invalidated for not respecting the Charter rights. In case of the *Digital Rights Ireland*, the interference with the fundamental right at issue was rather direct, as the Directive required the retention of data by telecom operators. It was therefore a clear example of State interference. In the case of the E-Commerce Directive, the interference with the right to freedom of expression is not direct. The liability exemptions do not require the hosting service providers to remove content. It does occur however, as a result of the provision in Article 14 of the E-Commerce Directive. It is a situation of a horizontal interference resulting from a failure of the legislator (EU) on the vertical level to effectively protect the right to freedom of expression – a form of "State interference by proxy". This situation could be remedied by providing procedural safeguards for freedom of expression in the E-Commerce Directive.

---

939 *Ibid.*, para. 91.
940 *Ibid.*, para. 95.
941 *Ibid.*, paras. 97, 98, 104, 105.

3. INTERIM CONCLUSION

STAYING POSITIVE – The doctrine of positive obligations does not enjoy the same status under the Convention and the Charter. States signatory to the Convention clearly have positive obligations to ensure effective enjoyment of the Convention rights. In that sense, the doctrine of positive obligations is '*the hallmark of the European Convention on Human Rights, and mark it out from other human rights instruments (...)*.'[942] The European Court of Human Rights has recognized that States have certain positive obligation in relation to Article 10. Under the Charter the doctrine is less developed. There exists, however, an obligation to ensure an effective protection of the Charter rights. The theories of positive obligations and effective protection may require States to take measures to protect the right to freedom of expression from interference by other private individuals. For example, States should ensure that they do not place intermediaries under such a fear of liability claims that they come to impose on themselves measures that are '*appropriate for making them immune to any subsequent accusation but is of a kind that threatens the freedom of expression of Internet users*'.[943]

TOWARDS PROCEDURAL SAFEGUARDS – Under the three conditions specified in the Convention and the Charter, interference with freedom of expression may be permitted. If the States delegate their powers to make decisions regarding fundamental human rights, such as freedom of expression, they should ensure that certain protective measures are in place. A requirement to take action necessary to ensure effective enjoyment of a right and prevent its abuse stems from the positive obligation theory. The idea of positive obligations in the context of Article 10 ECHR has not been developed so far to the same extent as the positive obligation in connection to Articles 2, 3, 4 and 8 ECHR.[944] As is evident from the Strasbourg case law, such obligations nevertheless exist. The same could be argued in the context of the Charter, even if the phenomenon is branded differently, as 'effective protection'. States could satisfy the requirement to ensure effective protection by implementing procedural safeguards into the legislation, which provides a basis for the notice and action mechanisms. Such procedural safeguards are missing in the EU legislation currently in force. Therefore, this book argues that States are currently not complying with their positive obligation to protect the right to freedom of expression from interference by private entities in the context of the notice and action mechanisms. In other words, States could become responsible for violations of freedom of expression by private entities because there is a failure in the legal order, which in this case amounts to an absence of sufficient protective measures.

---

942 K. Starmer, "Positive Obligations Under the Convention" in J. Jowell and J. Cooper (eds) *Understanding Human Rights Principles*, Oxford, Hart Publishing, 2001, p. 159.

943 E. Montero and Q. Van Enis, "Enabling freedom of expression in light of filtering measures imposed on Internet intermediaries: Squaring the circle", *o.c.*, p. 34.

944 J.-F. Akandji-Kombe, *Human rights handbook, No. 7. o.c.*, p. 48.

CHAPTER 4

CRITERIA FOR SAFEGUARDS FOR FREEDOM OF EXPRESSION ONLINE

1. METHODOLOGY

RESEARCH OBJECTIVE – The aim of this book is to propose safeguards for notice and action procedures that promote compliance with the right to freedom of expression. In order to determine which safeguards might be appropriate, a set of criteria is required. This Chapter provides an inventory of criteria that should be taken into account when designing notice and action mechanisms that respect the right to freedom of expression.

OUTLINE – Notice and action mechanisms should advance the three guiding principles for this book, namely (a) legal certainty, (b) legitimacy, and (c) proportionality. The analysis of the issues with the intermediary liability regimes and the E-Commerce Directive specifically showed that these three principles are currently at a disadvantage.[945] The assessment criteria proposed in this Chapter aim to contribute to the realization of the guiding principles. In the following sections, the book defines each principle separately and identifies the relevant criteria that will serve as the positive assessment framework. Every criterion consists of several elements that help understand the meaning of the criterion. The role of the elements, however, is secondary. The assessment, which will be carried out in Part III shall be focused on the general advancement of the criteria, rather than the presence of each specific element in the analysed response mechanisms.

INTERDEPENDENCIES – It should be noted that a number of criteria are closely linked to each other and may be overlapping. A particular assessment criterion might therefore, in practice, advance more than one guiding principle at the same time. With this in mind, the assessment criteria developed below are not categorized according to the guiding principles. Instead, existing interdependencies or interactions between the criteria and the guiding principles are highlighted.[946]

[945] See Part I Chapter 6.

[946] Arguably, the categorization presented here is subjective and there may be different ways to arrange the same criteria. Linking the criteria to the specific guiding principle, however, is less relevant than presenting the criteria in a clear and structured manner.

RELEVANT SOURCES – The criteria enumerated in this Chapter have been selected in light of the issues in the EU intermediary liability regime identified in Part I of the book. The criteria themselves have been developed on the basis of the case-law of the ECtHR and CJEU. Guidance was also obtained by analysing the procedural provisions of these human rights instruments, specifically Articles 6 (right to fair trail) and 13 (right to effective remedy) of the ECHR, as well as Article 47 (right to an effective remedy and to a fair trial) of the CFEU. It should be highlighted that the procedural provisions of both instruments are directed to States, instructing them how to design their judicial system. The case-law interpreting the procedural rights, therefore, refers specifically to the context of formal legal proceedings. In this book the procedural provisions, however, function in a different context. In a situation where certain decisions about fundamental rights are delegated to intermediaries (which are private entities), full compliance with the procedural provisions cannot be expected. They could, however, serve as a source of inspiration for safeguards as they provide essential key factors that could make notice and action mechanisms certain, legitimate, and proportionate. Moreover, if the safeguards were to be provided by States in a formal legal framework, as is argued in this book, they should be designed with the utmost attention to the procedural provisions of the human rights instruments.

POSITIVE ASSESSMENT FRAMEWORK – The criteria developed in this Chapter are applied as a *positive assessment framework*[947], against which existing notice and action mechanisms to infringing online content – currently used around the world – are measured (Part III). The aim of the assessment is to inform a selection of safeguards that are best suited to ensure that content removal is undertaken with adequate consideration for the right to freedom of expression. The selection of safeguards is based on an assessment of how the existing mechanisms address the established criteria. The purpose of the exercise is to draw conclusions on how they realize the three guiding principles.

2. GUIDING PRINCIPLES

GUIDING THE RESEARCH – The conditions for lawful interference can be linked to three fundamental human rights principles, namely the principle of a) legal certainty, b) legitimacy, c) and proportionality. The three principles represent values underlying the human rights instruments of the EU. These three

---

947 *A 'positive assessment framework' contains a set of criteria that are being formulated in a 'positive way'. This implies that the outcome of the evaluation will be positive or favourable when the legal phenomenon meets (nearly) all criteria.* L. Kestemont, "Methods For traditional legal research", *Reader 'Methods of Legal Research'*, Research Master In Law, KU Leuven University Of Tilburg, 2014–2015, p. 32.

principles shall be the guiding principles for the research conducted in this book. While they do remain on a somewhat abstract level, this is exactly their benefit. According to De Schutter and Tulkens, '*in order to be effective (...), principles need not take the form of explicit rules or preestablished criteria: they may remain unstated, or (...), stated only at a very general level, and their content progressively clarified in the very process of their application to specific instances*'.[948]

2.1. LEGAL CERTAINTY

INTRODUCTION – The principle of legal certainty is the first of the three guiding principles. It is derived from the first requirement of Article 10.2 ECHR, which stipulates that every interference with freedom of expression must be "prescribed by law".[949]

DEFINITION – According to the case law of the ECtHR[950], any interference with the exercise of freedom of expression should be lawful, that is, must have a basis in law.[951] A law allowing for interference must moreover be adequately accessible and foreseeable.[952] The main point is that everyone should be able to predict, with a sufficient degree of certainty, what behaviour is expected of them and what to expect when the rules are not followed.

The principle of legal certainty is one of the general principles of EU law.[953] Legal certainty exists when '*subjects can rely on the law and can foresee application of state power*'.[954] In other words, the principle means that '*those subject to the law must know what the law is so that they can abide by it and plan their actions accordingly.*'[955]

Legal certainty, listed as a principle of EU administrative procedural law, is corollary to the rule of law.[956] The principle requires legal rules to be clear and

---

948 O. De Schutter, F. Tulkens, "The European Court of Human Rights as a Pragmatic Institution", *o.c.*, p. 197.

949 See Part II Chapter 2.1.2.

950 See Part II Chapter 2.1.2.

951 See for example ECtHR, *Sunday Times v. the United Kingdom*, 26 April 1979, para. 47; ECtHR, *Groppera Radio AG and others v. Switzerland*, 28 March 1990, para. 68; ECtHR, *Barthold v. Germany*, 25 March 1985, para. 46.

952 See ECtHR, *Sunday Times v. the United Kingdom*, 26 April 1979, para. 49.

953 T. Tridimas, *The General Principles of EU Law*, *o.c.*, p.242. See also, to that effect, the judgment in CJEU, Joined Cases 205/82 to 215/82 *Deutsche Milchkontor and Others v Germany* [1983] ECR 2633, para. 30.

954 J. R. Maxeiner, "Legal Certainty: A European Alternative to American Legal Indeterminacy?", *o.c.*, p. 546.

955 T. Tridimas, *The General Principles of EU Law*, *o.c.*, p.242.

956 The European Parliament resolution of 15 January 2013 on a Law of Administrative Procedure of the European Union (2012/2024(INL)),includes a Recommendation on the general principles which should govern the Union's administration (Annex, Recommendation 3). In 2015 an in-depth analysis was prepared for the Committee on Legal Affairs of the European

precise, according to the interpretation of the CJEU.[957] Its aim is to ensure that situations and legal relationships are foreseeable '*in that individuals must be able to ascertain unequivocally what their rights and obligations are and be able to take steps accordingly.*'[958] This definition corresponds to the clarification of the ECtHR that laws must be sufficiently precise for the people to foresee the consequences of their actions.[959]

2.2. LEGITIMACY

INTRODUCTION – The principle of legitimacy is the second of the three guiding principles. It is derived from the second requirement of Article 10.2 ECHR, which stipulates that restrictions to the right to freedom of expression may be permitted in the interest of one or more of the legitimate aims listed in the provision.[960] National authorities may not legitimately rely on any other ground that falls outside the list provided for in paragraph 2.[961]

DEFINITION –In legal theory, legitimacy is defined by reference to values.[962] Translating this into the human rights context, it means that interference with a right may be accepted if it pursues a goal that is considered worthy of protection. The goals worthy of such status are those enumerated in paragraph 2 of Article 10 ECHR, that is

> '(...) in the interests of national security, territorial integrity or public safety, for the prevention of disorder or crime, for the protection of health or morals, for the protection of the reputation or rights of others, for preventing the disclosure of

Parliament. The Analysis puts forward drafting proposals for the general principles of EU administrative procedural law to be included in the Recitals of a draft Regulation on EU Administrative procedures. D.-U. Galetta, H. C. H. Hofmann, O. Mir Puigpelat, and others, "The General Principles of EU Administrative Procedural Law, In-depth Analysis", Study commissioned by the European Parliament, Directorate-General for Internal Policies, Policy Department C – Citizen's Rights and Constitutional Affairs, the JURI Committee on Legal and Parliamentary Affairs, PE 519.224, June 2015.

957 For example: CJEU, *Gebroeders van Es Douane Agenten vs Inspecteur der Invoerrechten en Accijnzen*, C-143/93, para. 27;, CJEU, *Gondrand Frères*, C-169/80, para. 17; and CJEU, *Commission v France and United Kingdom*, Joined Cases 92/87 and 93/87, para. 22.

958 D.-U. Galetta, H. C. H. Hofmann, O. Mir Puigpelat and others, "The General Principles of EU Administrative Procedural Law, In-depth Analysis", *o.c.*, p. 19.

959 ECtHR, *Sunday Times v. the United Kingdom*, 26 April 1979, para. 49. ECtHR, *Korchuganova v. Russia*, 8 June 2006, para. 47.

960 See Part II Chapter 2.1.3.

961 M. Macovei, *Freedom of expression – A guide to the implementation of Article 10 of the European Convention of Human Rights*, *o.c.*, p. 28.

962 N. Luhmann, *Law as a social system*, Translated by Ziegert K. A., *Oxford Socio-Legal Studies*, Oxford University Press, 2009, p. 69.

information received in confidence, or for maintaining the authority and impartiality of the judiciary'.[963]

Those are the aims which a State may legitimately pursue, and which may justify restrictions to the rights and freedoms of the Convention to the extent that such restrictions are necessary.[964]

In the EU, restrictions on rights protected by the CFEU are allowed if they 'genuinely meet objectives of general interest recognised by the Union or the need to protect the rights and freedoms of others'.[965] The CFEU ensures consistency with the ECHR through Article 52.3 CFEU. According to this provision, in so far as the Charter 'contains rights which correspond to rights guaranteed by the Convention for the Protection of Human Rights and Fundamental Freedoms, the meaning and scope of those rights shall be the same as those laid down by the said Convention'.[966] This means that Article 11 CFEU and Article 10 ECHR should have the same scope of protection and meaning, which includes the grounds for restrictions listed in Article 10.2 ECHR.

2.3. PROPORTIONALITY

INTRODUCTION – The principle of proportionality is the third of the three guiding principles. It is derived from the third requirement of Article 10.2 ECHR, which stipulates that the exercise of the right to freedom of expression may be subject to such formalities, conditions, restrictions or penalties as are necessary in a democratic society.[967] In other words, interference with freedom of expression must be justified by the existence of a "pressing social need".[968] The reasons for the interference should be "relevant and sufficient" and the administered measure must be "proportionate to the legitimate aims pursued".[969]

DEFINITION – The principle of proportionality 'expresses clearly the idea of balance, reasonability but also of adjusting the measures ordered by the state's authorities to the situation in fact, respectively to the purpose for which they

963 Article 10. 2 ECHR.

964 O. De Schutter, F. Tulkens, "The European Court of Human Rights as a Pragmatic Institution", *o.c.*, p. 177.

965 Article 52.1 CFEU.

966 Article 52.3 CFEU.

967 See Part II Chapter 2.1.3.

968 ECtHR, *Observer and Guardian v. the United Kingdom*, 26 November 1991, para. 57. See also: Council of Europe, *Freedom of expression in Europe: case-law concerning article 10 of the European Convention on Human Rights*, *o.c.*, p. 9.

969 P. Van Dijk, F. Van Hoof, A. Van Rijn, L. Zwaak (eds), *Theory and practice of the European Convention on Human Rights*, *o.c.*, p. 775. See for example ECtHR, *Stoll* v. *Switzerland*, 10 December 2007; ECtHR, *Féret* v. *Belgium*, 16 July 2009.

have been conceived'.[970] Moreover, the principle can be 'procedurally determined and used to delimit the discretionary power and power abuse'.[971]

The principle of proportionality requires that decisions affecting rights and interests are taken only when necessary and to the extent required to achieve the aim pursued.[972] According to this principle, any measure that affects a fundamental right should be suitable and necessary in order to achieve the objective.[973] In cases where the exercise of a Convention right is interfered with, the proportionality test requires balancing of interests between the objectives pursued by the measure and its adverse effects on individual freedom.[974]

For a restriction to be proportionate, it must strike a fair balance between the competing interests at stake. It could amount to the balancing of a fundamental right protected by the ECHR with the legitimate interests listed as possible grounds for restrictions (for example in Article 10.2 ECHR), or with another fundamental right protected by the ECHR. The search for a fair balance of interests is inherent in the Convention.[975] The CJEU also recognizes the need to find a balance between different rights at stake. In *Promusicae,* for example, the CJEU declared that Member States must rely on an interpretation of the directives '*which allows a fair balance to be struck between the various fundamental rights protected by the Community legal order*'.[976]

The "necessity test", as explained by the ECtHR on numerous occasions, requires the Court to determine whether the interference corresponded to a "pressing social need", whether it was proportionate to the legitimate aim pursued and whether the reasons given by the national authorities to justify it were relevant and sufficient.[977] In cases where the right to freedom of expression and the right to private life are in conflict, the Court has laid down a number of criteria to guide the balancing exercise that must be performed.[978] The criteria refer to the content and context of the publication. They are useful in instances

970 M. Andreescu, "Principle of Proportionality, Criterion of Legitimacy in the Public Law", *Challenges of the Knowledge Society,* Vol.1, April 2011, pp. 524–530, p. 524.

971 *Ibid.*

972 European Parliament Resolution of 15 January 2013 with recommendations to the Commission on a Law of Administrative Procedure of the European Union, *o.c.*, p. 5.

973 See T. Tridimas, The General Principles of EU Law, *o.c.*, p. 139.

974 *Ibid.*

975 For example ECtHR, *Soering v. UK,* 07 July 1989, para. 89; ECtHR, *Verein gegen Tierfabriken Schweiz (VgT) v. Switzerland* (No. 2), 30 June 2009, para. 81.

976 CJEU, *Promusicae v. Telefonica de Espana,* C 275/06, 29 January 2008, para. 70.

977 For example in ECtHR, *Couderc and Hachette Filipacchi Associés v. France,* 10 November 2015, para. 92 and ECtHR, *The Sunday Times v. the United Kingdom (no. 1),* 26 April 1979, para. 62.

978 The relevant criteria are: contribution to a debate of public interest, the degree of notoriety of the person affected, the subject of the news report, the prior conduct of the person concerned, the content, form and consequences of the publication, and, where appropriate, the circumstances in which the photographs were taken. Where an application was lodged under Article 10, the Court will also examine the way in which the information was obtained and its veracity, and the gravity of the penalty imposed on the journalists or publishers. ECtHR, *Couderc and Hachette Filipacchi Associés v. France,* 10 November 2015, para. 93, and

where a decision must be taken regarding whether specific information should be "taken down". They are not, however, of a procedural nature and therefore are not included in the positive assessment framework proposed in this book.

The principle of proportionality has been elevated to a fundamental principle of the EU constitutional order. According to Article 5(4) TEU '*Under the principle of proportionality, the content and form of Union action shall not exceed what is necessary to achieve the objectives of the Treaties [...]*'. The CJEU has interpreted the principle of proportionality, in the context of the European administration, to mean that any measure must be appropriate and necessary for meeting the objectives legitimately pursued by the act in question; where there is a choice among several appropriate measures, the least onerous measure must be used; and the charges imposed must not be disproportionate to the aims pursued.[979]

3. ASSESSMENT CRITERIA

INTRODUCTION – This Chapter provides an inventory of criteria that should be taken into account when designing a removal mechanism that respects the right to freedom of expression in the online environment. The selection of the assessment criteria has been informed by the problems haunting the EU intermediary liability regime. The criteria have been developed on the basis of the two leading sources of law for this book, the ECHR and the CFEU, as well as the case-law of the ECtHR and CJEU.

The assessment criteria for this book are:

1. Quality of law
2. Protection of democratic society
3. Tailored response
4. Procedural fairness
5. Effective remedy

The aforementioned criteria shall serve the function of a positive assessment framework, which will be used to evaluate the currently existing notice and

ECtHR, *Axel Springer AG v. Germany* [GC], 7 February 2012, paras. 90–95. See also ECtHR, *Von Hannover v. Germany* (no. 2), 7 February 2012.

979 See for example CJEU, *Schräder v Hauptzollamt Gronau,* C-265/87, para 21. See also CJEU, *Afton Chemical v Secretary of State for Transport,* C-343/09, para 45, and CJEU, *Nelson and Others v Deutsche Lufthansa AG,* C-581/10 and CJEU, *TUI Travel and Others v Civil Aviation Authority,* C-629/10, Joined Cases C-581/10 and C-629/10 published in the electronic Reports of Cases, para 71; as referenced in D.-U. Galetta, H. C. H. Hofmann, O. Mir Puigpelat, and others, "The General Principles of EU Administrative Procedural Law, In-depth Analysis", *o.c.*, p. 18.

action mechanisms in Part III. The criteria advance the guiding principles in the following way:

Figure 3 – Interdependencies between the criteria and the guiding principles

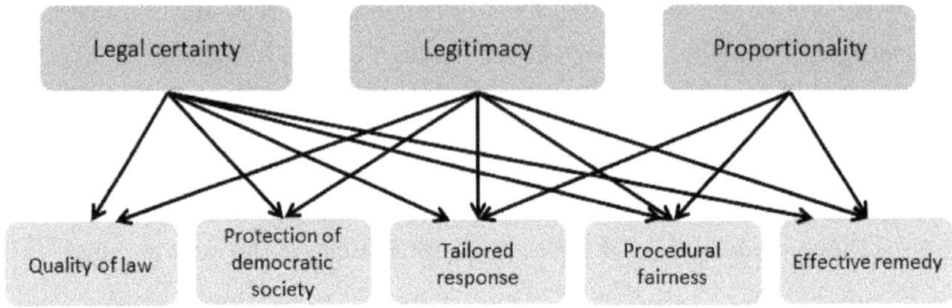

3.1. QUALITY OF LAW

OUTLINE – The legal basis constituting the interference must meet certain requirements of "quality".[980] Mainly, it should provide sufficient guarantees against arbitrariness and abuse of power.[981] When referring to the quality of law in *Yildrim v. Turkey* and *Dink v. Turkey*, the ECtHR specified that the law '*should be accessible to the person concerned, who must moreover be able to foresee its consequences, and that it should be compatible with the rule of law*'.[982]

In the context of this book, quality of law is a criterion linked to the principle of legal certainty. The criterion encompasses the idea that any rules allowing for content regulation should be clear, precise and known to those who might be affected by them. The criterion consists of qualities such as foreseeability (also referred to as predictability) and accessibility.

A. *Accessibility*

MEANING – The ECtHR requires that the law on which a restriction is based must be accessible.[983] This means that it must be possible to know the rules, because only then can they be predictable. As provided in Sunday Times,

---

980 ECtHR, *Editorial Board of Pravoye Delo and Shtekel v. Ukraine*, 5 May 2011, para. 51. See more in Part II Chapter 2.1.1.

981 ECtHR, *Glas Nadezhda and Elenkov v. Bulgaria*, 11 October 2007, paras. 45–53.

982 ECtHR, *Ahmet Yıldırım v. Turkey*, 18 March 2013, para. 57; ECtHR, *Dink v. Turkey*, 14 September 2010, para. 114.

983 ECtHR, *Rotaru v. Romania* [GC], 4 May 2000, para. 52; ECtHR, *Gorzelik v. Poland*, 17 February 2004, para. 64.

> 'Firstly, the law must be adequately accessible: the citizen must be able to have an indication that is adequate in the circumstances of the legal rules applicable to a given case'.[984]

The ECtHR finds the accessibility condition satisfied, for example, when a law is duly published.[985] In certain circumstances, the condition may also be satisfied where rules are not generally published, but available for the members of a particular group that needs to abide by them i.e. when they are '*readily accessible to the applicant on account of his profession*'.[986] Accessibility is also satisfied when a binding decision of a national constitutional court had been published in the state official gazette.[987]

The CJEU considers that a legal act, which has not been the subject of official publication, cannot be considered a satisfactory transposition of a Directive.[988] Moreover, the CJEU points out that the adopted rules of law must be '*capable of creating a situation which is sufficiently precise, clear and transparent to allow individuals to know their rights and rely on them before the national courts*'.[989] Finally, accessibility and legal clarity of procedure and outcome can also be linked to the notion of openness, which can be found in the TFEU.[990]

B. Foreseeability

MEANING – The CJEU explained on several occasions that the aim of the principle of legal certainty is to '*ensure that situations and legal relationships governed by Community law remain foreseeable*'.[991] The CJEU repeated in several cases that '*Community legislation must be certain and its application foreseeable by those subject to it*'.[992]

Strictly speaking, foreseeability requires that rules that allow for interference must be formulated with sufficient precision '*to enable any individual – if need be*

984 ECtHR, *Sunday Times v. the United Kingdom*, 26 April 1979, para. 49.
985 See also ECtHR, *Verein gegen Tierfabriken Schweiz (VgT) v. Switzerland*, 28 June 2001, para. 54.
986 ECtHR, *Maestri v. Italy*, 17 February 2004, para. 33.
987 ECtHR, *Leyla Şahin v. Turkey*, 10 November 2005, para. 93.
988 CJEU, *Commission v. Luxembourg*, Case 220/94, 15 June 1995, para. 9.
989 *Ibid.*, para. 10; see also CJEU, *Commission v Germany*, Case 361/88, 30 May 1991, para. 24.
990 Article 298.1 TFEU states that '[i]n carrying out their missions, the institutions, bodies, offices and agencies of the Union shall have the support of an open, efficient and independent European administration.' See H.C.H. Hofmann, J.-P. Schneider, J. Ziller, Administrative Procedures and the Implementation of EU Law and Policies, Contribution by the Research Network on EU Administrative Law (ReNEUAL) project on administrative procedure to the EU Commission's 'Assises de la Justice' conference in Brussels 21–22 November 2013 to the topic of EU ADMINISTRATIVE LAW, Law Working Paper Series, Paper number 2014–09, p. 12.
991 CJEU, C-199/03 *Ireland v Commission* [2005] ECR I-8027, para. 69; CJEU, C-63/93 *Duff and Others* [1996] ECR I- 569, para. 20.
992 CJEU, *Netherlands* v *Council* C301/97 [2001] ECR I8853, para. 43, and CJEU, *Halifax and Others* Case C255/02 [2006] ECR I1609, para. 72.

with appropriate advice – to regulate his conduct'.[993] In other words, as expressed by the ECtHR in *Maestri v. Italy*, an individual must be able '*to foresee, to a degree that is reasonable in the circumstances, the consequences which a given action may entail*'.[994] The rules, therefore, must be clear and precise to be foreseeable as to their effects.[995]

The risk posed by a lack of foreseeability is not trivial, also in the context of the right to freedom of expression. As stated by judges Sajó and Tsotsoria in *Delfi v. Estonia* '*[v]aguely worded, ambiguous and therefore unforeseeable laws have a chilling effect on freedom of expression*'.[996]

The effects of the law need not be foreseeable with absolute certainty.[997] Although it is desirable, certainty may result in 'excessive rigidity and the law must be able to keep pace with changing circumstances. Accordingly, many laws are inevitably couched in terms which, to a greater or lesser extent, are vague, and whose interpretation and application are questions of practice.'[998]

Domestic law prescribing a possibility of interference must, nevertheless, '*afford a measure of legal protection against arbitrary interferences by public authorities*' with the Convention rights.[999] For this reason, the law must '*indicate with sufficient clarity the scope of any such discretion and the manner of its exercise*'.[1000] This means that a legal framework is required that would ensure both tight control over the scope of bans and effective judicial review to prevent any abuse of power.[1001] The ECtHR found the judicial review of a prescribed measure inconceivable '*without a framework establishing precise and specific rules regarding the application of preventive restrictions on freedom of expression*'.[1002]

The CJEU also addresses the principle of legal certainty (together with the principle of protection of legitimate expectations) but often chooses different vocabulary when doing so. According to the CJEU, these principles require that '*the effect of Community legislation must be clear and predictable for those who are subject to it*'.[1003]

---

993 ECtHR, *Ahmet Yıldırım v. Turkey*, 18 March 2013, para. 57; ECtHR, *RTBF v. Belgium*, 2011, para. 103 and ECtHR, *Altuğ Taner Akçam v. Turkey*, 25 October 2011, para. 87.

994 ECtHR, *Maestri v. Italy*, 17 February 2004, para. 27.

995 See ECtHR, *Ahmet Yıldırım v. Turkey*, 18 March 2013, para. 60 and ECtHR, *Verein gegen Tierfabriken Schweiz (VgT) v. Switzerland*, 28 June 2001, para. 54.

996 ECtHR, *Delfi AS v. Estonia*, Grand Chamber, 16 June 2015, joint dissenting opinion of judges Sajó and Tsotsoria, para. 20.

997 ECtHR, *Verein gegen Tierfabriken Schweiz (VgT) v. Switzerland*, 28 June 2001, para. 55.

998 *Ibid.*, para. 55.

999 ECtHR, *Ahmet Yıldırım v. Turkey*, 18 March 2013, para. 59.

1000 *Ibid.* See also ECtHR, *Maestri v. Italy*, 17 February 2004, para. 30.

1001 ECtHR, *Ahmet Yıldırım v. Turkey*, 18 March 2013, para. 64, ECtHR, *Association Ekin v. France*, 17 July 2001, para. 58 and, *mutatis mutandis*, ECtHR, *Editorial Board of* Pravoye Delo *and Shtekel v. Ukraine*, May 2011, para. 55.

1002 ECtHR, *Ahmet Yıldırım v. Turkey*, 18 March 2013, para. 64, ECtHR, *RTBF v. Belgium*, 28 March 2011, para. 114.

1003 CJEU, *Meridionale Industria Salumi and Others*, Joined cases 212 to 217/80, 12 November 1981, para. 10.

The requirements of predictability and clarity of law[1004] express the same idea that '*legal rules should be worded unequivocally so as to give the persons concerned a clear and precise understanding of their rights and obligations*'.[1005] The concepts of clarity and predictability are used interchangeably with the concept of foreseeability. All these terms constitute yet another expression of the principle of legal certainty, therefore, in this book, they fall under the same criterion.

C. Practical implications

QUALITY OF LAW CRITERION – Quality of law is a substantive criterion. In the context of this book, the criterion signifies that a legal basis providing for interference with the right to freedom of expression must:

- be adequately accessible;
- be formulated with sufficient precision;
- be foreseeable as to its effects;
- clearly indicate the scope of any such discretion and the manner of its exercise; and
- establish precise and specific rules regarding the application of preventive restriction.

The specified elements contribute additionally to the overall transparency of a process and outcome; therefore they also contribute to the forthcoming criteria, such as procedural fairness and effective remedy.

3.2. PROTECTION OF DEMOCRATIC SOCIETY

OUTLINE – In its case law, the ECtHR traditionally refers to the concept of democratic society.[1006] As the Court pointed out in *Young, James and Webster*,

> '[a]lthough individual interests must on occasion be subordinated to those of a group, democracy does not simply mean that the views of a majority must always prevail: a balance must be achieved which ensures the fair and proper treatment of minorities and avoids any abuse of a dominant position'.[1007]

1004 Especially in case of rules which can entail financial consequences. See CJEU, *Ireland v. Commission*, Case 325/85, 15 December 1987, para. 18, and CJEU, *Commission v. France*, Case 30/89, 13 March 1990.

1005 CJEU, *Commission of the European Communities v Italian Republic*, Case 257/86, 21 June 1988.

1006 ECtHR, Handyside v. the United Kingdom, 7 December 1976, para. 49; ECtHR, *Young, James and Webster v. the United Kingdom*, 13 August 1981, para. 63; ECtHR, *Chassagnou and Others v. France*, 29 April 1999, para. 112; ECtHR, *Associated Society of Locomotive Engineers & Firemen (ASLEF) v. the United Kingdom*, 27 February 2007, para. 43.

1007 ECtHR, *Young, James and Webster v. the United Kingdom*, 13 August 1981, para. 63.

For the democratic society to function, certain rights and interests need to be protected. This idea entails, for example, protection of expression that offends, shocks or disturbs the State or any sector of the population.[1008]

In a democratic society, it is required 'that all decisions, even those adopted according to democratic procedures, be justified in regard of the public interest they pursue, and that they only impose restrictions on the rights of individuals to the extent strictly necessary for the pursuance of that interest'.[1009] In the context of this book, protection of democratic society is a substantive criterion linked to the principle of legal certainty and legitimacy. The criterion allows for evaluation of the substance of rules prescribing a possibility of interference, for example by removal of online content, with the right to freedom of expression. Such rules can only be allowed if they protect one (or more) of the values listed in Article 10.2 ECHR. In this book they are called the "democratic values". Even though there is no hierarchy between the rights and values, some of them may be considered especially worthy of protection. If violations of such values are manifest, some States allocate more responsibility on those who have knowledge of it and require a swift reaction. This could result in the creation of a stricter regime, with regard to removals of certain types of infringing content. The criterion of protection of democratic society, therefore, consists of two elements: democratic values and manifest illegality.

A. *Democratic values*

MEANING – Recognized democratic values are the values listed in Article 10.2 ECHR. The list is exhaustive. This means that the interest or value which is being protected through the interference must correspond with one of those enumerated in paragraph 2 of Article 10 ECHR.[1010]

The CFEU ensures consistency with the ECHR through Article 52.3, which provides that_the meaning and scope of the Charter rights, which are also protected by the ECHR, should be the same as provided for in the latter instrument. Therefore, the public interests worthy of protection and the general interests recognised by the Union are those listed in Article 10.2 ECHR – in this book referred to as the "democratic values".

B. *Manifest illegality*

MEANING – Certain types of expression, for example hate speech, fall outside of the scope of Article 10 ECHR.[1011] As the ECtHR stated in *Gündüz v. Turkey*, *'as a*

1008 ECtHR, *Handyside v. the United Kingdom*, 7 December 1976, para. 49.

1009 O. De Schutter, F. Tulkens, "The European Court of Human Rights as a Pragmatic Institution", *o.c.*, p. 215.

1010 See more in Part II Chapter 2.1.2.

1011 For example ECtHR, *Gündüz v. Turkey*, 04 December 2003; and ECtHR, *Perinçek v. Switzerland*, 15 October 2015.

matter of principle it may be considered necessary in certain democratic societies to sanction or even prevent all forms of expression which spread, incite, promote or justify hatred based on intolerance'.[1012] Interference with this type of expression is therefore not considered a violation of the right to freedom of expression.[1013] In case of hate speech, for example, a service provider may be required to remove it on its own initiative without such requirement constituting a violation of Article 10 ECHR, as stated by the ECtHR in *Delfi As v. Estonia*.[1014] It is crucial, however, that the establishment of the unlawful nature of the expression in such cases does not require any linguistic or legal analysis, i.e. that the remarks are on their face manifestly unlawful.[1015] The ECtHR clarified in *MTE and Index.hu* that the requirement for the service provider to remove content on his own initiative cannot be the same when the content is offensive and vulgar, but '*the incriminated comments did not constitute clearly unlawful speech; and they certainly did not amount to hate speech or incitement to violence*'.[1016] The same line was followed in the 2017 decision of the ECtHR on inadmissibility in *Pihl v. Sweden*.[1017] The Court found that the national authorities had struck a fair balance when refusing to hold an association who published a story about the applicant liable for the anonymous defamatory comment posted under the story. In particular, this was because the comment had been offensive, but did not amount to hate speech or an incitement to violence. It had been posted on a small blog run by a non-profit association, and had been taken down the day after the applicant made a complaint.

Under the E-commerce Directive intermediary liability regime, the main question is not whether the expression is protected as such, but rather whether the service provider has knowledge or awareness of the illegal content or activity and may therefore be required to act in order to retain the immunity. The CJEU analysed the issue in *L'Oréal v. eBay*, which concerned copyright infringements by the users of online marketplaces.[1018] According to Article 14 of the E-Commerce Directive, a hosting provider is exempted from liability for third party content on the condition that the service provider has not had '*actual knowledge of illegal activity or information*' and, as regards claims for damages, has not been '*aware of facts or circumstances from which the illegal activity or information is apparent*' (i.e. constructive knowledge).[1019] Upon obtaining such knowledge or awareness, the service provider has to act expeditiously to remove or disable access to, the information. Apparent illegality occurs, according to the

---

1012 *Ibid.*, para. 40.

1013 See ECtHR, *Delfi As v. Estonia*, (GC), 16 June 2015.

1014 *Ibid.*, para. 153.

1015 *Ibid.*, para. 117.

1016 ECtHR, *Magyar Tartalomszolgáltatók Egyesülete and Index.hu Zrt v. Hungary (MTE and Index.hu)*, 2 February 2016, para. 64.

1017 ECtHR, *Rolf Anders Daniel Pihl v. Sweden*, 7 February 2017.

1018 See Part II Chapter 2.2.

1019 See Article 14 E-Commerce Directive 2000/31/EC.

CJEU, when *'any diligent economic operator should have identified the illegality in question'*.[1020] The standard articulated by the ECtHR in *Delfi* that the remarks should be on their face manifestly unlawful is actually not very different from the CJEU standard pronounced in *L'Oréal v. eBay*.

The legislator may consider certain types of content and activities as worthy of special protection (e.g. protection of minors or the prevention of serious harm). Such special status may lead to a stricter regime raising the bar for immunity when violation of the content is manifest. Manifest illegality occurs where the content is easily recognizable as such, without any additional legal or factual analysis. It refers mainly to the facility of recognizing content as illegal. In case of manifest illegality the legislator may, for example, require intermediaries not only to react to notification from third parties, but also to act on their own initiative.

C. *Practical implications*

PROTECTION OF DEMOCRATIC SOCIETY CRITERION – The protection of democratic society, in the context of this book, signifies that restrictions can only be allowed if they protect one of the values listed in Article 10.2 ECHR. Certain types of content or activities may require a different response from intermediaries. States may introduce a stricter regime with regard to manifest violations online of certain rights and values considered worthy of special protection. In such a case, the rights and values justifying a higher threshold for immunity should be specified clearly. The criterion of protection of democratic society is of a substantive nature and it allows for an evaluation of the substance of laws allowing for restrictions on expression.

3.3. TAILORED RESPONSE

OUTLINE – Where there is a choice among several appropriate measures, the least onerous measure should be preferred. Even though the ECtHR has generally rejected the strict necessity test[1021], the requirement of the least restrictive mean is very relevant in the context of online expression. In case of removals of or blocking access to online content, the solution preferred by national authorities often consists of overly broad measures (e.g., blocking access at the level of an Internet service provider or even an Internet access provider).[1022] Moreover, when assessing the severity of an interference with online expression, the potential chilling effect of a restrictive measure should be taken into account.

1020 CJEU, *L'Oreal SA v. eBay*, Case C324/09, 12 July 2011, para. 120.

1021 ECtHR, *James and Others v. the UK*, 21 February 1986, para. 51. See more in Part II Chapter 2.1.3.

1022 See for examples *ECtHR, Ahmet Yıldırım v. Turkey, 18 March 2013,* which concerned wholesale blocking of access to the Internet as a preventive measure.

In other words, it should be considered whether the restrictive measure might have a detrimental effect towards exercising freedom of expression in the future, especially when less intrusive alternatives may be possible.[1023]

The rejection of the strict necessity test by the ECtHR means that national authorities are not obliged to find the least intrusive solution to a particular problem.[1024] Consequently, the availability of a better solution is not decisive and does not *per se* imply a violation of the ECHR.[1025] Nevertheless, the possibility of less restrictive means can still be taken into account when assessing the overall adequacy of a measure.[1026]

In the context of this book, the criterion of tailored response means that the interfering measure should ideally consist of the least restrictive means and impose a minimum impairment of the rights at stake. The criterion of tailored response advances the principles of legitimacy and proportionality. As has been explained earlier, legitimacy is based on a belief of individuals about the rightfulness of a rule. In that sense, only a proportionate response, so one that is not excessive, will lead to acceptance of the decision taken.

A. *Least restrictive means*

MEANING – According to the ECtHR, there should be a 'reasonable relationship of proportionality between the means employed and the aim sought to be achieved'.[1027]

One way to assess the relationship is through the means-and-end test of the least restrictive means, which allows for assessment of the adequacy of the interference with respect to the aim pursued.[1028] As the ECtHR stated in *Soltsyak v. Russia*, testing a measure involves demonstrating that it was taken in pursuit of a legitimate aim *'and that the interference with the rights protected was no greater than was necessary to achieve it'*.[1029] The ECtHR does not consider the availability of alternative measures a decisive element. Nevertheless, an interference may be considered excessive if a less intrusive (but equally effective) measure existed.[1030] The test of the less intrusive measure *'envisages the minimal impairment of the right or freedom at stake, by asking if there is an equally effective but less restrictive means available to further the same social need'*.[1031]

1023 See ECtHR, *Mosley v the United Kingdom*, 10 May 2011, para. 129.

1024 ECtHR, *James and Others v. the UK*, 21 February 1986, para. 51. See also ECtHR, *Belgian Linguistic case*, 23 July 1968, para. 13 (question 2).

1025 J. Christoffersen, *Fair Balance: Proportionality, Subsidiarity and Primarity in the European Convention on Human Rights*, *o.c.*, p. 132–135.

1026 See ECtHR, *Roman Zakharov v. Russia*, 4 December 2015.

1027 ECtHR, *Ashingdane v. the United Kingdom*, 28 May 1985, para. 57, Series A no. 93.

1028 See more in Part II Chapter 2.1.3.

1029 ECtHR, *Soltsyak v. Russia*, 10 February 2011, para. 48.

1030 See for example ECtHR, *Ürper and Others v. Turkey*, 20 October 2009, para. 43.

1031 ECtHR, *Mouvement Raëlien Suisse v. Switzerland*, dissenting opinion of Judge Pinto De Albuquerque, footnote 31.

The CJEU also takes into account the intrusiveness of a measure. Generally, the preferred measure is one that is least problematic from the perspective of the individual rights at stake.[1032] In *Telekabel Wien, for example,* the CJEU specified that the measures blocking access should '*not unnecessarily deprive internet users of the possibility of lawfully accessing the information available*'.[1033]

B. Practical implications

TAILORED RESPONSE CRITERION – In the context of this book, tailored response means that a restricting measure should not be excessive and ideally, the least restrictive option should be preferred.

3.4. PROCEDURAL FAIRNESS

OUTLINE – Finding the fair balance between rights and interests at stake can be aided by the incorporation of procedural standards. In *Steel and Morris,* the ECtHR stated that in order to safeguard the countervailing interests (in this case free expression and open debate) it is essential '*that a measure of procedural fairness and equality of arms is provided for*'.[1034]

Procedural fairness, also called procedural justice, can facilitate desired outcomes such as proportionality and fair balance. But the concept mainly refers to the way in which the case is handled rather than its outcome.[1035] Ensuring that the process of resolving conflicts is handled in a fair manner can improve the perception of the legitimacy of an institution, which in consequence contributes to the acceptance of the decisions taken.[1036]

Equality of arms is one of the implicit rights included in the right to a fair trial.[1037] The right to a fair trial is provided by Article 6 ECHR and Article 47 CFEU. The latter implements in European Union law the protection afforded by Article 6(1) of the ECHR.[1038] The right to a fair trial constitutes a procedural

1032 J. Gerards, "How to improve the necessity test of the European Court of Human Rights", *o.c.*, p. 482.

1033 CJEU, *UPC Telekabel Wien GmbH v. Constantin Film Verleih GmbH, Wega Filmproduktionsgesellschaft mbH*, C 314/12, 27 March 2014, p. 64.

1034 ECtHR, *Steel and Morris v. the United Kingdom*, 15 February 2005, para. 95.

1035 See E. Brems, L. Lavrysen, "Procedural Justice in Human Rights Adjudication: The European Court of Human Rights", *Human Rights Quarterly*, Vol. 35, 2013, pp. 176–200, p. 177 referring to J. Thibaut, L. Walker, *Procedural Justice: A Psychological Analysis*, 1975.

1036 See E. Brems, L. Lavrysen, "Procedural Justice in Human Rights Adjudication: The European Court of Human Rights", *o.c.*, p. 177 referring to T. R. Tyler, *Why People Obey the Law*, 2006.

1037 R. Clayton, H. Tomlinson, *Fair Trial Rights*, 2nd Edition, Oxford University Press, 2010, p. 121.

1038 CJEU, *Chalkor AE Epexergasias Metallon*, Case C-386/10 P, 8 December 2011, para. 51. See also CJEU, *DEB Deutsche Energiehandels- und Beratungsgesellschaft mbH v. Bundesrepublik Deutschland*, Case C-279/09, 22 December 2010, para. 32.

right composed of several elements that, in the context of this book, can serve as guidance in obtaining procedural fairness in the process of content removal. The relevant elements of the two provisions, if introduced into the content removal mechanisms, could add an element of due process that is currently missing (see *Supra*). Moreover, to solve conflicts between rights, certain requirements for the decision-making process should be employed.[1039]

It should be highlighted that the procedural provisions, such as the right to a fair trial but also the right to an effective remedy, are directed to States, prescribing them how to organize their judicial system. The specific elements of the rights are interpreted by the ECtHR in relation to legal proceedings. In this book, the procedural provisions function in a different context. When the procedure is conducted (and often also designed) by private entities such as hosting service providers, strict compliance with the provision cannot be expected. Certain elements of the provision can, however, be applied by analogy and used as inspiration to introduce due process safeguards into the removal process.

The criterion of procedural fairness is complex. It consists of two main elements, namely (A) due process and (B) requirements for the decision making process. The principle of procedural fairness advances the principles of legitimacy and proportionality, as it contributes to the acceptance of the decisions taken and helps to reach a proportionate outcome.

A. *Due process*

MEANING – The right to a fair trial is comprised of explicit rights, such as '*a fair and public hearing within a reasonable time by an independent and impartial tribunal established by law*'.[1040] The right also encompasses several implicit rights, derived from the provision through the teleological interpretation, such as the right to equality of arms, to adversarial proceedings, and to a reasoned judgement.[1041]

1. Explicit rights

FAIR HEARING – The right to fair hearing includes the right to participate effectively in the hearing[1042], that is, '*to hear and follow the proceedings*'.[1043]

1039 See ECtHR, *Hatton and Others v. the United Kingdom*, 8 July 2003, para. 128.

1040 Article 6 ECHR.

1041 See D. Vitkauskas, G. Dikov, *Protecting the right to a fair trial under the European Convention on Human Rights*, Council of Europe human rights handbooks, Council of Europe Strasbourg, 2012, p. 45.

1042 See E. Brems, L. Lavrysen, "Procedural Justice in Human Rights Adjudication: The European Court of Human Rights", *o.c.*, p. 190.

1043 ECtHR, *Stanford v. The United Kingdom*, 23 February 1994, para. 26.

The right has two aspects: the right to hear what is said about the case (and the defendant) and the right to respond to the arguments given by the other party. In that sense the right to fair hearing is further complemented by the rights to equality of arms and to adversarial proceedings.

According to the ECtHR, Article 6 'does not guarantee the right to personal presence before a civil court but rather a more general right to present one's case effectively before the court and to enjoy equality of arms with the opposing side'.[1044]

The right to a fair trial can only be seen to be effective if the observations are actually "heard", that is to say are duly considered by the trial court.[1045] In *Perez v. France*, the Court specified that

> 'the effect of Article 6 is, among others, to place the 'tribunal' under a duty to conduct a proper examination of the submissions, arguments and evidence adduced by the parties, without prejudice to its assessment of whether they are relevant'.[1046]

In the context of administrative procedures a right to express one's views takes the form of the right to be heard. The CJEU linked this right to the right to good administration.[1047] The right to be heard '*guarantees every person the opportunity to make known his views effectively during an administrative procedure and before the adoption of any decision liable to affect his interests adversely*'.[1048]

Moreover, the right 'also requires the authorities to pay due attention to the observations thus submitted by the person concerned, examining carefully and impartially all the relevant aspects of the individual case and giving a detailed statement of reasons for their decision'.[1049]

REASONABLE TIME – The right to a hearing within a reasonable time requires States to 'organise their legal systems in such a way that their courts can guarantee to everyone the right to a final decision within a reasonable time in the determination of his civil rights and obligations'.[1050] The right is closely linked to the right to effective remedy.[1051]

1044 ECtHR, *Gladkiy v. Russia*, 6 March 2014, para. 103; See also ECtHR, *Steel and Morris v. The United Kingdom*, 15 February 2005, para. 59.

1045 ECtHR, *Donadze v. Georgia*, 7 March 2006, para. 35. See also ECtHR, Guide on Article 6 of the European Convention on Human Rights, Right to a fair trial (civil limb), Updated to 31 December 2017, https://www.echr.coe.int/Documents/Guide_Art_6_ENG.pdf.

1046 ECtHR, *Perez v. France*, 12 February 2004, para. 80.

1047 CJEU, *M. M. v. Minister for Justice, Equality and Law Reform, Ireland*, Case C-277/11, 22 November 2012, para. 82.

1048 *Ibid.*, para. 87; see also CJEU, *Spain* v *Commission*, Case C287/02, 9 June 2005, para. 37 and caselaw cited; CJEU, *Sopropé*, Case C-349/07, 18 December 2008, para. 37; CJEU, *Foshan Shunde Yongjian Housewares & Hardware* v *Council*, Case C141/08 P, 1 October 2009, para. 83.

1049 CJEU, *M. M. v. Minister for Justice, Equality and Law Reform, Ireland*, Case C-277/11, 22 November 2012, para. 88.

1050 ECtHR, *Frydlender v. France*, 27 June 2000, para. 45; and ECtHR, *Salesi v. Italy*, 26 February 1993, para. 24.

1051 ECtHR, *Kudla v. Poland*, 26 October 2000, para. 156.

The purpose of the right to a hearing within a reasonable time is to provide protection against excessive delays in rendering justice, '*which might jeopardise its effectiveness and credibility*'.[1052] The reasonableness of the time required to adjudicate a case is examined on a case-by-case basis, according to the facts of the case.[1053] The Court has laid down the criteria that it takes into account when assessing the reasonableness of the length of the proceedings: '*the complexity of the case, the conduct of the applicant and of the relevant authorities and what was at stake for the applicant in the dispute*'.[1054]

Similarly, the CJEU ruled that '*everyone is entitled to legal process within a reasonable period*'.[1055] Moreover, the CJEU confirmed the case-by-case approach and the criteria to be used by stating that

> 'it is clear from the case-law of both the Court of Justice and the European Court of Human Rights that the reasonableness of the length of proceedings is to be determined in the light of the circumstances specific to each case and, in particular, the importance of the case for the person concerned, its complexity and the conduct of the applicant and of the competent authorities'.[1056]

INDEPENDENT AND IMPARTIAL TRIBUNAL – The ECtHR explained in *Campbell and Fell v the UK* that the word "tribunal" in Article 6.1 'is not necessarily to be understood as signifying a court of law of the classic kind, integrated within the standard judicial machinery of the country'.[1057] The term can describe a body equipped with power to decide matters 'on the basis of rule of law, following proceedings conducted in a prescribed manner'.[1058] Moreover, such a body must be independent from the parties and the executive power, and offer guarantees of a judicial procedure.[1059]

Freedom from external intervention or pressure liable to jeopardise the judgement[1060] is the main requirement for independence. According to the

1052 ECtHR, *Katte Klitsche de la Grange v. Italy*, 27 October 1994, para. 61.

1053 ECtHR, *Gast and Popp v. Germany*, 25 February 2000, para. 70; also P. Leanza, O. Pridal, *The right to a fair trial: Article 6 of the European Convention on Human Rights*, Alphen aan den Rijn: Kluwer law international, 2014, p. 145.

1054 ECtHR, *Frydlender v. France*, 27 June 2000, para. 43. See also ECtHR, *Gast and Popp v. Germany*, 25 February 2000, para. 70.

1055 CJEU, *Z v. Parliament*, C-270/99 P, 27 November 2001, para. 24; see also CJEU, *P Baustahlgewebe v Commission*, Case C-185/95, 17 December 1998, para. 21.

1056 CJEU, *Z v. Parliament*, C-270/99 P, 27 November 2001, para. 24; see also CJEU, P *Baustahlgewebe* v *Commission*, 17 December 1998, Case C-185/95, para. 29.

1057 ECtHR, *Campbell and Fell v. the United Kingdom*, 28 June 1984, para. 76.

1058 ECtHR, *Sramek v. Austria*, 22 October 1984, para. 36, as referenced by L. Pech, "Article 47(2)", in S. Peers et al. (eds.), *The EU Charter of Fundamental Rights – A Commentary*, Hart Publishing, Oxford and Portland, Oregon, 2014, p. 1253.

1059 See *mutatis mutandis* with regard to Article 5.4 ECHR, ECtHR, *X v. the United Kingdom*, 5 November 1981, para. 53, as referenced by P. Leanza, O. Pridal, *The right to a fair trial: Article 6 of the European Convention on Human Rights*, *o.c.*, p. 129.

1060 See to that effect CJEU, *Abrahamsson and Anderson*, C-407/98, 6 July 2000, para. 32 and 36; see also L. Pech, "Article 47(2)", *o.c.*, p. 1256.

CJEU, that essential freedom from external factors '*requires certain guarantees sufficient to protect the person of those who have the task of adjudicating in a dispute, such as guarantees against removal from office*'.[1061] To establish whether a tribunal is independent from the parties and the executive power, the ECtHR examines additional factors, such as the composition of the tribunal, the appointment procedure for its members and the duration of their office.[1062] When determining independence of a tribunal '*regard must be had, inter alia, to the existence of safeguards against outside pressures and the question whether it presents an appearance of independence*'.[1063] This is because '*justice must not only be done; it must also be seen to be done*'.[1064]

The Court considers that while '*impartiality normally denotes absence of prejudice or bias*'[1065], there are two ways to test impartiality. As pointed out in *Piersack v. Belgium*, a distinction can be made between '*a subjective approach, that is endeavouring to ascertain the personal conviction of a given judge in a given case, and an objective approach, that is determining whether he offered guarantees sufficient to exclude any legitimate doubt in this respect*'.[1066]

According to the CJEU, impartiality requires objectivity[1067] and '*the absence of any interest in the outcome of the proceedings apart from the strict application of the rule of law*'.[1068] The requirements of independency and impartiality are connected and the ECtHR often examines these two aspects together.[1069]

Personal impartiality of the members of the tribunal will be difficult to assess when analysing different response mechanisms in Part III of the book. Nevertheless, impartiality understood as an element of independence of the decision-making body is without any doubt relevant. In the context of this book, the main factor to consider in the analysis is whether the removal decisions are taken by courts, administrative authorities, or the intermediaries involved in the conflict.

1061 CJEU, *Wilson v. Ordre des avocats du barreau de Luxembourg*, C-506/04, 19 September 2006, para. 51.

1062 P. Leanza, O. Pridal, *The right to a fair trial: Article 6 of the European Convention on Human Rights*, *o.c.*, p. 129.

1063 For example ECtHR, *Findlay v. the United Kingdom*, 25 February 1997, para. 73; ECtHR, *Coëme and Ohters v. Belgium*, 22 June 2000, para. 120.

1064 ECtHR, *Delcourt v. Belgium*, 17 January 1970, para. 31; also ECtHR, *Piersack v. Belgium*, 1 October 1982, para. 27.

1065 ECtHR, *Piersack v. Belgium*, 1 October 1982, para. 30.

1066 *Ibid.*

1067 See to that effect CJEU, *Abrahamsson and Anderson*, C-407/98, 6 July 2000, para. 32.

1068 CJEU, *Wilson v. Ordre des avocats du barreau de Luxembourg*, C-506/04, 19 September 2006, para. 52.

1069 P. Leanza, O. Pridal, *The right to a fair trial: Article 6 of the European Convention on Human Rights*, *o.c.*, p. 129.

2. Implicit rights

EQUALITY OF ARMS AND ADVERSARIAL PROCEEDINGS – The fundamental aspect of the right to a fair trial (in criminal proceedings) is that the proceedings '*should be adversarial and that there should be equality of arms between the prosecution and defence*'.[1070]

The rights to equality of arms and to adversarial proceedings are closely linked as they are both derived from the right to a fair hearing. Equality of arms is understood as a requirement that every party to the proceedings '*shall have a reasonable opportunity of presenting his case to the [c]ourt under conditions which do not place him at a substantial disadvantage vis-à-vis his opponent*'.[1071] The same wording is used by the CJEU[1072], which, additionally, describes equality of arms as a corollary of the very concept of a fair hearing.[1073]

The right to adversarial proceedings means that each party shall have the opportunity to have knowledge of and comment on the evidence adduced and on the observation filed by the other party.[1074] According to the CJEU, adversarial proceedings means that '*the parties to a case must have the right to examine all the documents or observations submitted to the court for the purpose of influencing its decision, and to comment on them*'.[1075]

REASONED JUDGEMENT – According to the Court's established case-law reflecting a principle of the proper administration of justice, '*judgments of courts and tribunals should adequately state the reasons on which they are based*'.[1076] However, Article 6.1 ECHR '*cannot be understood as requiring a detailed answer to every argument*'.[1077] The extent to which the duty to give reasons applies may vary according to the nature of the decision.[1078]

The right to a fair trial, therefore, places a duty on a court or a tribunal to provide reasoned judgements that adequately outline the legal and factual basis of the decision.[1079] The right to a reasoned judgement aims to protect the parties from arbitrary decisions concealed behind ambiguous and incomplete

---

1070 ECtHR, *Rowe and Davis v. the United Kingdom*, 16 February 2000, para. 60.

1071 For example ECtHR, *Ankerl v. Switzerland*, 23 October, 1996, para. 38.

1072 CJEU, *Europese Gemeenschap v. Otis NV and others*, C-199/11, 6 November 2012, para. 71.

1073 *Ibid.*; see also CJEU, *Sweden and Others v API and Commission*, Joined Cases C514/07 P, C528/07 P, 21 September 2010; and CJEU, *Commission v API*, C532/07 P, 21 September 2010, para. 88.

1074 ECtHR, *Vermeulen v. Belgium*, 20 February 1996, para. 33; see also ECtHR, *Rowe and Davis v. the United Kingdom*, 16 February 2000, para. 60.

1075 CJEU, *ZZ v. Secretary of State for the Home Department*, C-300/11, 4 June 2013, para. 55; see also CJEU, *Varec*, Case C-450/06, 4 June 2009, para. 45; CJEU, *Commission* v *Ireland and Others*, Case C-89/08 P, 2 December 2009, para. 52; and CJEU, *Banif Plus Bank*, Case C-472/11, 21 February 2013, para. 30.

1076 ECtHR, *Suominen v. Finland*, 1 July 2003, para. 34.

1077 *Ibid.*

1078 *Ibid.*

1079 P. Leanza, O. Pridal, *The right to a fair trial: Article 6 of the European Convention on Human Rights*, *o.c.*, p. 151.

reasoning.[1080] Moreover, it is meant to provide sufficient information that might be required to file an appeal.[1081]

B. Requirements for decision-making processes

MEANING – Procedural fairness first appeared in the ECtHR decisions in cases concerning custody of minors under Article 8 (right to private life).[1082] Despite the fact that Article 8 contains no explicit procedural requirements, the ECtHR, nevertheless, started expressing its views on the decision-making process that leads to a decision.[1083] In *W. v. the UK*, the ECtHR stated that

> '[t]he (...) authority's decision-making process clearly cannot be devoid of influence on the substance of the decision, notably by ensuring that it is based on the relevant considerations and is not one-sided and, hence, neither is nor appears to be arbitrary'.[1084]

The Court highlighted procedural justice concerns such as accuracy, neutrality and participation.[1085] Regarding parents' involvement in the custody proceedings, the ECtHR declared that

> '[t]he decision-making process must therefore, in the Court's view, be such as to secure that their views and interests are made known to and duly taken into account by the (...) authority and that they are able to exercise in due time any remedies available to them'.[1086]

The Court's views that 'the decision-making process leading to measures of interference must be fair and such as to afford due respect for the interests safeguarded to the individual'[1087] started appearing in other cases under Article 8, for example regarding spatial planning and environment.

In *Buckley v. the UK*, which concerned the refusal to grant a permission to live in caravans on one's own land, the Court addressed the relevance of procedural safeguards, stating that

> '[w]henever discretion capable of interfering with the enjoyment of a Convention right such as the one in issue in the present case is conferred on national authorities,

1080 *Ibid.*
1081 See to that effect CJEU, *ASML Netherlands BV v. Semiconductor Industry Services GmbH (SEMIS)*, C-283/05, 14 December 2006, para. 28.
1082 For example ECtHR, *W. v. The United Kingdom*, 8 July 1987; ECtHR, *Buscemi v. Italy*, 16 September 1999; ECtHR, *Kutzner v. Germany*, 26 February 2002.
1083 ECtHR, *W. v. The United Kingdom*, 8 July 1987, para. 62.
1084 *Ibid.*
1085 E. Brems, L. Lavrysen, *Procedural Justice in Human Rights Adjudication: The European Court of Human Rights*, *o.c.*, p. 192.
1086 ECtHR, *W. v. The United Kingdom*, 8 July 1987, para. 63.
1087 For example ECtHR, *Hatton v. The United Kingdom*, 8 July 2003; and ECtHR, *Buckley v. the United Kingdom*, 29 September 1996.

the procedural safeguards available to the individual will be especially material in determining whether the respondent State has, when fixing the regulatory framework, remained within its margin of appreciation'.[1088]

The issue of a decision-making process was extensively addressed in *Hatton and others v. United Kingdom*, which addressed night flights at Heathrow Airport.[1089] When reviewing the procedural elements of the case,

> 'the Court is required to consider all the procedural aspects, including the type of policy or decision involved, the extent to which the views of individuals (including the applicants) were taken into account throughout the decision-making procedure, and the procedural safeguards available'.[1090]

The decision-making process, therefore, can also be taken into account in other cases where the Court grants the States a wide margin of appreciation, such as cases concerning spatial planning and religious freedom.[1091] In *Leyla Şahin v. Turkey*, which concerned a ban on headscarves at university grounds, the Court confirmed that even in cases where the decision about interference is left to the States' own discretion, it is still possible for the Court to check how such a decision was taken. Specifically, the Court may scrutinise the decision-making process to check whether the national authorities accorded due weight to the interests of the individual.[1092]

C. *Practical implications*

PROCEDURAL FAIRNESS CRITERION – The criterion of procedural fairness is more complex as it refers to the core issue of this book – the procedural safeguards. In the context of the book, the criterion of procedural fairness signifies that the procedure that gives rise to the interference should address certain due process rights, such as:

- the right to present one's case effectively before the decision-making body;
- the right to a proper examination by the decision-making body of the submissions, arguments and evidence adduced by the parties, without prejudice to its assessment;
- the right to obtain a decision within a reasonable time, according to the facts of the case;

1088 ECtHR, *Buckley v. the United Kingdom*, 29 September 1996, para. 76; and ECtHR, *Chapman v. The United Kingdom*, 18 January 2001.
1089 ECtHR, *Hatton and Others v. the United Kingdom*, 8 July 2003.
1090 *Ibid.*, para. 104.
1091 For example ECtHR, *Leyla Şahin v. Turkey*, 10 November 2005.
1092 ECtHR, *Hatton and Others v. the United Kingdom*, 8 July 2003, para. 99.

- the right to have one's case resolved by a decision-making body which is independent from the parties and the executive power;
- the right to equality of arms, i.e., the right to have a reasonable opportunity to present one's case to the decision-making body under conditions which do not place one at substantial disadvantage vis-à-vis the opponent;
- the right to adversarial proceedings, i.e., the right to obtain knowledge of and to comment on the evidence and observations presented by the opponent;
- the right to receive a reasoned judgement that adequately outlines the legal and factual basis of the decision.

Moreover, when deciding about measures of interference, the decision-making process should comply with the requirements specified by the ECtHR. Specifically, the decision-making body should afford due weight to the interests of the parties involved, and ensure that procedural safeguards are available.

The procedural fairness criterion is focused more on the process of reaching a decision, rather than on its outcome. The elements and sub-elements identified within this criterion overlap on several occasions. For example, the right to a fair hearing, the right to adversarial proceeding and the right to equality of arms are meant to ensure that the decision is fair and that due weight is given to the interests of the parties involved. However, the overlap is not problematic from the point of view of the assessment to be made, since the conducted assessment of the existing response mechanisms focuses on the overall satisfaction of the criteria, rather than their specific elements.

3.5. EFFECTIVE REMEDY

OUTLINE – The criterion of effective remedy is based on Article 13 ECHR and Article 47 CFEU. The right to an effective remedy may apply not only in disputes between individuals and public authorities but also in disputes between individuals.

Article 13 ECHR guarantees the right to an effective remedy before a national authority '*to everyone who claims that his rights and freedom under the Convention have been violated*'.[1093] In European Union law, the protection is more extensive since it guarantees the right to an effective remedy before a court.[1094] The scope of the right under the CFEU, moreover, extends to all rights arising from EU law.[1095] Specifically, as stated by the CJEU, the right extends to '*any provision of a national legal system and any legislative, administrative or judicial practice which might*

1093 For example ECtHR, *Klass and Others v. Germany*, 6 September 1978.

1094 Praesidium of the Convention, Explanations relating to the Charter of Fundamental Rights, *o.c.* Explanation on Article 47.

1095 H. CH. Hofmann, "Art. 47 – Right to Effective Remedy" in S. Peers et al. (eds.), *The EU Charter of Fundamental Rights – A Commentary*, Hart Publishing, Oxford and Portland, Oregon, 2014, p. 1214, ft. 81.

impair the effectiveness'[1096] of EU law and which '*might prevent, even temporarily, Community rules from having full force and effect*'.[1097]

The purpose of the right to an effective remedy is to allow a victim of a violation appropriate relief.[1098] Appropriate relief involves a measure that is capable of stopping the violation, or allows the victim to obtain adequate redress, including compensation.[1099]

In the context of online expression, the right to an effective remedy comes into play on two separate occasions. First, when a victim of infringing expression attempts to stop it, for example by requesting removal. Second, in case of successful removal, the right may be of use when the author tries to contest the removal and asks for the expression to be reinstated. It can be used, therefore, by both sides of a conflict to remedy possible infringements of their rights. In any case, for the right to an effective remedy to become applicable, the existence of an "arguable claim" of a violation is required.[1100]

The criterion of effective remedy in case of online rights violations can be manifested by the presence of two elements: a possibility to appeal a decision of the hosting provider, and a judicial redress. Defining these two elements, for the purpose of this study, requires examination of the effectiveness of a remedy and of types of remedies recognized by the European courts. It should be highlighted, however, that even though inspiration for the criterion is found in the provisions of the ECHR and the CFUE and the accompanying case law, their application is not strict but is rather based on analogy, as full compliance with the two provisions cannot be achieved in the private enforcement context. The criterion of effective remedy is closely linked to the elements of the procedural fairness criterion. The criterion of effective remedy advances mainly the principle of proportionality but also the principle of legitimacy.

A. *Possibility to appeal*

MEANING – Neither Article 13 ECHR nor any other provision of the Convention lay down any given manner for ensuring the effective implementation of any of the provisions of the Convention.[1101] In general, applicants should have a remedy before a national authority in order to have their claim decided and, if appropriate, to obtain redress.[1102] Article 13 ECHR

1096 CJEU, *The Queen v Secretary of State for Transport, ex parte: Factortame Ltd and others*, C-213/89, 19 June 1990, para. 19.

1097 *Ibid.*

1098 See ECtHR, *Vilho Eskelinen and Others v. Finland*, 19 April 2007, para. 80.

1099 For example ECtHR, *Kaya v. Turkey*, 19 February 1998.

1100 ECtHR, *Silver and Others v United Kingdom*, 25 March 1983, p. 113. See also H. CH. Hofmann, "Art. 47 – Right to Effective Remedy", *o.c.*, p. 1215.

1101 See ECtHR, *Silver and Others v United Kingdom*, A.61. (1983), p. 113.

1102 ECtHR, *Leander v. Sweden*, 26 March 1987, para. 77.

does not necessarily require judicial remedies in place. As the ECtHR clarified in *Klass and Others v. Germany*, Article 13 must guarantee an "effective remedy before a national authority".[1103]

The "authority" referred to in Article 13 does not necessarily have to be a judicial one.[1104] If it is not, however, its powers and the guarantees which it affords are relevant in determining whether the remedy is effective.[1105] For example in *Peck*, the ECtHR declared that the lack of legal power of the commissions to award damages to the applicant meant that those bodies could not provide an effective remedy.[1106]

The available remedy should be effective in practice and in law.[1107] This means, that the available remedy should allow for either '*preventing the alleged violation or its continuation, or (...) providing adequate redress for any violation that had already occurred*'.[1108] Moreover, '*its exercise must not be unjustifiably hindered by the acts or omissions of the authorities of the respondent State*'.[1109]

The "effectiveness" of a "remedy" within the meaning of Article 13 does not depend on the certainty of a favourable outcome for the applicant, as the ECtHR explained in *M.S.S. v. Belgium and Greece*.[1110] Moreover, '*even if a single remedy does not by itself entirely satisfy the requirements of Article 13, the aggregate of remedies provided for under domestic law may do so*".[1111]

Under European Union law, '*Member States shall provide remedies sufficient to ensure effective legal protection in the fields covered by Union law*'.[1112] Moreover, Article 4(3) [TEU] requires Member States to take all measures necessary to guarantee the application and effectiveness of Community law.[1113] As stated by the CJEU on numerous occasions, this means that the enforcement of EU rights at national level must not be '*virtually impossible or excessively difficult*'.[1114] To evaluate whether this requirement has been met, each case must be analysed

1103 ECtHR, *Klass and Others v. Germany*, 6 September 1978, 6 September 1978, para. 64.
1104 ECtHR, *M.S.S. v. Belgium and Greece*, 21 January 2011, para. 289. Also, ECtHR, *Gebremedhin [Gaberamadhien] v. France*, 26 April 2007, para. 53.
1105 ECtHR, *M.S.S. v. Belgium and Greece*, 21 January 2011, para. 289. Also, ECtHR, *Gebremedhin [Gaberamadhien] v. France*, 26 April 2007, para. 53. See also ECtHR, *Silver and Others v United Kingdom*, 25 March 1983; and ECtHR, *Chahal v United Kingdom*, 15 November 1996.
1106 ECtHR, Peck v. the United Kingdom, 28 January 2003, para. 109.
1107 ECtHR, *Kudla v. Poland*, 26 October 2000, para. 157.
1108 *Ibid.* para. 158.
1109 ECtHR, *M.S.S. v. Belgium and Greece*, 21 January 2011, para. 290. Also ECtHR, *Çakıcı v. Turkey* [GC], 8 July 1999, para. 112.
1110 ECtHR, *M.S.S. v. Belgium and Greece*, 21 January 2011, para. 289. Also, ECtHR, *Gebremedhin [Gaberamadhien] v. France*, 26 April 2007, para. 53.
1111 *Ibid.*
1112 Article 19(1) TEU, second subparagraph.
1113 CJEU, *Nunes et de Matos*, C-186/98, 8 July 1999, para. 9.
1114 See CJEU, *Fisscher*, C-128/93, para. 37; CJEU, *Palmisani*, C-261/95, para. 27; CJEU, *Preston and Others*, C-78–98, para, 39; CJEU, *Adeneler and Others*, C-212/04, para. 95.

> 'by reference to the role of [the national procedural] provision in the procedure, its progress and its special features, viewed as a whole, before the various national bodies. For those purposes, account must be taken, where appropriate, of the basic principles of the domestic judicial system, such as protection of the rights of the defence, the principle of legal certainty and the proper conduct of procedure'.[1115]

As the CJEU stated in *Inuit Tapiriit*, it is therefore 'for the Member States to establish a system of legal remedies and procedures which ensure respect for the fundamental right to effective judicial protection'.[1116] The CJEU further explained that in the absence of European Union rules governing the matter, it is for the domestic legal system of each Member State 'to lay down the detailed procedural rules governing actions brought to safeguard rights which individuals derive from European Union law'.[1117] Compliance with the right to an effective remedy depends on whether the State offers procedural rules guaranteeing fair prospects for a case to be instituted and provides admissibility criteria allowing actual access to a court.[1118] Moreover, it requires the provision of a remedy which is capable of addressing the violation of the right.[1119]

B. *Judicial redress*

MEANING – The scope of the obligation under Article 13 varies depending on the nature of the applicant's complaint under the Convention.[1120] Remedies should be available to everyone whose substantive rights have been interfered with. Effective remedy should also be available for interference with procedural rights, for example '*for an alleged breach of the requirement under Article 6.1 to hear a case within a reasonable time*'.[1121] Remedies discussed by the ECtHR include an obligation to conduct effective prosecution, full access by the victims

1115 CJEU, *Peterbroeck, Van Campenhout & Cie SCS v Belgian State*, C-312/93, 14 December 1995, para. 14; CJEU, *Jeroen van Schijndel and Johannes Nicolaas Cornelis van Veen v Stichting Pensioenfonds voor Fysiotherapeuten*, Joined cases C-430 and 431/93, 14 December 1995, para. 19.

1116 CJEU, *Inuit Tapiriit Kanatami and Others v Parliament and Council*, C-583/11 P, para. 100. See also CJEU, *Unión de Pequeños Agricultores v Council*, para. 41, and CJEU, *Commission v Jégo-Quéré*, para. 31.

1117 CJEU, *Inuit Tapiriit Kanatami and Others v Parliament and Council*, C-583/11 P, para. 102. See also to that effect CJEU, *Impact*, Case C-268/06, para. 44 and the case-law cited; CJEU, *Transportes Urbanos y Servicios Generales*, Case C-118/08, para. 31; and CJEU, *Alassini and Others*, Joined Cases C-317/08 to C-320/08, paras. 47 and 61.

1118 See H. CH. Hofmann, "Art. 47 – Right to Effective Remedy" *o.c.*, p. 1216.

1119 *Ibid.*

1120 ECtHR, *Isayeva and Others v. Russia*, 24 February 2005, para. 237.

1121 ECtHR, *Kudla v. Poland*, 26 October 2000, para. 156. See more case-law on the ECtHR, *Scordino (No. 1), Riccardi Pizzati, Musci, Giuseppe Mostacciuolo (Nos. 1 and 2), Cocchiarella, Apicella, Ernestina Zullo, Giuseppina and Orestina Procaccini v. Italy*, 29 Mar. 2006.

to the investigation and appropriate compensation for the loss and damage suffered.[1122]

According to the CJEU, the 'very existence of effective judicial review designed to ensure compliance with provisions of EU law is inherent in the existence of the rule of law'.[1123] According to the principle ubi ius ibi remedium, where there is a right conferred on individuals, there must be an accompanying remedy to ensure its enforcement.[1124] In case of violation of an EU right, national courts must be empowered to grant injunctive and monetary relief.[1125] Availability of an effective remedy, in that sense, depends on access to the court, effective judicial review and judicial supervision.[1126]

Examples of decisions on the right to an effective remedy include instances where the CJEU addressed procedural obligations (stemming from the right to a fair trial), such as an obligation of public bodies to reason their acts.[1127] Substantive remedies capable of effectively enforcing EU law rights include the obligation to pay damages for non-compliance with EU law, for example in case of a failure to implement a directive.[1128] Other forms of remedies include an obligation for the courts to order repayment of unduly levied sums by States[1129], or an order to reopen a final administrative decision.[1130] The effective remedy also includes a right to thorough review by the national courts of the final decisions on the implementation of EU law.[1131] In case of conflicts between individuals, the CJEU ruled that when implementing a directive (e.g. on equality of sexes) States should do so in a way that grants sanctions '*as to guarantee real and effective judicial protection*' of the right arising from the directive.[1132]

1122 ECtHR, *Isayeva and Others v. Russia*, 24 February 2005, para. 237, in in the context of violations of Articles 2 and 3.

1123 CJEU, *Schrems v. Data Protection Commissioner*, C-362/14, para. 95. See also to this effect, judgments in CJEU, *Les Verts v Parliament*, 294/83, para. 23; CJEU, *Johnston*, 222/84, para. 18 and 19; CJEU, *Heylens and Others*, 222/86, para. 14; and CJEU, *UGT-Rioja and Others*, C-428/06 to C-434/06, para. 80.

1124 See H. CH. Hofmann, "Art. 47 – Right to Effective Remedy", *o.c.*, p. 1214.

1125 K. Lenaerts, Effective judicial protection in the EU, Intervention at the Conference 'Assises de la Justice – What role for Justice in the European Union?' hosted by the European Commission on 21–22 November 2013 in Brussels, p. 3.

1126 See *Ibid.*

1127 CJEU, *Evropaïki Dynamiki – Proigmena Systimata Tilepikoinonion Pliroforikis kai Tilematikis AE v European Investment Bank (BEI)*, T-461/08, 20 September 2011, para. 122.

1128 For example CJEU, *Andrea Francovich and Danila Bonifaci and others v Italian Republic*, Joined cases C-6/90 and C-9/90, 19 November 1991, paras. 40 – 43.

1129 For example CJEU, *Marks & Spencer plc v Commissioners of Customs & Excise*, C-309/06, 10 April 2008, paras. 41 – 44.

1130 For example CJEU, *Hristo Byankov v Glaven sekretar na Ministerstvo na vatreshnite raboti*, C-249/11, 4 October 2012.

1131 For example, CJEU, *Brahim Samba Diouf v Ministre du Travail, de l'Emploi et de l'Immigration*, C-69/10, 28 July 2011, para. 56.

1132 CJEU, *Sabine von Colson and Elisabeth Kamann v Land Nordrhein-Westfalen*, C- 14/83, 10 April 1984, para. 23.

Moreover, such sanctions must have '*a real deterrent effect*' on those breaching the objectives of the directive.[1133]

However, 'neither the FEU Treaty nor Article 19 TEU intended to create new remedies before the national courts to ensure the observance of European Union law other than those already laid down by national law'.[1134] The position is different only if the structure of the domestic legal system provides no remedy making it possible, even indirectly, to ensure respect for the individuals' rights derived from European Union law.[1135]

C. *Practical implications*

EFFECTIVE REMEDY CRITERION – In the context of the book, the criterion of effective remedy means that everyone whose rights have been interfered with should have an effective remedy available. This means, an appropriate relief that could stop the violation or allow them adequate redress. The available remedy should be effective in practice and in law. The criterion of effective remedy refers to the core issue of this book – the procedural safeguards which should be introduced to ensure the availability of a remedy.

In the context of online content removals, the requirement of an effective remedy would mean that, as a first step, there should be a possibility to launch an appeal to a decision about removal of content. Even though such an appeal would be, in most cases, handled by the hosting provider and not a national or judicial authority, it certainly has the advantage of being an effective (and efficient) measure. Regardless of what response mechanism States provide, and whether decisions about removals are taken solely by intermediaries themselves or by a State body, judicial redress should always be available as a second step, to ensure independent review and effective legal protection of the right to freedom of expression.

From the CJEU case-law it can be concluded that when such rules are lacking at the EU level, it is for the States to establish a system of legal remedies and procedures which ensure respect for the fundamental right to effective judicial protection.[1136] In this book, however, it is argued that such a system of remedies and procedures should exist at the EU level on the basis of the EU's duty to ensure effective protection of fundamental rights. Giving the power to private entities to make decisions that are binding on others, regarding fundamental human rights, such as freedom of expression, requires ensuring that appropriate protective measures are in place.

1133 *Ibid.*

1134 CJEU, *Inuit Tapiriit Kanatami and Others v Parliament and Council*, C-583/11 P, para. 103. Also CJEU, *Unibet*, C-432/05, para. 40.

1135 CJEU, *Inuit Tapiriit Kanatami and Others v Parliament and Council*, C-583/11 P, para. 104.

1136 For example CJEU, *Inuit Tapiriit Kanatami and Others v Parliament and Council*, C-583/11 P, para. 100. See also CJEU, *Unión de Pequeños Agricultores v Council*, para. 41, and CJEU, *Commission v Jégo-Quéré*, para. 31.

CHAPTER 5
CONCLUSION

STATE INTERFERENCE BY PROXY – Under the current legislation in the EU, that is the E-Commerce Directive and the laws implementing the act at national level, Internet intermediaries are in a position to decide which content can remain online and which should be removed. They may be considered as gatekeepers, who are able to regulate the behaviour (and speech) of their users. By providing conditional liability exemptions for third parties' illegal content or activities, the States enlist the intermediaries to enforce the public policy objectives. As a result, the intermediaries are incentivized to remove content from their platforms without the proper balancing of rights at stake. Such indirect responsibilization can be explained by the practicality and efficiency purposes. It nevertheless creates a situation where States provide an incentive and allow for interference with the freedom of expression of the Internet users by private entities. It is therefore a question of the role of the legislator that indirectly contributes to the interference by private individuals – a type of "State interference by proxy".

MISSING PROCEDURAL SAFEGUARDS – In Chapter 2 of Part II, I argued that freedom of expression is not an absolute right, neither under the Convention, nor under the Charter. Interference is allowed, when it satisfies the conditions specified by each instrument. In Chapter 3 of Part II, I argued that the EU legislature currently does not comply with its positive obligation to protect the right to freedom of expression from interference by private entities in the context of notice and take down mechanisms. The absence of sufficient protective measures could be amended by introducing into the relevant legislation precise and specific rules regarding the application of restrictions on freedom of expression, including procedural safeguards.

The availability of adequate procedural safeguards to protect the interests of the parties involved is becoming one of the main points of interest of both the ECtHR and CJEU when analysing conflicts of interests. Procedural safeguards available to the individual are material in determining whether the State, when establishing a regulatory framework, has remained within its margin of appreciation. Procedural safeguards are also considered a crucial instrument to achieve procedural fairness and can contribute to the proper decision-making process, which are capable of operationalizing the guiding principles of this book that is (a) legal certainty, (b) legitimacy, and (c) proportionality.

CRITERIA FOR ASSESSMENT – The aim of this book is to propose safeguards for notice and take down procedures that promote compliance with the right to freedom of expression. In order to determine which safeguards would be best to achieve such a goal, a set of criteria is necessary. Chapter 4 of Part II proposed the following set of criteria:

1. Quality of law
2. Protection of democratic society
3. Tailored response
4. Procedural fairness
5. Effective remedy

The assessment criteria will be applied in Part III of the book to analyse the currently existing types of notice and action mechanisms.

PART III

EVALUATION OF EXISTING NOTICE AND ACTION MECHANISMS

CHAPTER 1
INTRODUCTION

1. METHODOLOGY

RESEARCH OBJECTIVE – The aim of this book is to propose safeguards for notice and action procedures that promote compliance with the right to freedom of expression. Such safeguards are currently missing from the EU legal regime addressing liability of Internet intermediaries for third party content. The lack of the safeguards constitutes a failure of the EU legislature of its positive obligation to ensure effective protection of the fundamental rights and specifically to the right to freedom of expression.

METHOD – In order to determine which safeguards might be appropriate, a set of criteria was developed in Part II. The criteria shall now be applied as a *positive assessment framework*[1137], to assess the existing notice and action mechanisms with a view of identifying best practices. The purpose of the assessment is to evaluate whether and how the existing notice and action mechanisms address the established criteria and draw conclusions on how they advance the three guiding principles. Part III presents specific notice and action mechanisms through illustrative examples of implementation at national level. The mechanisms are measured against the assessment criteria, to identify best practices worth following and to inform the subsequent selection of safeguards that should be introduced.

QUALITATIVE ASSESSMENT – The assessment conducted in this Part is qualitative rather than quantitative in nature. It is not the aim, therefore, to select a mechanism that scores the highest in the number of fulfilled criteria, or to choose the best notice and action mechanism or its best national version. Instead, the aim is to learn from the available examples how the criteria should and should not be pursued, and what best practices are employed to help advance the legal certainty, legitimacy, and proportionality of the mechanism.[1138]

1137 See Part II Chapter 3.

1138 Neither is this exercise aimed at providing an exhaustive analysis of the national legislations addressing the issue of content removal from the Internet. For a detailed analysis of the national approaches to the problem of content regulation on the Internet see, for example, the

Moreover, the focus of the analysis is on the *overall* performance in light of the selected criteria. This means that, depending on the mechanism, not all the elements identified within each criterion are relevant and need to be taken into account.

The ultimate goal of this exercise is to examine which best practices are best suited to their function; that is, to ensure that content removal is undertaken with adequate consideration for the right to freedom of expression. This exercise will help to identify which safeguards should be introduced to ensure that the EU legislature complies with its positive obligation to ensure adequate balance and effective protection of the fundamental right to freedom of expression.

OUTLINE – This Part of the book provides

(1) an analysis of the existing forms of notice and action mechanisms;
(2) proposed safeguards for freedom of expression in notice and action mechanisms.

2. DIFFERENT FORMS OF 'NOTICE AND ACTION'

NOTICE AND ACTION – 'Notice and action' (N&A) is an umbrella term for a range of mechanisms designed to eliminate illegal or infringing content from the Internet. According to the European Commission,

> '[t]he notice and action procedures are those followed by the intermediary internet providers for the purpose of combating illegal content upon receipt of notification. The intermediary may, for example, take down illegal content, block it, or request that it be voluntarily taken down by the persons who posted it online'.[1139]

REMOVAL OR BLOCKING – This book focuses on the response mechanisms aimed at removal of content from the Internet. Removal leads to deletion of content and effectively erases it from the free flow of information on the Internet. Although the removal is implemented by a hosting service provider residing within the territory of one State, it brings an end to the dissemination of content also in other States.[1140] As a permanent solution, removal has serious consequences for the right to freedom of expression, including access to information.

---

country reports accompanying two reports: Swiss Institute of Comparative Law, Comparative Study on Filtering, blocking and take-down of illegal content on the Internet, *o.c*; and T. Verbiest, G. Spindler *et al.*, "Study on the Liability of Internet Intermediaries", *o.c.*

1139 Commission Communication, A coherent framework for building trust in the Digital Single Market for e-commerce and online services, *o.c.*

1140 Swiss Institute of Comparative Law, Comparative Study on Filtering, blocking and take-down of illegal content on the Internet – comparative considerations, *o.c.*, p. 794.

Blocking is a technical measure that leads to disabling access to content by creating restrictions on access according to predefined conditions, e.g. from certain locations. The information remains in the network, however, and can be accessed from different locations. Blocking comes into play when takedown is not possible because the illegal activity or information is stored outside the European Union.[1141] Moreover, blocking is requested mainly from access providers or hosting service providers that operate at the infrastructure level. These service providers usually have no means to remove a single piece of content from a platform or a website they provide access to or host. Granular removal of content can in principle only be done by the providers of the platform or a website operating at the application level.

Blocking is considered problematic for similar, albeit not the same reasons as removal of content.[1142] Blocking raises concerns regarding its legality, legitimacy and possible chilling effects on speech.[1143] Moreover, blocking often takes the form of a wholesale measure.[1144] Despite the fact that blocking does not lead to permanent removal of online content, it does have an impact on the free flow of information, therefore, it should not be excluded completely from the analysis. As will become apparent in the following sections of this Chapter, countries use a variety of technical measures to eliminate infringing content from circulation. The focus of the analysis, however, shall be on response mechanisms rather than specific technical measures.

STATE OR NON-STATE – In this book I focus primarily on non-state response mechanisms. Non-state response mechanisms are mechanisms where the State authorities are, generally, not actively involved but rather the whole interaction occurs between private entities (Internet intermediaries, their users, and other interested parties protecting their rights). Internet intermediaries can also be called upon by public authorities, for example courts or regulatory bodies, to remove or block access to online content. Because of the direct State involvement, I refer to these mechanisms as state response mechanisms. This book assumes that state response mechanisms follow the rule of law and provide sufficient safeguards for protection of human and constitutional rights. While

---

1141 European Commission, Online Services, Including e-commerce in Single Market, Commission Staff Working Paper, *o.c.*, p. 39.

1142 See Swiss Institute of Comparative Law, Comparative Study on Filtering, blocking and take-down of illegal content on the Internet – comparative considerations, *o.c*; and T. Verbiest, G. Spindler *et al.*, "Study on the Liability of Internet Intermediaries", *o.c*; P. Van Eecke, M. Truyens, EU Study on the Legal Analysis of A Single Market for the Information Society – New Rules for a New Age?, *o.c.*

1143 See more in OSCE, Organisation for Security and Co-operation in Europe, The Office of the Representative on Freedom of the Media, REPORT Freedom of Expression on the internet, Study of legal provisions and practices related to freedom of expression, the free flow of information and media pluralism on the internet in OSCE participating states, 15 December 2011.

1144 See for example ECtHR, *Ahmet Yıldırım v. Turkey*, 18 March 2013.

the safeguards might not always work perfectly, an assessment of the functioning of the judiciary system in each State is outside of the scope of this book.

The distinction between state and non-state response mechanisms is not always easy to make. As has been shown by two separate studies, a significant number of countries have no specific legal framework aimed at the blocking, filtering and takedown of illegal Internet content.[1145] The deliberate lack of legislative intervention can be explained by States' preference to rely on general rules of law, their legal traditions, or their concern that specific legislation would not keep up with the technical developments.[1146] Instead, these States use different models to approach the problem of illegal online content, creating diverse, often novel, mechanisms and combining approaches to fill the regulatory gap.[1147] In 2007, the authors of a report drafted for the European Commission distinguished between three models, namely, codified NTD-procedures, self-regulation, and co-regulation.[1148] In the 2015 study on filtering, blocking and removal of illegal online content commissioned by the Council of Europe, the authors distinguished between three different models, namely, the co-perpetrator model (with the host provider privilege), self-regulation, and notice and take down procedures provided for by law.[1149] Both studies show that States "mix and match" the models and their response methods depending on their needs and the type of content which is targeted. The division between non-state and state response mechanism may become blurry in practice. For example, a mechanism can be initiated as non- state but courts may become involved at a later stage of the procedure. Therefore, it is not possible to strictly limit the analysis to non-state mechanisms. For this reason the analysis below includes instances of notice and action where additional state involvement elements can be identified, if necessary for the completeness of the assessment.

TYPES OF CONTENT AND ACTIVITIES – The types of content and activities targeted by notice and action mechanisms can vary significantly. In the EU, the notice and take down mechanism is not provided directly but implied in the E-Commerce Directive. Nevertheless, EU countries do not restrict themselves only to this type of response mechanism. The E-Commerce Directive provides conditions for the liability exemption for hosting service providers. The scope of

---

1145 Swiss Institute of Comparative Law, Comparative Study on Filtering, blocking and take-down of illegal content on the Internet – comparative considerations, *o.c.*, p. 775.

1146 *Ibid.*, p. 775. See also T. Verbiest, Spindler G, et al., Study on the liability of Internet Intermediaries – General trends in Europe, *o.c.*, p. 12.

1147 Swiss Institute of Comparative Law, Comparative Study on Filtering, blocking and take-down of illegal content on the Internet – comparative considerations, *o.c.*, p. 775.

1148 See T. Verbiest, G. Spindler *et al.*, Study on the Liability of Internet Intermediaries, *o.c.* P. Van Eecke, M. Truyens, EU Study on the Legal Analysis of A Single Market for the Information Society – New Rules for a New Age?, *o.c.*

1149 Swiss Institute of Comparative Law, Comparative Study on Filtering, blocking and take-down of illegal content on the Internet – comparative considerations, *o.c.*, p. 795.

the liability exemptions in the Directive is horizontal in nature. This means that the liability exemptions cover various types of illegal content and activities (copyright infringements, defamation, child sexual abuse material, unfair commercial practices, etc.) and different kinds of liability (criminal, civil, direct, indirect).[1150] Most of the national acts implementing the Directive into their national legal orders copy its text nearly verbatim.[1151] Countries that have introduced additional N&A procedures usually restrict them to a specific type of content (e.g. material encouraging terrorism in the UK or copyright infringements in Finland).[1152] Outside of the EU, countries have generally opted for a vertical approach focusing on one type of illegal content or activity. In the US, for example, the DMCA was enacted specifically for copyright infringements and does not address other types of infringing activities or content, which are covered by Section 230 CDA.

SELECTED NOTICE AND ACTION MECHANISMS – The selection below consists of the currently existing forms of non-judicial response mechanisms to infringing online content. Broadly described as notice and action, these mechanisms result in some type of action in response to a complaint regarding illegal or infringing online content. The selected mechanisms are the most commonly encountered notice and action mechanisms around the world, although they might appear in different versions or in combinations with one another. The selected notice and action mechanisms are the following:

- Notice and take down (NTD)
- Notice and stay down (NSD)
- Notice and notice (including graduated response) (N&N)
- Full immunity

OUTLINE – In the following sections, each notice and action mechanism is first defined in order to clarify its meaning. For each mechanism, one or more examples of national implementations are provided as an illustration (ordered alphabetically). The examples consist of national legislations from around the world that are the most informative, or the most innovative from the perspective of the research question. Since the research question focuses on State's (indirect) role in content regulation the primary factor in the selection of countries was an existence of codified notice and action procedures. It should be noted, however, that this requirement was not followed strictly – some mechanisms operate

1150 See T. Verbiest, Spindler G, et al., Study on the liability of Internet Intermediaries – General trends in Europe, *o.c.*, p. 4.

1151 T. Verbiest, G. Spindler *et al.*, Study on the liability of Internet Intermediaries – General trends in Europe, *o.c.*; P. Van Eecke, M. Truyens, EU Study on the Legal Analysis of A Single Market for the Information Society – New Rules for a New Age?, *o.c.*, p. 34.

1152 Swiss Institute of Comparative Law, Comparative Study on Filtering, blocking and take-down of illegal content on the Internet – comparative considerations, *o.c.*, p. 797.

successfully on the basis of case-law, rather than codified procedures. Another factor that played a role in the selection was a diversity of legal traditions. Therefore, the example countries are not limited to the EU countries but include countries from Asia, North America, and South America.

For each national example, a concise legislative background, or a focused country profile, is provided to set a context for the analysis. First, the applicable legislation is presented introducing the mechanism, then specification is given for which types of content it is used. The detailed procedure of the mechanism is described in the Annex to this book. For each country the most relevant case-law is provided (where available – for some countries there is no case law on the topic).[1153] Next, an assessment is conducted according to the criteria developed in Part II Chapter 4. Finally, for each mechanism, lessons learned from the evaluation are provided.

1153 The national background should not be considered a country report as it is focused solely on a specific element of the national legislation.

CHAPTER 2

ANALYSIS OF DIFFERENT RESPONSE MECHANISMS

1. NOTICE AND TAKE DOWN

1.1. DEFINITION

MAIN CHARACTERISTICS – In this book, the notice and take down (NTD) is defined as a mechanism where an Internet intermediary is called upon by a private entity (individual, company, rights holders organization, etc.) to remove or disable access to information in breach of their rights (or of the law more generally). Removal erases the information from its location, and unless previously copied, eliminates it completely from the free flow of information on the Internet. Blocking solely limits access to the content according to predefined conditions (e.g. location or age).

In multiple jurisdictions around the world, Internet intermediaries can benefit from a liability exemption provided that they react expeditiously to remove or disable access to infringing content upon obtaining knowledge about the illegal character of the impugned information. The provider of a hosting service can obtain knowledge about the illegal character of hosted content in a number of ways. He could find such content through his own activities or he could be notified about the situation by a third party. Notifications could stem either from private entities (classic NTD mechanism) or from public authorities, for example administrative bodies or courts (other forms of N&A). In the former case, public authorities are not involved. Instead, the provider of the hosting service is called upon directly by a private individual to take down the content in question. It is the provider's task to assess whether such a complaint is credible and whether the character of the content is in fact infringing. As a result, the provider must make a decision either to remove the disputed content or to maintain it.

1.2. COUNTRY PROFILES

NATIONAL EXAMPLES – Notice and take down mechanisms can be found in several regulatory instruments at both regional and national level. In the EU, it is implied, but not directly provided, in Article 14 of the E-Commerce Directive 2000/31/EC. The Member States implemented the Directive into their national legislations; however, the Directive provided no guidelines on how the resulting notice and take down should look like. Instead, the Directive leaves the subject matter to the discretion of the Member States.[1154] In Article 16 and recital 40, the Directive encourages self-regulation in this field. The majority of the Member States chose for a verbatim transposition of the Directive, often following the same self-regulatory approach.[1155] Yet, in most of the countries no self-regulatory measures came into existence. Moreover, a significant number of countries have no specific legal framework for content removal and rely on the general rules of law. Only a few countries introduced codified NTD procedures, most notably Finland, France, Hungary, Lithuania, Sweden and partially the UK.[1156] The result is a lack of harmonization on the matter and a lack of firm safeguards in most of the EU countries.[1157] For this reason, the examples of EU notice and take down mechanisms, which are discussed below, are not limited to one country, but rather look at different national laws implementing the E-Commerce Directive which effectively provide additional procedures clarifying the functioning of the NTD mechanism. To complement the picture, examples of NTD mechanism from other legal traditions are provided, specifically from the US and South Korea. The following sections provide a brief delineation of the country profiles, while more detailed information on the applicable laws and procedures are provided in the Annex.

A. *Finland*

LEGISLATION – A general liability exemption for hosting services is provided in Section 184 of the Finnish Information Society Code, which entered into force on 1 January 2015.[1158] There is, however, a notable exception in relation to certain types of manifestly illegal content. The service provider is not liable if it acts expeditiously to disable access to the information upon '*otherwise obtaining*

1154 Recital 46 E-commerce Directive.

1155 T. Verbiest, G. Spindler *et al.*, Study on the Liability of Internet Intermediaries, *o.c.* P. Van Eecke, M. Truyens, EU Study on the Legal Analysis of A Single Market for the Information Society – New Rules for a New Age?, *o.c.*, p. 14–16.

1156 See T. Verbiest, G. Spindler *et al.*, Study on the Liability of Internet Intermediaries, *o.c.* P. Van Eecke, M. Truyens, EU Study on the Legal Analysis of A Single Market for the Information Society – New Rules for a New Age?, *o.c.*; and Swiss Institute of Comparative Law, Comparative Study on Filtering, blocking and take-down of illegal content on the Internet – comparative considerations, *o.c.*, p. 797.

1157 European Commission, Online Services, Including E-commerce in Single Market, Commission Staff Working Paper, *o.c.*

1158 The Finnish Information Society Code (2014/917), which entered into force on 1 January 2015, Tietoyhteiskuntakaari, 7.11.2014/917, available: www.finlex.fi/en/laki/kaannokset/2014/en20140917.pdf, Chapter 22.

actual knowledge of the fact that the stored information is clearly contrary to' legal provisions regarding specified types of content.[1159]

Additionally, Finland implemented a specific NTD procedure aimed at preventing access (which includes both removal and blocking) to material infringing copyright or neighbouring rights, without a court order.[1160] The procedure is provided in Section 189 and further regulated in Section 191 of the Finnish Information Society Code. Other types of content removals and blocking of content in Finland generally require a court order (Section 184 and 185 of the Finnish Information Society Code).

B. *France*

LEGISLATION – In France, the main legislation addressing removal (and blocking) of content is enshrined in Law No. 2004–575 of 21 June 2004 on ensuring confidence in the digital economy (hereinafter the "LCEN").[1161] Apart from the court and administrative removals, LCEN also provides an optional notification procedure in Article 6-I-5. Together with Article 6-I-2 providing conditions for civil liability exemptions for the hosts, and Article 6-I-3 providing similar conditions for criminal liability exemption, the three articles of LCEN constitute the notice and take down procedure.[1162] The French NTD procedure is of general application and can be applied to any type of content violating national law.[1163] When interpreting Article 6-I-2 LCEN, the *Conseil Constitutionnel* declared that hosting providers are only under an obligation to remove notified content when it is: (a) manifestly unlawful; or (b) its removal has been ordered by a court.[1164] If there is no court order (and the content is not manifestly unlawful)

1159 *Ibid.*, Section 184.

1160 *Ibid.*, Chapter 22. See also T. Verbiest, G. Spindler *et al.*, Study on the Liability of Internet Intermediaries, *o.c.*; P. Van Eecke, M. Truyens, EU Study on the Legal Analysis of A Single Market for the Information Society – New Rules for a New Age?, *o.c.*, General Trends in the EU, p. 28.; and Swiss Institute of Comparative Law, Comparative Study on Filtering, blocking and take-down of illegal content on the Internet – Finland country report, 20 December 2015, available at: www.coe.int/en/web/freedom-expression/country-reports, p. 221.

1161 Loi n° 2004–575 du 21 juin 2004 pour la confiance dans l'économie numérique, www.wipo.int/wipolex/en/text.jsp?file_id=276258.

1162 N. van Eijk, C. Jasserand, C. Wiersma and T. M. van Engers, Moving towards Balance: A Study into Duties of Care on the Internet, Institute for Information Law & Leibniz Center for Law, University of Amsterdam, p. 100.

1163 See C. Rubin, Ministère de l'Economie, des Finances et de l'Industrie, Presentation of France concerning national legislative approach to notice and action, EC Expert group on electronic commerce (E01636), 27 April 2017, http://ec.europa.eu/transparency/regexpert/index.cfm?do=groupDetail.groupDetail&groupID=1636; see also Swiss Institute of Comparative Law, Comparative Study on Filtering, blocking and take-down of illegal content on the Internet – France country report, *o.c.*, p. 243.

1164 Conseil Constitutionnel, Décision No 2004–496 DC du 10 juin 2004, Journal officiel du 22 juin 2004, p. 11182.

the hosting providers enjoy a certain margin of appreciation and can decide how to respond to a notification without risking their own liability.[1165]

C. Germany

LEGISLATION – In Germany, the E-Commerce Directive and its safe harbours were implemented into German law through the *Telemediengesetz* (TMG) of 26 February 2007.[1166] The transposition is almost verbatim with some exceptions for providers who work together with a recipient of the service to act illegally.[1167] Until recently, there were no specific legislations about blocking, filtering or taking down of content. The German system relied on general rules of law used to order hosting providers to take down and filter illegal content.[1168]

In 2017, a new law was introduced to help combat fake news and hate speech on social media. The Act to Improve Enforcement of the Law in Social Networks (Network Enforcement Act – Netzdurchführungsgesetz – NetzDG) entered into force on 1 October 2017.[1169] Since the law only recently came into force there is not much information about the application, interpretation or effects it may lead to. Moreover, no case law is available at this point.

D. Hungary

LEGISLATION – In Hungary, the NTD procedure is regulated in Article 13 of Act CVIII of 2001 on certain issues of electronic commerce services and information society services.[1170] The provisions on NTD in the Hungarian Act apply to copyright infringements on any copyrighted work, performance, recording, audiovisual work or database, or of an exclusive right arising from trademark protection under the Act on the Protection of Trademarks and Geographical Indications of Origin (Article 13.1 of the Hungarian Act CVIII). In 2014, the mechanism was extended to cover the personal rights of minors as well.[1171] The

1165 See C. Jasserand, "Régime français de la responsabilité des intermédiaires techniques", *Les Cahiers de la propriété intellectuelle*, Vol. 25, Issue 3, 2013, p. 1135, as referenced by C. Angelopoulos, *European intermediary liability in copyright: A tort-based analysis*, *o.c.*, p. 121.

1166 *Telemediengesetz*, 26 February 2007, BGBl. I S. 179.

1167 C. Angelopoulos, *European intermediary liability in copyright: A tort-based analysis*, *o.c.*, p. 149.

1168 Swiss Institute of Comparative Law, Comparative Study on Filtering, blocking and take-down of illegal content on the Internet – Germany country report, *o.c.*, p. 261.

1169 Gesetz zur Verbesserung der Rechtsdurchsetzung in sozialen Netzwerken [Netzdurchführungsgesetz – NetzDG], Drucksache 536/17, 30 June 2017. See German Federal Ministry of Justice and Consumer Protection, unofficial translation, https://www.bmjv.de/SharedDocs/Gesetzgebungsverfahren/Dokumente/NetzDG_engl.pdf.

1170 Act CVIII of 2001 on certain issues of electronic commerce services and information society services, Promulgated: 24 December, 2001, available at: www.neuronit.com/documents/108_2001_el_comm_torv_20070502.pdf.

1171 See Swiss Institute of Comparative Law, Comparative Study on Filtering, blocking and take-down of illegal content on the Internet – Hungary country report, *o.c.*, p. 310.

change was introduced as the government made it a priority to ensure the protection of personality rights of minors and to eliminate cyber bullying in particular.[1172]

E. South Korea

LEGISLATION – South Korea has taken a "vertical" approach to intermediaries' liability. Multiple laws, provisions and procedures regulate issues of copyright, telecommunications, protection of children and juveniles as well as matters related to election.[1173] NTD mechanisms can be found in the Copyright Act, and in the Information and Communications Network Act (ICNA).[1174] The Korean intermediary liability regime foresees, effectively, two NTD procedures, for copyright infringements (Article 103 of the Copyright Act) and for other types of content that infringes the rights of others (privacy infringements, defamation, and others – Article 44-2 ICNA). In 2009, the Copyright Act introduced the graduated response (three strikes) in Articles 133-2 and 133-3 (see Chapter 2.2 notice and notice section). The procedure provided in ICNA, also has two variations, where take-downs are requested either by the victims of the infringements or by the Korea Communications Commission.

F. United Kingdom

LEGISLATION – The general liability exemptions for Internet intermediaries are included in the Electronic Commerce Regulations 2002, which transposes the E-Commerce Directive into the UK law.[1175] There is no legislation specifically regulating the removal, blocking or filtering of infringing online content. However, some specific provisions addressing content removal have been included in Acts of Parliament and secondary legislation addressing copyright, defamation and terrorist activities.[1176] Two separate statutory NTD procedures

---

1172 See G. Csiszér, Ministry of National Development, Presentation of Hungary concerning national legislative approach to notice and action, EC Expert group on electronic commerce (E01636), 27 April 2017, http://ec.europa.eu/transparency/regexpert/index.cfm?do=groupDetail.groupDetail&groupID=1636.

1173 See Annex.

1174 Copyright Act, Amended by Act No. 9625, Apr. 22, 2009; Act No. 10807, Jun. 30, 2011; Act No. 11110, 2 Dec. 2011 http://elaw.klri.re.kr/kor_service/lawView.do?hseq=25455&lang=ENG; Act on Promotion of Information and Communications Network Utilization and Information Protection, etc. (ICNA, Information and Communications Network Act), last amended by Act No. 11322, February 17, 2012. See: http://elaw.klri.re.kr/kor_service/lawView.do?hseq=25446&lang=ENG.

1175 Electronic Commerce (EC Directive) Regulations 2002 (Statutory Instrument 2013/2002), available at www.legislation.gov.uk/uksi/2002/2013/contents/made

1176 Swiss Institute of Comparative Law, Comparative Study on Filtering, blocking and take-down of illegal content on the Internet – United Kingdom country report, *o.c.*, p. 753.

exist targeting specific types of content: offences under the Terrorism Act 2006[1177] and offences under the Defamation Act 2013.[1178]

Additionally in the UK, a special arrangement exists that is targeted at child abuse content. It is administered through a partnership between the ISPs and an industry regulatory body known as the Internet Watch Foundation (IWF).[1179] The IWF is a regulatory body with broad membership from the Internet Industry, including ISPs, mobile operators, search engines, content providers, and filtering companies.[1180] The IWF operates on the basis of a memorandum of understanding between the Association of Chief Police Officers and the Crown Prosecution Service.[1181] The IWF's remit is to remove or block child sexual abuse content.

G. *United States*

LEGISLATION – In the US Section 202 of the Digital Millennium Copyright Act (codified at 17 U.S.C. §512) (hereafter: 'DMCA') provides a NTD procedure.[1182] The procedure in the DMCA is aimed solely at copyright infringing content.[1183] The DMCA describes the procedure for removal of copyright infringing information in detail.

1.3. ASSESSMENT

A. *Quality of law*

ACCESSIBILITY – In the EU, providing more detailed regulation is optional for the Member States. Several countries opted for the opportunity provided by Article 14.3 of the E-Commerce Directive to introduce more detailed measures for removal of online content and codify them. For example, such specific laws are provided in Finland in the Information Society Code[1184], in France

1177 Terrorism Act 2006, available at www.legislation.gov.uk/ukpga/2006/11/contents.

1178 Defamation Act 2013, available at www.legislation.gov.uk/ukpga/2013/26/contents/enacted.

1179 See Internet Watch Foundation, https://www.iwf.org.uk/. See also Swiss Institute of Comparative Law, Comparative Study on Filtering, blocking and take-down of illegal content on the Internet – United Kingdom country report, *o.c.*, p. 754.

1180 See https://www.iwf.org.uk/what-we-do/why-we-exist/our-history; and E. B. Laidlaw, "The responsibilities of free speech regulators: an analysis of the Internet Watch Foundation", *International Journal of Law and Information Technology*, Vol. 20, No. 4, 2012, pp. 312 – 345, p. 315.

1181 Memorandum of Understanding Between Crown Prosecution Service (CPS) and the Association of Chief Police Officers (ACPO) concerning Section 46 Sexual Offences Act 2003, https://www.iwf.org.uk/sites/default/files/inline-files/CPS%20ACPO%20S46%20MoU%20 2014%202.pdf

1182 Section 202 of the Digital Millennium Copyright Act (codified at 17 U.S.C. §512), available: https://www.law.cornell.edu/uscode/text/17/512

1183 *Ibid.*

1184 The Finnish Information Society Code (2014/917), *o.c.*, Chapter 22

in the LCEN Law No. 2004-575 of 21 June 2004 on ensuring confidence in the digital economy[1185], and in Hungary in Act CVIII of 2001 on certain issues of electronic commerce services and information society services.[1186] In Germany the new Network Enforcement Act regarding the removal and blocking of hate speech (and indirectly "fake news") does not establish procedures, but specifies requirements for the procedures provided by the social media networks.[1187] In South Korea, one NTD procedure is provided in the Copyright Act[1188] and another one, for types of content infringing rights other than copyright, in the Information and Communications Network Act (ICNA).[1189] In the US the rules on the NTD mechanism are also provided by law – the Digital Millennium Copyright Act (the DMCA). Often, the specific rules address only one type of illegal or infringing content and activity, leaving removals of other types of infringements unaddressed.

There is also the example of the IWF in the UK. The IWF operates on the basis of a memorandum of understanding between the Association of Chief Police Officers and the Crown Prosecution Service.[1190] It is not a government body nor a law enforcement agency but a registered charity. The notice and take down procedure operated by the IWF is only described in the Code of Practice, directed to the members. The Code does not require for site owners to be notified that their sites have been blocked.[1191] Other than the Code, there is no legislative underpinning regulating the procedure.[1192] Moreover, the IWF is not subject to any kind of parliamentary or judicial oversight.[1193] This means that there are no safeguards in law to protect against arbitrary interference by the organization.[1194] Together with a lack of transparency, this results in the IWF's operations being conducted largely in secret with minimal oversight.[1195] As pointed out by the Open Rights Group, *'the legality of the materials added*

1185 Loi n° 2004-575 du 21 juin 2004 pour la confiance dans l'économie numérique, *o.c.*

1186 Act CVIII of 2001 on certain issues of electronic commerce services and information society services, *oc.*

1187 Gesetz zur Verbesserung der Rechtsdurchsetzung in sozialen Netzwerken [NetzDG], *o.c.*

1188 Copyright Act, *o.c.*

1189 Act on Promotion of Information and Communications Network Utilization and Information Protection, etc. (ICNA), *o.c.*

1190 See Internet Watch Foundation, *o.c.* See also Swiss Institute of Comparative Law, Comparative Study on Filtering, blocking and take-down of illegal content on the Internet – United Kingdom country report, *o.c.*, p. 754.

1191 TJ McIntyre and C Scott, "Internet Filtering: Rhetoric, Legitimacy, Accountability and Responsibility'" in R Brownsword and K Yeung (eds), *Regulating Technologies: Legal Future, Regulatory Frames and Technological Fixes*, Hart Publishing 2008, pp. 109 – 124, p. 121.

1192 *Ibid.*, p. 122.

1193 Open Rights Group web pages, Internet Watch Foundation, available at https://wiki. openrightsgroup. org/wiki/Internet_Watch_Foundation.

1194 See E. B. Laidlaw, "The responsibilities of free speech regulators: an analysis of the Internet Watch Foundation", *o.c.*, p. 327.

1195 See *Ibid.*, p. 328. See also L. Edwards, "From Child Porn to China, in one Cleanfeed" *Script-ed, Vol.* 3, Issue 3, 2006, p.174, 175; and J. Riordan, "Website Blocking Injunctions under United

to the IWF's blacklist has never been assessed by a court or other qualified and accountable legal body, and there is nothing stopping legal material being included on the list, neither inadvertently nor deliberately'.[1196] Since the IWF's powers to censor have no basis in law, it could be questioned whether their interference with expression should be considered as prescribed by law.[1197] There is no doubt that by protecting children from abuse the IWF serves a number of legitimate aims such as the prevention of crime, the protection of reputation and the protection of health or morals or public safety.[1198] Even though the IWF is not, strictly speaking, a public authority, it may qualify as such by virtue of its public functions.[1199] The Crown Prosecution Service agreed not to prosecute the IWF, for intentionally accessing and viewing child abuse content as this is done for legitimate purposes.[1200] It is clear, therefore, that its legitimacy and role is government driven.[1201] According to the IWF Human Rights Audit, '*it is highly likely that IWF's acts would be construed by the Courts as public acts, so that its policies and decision-making are in reality susceptible to judicial review, and may be overturned by the Courts were it ever to be found that the IWF was exercising them in a manner incompatible with human rights law*'.[1202]

FORESEEABILITY – The rules providing liability exemptions for intermediaries continue to present difficulties with interpretation. Most of the issues, however, concern their application, especially when it comes to new types of online services, rather than procedural aspects. Moreover, the same online services have on several occasions been granted protection in one Member State but denied it in another.[1203] Qualification as an intermediary was the problem with the Hungarian *MTE and Index.hu case* and multiple French cases, such as *Lafesse v.*

Kingdom and European Law", in in G. B. Dinwoodie, *Secondary Liability of Internet Service Providers*, Ius Comparatum – Global Studies in Comparative Law, Springer, 2018, p. 298.

1196 Open Rights Group web pages, Internet Watch Foundation, *o.c.*

1197 See Swiss Institute of Comparative Law, Comparative Study on Filtering, blocking and take-down of illegal content on the Internet – UK report, *o.c.*, p. 776.

1198 E. B. Laidlaw, "The responsibilities of free speech regulators: an analysis of the Internet Watch Foundation", *o.c.*, p. 327.

1199 See Swiss Institute of Comparative Law, Comparative Study on Filtering, blocking and take-down of illegal content on the Internet – UK report, *o.c.*, p. 776.

1200 Open Rights Group web pages, Internet Watch Foundation, *o.c.*

1201 E. B. Laidlaw, "The responsibilities of free speech regulators: an analysis of the Internet Watch Foundation", *o.c.*, p. 324.

1202 IWF, A Human Rights Audit of the Internet Watch Foundation, by Lord MacDonald of River Glaven QC, 2014, https://www.iwf.org.uk/sites/default/files/inline-files/Human_Rights_Audit_web.pdf, p. 5.

1203 For example eBay was able to benefit from Article 14 of the e-Commerce Directive in Belgium but no in France. See *Lancôme Parfums & Beauté & Cie v eBay International AG, eBay Europe SARL, eBay Belgium*, Bruxelles, 7th chamber, n° A/07/06032, 31 July 2008; and *Parfums Christian Dior and others v eBay Inc., eBay International AB AG*, Paris, 1st chamber, B, 30 June 2008; See S. Stalla-Bourdillon, "Internet Intermediaries as Responsible Actors? Why It Is Time to Rethink the e-Commerce Directive as Well…", *o.c.*, ft. 33 and 34.

MySpace[1204], *Tiscali v Lucky Comics*[1205], or *Louis Vuitton Malletier c. Google.*[1206, 1207] The problem with interpreting the provisions of the E-Commerce Directive, and therefore the national rules implementing the act, was taken up but not entirely clarified by the CJEU in two cases, *Google France*[1208] and *L'Oréal v. eBay.*[1209, 1210] The former established that to qualify for a liability exemption a hosting service provider must be '*merely technical, automatic and passive*' in nature.[1211] The latter seemingly reduced the standard by replacing the "neutrality" requirement with "lack of knowledge". The CJEU ruled that Article 14 of the Directive applies to hosting providers if they do not play an active role that would allow them to have knowledge or control of the stored data.[1212] To this day, the differentiation between active and passive hosts, and applicability of the liability exemption to the latter, remains unclear. The problem basically boils down to the question of how much involvement in content moderation is too much to maintain that hosting provider is still passive. This is particularly problematic as the EU makes moves to "encourage" the online intermediaries to take more pro-active steps to moderate the content that they host.[1213]

The US case law has dealt with this problem in *Universal Music Group v. Shelter Capital Partners*[1214] in the Ninth Circuit and *Viacom International, Inc. v. YouTube, Inc.*[1215] in the Second Circuit. In both cases, plaintiffs argued for an interpretation of Section 512(c) safe harbour that would limit the protection to passive hosts (e.g. cyberlockers), while leaving active hosts (e.g., video-sharing services like YouTube and Vimeo) unprotected by the DMCA.[1216] The US courts

1204 *Jean Yves L. dit Lafesse c. Myspace,* Tribunal de Grande Instance de Paris, Ordonnance de référé 22 juin 2007.

1205 *Tiscali Media c. Dargaud Lombard, Lucky Comics,* Cour d'appel de Paris, 7 June 2006.

1206 *Louis Vuitton Malletier c. Google,* Tribunal de Grande Instance de Paris, 4 February 2005 and Cour d'appel de Paris, 28 June 2006.

1207 See also S. Stalla-Bourdillonm, "Sometimes one is not enough!" *o.c.*, ft. 36.

1208 CJEU, *Google France Inc.* v. *LouisVuitton Malletier e.a.*, Joined Cases C-236, 237 & 238/08, 23 March 2010.

1209 CJEU, *L'Oreal SA v. eBay,* Case C324/09, 12 July 2011.

1210 See more in S. Stalla-Bourdillonm, "Sometimes one is not enough!" *o.c.*; and Opinion of Advocate General Poires Maduro delivered on 22 September 2009, *Google France Inc.* v. *LouisVuitton Malletier e.a.* in Joined Cases C-236, 237 & 238/08.

1211 CJEU, *Google France Inc.* v. *LouisVuitton Malletier e.a.*, Joined Cases C-236, 237 & 238/08, 23 March 2010, paras. 113–114.

1212 CJEU, *L'Oreal SA v. eBay,* Case C324/09, 12 July 2011, paras. 112–116.

1213 See more in European Commission, Communication on Tackling Illegal Content Online, Towards an enhanced responsibility of online platforms, *o.c.* In the Communication the EC attempts to '*provide clarifications to platforms on their liability when they take proactive steps to detect, remove or disable access to illegal content (the so-called "Good Samaritan" actions)*', p. 3. See more in Part I Chapter 6.

1214 *Universal Music Group v. Shelter Capital Partners, 718 F.3d 1006 (9th Cir. 2013).*

1215 *Viacom International, Inc. v. YouTube, Inc., 676 F.3d 19 (2d Cir. 2012).*

1216 A. Bridy, D. Keller, U.S. Copyright Office Section 512 Study: Comments in Response to Notice of Inquiry, 31 March 2016, p. 6. See also *UMG Recordings, Inc. v. Shelter Capital Partners LLC,* 718 F.3d 1006, 1015–16 (9th Cir. 2013).

have unequivocally rejected this reasoning, basing their opinion on statutory text, architecture, and public policy.[1217]

Specific NTD regimes, if present, clarify the measures which a host may take out of its own power and the measures which it may only take after a court order or order by an administrative authority.[1218] The laws providing the NTD procedures describe the order of events in detail, which starts with the notification to the service provider (for example in the Hungarian or US procedure). Moreover, they specify the timeframes for different actions in the procedure and the formal requirements for a valid notice. In particular, rules regulating the latter are relevant because the validity of notice often determines the existence of actual knowledge.[1219] This has been recognized by the example countries that all took steps to explicitly list the requirements for a valid notice. This approach is consistent with the CJEU ruling in *L'Oreal SA v. eBay*, which stated that notification should be sufficiently precise and adequately substantiated.[1220]

There is also the case of the new German law targeting hate speech, the Network Enforcement Act. It was announced to the European Commission in March 2017 and it entered into force on 1 October 2017.[1221] The Act has been criticized from the start by academics and civil societies pointing out its potential non-compliance with the E-Commerce Directive.[1222] Specifically, the commentators observed that the Act does not differentiate between domestic and EU companies, which creates a conflict with the "country of origin" principle.[1223] This principle provides that '*Member States may not, for reasons falling within the coordinated field, restrict the freedom to provide information society services*

1217 *Viacom Int'l, Inc. v. YouTube, Inc.*, 676 F.3d 19, 39 (2d Cir. 2012) (holding that it 'would eviscerate the protection afforded to service providers by §512(c)" to exclude YouTube's transcoding, playback, and 'related video' functions, given that the functions are "performed for the purpose of facilitating access to user-stored material'). A. Bridy, D. Keller, U.S. Copyright Office Section 512 Study: Comments in Response to Notice of Inquiry, *o.c.*, p. 6.

1218 Swiss Institute of Comparative Law, Comparative Study on Filtering, blocking and take-down of illegal content on the Internet – comparative considerations, *o.c.*, p. 798.

1219 T. Verbiest, G. Spindler *et al.*, Study on the Liability of Internet Intermediaries, *o.c.*; P. Van Eecke, M. Truyens, EU Study on the Legal Analysis of A Single Market for the Information Society – New Rules for a New Age?, *o.c.*, p. 14 and 41.

1220 CJEU, *L'Oreal SA v. eBay*, Case C324/09, 12 July 2011, para. 122.

1221 See Notification to the European Commission, Number 2017/0127/D – SERV60, Act improving law enforcement on social networks [NetzDG], http://ec.europa.eu/growth/tools-databases/tris/en/search/?trisaction=search.detail&year=2017&num=127.

1222 See G. Spindler, "Internet Intermediary Liability Reloaded – The New German Act on Responsibility of Social Networks and its (In-) Compatibility with European Law", *JIPITEC*, Vol. 8, 2017, p. 166; J. McNamee, German Social Media law – sharp criticism from leading legal expert, 19 April 2017, https://edri.org/german-social-media-law-sharp-criticism-from-leading-legal-expert/; and Article 19, Germany: Act to Improve Enforcement of the Law on Social Networks – Legal Analysis, August 2017, https://www.article19.org/data/files/medialibrary/38860/170901-Legal-Analysis-German-NetzDG-Act.pdf.

1223 EDRI, Recommendations on the German bill "Improving Law Enforcement on Social Networks" (NetzDG), 20 June 2017, https://edri.org/files/consultations/tris_netzdg_edricontribution_20170620.pdf, p. 7; see also G. Spindler, "Internet Intermediary Liability Reloaded – The New German Act on Responsibility of Social Networks and its (In-) Compatibility with European Law", *o.c.*, p. 167–170.

from another Member State'.[1224] The Act raises concerns, moreover, about its compatibility with the Article 14 of the E-Commerce Directive.[1225] This is because the Act calculates the period for removal starting with the reception of the complaint and not from the moment of obtaining the actual knowledge.[1226] At the moment, it is too soon to assess the impact and legal consequences of the Act. However, a possible conflict with the Directive creates a serious problem for the foreseeability and legal certainty of the Act.

B. *Protection of democratic society*

DEMOCRATIC VALUES – National rules describing the NTD procedure differ widely when it comes to specifying which rights and interests are worthy of such particular protection as to justify interference with the right to freedom of expression. For example, the Finnish NTD procedure described in the Information Society Code applies specifically to the content infringing copyright or neighbouring rights.[1227] Similarly, the NTD procedure in the U.S. DMCA is aimed solely at copyright infringing content.[1228] The provisions on the NTD in the Hungarian Act apply to the copyright infringements[1229] but in 2014 it was extended to additionally cover the personal rights of minors.[1230] In the UK, which generally opted for a self-regulatory model, two instances of statutory NTD exist, one addressing content encouraging terrorism and one dealing with defamatory content.[1231] Moreover, there is a NTD procedure operated by the IWF for child sexual abuse content and criminally obscene adult content.[1232] South Korea foresees two separate NTD procedures, one of them specifically applicable for copyright infringements.[1233]

1224 Art. 3.2 of the E-commerce Directive, 2000/31/EC.

1225 G. Spindler, "Internet Intermediary Liability Reloaded – The New German Act on Responsibility of Social Networks and its (In-) Compatibility with European Law", 8 (2017) JIPITEC 166, p. 170.

1226 *Ibid.*, p. 171.

1227 The Finnish Information Society Code (2014/917), *o.c.*, Chapter 22.

1228 Section 202 of the Digital Millennium Copyright Act, *o.c.*

1229 Article 13.1 of the Hungarian Act CVIII of 2001 on certain issues of electronic commerce services and information society services, *o.c.*

1230 See Swiss Institute of Comparative Law, Comparative Study on Filtering, blocking and take-down of illegal content on the Internet– Hungary country report, *o.c.*, p. 310.

1231 Section 3 of the UK Terrorism Act 2006, *o.c;* and Section 13 of the Defamation Act 2013, *o.c.*. In the case of content encouraging terrorism the notification is sent to an agency (the Counter Terrorism Internet Referral Unit – CTIRU) which verifies them and if necessary, notifies the service providers. In case of defamatory content, successful claimants can request a removal order from the court (an "order to remove statement or cease distribution"). Both instances, therefore, are not, strictly speaking, non-judicial NTD procedures. They do, nevertheless, define explicitly the rights and values they aim to protect.

1232 See more: IWF, The laws and assessment levels, https://www.iwf.org.uk/what-we-do/how-we-assess-and-remove-content/laws-and-assessment-levels.

1233 Copyright Act, *o.c.*

The rights and values that different countries choose to protect through the NTD procedure generally do fit within the list of grounds for restrictions in Article 10.2 ECHR. The right to protection of one's intellectual property, as well as the personal rights of minors and protection against defamation, fall under the broad category of the "reputation or rights of others". Content related to terrorist activities is removed in the interests of national security, territorial integrity or public safety, and for the prevention of disorder or crime. Protection of children from abuse qualifies as the prevention of crime, the protection of reputation and the protection of health or morals or public safety.

Not all the countries, however, specify in detail the values they wish to protect through the available procedures. The NTD procedure implemented in France does not contain such a delineation. The removal can be requested with regard to any content in violation with the national law.[1234] The French NTD procedure requires the providers to remove the content that is manifestly unlawful. Also, the second NTD procedure available in South Korea is broader in scope, applying to privacy infringing content, defamatory content, or content otherwise violating rights of others.[1235]

MANIFEST ILLEGALITY – Some countries specifically distinguish situations when the online content is of a particular nature. Usually, this refers to hate speech and child sexual abuse material, sometimes also incitement to violence and Holocaust denial. The specified type of content, however, should be clearly recognizable as such, or as is sometimes described, "manifestly illegal". The illegality should be easily assessed, even by laymen and non-lawyers.[1236] In case of such types of illegal content, some countries raise the bar for liability exemption for intermediaries and require them to remove such content on their own initiative after obtaining knowledge of its existence.[1237]

In Finland, for example, hosting providers are obliged to act based upon their knowledge when the content in question consists of hate speech, or pictures with child pornography, sexual violence or intercourse with an animal.[1238] The content must be "clearly contrary" to the Criminal Code's provisions on this type of content.[1239] This condition was based on the principle of legality in criminal

---

1234 See Swiss Institute of Comparative Law, Comparative Study on Filtering, blocking and take-down of illegal content on the Internet – France country report, *o.c.*, p. 244.

1235 Act on Promotion of Information and Communications Network Utilization and Information Protection, etc. (ICNA), *o.c.*

1236 T. Verbiest, G. Spindler *et al.*, Study on the Liability of Internet Intermediaries, *o.c.*; P. Van Eecke, M. Truyens, EU Study on the Legal Analysis of A Single Market for the Information Society – New Rules for a New Age?, *o.c*, p. 17.

1237 See T. Verbiest, G. Spindler *et al.*, Study on the Liability of Internet Intermediaries, *o.c.*; P. Van Eecke, M. Truyens, EU Study on the Legal Analysis of A Single Market for the Information Society – New Rules for a New Age?", *o.c.*, p. 36 and 37 – 41.

1238 Section 184 of the Finnish Information Society Code, *o.c.*

1239 The Constitutional Committee of the Parliament (report 60/2001), as referred by Swiss Institute of Comparative Law, Comparative Study on Filtering, blocking and take-down of

procedure and the presumption of innocence until proven guilty.[1240] The provision is considered to be complaint with the CJEU's standard of a diligent economic operator (CJEU, *L'Oreal v eBay*) used to determine when illegality should have become apparent for the hosting service.[1241]

In France, hosting providers are only required to remove content once they obtain actual knowledge of its illegal character. This means that without a court order, they are not obliged to disable access to unlawful content unless it is of manifestly unlawful nature. As a result, the hosting service will not be punished for failing to remove content which was not obviously unlawful.[1242] Child sexual abuse material, incitement to racial hatred or condoning crimes against humanity are considered to be manifestly unlawful, but the same qualification can also extend to other categories, such as defamation, and possibly content inciting or condoning terrorism. The provisions on liability of hosting service providers, according to the Constitutional Council,

> 'should not have the effect of incurring the liability of a hosting service that has not removed information notified as being unlawful by a third party if such information is not manifestly unlawful or if its removal has not been ordered by a court.'[1243]

In Germany, the new Act on Network Enforcement requires social media networks with over 2 million users in Germany to remove manifestly unlawful content within 24 hours of receiving the complaint (Section 3(2)2 NetzDG). The German legislator, however, did not give any indication on how to recognise manifestly unlawful content.[1244] It is also not clear how to differentiate between manifest and not manifest unlawful content, for which the removal period is 7 days.[1245] It could lead to a situation where social media networks will argue that content is not manifestly unlawful, or they will treat all content under complaint as manifestly unlawful to avoid a fine.[1246] According to civil societies, both situations create a risk of over-compliance and arbitrary censorship.[1247]

---

illegal content on the Internet – Finland country report, *o.c.*, p. 222.

1240 Swiss Institute of Comparative Law, Comparative Study on Filtering, blocking and take-down of illegal content on the Internet – Finland country report, *o.c.*, p. 222.

1241 *Ibid.*, p. 220.

1242 Swiss Institute of Comparative Law, Comparative Study on Filtering, blocking and take-down of illegal content on the Internet – France country report, *o.c.*, p. 243.

1243 Constitutional Council, 10 June 2004, No. 2004–496 DC, available (in French only) on www.conseil-constitutionnel.fr as referenced by Swiss Institute of Comparative Law, Comparative Study on Filtering, blocking and take-down of illegal content on the Internet – France country report, *o.c.*, p. 243.

1244 EDRI, Recommendations on the German bill "Improving Law Enforcement on Social Networks" (NetzDG), *o.c.*, p. 5.

1245 Article 19, Germany: Act to Improve Enforcement of the Law on Social Networks – Legal Analysis, *o.c.*, p. 19.

1246 EDRI, Recommendations on the German bill "Improving Law Enforcement on Social Networks" (NetzDG) *o.c.*, p. 6.

1247 *Ibid.*, p. 6.

C. *Tailored response*

LEAST RESTRICTIVE MEANS – National legislatures strive to limit excessive content removal mainly through two measures. Some of them describe in their national NTD procedures the order in which the providers of different intermediary services are called into action. The "chain of responsibility" usually starts with removal requests addressed to hosting service providers before moving on to access service providers who can solely filter and block at the network level. Moreover, many national rules on content removal require that the notice filed to the hosting service provider by a private entity includes a confirmation that they had tried, unsuccessfully, to request a removal from the content provider (e.g. publisher or author of the infringement). By introducing such elements of subsidiarity, legislatures try to avoid escalating the conflict and unnecessarily involving the intermediaries.

In the Finnish NTD procedure, a request must first be submitted to the content provider of the impugned material. If the content provider could not be identified or they did not remove the material or prevent access to it, the request may be submitted to the hosting provider by notification (Section 191 of the Finnish Information Society Code). The French LCEN similarly requires a copy of a request for removal (or modification of the content) sent to the author or editor to be filed with a notice. In case it was impossible to contact the author or editor, evidence supporting that claim should be attached (Article 6-I-5 LCEN).

In Hungary, another form of tailored response exists. It is, however, reserved for judicial mechanisms. The Criminal Proceedings Act (CPA) in Article 158/B. (4) foresees a possibility of 'rendering electronic data temporarily inaccessible'.[1248] The measure is aimed at criminal proceedings that have been instigated to combat specific types of crimes.[1249] The measure actually consists of two steps, in a graduated system of response: (1) the temporary removal of electronic data (directed to the web hosting providers), and (2) the temporary prevention of access to electronic data (directed to ISPs). If the hosting provider fails to comply with the order for temporary removal (or where a letter rogatory by a foreign government

---

1248 Act. XIX of 1998 on Criminal Proceedings Act (hereinafter: CPA) 158/B-158/D and 596/A. regulates 'Rendering electronic data temporarily inaccessible' and 'the temporary removal of electronic data' as a subcategory of the former, as referenced by Swiss Institute of Comparative Law, Comparative Study on Filtering, blocking and take-down of illegal content on the Internet – Hungary country report, *o.c.*, p. 303.

1249 That is: Drug Trafficking (Art. 176–177 of the CC), Inciting Substance Abuse (Art. 181. of the CC), Aiding in the Manufacture or Production of Narcotic Drugs (Art. 182 of the CC), Criminal Offenses with Drug Precursors (Art. 183 of the CC), Illegal Possession of New Psychoactive Substances (Art. 184–184/A. of the CC), Child Pornography (Art. 204 of the CC), Criminal Acts Against the State (Chapter XXIV of the CC), Terrorist Act (Art. 314–316 of the CC), Terrorist Financing (Art. 318 of the CC), and the electronic data are connected to these forms of criminality. See Swiss Institute of Comparative Law, Comparative Study on Filtering, blocking and take-down of illegal content on the Internet – Hungary country report, *o.c.*, p. 304.

agency seeking the temporary removal fails to achieve its intended purpose within a period of thirty days), the court can issue an order to ISPs to temporarily disable access to that electronic data.[1250] Both measures can further develop into permanent removal or inaccessibility, if the reason for the measure continues to exist. A possibility to issue an order to render electronic data irreversibly inaccessible is regulated under Article 77 of the Criminal Code (CC).[1251]

D. *Procedural fairness*

DUE PROCESS – The right to due process instructs States how to design their judicial system. It must be complied with in legal proceedings when decisions about content removals are taken by courts. In case of NTD procedures, however, when decisions about removals are left to private intermediaries, there is a strong contextual difference. Because the procedural provisions of both the ECHR and CFEU are directed to States, there is no legal justification to require full compliance with all due process requirements by intermediaries. Nevertheless, the introduction of due process elements in the NTD procedure is generally considered desirable and highly beneficial as it advances the principles of proportionality and fair balance as well as legitimacy of the procedure. When intermediaries are allowed (and requested) to interfere with the right to freedom of expression, the existence of (at least some level of) due process can help reduce the risk of excessive interference with the right to freedom of expression.

One way to introduce elements of due process into the NTD procedures is by requiring notification to the content provider. Such a notification informs content providers that there has been a complaint made about their content. Depending on the procedure, the role of the notification may be limited to informing the content providers that their content is about to be removed or already has been removed (or made inaccessible), but it might go further and allow them to respond with a defence of the use of the content. Such counter-notification introduces elements of fair hearing, but also elements of equality of arms and of adversarial proceedings as it allows all the involved parties to have knowledge of and comment on the evidence and the observations made by the other party. The notification and the possibility to respond, moreover, enable the content provider to present his or her case without (substantial) disadvantage vis-à-vis the opponent. In theory, counter-notification might come into play before or after the hosting provider takes action. In the former case, the response of the content provider would, ideally, be taken into account by the hosting provider when deciding whether or not to remove the impugned content. It

---

[1250] Swiss Institute of Comparative Law, Comparative Study on Filtering, blocking and take-down of illegal content on the Internet – Hungary country report, *o.c.*, p. 304.

[1251] Act C of 2012 on Criminal Code (CC) Art 63. (1) g) lists and Art 77 regulates 'irreversibly rendering electronic communication inaccessible'.

seems, however, that most of the existing NTD legislations require the content first to be removed (or made inaccessible) before allowing the content provider to defend his or her position.

This is the case, for example, in the NTD procedures in Finland, Hungary and the US, where notification of the content provider takes place after the removal (or blocking of access). The response times are specified. The main difference is whether the counter-notification is delivered to the service provider, who consecutively forwards it to the original notice provider (Hungary, the US), or it is delivered directly to the notice provider while the service provider receives a copy (Finland). South Korea foresees notification to the content providers for both types of the NTD, but counter-notification and restoration of content is only possible in the copyright NTD, not in the ICNA NTD. Interestingly, if the procedure is initiated by the Korea Communications Commission, intermediaries and users may not have an opportunity to object or to defend their position on the matter. The KCC may forego this element of the procedure, for example, if the matter is urgent for public safety or if there is a reason to believe that it is "evidently unnecessary" to hear an opinion (Article 44-7 (4) ICNA).

The Finnish procedure provides a further element of fair hearing, equality of arms and adversarial proceedings that is rarely found in NTD procedures. According to the Information Society Code, the notification must be made in the mother tongue of the content provider, in Finnish or in Swedish (the two official languages). But additionally the notification may also be made in another language agreed with the content provider (Section 187 of the Finnish Information Society Code).

Another interesting element can be found in the US NTD procedure, that is, a possibility of a punishment for misrepresentations of facts in the notification and in the counter-notification. According to Section 512(f) DMCA,

> 'any person who knowingly materially misrepresents that material or activity is infringing, or that material or activity was removed or disabled by mistake or misidentification, shall be liable for any damages, including costs and attorneys' fees, incurred by the alleged infringer, by any copyright owner or copyright owner's authorized licensee, or by a service provider'.[1252]

These penalties apply only when the misrepresentation is material and knowing.[1253] A statement about accuracy of the information and the notifying party's good faith must be included in both the notification and counter-notification. There is, however, a major difference between statements required

1252 Section 512(f) DMCA.

1253 See A. Holland et al., Online Intermediaries Case Studies Series: Intermediary Liability in the United States, *o.c.*, p. 13.

for a notification and a counter-notification. The former must contain a statement that the complaining party has a good faith belief that use of the material is not authorized and, under penalty of perjury, that the complaining party is authorized to act on behalf of the owner of an exclusive right that is allegedly infringed.[1254] The latter must contain a statement under penalty of perjury that the subscriber has a good faith belief that the material was removed or disabled as a result of mistake or misidentification.[1255] The chosen wording suggests that the counter-notification procedure is biased against the content provider.[1256] Moreover, '*the risk involved with filing a counter-notification is made to appear greater than the risk of initial posting*'.[1257] This is because the penalty of perjury refers to different elements, which discourages private individuals from exercising their right to appeal the initial take down.

Research on the DMCA NTD showed that counter-notice is rarely used in practice.[1258] This is because such counter-notification is considered an added cost, which individuals are not willing to take when exercising their right to speech.[1259] What is even more disconcerting, is that users are too afraid to file counter-notifications because of threat of a lawsuit that could follow.[1260] According to Bridy and Keller, the counter notice process is intimidating.[1261] Specifically, they argue that the process '*is likely to be far more intimidating to individual users responding without benefit of counsel. And the cost of error for a user if she is mistaken about her copyright defenses is much higher than the cost of error for a copyright owner who is mistaken about her claims*'.[1262]

Despite the intention, Section 512(f) DMCA does not actually provide sufficient protection from bogus claims.[1263] Complaints against notification senders under Section 512(f) are rarely successful and often considered futile.[1264]

1254 Section 512(c)(3)(A)(v)(vi) DMCA.

1255 Section 512(g)(3)(C) DMCA.

1256 W. Seltzer, "Free Speech Unmoored in Copyright's Safe Harbor: Chilling Effects of the DMCA on the First Amendment", *o.c.*, p. 191.

1257 *Ibid.*

1258 J. Urban, J. Karaganis, and B. L. Schofield, "Notice and Takedown in Everyday Practice", *o.c.*, p. 42; J. Urban and L. Quilter, "Efficient Processes or Chilling Effects?" *o.c.*, p. 679.

1259 See more in: W. Seltzer, "The Politics of Internet Control and Delegated Censorship", *o.c.*; Seltzer W., "Free Speech Unmoored in Copyright's Safe Harbor: Chilling Effects of the DMCA on the First Amendment", *o.c.*

1260 See J. Urban, J. Karaganis, and B. L. Schofield, Notice and Takedown in Everyday Practice, *o.c.*, p. 45.

1261 A. Bridy, D. Keller, U.S. Copyright Office Section 512 Study: Comments in Response to Notice of Inquiry, *o.c.*, p. 29.

1262 *Ibid.*

1263 See W. Seltzer, "Free Speech Unmoored in Copyright's Safe Harbor: Chilling Effects of the DMCA on the First Amendment", *o.c.*, p. 178. See also J. Urban, J. Karaganis, and B. L. Schofield, Notice and Takedown in Everyday Practice, *o.c.*, p. 42.

1264 See *Online Policy Group v. Diebold, Inc.*, 337 F. Supp. 2d 1195 (N.D. Cal. 2004) (granting plaintiff's claim); and *Rossi v. Motion Picture Assoc. of Am.*, 391 F.3d 1000 (9th Cir. 2004) (dismissing plaintiff's claim); see also E. Goldman, Section 512(f) Complaint Survives Motion

There are, however, some notable exemptions to this trend. Perhaps the most famous example of a successful defence against an abusive notice is *Lenz v. Universal,* also known as the "Dancing Baby" case.[1265] The case concerned a take-down notice filed by Universal to remove from YouTube a 30 sec. video of a baby dancing to the song "Let's go crazy" by Prince. The mother contested the removal, and the video was eventually restored. Nevertheless, she sued Universal for damages under Section 512(f) DMCA arguing that the notice was abusive. The case went on for ten years. It has become a test case over bad DMCA takedown requests and helped determine the boundaries of "fair use."[1266] The court noted that the case '*boils down to a question of whether copyright holders have been abusing the extrajudicial takedown procedures provided for in the DMCA by declining to first evaluate whether the content qualifies as fair use*'.[1267] As a result, the Ninth Circuit Court of Appeals ruled that copyright owners need not make the right call on fair use, but they must at least consider fair use before they issue the DMCA takedown request.[1268]

Recently, a claim under Section 512(f) DMCA survived motion to dismiss, which is already considered unusual.[1269] The Court stated that the claimant '*has presented facts sufficient for the Court to draw the reasonable inference that Defendants knowingly misrepresented copyright infringement*'.[1270] This, however, rarely happens and the claimant still faces a long way to reach a favourable judgement.[1271] These factors contribute to the opinion that counter-notification in the DMCA is '*a visible and concrete*' yet '*largely symbolic acknowledgment of the importance of users' expressive rights*'.[1272]

The Finnish legislation also contains a provision about false information, but is more light-handed in its approach. According to Section 194, a person who gives false information in the notification or in the plea with objection shall be liable to compensate for the damage caused. However, there is no liability to

---

to Dismiss–Johnson v. New Destiny Church, 30 August 2017, http://blog.ericgoldman.org/archives/2017/08/section-512f-complaint-survives-motion-to-dismiss-johnson-v-new-destiny-church.htm.

1265 *Lenz v. Universal Music Corp.*, 801 F.3d 1126 (2015), (9th Cir. 2015).

1266 See J. Mullin, Supreme Court turns down EFF's "Dancing Baby" fair use case, 20 June 2017, https://arstechnica.com/tech-policy/2017/06/supreme-court-wont-hear-dancing-baby-copyright-case/.

1267 *Lenz v. Universal Music Corp.*, 801 F.3d 1126 (2015), (9th Cir. 2015).

1268 M. J. Randazza, "Lenz v. Universal: A Call to Reform Section 512(f) of the DMCA and to Strengthen Fair Use", *Vanderbilt Journal of Entertainment & Technology Law*, Vol. 18, No. 3, 2016, p. 103.

1269 See *Johnson v. New Destiny Christian Center Church*, 2017 WL 3682357 (M.D. Fla. Aug. 25, 2017).

1270 *Ibid.*

1271 E. Goldman, Section 512(f) Complaint Survives Motion to Dismiss–Johnson v. New Destiny Church, 30 August 2017, http://blog.ericgoldman.org/archives/2017/08/section-512f-complaint-survives-motion-to-dismiss-johnson-v-new-destiny-church.htm.

1272 A. Bridy, D. Keller, U.S. Copyright Office Section 512 Study: Comments in Response to Notice of Inquiry, *o.c.*, p. 30.

compensate or it may be adjusted if the notifying party had reasonable grounds to assume that the information was correct or if the false information was only of minor significance, when taking into account the entire content of the notification or the plea (Section 194 of the Finnish Information Society Code).

REASONABLE TIME – Due process implies that a final decision determining the rights and obligations of parties to a dispute shall be issued within a reasonable time. This element is also relevant for the criterion of effective remedy. What constitutes a "reasonable time" is defined on a case-by-case basis. Factors that should be taken into account include the complexity of the case, the conduct of the parties involved, and the importance of what is at stake. The NTD procedures discussed in the examples above do not strictly specify the time for a final decision, which is not necessary. They generally do provide, however, indications about timeframes for different actions within the NTD procedure. Some of them limit themselves to requesting that a removal is conducted "expeditiously" from the moment of receiving a valid notice (Finland, US). Others specifically define the number of days or even hours to remove content, notify the content provider, file a counter-notification and reinstate the content (e.g. Hungary and partially Finland and the UK).

REASONED JUDGEMENT – The right to due process also requires that decisions about rights and obligations should adequately state the reasons on which they are based. In the context of NTD procedures, where decisions are being taken by private intermediaries, this requirement can only be applied by analogy. It is not, however, unreasonable to expect intermediaries to state the reasons for removing or disabling access to content. Such a requirement exists, for example, in Finland where the Information Society Code provides that the notification to the content provider must state the reason for removal or blocking (Section 187 of the Finnish Information Society Code). In a way, the goal of informing the content provider about the reasons for removal is also achieved by forwarding them a copy of the original notification. The new German Network Enforcement Act provides that the social media network must immediately notify both the person submitting the complaint and the user about any decision taken. Moreover, the notification should include reasons for the decision (Section 3(2)5 NetzDG).

INDEPENDENT AND IMPARTIAL TRIBUNAL – Decisions impacting fundamental human rights should ideally be taken by an independent and impartial tribunal. Such a tribunal does not necessarily have to be a court of law. It could be any body that is equipped with power to decide matters on the basis of rule of law, following proceedings conducted in a prescribed manner.[1273] Such

1273 See Part II Chapter 4.3.4.

a body, nevertheless, must be independent from the parties and the executive power, and offer guarantees of a judicial procedure.

In most of the NTD procedures described in this section, the decisions are taken by the intermediaries. Since the intermediaries can potentially become a party of a subsequent conflict, they cannot reasonably be considered as independent. In the context of the existing NTD mechanisms, bodies that could fulfil the criteria, other than courts, are not commonly found. One interesting example is the Internet Watch Foundation (IWF) operating in the UK (see *Supra*). The organization draws its legitimacy from member trade associations and associated internal codes of conduct.[1274] For example ISPA – the UK Internet Service Providers Association – defers to the IWF with regard to filtering of unlawful content in its Code of Practice.[1275] The Code states that membership of the IWF is not mandatory, but it also makes clear that the ISPA co-operates with the IWF and that its procedures in this regard are mandatory for ISPA members.[1276] This means that ISPA members must follow the IWF orders and procedures, regardless of whether they are members of the IWF or not.[1277]

The question is whether the IWF can be classified as an independent and impartial body. Its status is not obvious. Is it a public authority bound directly by the Human Rights Act or is it a self-regulatory body that voluntarily undertakes some human rights responsibilities?[1278]As pointed out by Laidlaw, '*a fundamental issue with the IWF is that it has evolved to the point that it is unclear what it is in law*'.[1279] It could be classified as a hybrid public authority, which according to the UK Human Rights Act is '*any person certain of whose functions are functions of a public nature*'.[1280] The IWF maintains that it is independent of government, but has a good working relationship with the Home Office, the Ministry of Justice, the Department for Education, etc.[1281] The actual set-up, however, is less clearly self-regulatory.[1282] The IWF was created as a result of direct government threats and is carrying out a function that is governmental in nature.[1283] Laidlaw has no doubts that the organization's legitimacy and role is government driven.[1284] Others also point out that the threat of government regulation as motivation

1274 E. B. Laidlaw, "The responsibilities of free speech regulators: an analysis of the Internet Watch Foundation", *o.c.*, p. 317.

1275 See https://www.ispa.org.uk/about-us/ispa-code-of-practice/.

1276 See https://www.ispa.org.uk/about-us/ispa-code-of-practice/, point 5.

1277 E. B. Laidlaw, "The responsibilities of free speech regulators: an analysis of the Internet Watch Foundation", *o.c.*, p. 317.

1278 *Ibid.*, p. 314.

1279 *Ibid.*

1280 UK Human Rights Act, ss 6(3)(b) and 6(5).

1281 See IWF, https://www.iwf.org.uk/what-we-do/how-we-assess-and-remove-content/our-political-engagement.

1282 E. B. Laidlaw, "The responsibilities of free speech regulators: an analysis of the Internet Watch Foundation", *o.c.*, p. 324.

1283 *Ibid.* See also L. Edwards, "From Child Porn to China, in one Cleanfeed", *o.c.*, p. 175.

1284 E. B. Laidlaw, "The responsibilities of free speech regulators: an analysis of the Internet Watch Foundation", *o.c.*, p. 324.

for development of a self-regulatory mechanism can be considered government involvement, which precludes the 'pure' self-regulation label.[1285] Moreover, according to the Memorandum of Understanding '*reports made to the IWF in line with its procedures will be accepted as a report to a relevant authority*'.[1286] Consequently, it is unclear if the IWF is truly independent from the executive power yet it operates without any legislative underpinning (see *Supra*).[1287]

In Germany, the new Network Enforcement Act provides a possibility of delegating the decisions about unlawfulness of content to a "recognised self-regulation institution". If this is the case, however, the social media network must agree and accept the decision of that institution (Section 3(2)3.b NetzDG). The Act provides additional provisions regarding such institutions. To qualify, an institution, among others, must 1) possess expertise in analysing content and be independent; 2) have appropriate facilities in place and guarantee prompt analysis within a 7-day period; 3) have rules of procedure regulating the scope and structure of the analysis, and provide for the possibility to review decisions. Most interestingly, the Act also requires that such an institution is funded by several social network providers or establishments. In addition, the institution must remain open to the admission of further providers of social networks (Section 3(6)5 NetzDG). The status of a "recognised self-regulation institution" can be wholly or partly withdrawn or tied to supplementary requirements if any of the conditions for recognition are subsequently no longer met (Section 3(8) NetzDG). Article 19 observes that the social media networks, according to the Act, can delegate the decisions about unlawfulness of the content, but not about manifest unlawfulness.[1288] Moreover, such a delegation does not provide an alternative model for resolving disputes but merely delays some of the decisions.[1289] In the end, content is still removed without an assessment of legality by a judicial body.

REQUIREMENTS FOR DECISION MAKING PROCESS – The decision-making process leading to interference with the right to freedom of expression must be fair and such as to afford due respect for the interests of the individual. To assess the decision-making process it is important to look at several aspects, such as the type of decision involved, the extent to which the views of individuals were taken into account throughout the procedure, and the available procedural safeguards.

1285 See M. Price and S. Verhulst, "In search of the self: charting the course of self-regulation on the Internet in a global environment", in C. Marsden, *Regulating the global information society*, London, Routledge, 2000, p. 66. See also E. Lievens, *Protecting Children in the Digital Era – the Use of Alternative Regulatory Instruments*, *o.c.*, p. 194.

1286 Memorandum of Understanding Between the Crown Prosecution Service (CPS) and the Association of Chief Police Officers, *o.c.*, p. 6.

1287 E. B. Laidlaw, "The responsibilities of free speech regulators: an analysis of the Internet Watch Foundation", *o.c.*, p. 324.

1288 Article 19, Germany: Act to Improve Enforcement of the Law on Social Networks – Legal Analysis, *o.c.*, p. 20.

1289 *Ibid.*, p. 21.

In the context of NTD procedures that do not involve state authorities the decision to remove content is made entirely by a private entity – the intermediary. The existence of additional safeguards, as well as the possibility for all parties involved to express their views, can be linked to the existence of a counter-notification and the so-called put-back procedure.[1290] The views of the complaining party are expressed in the original notification, while the content provider can only defend his stance through a counter-notification. It is difficult to assess, however, to what extent the arguments presented in counter-notifications are actually given any consideration by intermediaries. For the arguments in the counter-notification to be truly taken into account the NTD procedure would need to ensure that intermediaries are not punished for reinstating the content. Similarly, they should not be punished if they decide not to remove content because they find the arguments in the notification unconvincing. Only then can hosting service providers have an incentive to evaluate the notice without the risk of falling into the trap of over compliance. Such freedom is granted to the intermediaries, for example, in the French NTD procedure where they can, but are not obliged, to remove the impugned content, unless it is manifestly illegal. Other national NTD procedures (e.g. Finland, Hungary and the US) require an expeditious removal when the notice is filed and only in case of counter-notification, can they provide a possibility to reinstate the content.[1291] In Finland and in the US, the reinstating of content depends on whether the counter-notification is filed timely and in accordance with the specified requirements. In Hungary, the service provider shall expeditiously make the relevant information accessible again upon receiving the objection. The Hungarian law provides another interesting safeguard. Specifically, the service provider shall refuse to remove the content, if they have already previously taken the requested measures in relation to the same content based on the notice of the same rights holder (or the proxy thereof), unless the removal was ordered by a court or authority.[1292] Such a measure protects the reinstated content from a new notification. Moreover, the Hungarian NTD provides explicitly that the service provider is not liable for the successful removal of, or disabling access to the relevant information, when the service provider has acted in accordance with the law in good faith.[1293] Similar protection from liability for the undertaken removals exists in the US NTD procedure which provides that

1290 See T. Verbiest, G. Spindler *et al.*, Study on the Liability of Internet Intermediaries, *o.c.*; P. Van Eecke, M. Truyens, EU Study on the Legal Analysis of A Single Market for the Information Society – New Rules for a New Age?, *o.c.*, p. 16.

1291 See T. Verbiest, G. Spindler *et al.*, Study on the Liability of Internet Intermediaries, *o.c.*; P. Van Eecke, M. Truyens, EU Study on the Legal Analysis of A Single Market for the Information Society – New Rules for a New Age?, *o.c.*, p. 16.

1292 Article 13.5 of the Hungarian Act CVIII of 2001 on certain issues of electronic commerce services and information society services, *o.c.*

1293 Article 13.12 of the Hungarian Act CVIII of 2001 on certain issues of electronic commerce services and information society services, *o.c.*

> 'a service provider shall not be liable to any person for any claim based on the service provider's good faith disabling of access to, or removal of, material or activity claimed to be infringing or based on facts or circumstances from which infringing activity is apparent, regardless of whether the material or activity is ultimately determined to be infringing'.[1294]

It is notable that in all these jurisdictions not taking down content does not automatically mean that the service provider becomes liable. In South Korea, however, the approach is different. The Korean copyright law requires compliance with the take-down procedure before an OSP can be exempted from the liability.[1295] Under the ICNA NTD, even in case of compliance with the request, the liability exemption is merely optional.[1296] For this reason the service providers in Korea interpret these provisions as obligatory rather than exempting them from liability.[1297]

The German Network Enforcement Act provides a possibility of regulatory fines up to 5 million Euros for non-compliance with its provisions, for example, a failure to provide a procedure for content removal and its correct implementation. Even though it is too early to assess, the risk is that the effect might be similar as in Korea, and that the social media networks will generally comply with the removal requests to avoid liability. The German Act includes a number of safeguards that are commendable. For example, the Act requires a notification to both the submitter of a request and the user, informing them of the decision taken, including the reasons. Moreover, the Act contains several provisions that improve transparency of the process. The efforts of the German government to request for more mandatory reporting and more transparency by the social media networks are laudable, however, these safeguards might not be enough to prevent the potential detriment to the right to freedom of expression posed by the Act.[1298]

E. *Effective remedy*

DOUBLE-EDGED SWORD – In case of content removals from the Internet, the right to effective remedy is equally relevant for both sides of the conflict. Both the party whose rights were possibly violated by the posted content and the content provider are potentially in a situation where their rights have been

---

1294 Section 512(g)(1) DMCA.

1295 See The Center for Internet and Society, World Intermediary Liability Map: South Korea, http://cyberlaw.stanford.edu/page/wilmap-south-korea.

1296 See K. S. Park, Intermediary Liability: Not just Backwards but Going Back, NoC Online Intermediaries Case Studies Series – South Korea, https://publixphere.net/i/noc/page/OI_Case_Study_Intermediary_liability__Not_Just_Backward_but_Going_Back.

1297 *Ibid.*

1298 See EDRI, Recommendations on the German bill "Improving Law Enforcement on Social Networks" (NetzDG), *o.c.*, p. 8.

infringed. In the first case, the victim of the infringing expression should have access to an effective remedy to stop the infringement, for example by requesting removal. In the second case, the content provider (and possibly the author of the impugned content) whose content was wrongfully removed should have the possibility to contest the removal and request reinstating the content.

The requirement of effective remedy is realized in the jurisdictions under analysis by providing a possibility to appeal a decision by the intermediary and by providing a possibility of judicial redress. In some jurisdictions these two elements appear together.

POSSIBILITY TO APPEAL THE DECISION – Existence of a NTD mechanism provides a possibility of remedying online infringement of rights. By complaining to the intermediary, the rights holder can stop the interference from continuing. The NTD mechanisms, such as the DMCA safe harbours, '*provide copyright owners with a direct and efficient remedy against infringing conduct on the massive scale*'.[1299] The NTD mechanism allows removal of infringing content from circulation through a process that '*avoids costly and time-consuming adjudication while simultaneously providing due consideration of the interests of all parties involved*'.[1300]

The possibility to appeal a removal decision exists in several national NTD procedures. As indicated above, measures that allow parties to file an objection to a removal or a counter-notification also contribute to procedural fairness. Such measures are provided by the NTD procedures in Finland, Hungary and the United States. According to the legislations of these countries, the appeal must meet certain specified requirements to be considered valid, just like the original notification. Depending on the way counter-notifications are implemented, however, they might fulfil their role or become a mere symbol of attempted balance between copyright holder rights and users' information rights.[1301]

The new German Act on Network Enforcement does not provide any indication of an appeal procedure. This is somewhat surprising for a law developed recently when multiple discussions have been held on over-compliance with removal requests and risks to the right to freedom of expression. Article 19 points out that administrative authorities are only required to intervene in case of failures to remove or block content but the Act provides no recourse for

1299 A. Bridy, D. Keller, U.S. Copyright Office Section 512 Study: Comments in Response to Notice of Inquiry, *o.c.*, p. 12.

1300 *Ibid.*, p. 12. See *also Viacom Int'l Inc. v. YouTube, Inc.*, 718 F. Supp. 2d 514, 524 (S.D.N.Y. 2010) (stating that the case shows that the DMCA notification regime works efficiently), aff'd in part and vacated in part, 676 F.3d 19 (2d Cir. 2012).

1301 See A. Bridy, D. Keller, U.S. Copyright Office Section 512 Study: Comments in Response to Notice of Inquiry, *o.c.*, p. 30.

users whose lawful content is removed.[1302] This omission, according to EDRI, is unacceptable and prevents access to effective remedy.[1303]

If available, the appeals are filed to and resolved by the hosting providers. This type of remedy, therefore, does not exactly comply with the provision of Article 13 ECHR, which require that effective remedy is available before a national authority. But as has been indicated already, in the context of this book, Article 13 is applied by analogy and serves mainly as an inspiration for introducing proportionality and fair balance elements into the removal procedures. Therefore the lack of full compliance with Article 13 ECHR is not considered problematic. According to the ECtHR jurisprudence, the authority involved should have powers to guarantee that the remedy is effective. In that sense a notification and a counter-notification may serve the purpose as they can effectively stop the interference (by removing content or by reinstating it). After all, a single remedy by itself does not have to entirely satisfy the requirements of Article 13, as long as the combined collection of remedies available under domestic law does so.[1304] This means, however, that the appeal cannot constitute a final step in the process, but should always leave the door open for a judicial review.

JUDICIAL REDRESS – The right to effective remedy includes a right to thorough review by the national courts of final decisions interfering with rights. National courts must be empowered to grant injunctive and possibly also monetary relief.[1305]

The concept of injunctive relief can be found in the E-Commerce Directive. Article 14.3 of the Directive provides that the liability exemption for hosting providers should not affect the possibility for a court or administrative authority of requiring the service provider to terminate or prevent an infringement.[1306] This means that the injunctive relief should be available irrespective of the intermediary's liability (e.g. for not removing the infringing content). If the Directive is implemented correctly into the national legal system of the EU countries, such a form of judicial redress to obtain an injunctive relief should always be possible, even if there is no specific procedure introduced at the national level. This is because the Directive provides conditions solely for liability exemption, but does not determine when the intermediaries are actually liable, which means that where liability is not exempted, normal rules of civil

---

1302 Article 19, Germany: Act to Improve Enforcement of the Law on Social Networks – Legal Analysis, *o.c.*, p. 19.

1303 EDRI, Recommendations on the German bill "Improving Law Enforcement on Social Networks" (NetzDG), *o.c.*, p. 6.

1304 See ECtHR, *M.S.S. v. Belgium and Greece*, 21 January 2011, para. 289. Also, ECtHR, *Gebremedhin [Gaberamadhien] v. France*, 26 April 2007, para. 53.

1305 K. Lenaerts, Effective judicial protection in the EU, *o.c.*, p. 3.

1306 Article 14.3 E-Commerce Directive 2000/31/EC.

and criminal liability apply. This provision, however, refers only to the situation when content is (or is not) removed on the request of the rights holder. There is no similar provision that would indicate a possibility of an injunctive relief in case of wrongful content removal. In theory, applying standard liability provisions does not exclude seeking this type of redress in a court, even if the Directive remains silent in this aspect. Examples of court orders to remove content from the Internet can be found all over the EU, but it is harder to find examples of court orders to reinstate content.[1307] Recently, a Berlin court has ordered Facebook not to block a user and not to delete a comment made by that user, even though it breached the social network's community standards.[1308] The case is ongoing.

In theory, judicial redress should always be possible when there is interference with one's rights. This possibility, however, is not always mentioned in the notice and takedown procedures. From the EU countries that introduced specific NTD procedure, Finland is a good example when it comes to ensuring judicial redress. In the Finnish Information Society Code, the procedure is designed to ensure the content providers' due process by providing them with a possibility to challenge the grounds for removal and have online content reinstated.[1309] For example, the Code provides a reversal procedure if the content is removed upon a court order, rather than a private complaint (Section 185 of the Finnish Information Society Code). In such case, the rules of the general Code of Judicial Procedure apply. In case of a NTD procedure with a private notice, the notification that is sent by the hosting provider to the content provider must provide information on the right of the content provider to bring the matter for a court hearing within 14 days from the receipt of the notification (Section 187 of the Finnish Information Society Code).

Hungary also clearly indicates a possibility of judicial redress in its NTD procedure. The possibility of redress, however, is foreseen for the rights holders

---

1307 It is very easy to prevent such rulings as intermediaries can just put the content back online if there is a reasonable case against them. Often, content is put back not as a result of a court order but a public outcry and negative media attention. For example, this happened in case of removal of the iconic "Vietnam napalm girl" picture or the prehistoric "Venus of Willendorf" figurine. See more in S. Levin, J. Carrie Wong, L. Harding, Facebook backs down from 'napalm girl' censorship and reinstates photo, 9 September 2016, https://www.theguardian.com/technology/2016/sep/09/facebook-reinstates-napalm-girl-photo; and Phys.org, Facebook apologises for censoring prehistoric Venus statue, 1 March 2018, https://phys.org/news/2018-03-facebook-apologises-censoring-prehistoric-venus.html. Currently, there is ongoing case in France about Facebook deleting a user's account because he posted a picture of a 19th-century painting of a woman's genitals ("L'Origine du Monde", an 1866 oil painting by Gustave Courbet). See more in J. Schmid, S. Bouderbala, Facebook denies 'censoring' 19th-century vagina painting, 1 February 2018, https://phys.org/news/2018-02-facebook-denies-censoring-19th-century-vagina.html.

1308 D. Meyer, Court tells Facebook: Stop deleting 'offensive' comment, 13 April 2018, https://www.zdnet.com/article/court-tells-facebook-stop-deleting-offensive-comment/.

1309 Swiss Institute of Comparative Law, Comparative Study on Filtering, blocking and take-down of illegal content on the – Finland country report, *o.c.*, p. 222.

whose content was reinstated online, and not, like in the Finnish procedure, for the content providers. After the content is put back online, the rights holder can re-enforce his claim by requesting an injunction for abandonment and prohibition, an order of payment or file a criminal report with the police (Article 13.9 of the Hungarian Act CVIII). Within 12 hours of receiving the court decision ordering interim measures to that effect, the service provider should once again disable access to, or remove the information identified in the notice. In such cases, the service provider should again notify the affected content provider of the measure that it has taken by supplying a copy of the court decision (Article 13.9 of the Hungarian Act CVIII). Moreover, the Act on electronic commerce requires the rights holder to inform the service provider without delay of the final decisions delivered in the course of the procedure – including an order for interim measure or the dismissal of the claim. The service provider shall expediently obey such decisions (Article 13.10 of the Hungarian Act CVIII). The provided NTD procedure does not address a possibility of judicial redress for content providers whose content was wrongfully removed.

Similarly, in the United States, the focus of the legislation is on providing a judicial redress and a possibility of injunctions to the rights holders. The DMCA specifies that in case of counter-notification the content is reinstated within a specified time (but not earlier than 10 days), unless the service provider first receives notice from the person who submitted the original notification that such person has filed an action seeking a court order to restrain the content provider from engaging in infringing activity relating to the content (Section 512(g)(2)(c) DMCA). Moreover, the DMCA contains a specific provision on injunctions. In Section 512(j), the Act distinguishes between conduct other than that which qualifies for the limitation on remedies and situations where the service provider qualifies for the limitation on remedies. In the first case, the possible injunctions include an order restraining the service provider from providing access to the content; an order restraining the service provider from providing access to the content provider (or account holder) engaged in the infringing activity by terminating their account; and any other injunctive relief that the court may consider necessary to prevent or restrain infringement of the copyrighted material specified, if such relief is the least burdensome to the service provider among the forms of relief comparably effective for that purpose (Section 512(j)(1)(A) DMCA). In the latter case, only two types of injunctions are possible, separately or jointly: termination of the account of the content provider (or account holder); and an order restraining the service provider from providing access, by taking reasonable steps specified in the order to block access, to a specific, identified, online location outside the United States (Section 512(j)(1)(B) DMCA). The DMCA also provides a list of relevant criteria that the court should take into account when considering an injunctive relief under applicable law.[1310] The criteria mainly focus on the impact of the relief and its proportionality aspects such as significant burden to the provider, magnitude of the harm likely to be suffered by the copyright holder if the steps are not taken, technical feasibility and effectiveness of the relief, and availability of comparably effective but less burdensome means (Section 512(j)(2)DMCA).

1.4. LESSONS LEARNED

EXISTING SAFEGUARDS – The existing NTD mechanisms contain a number of safeguards already. Countries that developed specific NTD procedures clearly designed the mechanisms to include protective measures against certain risks linked to privatized censorship. It is not necessary, therefore, to invent all the safeguards from scratch. The conducted assessment indicates, however, that functioning of the safeguards depends very much on their implementation and accompanying conditions. They can either achieve their goal, or completely miss the point.

CODIFIED AND CLEAR PROCEDURES – The countries presented in this research provided some type of NTD mechanism codified in law, ensuring they are accessible. All these countries describe the procedures for their NTD mechanisms rather in detail, which improves their foreseeability. For example, they specify the timeframes for different actions in the procedure and the formal requirements for a valid notice, which is relevant to determine the existence of actual knowledge. Clear requirements and rules of application certainly improve legal certainty and legitimacy of the mechanisms. There still remain issues with application of the mechanisms but they refer mainly to the question whether the mechanisms apply to specific, often novel, services rather than procedural aspects (for example the case of MTE and Index.hu in Hungary).

TARGETED SCOPE – Most of the analysed NTD mechanisms apply to a specific type of content or infringement. It is indicative that many of the existing NTD mechanisms apply only to the copyright infringements (Finland, US). This could be interpreted in two ways. The copyright holders managed to convince policymakers that due to a severe impact on their interests they need a simple yet efficient mechanism to combat infringements. At the same time, copyright infringements were possibly seen as easy cases, the resolution of which could be dealt by private entities, while other types of infringing content should be resolved by more traditional approaches. Some countries, over time, broadened the reach of the provided mechanisms to other types of infringements also. Few countries actually took a horizontal approach, following the E-Commerce

[1310] See Section 512(j)(2)DMCA.

Directive, and apply the mechanism to any type of content or activity in violation of law.

SPECIAL PROTECTION CONTENT – Several countries distinguish types of content that violates certain rights and values particularly worthy of protection. These usually include child abuse content and hate speech, and sometimes also Holocaust denial. The crucial factor, however, is that such content has to be manifestly unlawful, which means it must be easily recognized by laymen (Finland, France). These countries raise the bar for liability exemption for intermediaries and require them to remove such content on their own initiative after obtaining knowledge of its existence.

SUBSIDIARITY – There are several means that countries employ to ensure that the response is not excessive. For example, the procedures may require the notice to include a confirmation that the notifier had tried, without success, to request a removal from the content provider. If a removal by the content provider was not possible, the notifier can turn to intermediaries for help. In such a case, the procedures may describe the order in which the providers of different intermediary services are called into action – the so-called "chain of responsibility". Usually, it starts with removal requests addressed to hosting service providers before moving on to access service providers who can solely filter and block entire websites. Both measures follow the idea of subsidiarity that decisions should always be taken at the lowest possible level, or as close to the citizen as possible.[1311] By introducing elements of subsidiarity, the countries aim to avoid escalating the conflict (Finland, France).

NOTIFICATIONS AND COUNTER-NOTIFICATIONS – The existing procedures introduce elements of due process and requirements of the decision making process in several ways. The main element is a requirement of a notification to the content provider, to inform him of a complaint made against him. By informing the content provider of charges against him, the notifications bring the right to fair hearing into the process. Moreover, most of the analysed procedures allowed for a certain form of objection or counter-notification. The possibility of a counter-notification allows the parties to respond to the complaint and defend their use of the content. The role this measure can play depends largely on the timing of such counter-notification – whether it should happen before or after the take down. In the first case it allows the defence of the content provider to be taken into account in the decision-making process, while in the second case it is rather to inform about the takedown and about any possibility to appeal it. Moreover, it becomes clear that counter-notification can

[1311] European Parliament, Fact Sheets on the European Union, www.europarl.europa.eu/atyourservice/en/displayFtu.html?ftuId=FTU_1.2.2.html.

only influence the decision-making process if the intermediary is actually able to assess the arguments without becoming automatically liable for keeping the content online. This is the case in France, however other countries, like South Korea, effectively require content removal.

MEASURES AGAINST ABUSIVE REQUESTS – To discourage abusive requests, some procedures foresee penalties for misrepresentations. The examples can be found in the US, which present a strict approach with penalties of perjury, and Finland, with a more lenient approach limited to compensation for damage. Penalties for misrepresentations in a notice, as implemented in the US, are not a successful deterrent against abusive notices. On the other hand, penalties of perjury in the counter-notification intimidate the users who do not want to risk a lawsuit and, as a result, do not dare to exercise their rights. As indicated in the assessment, a strict approach can have a limiting effect on the usability and effectiveness of counter-notifications. Essentially, penalties for perjury in the counter-notification, as implemented in the US, turn counter-notification – a potentially great tool, into an empty, symbolic measure. This is unfortunate because counter-notification could help to bring elements of due process, right to a fair hearing, equality of arms and adversarial proceedings into the NTD mechanisms.

(IN)DEPENDENT BODIES – In most of the analysed NTD procedures, the takedown decisions are taken by intermediaries, which are not exactly independent and impartial if they can possibly become liable as a result of the decisions they take. In some of the countries, a public authority might become involved at a certain stage of the procedure. For example, in France the actual knowledge is only obtained through a court order. In many cases, however, it is hard to argue that the authorities involved are entirely independent. In the UK, there is a procedure involving the IWF, which claims it is self-regulatory and independent of the government but nevertheless its legitimacy and role is government driven. The Korea Communication Commission (KCC) has the power to order service providers to suspend, or restrict processing of content. It is a media regulation agency but subordinate to the president so part of the executive branch.

APPEAL AND REDRESS – The requirement of effective remedy dictates that there should be a possibility to appeal a decision about removal of content. This can be achieved through the objections or counter-notifications. Such appeals are resolved by the hosting providers, which can effectively stop the interference (by removing content or by reinstating it). Moreover, there should always exist a possibility of judicial redress to ensure effective legal protection of the rights in conflict. According to the E-Commerce Directive, the injunctive relief of removal should be available irrespective of the intermediary's liability. There is no similar provision in the Directive, however, that would indicate a possibility of a relief in case of wrongful content removal. Some countries provide such a safeguard (Finland). In theory, seeking this type of redress in a court should be possible. It is, however, difficult to find examples of court orders to reinstate content.[1312]

2. NOTICE AND STAY DOWN

2.1. DEFINITION

MAIN CHARACTERISTICS – Under a notice and stay down mechanism (NSD) the intermediary receives a notification about illegal or infringing character of hosted content, similar to notice and take down. In this case, however, the intermediary is required not only to remove the information, but also to take additional measures to ensure that it is not subsequently reposted, either by the same user or by other users.[1313] The identification of recurring postings of content previously notified as unlawful requires the implementation of systems that monitor all user-submitted information. Such systems can take the form of manual human supervision or automated systems.[1314] In both cases, however, the intermediaries must filter everything, that is, the entirety of content to detect a re-posting of once removed (or blocked) content.[1315] The mechanism, therefore, requires mandatory filtering initiated by the first notification.[1316]

2.2. COUNTRY PROFILES

A JURISPRUDENTIAL CONSTRUCT – Notice and stay down goes further than 'traditional' notice and take down mechanisms. This is because a submitted notice not only refers to a one-time illegality, but starts an ongoing obligation on the side of the intermediary to prevent the same illegality from occurring in the future. Such an approach can stem from an extensive interpretation of the same provisions that constitute the basis of a notice-and-take down mechanism. There are instances of NSD mechanisms in several EU countries, however, they are found in case-law, rather than explicitly in the law.

1312 See more in ft. 1307 and 1308.

1313 C. Angelopoulos, S. Smet, "Notice-and-fair-balance: how to reach a compromise between fundamental rights in European intermediary liability", *o.c.*, p. 288.

1314 *Ibid.*

1315 E. Harmon, "Notice-and-Stay-Down" Is Really "Filter-Everything", 21 January 2016, https://www.eff.org/deeplinks/2016/01/notice-and-stay-down-really-filter-everything.

1316 See M. Husovec, "Accountable, Not Liable: Injunctions Against Intermediaries", *TILEC Discussion Paper No. 2016-012*, 2 May 2016, https://papers.ssrn.com/sol3/papers.cfm?abstract_id=2773768, p. 70.

A. France

LEGISLATION – The French law LCEN does not contain a specific provision which explicitly requires the introduction of a notice and stay down mechanism. The safe harbour for the hosting providers in Article 6-I-2 LCEN has, at one point however, been interpreted expansively by lower courts in a way that led to de-facto introduction of such a mechanism through jurisprudence.[1317] The case-law indicates that the regime was mainly targeted at copyright infringing content.

In 2011 the Paris Court of Appeal confirmed the notice and stay down approach in four judgements handed down on the same day.[1318] In each of the judgements, the Court held Google Video liable for copyright infringements by its users. In the previous instance the *Tribunal de Commerce* had recognized Google's eligibility for the safe harbour protection but had issued an injunctive order for Google to refrain from future reproduction or communication to the public of the films in question, as well as from referencing any link allowing them to be viewed or downloaded.[1319] In the appeal, the Court ruled that the hosting service provider should not limit itself to the removal of the notified content, but also implement every possible technical measure to prevent future access to the disputed content through its search engine.[1320] In the Court's opinion, when the protected status of the video is notified to the provider, each new upload by the same user or by different users does not require a separate notification.[1321] At that time the CJEU was deliberating on the *SABAM v. Netlog* case[1322], but the French Court refused to delay the proceedings.

In three judgements issued in 2012, the Court of Cassation ended the stay down regime by declaring that the stay down obligation cannot be fulfilled by

1317 See C. Jasserand, France -Youtube guilty but not liable? some more precisions on the status of hosting providers, stating that 'French Courts have a tendency to impose such an obligation on hosting providers shifting from a notice and take down rule to a notice and stay down rule'. 18 June 2012, http://copyrightblog.kluweriplaw.com/2012/06/18/france-youtube-guilty-but-not-liable-some-more-precisions-on-the-status-of-hosting-providers/.

1318 *Google Inc. c. Compagnie des phares et balises,* Cour d'appel de Paris, 14 January 2011; *Google Inc. c. Bac Films, The Factory,* Cour d'appel de Paris, 14 January 2011; *Google Inc. c. Bac Films, The Factory,* Cour d'appel de Paris, 14 January 2011; *Google Inc. c. Les Films de la Croisade, Goatworks Films,* Cour d'appel de Paris, 14 January 2011.

1319 C. Angelopoulos, *European intermediary liability in copyright: A tort-based analysis, o.c.,* p. 126.

1320 See C. Jasserand, Recent decisions of the Paris Court of Appeal: towards an extra duty of surveillance for hosting providers? 29 March 2011, http://copyrightblog.kluweriplaw.com/2011/03/29/recent-decisions-of-the-paris-court-of-appeal-towards-an-extra-duty-of-surveillance-for-hosting-providers/.

1321 The Court repeated this reasoning in André Rau v Auféminin. See *Google France et Google Inc., Auféminin.com v. H&K SARL, André Rau,* Cour d'appel, 4 February 2011.

1322 CJEU, *Belgische Vereniging van Auteurs, Componisten en Uitgevers CVBA (SABAM) v. Netlog NV,* Case C 360/10, 16 February 2012.

online providers without conducting general monitoring of content.[1323] These decisions brought an end to the judge-made notice and stay down mechanism in France.[1324]

B. Germany

LEGISLATION – Until recently, no specific legislation existed in Germany about blocking, filtering or taking down of content. Instead, Germany relied on the implementation of the E-Commerce Directive – the *Telemediengesetz* (TMG)[1325] and general rules of law in the areas of copyright, trademark and unfair competition, which allow granting general injunctive relief.[1326] In 2017, the new law to help combat fake news and hate speech on social media was introduced. Additionally, German courts have created a special notion of "disturbance liability" (*Störerhaftung*), which is applied in the online context to hold the hosting providers liable for third party illegal content.[1327]

The disturber liability in Germany involves the duty to review (monitor) content to prevent future infringements. The approach was developed through jurisprudence of the German courts by analogy to the regulation on infringements of corporeal property (§1004 German Civil Code).[1328] It is based on responsibility for nuisance, and not on responsibility for unlawful acts.[1329] The disturbance liability is generally used for private law issues, as the main element of the approach is that someone's property (also intellectual) is being disturbed. Most of the cases, therefore, deal with unfair competition disputes, as well as copyright, and trademark law.[1330] Interestingly, the duty to review does not apply only to identical copies of the content, or to copies uploaded by the same users.[1331] On the contrary, the duty extends to all following infringing acts

1323 *La société Google France* c. *la société Bach films (L'affaire Clearstream)* (11–13.669), Cour de cassation, 12 July 2012; *La société Google France c. La société Bac films (Les dissimulateurs)* (11–13666), Cour de cassation, 12 July 2012; *La société Google France c. André Rau* (Auféminin) (11–15.165; 11–15.188) Cour de cassation, 12 July 2012.

1324 See C. Jasserand, France: The Court of Cassation puts an end to the Notice and Stay Down Rule, 14 August 2012, http://copyrightblog.kluweriplaw.com/2012/08/14/france-the-court-of-cassation-puts-an-end-to-the-notice-and-stay-down-rule/.

1325 *Telemediengesetz*, 26 February 2007, BGBl. I S. 179.

1326 Swiss Institute of Comparative Law, Comparative Study on Filtering, blocking and take-down of illegal content on the Internet – Germany country report, *o.c.*, p. 261.

1327 *Ibid.*

1328 J. B. Nordemann, "Liability for Copyright Infringements on the Internet: Host Providers (Content Providers) – The German Approach", *Journal of Intellectual Property, Information Technology and Electronic Commerce Law (JIPITEC)*, Vol. 2, Issue 1, 2011, p. 39.

1329 Swiss Institute of Comparative Law, Comparative Study on Filtering, blocking and take-down of illegal content on the Internet – Germany country report, *o.c.*, p. 266.

1330 See M. Leistner," Structural aspects of secondary (provider) liability in Europe", *Journal of Intellectual Property Law & Practice*, Vol. 9, No. 1, 2014, p. 82.

1331 J. Bornkamm, "E-Commerce Directive vs. IP Rights Enforcement – Legal Balance Achieved?", *GRUR Int*, 2007, p. 642.

of a similar nature that are easily recognisable.[1332] In short, the infringements must be '*similar in their core*' (the "*Kerntheorie*").[1333] According to Angelopoulos, the doctrine essentially achieves the same, or even a slightly broader effect as the French judge-made notice and stay down regime.[1334]

2.3. ASSESSMENT

A. *Quality of law*

ACCESSIBILITY – Any rules regulating behaviour must be known to the public to inform them of the expected behaviour. This usually means that the rules should be described in a law that has been duly published. This is not the case in any of the example countries provided above. In the case of both France and Germany, the notice and stay down mechanism was developed through jurisprudence, by the judges interpreting the provisions transposing the E-Commerce Directive and its liability exemption for hosting providers in an expansive way. The notice and stay down mechanism, therefore, does have a basis in law. However, the details of the mechanisms in the two example countries are actually not described in any law. This arguably undermines the accessibility of the rules. At the same time, however, the ECtHR has held that the condition of accessibility is also satisfied when a binding decision of a national constitutional court has been published in the state official gazette and followed this court's previous case-law.[1335] In that sense, the German notice and stay down mechanism has been confirmed by several judgements of the German Federal Supreme Court (BGH) and published in the state official gazette. For this reason, the condition of accessibility should be considered as satisfied. In France, the *Cour de cassation* actually eliminated the lower court-made notice and stay down mechanism from the legal regime. It can be considered, therefore, that the decision of the *Cour de cassation* is accessible and provides information to the subjects on what behaviour is expected of them in terms of monitoring content to prevent future infringements.

FORESEEABILITY – Even though the notice and stay down mechanism, as it currently functions in the German legal system, can be considered as accessible, the matter of foreseeability is more complicated. There are certain

[1332] See *Ibid*.

[1333] M. Leistner, "Störerhaftung und mittelbare Schutzrechtsverletzung", GRUR-Beil 1, 2010, as referenced by C. Angelopoulos, *European intermediary liability in copyright: A tort-based analysis*, *o.c.*, p. 154.

[1334] C. Angelopoulos, *European intermediary liability in copyright: A tort-based analysis*, *o.c.*, p. 154.

[1335] ECtHR, *Leyla Şahin v. Turkey*, 10 November 2005, para. 93.

doubts about the compatibility of the mechanism with Article 15 of the E-Commerce Directive, which prohibits States from introducing general monitoring obligations.[1336] Article 15 was analysed by the CJEU in the *Sabam* rulings where it declared that the filtering of all electronic communications applied indiscriminately to all users as a preventive measure, at the expense of the intermediary and for an unlimited period of time, should be understood as general, and therefore not permitted by the Directive.[1337] The Court explained that preventive monitoring of this kind would require active observation of files stored by users with the hosting service provider and would involve almost all of the information stored and all of the service users of that provider.[1338] Moreover, the Court found problematic the fact that the requested monitoring was directed at all future infringements and was intended to protect not only existing works, but also works that have not yet been created.[1339] The measures administered by the German courts bear a strong resemblance to those rejected by the CJEU in the *Sabam* cases. The potential incompatibility of the German approach with the secondary EU law raises legitimate questions about predictability of a legal mechanism.

The German Federal Supreme Court (BGH) does not consider the review obligation to constitute a general monitoring obligation, but rather a specific monitoring obligation, which is permitted by the Directive.[1340] In *Rapidshare III*, the BGH considered the *Störerhaftung* approach as compatible with the CJEU judgement in *L'Oréal v eBay*.[1341] Specifically, the BGH declared that the '*appeal court rightly assumed that the defendant can be subjected not to a general but rather an incident-related monitoring obligation to trace an infringement already made and prevent further infringements*'.[1342]

According to Bornkamm, extending *Störerhaftung* to future infringements is not incompatible with the E-Commerce Directive because it does not impose *ex ante* monitoring, but only an *ex post* obligation to react.[1343] He argues that the prohibition in Article 15 of the E-Commerce Directive is limited to *ex ante* obligations, but that *ex post* injunctive relief relating to future infringements is permitted. Therefore, '*the directive does not rule out injunctive relief as to further*

1336 P. Valcke, A. Kuczerawy, P.-J. Ombelet, "Did the Romans get it right? What Delfi, Google, eBay, and UPC TeleKabel Wien have in common", *o.c.*, p. 109.

1337 See Part II Chapter 2.2.

1338 CJEU, *Belgische Vereniging van Auteurs, Componisten en Uitgevers CVBA (SABAM) v. Netlog NV*, Case C 360/10, 16 February 2012, para. 37.

1339 *Ibid.*, para. 45.

1340 See J. B. Nordemann, "Liability for Copyright Infringements on the Internet: Host Providers (Content Providers) – The German Approach", *o.c.*, p. 42.

1341 C. Angelopoulos, *European intermediary liability in copyright: A tort-based analysis*, *o.c.*, p.161.

1342 Translation from C. Angelopoulos, *European intermediary liability in copyright: A tort-based analysis*, *o.c.*, p. 161.

1343 J. Bornkamm, "E-Commerce Directive vs. IP Rights Enforcement – Legal Balance Achieved?" *o.c.*

infringements once an infringement has been shown'.[1344] Albeit interesting, such an interpretation of the Directive might just be wishful thinking. The Directive does not distinguish between *ex ante* and *ex post* monitoring. Nothing in the wording of the Directive suggests that timing determines the legality of a general monitoring obligation or a general obligation to actively seek facts or circumstances indicating illegal activity.[1345]

The BGH's statement in *Internetversteigerung I* shows a peculiar understanding of the monitoring problem. According to the Court, the provider

> 'cannot reasonably be expected to check every offer placed directly on the internet in an automated process for a possible infringement of third-party property rights. If a service provider acquires notice of a trade mark infringement, it must not only immediately block the specific sale but must also take technically feasible and reasonable measures to prevent further such infringements'.[1346]

The Court did not elaborate further how similar future infringements could be prevented without checking every offer for a possible infringement. After all, no matter how specific the content being targeted is, an obligation to prevent re-uploads means that a service provider must constantly monitor all uploads to catch re-uploads.[1347] Angelopoulos offers an interesting real-life analogy to illustrate the problem. According to her, '*it matters little if airport security services give airplane travellers routine pat-downs in search of any kind of weapon or only semi-automatic pistols – the pat down is still taking place*'.[1348] Of course, it would be convenient to only pat-down persons carrying the specified weapon, but identifying those individuals is the very objective of the pat-down.[1349] To achieve that purpose, the security services must conduct the pat-down of all travellers. It seems logical. This opinion, however, is not shared by German jurists, who often seem to confuse the purpose of the monitoring (identifying a specific infringement) with the subject of the monitoring (entirety of the stored content) when assessing its generality. For example, Nordemann explains that '*hosting providers are not obliged to use [audio and audiovisual] filters on all content uploaded by any user, as this would result in a general monitoring duty*', they may be obliged, however, to install '*audio-visual filters only for certain works*

[1344] *Ibid.*

[1345] C. Angelopoulos, *European intermediary liability in copyright: A tort-based analysis*, *o.c.*, p. 161.

[1346] Translation from Case comment, "Federal Supreme Court (Bundesgerichtshof): GERMANY", *International Review of Intellectual Property and Competition Law* (IIC), 2005, 573.

[1347] CDT, Cases Wrestle with Role of Online Intermediaries in Fighting Copyright Infringement, 26 June 2012, https://cdt.org/insight/cases-wrestle-with-role-of-online-intermediaries-in-fighting-copyright-infringement/.

[1348] C. Angelopoulos, *European intermediary liability in copyright: A tort-based analysis*, *o.c.*, p. 162.

[1349] *Ibid.*

upon knowledge that such works were made publicly available on the site'.[1350] The same author presents the opinion that the CJEU's ruling in *Netlog* '*does not mean that word filters may not be imposed on hosting providers. Word filters by their nature only search for certain film titles, game titles, audio book titles, music titles, band names etc.*'[1351] According to Angelopoulos, such an approach '*transplants the generality of the monitoring to the works the measure is intended to protect, rather than the content being filtered*'.[1352]

However, it is difficult to see how the requirements imposed by the German courts are different than the obligations rejected in SABAM cases.[1353] According to Hoeren and Yankova, an injunction to '*prevent future similar infringements refers neither to a specific field nor to a specific time period and can in no way represent a monitoring obligation in a specific case. This proactive duty establishes rather a monitoring obligation of a general nature*'.[1354] In such a case, compatibility of the mechanism with the E-Commerce Directive is highly doubtful. Some commentators have accused the German courts of '*misconceiving the main goals which national and European legislators have pursued when drafting the Telemedia Act and the E-Commerce Directive*'.[1355]

Disagreements about the nature of the monitoring obligations to prevent future infringements would benefit from clarification by the CJEU. The *Sabam* cases did not convince the German courts, which for a long time did not see a need to refer cases on this matter to the CJEU themselves. In 2014, the Munich district Court directed a reference for a preliminary ruling in *McFadden*.[1356] The case concerned application of the *Störerhaftung* doctrine to access provider (covered by Article 12 of the E-Commerce Directive), whose unprotected Internet connection was used by third parties to upload copyright-protected work without the permission of the copyright holder. The Court considered that granting an injunction, which requires the access provider to prevent third parties from making a particular copyright-protected work available to the general public

1350 J. B. Nordemann, "Internet Copyright Infringement: Remedies against Internet Intermediaries – the European Perspective on Host and Access Providers", *Journal of the Copyright Society of the USA, Vol.* 59, Issue 4, 2012, p. 773.

1351 *Ibid.*

1352 C. Angelopoulos, *European intermediary liability in copyright: A tort-based analysis, o.c.*, p. 162.

1353 See CDT, Cases Wrestle with Role of Online Intermediaries in Fighting Copyright Infringement, 26 June 2012, https://cdt.org/insight/cases-wrestle-with-role-of-online-intermediaries-in-fighting-copyright-infringement/.

1354 T. Hoeren and S. Yankova, "The Liability of Internet Intermediaries – The German Perspective", *International Review of Intellectual Property and Competition Law,* IIC 2012, p. 501.

1355 T. Hoeren, "German Law on Internet Liability of Intermediaries", LIDC Congress, Oxford 2011; J. Wimmers, "Who Interferes? Liability for Third Party Content on the Internet in Germany", *Intellectual Property Today,* August 2007, p. 32.

1356 CJEU, *Tobias Mc Fadden v. Sony Music Entertainment Germany GmbH*, Case C 484/14, 15 September 2016.

via the Internet connection, is not precluded by the E-Commerce Directive.[1357] In practice, the only measures which the provider may adopt to comply with an injunction consist of terminating or password-protecting the Internet connection or of examining all communications passing through it.[1358] The Court declared, that monitoring all of the information transmitted as a measure

> 'must be excluded from the outset as contrary to Article 15(1) of Directive 2000/31, which excludes the imposition of a general obligation on, inter alia, communication network access providers to monitor the information that they transmit'.[1359]

Even though the case addressed the issue of monitoring all content by access providers, and not hosting providers, it is yet another ruling, after the *Sabam* cases, indicative of the CJEU's close scrutiny of measures instituting monitoring obligations. Differing opinions about the nature of the required monitoring and its compatibility with the secondary EU law pose questions about the level of foreseeability of the German notice-and-stay down approach. The same question about the French system was resolved by the decision of the *Cour de cassation,* which decided to conform the French jurisprudence with the *Sabam* judgements and ended the stay-down regime.[1360]

B. Protection of democratic society

DEMOCRATIC VALUES – In France, when still operational, notice and stay down was used to target copyright infringements.[1361] In Germany, *Störerhaftung* is based on the idea that someone's property (including intellectual) is being disturbed. It is mostly used in cases involving unfair competition disputes, as well as copyright, trademark and patent law.[1362] In some cases it is also used when disputes involve aspects of the general personality right, for example libel.[1363] The right to protection of one's intellectual property, protection from

1357 *Ibid.*, para. 101.

1358 *Ibid.*, para. 80.

1359 *Ibid.*, para. 87.

1360 *La société Google France* c. *la société Bach films (L'affaire Clearstream)* (11–13.669), Cour de cassation, 12 July 2012; *La société Google France c. La société Bac films (Les dissimulateurs)* (11–13666), Cour de cassation, 12 July 2012; *La société Google France c. André Rau* (Auféminin) (11–15.165; 11–15.188) Cour de cassation, 12 July 2012.

1361 See for example: *Google Inc. c. Compagnie des phares et balises,* Cour d'appel de Paris, 14 January 2011; *Google Inc. c. Bac Films, The Factory,* Cour d'appel de Paris, 14 January 2011; *Google Inc. c. Bac Films, The Factory,* Cour d'appel de Paris, 14 January 2011; *Google Inc. c. Les Films de la Croisade, Goatworks Films,* Cour d'appel de Paris, 14 January 2011.

1362 See for example BGH, *Jugendgefährdende Medien bei eBay,* 12 July 2007, I ZR 18/04 and OLG Düsseldorf, *Rapidshare I,* 27 April 2010, I-20 U 166/09; OLG Hamburg, *Rapidshare II,* 14 March 2012, 5 U 87/09; OLG Düsseldorf, *Rapidshare III,* 21 December 2010, I-20 U 59/10; BGH, *Rapidshare I,* 12 July 2012, I ZR 18/11; BGH, *Rapidshare III,* 15 August 2013, I ZR 80/12.

1363 See for example BGH, *Katzenfreund,* July 23, 2007, VI ZR 101/06.

unfair competition and protection against defamation and libel fall under the broad category of the "reputation or rights of others".

The notice and stay down mechanisms that exist in the analysed countries are not regulated by a code but instead resulted from jurisprudence. Therefore, there is no clear description of the rights and values they are used to protect. It is also not obvious if the mechanism could be extended to other types of infringing content or activities. The mechanism is scoped by the case law, so the fact that until now it has not been used in relation to one type of right, does not mean it won't happen in the future. Without rules prescribing circumstances for a possible interference with the right to freedom of expression by continuous monitoring and removal, it is hard to argue that the principles of legal certainty are satisfied.

MANIFEST ILLEGALITY – The key characteristic of notice and stay down is that an intermediary, once notified about the infringing content, must continuously monitor its platform to prevent re-occurrence of the infringement in the future. The future infringements that the intermediary has to detect must be "clear". However, these clear infringements are not limited solely to instances where the same work is infringed by the same user. It may also apply to other works of the same kind by the same user but also to other works of different types infringed by a different user (if the service is particularly susceptible to infringements).

It will not always be possible for the hosting provider to immediately recognize whether an infringement has taken place, as the BGH acknowledged in *Blog-Eintrag*.[1364] Accordingly, a host provider is required to act only if the notice he received is sufficiently specific. The notice must enable identification of the infringement without excessive difficulty, i.e. without an in-depth legal and factual review.[1365] If, however, the original notification has to be detailed enough to indicate an infringement without a need for a thorough legal and factual examination, how can the host be required to recognize future infringements of other works of the same or even different kind by himself, when no new notification is issued? Clearly, such a task will require detailed legal and factual analysis to avoid overbroad removals.

The requirement that indications of infringements are "clear" '*is reminiscent of the French preoccupation with "manifest" unlawfulness*'.[1366] In the German version, however, it refers not to the gravity of the violated rights (which facilitates identification of the infringement), but to the ability of the intermediaries to recognize them without any specific clues. It is not obvious

1364 BGH, *Blog-Eintrag*, 25 October 2011, I ZR 93/10.

1365 C. Angelopoulos, *European intermediary liability in copyright: A tort-based analysis*, *o.c.*, p. 154.

1366 *Ibid.*

how the strict interpretation of the notification requirements by the German courts is consistent with the subsequent obligation to remove future undefined infringements.[1367]

C. *Tailored response*

LEAST RESTRICTIVE MEANS – The notice and stay down mechanism, as it was employed in France and still is in Germany, requires active searching for infringing content. The obligation applies not only to the same content reposted by the same users but also to content of a similar type, posted by other users. Court orders in Germany describe the obligation differently, depending on the circumstances of the case. The obligation, however, can be alarmingly broad. For example, in *GEMA v Rapidshare,* the provider of the service was ordered to take up a variety of preventive measures to eliminate future infringements.[1368] The Court found that Rapidshare should have installed a word filter to retrieve and remove all infringing files already in its system. The automated monitoring should have been supplemented with subsequent manual reassessment to avoid over-blocking. The Court acknowledged that these measures might not be entirely effective, but they would at least reduce the number of infringements. The order was considered '*a duty of care to be expected of [the website] according to reasonable judgement and set down in national legal regulations in order to discover and prevent specific types of illegal activity*'.[1369]

Moreover, Rapidshare was ordered to supervise not only its own platform, but also the entire Internet (albeit selectively). This was considered a general market monitoring duty to search (*Marktbeobachtungspflicht*), by use of general search engines '*such as Google, Facebook or Twitter*' and through web crawlers.[1370] The goal was to discover further illegal links to its service with regard to 4815 works at issue. Putting aside the fact that the Court referred to Facebook and Twitter as search engines, which does not suggest a good understanding of the technology at stake, one can wonder about the proportionality of such a measure.[1371] Even limiting the order to copies similar in their "core" does not address the risk of

---

[1367] See *Ibid.*

[1368] BGH, *Rapidshare III,* 15 August 2013, I ZR 80/12.

[1369] BGH, *Rapidshare III,* 15 August 2013, I ZR 80/12; see translation: https://stichtingbrein.nl/public/2013-08-15%20BGH_RapidShare_EN.pdf.

[1370] BGH, *Rapidshare III,* 15 August 2013, I ZR 80/12, para. 54. G. Frosio, "The Death of 'No Monitoring Obligations': A Story of Untameable Monsters", *Journal of Intellectual Property, Information Technology and E-Commerce Law (JIPITEC* – special Intermediary Liability & Human Rights Issue), Vol. 8 2017, p. 11.

[1371] See C. Angelopoulos, *European intermediary liability in copyright: A tort-based analysis, o.c.*, p.158. See also P. Doda, "Distinguishing Common Carriers from Common Thieves: Requiring Notice and Stay down for Structurally Infringing Host Sites That Discourage Legitimate Electronic Storage, Incentivize Copyright Infringement, and Exploit the DMCA 512 (c) Safe Harbor", *Journal of the Copyright Society of the USA*, Vol. 63, Issue 3, Summer 2016, pp. 515–534.

overbroad reach. The problem is especially difficult in copyright, where the same posting might be illegal when done by one person at one point in time and legal when done by another or at a different time.[1372] Similarly, the work might enter into the public domain since the original posting; it might have been released under an open-content license or it might simply have been posted by the rights holder.[1373]

The criterion of tailored response requires that the response should consist of a minimal intervention that would be able to address only the targeted wrongdoing with precision and accuracy. Considering the form in which the notice and stay down functions in the German legal order is, it is hard to argue that the mechanism follows the approach of the least restrictive interference. Requiring providers to monitor their platforms, or even other platforms of which they have no control, to detect other (both the same and merely similar) instances of infringements by the same user and by other users is neither specific nor precise. Such an application of the mechanism does not properly reflect the nuances of copyright law, which foresees possibilities of the same content having different legal statuses when posted by different users, or the fact that the status of content changes over time. Under the criteria followed in this book, the notice and stay down mechanism, as it currently functions in Germany, is considered excessive.

D. *Procedural fairness*

INDEPENDENT AND IMPARTIAL TRIBUNAL – The notice and stay down mechanism currently functions in Germany on the basis of case-law. This means that the mechanism is administered not by the hosting service providers but by independent and impartial tribunals of the judiciary system established by law. The decisions are taken by bodies that are independent from the parties and the executive power, and offer guarantees of a judicial procedure.[1374] It would be difficult to analyse whether in each case where the notice and stay down mechanism was administered, the court was in fact free from external intervention or pressure liable to jeopardise the judgement.[1375] Similarly, it would be difficult to analyse whether members of a tribunal were personally impartial.[1376] Such questions fall outside of the scope of this book. Moreover,

---

1372 C. Angelopoulos, *European intermediary liability in copyright: A tort-based analysis*, *o.c.*, p. 162.

1373 *Ibid.*

1374 See *mutatis mutandis* with regard to Article 5.4 ECHR, ECtHR, *X v. the United Kingdom*, 5 November 1981, para. 53, as referenced by P. Leanza, O. Pridal, *The right to a fair trial: Article 6 of the European Convention on Human Rights*, *o.c.*, p. 129.

1375 See to that effect CJEU, *Abrahamsson and Anderson*, C-407/98, 6 July 2000, para. 32 and 36; see also L. Pech, "Article 47(2)", *o.c.*, p. 1256.

1376 P. Leanza, O. Pridal, *The right to a fair trial: Article 6 of the European Convention on Human Rights*, *o.c.*, p. 132.

such claims cannot be supported without a specific judgement of the ECHR on the matter. It is, therefore, considered that the element of independent and impartial tribunal in the German approach to the notice and stay down mechanism is satisfied. in the same way, it is considered that the German judiciary is organized in compliance with the ECHR. Therefore, German courts, when applying the mechanism, follow the general requirement of due process guaranteeing a fair hearing within a reasonable time, and that the proceedings are adversarial with equality of arms between the prosecution and defence.[1377]

REQUIREMENTS FOR THE DECISION-MAKING PROCESS – Even though the notice and stay down mechanism is administered by the courts, it is interesting to look not only at the outcome, but also the way that the decisions are taken, for example, whether courts give due weight to the interests of the individuals. When applying the notice and stay down, courts generally consider the positions of the complainants and the service providers. The position of the content provider is usually not taken into account. The underlying reason is that the *Störerhaftung* doctrine, and the subsequent notice and stay down, is considered a different procedure, separate from the procedure regarding infringement by the content provider. *Störerhaftung* is a form of strict liability that is limited to injunctive relief. It is aimed only at third parties who have not themselves committed an infringement, but who are able to provide relief. The fine that might follow is a result of a breach of an injunction, which is considered contempt of court.[1378]

The fact that the injunction proceedings are considered in separation from any proceedings against the actual wrongdoer can be justified in case of the original infringing post. However, it is hard to justify such an approach in case of all future infringements. After all, no proceedings against the future infringements are necessary and the responsibility to recognize them falls entirely on the hosting service providers. As was pointed out above, in copyright the same content posted by a different user might have a different legal status. There is, however, no guarantee that the reposted content is actually infringing. Moreover, the views of the reposting individuals are at no point taken into account when deciding about removals of the re-posted content. It is, therefore, difficult to argue that the decision-making process leading to interference is fair and affords due respect for the interests safeguarded to the individual.[1379] It is also interesting to note that even though the application of the notice and stay down mechanism is reserved to independent and impartial tribunals, the decisions about future infringements are actually pushed back to the service

1377 See ECtHR, *Rowe and Davis v. the United Kingdom*, 16 February 2000, para. 60.

1378 See G. Spindler, "Country Report – Germany" for "Study on the Liability of Internet Intermediaries" (2006), available at: http://ec.europa.eu/internal_market/e-commerce/directive_en.htm.

1379 For example ECtHR, *Hatton v. The United Kingdom*, 8 July 2003; and ECtHR, *Buckley v. the United Kingdom*, 29 September 1996.

providers who must take the reposted content down or face a fine for contempt of court. There is no judicial oversight for decisions made regarding future infringements. Additionally, there are no safeguards protecting the users from the removal decisions taken by the service providers.

E. Effective remedy

JUDICIAL REDRESS – The notice and stay down mechanism in Germany is applied by courts. This means that the parties to the procedure can appeal a decision which would then be reviewed by a court of second instance. In that sense, the mechanism complies with the criterion of effective remedy.

POSSIBILITY TO APPEAL THE DECISION – Considering that all the future re-postings of the content once declared infringing are at risk of being removed by the service providers, the problem of effective remedy takes a different shape. As discussed above, content providers of the future re-postings do not have any way to express their view and defend their right to use the content. They have no measure that would allow for an appropriate relief. In theory they could of course direct a claim to court, but such cases rarely happen. From this perspective, therefore, the procedure fails to satisfy the criterion of effective remedy.

2.4. LESSONS LEARNED

(IN)COMPATIBILITY WITH THE DIRECTIVE – The notice and stay down mechanism is not a commonly used mechanism. The main reason is that most laws on intermediary liability prevent States from introducing general monitoring obligations. In Germany, the courts (and many scholars) believe, however, that an obligation to detect future infringements that are not only the same but merely similar does not constitute a general monitoring obligation, but rather a specific one, which is allowed by the E-Commerce Directive. The opinion stems from an alternative understanding of the difference between the purpose of the monitoring (detecting specific infringements) and the subject of the monitoring (entirety of the content) to achieve that purpose. The CJEU's rulings in the *Sabam* cases and the recent *McFadden* case did not convince German courts that what they administer on many occasions would qualify as general monitoring. This inconsistency and possible incompatibility with Article 15 of the E-Commerce Directive raises legitimate questions about the predictability of the German mechanism.

COURT-MADE CONSTRUCT – The notice and stay down mechanism is a judicial construct. It is not provided by any laws but based on the courts' interpretation of the liability exemption provision. The scope of application is, therefore, not clearly defined but depends on whether courts decide to extend it to new types of content. Currently, it is mainly applied to intellectual property infringements. The positive aspect of the mechanism is that it is always administered by independent tribunals – the courts of law. This ensures that due process rights and the requirements for the decision-making process are followed. Moreover, the fact that any order to remove current and future infringing content requires court decisions means that judicial redress in the form of an appeal is possible.

LIMITED REDRESS – An obligation to detect and prevent future infringements creates several issues that are currently not being addressed. Despite the fact that the mechanism is administered by courts following decision-making procedures, the only parties that get to express their opinion are the plaintiffs (right holders) and the intermediaries. The content providers do not take part in the process. They have, therefore, no say in the process that will effectively impact their rights by restricting their expression. Moreover, providers of any future infringing content will have no possibility to appeal the decisions. In their case, the decision will be made by the intermediary and not by the court. If the intermediary makes a wrong assessment, for example when the content changed its status, content providers of the future infringing content have limited chances to exercise their right to effective remedy.

3. NOTICE AND NOTICE

3.1. DEFINITION

MAIN CHARACTERISTICS – Under a notice and notice mechanism (N&N), an intermediary receives a notification with a complaint, which he then forwards to the content provider.[1380] At this point the intermediary's involvement ends.[1381] The notification to the content provider serves the purpose of a warning. The content provider is given an opportunity to correct his behaviour, which halts the procedure, or to defend it within a provided time limit, which may lead to further actions (notifications or sanctions).[1382] The mechanism is a variation of notice and take down. The main difference is that the remedy to a potential wrongdoing is not taken immediately but is spread

1380 OECD, The Role of Internet Intermediaries in Advancing Public Policy Objectives – Forging partnerships for advancing policy objectives for the Internet economy, *o.c.*, p. 57.

1381 C. Angelopoulos, S. Smet, "Notice-and-fair-balance: how to reach a compromise between fundamental rights in European intermediary liability", *o.c.*, p. 295.

1382 See *Ibid.*

over time. Usually, there are several notifications (warnings) to the content provider before the final response is delivered. The mechanism can be achieved in different ways: voluntarily, when intermediaries agree to participate without legal pressure; imposed by as a result of private court action; or imposed by legislation.[1383] Its goal, partially, is to educate users and to deter them from wrongdoings by demonstrating that they cannot hide from legal detection.[1384] It is meant, therefore, to persuade users to look instead for legal alternatives, for example to obtain music.[1385]

3.2. COUNTRY PROFILES

VARIATIONS – Several variations of the notice and notice mechanism exist, varying in how the conflict escalates or in the final outcome. Some authors discuss these variations separately as distinct mechanisms.[1386] However, here they are grouped together as different versions of a mechanism based on a system of warnings and a delayed response. The variations include, for example, notice and notice leading to a judicial take down and notice wait and take down.[1387] Responses might involve the suspension and termination of service, capping of bandwidth, blocking of sites, portals, and protocols.[1388] In the most extreme form, the content provider is disconnected from the Internet after the final warning has been issued. This version of the mechanism is known as graduated response or the "three-strikes-and-you're-out" approach, although the number of strikes might differ.[1389] Decisions on the matter could be taken by an ISP, an administrative authority or a court of law, depending on the country.

1383 See more L. Edwards, Role and responsibility of the internet intermediaries in the field of copyright and related rights, *o.c.*, p. 26.

1384 *Ibid.*, p. 29.

1385 *Ibid.*

1386 See for example C. Angelopoulos, S. Smet, "Notice-and-fair-balance: how to reach a compromise between fundamental rights in European intermediary liability", *o.c.*; OECD, The Role of Internet Intermediaries in Advancing Public Policy Objectives – Forging partnerships for advancing policy objectives for the Internet economy, *o.c.*

1387 See C. Angelopoulos, S. Smet, "Notice-and-fair-balance: how to reach a compromise between fundamental rights in European intermediary liability", *o.c.*, p. 294–300.

1388 See P. Yu, The Graduated Response, *62 Florida Law Review*, 2010, pp. 1373–1430, p. 1374.

1389 See *Ibid.*. In February 2013 in the US, Motion Picture Association of America (MPAA) and five major US internet service providers launched a 'six strikes' Copyright Alert system to deal with online copyright infringements. J. Panday et al., Comparative Study Of Intermediary Liability Regimes Chile, Canada, India, South Korea, UK and USA in support of the Manila Principles On Intermediary Liability, *o.c.*, p. 15. See also J. Hruska, Six Strikes' programs from ISPs & MPAA ignites in nine days: Here's what you need to know, Extreme Tech, 19 November 2012, www.extremetech.com/internet/140774-six-strikesprograms-from-isps-mpaa-ignites-in-nine-days-heres-what-you-need-to-know.

A. *Canada*

LEGISLATION – The Canadian notice and notice mechanism is a relatively new development.[1390] It was introduced in the Copyright Modernization Act SC 2012 (CMA), but the final provisions only took effect in January 2015.[1391] Section 31.1 of the CMA is actually a codification of the holding in *SOCAN v CAIP*, which requires neutrality as a condition for immunity.[1392] Section 41.25 of the CMA enacts the notice and notice procedure and the following sections specify the details related to notice. Interestingly, notice and notice has been effectively in place between ISPs and the music and cable industry since 2000 as a voluntary standard adopted to deal with copyright infringement.[1393]

B. *Chile*

LEGISLATION – In Chile, a regime limiting liability of intermediary service providers for copyright infringements of their users is provided in Law No. 20.435, amending Intellectual Property Law enacted on 4 May 2010 (Ley de Propiedad Intelectual, hereafter 'LPI').[1394] The scope of Law No. 20.435 LPI is limited to copyright infringements.[1395] The regime comes predominantly from the Intellectual Property Chapter of the Chile-US FTA.[1396] For this reason, the regime strongly follows the DMCA model, with one notable exception.[1397] Specifically, the decisions concerning content and content providers are taken by the courts. Service providers must comply with court injunctions, adopted before or during a judicial procedure.[1398] They can neither take down content nor disconnect a user on their own initiative or at rights holders' request.[1399]

1390 For the summary of the regime before the CMA see D. Seng, Comparative Analysis of National Approaches of the Liability of the Internet Intermediaries – Part I, WIPO, 2010, www.wipo.int/publications/en/details.jsp?id=4144&plang=EN.

1391 Copyright Modernization Act (S.C. 2012, c. 20), http://laws-lois.justice.gc.ca/eng/annualstatutes/2012_20/page-1.html.

1392 See J. Panday *et al.*, Comparative Study Of Intermediary Liability Regimes Chile, Canada, India, South Korea, UK and USA in support of the Manila Principles On Intermediary Liability, *o.c*, p. 26.

1393 *Ibid.*, p. 27.

1394 Ley no. 20.435, modifica la Ley no. 17.336 sobre propiedad intelectual, https://www.leychile.cl/Navegar?idNorma=1012827&idParte=&idVersion=2010–05–04

1395 See more on the Law 20.435 in D. Alvarez Valenzuela, "The Quest for a Normative Balance: The Recent Reforms to Chile's Copyright Law", POLICY BRIEF 12. December 2011, https://www.ictsd.org/sites/default/files/research/2012/03/the-quest-for-a-normative-balance-the-recent-reforms-to-chilee28099s-copyright-law.pdf.

1396 Chapter 17 of the Chile-US FTA, https://ustr.gov/sites/default/files/uploads/agreements/fta/chile/asset_upload_file912_4011.pdf.

1397 J. Panday et al., Comparative Study Of Intermediary Liability Regimes Chile, Canada, India, South Korea, UK and USA in support of the Manila Principles On Intermediary Liability, *o.c.* p. 29.

1398 A. Cerda Silva, "Cyber Law in Chile, in International Encyclopaedia of Laws", *Kluwer Law International*, The Netherlands, Suppl. 63, 2017, p. 126.

1399 *Ibid.*, p. 126.

C. *France*

LEGISLATION – Apart from LCEN, France has adopted a separate law to combat copyright infringements online: Law No. 2009-669 of June 12, 2009, Promoting The Dissemination and Protection Of Creative Works on The Internet (HADOPI law).[1400] The law created a new administrative authority – HADOPI (*Haute Autorité pour la Diffusion des Oeuvres et la Protection des Droits sur Internet*), in charge of enforcing copyright protection. Novel in its approach, the law introduced a policy of "graduated response", also known as "three strikes and you're out".[1401] The approach requires that after a specified number of warnings ("strikes") have been administered by the HADOPI agency, ISPs must apply certain sanctions to punish repeated misconducts by their users.[1402]

The scope of the law is limited to copyright infringements online as well as breaches of users' "duty of surveillance".[1403] The latter refers to the end-users' obligation to secure their Internet connection and monitor its use to prevent copyright infringements, as laid down in the French Code of Intellectual Property.[1404] At first, suspending access to the Internet was to be ordered directly by the HADOPI agency. However, in 2009 the law was supplemented with a new "HADOPI 2" Act[1405], according to which an actual suspension of the Internet connection could only be ruled by the criminal court.[1406] In 2013, the French Ministry of Culture issued a decree lifting the penalty of Internet access suspension for those who failed to secure their access to the network.[1407] It was decided that in future, only fines may be issued for Internet users in fault of gross negligence in securing their Internet connection. Internet suspension, however, may still be imposed on anyone found guilty of an actual infringement.[1408]

1400 Loi n° 2009-669 du 12 juin 2009 favorisant la diffusion et la protection de la création sur internet (HADOPI law), www.wipo.int/wipolex/en/text.jsp?file_id=179252.

1401 L. Edwards, Role and responsibility of the internet intermediaries in the field of copyright and related rights, *o.c.*, p. 30.

1402 *Ibid.*

1403 C. Angelopoulos, *European intermediary liability in copyright: A tort-based analysis*, *o.c.*, p. 148.

1404 N. van Eijk, C. Jasserand, C. Wiersma and T. M. van Engers, Moving towards Balance: A Study into Duties of Care on the Internet, *o.c.*, p. 26 and 112.

1405 *Loi n° 2009-1311 du 28 octobre 2009 relative à la protection pénale de la propriété littéraire et artistique, Journal officiel du 29 octobre 2009*, known as HADOPI 2.

1406 See P. de Filippi and D. Bourcier, "Three-Strikes Response to Copyright Infringement: The Case of HADOPI", in F. Musiani, D. L. Cogburn, L. DeNardis, N.S. Levinson, (eds.), *The Turn to Infrastructure in Internet Governance*, Palgrave-Macmillan, 2016, p. 141.

1407 *Décret n° 2013-596 du 8 juillet 2013 supprimant la peine contraventionnelle complémentaire de suspension de l'accès à un service de communication au public en ligne et relatif aux modalités de transmission des informations prévue à l'Article L. 331-21 du code de la propriété intellectuelle, Journal officiel n°0157 du 9 juillet 2013, page 11428, texte n° 60.* The decree also followed the recommendations of the Lescure report, see more: P. Lescure, Mission 'Acte II de l'exception culturelle' – Contribution aux politiques culturelles à l'ère numérique, May 2013.

1408 C. Angelopoulos, *European intermediary liability in copyright: A tort-based analysis*, *o.c.*, p. 148.

D. *South Korea*

LEGISLATION – South Korea presents a complex liability regime with a "vertical" approach to the problem, depending on the type of infringement.[1409] A graduated response is provided by the South Korean Copyright Act (Article 133-2 and 133-3).[1410] The mechanism functions in addition to the NTD procedures for copyright and other types of infringing content. The Copyright Act was amended in 2009 in order to introduce the graduated response, which was one of the requirements for entering into the US-Korea Free Trade Agreement.[1411]

Article 133-2 of the Copyright Act states that the Minister of Culture, Sports and Tourism (MCST) may order service providers to issue warnings to infringers or to websites hosting infringing content ('*reproducers and interactive transmitters*'), ordering them to cease transmission or to delete infringing material.[1412] According to Article 133-3, the procedure can be initiated by the Korea Copyright Protection Agency (KCPA) as a result of an investigation.[1413] The KCPA does not have the power to issue binding orders but it can recommend the same corrective measures as the MCST.

3.3. ASSESSMENT

A. *Quality of law*

ACCESSIBILITY – In each of the examples presented above, the notice and notice mechanism is provided by a legislative act. In Canada, it is the Copyright Modernization Act of 2012, in Chile it is the Law No. 20.435, amending Intellectual Property Law enacted of 2010, in France, it is the HADOPI law and HADOPI 2 Act, and in South Korea, it is the Copyright Act. In Canada, the notice and notice has actually been used between ISPs and the music and cable industry since 2000 as a voluntary measure adopted to deal with copyright infringement.[1414] The enactment of the Copyright Modernization Act codified the procedure, which improved its accessibility.

1409 See Annex.

1410 Copyright Act, *o.c.*

1411 C. Doctorow, South Korea's US-led copyright policy leads to 65,000 acts of extrajudicial censorship/ disconnection/ threats by govt bureaucrats, 26 October 2010, https://boingboing.net/2010/10/26/south-koreas-us-led.html.

1412 Article 133-2 (Orders, etc. for Deletion of Illegal Reproductions, etc. through Information and Communications Network) of the Copyright Act, *o.c.* See also OECD, The Role of Internet Intermediaries in Advancing Public Policy Objectives – Forging partnerships for advancing policy objectives for the Internet economy, *o.c.*, p. 63.

1413 In the former version of the Copyright Act the function was entrusted to the Korean Copyright Commission (KCC). See old version of the Copyright Act, (Act No. 11110, Dec. 2, 2011), Article 133-3, http://elaw.klri.re.kr/kor_service/lawView.do?hseq=25455&lang=ENG.

1414 J. Panday et al., Comparative Study Of Intermediary Liability Regimes Chile, Canada, India, South Korea, UK and USA in support of the Manila Principles On Intermediary Liability,

FORESEEABILITY – In Canada, the law introducing the notice and notice mechanism has been criticized for placing no clear controls over a warning letter's content.[1415] Specifically, it has been accused of failing to establish regulations prohibiting misleading content or the use of notice and notice to demand settlements.[1416] As a result, the mechanism is abused by copyright holders who use the notice and notice system to pressure recipients into paying large settlements.[1417] According to government sources, the law '*sets clear rules on the content of these notices*', but it does not restrict the possibility for rights holders to include information that goes beyond the statutory minimum.[1418] Moreover, ISPs cannot refuse to forward a notice which contains inaccurate or plainly misleading information. Users who receive such notices are often confused and feel pressured to pay to avoid legal action.[1419] According to the regulations on notice and notice, however, '*no one is under obligation to pay a settlement – not even a penny*'.[1420] A system where people are confused and even misled about their rights and obligations can hardly pass as foreseeable. Such '*education through fear*', which is currently a result of the missing restrictions, has been criticized by many, who urge the government to review the rules.[1421] The proposed solution to mitigate the problem would require implementing the missing regulations by establishing an appropriate fee for forwarding notices, prohibiting the use of notices to demand settlements, and giving ISPs the option to refuse to forward notices where they contain misleading or inaccurate information.[1422] The notice and notice mechanism in Canada is apparently up for a review in early 2018.

In Chile, the introduction of the intermediary liability regime was a process that took over three years of debates, consultations and campaigning. Unlike any

---

o.c. p. 27. See also Canada's Approach to Intermediary Liability for Copyright Infringement: the Notice and Notice Procedure, Berkley Technology Law Journal, 2 March 2014, http://btlj.org/2014/03/canadas-approach-to-intermediary-liability-for-copyright-infringement-the-notice-and-notice-procedure/.

1415 S. Harris, U.S. cancels internet piracy notices while Canadians still get notices demanding settlement fees, 1 February 2017, www.cbc.ca/news/business/notice-system-piracy-copyright-internet-1.3960462.

1416 M. Geist, Misuse of Canada's Copyright Notice System Continues: U.S. Firm Sending Thousands of Notices With Settlement Demands, 5 March 2015, www.michaelgeist.ca/2015/03/misuse-canadas-copyright-notice-system-continues-u-s-firm-sending-thousands-notices-settlement-demands/.

1417 *Ibid.*

1418 *Ibid.*

1419 S. Harris, 'Feels like blackmail': Canada needs to take a hard look at its piracy notice system, 2 November 2016, www.cbc.ca/news/business/copyright-infringement-notice-canada-piracy-1.3831492.

1420 *Ibid.*

1421 *Ibid.*

1422 M. Geist, Misuse of Canada's Copyright Notice System Continues: U.S. Firm Sending Thousands of Notices With Settlement Demands, *o.c.*

other issue, copyright law reform became a matter of public and civil concern.[1423] The intense public debate and the interest voiced by an unprecedented number of citizens allowed the shaping of a law that balances the rights of creators and industry with the rights of the users and consumers.[1424] The main feature of the Chilean legislation is that a court order is required to compel blocking or removal of infringing content.[1425] The approach shifts the task of evaluating notices from intermediaries to courts.[1426] No private entities were deemed fit to decide on the constitutional rights of individuals. As a result, it allows for greater certainty as the assessment of the content is conducted by an independent tribunal properly equipped for this task. By providing that an intermediary shall be deemed to have "actual knowledge" when a court has ordered that material be removed, the Law introduced a great level of foreseeability and legal certainty.[1427] The Chilean Law manages to address one of the most unclear issues of intermediary liability regimes, that being when "actual knowledge" actually starts.[1428] This solution has numerous other consequences, which will be visible in practically every criterion of this analysis.

The French law introducing the graduated response started with a firm idea of what it wanted to achieve and how. Over time, however, the law has grown weaker due to complaints about its constitutionality and respect for human rights. Already at the beginning of its existence, the law received a severe cool-down by the *Conseil Constitutionnel*, which declared that the power to suspend Internet access could not be exercised by an administrative body as it constituted a disproportionate restriction on the freedom of expression, as well as an unacceptable presumption of culpability.[1429] From severe punishments for copyright infringements and insufficient surveillance of one's own network, the law was reduced to a merely "pedagogical" system.[1430] Especially the surveillance obligation seemed to confuse too many people. According to the initial idea, Internet users were obliged to install efficient technical measures (listed by the HADOPI authority) to secure their Internet connection or else, face the consequences of their negligence. In a decree issued soon after

1423 D. Alvarez Valenzuela, "The Quest for Normative Balance: The Recent Reforms to Chile's Copyright Law," *o.c.*, p. 9.

1424 See *Ibid.*, p. 11.

1425 CDT, Chile's Notice-and-Takedown System for Copyright Protection: an Alternative Approach, August 2012, p. 2.

1426 *Ibid.*, p. 5.

1427 See Art. 85 Ñ, LPI.

1428 See CDT, Chile's Notice-and-Takedown System for Copyright Protection: an Alternative Approach, *o.c.*, p. 9.

1429 Conseil Constitutionnel, Décision n° 2009–580 DC du 10 juin 2009, Journal officiel du 13 juin 2009, page 9675, texte n° 3. As referenced by C. Angelopoulos, *European intermediary liability in copyright: A tort-based analysis*, *o.c.*, p. 148.

1430 See S. Columbus, France to disconnect first Internet users under three strikes regime, 27 July 2017, https://opennet.net/blog/2011/07/france-disconnect-first-internet-users-under-three-strikes-regime.

the HADOPI law, negligence was defined as *'not having put in place security measures'* or having *'lacked diligence in putting in place this measures'*.[1431] The critics pointed out, however, that the definition is unclear as it fails to specify what it means by "certified security measures".[1432] It appeared to be unclear enough for many people who received a second warning, but who claimed that they had not downloaded anything.[1433] In July 2013, the French Ministry of Culture issued a decree lifting the penalty of Internet access suspension for those who failed to secure their access to the network.[1434] Considering the tumultuous developments of the graduated response in France, it becomes clear that the law introducing the mechanism was not clear or sufficiently foreseeable, neither for the French Internet users nor for the French legislator. The quality of the law is one of the main reasons why the ambitious idea was eventually struck down.

The South Korean Copyright Act has also been criticized for the quality of the law implementing the "three strikes" approach. From the beginning, the law has been controversial and raised several constitutional concerns.[1435] The suspension of user's accounts was considered a possible violation of the right to the freedom of speech.[1436] It was questioned whether the power of an executive agency to order corrections should be considered as an unconstitutional violation of the separation of powers.[1437] Finally, commentators expressed concerns about compliance with the principle of due process.[1438] Moreover, the law left several issues unspecified, raising questions about its foreseeability. For example, the law did not set a timeframe of how the warnings should be spread in time.[1439] There is also no requirement that any particular infringement must be of a certain level of severity before a warning may be issued, despite the law being described as targeted at heavy infringers.[1440] In practice, however, the law has been broadly enforced against minor offenders.[1441] Moreover, the procedure of recommendation (in the earlier version by the Korea Copyright

1431 *Ibid.*

1432 G. Champeau, Hadopi: la négligence caractérisée est enfin définie... de manière très floue, 26 June 2010, www.numerama.com/magazine/16087-hadopi-la-negligence-caracterisee-est-enfin-definie-de-maniere-tres-floue.html.

1433 M. Rees, Suspension: les 10 premiers internautes convoqués par l'Hadopi, 1 July 2011, https://www.nextinpact.com/archive/64415-hadopi-tmg-abonnes-convoques-suspension.htm.

1434 *Décret n° 2013-596 du 8 juillet 2013, o.c.*

1435 S.-Y. Moon and D. Kim, "The 'Three Strikes' Policy in Korean Copyright Act 2009: Safe or Out?", *Washington Journal of Law, Technology & Arts*, Vol. 6, 2011, p. 173.

1436 *Ibid.*, p. 171.

1437 *Ibid.*

1438 *Ibid.*

1439 Centre for Law and Democracy, Analysis of the Korean Copyright Act, June 2013, www.law-democracy.org/live/wp-content/uploads/2013/06/Korea.Copyright.pdf, p. 6.

1440 *Ibid.*

1441 *Ibid.* See also P. Resnikoff, Three Strikes: A Complete & Total Failure In South Korea..., 1 April 2013, https://www.digitalmusicnews.com/2013/04/01/effkorea/; and Heesob's IP Blog, Facts and Figures on Copyright Three-Strike Rule in Korea, 24 October 2010, http://hurips.blogspot.be/2010/10/facts-and-figures-on-copyright-three.html.

Commission and in the most recent version by the Korea Copyright Protection Agency) seems to provide an alternative route to suspension of an account, without any independent oversight. The law also does not require the issuance of three warnings in the recommendation procedure. A recommendation for suspension may be issued without a warning if it has been alleged that multiple infringements had taken place.[1442] Technically, the OSPs are not obliged to follow the recommendations and no direct sanctions are foreseen in such an event.[1443] However, the Protection Agency (and earlier the KCC) may request the MCST to issue correction orders, in which case pre-consultation is not required.[1444] To avoid the issuance of correction orders recommendations have generally been followed.[1445]

B. *Protection of democratic society*

DEMOCRATIC VALUES – In the sample of countries analysed in this section, the notice and notice mechanism, even in its strictest form of a graduated response, applies solely to copyright infringements. Copyright falls under the category of "rights of others" therefore the protected value fits within the list of grounds for restrictions in Article 10.2 ECHR.

Despite strong differences in the severity of the response foreseen in each national implementation, they are grouped together here because they spread the response in time by gradually increasing the pressure on the infringer while giving them an opportunity to correct his behaviour. It is interesting, however, that this "delayed-response" model is so often preferred for copyright infringements.

C. *Tailored response*

LEAST RESTRICTIVE MEANS – The notice and notice mechanism knows many variations. Starting from the light-handed version, as present in Canada, through a moderate version in Chile, the spectrum goes all the way to its hard-handed version which can lead to user account suspension in South Korea

---

1442 Centre for Law and Democracy, Analysis of the Korean Copyright Act, *o.c.*, p. 6.

1443 S.-Y. Moon and D. Kim, "The 'Three Strikes' Policy in Korean Copyright Act 2009: Safe or Out?", *o.c.*, p. 177.

1444 See Annual Report 2009 Korea APAA Copyright Committee, Major Amendments to Korean Copyright Act – April, 2009, www.apaaonline.org/pdf/APAA_56th_&_57th_council_meeting/copyright/2-Korea%20Copyright%20Cttee%20Country%20Report%202009.pdf, p. 8.

1445 See M. Masnik, A Look At How Many People Have Been Kicked Offline In Korea On Accusations (Not Convictions) Of Infringement, 26 October 2010, https://www.techdirt.com/articles/20101025/18093711583/a-look-at-how-many-people-have-been-kicked-offline-in-korea-on-accusations-not-convictions-of-infringement.shtml; see also S.-Y. Moon and D. Kim, "The 'Three Strikes' Policy in Korean Copyright Act 2009: Safe or Out?", *o.c.*, p. 182.

and even Internet disconnection in France. Yet, despite strong differences in severity, each version is considered as an appropriate response to copyright infringements. Is it possible, therefore, that they are all proportionate to the aim pursued?

According to the criterion of the tailored response, a restricting measure should not be excessive and, if possible, should opt for the least restrictive intervention. This is definitely the case in Canada, where the only tasks of the ISPs are to forward the complaint and to retain records to be presented in court and to identify the infringer.[1446] The intermediary's involvement is therefore minimal as he is not obliged to take down the content, but only to assist the copyright holder in exercising the rights against the primary infringer.

In Chile, service providers cannot take down content or disconnect a user on their own initiative or at rights holders' requests.[1447] Similarly as in Canada, service providers must communicate the received notices to the concerned users.[1448] It is the courts that order removal of, or disabling access to the infringing content and termination of the accounts of the repeated offenders who have been clearly identified as copyright infringers.[1449] The measures can be ordered during a trial or prior to a trial, as a preliminary measure. If the order is requested as a preliminary measure, the court can rule without the presence of the content provider, however, in such a case the plaintiff must provide a bond.[1450] Requirement of a bond can act as prevention against abusive requests at the point when the content provider is not yet part of the proceedings and cannot defend his actions. The procedure contains another safeguard against abusive take down requests in the form of compensation for damages in case of removals resulting from false information.[1451] Some authors fear that it might not be a sufficient safeguard to prevent abuses of the system, as the compensation excludes any statutory or punitive damages and is limited to actual damages.[1452] The provision, however, also includes a reference to the Criminal Code. With the risk of imprisonment of up to five years and monetary fines for falsification of private documents, the sanctions seem to be dissuasive enough.[1453]

South Korea took a different approach, under the strong influence of the US, in the negotiation process of the US – Korea FTA.[1454] The Minister of Culture, Sports and Tourism (MCST) has the power to order service providers

1446 Article 41.26(1) of the Copyright Modernization Act (S.C. 2012, c. 20).

1447 A. Cerda Silva, "Cyber Law in Chile, in International Encyclopaedia of Laws, *o.c.*, p. 126.

1448 Art. 85 U, LPI.

1449 See A. Cerda Silva, Cyber Law in Chile, in International Encyclopaedia of Laws, *o.c.*, p. 131.

1450 Art. 85 Q, LPI.

1451 Art. 85 T, LPI.

1452 A. Cerda Silva, Cyber Law in Chile, in International Encyclopaedia of Laws, *o.c.*, p. 133.

1453 Criminal Code, Art. 197. See A. Cerda Silva, Cyber Cyber Law in Chile, in International Encyclopaedia of Laws, *o.c.*, p. 134.

1454 See C. Doctorow, South Korea's US-led copyright policy leads to 65,000 acts of extrajudicial censorship/ disconnection/ threats by govt bureaucrats, *o.c.*

to issue warnings to infringers and websites hosting infringing content and to order them to cease transmission or to delete infringing material.[1455] If the infringement continues after three warnings, the Minister (after consultation with the Deliberation Committee) may order the service provider to suspend an account of the infringer or a website for up to six months.[1456] The suspension does not apply to e-mail accounts but includes other accounts given by the relevant online service provider.[1457] The same measures can be recommended by the Korea Copyright Protection Agency, which does not have the power to issue binding orders, but has the power to request the MCST to issue binding orders.[1458] The measures foreseen by the Korean legislation can hardly be called a minimal intervention. Even though the MCST procedure requires three warnings before an order to remove content or disconnect, the alternative procedure by the KCPA does not contain such a requirement. This means that the KCPA could issue a recommendation much earlier, after detecting any instance of a repeated copyright infringement.[1459] The severity of the law can be seen by the early figures on the implementation. By the end of July 2010, there had been no suspension of an individual user or a web site resulting from the order of the MCST.[1460] However, there had been 31 cases of suspended accounts on the recommendation by the Korea Copyright Commission (the body issuing recommendations at that time).[1461] By the end of 2012, a total number of 408 users had had their accounts suspended.[1462] The disconnection measure, moreover, does not appear to be proportionate to the harm. Most of the suspended users were minor offenders.[1463] This is in stark contrast to the intention of the law, which had been supposedly aimed at "heavy uploaders" making illegal content sharing a profession.[1464] However, as discovered by the Korean politician Choi Jae-Cheon, half of those suspended were involved in infringement of material that would cost less than 90 US cents.[1465] The measure was also not very successful in achieving its purpose to curb online piracy.[1466]

1455 Article 133-2 (Orders, etc. for Deletion of Illegal Reproductions, etc. through Information and Communications Network) of the Copyright Act, *o.c.* See also OECD, The Role of Internet Intermediaries in Advancing Public Policy Objectives – Forging partnerships for advancing policy objectives for the Internet economy, *o.c.*, p. 63.

1456 Article 133-2(2) of the Copyright Act.

1457 Article 133-2(2) of the Copyright Act.

1458 See Article 133-3(3) of the Copyright Act.

1459 Centre for Law and Democracy, Analysis of the Korean Copyright Act, *o.c.*, p. 6.

1460 Heesob's IP Blog, Facts and Figures on Copyright Three-Strike Rule in Korea, *o.c.*

1461 *Ibid.*

1462 See Copyright Reform – Abolishing Three-Strikes-Out Rule from Copyright Law, https://opennet.or.kr/copyright-reform.

1463 See *Ibid.*

1464 See *Ibid.*

1465 D. O'Brien, M. Sutton, Korean Lawmakers and Human Rights Experts Challenge Three Strikes Law, Electronic Frontiers Foundation, 29 March 2013, https://www.eff.org/deeplinks/2013/03/korea-stands-against-three-strikes.

1466 *Ibid.*

As more users became subject to deletion, blocking or suspensions, the amount of detected infringements was constantly increasing.[1467] Considering the low effectiveness of the approach together with the widespread levity of the offenses, it is hard to consider the mechanism as proportionate. Also the severity of the sanction, which can lead to suspension of the user account is clearly not a least restrictive response to offer. It is true that the sanction does not lead to disconnection from the Internet, like in the French version of the graduated response. The accused infringer suffers "only" from suspension of his account(s) with a particular service provider. The law clearly excludes e-mail accounts from the scope. This means, that, unlike in France, the sanction is not a complete exile from the Internet. It is a small consolation which does not erase the fact that the sanction creates an obstacle to the exercise of the right to freedom of expression and access to information. It is therefore understandable that in 2013 the National Human Rights Commission of South Korea recommended re-evaluation of the Copyright Act and, and in particular, introduction of users' rights capable of offsetting abusive enforcement of copyright, providing more balance between intellectual property protection and the right to culture and information, and re-examination of the three-strikes approach from the perspective of the right to access to information and possibly its revocation.[1468] Unfortunately, the calls have not been very successful because after the last amendment of the Copyright Act in 2017, the three-strikes approach is still standing strong.

In France the notice and notice mechanism took the most extreme form. When introduced, the new law gave the HADOPI agency power to issue sanctions in the form of fines and temporary suspensions of Internet connection. The latter penalty was strengthened with a prohibition to subscribe to any other ISP for the period of the punishment. The period of suspension could range from three months to one year.[1469] In the last phase of the procedure, the user was given a chance to decrease the period of suspension (to a period between one month and three months) but he had to confess to committing the infringing act. The reduced penalty required a commitment of the user that they would not engage in similar activities in the future.[1470] It should be highlighted that disconnection from the Internet was initially foreseen as a sanction not only for copyright infringements but also for not securing one's Internet connection

1467 South Korea sees fewer crackdowns on copyright infringement: report, 13 August 2011, http://english.yonhapnews.co.kr/national/2011/08/13/43/0302000000AEN20110813001100315F.HTML.

1468 Heesob's IP Blog, National Human Rights Body Recommends Abolishing Three-Strike-Out Rule, 27 March 2013, http://hurips.blogspot.be/2013/03/national-human-rights-body-recommends.html.

1469 See P. de Filippi and D. Bourcier, "Three-Strikes" Response to Copyright Infringement: The Case of HADOPI", *o.c.*, p. 134.

1470 See *Ibid.*, p. 135.

which allowed it to be used for copyright infringements by others. Even if the user failed to follow the instructions from the ISP to secure the network, it seems that a penalty of disconnection, and therefore a strong interference with the right to freedom of expression, is grossly disproportionate to the wrongdoing – especially considering that the main wrongdoing was committed by someone else.

Similar arguments led the *Conseil Constitutionnel* to issue an opinion in 2009 that the power to sanction by suspending Internet access constituted a disproportionate interference with the right to freedom of expression and communication, as well as an unacceptable presumption of culpability.[1471] The sanction of disconnection by itself was considered permissible. The problem pointed out by the *Conseil Constitutionnel* was that such severe interference was issued by an administrative authority and not a court of law.[1472] As a solution, the law was supplemented with "HADOPI 2" Act[1473], which provided that the suspension of the Internet connection could only be ruled by the criminal court.[1474] This step, however, did not put the criticism of the law to rest. By 2013, the French Ministry of Culture lifted the penalty of Internet access suspension for the users who failed to secure their access to the network against infringement.[1475] Since then, only fines may be issued for those in fault of gross negligence in securing their Internet connection. Internet suspension still functions as a possible sanction, but it can be imposed only on those found guilty of an actual infringement.[1476]

According to the report of the Lescure commission by the government around the same time, the law failed to achieve its goals.[1477] By 2013, the law had resulted in conviction and a 15 days suspension of exactly one individual, who moreover, insists that he did not commit the infringement.[1478] In the same year, the penalty of suspension was abolished.[1479] By 2017, the law had led to 189 criminal convictions.[1480] The findings of the Lescure commission are consistent with other research, which showed that the three strikes law didn't stop or even

1471 Conseil Constitutionnel, Décision n° 2009–580 DC du 10 juin 2009, *o.c.*

1472 See P. de Filippi and D. Bourcier, "Three-Strikes" Response to Copyright Infringement: The Case of HADOPI", *o.c.*, p. 135.

1473 Loi n° 2009–1311 du 28 octobre 2009 (HADOPI 2), *o.c.*

1474 See P. de Filippi and D. Bourcier, "Three-Strikes" Response to Copyright Infringement: The Case of HADOPI", *o.c.*, p. 141.

1475 Décret n° 2013–596 du 8 juillet 2013, *o.c.*

1476 C. Angelopoulos, *European intermediary liability in copyright: A tort-based analysis*, *o.c.*, p. 148.

1477 See P. Lescure, "Mission 'Acte II de l'exception culturelle' – Contribution aux politiques culturelles à l'ère numérique", *o.c.*

1478 See S. Columbus, France to disconnect first Internet users under three strikes regime, *o.c.*

1479 HADOPI, Rapport d' activité 2016–2017, https://www.hadopi.fr/sites/default/rapportannuel/HADOPI-Rapport-d-activite-2016–2017.pdf, p. 34, ft. 28.

1480 Seven Years of Hadopi: Nine Million Piracy Warnings, 189 Convictions, 1 December 2017, https://torrentfreak.com/seven-years-of-hadopi-nine-million-piracy-warnings-189-convictions-171201/.

reduce piracy.[1481] The French attempt to fight copyright infringements online was not successful. With the intended severe response, France opted for the most restrictive measures available. Moreover, it contributed to the normalization of surveillance and to an increase of centralized control of the Internet.[1482] Due to continuous doubts about its constitutionality, proportionality and effectiveness, however, the law was gradually reduced to a mere shadow of itself.

D. *Procedural fairness*

DUE PROCESS – Installing elements of due process in a response mechanism helps to achieve procedural fairness, and as a result, to reach a proportionate and fair conclusion. Observance of due process is facilitated when the removal decisions are taken by courts, and not by private entities. Although not always with a perfect score, judiciary systems in democratic States have well established sets of rules of handling conflicts in front of the courts. This is the approach in Canada and Chile where the main focus in combating online infringements is on the primary wrongdoers and not on the intermediaries. Once the claim reaches the judiciary, it becomes the court's role to ensure that the right to fair hearing within a reasonable time is respected and the proceedings are adversarial and that there is equality of arms between the prosecution and defence. Nevertheless, both countries added elements of due process in their procedures at the level of intermediaries. In Canada, the notice of the copyright holder is forwarded to the content provider, which provides an opportunity to obtain knowledge about the accusations. The Canadian procedure allows the content provider to respond to the notification within a limited period of time.[1483] Both of these elements contribute to the fairness of the procedure by introducing elements of the right to fair hearing, adversarial proceedings and equality of arms. Even though the intermediary is not going to make any decisions about the case, from the very beginning of the procedure both parties are able to express their positions on the matter. In Chile the service provider also forwards the complaint from the copyright holder to the content provider. Moreover, the service provider has to attach the records provided by the copyright holder to the notice.[1484] This step strengthens the position of the content provider who knows exactly what he is accused of and what evidence exists to support the claim. The content provider in Chile, however, does not have

---

1481 See M. A. Arnold, et al., Graduated Response Policy and the Behavior of Digital Pirates: Evidence from the French Three-Strike (Hadopi) Law, 2014. Available at: https://ssrn.com/abstract=2380522 or http://dx.doi.org/10.2139/ssrn.2380522.

1482 See T. Meyer & L. Van Audenhove, "Surveillance and regulating code: an analysis of graduated response in France", *Surveillance & Society*, Vol. 4, Issue 9, pp. 365–377. See also T. Meyer, "Graduated Response In France: The Clash of Copyright and the Internet", *Journal of Information Policy*, Vol. 2, 2012, pp. 107–127.

1483 C. Angelopoulos, S. Smet, "Notice-and-fair-balance: how to reach a compromise between fundamental rights in European intermediary liability", *o.c.*, p. 295.

1484 A. Cerda Silva, "Cyber Law in Chile, in International Encyclopaedia of Laws", *o.c.*, p. 129.

an opportunity to respond to the notice before the conflict reaches the court. The requested measure is normally ordered during a trial, but it is also possible for the court to issue a preliminary measure.[1485] The content provider might not necessarily be present if preliminary measures are issued pre-trial, which is not ideal from the perspective of due process. Such a possibility must be justified, however, by serious circumstances and the plaintiff must provide a bond.[1486] The affected content provider can submit a counter-request to nullify the decision.[1487] Expeditious processing of the case is another due process element as it ensures that the conflict is resolved within a reasonable time.

Where decisions about content are taken by private entities or administrative authorities, a procedure should be provided to ensure that due process is respected by the decision-making parties. Absence of due process in private enforcement is a point of frequent criticism of the existing mechanisms. That is, for example, the case in South Korea where the law is criticized for not respecting the due process requirements.[1488] The main argument against the law is that the procedure is handled by the executive branch of the government, the Ministry of Culture, Sports, and Tourism. Under South Korean law, a possibility exists to "express an opinion" by those affected by the order.[1489] While expressing one's opinion on the matter undoubtedly inserts an element of fair hearing, the law does not specify whether such an opinion should be treated as an objection against the decision of the MCST, whether it must be taken into account in the decision-making process, or whether it leads to the review of the MCST's decision. In any case, the decision is not reviewed by the courts, only consulted with the Deliberation Committee, which is not an independent body. Lack of judicial review and a complete dependency on the public administration authority make the process less transparent and more vulnerable to arbitrary decision-making.[1490]

In France, the graduated response mechanism was criticised on multiple grounds from the very beginning. The initial procedure included attempts to introduce elements of due process. For example, the first warning had to inform the user about his right to request further clarification regarding the charges.[1491] The second warning gave the user a possibility to respond (within a specified time) and defend his behaviour.[1492] In the last phase the user was able to challenge

---

1485 Art. 85 Q, LPI.

1486 Art. 85 Q, LPI.

1487 A. Cerda Silva, "Cyber Law in Chile, in International Encyclopaedia of Laws", *o.c.*, p. 131.

1488 See C. Doctorow, South Korea's US-led copyright policy leads to 65,000 acts of extrajudicial censorship/ disconnection/ threats by govt bureaucrats, *o.c.*

1489 Article 133-2(7) of the Copyright Act.

1490 J. Y. Kim, South Korean Politician Moves to Repeal Biased Copyright Law, 28 March 2013, https://advox.globalvoices.org/2013/03/28/south-korean-politician-moves-to-repeal-biased-copyright-law/.

1491 Articles L. 335-7 and L. 335-7-1 of the HADOPI law.

1492 See P. de Filippi and D. Bourcier, " Three-Strikes Response to Copyright Infringement: The Case of HADOPI", *o.c.*, p. 134.

the decision in front of a judge, by demonstrating that he was not responsible for the alleged infringement (and that he took the necessary measures to secure the Internet connection). The law was, nevertheless, challenged in front of the *Conseil Constitutionnel*, which ruled that in such a form, the law allowed for a disproportionate interference with the right to freedom of expression and an unacceptable presumption of guilt.[1493] The Court ruled that such powers must be exercised by courts and not by administration authorities. In 2011, the *Conseil d'Etat* rejected the applications against the two HADOPI Acts accusing them of violating the right to a fair trial under Article 6 of the ECHR.[1494] Despite the rejection, it is clear that the criticism and the multiple challenges of the law had a strong influence on the procedure. The main impact on the due process rights was undeniably provided by the ruling of the *Conseil Constitutionnel*, which took away the power of the HADOPI agency to sanction users and confirmed that this type of punishment must be administered under judicial control.

INDEPENDENT AND IMPARTIAL TRIBUNAL – In Canada, the authority on online copyright infringements lays with the courts. Internet intermediaries are not obliged to remove content upon receiving the notice from the copyright holders.[1495] Copyright holders must seek relief from the courts when the content provider does not remove the content on their own, after being forwarded the notice by the intermediary. The Parliament Legislative Summary shows that the Canadian legislature was intensively discussing whether to adopt the notice and notice mechanism or the notice and take down (or even the graduated response).[1496] The Summary document pointed out that under Canadian law, the courts already have the ability to order the takedown of infringing material.[1497] The NTD, which requires no court order, however, raised concerns about creating incentives to remove content without warning or evidence, and as a result, could potentially lead to stifling free expression.[1498] The government was aware of the criticism and rejected the NTD approach because of insufficient protection to users' rights.[1499]

1493 Conseil Constitutionnel, Décision n° 2009–580 DC du 10 juin 2009, *o.c.*

1494 Conseil d'Etat, *Société Apple Inc et Société I-Tunes Sarl*, 19 October 2011, n° 339154 and *French Data Network*, 19 October, 2011, n°339279 and n° 342405.

1495 S. Kilpatrick and R. Black, Internet Intermediaries and Copyright Owners Take Notice: Canada's Notice-and-Notice Regime Comes into Force, January 2015, Intellectual Property Bulletin, http://mcmillan.ca/Internet-Intermediaries-and-Copyright-Owners-Take-Notice-Canadas-Notice-and-Notice-Regime-Comes-into-Force.

1496 D. Lithwick, M.-O. Thibodeau, Bill C-11: An Act to amend the Copyright Act, Library of Parliament Legislative Summary, Publication No. 41-1-C11-E, 14 October 2011, Revised 20 April 2012, p. 27.

1497 *Ibid.*, p. 27.

1498 M. Geist, Canada's 'Notice and notice', p2pnet.net, 16 February 2007, as referenced by D. Lithwick, M.-O. Thibodeau, Bill C-11: An Act to amend the Copyright Act, *o.c.*, p. 27.

1499 House of Commons Debates, 41st Parl, 1st Sess, No 31 (18 October 2011) at 1050 (Hon James Moore, Conservative Party of Canada), as referenced by P. Schabas, I. Fischer, C. DiMatteo,

In Chile, the decision to leave the takedown order to courts was less obvious. The amendment to the Copyright Law was implementing provisions of the US-Chile FTA, which is why the approach to content take downs resembles the DMCA.[1500] There is, however, one significant difference. In Chile, there is no private enforcement of the copyright infringements and the orders to take down content must be issued by the courts. The mechanism resulting from this approach is often called "notice and judicial takedown".[1501] The introduced judicial proceedings are simplified, as they authorize an expeditious court order provided that the specific requirements are met (see *Supra*). Initially, the proposal for the Law contained a mechanism of good faith that would allow a service provider to block allegedly infringing content without judicial intervention.[1502] The measure, however, was rejected by the National Congress which expressed a strong opposition against any non-judicial mechanisms, either administrative or private proceedings.[1503] Even though certain interest groups argued that judicial proceedings are impractical and timely, the National Congress rejected any provision that did not include the intervention of a judge.[1504] The approach taken was also criticized by the US Trade Representative as not efficient enough.[1505] Numerous stakeholders argued for implementation of the DMCA system, pointing out, for example, that it would be compatible with the commitment of the FTA signed with the US.[1506] The final decision of the Congress was based on a belief that any other option would seriously affect rights and freedoms guaranteed by the Chilean Constitution, which are enforceable against both State and non-State actors, and by the American Convention on Human Rights (ACHR).[1507] As

---

"Canada's Copyright Modernization Act: A Delicate Rebalancing of Interests", *MLRC Bulletin*, Issue 2, 2013, www.medialaw.org/component/k2/item/1820-canada%E2%80%99s-copyright-modernization-act-a-delicate-rebalancing-of-interests.

1500 See D. Alvarez Valenzuela, "The Quest for Normative Balance: The Recent Reforms to Chile's Copyright Law," *o.c.*

1501 See for example C. Angelopoulos, S. Smet, "Notice-and-fair-balance: how to reach a compromise between fundamental rights in European intermediary liability", *o.c.*, p. 299.

1502 D. Alvarez Valenzuela, "The Quest for Normative Balance: The Recent Reforms to Chile's Copyright Law," *o.c*; and CDT, Chile's Notice-and-Takedown System for Copyright Protection: an Alternative Approach, *o.c.*, p. 3.

1503 *Ibid.*

1504 See more in D. Alvarez Valenzuela, "The Quest for Normative Balance: The Recent Reforms to Chile's Copyright Law," *o.c*; and CDT, Chile's Notice-and-Takedown System for Copyright Protection: an Alternative Approach, *o.c*, p. 11.

1505 United States Trade Representative. 2013 Special 301 Report, p. 28. See also A. Cerda Silva, "Cyber Law in Chile", *o.c.* p. 131.

1506 For an overview of the arguments on both sides see: E. Walker Echenique, "Implementing the IP Chapter of the FTA between Chile and the USA: Criticism and Realities from a Developing Country Perspective", *SCRIPTED*, Volume 9, Issue 2, August 2012, pp. 233–257, at p. 251 and following.

1507 D. Alvarez Valenzuela, "The Quest for Normative Balance: The Recent Reforms to Chile's Copyright Law," *o.c.*; and CDT, Chile's Notice-and-Takedown System for Copyright Protection: an Alternative Approach, *o.c.*, p. 3. A. Cerda Silva, "Cyber Law in Chile", *o.c.*,

a result of that choice, in 2011, the US kept Chile on its Priority Watch List, expressing its negative opinion about the Law by declaring that Chile should '*amend its Internet service provider liability regime to permit effective action against any act of infringement of copyright and related rights*'.[1508] The choice made by the Chilean legislature was praised by the UN Special Rapporteur on the Promotion and Protection of the Right to Freedom of Opinion and Expression, who welcomed initiatives taken to protect intermediaries,

> 'such as the bill adopted in Chile, which provides that intermediaries are not required to prevent or remove access to user-generated content that infringes copyright laws until they are notified by a court order'.[1509]

In South Korea, the orders to suspend users' accounts are issued by the MCST, which is part of the executive branch. Moreover, another procedure exists where issuing warnings and suspension of accounts is recommended by the Korea Copyright Protection Agency (KCPA).[1510] The KCPA is a body that is tasked to provide support for the establishment and implementation of policies for the protection of copyrights, to provide support to the investigation and regulation of infringements on copyrights, to deliberate on corrective orders issued by the MCST, and to make recommendations to online service providers to take corrective measures.[1511] Moreover, it shall take care of any other affairs entrusted by the Minister of Culture, Sports and Tourism.[1512] The chairman of the KCPA is appointed by the MCST. The body includes a Deliberation Committee, which consists of equal representatives from rights holders and users.[1513] However, the members of the Committee are commissioned by the Minister, therefore, it is difficult to consider this body as independent from the executive power. Since the introduction of the graduated response in South Korea, the role of the government bodies in the suspension process has been one of the main points of its criticism.[1514]

In France, a question quickly emerged regarding whether an administrative authority can order a restriction on the freedom of expression in the form

p. 131. See also Human Rights and Internet Intermediary Regulation in Chile, Global Censorship Chokepoints, https://globalchokepoints.org/human-rights-and-internet-intermediary-regulation-chile.html.

1508 Ambassador Ronald Kirk, Office of the United States Trade Representative, 2011 Special 301 Report, p. 28. The "Special 301" Report is an annual review of the global state of intellectual property rights (IPR) protection and enforcement in 77 trading partner countries, conducted by the Office of the United States Trade Representative (USTR).

1509 F. La Rue, Report of the Special Rapporteur on the promotion and protection of the right to freedom of opinion and expression, United Nations. General Assembly. A/HRC/17/27, p. 13.

1510 See Article 133-3(1) of the Copyright Act.

1511 For the full list of tasks see Article 122-5 of the Copyright Act.

1512 Article 122-5.8 of the Copyright Act.

1513 See Article 122-6 of the Copyright Act.

1514 Centre for Law and Democracy, Analysis of the Korean Copyright Act, *o.c.*, p. 6 and 9.

of account suspension. Initially, suspending access to the Internet was to be ordered directly by the HADOPI agency, but this approach was challenged on the grounds of its constitutionality. The *Conseil Constitutionnel* declared granting the power to sanction by suspending Internet access to an independent administrative authority to be disproportionate.[1515] The Court ruled that such a decision required a judicial procedure so it could not be taken by an administrative body.[1516] The law, in result, was supplemented with "HADOPI 2" Act[1517], which gave the competence to the criminal court.[1518]

REQUIREMENTS FOR THE DECISION-MAKING PROCESS – Notice and notice procedures exist in a variety of forms. In some, the interfering measures are administered by courts, for example in Canada, Chile, and France (after HADOPI 2). In others, for example in South Korea (and originally in France), the measures are administered by administrative authorities. According to the requirements for the decision making process, the decision-making body should afford due weight to the interests of the parties involved, and ensure that procedural safeguards are available. In the context of this book, the requirements apply equally, irrespective of whether the decisions are made by the courts or by the administrative authorities.

Fair balancing of the interests at stake lies within competences of the courts in democratic States. Leaving the decision-making process to the courts, therefore, contributes to ensuring that the legitimate interests of creators and industry as well as those of the users and consumers are taken into account and adequately balanced.[1519] Nevertheless, both Chile and Canada introduced additional safeguards to ensure respect for procedural rights in their mechanisms. These safeguards include notification to the content provider and a possibility to file a response (Canada). They are discussed in the section on due process but the fact that they have been implemented in the procedure clearly fulfils the requirement for the decision-making process.

Countries in which the decisions are taken by the administrative authority attempted to introduce safeguards in the removal procedures. Both in South Korea and France (before HADOPI 2) the procedures included elements of notification and counter-notification.[1520] Yet, in both cases the safeguards did not manage to improve the level of the decision-making process nor did they address the widespread criticism. In South Korea, for example, it is still unclear if the

[1515] Conseil Constitutionnel, Décision n° 2009–580 DC du 10 juin 2009, *o.c.*

[1516] See P. de Filippi and D. Bourcier, "Three-Strikes Response to Copyright Infringement: The Case of HADOPI", *o.c.*, p. 135.

[1517] *Loi n° 2009–1311 du 28 octobre 2009* (HADOPI 2), *o.c.*

[1518] See P. de Filippi and D. Bourcier, "Three-Strikes Response to Copyright Infringement: The Case of HADOPI", *o.c.*, p. 141.

[1519] See more in D. Alvarez Valenzuela, "The Quest for Normative Balance: The Recent Reforms to Chile's Copyright Law," *o.c.*, p. 2 and 11.

[1520] See section C on Tailored response.

possibility to "express an opinion" should be considered an objection or counter-notification. Where the procedure is initiated by the KCPA, such a possibility is not mentioned at all.[1521] In France the original HADOPI Act contained a number of safeguards. However, the *Conseil Constitutionnel* did not consider them sufficient to ensure a proportionate outcome and took away the power of the HADOPI Agency to administer the sanctions without judicial review.

E. Effective remedy

POSSIBILITY TO APPEAL THE DECISION – In the context of this book, having the possibility to appeal a takedown (or suspension of an account) is relevant mainly when the decision is taken by bodies other than courts. For example, it could be a private body or, as in cases of the presented notice-and-notice mechanism, an administrative authority. As mentioned above, the existence of the possibility to appeal a decision is not always obvious. In South Korea, the possibility to "express an opinion" exists, but it is not clear if it actually constitutes an objection. Moreover, some of the procedures available in South Korea do not mention this option at all, which does not suggest that there is much attention to the right to effective remedy.[1522] In France, the original HADOPI procedure provided that the recipient of the second warning could respond within 15 days, providing a justification for the repeated misconduct.[1523] In the final stage of the procedure, they had a chance to challenge the decision in front of a judge, by demonstrating that they were not responsible for the alleged infringement and that they took the necessary measures to secure the Internet connection. It seems that by providing such safeguards the law intended to offer a possibility to appeal the decision. Even with those safeguards in place, however, the *Conseil Constitutionnel* did not find overall that the mechanism was able to replace a judicial procedure when a disproportionate interference with fundamental rights was at stake.[1524]

JUDICIAL REDRESS – Any form of the notice and notice mechanism should offer a possibility of judicial redress as a final form of remedy. In theory, the lack of a specific provision addressing this matter should not necessarily prevent seeking a redress in court. From the perspective of legal certainty as well as effectiveness of redress, however, a law allowing for interference with fundamental rights should be clear on this matter. The South Korean procedure does not mention

1521 See Article 133-3 of the Copyright Act.

1522 See Article 133-3 of the Copyright Act.

1523 P. de Filippi and D. Bourcier, "Three-Strikes Response to Copyright Infringement: The Case of HADOPI", *o.c.*, p. 134.

1524 See Conseil Constitutionnel, Décision n° 2009-580 DC du 10 juin 2009, *o.c.* See also P. de Filippi and D. Bourcier, "Three-Strikes Response to Copyright Infringement: The Case of HADOPI", *o.c.*, p. 135.

such a possibility. In France, the original HADOPI Act did foresee a possibility to challenge the decision of the HADOPI Agency in front of a judge. However, it was considered insufficient to ensure proportionality of the response. The mechanism was revised as a result and HADOPI 2 Act established that such a severe interference with the right to freedom of expression and communication must be administered by courts from the very beginning of the procedure.

In countries where the restricting measure is applied by the courts, the parties to the procedure can appeal a decision which would then be reviewed by a court of second instance. The mechanism applied in that form complies with the criterion of effective remedy.

3.4. LESSONS LEARNED

VARIATIONS OF THE MECHANISM – The N&N mechanism exists in many variations. Canada took a light-handed approach and the intermediaries are only required to forward the notice, while Chile opted for a moderate version where any decisions to take down or suspend an account are taken by the courts. South Korea chose a stricter version, where N&N can lead to user account suspension (but not the email account). The most severe approach was taken in France going all the way to Internet disconnection with prohibition to subscribe to a new ISP. It is interesting that, despite such strong differences in severity, each version is considered as an appropriate and proportionate response to copyright infringements in the respective country. Another distinction that can be made is between mechanisms that require the involvement of courts, and mechanisms that rely on the decisions made by administrative authorities. The consequences of this choice are visible throughout the analysis.

ACCESSIBLE BUT NOT ALWAYS CLEAR PROCEDURES – The analysed N&N mechanisms are provided in law, which makes them accessible. These laws aim to describe the procedures in detail, yet, they are not entirely free from issues regarding interpretation and application. For example, in Canada notices have to be forwarded by the intermediaries to the content providers. There are rules that describe what information the notice must contain but there are no restrictions limiting the content of the notice. This has allowed copyright holders to add information designed to intimidate users in order to demand settlements. Intermediaries, even if aware of the false claims, cannot refuse to forward the notice. Users who receive such abusive notices are often confused about their rights and obligations, which means that the procedure is not sufficiently clear and foreseeable for the users to anticipate its consequences.

COPYRIGHT INFRINGEMENTS ONLY – All N&N mechanisms analysed in this section applied only to copyright infringements. It is an interesting observation that a mechanism where the response is not provided in one step, but in several, is preferred for copyright infringements. In France, initially, it was also applicable to situations when a user failed to properly secure his Internet connection, creating a possibility for somebody else to commit a copyright infringement using his network. The approach was considered controversial and problematic from the perspective of human rights, which made France eventually give it up.

DECISIONS BY COURTS – Entrusting removal decisions to courts increases the level of procedural fairness, and as a result, the legitimacy of the procedure as well. It also improves the quality and proportionality of the decisions as they are made by bodies competent to resolve conflicts. This option was chosen in Canada and Chile. Still, these two countries added other elements of due process in their procedures, such as forwarding of a notification to the content provider and a counter-notification. Both these steps strengthen the fairness of the procedure by introducing elements of the right to a fair hearing, adversarial proceedings and equality of arms. Court involvement, moreover, ensures compliance with the right to effective remedy, as the right to appeal is generally available when the decisions are made directly by courts.

DECISIONS BY ADMINISTRATIVE AUTHORITIES – In countries where the decisions are made by public administration, lack of due process is one of the main criticisms. This is the case in Korea where the procedure is handled by the executive branch of the government and the decisions are not reviewed by courts. This makes the process untransparent and vulnerable to arbitrary decision-making. Even introducing safeguards, such as notification to the content provider, is not able to improve this assessment. South Korea provides an opportunity to the intermediaries and the users to present their opinion in advance of fulfilling the order, but it is not clear if the opinion is actually considered an appeal and whether it leads to a proper review. The lack of judicial redress, moreover, was one of the main reasons why the original HADOPI law was challenged and eventually significantly watered down. The procedures that concentrate all the decision-making power with administrative authorities, therefore, are considered problematic from the perspective of the right to effective remedy.

4. FULL IMMUNITY

4.1. DEFINITION

MAIN CHARACTERISTICS – Full immunity of Internet intermediaries places no liability on them for content provided by third parties. It also requires no actions to be taken by the intermediaries in relation to infringing or illegal content by third parties, even if they have the technical ability to do so. Strictly speaking, therefore, full immunity is not a response mechanism, as it does not foresee any response. In that sense it is not considered a type of notice and action because it requires no action from the intermediaries to qualify for the protection. Rather, it is a legislative approach, tilting the balance of interest at stake clearly to one side. Full immunity must be discussed in this Chapter as it provides insights useful in the search for safeguards. However, the goal is not to see how safeguards are implemented and functioning in this scenario but rather, to see what happens when there are no safeguards. The conducted analysis is, therefore, visibly different in nature. As there is no action, there is also no procedure, making it impossible to address some of the assessment criteria. The analysis focuses mainly on the existing case law on this matter.

4.2. COUNTRY PROFILE

ONE AND ONLY – Full immunity of Internet intermediaries can be found only in one country in the world: the US. This approach contributed to the rapid development of the Internet industry in this country. Yet, no other country decided to follow in the footsteps of the US.[1525]

A. *United States*

LEGISLATION – Full immunity in US law is provided in Section 230(c) of the Communications Decency Act (CDA).[1526] Section 230 was initially part of a greater law (addressing the transmission of offensive and obscene content to minors), which was struck down by the Supreme Court for its overbroad limitations on protected speech.[1527] Section 230 CDA addresses claims of defamation, invasion of privacy, tortious interference, civil liability for criminal law violations, and general negligence claims based on third-party content.[1528] It expressly excludes federal criminal law, intellectual property law (addressed in the DMCA), and the federal Electronic Communications Privacy Act or any state analogues.[1529]

Section 230 provides that Internet intermediaries ("interactive computer services") are not liable for the infringing or illegal content by third parties. They

1525 See D. Post, A bit of Internet history, or how two members of Congress helped create a trillion or so dollars of value, 27 August 2015, https://www.washingtonpost.com/news/volokh-conspiracy/wp/2015/08/27/a-bit-of-internet-history-or-how-two-members-of-congress-helped-create-a-trillion-or-so-dollars-of-value/.

1526 47 U.S. Code §230 – Protection for private blocking and screening of offensive material.

1527 See *Reno v. ACLU*, 521 U.S. 844 (1997). P. Ehrlich, "Communications Decency Act 230", *o.c.* See more on Section 230 CDA in Part I Chapter 4.3.

1528 D. Ardia, "Free Speech Savior or Shield for Scoundrels: an Empirical Study of Intermediary Immunity Under Section 230 of the Communications Decency Act", *o.c.*, p. 452.

1529 47 U.S.C §230(e)(1)–(4).

are not obliged to remove this type of content, even upon obtaining knowledge about the illegality. There is, therefore, no procedure for removal of content in Section 230 CDA. However, Section 230 is further analysed under the positive assessment framework to examine whether and how such a legislative approach satisfies the developed criteria.

4.3. ASSESSMENT

A. *Quality of Law*

FORESEEABILITY – Under Section 230 the online service providers are not required to take any action with regard to infringing content by third parties, even after obtaining knowledge about its existence on their platforms. There is, therefore, no procedure under Section 230 that would lead to removal or blocking of access to the infringing content. It is interesting to investigate, however, whether the effect of Section 230 immunizing the intermediaries from liability is foreseeable and predictable to those subject to it.

As has been pointed out by several authors, many claims are still brought against online intermediaries, and the question of their liability is often litigated extensively.[1530] Parties that feel injured by content posted online attempt to seek recourse from online service providers. According to Goldman, plaintiffs '*routinely seek to hold websites responsible for offline problems caused by the site's users*'.[1531] That would suggest that the immunizing effect is not necessarily the only possible outcome. The rich US case-law on the issue indicates that on some occasions plaintiffs are in fact successful, and that their claims are not always invalid. Some authors argue, actually, that US courts are increasingly reluctant to extend Section 230 protection to intermediaries that contributed to the harmful online content.[1532]

Starting with *Zeran*, the US courts applied a broad interpretation of the provisions of Section 230. The Court in *Zeran* reasoned that the statute '*creates a federal immunity to any cause of action that would make service providers liable for information originating with a third-party user of the service*'.[1533] Other courts followed the complete immunity approach. In some cases, courts applied the immunity even when they recognised that the end result was unfair.[1534] In

1530 A. Holland et al., "Online Intermediaries Case Studies Series: Intermediary Liability in the United States", *o.c.*, p. 8; and D. Ardia, "Free Speech Savior or Shield for Scoundrels: an Empirical Study of Intermediary Immunity Under Section 230 of the Communications Decency Act", *o.c.*, p. 381.

1531 E. Goldman, "The Ten Most Important Section 230 Rulings", *o.c.*, p. 4.

1532 J. Kosseff, Twenty Years of Intermediary Immunity: the US Experience, Scripted, Volume 14, Issue 1, June 2017, p. 9.

1533 *Zeran v America Online*, [1997] 129 F.3d 327 (4th Cir.).

1534 J. Kosseff, "Twenty Years of Intermediary Immunity: the US Experience", *o.c.*, p. 15.

Blumenthal v. Drudge, concerning a defamation lawsuit against Drudge (author of a gossip column) and AOL (online service provider), the latter had broad editing rights over the provided content. The Court held that '*it would seem only fair*' to hold AOL to the liability standards applied to a publisher or, at least, a distributor.[1535] Nevertheless, the Court applied Section 230 immunity.[1536] The ruling reinforced *Zeran*'s conclusion and showed that Section 230 equally protects passive conduits and editorially controlled publications.[1537]

Courts have also applied Section 230 in cases where the online service providers have modified the third-party content, providing that the modification was not the source of the harmful content.[1538] In *Batzel v. Smith*, the Court held that Section 230 '*necessarily precludes liability for exercising the usual prerogative of publishers to choose among proffered material and to edit the material published while retaining its basic form and message*'.[1539]

The immunizing effect of Section 230 has become so widespread that some websites rely on the provision as a basis for their operations. For example Ripoff Report, which allows consumers to anonymously post complaints about businesses, has frequently benefited from the immunity.[1540] In 2008, a defamation complaint against Ripoff Report was dismissed, even though it was obvious that Ripoff Report encouraged the publication of the defamatory content.[1541] A federal judge pointed out that '*there is no authority for the proposition that this makes the website operator responsible, in whole or in part, for the 'creation or development' of every post on the site*'.[1542] Ripoff Report, by now experienced in dismissed lawsuits, warns on their website that, '*[i]f you are considering suing Ripoff Report because of a report which you claim is defamatory, you should be aware that, Ripoff Report has had a long history of winning these types of cases*'.[1543]

Statements such as that by Ripoff Report suggest that service providers expect to receive the protection from Section 230. This means that they consider the results as relatively predictable and foreseeable. There is however a growing number of cases where courts did not grant the immunity to online service providers. Already in 2010, Ardia observed that in all cases since the introduction of the law, more than a third of the claims survived pre-emption.[1544] According

---

1535 *Blumenthal v Drudge*, [1998] 992 F. Supp. 44 (D.D.C.).

1536 E. Goldman, "The Ten Most Important Section 230 Rulings", *o.c.*, p. 6.

1537 *Ibid.*

1538 J. Kosseff, "Twenty Years of Intermediary Immunity: the US Experience", *o.c.*, p. 16.

1539 *Batzel v Smith*, [2003] 333 F.3d 1018 (9th Cir.).

1540 J. Kosseff, "Twenty Years of Intermediary Immunity: the US Experience", *o.c.*, p. 25.

1541 *Global Royalties, Ltd. v Xcentric Ventures, LLC*, [2008] 544 F. Supp. 2d 929 (D. Ariz.).

1542 *Ibid.*

1543 Ripoff Report, About Us: Want to sue Ripoff Report?, 2011, www.ripoffreport.com/consumers-say-thank-you/want-to-sue-ripoff-report.

1544 D. Ardia, "Free Speech Savior or Shield for Scoundrels: an Empirical Study of Intermediary Immunity Under Section 230 of the Communications Decency Act", *o.c.*, p. 382.

to Kosseff, between 2001 and 2002, US courts granted immunity in eight out of ten cases (the two cases concerned copyright infringements exempted from the scope of Section 230 CDA), while between 2015 and 2016, in 14 out of 27 cases the courts refused to provide intermediaries with full immunity.[1545] Kosseff is of the opinion that courts have become increasingly likely to deny Section 230 immunity to online intermediaries for user-generated content.[1546] This trend started with the 2008 ruling in *Fair Housing Council of San Fernando Valley v. Roommates.com.*[1547] In this case, the Court held the roommate-matching service provider liable for user content provided as a response to the questionnaire created by the provider, but not liable for user content freely provided in the "Additional Comments" section.[1548] The *Roommates.com* opinion is often cited as an exception to *Zeran*'s defence-favourable ruling.[1549] In 2012, however, the case came back to court, which ruled this time that the website was never covered by the housing anti-discrimination laws, therefore, it never had any illegal content at all.[1550] This finding made the previous ruling effectively pointless.[1551]

The original Roommates.com exception was, however, embraced and even extended in 2009.[1552] In *FTC v. Accusearch*, the Court held that 'a service provider is "responsible" for the development of offensive content only if it in some way specifically encourages development of what is offensive about the content'.[1553] The *Accusearch* ruling now sometimes contributes to the loss of defence, rather than the problematic Roommates.com.[1554] Another example of a case that did not recognize the immunity of an online service provider can be found in *Diamond Ranch Academy v Filer.* The website operator argued that a defamation lawsuit should be dismissed under Section 230, as she merely summarised and made editorial changes to some of the content provided by third parties.[1555] The court rejected the argument, stating that the posts on her website 'do not lead a person to believe that she is quoting a third party'.[1556] There are more examples of cases where the courts did not recognize the immunity of the online service providers.[1557] Ardia pointed out that 'judges have been haphazard

---

1545 J. Kosseff, "Twenty Years of Intermediary Immunity: the US Experience", *o.c.*, p. 29.

1546 *Ibid.*

1547 *Fair Housing Council of San Fernando Valley v Roommates.com*, [2008] 521 F.3d 1157 (9th Cir.) (en banc).

1548 See more in Part I Chapter 4.3.

1549 E. Goldman, "The Ten Most Important Section 230 Rulings", *o.c.*, p. 2.

1550 *Fair Housing Council of San Fernando Valley v. Roommate.com*, [2012] WL 310849 (9th Cir.).

1551 E. Goldman, "The Ten Most Important Section 230 Rulings", *o.c.*, p. 3.

1552 *Ibid.*, p. 4.

1553 *Fed. Trade Comm'n v. Accusearch Inc.*, 570 F.3d 1187 (10th Cir. 2009).

1554 See E. Goldman, "The Ten Most Important Section 230 Rulings", *o.c.*, p. 4.

1555 *Diamond Ranch Academy v Filer*, 2016 WL 633351 (D. Utah Feb. 17, 2016).

1556 *Ibid.*

1557 For example: *Amcol v Lemberg Law, LLC*, [2016] No. 3:15-3422-CMC, 2016 U.S. Dist. LEXIS 18131 (D.S.C.); *Congoo v Revcontent*, [2016] Civil Action No. 16-401 (MAS) (TJB), 2016 U.S. Dist. LEXIS 51051 (D.N.J.); *Consumer Cellular v ConsumerAffairs.com*, [2016]

in their approach to section 230, often ignoring important threshold questions or assuming that certain requirements are met'.[1558] Contradicting case law, such as in Roommates.com, is also adding to the confusion. Considering that the effect of Section 230 is not at all obvious and predictable, it is perhaps understandable that plaintiffs keep trying to find recourse from online intermediaries.

There is, however, another aspect of foreseeability of Section 230. Several authors argue that courts have extended the safe harbour far beyond the provision's words, context, and purpose and that the complete immunity is too sweeping.[1559] Specifically, they point out that the interpretation initiated in *Zeran* is far broader than what the Congress intended when introducing Section 230.[1560] This opinion refers to the original goals of the statute (see *Supra*) and specifically its "core policy" to protect Good Samaritan blocking and screening of offensive material.[1561] Critics argue that it was never the purpose of Section 230 to immunize services whose business is '*the active subversion of online decency*'.[1562] As noted by Judge Easterbrook, such a broad protection incentivizes online service providers to '*do nothing about distribution of indecent and offensive material*'.[1563] As a result of the broad interpretation, Section 230 awards immunity to businesses that are '*not merely failing to take "Good Samaritan" steps to protect users from online indecency but are actually being Bad Samaritans*'.[1564] This refers, for example to services such as Backpage.com which was protected from liability against a claim of deliberately structuring its service to enable sex trafficking.[1565]

According to Keats Citron and Wittes, the judiciary's insistence that the CDA reflected '*Congress' desire to promote unfettered speech on the Internet*'[1566] (as stated in *Zeran*) actually ignores its text, purpose and history.[1567] They argue that

3:15-CV-1908-PK (D. Or.); *Diamond Ranch Academy v Filer*, [2016] Case No. 2:14-CV-751-TC, 2016 U.S. Dist. LEXIS 18131 (D. Utah); *Doe v Internet Brands, Inc*, [2016] Case No. 12–56638 (9th Cir.); *E-Ventures Worldwide, LLC v Google*, [2016] Case No. 2:14-cv-646-FtM-29CM, 2016 U.S. Dist. LEXIS 62855 (M.D. Fla.).

1558 D. Ardia, "Free Speech Savior or Shield for Scoundrels: an Empirical Study of Intermediary Immunity Under Section 230 of the Communications Decency Act", *o.c.*, p. 381.

1559 D. Keats Citron and B. Wittes, "The Internet Will Not Break: Denying Bad Samaritans Section 230 Immunity", *o.c.*, p. 2. See also D. Keats Citron, "Cyber Civil Rights", *Boston University Law Review*, Vol. 89, Issue 61, 2009, p. 116.

1560 *See Barrett v. Rosenthal*, 114 Cal. App. 4th 1379, 1395 (2004) ('The view of most scholars who have addressed the issue is that Zeran's analysis of section 230 is flawed, in that the court ascribed to Congress an intent to create a far broader immunity than that body actually had in mind or is necessary to achieve its purposes.').

1561 *Doe v. Internet Brands*, 824 F.3d 846, 851–52 (9th Cir. 2016).

1562 D. Keats Citron and B. Wittes, "The Internet Will Not Break: Denying Bad Samaritans Section 230 Immunity", *o.c.*, p. 8.

1563 *Chicago Lawyers Comm. for Civil Rights v. Craigslist*, 519 F.3d 666, 670 (7th Cir. 2008).

1564 D. Keats Citron and B. Wittes, "The Internet Will Not Break: Denying Bad Samaritans Section 230 Immunity", *o.c.*, p. 8.

1565 *Jane Doe No. 1 v. Backpage.com*, 817 F.3d 12 (1st Cir. 2016).

1566 *Zeran v America Online*, [1997] 129 F.3d 327 (4th Cir.).

1567 D. Keats Citron and B. Wittes, "The Internet Will Not Break: Denying Bad Samaritans Section 230 Immunity", *o.c.*, p. 7.

the Internet businesses no longer need the same level of protection that they did 20 years ago, and that at this point they can be expected to act according to some enforceable standard of conduct.[1568] Others add that an online service provider '*should act like a 'good Samaritan' in order to enjoy Section 230 'good Samaritan' immunity status*'.[1569] The broad interpretation provided protection and (some) clarity for intermediaries, but it hindered judicial attempts to adapt the common law to the changing technology.[1570] The Supreme Court declined an opportunity to clarify the meaning of section 230. This caused a shift in interpretation, which would bring Section 230 closer to its text, context and history, unlikely to happen. Critics of the broad interpretation point out that the only course of action is a potential statutory fix that would help adjust the current liability environment to the reality of modern online business operations.[1571]

B. Protection of democratic society

DEMOCRATIC VALUES – Section 230 CDA addresses claims of defamation, invasion of privacy, tortious interference, civil liability for criminal law violations, and general negligence claims based on third-party content.[1572] Section 230 CDA, however, does not specify explicitly what values or types of content it covers. Instead, it specifies what is excluded from its scope: federal criminal law, intellectual property law, and the federal Electronic Communications Privacy Act or any state analogues.[1573] For everything else, Section 230 immunizes the intermediaries fully from any claims to act, for example to remove or block access to the content. This means that there is no mechanism provided by law to stem unlawful online content, even if it concerns content that could qualify as manifestly unlawful, for example allowing advertisements that facilitate prostitution and sex trafficking.

Two cases concerning the websites Craigslist and Backpage.com, provide an example of how Section 230 may pose a barrier to efforts by state governments to shut down content that violates state criminal laws.[1574] Both Craigslist and Backpage.com are online classified advertisements services, which include separate sections for "erotic services" and "adult entertainment services". Both services have been subject to intense attempts by state governments to

1568 *Ibid*, p. 9.
1569 A. M. Sevanian, "Section 230 of the Communications Decency Act: A 'Good Samaritan' Law Without the Requirement of Acting as a 'Good Samaritan'", *o.c.*, p. 144.
1570 See J. Zittrain, "A History Of Online Gatekeeping", *o.c.*, p. 262.
1571 See D. Keats Citron and B. Wittes, "The Internet Will Not Break: Denying Bad Samaritans Section 230 Immunity", *o.c.*, p. 13.
1572 D. Ardia, "Free Speech Savior or Shield for Scoundrels: an Empirical Study of Intermediary Immunity Under Section 230 of the Communications Decency Act", *o.c.*, p. 452.
1573 47 U.S.C §230(e)(1)–(4).
1574 See A. Holland *et al.*, "Online Intermediaries Case Studies Series: Intermediary Liability in the United States", *o.c.*, p. 19.

circumvent Section 230 immunity. Creative paths were explored, such as, for example, applying public pressure, initiating lawsuits or legislative attempts.[1575] For Craigslist, the trouble started in 2008 with a letter sent by the attorney general of Connecticut, Richard Blumenthal, on behalf of the attorneys general of 40 states, demanding that Craigslist clears out the site of ads for prostitution and illegal sex-oriented services.[1576] It was followed by negotiations and changes to the targeted listings[1577], a lawsuit in federal court (won by Craigslist)[1578], another letter by an attorney general threatening the company's management with criminal investigation and prosecution[1579], a subpoena sent by 39 states to reveal the site's revenue from sex-related advertisements[1580], and public pressure after an open letter by two teenagers who claimed that they had been victims of sex trafficking through the site.[1581] Following this series of events Craigslist shut down its "adult services" section, even though it was never held liable, due to the protection by Section 230.[1582] Backpage.com experienced a similar attack, which included public letters[1583], a petition[1584], and two states enacting laws that criminalized commercial advertising for sexual abuse of minors.[1585] Both laws were prevented from enforcement on the basis of Section 230 and the First Amendment.[1586] The failure of these laws led to demands upon

---

1575 See *Ibid.*

1576 V. Kopytoff, Craigslist gets heat for prostitution ads, 27 March 2008, http://blog.sfgate.com/techchron/2008/03/27/craigslist-gets-heat-for-prostitution-ads/.

1577 Joint Statement by Craigslist, the Attorneys General, and the National Center for Missing and Exploited Children ("NCMEC"), www.dmlp.org/sites/citmedialaw.org/files/2008–11–00-Craigslist%20AG%20Agreement.pdf. See also B. Stone, Craigslist Agrees to Curb Sex Ads, 6 November 2008, www.nytimes.com/2008/11/07/technology/internet/07craigslist.html.

1578 *Dart v. Craigslist, Inc.*, 665 F. Supp.2d 961 (N.D. Ill. 2009).

1579 See letter by H. McMaster, 5 May 2009, www.dmlp.org/sites/citmedialaw.org/files/2009–05–05-South%20Carolina%20AG%20Letter.pdf.

1580 J. Cheng, Craigslist "brothel business" under fire again, 4 May 2010, https://arstechnica.com/tech-policy/2010/05/craigslist-brothel-business-under-fire-again/.

1581 M. Saada Saar, Craigslist's shame: Child sex ads, 10 August 2010, http://edition.cnn.com/2010/OPINION/08/02/saar.craigslist.child.trafficking/index.html.

1582 See A. Holland *et al.*, "Online Intermediaries Case Studies Series: Intermediary Liability in the United States", *o.c.*, p. 20.

1583 *Ibid.*, p. 23.

1584 Village Voice Founder's Son Criticizes Company for Advertisements That Others Can Use for Sex Trafficking of Minors, Joins Groundswell Campaign, 12 January 2012, https://www.prnewswire.com/news-releases/village-voice-founders-son-criticizes-company-for-advertisements-that-others-can-use-for-sex-trafficking-of-minors-joins-groundswell-campaign-137170558.html.

1585 State of Washington Senate Bill 6251, 7 June 2012, http://apps.leg.wa.gov/documents/billdocs/2011–12/Pdf/Bills/Session%20Laws/Senate/6251-S.SL.pdf; and State of Tennessee Public Chapter No. 1075, 1 May 2012, www.dmlp.org/sites/dmlp.org/files/pc1075.pdf.

1586 See *Backpage.com v. Cooper, et al.*, 939 F.Supp.2d 805 (M.D. Tenn. 2013). See also J. Nix, Backpage.com sues state to halt law aimed at online child sex ads, 29 June 2012, http://nashvillecitypaper.com/content/city-news/backpagecom-sues-state-halt-law-aimed-online-child-sex-ads.

Congress to amend Section 230.[1587] In 2015, Congress passed the SAVE Act that aimed to expand federal trafficking law to cover advertising that supports sex trafficking.[1588] According to Goldman, it is too early to judge the SAVE Act's efficacy.[1589] Nevertheless, in 2017, two new bills were introduced, both of which are designed to accomplish the same policy goals as the SAVE Act.[1590] Backpage.com, in the meantime, refused to succumb to the pressure.[1591] In 2016 Backpage.com successfully defended its services in front of the First Circuit Court of Appeals.[1592] The Court declared that '*a website operator's decisions in structuring its website and posting requirements are publisher functions entitled to section 230(c)(1) protection*'.[1593]

These two examples show that states have significant difficulties to suppress online activities at the level of intermediaries.[1594] This seems to be the case, even when it concerns posting content advertising sex trafficking of minors or prostitution, therefore content that in some jurisdictions could be considered as manifestly unlawful. For a long time, Congress did not seem to show much interest in granting state authorities broad discretion to impose criminal sanctions on intermediaries for the behaviour of their users.[1595] Substantial changes to Section 230 seemed unlikely. Instead, case-by-case solutions targeted at a specific type of content or conduct, such as the SAVE Act, were being reached at the federal level.[1596]

In early 2018, however, an important change took place. In April 2018, the government seized the Backpage.com domain name, took the website offline

---

1587 See Open Letter by the National Association of Attorneys General, 23 July 2013, https://www.eff.org/sites/default/files/cda-ag-letter.pdf.

1588 Rep. Ann Wagner introduced H.R. 4225, the "Stop Advertising Victims of Exploitation (SAVE) Act of 2014" in the U.S. House of Representatives, 13 March 2014, https://wagner.house.gov/notforsale.

1589 E. Goldman, Senate's "Stop Enabling Sex Traffickers Act of 2017"–and Section 230's Imminent Evisceration, 31 July 2017, http://blog.ericgoldman.org/archives/2017/07/senates-stop-enabling-sex-traffickers-act-of-2017-and-section-230s-imminent-evisceration.htm.

1590 Rep. Ann Wagner's the "Allow States and Victims to Fight Online Sex Trafficking Act of 2017" bill, H.R. 1865, https://www.congress.gov/115/bills/hr1865/BILLS-115hr1865ih.pdf; and Senate's "Stop Enabling Sex Traffickers Act of 2017" bill, S. 1693, https://www.portman.senate.gov/public/index.cfm/files/serve?File_id=1DA519D4-4B37-4C5E-B8B9-4A205C5E488F. See more in E. Goldman, Senate's "Stop Enabling Sex Traffickers Act of 2017"–and Section 230's Imminent Evisceration, *o.c.*; and E. Goldman, The "Allow States and Victims to Fight Online Sex Trafficking Act of 2017" Bill Would Be Bad News for Section 230, 10 April 2017, http://blog.ericgoldman.org/archives/2017/04/the-allow-states-and-victims-to-fight-online-sex-trafficking-act-of-2017-bill-would-be-bad-news-for-section-230.htm.

1591 See A. Holland *et al.*, "Online Intermediaries Case Studies Series: Intermediary Liability in the United States", *o.c.*, p. 26.

1592 *Jane Doe No. 1 v. Backpage.com*, LLC, 817 F.3d 12 (1st Cir. 2016).

1593 *Ibid.*

1594 See A. Holland *et al.*, "Online Intermediaries Case Studies Series: Intermediary Liability in the United States", *o.c.*, p. 26.

1595 *Ibid.*

1596 *Ibid.*

globally, executed search warrants across multiple locations, and indicted 7 people affiliated with Backpage.[1597] The CEO of Backpage.com pleaded guilty to state and federal charges including conspiracy, money laundering, and human trafficking.[1598] A few days later, Congress passed a sex trafficking exception to Section 230's immunity (the Fight Online Sex Trafficking Act of 2017 – FOSTA/SESTA).[1599] The bill declares that Section 230 '*was never intended to provide legal protection to websites that unlawfully promote and facilitate prostitution and websites that facilitate traffickers in advertising the sale of unlawful sex acts with sex-trafficking victims*'. The bill was largely spurred by Backpage.com events, even though the site shut down its adult advertisement section by 2017.[1600] Interestingly, the new law was evidently not needed to shut down Backpage. The indictment cites the Travel Act and not FOSTA which was not yet adopted at that time. Moreover, Section 230 always has had a federal crimes exception, which in the end was used in this case. The new law has been criticized extensively for "eviscerating" Section 230.[1601] Its true impact on Section 230 protection and on the freedom of speech on the Internet remains to be seen.

FAILURE TO WARN – An interesting path to hold intermediaries liable for illegal actions of their users is developing in a situation where a website owner knows about possible risks of physical harm and fails to warn its users. In 2008, in *Doe v MySpace,* Section 230 immunized MySpace from liability for user-to-user communications which led to physical harm offline.[1602] In that case, an underage MySpace user exaggerated her age to access the MySpace service without protections normally imposed on young users' accounts. After meeting another MySpace user online, they agreed to meet in person, and he sexually assaulted her. The Fifth Circuit Court of Appeals held that MySpace's only contribution to the criminal assault was its provision of communication tools

1597 E. Goldman, 'Worst of Both Worlds' FOSTA Signed Into Law, Completing Section 230's Evisceration, 11 April 2018, https://blog.ericgoldman.org/archives/2018/04/worst-of-both-worlds-fosta-signed-into-law-completing-section-230s-evisceration.htm.

1598 D. Thompson, Backpage.com, CEO plead guilty to state, US charges, 13 April 2018, https://apnews.com/42a8140a1b3c49a8a2f454bf79283474/Backpage.com,-CEO-plead-guilty-to-state,-US-charges.

1599 U.S. Congress, Allow States and Victims to Fight Online Sex Trafficking Act of 2017 115th Congress (2017–2018) – H.R.1865, https://www.congress.gov/bill/115th-congress/house-bill/1865/text.

1600 See R. Hersher, Backpage Shuts Down Adult Ads In The U.S., Citing Government Pressure, 10 January 2017, https://www.npr.org/sections/thetwo-way/2017/01/10/509127110/backpage-shuts-down-adult-ads-citing-government-pressure.

1601 E. Goldman, 'Worst of Both Worlds' FOSTA Signed Into Law, Completing Section 230's Evisceration, 11 April 2018, https://blog.ericgoldman.org/archives/2018/04/worst-of-both-worlds-fosta-signed-into-law-completing-section-230s-evisceration.htm. See also A. Romano, A new law intended to curb sex trafficking threatens the future of the internet as we know it, 18 April 2018, https://www.vox.com/culture/2018/4/13/17172762/fosta-sesta-backpage-230-internet-freedom.

1602 *Doe v. MySpace, Inc.*, 528 F. 3d 413 (5th Cir. 2008).

to both users, therefore Section 230 applied. However, in 2016 *Doe v. Internet Brands*, Section 230 was not recognized as a defence. The case concerned a model, who was sexually abused after making a contact through a modelling industry networking website.[1603] The Ninth Circuit Court of Appeals concluded that her claim against the website is not prevented by Section 230 because the claim of "failure to warn" '*has nothing to do with Internet Brands' efforts, or lack thereof, to edit, monitor, or remove user-generated content*'.[1604]

Doe v. Internet Brands implicitly contradicts *Doe v. MySpace* of 2008, nevertheless, it has created an interesting precedent. Certain online service providers took notice and reacted by actually posting warnings on their websites. For example, the social media site Omegle[1605], which describes itself as '*a great way to meet new friends. When you use Omegle, we pick someone else at random and let you talk one-on-one*'.[1606] The website warns its users, however, that '*Predators have been known to use Omegle, so please be careful*'.[1607] It specifies further that the video chats are moderated, but '*moderation is not perfect. You may still encounter people who misbehave. They are solely responsible for their own behavior*'.[1608]

Section 230 does not distinguish between unlawful content and behaviour that falls within its scope. For everything that is covered intermediaries are given blanket immunity, and no procedure exists for removal of content, even if in some cases it could qualify as manifestly illegal. These developments suggest that even though Section 230 immunity stands strong, users who have become victims offline try other ways to hold the intermediaries responsible, and on some occasions, they are successful.

C. *Tailored response*

LEAST RESTRICTIVE MEANS – Provisions of Section 230 CDA do not require the intermediaries to take any action with regard to unlawful content by their users. It could be said, therefore, that Section 230 ensures that expression cannot be restricted by the government provided statute. In that sense, Section 230 provides truly the least restrictive means possible, or rather, no means of restriction at all.

ONLY PRIVATE MEANS – The fact that the State does not provide any procedure for removal or blocking access to unlawful online content does not mean that expression is not restricted in the online environment. After all, the

1603 *Doe #14 v. Internet Brands*, 824 F.3d 846 (9th Cir. 2016).
1604 *Ibid.*
1605 Omegle, https://www.omegle.com/
1606 *Ibid.*
1607 *Ibid.*
1608 *Ibid.*

main purpose of the CDA was to encourage private entities to take censoring actions online on their own initiative. And this they do, often without any pressure or intervention from the third parties, their users or the State. This is a consequence of the free-market, hands-off approach taken by the legislature when enacting Section 230 CDA.[1609]

Methods employed by the intermediaries to moderate user content include policies, procedures and technology.[1610] Most of the websites that deal with user content restrict a great amount of content in their content policies or in their terms of use. It could be, for example illegal activities in general, and specifically bullying, harassment, hate speech, nudity or violent content.[1611] Moreover, intermediaries introduce procedures to enforce these policies, for example a report button placed next to the content (e.g. Facebook). Such a report button effectively constitutes a form of private notice and action mechanism, which the intermediaries provide as a courtesy, entirely voluntarily. This means they can, and often do (but are not legally required to) provide some type of redress mechanism. Finally, intermediaries develop technologies to automatically filter content.[1612] These include, for example, tools for community moderation of online comments where users are asked to rate the civility of random comments by other users, or technology that scans their users' cloud data, emails and other content for child sexual abuse material.[1613] Other forms of response include prohibition of anonymous comments or elimination of the comments section altogether.[1614]

Even though intermediaries are not required to remove any content, they often do so, on their own initiative. As they are generally immune from claims for unlawful third party content, such moderating activities are a voluntary response to consumer demands of a friendly online environment free of illegal (but also just controversial) content.[1615] Some authors argue that in attempts to satisfy their customers, intermediaries '*have gone far beyond their legal duties to prohibit illegal and obscene content on their services*', as was intended by the creators of Section 230.[1616] It could very well be the case, but it does not change the fact that under Section 230 online expression is still restricted, just not by the State but by private entities. These private entities do not have to be transparent on the reasons for removal or accountable for their decisions. They also have no obligation to implement any safeguards against restrictions on speech. From the

---

1609 See J. Kosseff, "Twenty Years of Intermediary Immunity: the US Experience", *o.c.*, p. 13 and 30.

1610 *Ibid.*, p. 30.

1611 *Ibid.*, p. 31.

1612 *Ibid.*, p. 32.

1613 See *Ibid.*, p. 33–34.

1614 *Ibid.*, p. 33.

1615 *Ibid.*, p. 34.

1616 *Ibid.*, p. 34–35.

perspective of a content provider whose speech was removed, it might matter very little that their speech was not restricted by the State but "only" by a private entity. The distinction matters more, however, when it comes to exercising ones right to seek redress.

D. Procedural fairness

NO DUE PROCESS – As has been stated repeatedly, under Section 230 there is no procedure for removal or blocking access to unlawful online content. Nevertheless, such restrictions on expression online do take place on the private initiative of the intermediary service providers. For example, Google, which fought tirelessly against any obligation to comply with removal requests based on the EU data protection law[1617], provides avenues for reporting of certain types of sensitive information, defamatory material, and other harmful content.[1618] The whole process, however, is very opaque. Google provides little information about the requests it receives or how it responds to them.[1619] At the same time, Google repeatedly informs its users that the best way to remove content from a website, and consequently from Google search results, is to contact that website directly.[1620]

Since in the US the right to freedom of expression has no positive dimension, private entities are free to regulate the speech on their platform however they see fit. Generally, it is considered that private companies '*can do whatever they wish – within reason – when it comes to their business*'.[1621] Restriction of speech imposed by private entities is not considered a violation of the First Amendment rights.[1622] If private online companies provide any complaint mechanism that could lead to removal or blocking of content, they do so entirely on their own initiative. Under such circumstances, online companies have no obligation to ensure any due process rights or comply with any requirements for the decision-making process. They do not need to inform any party of the conflict or ask for their counter-arguments. They also do not need to be transparent about the number of requests (successful of not) or methods used to reach a decision.[1623]

1617 See more in A. Kuczerawy, J. Ausloos, "From Notice-and-Takedown to Notice-and-Delist: Implementing Google Spain", *Colorado Technology Law Journal*, Vol. 14, Issue 2, 2016, pp. 219–258.

1618 A. Haynes Stuart, "Google Search Results: Buried if not Forgotten", *North Carolina Journal of Law & Technology*, Vol. 15, Issue 3, Spring 2014, p. 496.

1619 *Ibid.*

1620 See Remove information from Google, https://support.google.com/websearch/troubleshooter/3111061#ts=2889054%2C2889099.

1621 M. Ingram, First they came for the mugshot, but I said nothing…, GIGAOM, 7 October 2013, http://gigaom.com/2013/10/07/first-they-came-for-the-mugshot-websites-but-i-said-nothing/.

1622 See *Langdon v. Google, Inc.*, 474 F. Supp. 2d 631 (D. Del. 2007).

1623 Google published transparency reports where it provides some information about removals, but only in categories of copyright removals, government requests to remove and removals under EU data protection law. See Google Transparency Report, https://transparencyreport.google.com/.

It is not within the scope of this research to engage in extensive analysis of the voluntary moderation measures taken by online intermediaries. The main goal is to look at removal procedures provided by States, which under Section 230 CDA do not exist. For the purpose of the analysis conducted in this chapter it shall suffice to say that procedural fairness, including due process elements and the requirements for decision-making process, are not present in a system that ensures (almost) full immunity for third party content online.

E. *Effective remedy*

POSSIBILITY TO APPEAL THE DECISION – Section 230 CDA effectively removed any duty for an interactive computer service to monitor content on its platforms and pushed all liability for content-based infringements to the content providers.[1624] Critics of the approach highlight, that in some cases the result of the protection by Section 230 '*unfairly burdens individuals who have been irreparably harmed by user-generated content*'.[1625] If they are not able to identify and sue the provider of the harmful content, they might be left without legal recourse.[1626] It is not uncommon, therefore, that Section 230 produces unjust results.[1627] In some cases, victims of harmful online content (e.g. revenge pornography) turn to other laws for help. One practical way to try to remove content is to use the provisions of the DMCA.[1628] This is only possible, however, when the victim is actually a copyright holder of the picture or video used to harm and embarrass them (e.g. it was taken as a "selfie" meaning that the author and the subject are the same).[1629] Such creative solutions are developed, because Section 230 CDA does not foresee any form of content removal mechanism.[1630] Online intermediaries can provide such mechanisms on their own initiative, and in many cases they do, very often as a result of the public outcry. For example, in 2015, Google started removing online revenge pornography on request, even though prior to 2015 it had not provided such a possibility. According to the announcement,

---

1624 See A. Holland *et al.*, "Online Intermediaries Case Studies Series: Intermediary Liability in the United States", *o.c.*, p. 7.

1625 J. Kosseff, "Twenty Year of Intermediary Immunity: the US Experience", *o.c.*, p. 23.

1626 See Z. Franklin, "Justice for Revenge Porn Victims: Legal Theories to Overcome Claims of Civil Immunity by Operators of Revenge Porn Websites", *California Law Review*, Vol. 102, 2014, p. 1314; See also J. Kosseff, "Twenty Year of Intermediary Immunity: the US Experience", *o.c.*, p. 23.

1627 See D. Keats Citron and B. Wittes, "The Internet Will Not Break: Denying Bad Samaritans Section 230 Immunity", *o.c.*, p. 12.

1628 A. Levandowski, "Using Copyright to Combat Revenge Porn", *NYU Journal of Intellectual Property & Entertainment Law*, Vol. 3, 2014, p. 426. See also D. Keats Citron, "Addressing Cyber Harassment: An Overview of Hate Crimes in Cyberspace", *Journal of Law, Technology & the Internet*, Vol. 6, 2015, p. 4.

1629 A. Levandowski, "Using Copyright to Combat Revenge Porn", *o.c.*, p. 426.

1630 See Z. Franklin, "Justice for Revenge Porn Victims: Legal Theories to Overcome Claims of Civil Immunity by Operators of Revenge Porn Websites", *o.c.*, p. 1310.

> 'Our philosophy has always been that Search should reflect the whole web. But revenge porn images are intensely personal and emotionally damaging, and serve only to degrade the victims – predominantly women. So going forward, we'll honor requests from people to remove nude or sexually explicit images shared without their consent from Google Search results. This is a narrow and limited policy, similar to how we treat removal requests for other highly sensitive personal information, such as bank account numbers and signatures, that may surface in our search results.'[1631]

It is entirely the intermediaries' decision to provide content moderation mechanisms and to specify what content it applies to, and what can safely remain online. It is also the intermediaries' own decision to remove (or demote) any type of content that they do not desire on their website, even if it is not unlawful, just merely in violation of their terms and conditions. Online intermediaries are known to exercise this right by administering punishments for certain behaviour of their users (e.g. using search engine optimizers).[1632] The punishment, for example, can take the form of hand-editing own search results, against which no appeal mechanism usually applies.[1633]

Appeal mechanisms provide a chance for an effective remedy to both victims of unlawful content (e.g. revenge porn) and victims of overbroad censorship (e.g. demoting in search results). Nevertheless, it is solely the intermediaries' decision to introduce an appeal mechanism for content that is kept online or for content that is removed. Either way, they are immune from liability for taking content moderation activities on their websites, thanks to Section 230 CDA.

JUDICIAL REDRESS – Section 230 CDA protects providers of online services from liability for all third party content that is not excluded from its scope. This refers to the majority of cases brought before courts against online service providers, for example cases concerning sex trafficking of minors[1634], online prostitution[1635] or "material support" for terrorists.[1636] The same applies to revenge pornography, where according to Goldman, cases are '*mostly dead*

1631 Google Public Policy Blog, "Revenge porn" and search, 19 June 2015, https://publicpolicy.googleblog.com/2015/06/.

1632 A. Haynes Stuart, "Google Search Results: Buried if not Forgotten", *o.c.*, p. 499. See also F. Pasquale, "Restoring Transparency to Automated Authority", *Journal on Telecommunications and High Technology Law*, Vol. 9, No. 235, 2011, p. 246; and J. Nocera, Stuck in Google's Doghouse, New York Times, 12 September 2008, www.nytimes.com/2008/09/13/technology/13nocera.html.

1633 See more E. B. Laidlaw, "Private Power, Public Interest: An Examination of Search Engine Accountability", *International Journal of Law and Information Technology*, Vol. 17 No. 1, 2008, p. 141.

1634 *Jane Doe No. 1 v. Backpage.com*, LLC, 2016 WL 963848 (1st Cir. March 14, 2016).

1635 *People v. Ferrer*, Case No. 16FE019224 (Cal. Super. Ct. Dec. 9, 2016).

1636 *Fields v. Twitter, Inc.*, 2016 WL 6822065 (N.D. Cal. Nov. 18, 2016); *Cohen v. Facebook, Inc.*, 2017 WL 2192621 (E.D.N.Y. May 18, 2017); *Gonzalez v. Google, Inc.*, 2017 WL 4773366 (N.D. Cal. Oct. 23, 2017).

on arrival', no matter how much the lawyers hype their lawsuit in the media, because all of the defendants – other than the users actually posting the revenge porn – are protected by Section 230.[1637] The diagnosis was confirmed (in appeal) in 2014 in *GoDaddy.com, Inc. v. Toups*[1638] and *Caraccioli v. Facebook*.[1639]

The US courts also dismiss cases against online intermediaries who remove or degrade third parties' content on their websites on their own initiative. Such content might not even be unlawful but merely in violation of the site's terms and conditions. The US courts addressed the issue in *Search King v. Google*[1640], *Langdon v. Google*[1641], and *Nieman v. Versuslaw*[1642], each time dismissing the claims and holding that the way Google organizes their search results are protected by the First Amendment.[1643]

Of course, examples exist where the protection of Section 230 was not successful. Such cases are still in the minority, although some argue that their number is growing.[1644] This trend demonstrates *'slow abrogation of Section 230's immunity, which in its early years appeared to be nearly impenetrable'*.[1645] Often, these cases take an innovative turn, for example by claiming that the found liability is not for hosting third party content but for a "failure to warn" as in *Doe v. Internet Brands*.[1646] Or, as in the case of *People v. Bollaert*, where the defendant was found liable for extortion and unlawful use of personal identifying information, resulting from his operation of a revenge porn website posting photographs along with the subjects' social media links and charging to have the information removed.[1647] Another example, *Barnes v. Yahoo!*, concerned a failure to take down a false profile of the plaintiff after a company employee assured that it would be removed.[1648] The Court refused to hold Yahoo liable for false accounts featuring the victim's name and nude pictures created by her ex-boyfriend but held that Section 230 would not bar a promissory estoppel claim. This was because *'liability here would come not from Yahoo's publishing conduct'*, but from the company's legally binding promise to do something, which happens to be removal of material from publication.[1649]

1637 E. Goldman, What Should We Do About Revenge Porn Sites Like Texxxan?, 9 February 2013, http://blog.ericgoldman.org/archives/2013/02/what_should_we.htm.

1638 *GoDaddy.com, Inc. v. Toups*, 2014 WL 1389776 (Tex. Ct. App. April 10, 2014). See also M. Masnick, Court Rightly Finds That GoDaddy Isn't Liable For Revenge Porn Site, 17 April 2014, https://www.techdirt.com/articles/20140416/11585926935/court-rightly-finds-that-godaddy-isnt-liable-revenge-porn-site.shtml.

1639 *Caraccioli v. Facebook, Inc.*, 2016 WL 859863 (N.D. Cal. March 7, 2016).

1640 *Search King v. Google*, No. CIV-02-1457-M, 2003 WL 21464568 (W.D. Okla. May 27, 2003).

1641 *Langdon v. Google, Inc.*, 474 F. Supp. 2d 622 (D. Del. 2007).

1642 *Nieman v. Versuslaw*, No. 12-3104, 2012 WL 3201931 (C.D. Ill. Aug. 3, 2012).

1643 A. Haynes Stuart, "Google Search Results: Buried if not Forgotten", *o.c.*, p. 489–490.

1644 J. Kosseff, "Twenty Year of Intermediary Immunity: the US Experience", *o.c.*, p. 35.

1645 J. Kosseff, "The Gradual Erosion of the Law that Shaped the Internet; Section 230's Evolution over two Decades", *Columbia Science and Technology Law Review*, Vol. 18, Issue 1, p. 34.

1646 *Doe #14 v. Internet Brands*, 824 F.3d 846 (9th Cir. 2016).

1647 *People v. Bollaert*, 2016 WL 3536550 (Cal. App. Ct. June 28, 2016).

1648 *Barnes v. Yahoo!, Inc.*, 2009 WL 4823840 (D. Or. Dec. 11, 2009).

1649 *Ibid.*

Victims of wrongdoings on the Internet must generally seek a remedy against the primary perpetrators: the content providers.[1650] In that process they may encounter several difficulties on their path. First of all, it could be impossible to identify the content provider because providers protective of their own users are unlikely to volunteer the information necessary to identify them.[1651] If that succeeds, however, it might occur that content providers are '*judgement-proof*', which means that it may be hard to recover much in the form of damages.[1652] This poses a problem for victims who have to invest significant amounts of time and money in a lawsuit. Moreover, an award of damages does not guarantee that websites will comply with requests to take down images.[1653] According to Keats Citron and Franks, civil litigation may be unable to achieve the removal of content, which is what most victims primarily desire.[1654] If successful, however, cases which rule injunctions on intermediaries create a whole set of free speech issues.[1655] For example, in *Hassell v. Bird* a lawsuit against the content provider resulted in injunctions against the intermediary Yelp, even though Yelp was not party to the lawsuit.[1656] The case was criticized extensively for disregarding Yelp's First Amendment and due process rights.[1657]

From the perspective of effective remedy, Section 230 CDA is a complicated piece of legislation. It is generally considered that Section 230 '*preempts all form of relief, both monetary and injunctive*'.[1658] On many occasions such an approach may pose an obstacle to remedy unlawfulness that occurred online. There are cases where a remedy was possible but they are often criticized for misinterpreting the provisions of Section 230. If applied properly, Section 230 may result in a situation where the courts are powerless to award the

---

1650 See K. Stafford, Michigan woman gets $500K in revenge-porn case, 26 August 2016, https://www.usatoday.com/story/news/nation-now/2016/08/26/michigan-revenge-porn-verdict/89393884/.

1651 See Z. Franklin, "Justice for Revenge Porn Victims: Legal Theories to Overcome Claims of Civil Immunity by Operators of Revenge Porn Websites", *o.c.*, p. 1314. See also M. Husovec, "Accountable, Not Liable: Injunctions Against Intermediaries", *o.c.*, ft. 310.

1652 D. Keats Citron, M.A. Franks, "Criminalizing Revenge Porn", *Wake Forest Law Review*, Vol. 49, 2014, pp. 345–391, p. 358.

1653 See *Blockowicz v. Williams*, No. 10-1167 (7th Cir. Dec. 27, 2010); and *Bobolas v. Does* 1–100, 2010 WL 3923880 (D. Ariz. Oct. 1, 2010).

1654 D. Keats Citron, M.A. Franks, "Criminalizing Revenge Porn", *o.c.*, p. 359.

1655 See C. Cohn, One Injunction to Censor Them All: Doe Injunctions Threaten Speech Online, 1 June 2016, https://www.knightfoundation.org/articles/one-injunction-censor-them-all-doe-injunctions-threaten-speech-online.

1656 *Hassell v. Bird*, 2016 WL 3163296 (Cal. App. Ct. June 7, 2016).

1657 See E. Goldman, Yelp Forced To Remove Defamatory Reviews–Hassell v. Bird, 8 June 2016, http://blog.ericgoldman.org/archives/2016/06/yelp-forced-to-remove-defamatory-reviews-hassell-v-bird.htm. See also E. Goldman, Dozen Amicus Briefs Oppose the Worst Section 230 Ruling of 2016 (and One Supports It)–Hassell v. Bird, 20 April 2017, http://blog.ericgoldman.org/2017/04/dozen-amicus-briefs-oppose-the-worst-section-230-ruling-of-2016-and-one-supports-it-hassell-v-bird/.

1658 E. Goldman, Blog Host Can't Be Bound by TRO for User Posts (Blockowicz redux)–Bobolas v. Does, 12 October 2010, http://blog.ericgoldman.org/2010/10/blog_host_cant/.

plaintiffs an effective remedy against harmful expression that has no First Amendment value.[1659]

4.4. LESSONS LEARNED

BROAD PROTECTION – Section 230 CDA offers broad protection to the providers of online services. It is considered a fundamental piece of legislation that contributed strongly to the development of the IT industry in the US and represents a cornerstone of protection of free speech online. The US Congress introduced the Act to support and encourage private entities to take up censoring activities without the risk of facing liability for them. Over time, however, courts have extended safe-harbour far beyond what Congress intended. Historically, therefore, CDA had little to do with protection of free speech.

Section 230 CDA currently protects all kinds of online service providers, whether they perform any moderating activities or not. Several commentators argue that the protection by Section 230 CDA is too broad. The protection that was crucial 20 years ago when the business was in its infancy is no longer necessary. Even though there are no plans to amend Section 230 CDA, the US lawmakers continually propose content-specific bills that would weaken the protection in certain cases and allow states to enforce their local criminal laws.

(UN)CLEAR OUTCOME – Protection offered by Section 230 CDA is extremely broad. The US courts extend the protection beyond what was intended by the policymakers, even if on some occasions it leads to results that are unjust. Such results are not easily accepted by those harmed by online activities or expression. For this reason, courts continue to adjudicate lawsuits brought by the victims, who, despite the immunity, make attempts to remedy situations that harmed them. There are numerous lawsuits against online service providers every year, and some of them are actually successful. Often, however, they rely on creative approaches to circumvent the protection of Section 230. The fact that lawsuits persist suggests that those harmed by online activities or expression do not necessarily accept the outcome of a legislation that arbitrarily sacrificed their rights on the altar of the freedom of speech.

NO EFFECTIVE REMEDY – Online service providers are not obliged to take any actions with regard to unlawful content, even if they have knowledge or have been requested to act by the rights holder. Section 230 CDA offers no procedure to requests of removal of content, even if it is manifestly unlawful. All liability

[1659] B. Sheffner, Court: 'no recourse' for victims of defamatory postings under Section 230, 22 December 2009, http://copyrightsandcampaigns.blogspot.be/2009/12/court-no-recourse-for-victims-of.html.

for content-based infringements is attributed to the content providers, which means the victims of online expression or activity should exercise their rights against the content providers. This, however, is not always possible, for example if the identity of the content provider cannot be uncovered. In many situations, victims are left without any recourse mechanism. Again, they can look for creative solutions, for example claim a copyright infringement to remove revenge pornography. These methods, however, do not always work. If the online service provider does not voluntarily offer a redress mechanism, on many occasions there is nothing to be done.

PRIVATE CENSORSHIP – The intention of Section 230 CDA was to encourage online service providers to take voluntary moderating actions against obscene content. They are, however, not obliged to take any such actions. If they do, it is entirely on their own initiative. There are no minimum requirements or procedural safeguards that such mechanisms should comply with. Often, such mechanisms are only provided as a response to consumer demand and public pressure. Leaving a choice about installing such mechanisms to the good will of the online service providers means that the responsibility for protecting users' rights is shifted entirely from the State to private entities. Online expression is indeed protected from interference by the State, but fully open to interference by private companies providing the online services. Moreover, the right to effective remedy is completely dependent on the private companies' business interests. This is, of course, in accordance with the US constitutional order, however, would be extremely problematic under the ECHR regime.

CHAPTER 3

SAFEGUARDS FOR FREEDOM OF EXPRESSION IN NOTICE AND ACTION

ALL TOGETHER NOW – Chapter 2 analysed a selection of notice and action mechanisms with a view of identifying best practices. The assessment criteria used during this analysis were developed on the basis of the issues surrounding the EU intermediary liability regime identified in Part I.[1660] The analysis was therefore designed to focus the attention on how these issues are addressed in different national laws and what solutions are offered to tackle them. The exercise was necessary to learn about the practical consequences of regulatory choices and implementation decisions made by different countries.

The next, and final, step is to synthesize the results and develop an answer to the central research question of this book. The answer consists of the **identification of safeguards** to promote compliance of the EU intermediary liability regime with fundamental rights, in particular the right to freedom of expression.

The identified safeguards are grouped by the assessment criteria developed in Part II in order to clarify which issues they seek to address and how.[1661] Keeping in mind the complexity of the problem of illegal and infringing online content, however, it should be noted that the proposed safeguards may not perfectly address all the particular concerns of content regulation. In some cases, safeguards may take a different form depending on the circumstances. For this reason, the identified safeguards also contain an analysis of the possible advantages and disadvantages associated with each option, as well as a description of the different forms it might take. Where appropriate, reference shall be made to recent initiatives concerning intermediary liability regimes, in particular the Manila Principles on Intermediary Liability, the EC Communication on Tackling Illegal Content Online, the EC Recommendation on Measures to Effectively Tackle Illegal Content Online and the CoE Recommendation on the Roles and Responsibilities of Internet Intermediaries, as well as the Report of the UN Special Rapporteur David Kaye on the promotion and protection of the right to freedom of opinion and expression.[1662]

1660 Part I Chapter 6.

1661 See Part II Chapter 4 (the assessment criteria are quality of law, protection of democratic society, tailored response, procedural fairness, effective remedy).

1662 Manila Principles on Intermediary Liability, Best Practices Guidelines for Limiting Intermediary Liability for Content to Promote Freedom of Expression and Innovation,

1. QUALITY OF THE LAW

OVERVIEW – Safeguards in the area of quality of law aim to ensure that the legal framework governing notice and action mechanisms is accessible, foreseeable and predictable and promote legal certainty and legitimacy. The proposed safeguards include (1) enacting a formal legal framework; (2) a clear delineation of scope; (3) a clear definition of the procedure; and (4) enhancing transparency. These safeguards are not of a procedural nature but rather of a substantive nature as they specify requirements for regulations implementing notice and action procedures in the legal regime.

1.1. ACCESSIBILITY

A FORMAL LEGAL FRAMEWORK – Safeguards to protect freedom of expression in the context of notice and action should be provided in a formal legal instrument. Rules established through jurisprudence, even though generally accepted by the ECtHR, have certain limitations. For example, their scope is defined only by the specific examples that have already been tried by the courts. Procedures for mechanisms permitting interference with expression and accompanying protective safeguards should be established through a democratic process, which is transparent and subject to public debate. Moreover, such procedures and safeguards should be provided in (ideally) one instrument that would serve as a "manual" for the general public, not only for legal professionals experienced in navigating national and international legislation and jurisprudence. Improving accessibility and awareness of notice and action procedures among the general public is crucial to effectively safeguard the right to the freedom of expression. Therefore, to ensure a comprehensive approach to the protection of freedom of expression, the safeguards should be provided in a formal legal instrument.

This recommendation is in line with the CoE Recommendation on the Roles and Responsibilities of Internet Intermediaries, which states that '*States should not exert pressure on internet intermediaries through non-legal means*'.[1663] This does not mean, however, that co-regulation should be excluded entirely.

A Global Civil Society Initiative, Version 1.0, March 24, 2015, https://www.eff.org/files/2015/10/31/manila_principles_1.0.pdf. European Commission, Tackling Illegal Content Online – Towards an enhanced responsibility of online platforms, *o.c.* European Commission, Recommendation on measures to effectively tackle illegal content online, *o.c.* Council of Europe, Recommendation CM/Rec(2018)2 of the Committee of Ministers to member states on the roles and responsibilities of internet intermediaries, *o.c.* United Nations, Report of the Special Rapporteur David Kaye on the promotion and protection of the right to freedom of opinion and expression, *o.c.*

1663 Council of Europe, Recommendation CM/Rec(2018)2 of the Committee of Ministers to member states on the roles and responsibilities of internet intermediaries, *o.c.*, p. 5.

Rather, it means that any co-regulatory mechanism, should be based on a legal framework set up by the State. Such a framework should define clear limits and provide safeguards (as proposed in this book) to prevent arbitrary decisions by non-state agents. As a result, co-regulatory initiatives, such as the Code of Conduct on Countering Illegal Hate Speech Online and the operations of the IWF, should be based on a legal act defining the division of roles between State and non-state agents.

AT EUROPEAN LEVEL – To achieve an effective protection of the right to freedom of expression, a set of minimum safeguards should be provided at the EU level. As has been argued throughout this book, this is an obligation of the EU acting as legislator incentivizing interference with the right to the freedom of expression by private entities. In particular, the EU should adopt a regulation on safeguards in notice and action mechanisms. It should be highlighted, however, that to provide a meaningful solution to the problem of tackling illegal content online, the regulation would have to be sufficiently specific to be implemented uniformly across the EU.

WHY A REGULATION? – When considering the range of regulatory instruments available at EU level, a regulation appears to be the most appropriate legal instrument. As observed in Part I, the current EU intermediary liability regime suffers from a high level of legal fragmentation. This book argues, therefore, that the safeguards should be provided in a regulation, to avoid repeating the same mistake, which resulted from approaching the problem through a directive. Only through a regulation which provides a single set of rules, can safeguards be applied uniformly across the EU and fulfil their goal of eliminating legal fragmentation and improving legal certainty. A regulation would provide a consistent level of protection and enhance transparency towards all stakeholders. Uniform safeguards would benefit Internet users willing to exercise their rights, as well as companies, especially smaller ones, willing to provide services across the EU. Harmonized procedures for content removal and reinstatement would, therefore, effectively help the users, facilitate business operations and strengthen the Digital Single Market.

A similar argumentation was presented in the context of the EU data protection reform explaining the shift from a directive to a regulation.[1664] It can be also found in the recently proposed EU Regulation on promoting fairness and

---

[1664] See Regulation (EU) 2016/679 of the European Parliament and of the Council of 27 April 2016 on the protection of natural persons with regard to the processing of personal data and on the free movement of such data, and repealing Directive 95/46/EC (General Data Protection Regulation), Official Journal of the European Union L 119/1, 4 May 2016, Recital (13); and European Commission, Communication from the Commission to the European Parliament and the Council Stronger protection, new opportunities – Commission guidance on the direct application of the General Data Protection Regulation as of 25 May 2018, Brussels,

transparency for business users of online intermediation services.[1665] The impact assessment for the latter instrument observes that in the inherently cross-border online intermediated environment a regulation is preferred, as it is directly applicable in Member States, establishes the same level of obligations for private parties and enables the coherent application of rules.[1666]

The question of liability for specific types of illegal or infringing content or activities online would still be regulated by national laws. It is not the purpose of the proposed minimum safeguards to alter substantive sector-specific national laws defining when a party may be considered liable (e.g. under defamation law, hate speech, gambling regulation, etc.).

GENERAL AND SPECIFIC – The regulation should contain a baseline of protection that would have to become a part of any notice and action mechanism, regardless of which specific mechanism is used. Considering that some of the safeguards proposed below could take a different form, depending on which type of content or activity they aim to address, the regulation could contain a general section with uniformly applicable safeguards (e.g. judicial redress) and specific sections addressing different types of content or activities (e.g. child abuse content, hate speech, defamation, copyright infringements). Such an approach would be compatible with the sectorial, problem-driven approach currently pursued by the European Commission. For example, it can be found in the recent EC Recommendation on Measures to Effectively Tackle Illegal Content Online, which delineates sections with general recommendations relating to all types of illegal content, and sections with specific recommendations relating to terrorist content.[1667] Alternatively, the regulation could limit itself to providing generally applicable safeguards for all types of notice and action mechanisms and all types of content and activities. This general baseline could be further complemented with specific sectorial instruments calibrating the safeguards according to the context, depending on the type of illegal content or activity at issue. In theory, sections listing the specific safeguards could be added to instruments addressing illegal content online in different policy areas (such as Copyright in the Digital Single Market and AVMS). If this option was preferred

---

24.1.2018 COM(2018) 43 final, http://eur-lex.europa.eu/legal-content/EN/TXT/PDF/?uri=CELEX:52018DC0043&from=EN.

1665 European Commission, Regulation on promoting fairness and transparency for business users of online intermediation services, 26 April, https://ec.europa.eu/digital-single-market/en/news/regulation-promoting-fairness-and-transparency-business-users-online-intermediation-services.

1666 European Commission, Impact assessment of the Proposal for a Regulation of the European Parliament and of the Council on promoting fairness and transparency for business users of online intermediation services, 26 April 2018, https://ec.europa.eu/digital-single-market/en/news/impact-assessment-proposal--promoting-fairness-transparency-online-platforms, p. 5.

1667 See European Commission, Recommendation on Measures to Effectively Tackle Illegal Content Online, *o.c.*

and the currently proposed instruments (and amendments) were adopted, this would mean that the safeguards would most likely be provided in the form of a directive, and not a regulation.

POLICY INCOHERENCE – Adopting a regulation at EU level would have the added benefit of significantly reducing issues relating to policy incoherence. As discussed in Part I, there is policy incoherence within the EU intermediary liability regime at both vertical and horizontal levels.[1668] The former arises because the EU intermediary liability regime does not actively safeguard the right to freedom of expression – other than vaguely mentioning it in the preamble to the E-Commerce Directive. The latter is a result of EU institutions introducing initiatives that may work at cross purposes, leading to contradictory results. For example, this is the case with the E-Commerce Directive (with the goal of limiting liability exposure of intermediaries), the Communication on Tackling Illegal Content Online, and the proposed Copyright in the DSM Directive (with the goals of employing intermediaries to fight hate speech and copyright infringements online, respectively). Eliminating, or at least reducing the level of policy incoherence, both vertical and horizontal, should be an ambition of EU policy makers.

CURRENT APPROACH – The need for greater coherence of public policy responses across geographical borders in the Digital Single Market is mentioned in the EC Communication on Tackling Illegal Content Online.[1669] The EC considers the Communication a first step towards addressing the problem of policy incoherence by providing guidelines on how to address the challenge of illegal content removal. The guidelines provided, however, as well as the tone of the Communication in general, clearly emphasize that the responsibility to tackle the problem of illegal content online resides mainly with intermediaries. The Commission plans to continue engaging with stakeholders and to monitor the intermediaries' progress. It will also assess whether additional measures are needed, including possible legislative measures to complement the existing regulatory framework. The Commission has continued this approach, which has materialized in issuing of a Recommendation on Measures to Effectively Tackle Illegal Content Online. The Recommendation is a follow-up to the Communication, providing more details on the Commission's vision on tackling illegal content online.[1670] The Recommendation, interestingly, reminds that '*[i] llegal content online should be tackled with proper and robust safeguards to ensure*

[1668] Part I Chapter 6.1.

[1669] European Commission, Tackling Illegal Content Online – Towards an enhanced responsibility of online platforms, *o.c.*, p. 20.

[1670] European Commission, Recommendation on Measures to Effectively Tackle Illegal Content Online, *o.c.*, p. 2.

protection of the different fundamental rights at stake of all parties concerned'.[1671] As a recommendation, however, the instrument is not binding and does not impose any legal obligations.[1672] The recent Recommendation, therefore, is another expression of the Commission's ideas but not itself a legal instrument, as was suggested in the Communication. The Commission plans to assess the effects of the newest Recommendation to determine whether additional steps, including binding acts of Union law, are required.[1673]

1.2. FORESEEABILITY

A. *Defined scope*

CLEAR AND PRECISE LAW – Laws allowing for interference with content dissemination should be clear and precise. The legislature must ensure that laws affecting freedom of expression are clear and predictable. Only then can such laws allow subjects to know what behaviour is expected of them so they can act accordingly or face the prescribed consequences. This is a basic requirement of quality law-making. The same point is made in the CoE Recommendation on the Roles and Responsibilities of Internet Intermediaries, which states that '*legislation applicable to internet intermediaries and to their relations with states and users must be accessible and foreseeable*'.[1674] Moreover, all '*laws should be clear and sufficiently precise to enable intermediaries, users and affected parties to regulate their conduct*'.[1675] The so-called Manila principles on Intermediary Liability similarly argue that '*[g]overnments must publish all legislation, policy, decisions and other forms of regulation relevant to intermediary liability online in a timely fashion and in accessible formats*'.[1676]

ACTORS AND ACTIVITIES – The scope of the law should be precise. It should define what actors and activities it is aimed at. Maintaining the existing typology of the E-Commerce Directive would undoubtedly promote consistency of terminology. However, in the rapidly developing IT environment where the disruption of traditional service models is often a recipe for success, an

---

1671 *Ibid.*, p. 3.

1672 European Union, Regulations, Directives and other acts, https://europa.eu/european-union/eu-law/legal-acts_en.

1673 European Commission, Recommendation on Measures to Effectively Tackle Illegal Content Online, *o.c.*, p. 9.

1674 Council of Europe, Recommendation CM/Rec(2018)2 of the Committee of Ministers to member states on the roles and responsibilities of internet intermediaries, *o.c.*, p. 6.

1675 *Ibid.*

1676 Manila Principles on Intermediary Liability, Best Practices Guidelines for Limiting Intermediary Liability for Content to Promote Freedom of Expression and Innovation, *o.c.*, p. 6.

updated classification of intermediaries should be considered. Primarily, such a classification should clarify which types of activities are covered by the liability exemption. Developing new definitions to describe actors that participate in the intermediation process could be useful, mainly to address the situation of intermediaries not specifically covered by the liability exemptions of the E-Commerce Directive. This refers specifically to search engines (information location tools), which now have to rely on the hosting exemption, but whose position as hosts is still debated. The main focus, however, should be on the functional aspect of the activities performed by intermediaries. In that sense, it might be worth looking into the terminology employed in the US DMCA, which does not refer to hosting providers, but uses a broader term of "information residing on systems or networks at direction of users". This term seems to be easier to understand, and easier to apply by eliminating the problematic distinction between active and passive hosts.

ACTIVE HOSTING – The liability exemption is only available to providers of hosting services who meet the conditions set out in Article 14 of the E-Commerce Directive. As indicated in the EC Communication on Tackling Illegal Content, such service providers are those whose activities consist of the storage of information at the request of third parties and which do not play an active role of such a kind as to give it knowledge of, or control over, that information.[1677] This is a reference to Recital (42) of the Directive, which informed the judgement in *L'Oréal v. eBay*. Interestingly, the EC Communication refers to recital (42) as an argument that proactive measures to detect and remove illegal content online would not put the intermediaries who engage them in the position of active hosts. In the view of the Commission such proactive measures should be understood as taken for the application of the terms of services. In that way, taking proactive measures would fall within the interpretation of the CJEU, providing that

> 'the mere fact that [an intermediary] stores offers for sale on its server, sets the terms of its service, is remunerated for that service and provides general information to its customers cannot have the effect of denying it the exemptions from liability provided for by [Article 14 of the E-Commerce Directive]'.[1678]

According to the Commission, therefore, the mere fact that an intermediary 'takes certain measures relating to the provision of its services in a general manner does not necessarily mean that it plays an active role in respect of the individual content items it stores'.[1679] This is an attempt by the Commission to convince the

---

1677 European Commission, Tackling Illegal Content Online – Towards an enhanced responsibility of online platforms, *o.c.*, p. 11.

1678 CJEU, *L'Oréal v. eBay*, Case C-324/09, 12 July 2011, para. 115.

1679 European Commission, Tackling Illegal Content Online – Towards an enhanced responsibility of online platforms, *o.c.*, p. 11.

intermediaries that taking proactive measures would not make them active hosts. This interpretation, however, appears to be stretching the CJEU's words a bit too far. It is questionable whether the Court would agree that employing proactive measures to detect and remove illegal content as an enforcement of the terms of service is similarly passive as merely setting the terms of service. Moreover, taking proactive measures would most likely give intermediaries (at least constructive) knowledge of, or control over information.[1680] Instead of engaging in interpretational gymnastics, the Commission should consider abolishing the distinction between active and passive hosts altogether.

As has been demonstrated above in Part I, the problem with application of Article 14 to passive and active hosts is based on the expansive application of Recital (42).[1681] In fact, however, Article 14 does not require a passive role of the hosting provider in order for the protection regime to apply – as long as it does not have knowledge or control over the data which are being stored.[1682] The EU legislature should finally resolve this problem by clearly including the active hosting providers in the scope of the exemption, under the condition that they are not the creators the content and that they have no knowledge about its illegal or infringing character. Explicitly clarifying the broad scope of the exemption is necessary in light of the constant development of new types of online services. In the online environment with multi-layered platforms, the traditional hosts that play a static role solely storing content concerns a very small subset of service providers. New types of platforms often adopt a more innovative approach to attract and engage users. If it is not clear whether they can benefit from the intermediary liability exemption for third party content; they may be forced to adopt a cautionary approach. The EU should take a clear position clarifying the situation of the active hosting services in order to preserve the role of the E-Commerce Directive in stimulating and facilitating innovation of the online services in the EU. One way to achieve this objective would be to move from the term "host" to the broader term of "information residing on systems or networks at direction of users". This claim in no way negates, however, the basic requirements for service providers to assume responsibility for content that they created, and to act after having been duly informed of the illegal or infringing character of content, which is being made available through their services.

GOOD SAMARITAN 0.5 – Hosts that want to engage actively as part of their service provision may wish to take proactive steps to detect, remove or disable access to illegal content. Proactive involvement is encouraged by the EC Communication on Tackling Illegal Content, which aims to clarify intermediaries' liability in such circumstances. Specifically, the EC argues that taking such

[1680] See more below in section Good Samaritan 0.5.

[1681] Part I Chapter 6.2.

[1682] P. Van Eecke, "Online Service Providers and Liability: a Plea for a Balanced Approach", *o.c.*, p. 1463.

voluntary, proactive measures does not automatically lead to the online platform losing the benefit of the liability exemption provided for in Article 14 of the E-Commerce Directive.[1683] With this reading, the EC seems to advocate for a "European version" of the Good Samaritan protection.[1684] According to the EC, proactive measures taken by an intermediary to detect and remove illegal content may indeed result in obtaining knowledge or awareness of illegal activities or illegal information, which could lead to the loss of the liability exemption. However, the EC argues that in such cases, the intermediary '*continues to have the possibility to act expeditiously to remove or to disable access to the information in question upon obtaining such knowledge or awareness*'.[1685] If the intermediary does so, he continues to benefit from the liability exemption, therefore, he should not be concerned about implementing proactive voluntary measures.

The presented interpretation of Article 14 of the E-Commerce Directive is interesting, but somewhat confusing and perhaps even misleading. Specifically, the EC argues that intermediaries should not worry about losing immunity because under Article 14 they already have an obligation to act expeditiously when they obtain knowledge or awareness. This includes situations when the knowledge or awareness is obtained '*as the result of an investigation undertaken on its own initiative*'.[1686] The fact that intermediaries can "choose" whether they comply with that obligation to maintain the immunity, according to the EC, is equivalent to the continuous benefit from the liability exemption. Arguably, this is the case under the assumption that they always "choose" to remove or block access. In other words, the EC attempts to convince intermediaries that they will not lose the protection – as long as they act according to the expectations of policy makers. The conditional character of the immunity is omitted in that argumentation. Moreover, the EC overlooks the difference in scale between the situation when intermediaries stumble upon illegal content occasionally, and when they would regularly find illegal content as a result of using proactive measures. After all, the more intermediaries look, the more they will find. The chances of missing a particular illegality, and therefore losing the immunity, grow significantly with increased searching. In any event, the proposed interpretation is not a "true" Good Samaritan protection, at least not in the meaning of Section 230 CDA. This is because Section 230 CDA protects intermediaries when they take any voluntarily measures to restrict access to or availability of certain content but also, and most importantly, when they miss such content and do not take any action at all. After all, the specific purpose for introducing this section was to overrule *Stratton-Oakmont v. Prodigy*.[1687]

1683 European Commission, Tackling Illegal Content Online – Towards an enhanced responsibility of online platforms, *o.c.*, p. 10.

1684 *Ibid.*, p. 3.

1685 *Ibid.*, p. 12.

1686 CJEU, *L'Oréal v. eBay*, Case C-324/09, 12 July 2011, paras. 120–121.

1687 See Part I Chapter 4.3.

The Good Samaritan protection in Section 230 CDA has several disadvantages. Mainly, it provides no effective remedy to complainants whose rights were infringed while at the same time encourages excessive take-downs on the intermediary's own initiative. It does, however, clarify that intermediaries will not be punished if they make their best effort to moderate content but fail to detect all instances of undesirable content. By providing this assurance the US Congress effectively encouraged intermediaries to implement proactive measures. The Commission's argumentation is actually only half of the Good Samaritan protection – intermediaries in the EU will not lose the immunity if they take voluntary action, but there is no protection if they fail to do so.

NO GENERAL MONITORING – The E-Commerce Directive is clear that States may not impose a general monitoring obligation on intermediaries or an obligation to actively look for facts or circumstances indicating illegal activity.[1688] This approach is generally accepted, as was illustrated for example in the *Sabam* cases. It is also present in several guidelines and recommendations in the area of intermediary liability. For example, the Manila Principles argue that intermediaries should never be required to monitor content proactively as part of an intermediary liability regime.[1689] The CoE Recommendation likewise provides that State authorities '*should not directly or indirectly impose a general obligation on intermediaries to monitor content which they merely give access to, or which they transmit or store, be it by automated means or not*'.[1690] The UN Special Rapporteur David Kaye, in his report on the promotion and protection of the right to freedom of opinion and expression, clarifies that States should refrain from establishing laws or arrangements that would require the "proactive" monitoring or filtering of content, as it would be both inconsistent with the right to privacy and likely to amount to pre-publication censorship.[1691]

GENERAL VS. SPECIFIC MONITORING – General monitoring obligations are not allowed. Specific monitoring obligations, on the other hand, are not precluded. Recital (47) of the E-Commerce Directive clarifies that the prohibition of general monitoring leaves room for monitoring in "specific cases".[1692] Voluntary monitoring, even if general, is also not prohibited. Recital (40) of the

1688 See Part I Chapter 4.1.

1689 Manila Principles on Intermediary Liability, Best Practices Guidelines for Limiting Intermediary Liability for Content to Promote Freedom of Expression and Innovation, *o.c.*, p. 2.

1690 Council of Europe, Recommendation CM/Rec(2018)2 of the Committee of Ministers to member states on the roles and responsibilities of internet intermediaries, *o.c.*, p. 7.

1691 United Nations, Report of the Special Rapporteur David Kaye on the promotion and protection of the right to freedom of opinion and expression, *o.c.*, p. 20.

1692 Modern Poland Foundation, Commission claims that general monitoring is not general monitoring, 10 January 2018, https://edri.org/commission-claims-that-general-monitoring-is-not-general-monitoring/.

E-Commerce Directive acknowledges the importance of voluntary measures. The matter becomes blurry, when it comes to distinguishing between general monitoring obligation, specific monitoring obligation, and defining when either of them are voluntary or not. The Commission is juggling these terms, creatively arguing that the promoted measures are not general but specific, therefore not prohibited. However, if they would effectively lead to a general monitoring obligation, this should not be problematic because they are actually taken voluntarily. The presented argumentation, nevertheless, is confusing.

As explained in the EC Communication on Tackling Illegal Content online, sector-specific legislation can establish mandatory rules for intermediaries to take measures (e.g., on copyright) to help ensure the detection and removal of illegal content.[1693] This information is mixed in the argumentation promoting voluntary measures. It refers, most likely, to the currently debated provisions of the Copyright Directive in the Digital Single Market, which would not be voluntary at all. Article 13 of the proposed Copyright Directive provides that

> 'Information society service providers that store and provide to the public access to large amounts of works or other subject-matter uploaded by their users shall, in cooperation with rightholders, (…) prevent the availability on their services of works or other subject-matter identified by rightholders through the cooperation with the service providers.'[1694]

Such measures would consist of content recognition technologies. As pointed out by multiple academics and NGOs, introducing such measures would in fact lead to imposing obligations on service providers to prevent the upload of infringing content.[1695] Moreover, ordering specific monitoring in this context would lead to a general monitoring obligation. This is because specific monitoring still requires searching through everything, disregarding the different contexts of a posting (e.g. exceptions, timing, etc.). Specific monitoring obligations, therefore, may effectively allow the circumvention of the prohibition of Article 15 of the E-Commerce Directive. In that sense the discussion is a reminiscence of the notice-and-stay down analysis.[1696] The result of this approach would be an indirect imposition of a general obligation to monitor content on intermediaries – which is exactly what the CoE Recommendations (and this book) advise against.

1693 European Commission, Tackling Illegal Content Online – Towards an enhanced responsibility of online platforms, *o.c.*, p. 12.

1694 European Commission, Proposal for a Directive of the European Parliament and of the Council on copyright in the Digital Single Market, *o.c.*

1695 See in S. Stalla-Bourdillon et al., Open Letter to the European Commission – On the Importance of Preserving the Consistency and Integrity of the EU Acquis Relating to Content Monitoring within the Information Society, *o.c.*; and S. Stalla-Bourdillon et al., A Brief Exegesis of the Proposed Copyright Directive, *o.c.*. See also Modern Poland Foundation, Commission claims that general monitoring is not general monitoring, *o.c.*

1696 See Part III Chapter 2.2.

B. *Defined procedure*

CLEAR PROCESS – Apart from clarifying the scope of liability exemptions, the law should also provide a clear procedure describing the notification mechanisms, the order of events, and steps that have to be taken by the involved parties. Notification mechanisms should generally be visible, easily accessible, user-friendly and contextual.[1697] They should also allow for easy notification of different content types, for example by providing a list of categories of reasons for notifying content. Such notification mechanisms should be available to the general public, without being signed-in as a user, where the content is publicly available.[1698]

At present, few countries define the details of notice and takedown procedure while others leave it to the intermediaries themselves. However, in order to ensure a high quality of law, the details of the procedure should be defined by the legislature.

OBTAINING ACTUAL KNOWLEDGE – Intermediaries may become aware of the existence of illegal content in a number of different ways. Different channels for notifications include (1) court orders or administrative decisions; (2) notices from competent authorities (e.g. law enforcement bodies), (3) specialised "trusted flaggers", intellectual property rights holders or ordinary users, or (4) through the platforms' own investigations or knowledge.[1699] Keeping in mind the existing lack of legal certainty regarding actual knowledge, the law should clarify minimum standards establishing when this type of knowledge is obtained by intermediaries. Specifically, orders issued by a court or independent administrative body should always establish actual knowledge and require expeditious reaction. This clarification would lead to a strong safeguard for content removals requested by States, improving not only legal certainty for intermediaries, but also advancing legitimacy and proportionality of such requests.

EXPECTED BEHAVIOUR – The law should also clarify what behaviour is expected of intermediaries. In particular, the law should define how they should react to a notification of the infringing or illegal character of content by a third party. Ideally, intermediaries should not be held liable simply for not taking down content after receiving a private notification. They should, however, comply with

---

[1697] European Commission, Tackling Illegal Content Online – Towards an enhanced responsibility of online platforms, *o.c.*, p. 10. See also European Commission, Recommendation on Measures to Effectively Tackle Illegal Content Online, *o.c.*, p. 4.

[1698] European Commission, Tackling Illegal Content Online – Towards an enhanced responsibility of online platforms, *o.c.*, p. 9.

[1699] European Commission, Tackling Illegal Content Online – Towards an enhanced responsibility of online platforms, *o.c.*, p. 7.

court orders or administrative orders, which would establish actual knowledge. In that sense, this recommendation follows the line taken in the French LCEN law. One exception constitutes content that is manifestly, i.e. in a way clearly recognizable by a diligent operator, illegal (see more *infra*). In such cases, the intermediary should be required to take down illegal content upon obtaining knowledge of the content also through a private notification. At the same time the intermediary should not be required to actively search for these types of content on the platform. Types of illegal content that would require a swift reaction of the intermediaries (e.g. child sexual abuse material or incitement to violence) should be clearly defined by the legislator.[1700] This safeguard would further promote due process as it ensures that the content remains in place until it has been held illegal by a court or administrative authority, without the risk of liability for the intermediary (except in cases that involve manifestly illegal content).[1701]

VALID NOTICE – The legal framework providing safeguards for the notice and action mechanisms procedure should specify the formal requirements for a valid notice, i.e. what information must be included to put the mechanisms in motion. As stated in the CoE Recommendation, notices should contain sufficient information for intermediaries to act upon.[1702] As clarified by the CJEU in *L'Oreal Ebay*, a notice should be "sufficiently precise and adequately substantiated".[1703] The actual meaning of those terms in the context of online content regulation, however, should be specified by the legislature.

The level of detail required to expeditiously take informed decisions may, however, vary considerably from one type of content to the other.[1704] Nevertheless, requirements for valid notice should be specified, and include basic elements such as: (1) reason for a complaint (including legal basis for the assessment of content); (2) location of the content; and (3) evidence for the claim.[1705] Interesting elements are proposed additionally by the Manila Principles, which add (4) consideration on limitations, exceptions, and defences available to the content provider, and (5) declaration of good

1700 See also Section 2.2 Manifest Illegality.

1701 C. Angelopoulos, S. Smet, "Notice-and-fair-balance: how to reach a compromise between fundamental rights in European intermediary liability", *o.c.*, p. 285. See also Article 19, 'Promoting Free Expression and Access to Information: 2010 Implementation Report', www.article19.org/data/files/annual_reports_and_accounts/2010-annual-report.pdf.

1702 Council of Europe, Recommendation CM/Rec(2018)2 of the Committee of Ministers to member states on the roles and responsibilities of internet intermediaries, *o.c.*, p. 7.

1703 See also European Commission, Recommendation on Measures to Effectively Tackle Illegal Content Online, *o.c.*, p. 4 and p. 11.

1704 European Commission, Tackling Illegal Content Online – Towards an enhanced responsibility of online platforms, *o.c.*, p. 10.

1705 See also European Commission, Recommendation on Measures to Effectively Tackle Illegal Content Online, *o.c.*, p. 11.

faith that the information provided is accurate.[1706] Additionally, the Manila Principles suggest requiring contact details of the issuing party or their agent, unless this is prohibited by law. This is a requirement commonly found in the existing notice and action procedures. As pointed out in the EC Communication, however, in some cases identification of the notifying party may put their safety at risk or could have legal implications. For this reason, the EC Communication recommends that users should normally not be obliged to identify themselves when reporting content, unless this information is required to determine the legality of the content (e.g. asserting ownership for intellectual property rights).[1707] The EC Recommendation clarifies that intermediaries generally do not need the contact details of the notice provider to be able to take an informed and diligent decision.[1708] Making the provision of contact details a prerequisite for the submission of a notice, the Commission observes, would entail an obstacle to notification.[1709] Instead, the Commission argues, users should be encouraged to raise their notification via trusted flaggers, where these exist, if they wish to maintain anonymous vis-à-vis platforms (see further below).[1710] At the same time, notice providers should have the opportunity to voluntarily submit their contact details in a notification.[1711] Such a solution would allow the online platform to ask for additional information or to inform the notice provider about any intended follow-up.[1712] The EC Recommendation suggests that the intermediary should send a confirmation of receipt to the notice provider if his contact details are known.[1713]

Moreover, the law should also set limitations on the content of the notifications. This is especially relevant if notices are to be forwarded by intermediaries to the content providers, as in the case of notice-and-notice mechanisms. The purpose of introducing limitations would be to avoid a situation such as in Canada, where adding additional (often misleading) content to the notice by copyright holders intimidates and pushes Internet users into unfavourable settlements.[1714]

1706 Manila Principles on Intermediary Liability, Best Practices Guidelines for Limiting Intermediary Liability for Content to Promote Freedom of Expression and Innovation, *o.c.*, p. 4.

1707 European Commission, Tackling Illegal Content Online – Towards an enhanced responsibility of online platforms, *o.c.*, p. 10.

1708 European Commission, Recommendation on Measures to Effectively Tackle Illegal Content Online, *o.c.*, p. 5.

1709 *Ibid.*

1710 European Commission, Tackling Illegal Content Online – Towards an enhanced responsibility of online platforms, *o.c.*, p. 10.

1711 *Ibid.*

1712 See also European Commission, Recommendation on Measures to Effectively Tackle Illegal Content Online, *o.c.*, p. 5.

1713 See *Ibid.*, p. 11.

1714 See Part III Chapter 2.3.

TRUSTED FLAGGERS – The EC Communication recommends the creation of privileged channels for high-quality notice providers.[1715] Notices from such privileged channels could be fast-tracked by intermediaries. The Commission refers to providers of high-quality notices as "trusted flaggers". They are entities with specific expertise and dedicated structures for detecting and identifying illegal online content.[1716] Introducing trusted flaggers, according to the Commission, would help to improve the quality of notices as well as speed up take-downs. The EC Communication encourages intermediaries to use existing networks of trusted flaggers, for example, the Europol Internet Referral Unit for terrorist content and the INHOPE network for reporting child sexual abuse material.[1717]

The idea of trusted flaggers requires the development of criteria based notably on respect for fundamental rights and on democratic values.[1718] The criteria should state when a particular entity can be considered a trusted flagger and may include internal training standards, process standards, and quality assurance. They should also include legal safeguards regarding independence, conflicts of interest, accountability, and protection of privacy and personal data. Trusted flaggers could be audited against the criteria to receive trusted status through a certification scheme.[1719] The Commission continues by clarifying that the criteria could be agreed by the industry at EU level, through self-regulatory mechanisms or within the EU standardisation framework. Moreover, the Commission states that

> 'a reasonable balance needs to be struck between ensuring a high quality of notices coming from trusted flaggers, the scope of additional measures that companies would take in relation to trusted flaggers and the burden in ensuring these quality standards'.[1720]

Arguably, introducing trusted flaggers could improve the quality of notices. If the experts were independent, it could also provide a very subtle hint of an independent tribunal, as required in Article 13 ECHR. Being independent would increase the chances of proper balancing decisions since the flaggers would not risk liability for a wrong assessment – although they could lose their status.

While the concept of trusted flaggers has a certain appeal, certain elements require further consideration. In theory, third parties specialized in recognizing

1715 European Commission, Tackling Illegal Content Online – Towards an enhanced responsibility of online platforms, *o.c.*, p. 8.

1716 *Ibid.* European Commission, Recommendation on Measures to Effectively Tackle Illegal Content Online, *o.c.*, p. 10.

1717 European Commission, Tackling Illegal Content Online – Towards an enhanced responsibility of online platforms, *o.c.*, p. 8.

1718 *Ibid.*, p. 8.

1719 *Ibid.*, p. 9.

1720 *Ibid.*

specific types of illegal content should have greater expertise than intermediaries. This is not always the case, however. For example, Google implements the idea through its Trusted Copyright Removal Program. In January 2017 Google submitted information to the Copyright Office which demonstrated that in total, 99.95% of all URLs processed from the Program were not even in their index.[1721] Trust in trusted flaggers should therefore not be unlimited. An additional concern regarding the Commission's proposal is that the criteria, standards, assurances and safeguards should be developed by the industry. As has been argued throughout this book, rules and procedures allowing for interference with the right to freedom of expression by private entities should not be delegated to them but provided by States. From the wording used in the EC Communication, it is evident that there is already a certain awareness about the burdens associated with ensuring quality standards. If the quality of standards was to be sacrificed in order not to burden intermediaries with the development, perhaps a different approach would be needed. If the standards were to be provided for by law (possibly subject to further development within the EU standardisation framework), the proposal would certainly fit better within the principles of legal certainty, legitimacy and proportionality. It would also avoid appearing as further delegation of enforcement to dilute responsibility.

1.3. TRANSPARENCY

FUNCTIONING OF THE RULES – The law providing the procedure for notice and action should be transparent. This means, that it should be accessible, clear and known. The same refers to the internal rules of intermediaries, usually described in their content policies. But transparency of the rules refers also to the information about the functioning of the law. It allows the gathering of evidence on the implementation and application of the law. Only through a collection of certain practical information would it be possible to monitor whether the law fulfils its objectives and whether any corrective measures are necessary to address identified weaknesses.

TRANSPARENCY REPORTS – The information necessary to assess the functioning of the law can be provided through transparency reports, to be issued by the intermediary at periodic intervals. Such reports should include information on (1) the number of notices; (2) types of entities that file them (private notices, court or administrative orders); and (3) the character of illegal or infringing content subject to complaints, as well as (4) the response time (time it took to

1721 T. Geigner, Google Report: 99.95 Percent Of DMCA Takedown Notices Are Bot-Generated Bullshit Buckshot, 23 February 2017, https://www.techdirt.com/articles/20170223/06160336772/google-report-9995-percent-dmca-takedown-notices-are-bot-generated-bullshit-buckshot.shtml.

notify the content provider, time given to file counter-notification, time until take down of content, etc.); and (5) the number of appeals, etc.[1722] An obligation to file regular transparency reports on the handling of notices should cover providers of intermediary services that receive a certain number of notices per year.[1723] The new German law, NetzDG, for example, provides strict provisions on transparency and accountability. The Commission encourages the publication of transparency reports on a regular basis and at least once per year.[1724]

The CoE Recommendation provides that States should require intermediaries to disclose clear (simple and machine-readable), easily accessible and meaningful information about interferences with the exercise of rights and freedoms in the digital environment.[1725] The Commission points out that transparency reports would benefit from some standardisation across the Digital Single Market. The Commission is right to observe that standardisation would allow for '*better monitoring, facilitate the electronic aggregation of such information and could help avoid unnecessary barriers to the cross-border provision of hosting services*'.[1726] There is no indication, however, who should provide such standards. It seems obvious, and in line with the main idea in this book, that minimum content of transparency reports across the Digital Single Market should be provided for by EU law.

Transparency reports, however, should not only be provided by intermediaries, but also by States. This recommendation specifically applies to situations where content restrictions are requested by States.[1727] As indicated in the CoE Recommendation, States should make available publicly and in a regular manner, comprehensive information on the number, nature and legal basis of content restriction requests sent to intermediaries and on the actions taken as a result of those requests.[1728] The information should include content restrictions based on international mutual legal assistance treaties.[1729] The Report of the Special Rapporteur David Kaye also argues that States should publish detailed transparency reports on all content-related requests issued to intermediaries.[1730] Only such reports, in combination with the reports by

1722 See also European Commission, Tackling Illegal Content Online – Towards an enhanced responsibility of online platforms, *o.c.*, p. 16.

1723 See *Ibid.*

1724 European Commission, Recommendation on Measures to Effectively Tackle Illegal Content Online, *o.c.*, p. 12.

1725 Council of Europe, Recommendation CM/Rec(2018)2 of the Committee of Ministers to member states on the roles and responsibilities of internet intermediaries, *o.c.*, p. 6.

1726 See also European Commission, Tackling Illegal Content Online – Towards an enhanced responsibility of online platforms, *o.c.*, p. 16.

1727 See also Manila Principles on Intermediary Liability, Best Practices Guidelines for Limiting Intermediary Liability for Content to Promote Freedom of Expression and Innovation, *o.c.*, p. 5.

1728 Council of Europe, Recommendation CM/Rec(2018)2 of the Committee of Ministers to Member States on the roles and responsibilities of internet intermediaries, *o.c.*, p. 6.

1729 *Ibid.*

1730 United Nations, Report of the Special Rapporteur David Kaye on the promotion and protection of the right to freedom of opinion and expression, *o.c.*, p. 20.

intermediaries, can provide a comprehensive picture on the trends and patterns in content restriction and on the effectiveness of the rules, which is necessary to engage in evidence based policy-making.

2. PROTECTION OF DEMOCRATIC SOCIETY

OVERVIEW – Safeguards in the area of protection of democratic society aim to ensure that the legal regime governing notice and action mechanisms protects democratic values and promotes legitimacy. The same safeguards also serve to advance legal certainty. The proposed safeguards include (1) definition of the types of content or activities concerned; (2) clarification of the application; and (3) definition of types of illegal content and activities for which stricter conditions for immunity may apply. Safeguards related to the protection of democratic society are not, strictly speaking, of a procedural nature but rather of a substantive nature. Similar to the quality of law safeguards, they specify substantive requirements for the legal regime governing notice and action mechanisms.

2.1. DEMOCRATIC VALUES

A. Types of content and activities

VALUES AND INTERESTS – Interference with freedom of expression may be permitted only in the interest of specific values and interests.[1731] The legal framework describing procedures for the notice and action mechanisms should define which specific values and interests they aim to protect by allowing interference with the freedom of expression. The matter should not be left to jurisprudence, because the courts' interpretation and application varies, even within the same jurisdiction. Such inconsistencies undermine the legal certainty and legitimacy of the laws. In particular, the law should clearly define whether their application is horizontal – to any type of content or activity endangering the protected values and interests, or only to specific types of content or activities infringing those values and interests.

B. Application

HORIZONTAL APPLICATION – The safeguards proposed in this book, ideally, should apply horizontally. Horizontal application would provide legal certainty regarding all types of infringing and illegal online content. The EU legal framework should avoid the legal fragmentation that is currently

1731 As recognized by Article 10. 2ECHR and Article 52.1CFEU. See more in Part II Chapter 1.

found in a number of national laws. As observed in the EC Communication, a harmonised and coherent approach to removing illegal content does not currently exist in the EU.[1732] Chapter 2 clearly illustrated that different approaches exist depending on the country, content category, or type of intermediary. For example, Finland, Hungary, Chile and the US provide detailed take down procedures, but only do so for copyright infringing content. The Commission rightly points out that a '*more aligned approach would make the fight against illegal content more effective*'.[1733] If the rules are to fulfil the goal of the E-Commerce Directive and provide legal certainty, they should clarify the treatment of all kinds of infringing and illegal content, not only some of them. After all, the E-Commerce Directive constitutes an overarching framework that covers different types of illegal content.[1734] It cannot be excluded, however, that certain differences may persist, depending on which types of content or activity is at stake.[1735] By now, it should be clear that a one-size-fits-all solution may not be attainable to properly address the wide variety of infringing or illegal content and activities. At the same time, there exists a set of procedural safeguards derived from the general principles of law and fundamental rights that should be applied uniformly, regardless of which type of illegality it refers to. For this reason, the legal framework providing safeguards for notice and action mechanism should make a distinction between generally applicable safeguards, and safeguards tailored to specific types of illegal content or activities.

2.2. MANIFEST ILLEGALITY

VALUES AND INTERESTS WORTHY OF SPECIAL PROTECTION – The legal framework governing notice and action mechanisms should specify whether certain types of values and interests are considered worthy of special protection (e.g. protection of minors or the prevention of serious harm). Such a special status may require the intermediary to take extra measures and react categorically. For example, the law could require the intermediary to remove certain content upon obtaining knowledge, but before obtaining a court or administrative order, particularly when the illegality is manifest. Manifest illegality occurs when the content is easily recognizable as such, without any additional legal or factual analysis, by a diligent operator. The CoE Recommendation describes this type of content as "illegal irrespective of context", for example content involving child sexual abuse

1732 European Commission, Tackling Illegal Content Online – Towards an enhanced responsibility of online platforms, *o.c.*, p. 5.
1733 *Ibid.*
1734 *Ibid.*, p. 6.
1735 See also *Ibid.*

material.[1736] The EC Communication gives an additional example of incitement to terrorism acts, where fast removal is particularly important.[1737] The list should be specific, for example as in Finland, where the requirement refers to a particular provision of the Criminal Code concerning depictions of child pornography, sexual violence and intercourse with animals. Following the LCEN example from France, failure to remove such content after a private notification by a third party would be the only situation when the intermediary might be held liable for not removing content without a court order. As a result, the intermediary would not be punished for failing to remove content which was not manifestly unlawful. Such a safeguard would prevent over-compliance and limit the effect of abusive notices.

3. TAILORED RESPONSE

OVERVIEW – Safeguards in the area of tailored response prescribe how notice and action mechanisms should be designed to minimize the interference with the right to freedom of expression.[1738] In order to comply with the principles of proportionality and legitimacy, the interference should be tailored to the aim pursued. The proposed safeguards include (1) the selection of proportionate response mechanisms; and (2) limiting intrusiveness of the applied mechanism. Safeguards in the area of tailored response are procedural in nature, because they focus on how notice and action mechanisms should be designed, rather than focusing on the legal framework which governs them.

3.1. LEAST RESTRICTIVE MEANS

A. *Proportionate response*

CHAIN OF RESPONSIBILITY – A first safeguard to avoid excessive interference is based on the concept of a "responsibility chain".[1739] Following this chain, certain actors would not be called into action prematurely, as their involvement would not be precise and accurate, i.e. limited to a particular infringing element on the whole website. In other words, an "escalation path" should be defined in

---

1736 Council of Europe, Recommendation CM/Rec(2018)2 of the Committee of Ministers to member states on the roles and responsibilities of internet intermediaries, *o.c.*,, p. 6. See also European Commission, Tackling Illegal Content Online – Towards an enhanced responsibility of online platforms *o.c.*, p. 14.

1737 European Commission, Tackling Illegal Content Online – Towards an enhanced responsibility of online platforms, *o.c.*, p. 14.

1738 See also Manila Principles on Intermediary Liability, Best Practices Guidelines for Limiting Intermediary Liability for Content to Promote Freedom of Expression and Innovation, *o.c.*, p. 4.

1739 See Part III Chapter 2.1.

order to minimize interference.[1740] To the extent that it is possible, practical and safe, complaining parties should attempt to resolve conflicts without involving intermediaries. If such a solution is not attainable (for example the content provider is not known, is not responding, or a request could hamper criminal investigations or put the complainant at risk), the next actor called into action should be the hosting provider at application level. This type of hosting provider has the technical ability to remove a specific infringing item, without affecting the rest of the (lawful) content.[1741] To be proportionate, any restriction of content should be limited to the specific content at issue.[1742] Only if the host at application level is not able or not willing to react, could other actors in the communication network be called into action, for example hosting providers at network level or ISPs who could filter or block access to the site in question (while also applying appropriate safeguards).

TEMPORARY MEASURES – Another safeguard that would help prevent excessive interference would be to introduce temporary measures. For example, if content is restricted because of its unlawfulness for a limited duration, the restriction must not last beyond this duration.[1743] Moreover, the procedure should allow for a preventive measure for certain (clearly specified) types of content. This safeguard follows the examples of legislation in Hungary and in the US, where certain removal or blocking measures can be taken pending resolution of a conflict.[1744] For example, content is removed or access is blocked while awaiting a response from the content provider or a decision of a court. Depending on the result, the action may be reversed or become permanent. Such "emergency" measures should be reserved for particular types of illegal content, which might not be manifest in nature but where a high level of harm, other than merely economic, could result from the content remaining online. Copyright infringing content should generally not be subject to emergency measures, with one possible exception. Temporary blocking or removal could be applied in situations where an infringement is time sensitive, for example illegal streaming of a live sports event.

SANCTIONS – States should ensure that any sanctions imposed on intermediaries for non-compliance with removal requests are proportionate.[1745] As pointed out by the CoE Recommendation, disproportionate sanctions

---

1740 See Internet and Jurisdiction Policy Network, Cross-border Content Restrictions, Input Document for Workstream II of the second Global Internet and Jurisdiction Conference, November 2017, p. 7.

1741 The hosting provider at application level is typically also the provider who has a direct relationship with the content provider. See Introduction.

1742 Manila Principles on Intermediary Liability, Best Practices Guidelines for Limiting Intermediary Liability for Content to Promote Freedom of Expression and Innovation, *o.c.*, p. 4.

1743 *Ibid.*

1744 See Part III Chapter 2.1.3.E.

1745 Council of Europe, Recommendation CM/Rec(2018)2 of the Committee of Ministers to member states on the roles and responsibilities of internet intermediaries, *o.c.*, p. 7. See

are likely to lead to over-compliance and have a chilling effect on the right to freedom of expression.[1746] The Manila Principles argue that any liability imposed on an intermediary must be proportionate and directly correlated to his wrongful behaviour in failing to comply with the content restriction order.[1747] This book argues that the only situation when an intermediary might be held liable for not removing content without a court order is when he disregards a private notification by a third party of manifestly unlawful content.

An additional element to consider is the gravity of the punishment for the content provider. This element will predominantly depend on the specific national legislations. However, it should be clear that a complete ban from the Internet, or a total disconnection, as found in the French and South Korean examples of graduated response, should generally be avoided as they are overly excessive and disproportionate.

B. *Limiting intrusiveness*

ADEQUATE SELECTION OF MECHANISMS – The law should ensure that the most appropriate notice and action mechanism is applied. States must evaluate possible unintended effects of any restrictions before and after applying them. Most importantly, they should seek to apply the least intrusive measure necessary to meet the policy objective.[1748] It has become clear by now, that a uniform response to unlawful online content does not guarantee a proportionate outcome. Different types of illegal online content and activities may require distinct responses.[1749] All types of responses, nevertheless, should have adequate safeguards – developed by the State – built into them.[1750]

As has been demonstrated, different notice and action mechanisms are preferred by different countries to address various types of illegalities online. It is possible to arrange commonly found mechanisms in the order of their intrusiveness. From the least intrusive, the mechanisms are: (1) full immunity; (2) notice and notice; (3) notice-wait-and take down (giving the content provider the possibility and time to file a counter-notification); (4) notice and judicial take down (where a court order is necessary to take down content); (5) notice and take down (when content is manifestly illegal); and (6) notice and stay down.

---

also United Nations, Report of the Special Rapporteur David Kaye on the promotion and protection of the right to freedom of opinion and expression, *o.c.*, p. 19.

1746 *Ibid.*

1747 Manila Principles on Intermediary Liability, Best Practices Guidelines for Limiting Intermediary Liability for Content to Promote Freedom of Expression and Innovation, *o.c.*, p. 2.

1748 Council of Europe, Recommendation CM/Rec(2018)2 of the Committee of Ministers to member states on the roles and responsibilities of internet intermediaries, *o.c.*, p. 6.

1749 See also European Commission, Tackling Illegal Content Online – Towards an enhanced responsibility of online platforms, *o.c.*, p. 5.

1750 See also *Ibid.*, p. 6.

Due to different levels of intrusiveness, the mechanisms should be applied adequately to the aim pursued and the potential risk to the protected rights. The two mechanisms at the opposite ends of the spectrum, i.e. full immunity and the notice and stay down, are not recommended here. The former, although it does not provide any interference with freedom expression, does not allow for any form of effective remedy in cases where certain rights of the complainants have in fact been violated. The latter, as has been argued over the course of the analysis, is considered disproportionate and at odds with the provisions of the E-Commerce Directive (no general obligation to monitor). The remaining four mechanisms should be applied in a way that would best address the infringement at stake. The choice requires a certain degree of calibration. For example, hate speech and incitement to violence may require a stronger response than merely offensive comments.[1751]

As proposed by Angelopoulos and Smet, the notice and action mechanisms should be applied in a way that allows the achievement of a compromise between rights at stake, a concept they call "fair-balance-as-compromise".[1752] These authors propose, convincingly, that the mechanisms should be applied as follows: (1) notice-and-notice for intellectual property rights' infringements; (2) notice-wait-and-takedown for defamation; and (3) notice-and takedown, combined with occasional notice-and-suspension, for hate speech.[1753] Additionally, they propose that notice-and-judicial-takedown should be available in all cases.[1754]

AUTOMATED MEASURES – The use of automatic detection and filtering technologies is becoming an increasingly popular tool in the fight against illegal content online. It is often used to ensure that previously removed content is not re-uploaded. The EC Recommendation supports the use of such technologies.[1755] Specifically, the Commission argues that it can be appropriate to take such measures '*where the illegal character of the content has already been established or where the type of content is such that contextualisation is not essential*'.[1756] Moreover, the Commission encourages industry to take up innovations which may contribute to increased efficiency and effectiveness of automatic detection

1751 C. Angelopoulos, S. Smet, "Notice-and-fair-balance: how to reach a compromise between fundamental rights in European intermediary liability", *o.c.*, p. 285.

1752 *Ibid.* The authors refer to their proposal as a move from a horizontal to a vertical approach by specifying which mechanisms are best to tackle different categories of wrongdoings. In this thesis, however, the approach is still considered horizontal, as all the mechanisms fall within the definition of notice and action mechanisms.

1753 *Ibid.*, p. 293.

1754 *Ibid.*, p. 293.

1755 See European Commission, Recommendation on Measures to Effectively Tackle Illegal Content Online, *o.c.*, p. 6.

1756 European Commission, Recommendation on Measures to Effectively Tackle Illegal Content Online, *o.c.*, p. 6.

procedures.[1757] The Commission supports further research and innovative approaches aimed at improving the accuracy of technical means to identify illegal content.[1758] As with the use of proactive measures, the Commission does not consider that using automatic detection tools would automatically lead to a loss of immunity by making hosts active (see section on active hosts and general monitoring).[1759] When promoting the use of automated means, however, States should consider that existing automated measures have limited capacity to assess context.[1760] Automated measures can therefore easily result in preventing the legitimate use of identical or similar content in other contexts. To prevent this effect, the Commission suggests using automatic tools to narrow down the set of contentious content for vetting by human experts. These human experts would then assess the nature of the selected content. The Commission observes that the "human-in-the-loop" principle is an important element of automated measures to determine the illegality of content, especially in areas where errors are common or where contextualisation is necessary.[1761] It is difficult to agree with the Commission that intermediaries using such tools could continue to claim that they remain "passive". Especially participation of humans assessing the content would most likely lead to obtaining constructive knowledge of illegality. The only reasonable way the Commission's proposal could work, would be by abolishing the distinction between active and passive hosting providers. Clearly including active hosting providers in the scope of the exemption (on the condition that they did not create the content and have no knowledge about its illegal or infringing character) appears to be the only way to encourage intermediaries to take up voluntary measures without risking the loss of immunity.

4. PROCEDURAL FAIRNESS

OVERVIEW – Safeguards in the area of procedural fairness prescribe how notice and action procedures should be administered, and in particular, how decisions are taken. They promote legal certainty, legitimacy and proportionality. The proposed safeguards include (1) ensuring due process; and (2) ensuring timely and reasoned decisions. Safeguards in the area of procedural fairness are,

---

1757 European Commission, Tackling Illegal Content Online – Towards an enhanced responsibility of online platforms, *o.c.*, p. 13.

1758 *Ibid.*

1759 See *Ibid.*, p. 12. European Commission, Recommendation on Measures to Effectively Tackle Illegal Content Online, *o.c.*, p. 6.

1760 Council of Europe, Recommendation CM/Rec(2018)2 of the Committee of Ministers to Member States on the roles and responsibilities of internet intermediaries, *o.c.*, p. 7.

1761 See European Commission, Tackling Illegal Content Online – Towards an enhanced responsibility of online platforms, *o.c.*, p. 12.

perhaps unsurprisingly, procedural in nature. Their existence can influence the outcome of the decision-making process by bringing in elements of due process and procedural justice. The proposed safeguards rely strongly on the (explicit and implicit) rights contained in the right to a fair trial, such as the right to a fair public hearing and a decision in a reasonable time, by an independent and impartial tribunal established by law, as well as the right to adversarial proceedings, to equality of arms and to a reasoned judgement.[1762]

4.1. DUE PROCESS

NOTIFICATION TO THE CONTENT PROVIDER – The first safeguard proposed here consists of a mandatory notification to the content provider, in which he is informed that a complaint has been filed against "his" content. The notification should inform the content provider what is the nature of the objection about the content. A similar safeguard can be found in the Manila Principles, which provide that intermediaries may be required by law to respond to content restriction requests by either forwarding lawful and compliant requests to the content provider, or by notifying the complainant of the reason it is not possible to do so.[1763] The EC Recommendation suggests that content providers should, as a matter of principle, be informed of the decision to remove or disable access to their content.[1764] Such notifications, the Commission argues, would help to ensure transparency and fairness and avoid the unintended removal of content which is not illegal content.[1765] Notification to the content provider is the key component of the notice and notice mechanism, however, it may be present also in the other notice and action mechanisms (e.g. notice-wait-and takedown).

Ideally, notification should be sent before any decision about the content is taken, unlike the current approach in many jurisdictions (e.g., Finland, Hungary and the US), where notification takes place after the action against the content is taken. The proposed procedure should allow, however, for exceptions to the general rule, for example where the content at stake is manifestly illegal, or when the infringement is particularly time sensitive.[1766]

1762 These rights instruct States how to design their judiciary systems and therefore cannot be automatically transposed to systems of privatised enforcement. However, notice and action procedures established by EU legislature – as is advocated in this thesis, should take these requirements into the utmost account in the design process. See Part II Chapter 3.

1763 Manila Principles on Intermediary Liability, Best Practices Guidelines for Limiting Intermediary Liability for Content to Promote Freedom of Expression and Innovation, *o.c.*, p. 3.

1764 See also European Commission, Recommendation on Measures to Effectively Tackle Illegal Content Online, *o.c.*, p. 5 and p. 11.

1765 See also *Ibid.*, p. 5.

1766 See Part III Chapter 3.3.1 – Temporary measures

The Commission advises against providing such notifications and allowing to contest the decision where the content in question is manifestly illegal and relates to serious criminal offences involving a threat to the life or safety of persons.[1767] This book argues, however, that even in cases of particularly grave and manifest illegalities, or especially in those cases, the content provider should be informed about the accusations and given the possibility to defend himself. In Finland, for example, the intermediary must notify the content provider even in cases where the content consists of hate speech, or pictures with child pornography, sexual violence or intercourse with an animal. The notification must state the reason for removal (or blocking) and provide an explanation of the rights of the content provider as well as any possibility to appeal the decision or to bring the matter for a court hearing.[1768] The notification to the content provider should be delivered as early as possible in the procedure. Exceptions to this safeguard should be foreseen, however, for situations when sending the notification would hamper ongoing law enforcement activities, in particular the prevention, investigation, detection and prosecution of criminal offences.[1769] Moreover, intermediaries should not limit themselves to the removal of criminal content (e.g. child sexual abuse). They should, additionally, report to law enforcement authorities whenever they are made aware of or encounter evidence of criminal or other offences to enable the relevant authorities to investigate and prosecute individuals generating such content.[1770] The EC Recommendation mentions a similar possibility of establishing reporting obligations for intermediaries, according to Article 15.2 of the E-Commerce Directive, to effectively tackle certain particularly serious criminal offences.[1771] The Commission, however, is more cautious in its approach, merely suggesting that Member States should be encouraged to make use of this possibility. In any case, however, such notifications should be taken up in accordance with applicable data protection requirements.

DATA PROTECTION – Intermediaries should not be required to ensure they have the capacity to identify users purely for the purpose of notification.[1772] In order to protect the personal data of the involved parties, the notification could

1767 European Commission, Recommendation on Measures to Effectively Tackle Illegal Content Online, *o.c.*, p. 5 and p. 11.

1768 See also Manila Principles on Intermediary Liability, Best Practices Guidelines for Limiting Intermediary Liability for Content to Promote Freedom of Expression and Innovation, *o.c.*, p. 3.

1769 Council of Europe, Recommendation CM/Rec(2018)2 of the Committee of Ministers to member states on the roles and responsibilities of internet intermediaries, *o.c.*, p. 7. European Commission, Recommendation on Measures to Effectively Tackle Illegal Content Online, *o.c.*, p. 5.

1770 European Commission, Tackling Illegal Content Online – Towards an enhanced responsibility of online platforms, *o.c.*, p. 15.

1771 European Commission, Recommendation on Measures to Effectively Tackle Illegal Content Online, *o.c.*, p. 7.

1772 Manila Principles on Intermediary Liability, Best Practices Guidelines for Limiting Intermediary Liability for Content to Promote Freedom of Expression and Innovation, *o.c.*, p. 3.

be forwarded to the content provider by the intermediary without revealing the contact information of either party. Intermediaries should not be compelled by law to disclose personal data about a user without an order by a judicial authority.[1773]

COUNTER-NOTIFICATION – The notice and action procedure should allow the content provider to file a counter-notification.[1774] The ability to file a counter-notification would allow content providers to file an objection to the complaints made against their content, and therefore, operationalize the rights to a fair hearing, to adversarial proceedings and to equality of arms. Moreover, it would provide an opportunity to clarify in case the content had not been provided by him – which may be particularly relevant in cases of criminal charges. Only when the content provider is given an opportunity to express his views and to present his defence, can the decision-making process be considered fair.

Taking removal decisions without hearing from the content provider, and possibly also without his knowledge, should only be done in exceptional circumstances. For example, the possibility of counter-notification could be foregone when it might harm ongoing law enforcement activities (e.g. in the case of child sexual abuse material).[1775] These exceptions, however, must be crafted carefully and defined explicitly in the legal framework. The fact that the content or activity in question constitutes serious illegality should not be the sole reason to deny content providers the possibility to defend themselves by filing a counter-notification. To the contrary, one could argue that especially when notification concerns manifest or grave illegality that could lead to criminal charges, an easily available defence mechanism should be provided. Counter-notification should also not be excluded merely for the purpose of simplifying and speeding up the procedure.

Ideally, a possibility to file a counter-notification should be available before any potential actions against the content are decided. Only then, can the information in the counter-notifications be taken into account in the decision-making process prior to interference and only then, can the safeguard actually become a meaningful manifestation of due process, procedural justice and the presumption of innocence until proven guilty.

Counter-notifications exist as part of the DMCA procedure in the US. The manner in which this version of the safeguard currently functions provides important insights on how the safeguard should be implemented. Several research studies have shown that the use of counter-notifications is marginal. Although great in theory, it proves merely symbolic in practice. Because of

---

1773 *Ibid.*

1774 See also European Commission, Recommendation on Measures to Effectively Tackle Illegal Content Online, *o.c.*, p. 11.

1775 European Commission, Tackling Illegal Content Online – Towards an enhanced responsibility of online platforms, *o.c.*, p. 17.

the accompanying conditions, such as a statement about accuracy of the information and the notifying party's good faith and a possible punishment for misrepresentations of facts, content providers are discouraged from exercising their rights. This refers especially to private users who do not have a legal counsel and do not want to risk involvement in lengthy and expensive legal proceedings. The DMCA approach therefore clearly has a chilling effect on the use of counter-notification and should therefore not be followed. In order to achieve a more satisfactory result, counter-notification should not create undue obstacles to exercise one's rights or function as a mere smoke-screen to cover the absence of procedural justice and due process.

MISREPRESENTATIONS – Punishment for misrepresentation is considered a protective safeguard against abusive notifications and counter-notifications. It is recommended, for example, in the Manila Principles, which state that abusive or bad faith content restriction requests should be penalized.[1776] To fulfil this purpose, however, penalties must be designed carefully to avoid intimidating individuals and creating a chilling effect on their right to effective remedy.

It must be highlighted that punishment for misrepresentation should apply equally to complaining parties and those who wish to file a counter-notification. A situation when one is seemingly easier than the other creates an asymmetry of power. It cannot be, therefore, that both parties have to submit a statement referring to the accuracy of the submission, but regarding different elements. This is a problem in the context of the DMCA, where the penalty of perjury refers to different elements of the submissions, which creates the impression that the risk involved with filing a counter-notification is greater than the risk of filing an initial notification. If that is the case, the counter-notification does not balance out the positions of the parties and does not prevent the abusive notifications.[1777]

Possibly, a more light-handed approach could be considered, modelled after the Finnish legislation. Under Finnish law, a person who provides false information in the notification or counter-notification shall be liable to compensate for the damage caused. The punishment may be forgone or adjusted, however, if the notifying party had reasonable grounds to assume that the information was correct or if the false information was only of minor significance, when taking into account the entire content of the submission. Such an approach, although less strict, may actually prove more fair to those who wish to object to their content being taken down.

1776 Manila Principles on Intermediary Liability, Best Practices Guidelines for Limiting Intermediary Liability for Content to Promote Freedom of Expression and Innovation, *o.c.*, p. 3.

1777 See Part III Chapter 2.1.3.D.

4.2. REQUIREMENTS FOR DECISION-MAKING PROCESSES

SPECIFIED TIME-FRAMES – The notice and action procedure should specify time-frames for the different steps to be taken by the involved parties. Anyone who wishes to initiate the procedure, or seek to protest an unjust removal, should be able to find out what steps he must take, and when. The intermediary should also have a clearly defined procedure and time-frame to follow. Information should be provided about: (1) the time to forward the notification to the content provider; (2) the time for the content provider to respond with a counter-notification; (3) the time to make a decision about removing content or maintaining it online; (4) the time to inform the involved parties about the decision taken; and (5) the time to initiate a review of the decision by the courts. The timeframes, however, cannot be too short, as this is likely to incentivize take downs of legal content.[1778] This safeguard specifying time-frames helps to ensure that a decision will be made within a reasonable time. It also contributes to the legal certainty and legitimacy of the mechanism. It stands, however, in stark contradiction to the recent demands of the European Commission, which argued that take downs by tech firms should not take longer than 120 minutes.[1779] In the EC Recommendation on Measures to Effectively Tackle Illegal Content Online, the Commission shortens the period even further, demanding take downs for terrorist content within one hour, as a general rule.[1780]

REASONED DECISION – The decision of the intermediary to remove content or to keep it online should be communicated to both parties involved in the procedure. The decision should provide reasons explaining why the intermediary gave effect to the notification or not.[1781] It should also contain an explanation of the rights of the content provider, and any possibility to appeal the decision.[1782] Similarly, when a counter-notice is rejected, the reasons should be specified in a reply to the notice giver.[1783]

Requiring a reasoned decision contributes to the legal certainty and legitimacy of notice and action mechanisms as it allows the parties to understand the grounds motivating the intermediary's decision. The explanation provided

---

1778 Council of Europe, Recommendation CM/Rec(2018)2 of the Committee of Ministers to member states on the roles and responsibilities of internet intermediaries, *o.c.*, p. 7.

1779 N. Nielsen, Commission: 120 minutes to remove illegal online content, 9 January 2018, https://euobserver.com/justice/140482.

1780 European Commission, Recommendation on measures to effectively tackle illegal content online, *o.c.*

1781 See also Manila Principles on Intermediary Liability, Best Practices Guidelines for Limiting Intermediary Liability for Content to Promote Freedom of Expression and Innovation, *o.c.*, p. 3.

1782 See also *Ibid.*

1783 European Commission, Tackling Illegal Content Online – Towards an enhanced responsibility of online platforms, *o.c.*, p. 17.

can help to draft an appeal, either to the intermediary or to a court, in cases where either party does not agree with the decision. Here again the example of the Finnish legislation could be given, which foresees a reasoned decision that should be delivered to the parties even in cases where the removal involved a particularly serious offence or manifest illegality.

5. EFFECTIVE REMEDY

OVERVIEW – Safeguards in the area of effective remedy aim to ensure that appropriate relief is available in case of an undue interference with the right to freedom of expression. The safeguards come into play after the interference with rights has taken place. The proposed safeguards include: (1) a possibility to appeal a decision about removal (or non-removal) of content; and (2) a possibility of judicial redress, regardless of which response mechanism is applied. Safeguards for effective remedy are procedural in nature.

5.1. THE POSSIBILITY TO APPEAL

APPEAL TO THE INTERMEDIARY – The procedure that requires intermediaries to make decisions about content should include a step allowing for correction of any initial decision. It is clear that decisions that involve balancing between the right to the freedom of expression and other fundamental rights (e.g. the right to privacy) may be difficult. Mistakes resulting from inaccurate assessments may happen but in such cases, a path for a relief should be available. Procedures for notice and action should provide users with the right to appeal decisions honouring removal requests, but also decisions denying such requests. In case an appeal against the removal of content is successful, intermediaries should reinstate the content.[1784] This is usually the main objective of those who protest against content removal. Other possible forms of remedies include apology, rectification and damages.[1785]

An appeal mechanism provided by intermediaries should comply with certain procedural safeguards, such as those listed under "procedural fairness". Moreover, the appeal mechanism should be accessible, equitable, rights-compatible, affordable and transparent.[1786] The appeal mechanism does not amount to a judicial remedy. As indicated before, however, this is not considered problematic, as long

[1784] Manila Principles on Intermediary Liability, Best Practices Guidelines for Limiting Intermediary Liability for Content to Promote Freedom of Expression and Innovation, *o.c.*, p. 4.

[1785] Council of Europe, Recommendation CM/Rec(2018)2 of the Committee of Ministers to member states on the roles and responsibilities of internet intermediaries, *o.c.*, p. 9.

[1786] *Ibid.*, p. 13.

as a second step of judicial redress is available.[1787] An effective remedy, after all, does not have to consist of a single type of remedy, but may be a combination of a collection of remedies. The CoE Recommendation lists remedies such as inquiry, explanation, reply, correction, apology, reinstatement, deletion, reconnection and compensation.[1788] The crucial element of the safeguard is that the remedy is effective. In that sense, an appeal to the intermediary, who can effectively stop the interference (by removing content or by reinstating it), provides an adequate solution.

The possibility to appeal a decision of an intermediary is offered in several jurisdictions at the moment, for example in Finland, Hungary, and the US. Usually, it takes the form of a counter-notification that can be filed by the content-provider. The safeguard, therefore, advances both the criteria of effective remedy and procedural fairness. For this reason, observations made about the implementation of counter-notification safeguards apply here as well.[1789] As has been pointed out above, appeal through a counter-notification should not favour one side of the conflict, for example by installing different conditions or different punishments for the same actions. Moreover, a possibility to appeal should be available not only to anyone whose content was unjustifiably removed but also to anyone whose initial notification was ignored or refused. In both cases, the parties of the conflict should be able to request a reassessment of the content in question. It would go against the principles of procedural fairness if one side of the conflict was offered an appeal mechanism but the other was not. This is, unfortunately, often the case at the moment.

DEFINED APPEAL PROCEDURE – Information about the possibility to appeal a decision should be provided in the notification to the content provider informing him about the existence of a complaint.[1790] Similar to the procedure for removal, the counter-notification procedure should be clearly defined. This means describing the order of events, and steps that can be taken by the parties involved. The procedure should specify the formal requirements for a valid counter-notice, i.e. what information must be included by the content provider to present his arguments and convince the intermediary not to take down the content, or to revise the decision if it has been taken down already. Moreover, it should clearly inform the parties about the timeframes that should be followed.

5.2. JUDICIAL REDRESS

EFFECTIVE JUDICIAL REVIEW – Judicial redress is an integral part of the rule of law. In the context of online content regulation, judicial redress should always

1787 See more in Part III Chapter 2.

1788 Council of Europe, Recommendation CM/Rec(2018)2 of the Committee of Ministers to member states on the roles and responsibilities of internet intermediaries, *o.c.*, p. 13.

1789 See Part III Chapter 3.4.1.

1790 See section 4.1 on the notification to the content provider.

be available as a second step in providing an effective remedy to an interference with one's rights. As stated by the CoE Recommendation, judicial review must remain available, when dispute settlement mechanisms prove insufficient or where the affected parties opt for judicial redress.[1791] This safeguard should be provided as a final element of any procedure, regardless of which notice and action mechanism is employed. In theory, judicial redress is always an option; however, only some of the analysed national procedures actually mention this possibility. From the perspective of legal certainty, legitimacy and proportionality, the safeguard of judicial redress should be clearly stated in the legal framework governing notice and action procedures.

INJUNCTIVE RELIEF – Injunctive relief should be available irrespective of the intermediary's liability (e.g. for not removing the infringing content). A provision to this effect is already included in the E-Commerce Directive.[1792] The provision, however, refers only to the situation when content is (or is not) removed on the request of the rights holder. There is no similar provision that would indicate a possibility of an injunctive relief in case of wrongful content removal. Nevertheless, injunctive relief should always be possible in case of wrongful removal, even if there is no specific procedure introduced at the national level. This stems from the principle that where there is a right, there must be a remedy to ensure its enforcement. By explicitly including this safeguard in the legal framework governing notice and action procedures, it would be clear that content providers whose content has been removed can seek judicial redress to reinstate their content.

1791 Council of Europe, Recommendation CM/Rec(2018)2 of the Committee of Ministers to member states on the roles and responsibilities of internet intermediaries, *o.c.*, p. 9. See also European Commission, Recommendation on Measures to Effectively Tackle Illegal Content Online, *o.c.*, p. 5.

1792 Art. 14.3 of the E-Commerce Directive.

CONCLUSION AND OUTLOOK

SUMMARY OF THE RESEARCH AND CONCLUSIONS

MAIN RESEARCH QUESTION – The book started from the observation that the liability regime of Article 14 of E-Commerce Directive incentivizes internet intermediaries to take down content from their platforms without proper balancing of rights at stake. At the same time, Internet intermediaries are increasingly enlisted to assist in the realization of public policy objectives. The research hypothesis of this book was that, when States assign Internet intermediaries with such a role, they have a positive obligation to ensure that the necessary safeguards are in place. Specifically, States must provide for adequate procedural safeguards for the effective exercise of the human rights enshrined in the European Convention of Human Rights, and the Charter of Fundamental Rights of the European Union and particularly freedom of expression. These observations led to the following main research question:

> Which safeguards should be implemented to ensure compliance of the notice and action mechanism implied in Article 14 E-Commerce Directive with the right to freedom of expression?

In developing an answer to this question, the following research questions guided the research:

- Is the notice and action mechanism under EU law compatible with the right to freedom of expression, as recognized by Article 10 ECHR, and Article 11 EU Charter?
- Is there a positive obligation derived from the relevant human rights law instruments (in particular Article 10 ECHR, and Article 11 EU Charter) for States to establish a formal legal framework for notice and action procedures?
- If yes, what are the minimum safeguards (substantive and procedural) necessary to ensure effective protection of human rights in the context of notice and action procedures?

ONLINE GATEKEEPING – Part I provided contextual background and the normative framework. Chapter 1 focused on the concept of gatekeeping. According to K. Lewin, gatekeepers are those who decide what to reject or allow through a gate, effectively controlling movement within the channel.[1793] The concept was first introduced in 1947 to describe the role of women who decide what foods to place on the dinner table. The concept, however, is broader and became particularly useful to depict the traveling of a news item through communication channels. Gatekeeping, as a result, has become a metaphor for the way the traditional media make decisions about what information to run or discard – the role played by editors and publishers. With the arrival of new media, in particular the Internet, the locus of gatekeeping has shifted. The Internet was predicted to give individuals the ability to communicate directly with each other, resulting in "disintermediation" of communication. Eliminating the "middle man" was foreseen to become the great "equalizer", giving everyone the same opportunity to shape public discourse. This has not turned out to be the case. Instead, one set of intermediaries (e.g., newspaper publishers and broadcast stations) has been exchanged for another set of intermediaries (e.g., Internet service providers, content hosts, and search providers). The concept of gatekeeping, therefore, remains relevant.

The concept of gatekeeping has been applied by R.H. Kraakman to characterize the liability that is imposed on private parties who have the ability to prevent wrongdoing by withholding cooperation from wrongdoers.[1794] Kraakman's work on gatekeeping liability constituted the starting point for the research presented in this book. The concept of gatekeeping liability can be applied to Internet intermediaries, who have the ability to disrupt misconduct of third parties on the intermediaries' platforms.

INTERMEDIARY LIABILITY REGIME – Internet intermediaries, typically, are private entities that provide commercial and technical services that enable the Internet to function. They intermediate the relationship between two or more parties by providing the infrastructure and the software through which information is exchanged. Internet Intermediaries are, therefore, the actual enablers of Internet communications. Because of their enabling role and technical capabilities, they hold a powerful position. They can eliminate access to service, objectionable material and, quite often, identify wrongdoers. They are capable of affecting, directly and indirectly, the behaviour of their users and for this reason, they are often seen as natural points of control for online content. With such power at their hands, they are certainly eligible to fulfil the role of gatekeepers.

States are increasingly delegating traditional regulatory and police functions to Internet intermediaries as a means of fulfilling public policy objectives. The delegation is achieved by providing different types of incentives. The first type of incentive is a conditional liability exemption. Intermediaries are in principle not

1793 See K. Lewin, "Frontiers in group dynamics. II. Channels of group life; social planning and action research". *Human Relations*, Vol. 1, No 2, 1947, pp. 143–153.

1794 See H.R. Kraakman, "Gatekeepers: The Anatomy of a Third-Party Enforcement Strategy", *Journal of Law, Economics, and Organization*, Vol. 2, No. 1, 1986, pp. 53–105.

liable for third party content, but only under specifically designed conditions. The first condition is that the intermediary does not modify the content in question and is not aware of its illegal character. Intermediaries receiving notification that certain content is illegal, are therefore incentivized to react in order to avoid potential liability. A mechanism providing rights holders with the ability to directly call upon an intermediary to remedy an alleged wrongdoing, is typically called notice and take down. This book, however, takes a broader perspective and refers to the mechanism as notice and action, because of a variety of actions that are possible in response to the notification.

Notice and action mechanisms place intermediaries in a position to decide which content can remain online and which content should be removed. Notice and action has gradually made its way into regulatory instruments at both the national and regional level. Part I provided details of the EU E-Commerce Directive 2000/31 as well as the US DMCA and Section 230 CDA.

REVIEW – Ten years after the adoption of the E-Commerce Directive, the European Commission initiated a periodic review process. Part of the process consisted of public consultations and policy documents to address the problem of illegal content online. These initiatives led to a thorough analysis of the problems surrounding notice and action. The analysis showed that there are fundamental problems in three areas: quality of law (uncertainty and fragmentation), the decision-making process (lack of due process), and the exercise of the right to effective remedy. Part I described the review process of the Directive (Chapter 5) and analysed the relevant issues (Chapters 6). Part I also revealed that there is a significant degree of policy incoherence, both vertical and horizontal, within the EU intermediary liability regime. All of these factors can have a negative impact on the freedom of expression of content providers and content receivers. The categories of issues identified were used in Part III to develop assessment criteria necessary to analyse safeguards in the existing national regulations that provide notice and action mechanisms.

INDIRECT INTERFERENCE – Notice and action mechanisms require intermediaries to decide on issues that do not fall within their competence. Intermediaries are essentially called upon to decide about human rights. Decisions by intermediaries following a complaint have a direct effect on the right to freedom of expression and the right to effective remedy. Notice and action mechanisms lead either to removal of online content (or alternatively a reduction of its visibility), or allows the content to remain online, in which case the rights holder's request is denied.

Strictly speaking, the intermediary liability regime of the E-Commerce Directive does not require intermediaries to take action, but offers them immunity if they play along. Such indirect responsibilization of intermediaries allows States to maintain a certain degree of control over online content without attracting too much attention and having to confront claims of States' interference. Delegation of enforcement measures to private entities, however, can give rise to various legal issues that affect the fundamental rights of Internet users. Notice and action mechanisms can provide a quick, effective and accessible redress mechanism for online infringements. They should come equipped, however, with certain safeguards to protect freedom of expression. Currently, such safeguards are missing in the EU. The legislature therefore is indirectly contributing to the interference by private individuals – a type of "State interference by proxy".

FREEDOM OF EXPRESSION IN ONLINE COMMUNICATION – Part II focused on the compatibility of the intermediary liability regime with the relevant human rights instruments (in particular the ECHR and the EU Charter). Specifically, Part II analysed the right to freedom of expression in light of the posed research questions to discover (1) whether the notice and action mechanisms resulting from the E-Commerce Directive are compliant with Article 10 ECHR and Article 11 EU Charter, and (2) whether there exists a positive obligation for States to introduce procedural safeguards for freedom of expression in the context of notice and action.

NEGATIVE AND POSITIVE OBLIGATIONS – Freedom of expression is not an absolute right, neither under the Convention, nor under the Charter. Interference may be permitted, provided it satisfies the conditions specified by each instrument. In response to the first research question, this book argues that the notice and action mechanisms resulting from the E-Commerce Directive are not, *per se*, incompatible with Article 10 ECHR and Article 11 EU Charter. The conditions put forward by both the Convention and the Charter can be linked to three fundamental rights principles, which became the guiding principles of this book, namely the principle of a) legal certainty, b) legitimacy, and c) proportionality.

According to the Convention and the Charter, States should respect the right to freedom of expression (negative obligation). The States, however, should also protect freedom of expression against interference by private actors, even more so if such interference is encouraged by the States (positive obligation). The doctrine of positive obligations does not enjoy the same status under the Convention and the Charter. States signatory to the Convention clearly have a positive obligation to ensure effective enjoyment of the Convention rights. Under the Charter, nevertheless, an obligation exists to ensure an effective protection of the Charter rights.

Therefore, in response to the second research question, this book argues that the theories of positive obligations and effective protection may require the States to take measures to protect the right to freedom of expression from interference by private actors. This book argues, moreover, that States can satisfy the requirement to ensure effective protection by implementing substantive and procedural safeguards into the legal framework that governs notice and action mechanisms. The EU legal framework currently lacks such procedural safeguards. Part II argues that the EU currently does not fulfil its positive obligation to protect the right to freedom of expression from interference by private entities in the context of the notice and action.

POSITIVE ASSESSMENT FRAMEWORK – The aim of this book was to propose safeguards for notice and action procedures that promote compliance with the right to freedom of expression. In order to determine which safeguards might be appropriate, a set of criteria was required. Part II provided an inventory of assessment criteria that should be taken into account when designing notice and action mechanisms to protect the right to freedom of expression. The assessment criteria were the following:

1. Quality of law
2. Protection of democratic society
3. Tailored response
4. Procedural fairness
5. Effective remedy

The assessment criteria have been selected in light of the problems surrounding notice and action identified in Part I. The criteria were developed on the basis of the case-law of the ECtHR and CJEU. Guidance was also obtained by reviewing the procedural provisions of these human rights instruments, specifically Articles 6 (right to fair trail) and 13 (right to effective remedy) of the ECHR, as well as Article 47 (right to an effective remedy and to a fair trial) of the CFEU. The procedural provisions of both instruments are directed to the States, instructing them how to design their judicial system. Full compliance with the procedural provisions, therefore, cannot be expected in the context of notice and action, where decisions about fundamental rights are delegated to private entities. Nevertheless, they provided a useful source of inspiration when developing safeguards that should be introduced by the States. The assessment criteria were applied as a positive assessment framework, against which existing response mechanisms to infringing online content – currently used around the world – were measured (Part III). The aim of the assessment was to identify and examine best practices implemented in different jurisdictions when regulating liability of Internet intermediaries. Furthermore, the aim was to inform a selection of safeguards that are best suited to ensure that content removal is undertaken with adequate consideration for the right to freedom of expression.

EVALUATION OF NOTICE AND ACTION MECHANISMS – The assessment conducted in Part III of the book was qualitative rather than quantitative in nature. It was not the aim, therefore, to select a mechanism that scores the highest in relation to the criteria, or to choose the "best" national notice and action mechanism. Instead, the aim was to learn from the available examples how the criteria should (or should not) be addressed, and what are best practices to advance legal certainty, legitimacy, and proportionality. The ultimate goal of this exercise was to examine best practices that are most suitable to their function; that is, to ensure that content removal is undertaken with adequate consideration for the right to freedom of expression.

The analysed mechanisms are among the most commonly encountered notice and action mechanisms around the world, although they might appear in different versions or in combination with one another. The following mechanisms were analysed:

- Notice and take down
- Notice and stay down
- Notice and notice (including graduated response)
- Full immunity

For each mechanism, one or more examples of national implementations were provided as an illustration (ordered alphabetically). The selected examples are considered to be the most informative, or the most innovative from the perspective of the research question. Since the research question focuses on the State's (indirect) role in online content regulation, the primary factor in the selection was the existence of a formal legal framework governing notice and action. It should be noted, however, that this requirement was not followed strictly – some mechanisms operate solely on the basis of case-law, rather than statutory procedures. Another factor that played a role in the selection was the diversity of legal traditions. The examples were not limited to the EU countries but also included countries from Asia, North America and South America.

For each national example, a concise legislative background, or a focused country profile, was provided to set a context for the analysis. First, the legislation introducing the notice and action mechanism was presented, specifying for which types of content it is used. The details of the notice and action procedure are provided in the Annex to this book. For each country, the most relevant case-law was cited (where available – for some countries there is no case law on the topic). Next, an assessment was conducted according to the criteria developed in Part II. Finally, for each mechanism a number of lessons learned were provided.

RECOMMENDED MINIMUM SAFEGUARDS – Part III synthesized the results of the research and proposed an answer to the main research question. The answer was provided by analysing and recommending a selection of safeguards to achieve compliance of the EU intermediary liability regime with the fundamental rights framework and specifically the right to freedom of expression. The recommendations focused on three guiding principles: legal certainty, legitimacy and proportionality of the regime. The proposed safeguards were grouped according to the assessment criteria to indicate the issues they could address. In some cases, safeguards may take a different form depending on the circumstances. The recommendation of the safeguards, for this reason, also provided an analysis of possible advantages and disadvantages, depending on the form that they might take. Moreover, the recommendations referred to other instruments or initiatives, proposing guidelines or recommendations for the intermediary liability regimes, for example the Manila Principles on Intermediary Liability, the EC Communication on Tackling Illegal Content Online, the EC Recommendation on Measures to Effectively Tackle Illegal Content Online and the CoE Recommendation on the Roles and Responsibilities of Internet Intermediaries.

QUALITY OF THE LAW – Safeguards in the area of quality of law aim to ensure that the legal framework governing notice and action mechanisms is accessible, foreseeable and predictable and promote legal certainty and legitimacy. The proposed safeguards include (1) enacting a formal legal framework; (2) a clear delineation of scope; (3) a clear definition of the procedure; and (4) enhancing transparency.

Safeguards to protect freedom of expression in the context of notice and action should be provided in a formal legal instrument. Procedures for mechanisms permitting interference with expression and accompanying protective safeguards should be established through a democratic process, which is transparent and subject to public debate. Moreover, a set of minimum safeguards should be provided at the EU level, preferably through a regulation. Only then, could safeguards be applied uniformly across the EU. Further recommendations addressed the need to provide a defined scope of the law, for example, to clarify the situation of active hosts and prevent indirect imposition of general monitoring obligations. The book also advises against introducing the Good Samaritan protection, both in the version existing in the US, and in the version proposed by the European Commission in the Communication on Tackling Illegal Content. The former provides no effective remedy to complainants whose rights were infringed while at the same time encourages excessive take-downs on the intermediary's own initiative. The latter ensures protection to intermediaries only if they act according to the expectations of the policy makers and take down content. Other safeguards recommended in this section advocated for the introduction of a defined procedure with specifications for a valid notice and for transparency measures, such as obligatory transparency reports (for both intermediaries and States). The proposed safeguards would help to diminish policy incoherence, both at vertical and horizontal level, that troubles the EU intermediary liability regime.

PROTECTION OF DEMOCRATIC SOCIETY – Safeguards in the area of protection of democratic society specify requirements for implementing notice and action procedures in the legal regime. The proposed safeguards include (1) definition of the types of content or activities concerned; (2) definition of types of illegal content and activities for which stricter conditions for immunity may apply.

The aforementioned safeguards should apply horizontally. If the rules are to provide legal certainty, they should clarify the treatment of all kinds of infringing and illegal content, not only some of them. At the same time, not all the safeguards will be appropriate for all types of illegal content or activities. For this reason, the legal framework governing the notice and action mechanism should make a distinction between generally applicable safeguards, and safeguards tailored to specific types of illegal content or activities. Moreover, the law should specify if it distinguishes any types of values and interests that are considered worthy of special protection (e.g. protection of minors or prevention of serious harm). Such a special status may require the intermediary to remove certain content upon obtaining knowledge of its illegal character, provided the illegality is manifest. Failure to remove such content after a private notification by a third party would be the only situation when the intermediary might be held liable for not removing content without a court or administrative order. As a result, the intermediary would not be punished for failing to remove content which was not obviously unlawful. Such a safeguard would prevent over-compliance and limit the effect of abusive notices.

TAILORED RESPONSE – Ideally, measures interfering with online expression should be the least intrusive and impose a minimum impairment of the rights at stake. Only mechanisms that are proportionate (i.e. not excessive) will prevent a potential chilling effect and detriment of the right to freedom of expression, and will ensure acceptance of the measures. The proposed safeguards include (1) the selection of proportionate response mechanisms; and (2) limiting intrusiveness of the applied mechanism. To be proportionate, the law should choose the most appropriate notice and action mechanism to address the illegal content or activity in question. Moreover, any restriction of content should be limited to the specific content at issue. The recommended safeguards advocate for the introduction of a "chain of responsibility" to prevent actors being called into action prematurely. Another safeguard that would help prevent excessive interference would be the introduction of temporary measures.

PROCEDURAL FAIRNESS – Safeguards in the area of procedural fairness focus mainly on the way the notice and action procedures are handled, and in particular, how decisions are taken. The proposed safeguards include (1) ensuring due process; and (2) ensuring timely and reasoned decisions. The safeguards rely heavily on the (explicit and implicit) rights contained in the right to a fair trial, such as the right to fair public hearing and a decision in a reasonable time by an independent and impartial tribunal established by law, as well as the rights to adversarial proceedings, to equality of arms and to a reasoned judgement. States should take these rights into the utmost account when designing notice and action procedures. Safeguards in the area of procedural fairness can also help to balance the distribution of power among parties involved in the procedure. Specific safeguards include notification to the content provider and counter-notification. The latter, however, should not be shaped after the US example from the DMCA. The book also recommends how to approach the problem of misrepresentations in notifications and how to ensure timely and reasoned decisions.

EFFECTIVE REMEDY – Finally, the book proposes safeguards for ensuring effective remedy. The safeguards in this area are aimed at rectifying violations and ensuring appropriate relief is possible once interference has taken place. The proposed safeguards include: (1) a possibility to appeal a decision about removal (or non-removal) of content; and (2) a possibility of judicial redress. States should guarantee accessible and effective judicial and non-judicial procedures that allow for the review of all claims concerning rights violations. They should ensure, in particular, that intermediaries provide affected individuals with access to a prompt, transparent and effective appeal mechanism. Any procedure that requires intermediaries to make decisions about content should include a step allowing for an initial decision to be corrected. A variety of remedies could come into play. In case an appeal against the removal of content is successful, intermediaries should reinstate the content.

Safeguards to ensure effective remedy should be available to both sides of a conflict. This refers to both the party whose rights have been violated by an initial posting and the party whose initial posting has been removed. Both parties should have a possibility to appeal a decision and to seek judicial redress. Judicial review must remain available when dispute settlement mechanisms prove insufficient or when the affected parties choose this path. This safeguard should be provided as a final element of any procedure, regardless of which notice and action mechanism is employed.

OUTLOOK

NEXT STEPS – The European Commission has been working on several proposals to tackle illegal and infringing online content, all of which rely heavily on online gatekeeping. For example, this approach can be found in the 2016 Code of Conduct on Countering Illegal Hate Speech Online, the legislative proposals for a new Copyright Directive in DSM and for amending the AVMS Directive, the 2017 Communication on Tackling Illegal Content Online, and the 2018

Recommendation on Measures to Effectively Tackle Illegal Content Online. Each of these initiatives rely strongly on private enforcement mechanisms that require different degrees of monitoring, filtering, and evaluating, as well as ranking, blocking and removal of content. None of these initiatives, however, incorporate robust safeguards necessary to ensure effective protection of freedom of expression online. One can only hope that the European Commission will take its positive obligations under the CFEU more seriously going forward.

BROADER FOCUS – Policy makers increasingly enlist private entities to police online content. The research presented in this book focused mainly on the safeguards necessary to ensure effective protection of freedom of expression. Future research should look beyond the right to freedom of expression and analyse the impact of delegated private enforcement mechanisms on other human rights. Delegating enforcement of public policy objectives to private entities effectively gives those entities power to decide what content to remove, degrade or block online. This power is used in practice, for example, to remove controversial speech or to ban speakers, while keeping online harassment or hate speech available.[1795] The same power is also used to adjust content according to the profiles of users construed on the basis of their personal data.[1796] Recent revelations on Facebook and Cambridge Analytica have illustrated that this power can be misused to turn private platforms into tools for misinformation, propaganda and manipulation.[1797] The activities of online gatekeepers can therefore also directly impact other fundamental human rights, such as the right to freedom of assembly and association, the right to effective remedy and the right to privacy and data protection.

RULE OF LAW – Future research should also analyse the effects of the delegated private enforcement mechanisms on the rule of law. Involvement of private entities in the policing of online content seems inevitable due to the *supra*-national and decentralized nature of the Internet. This approach, however, challenges the traditional distinction between "public" and "private" spheres. Such a shift in the locus of the activity of "regulating" from the State to other actors is called a

---

1795 S. Jeong, The History of Twitter's Rules, Motherboard, 14 January 2016, https://motherboard.vice.com/en_us/article/z43xw3/the-history-of-twitters-rules; and S. Emerson, Here's Twitter's Response to the Racist Harassment of Leslie Jones, Motherboard, 19 July 2016, https://motherboard.vice.com/en_us/article/pgkz37/heres-twitters-response-to-the-racist-harassment-of-leslie-jones.

1796 J. Winston, How the Trump Campaign Built an Identity Database and Used Facebook Ads to Win the Election, Medium, 18 November 2016, https://medium.com/startup-grind/how-the-trump-campaign-built-an-identity-database-and-used-facebook-ads-to-win-the-election-4ff7d24269ac; and C. Cadwalladr, British courts may unlock secrets of how Trump campaign profiled US voters, The Guardian, 1 October 2017, https://www.theguardian.com/technology/2017/oct/01/cambridge-analytica-big-data-facebook-trump-voters.

1797 C. Cadwalladr and E. Graham-Harrison, Facebook and Cambridge Analytica face mounting pressure over data scandal, 19 March 2018, https://www.theguardian.com/news/2018/mar/18/cambridge-analytica-and-facebook-accused-of-misleading-mps-over-data-breach.

situation of "decentred regulation".[1798] The situation, however, is at odds with the long established theory that the functioning of States should be based on the rule of law. The rule of law is considered a defining characteristic of liberal democracies and the most important trait of a free society.[1799] Despite its long history, the rule of law is still considered an 'elusive notion' with more than one conception.[1800] According to Dicey, who popularized the term in 1885, the rule of law is based on three principles: (1) that legal duties and responsibilities are determined by law and not any arbitrary or discretionary powers; (2) that disputes with citizens are resolved by courts applying the law; and (3) that fundamental rights of the citizens (e.g. right to freedom of expression, right to privacy, right to effective remedy) are always protected because they are rooted in the natural law.[1801] Rawls, on the other hand, focused on predictability and certainty of law.[1802] Application of the theory of the rule of law, however defined, in the delegated private enforcement model poses several difficulties. Non-state agents are expected to serve the public interest, but they are not subject to the professional norms in public service normally imposed on such institutions.[1803] Private entities make decisions based primarily on their own objectives and rules, which are not always predictable or accessible, and do not foresee the involvement of courts. Private enforcement mechanisms, moreover, do not contain clear safeguards to ensure compliance with the fundamental human rights. The search for an efficient solution to the problem of illegal online content may result, therefore, in circumvention of the rule of law.

Future research should analyse the limits of private enforcement mechanisms on the Internet from the perspective of the rule of law and the protection of human rights. The legality and legitimacy of private enforcement mechanism can be enhanced through the development of procedural and substantive safeguards. This book has already developed a set of procedural and substantive safeguards for the right to freedom of expression, in the context of specific online content removal mechanisms (so called "notice and action"). Future research should examine whether the identified safeguards can also be used to effectively address concerns related to the risks for other human rights in light of the regulatory trend of entrusting public State roles to private entities. Finally, future research should examine whether different sets of safeguards are needed for different content regulation mechanisms, for example, depending on their material scope or technology applied.

1798 See J. Black, "Decentring Regulation: Understanding the Role of Regulation and Self-Regulation in a 'Post-Regulatory' World", *o.c.*

1799 See B. Z. Tamanaha, "The Rule of Law for Everyone?", *St. John's Legal Studies Research Paper*, 2003, https://papers.ssrn.com/sol3/papers.cfm?abstract_id=312622.

1800 See B. Z. Tamanaha, *On the Rule of Law*, Cambridge University Press, 2004.

1801 See V. Dicey, & E. C. S. Wade, *Introduction to the study of the law of the constitution*, 10e ed., London: Macmillan, 1985.

1802 See J. Rawls, *A theory of Justice*, Cambridge, Massachusetts: The Belknap Press of Harvard University Press, 1999.

1803 See J. Freeman, "Private Parties, Public Functions and the New Administrative Law", *o.c.*

ANNEX
DETAILED COUNTRY PROFILES

1. NOTICE AND TAKE DOWN

A. FINLAND

LEGISLATION – Finland was one of the early adopters of the notice and take down procedure in the EU. In 2002, a detailed NTD procedure was introduced in the Act 458/2002, on Information Society Services and Electronic Commerce.[1804] The 2002 NTD procedure was hardly used at all.[1805] There are few examples of case-law from that period. In 2010, the Supreme Court in Finland held the operators and administrators of Bittorrent tracker "Finreactor" jointly criminally liable, including compensation and remuneration, for users' copyright infringement.[1806] The hosting exemption was not applicable as a result of the awareness, knowledge and participation of Finreactor to the infringing activities.[1807]

The 2002 Act was replaced by the Finnish Information Society Code, which entered into force on 1 January 2015.[1808] The new Act provides a general liability exemption for hosting services in Section 184. There is, however, a notable exception in relation to certain types of manifestly illegal content. The service provider is not liable if it acts expeditiously to disable access to the information upon '*otherwise obtaining actual knowledge of the fact that the stored information is clearly contrary to*' legal provisions regarding specified types of content.[1809]

1804 Act on provision of information society services (458/2002), 5 June 2002, www.finlex.fi/fi/laki/kaannokset/2002/en20020458.pdf.

1805 See T. Verbiest, G. Spindler *et al.*, Study on the Liability of Internet Intermediaries, *o.c.*; P. Van Eecke, M. Truyens, EU Study on the Legal Analysis of A Single Market for the Information Society – New Rules for a New Age?, *o.c.*, p. 107, ft. 475: Comments from Mr Antti Kotilainen, Managing Director of the Finnish Copyright Information and Anti- Piracy Centre (CIAPe).

1806 Supreme Court, *Finreactor*, KKO 2010:47, 30 June 2010. See more in K. Lindroos, "Intermediary Liability for IP Infringement in Finland: CopyRight vs. CopyLeft – A Series of Legislative Proposals and Decade of Debates", in G. B. Dinwoodie, *Secondary Liability of Internet Service Providers*, *o.c.*, p. 194.

1807 See The Center for Internet and Society, World Intermediary Liability Map: Finland, https://cyberlaw.stanford.edu/page/wilmap-finland.

1808 Chapter 22 of the Finnish Information Society Code (2014/917), *o.c.* See more in K. Lindroos, "Intermediary Liability for IP Infringement in Finland: CopyRight vs. CopyLeft – A Series of Legislative Proposals and Decade of Debates", in G. B. Dinwoodie, *Secondary Liability of Internet Service Providers*, *o.c.*

1809 Section 184 of the Finnish Information Society Code (2014/917), *o.c.*

Additionally, Finland implemented a specific NTD procedure aimed at preventing access (which includes both removal and blocking) to material infringing copyright or neighbouring rights, without a court order.[1810] The procedure is provided in section 189 and further regulated in section 191 of the Finnish Information Society Code. Other types of removal or blocking of content generally require a court order (Section 184 and 185 of the Finnish Information Society Code).

TYPES OF CONTENT – The Finnish NTD procedure described in the Information Society Code applies specifically to the content infringing copyright or neighbouring rights.[1811]

The Code specifies, however, that hosting providers are obliged to act based upon their knowledge when the content in question consists of hate speech, or pictures with child pornography, sexual violence or intercourse with an animal (Section 184 of the Finnish Information Society Code). As specified by the Constitutional Committee of the Parliament, the content must be clearly contrary to the Criminal Code's provisions on this type of content (regulated in Section 10 and 10(a) of Chapter 11 of the Criminal Code and Section 18 and 18(a) of Chapter 17 of the Criminal Code).[1812]

THE PROCEDURE – In order to qualify for the liability exemption, when dealing with content infringing copyright or neighbouring rights, the hosting provider upon receiving a notification must act expeditiously to disable access to the stored content (Section 184 of the Finnish Information Society Code). The Finnish NTD regulation explicitly defines what type of information must be provided in the notice for it to be considered valid. Specifically, the notification must include: (1) the name and contact information of the notifying party; (2) an itemisation of the material, for which removal is requested, and the location of the material; (3) confirmation by the notifying party that the material which the request concerns is, in their sincere opinion, illegally accessible in the communications network; (4) information concerning the fact that the notifying party has unsuccessfully submitted its request to the content provider or that the content provider could not be identified; (5) confirmation by the notifying party that they are the holder of copyright or neighbouring right (or entitled to act on

1810 See Swiss Institute of Comparative Law, Comparative Study on Filtering, blocking and take-down of illegal content on the Internet – Finland country report, *o.c.*, p. 221.

1811 Chapter 22 of the Finnish Information Society Code (2014/917), *o.c.* See also T. Verbiest, G. Spindler *et al.*, Study on the Liability of Internet Intermediaries, *o.c*; P. Van Eecke, M. Truyens, EU Study on the Legal Analysis of A Single Market for the Information Society – New Rules for a New Age?, General Trends in the EU, *o.c.*, p. 28.

1812 The Constitutional Committee of the Parliament (report 60/2001), as referred by Swiss Institute of Comparative Law, Comparative Study on Filtering, blocking and take-down of illegal content on the Internet – Finland country report, *o.c.*, p. 222.

behalf of the holder of the right); (6) signature of the notifying party (Section 191 of the Finnish Information Society Code). The notice shall be made in writing or electronically so that the content of the notification cannot be unilaterally altered and it remains available to the parties (Section 191 of the Finnish Information Society Code).

Furthermore, the Finnish Information Society Code specifies the exact the order of events once the NTD procedure is initiated through a notice. First, the impugned content is taken offline and the host must notify the content provider immediately, in writing or electronically, and provide them with a copy of the notice (Section 187 of the Finnish Information Society Code). The notification must state the reason for removal (or blocking access) and provide information on the right of the content provider to bring the matter for a court hearing within 14 days from the receipt of the notification (Section 187 of the Finnish Information Society Code). If the content provider considers that the complaint is groundless, they may object to the removal within 14 days. The plea with the objection must also meet specified requirements and must be delivered to the notifying party in writing or electronically (Section 192 of the Finnish Information Society Code). The plea must include, among others, the facts and other reasons under which prevention is considered groundless (Section 192 of the Finnish Information Society Code). A copy of the plea should be delivered to the service provider. If the plea meets the requirements and is delivered in time, the service provider '*must not prevent the material specified in the plea from being returned and kept available unless otherwise provided by an agreement between the service provider and the content provider or by an order or decision by a court or by any other authority*'.[1813]

The procedure, despite being thoroughly elaborated, does not seem to be used often in practice. A different phenomenon, however, began to occur in Finland. Instead of targeting hosting providers, law firms started going directly after Internet users accused of copyright violations.[1814] The actions are based on the provisions of the 2006 copyright law. The firms file petitions with the Market Court of Finland to obtain contact details of the users and later send out threatening letters on behalf of the copyright holders demanding the accused to pay a settlement fee.[1815] The practice attracted the attention of the Ministry of Education and Culture, which expressed concern about the intimidation practices as well as the number of the letters sent.[1816] The Ministry appointed a

1813 Section 193 of the Finnish Information Society Code (2014/917), *o.c.*

1814 D. Anderson, Finnish law firms are using intimidation to profit from internet piracy, 4 May 2017, www.helsinkitimes.fi/finland/finland-news/domestic/14734-finnish-law-firms-are-using-intimidation-to-profit-from-internet-piracy.html.

1815 *Ibid.*

1816 A. Teivainen, Finnish authorities receive complaints about "piracy letters", 25 July 2017, www.helsinkitimes.fi/finland/finland-news/domestic/14917-finnish-authorities-receive-complaints-about-piracy-letters.html.

task force to develop good practices for copyright monitoring and to address any possible violations of law.[1817] Recently, the Market Court of Finland addressed the issue in a ruling and imposed stricter evidentiary requirements on law firms demanding identification of subscribers involved in alleged downloading or sharing of copyright protected content.[1818] The Court specified that from now on the petitions for identity disclosure will only be considered if a subscriber is suspected of "substantial" copyright violations.[1819]

When dealing with content that consists of hate speech, or pictures of child pornography, sexual violence or intercourse with an animal, the hosting provider upon obtaining actual knowledge (but before court order), must act expeditiously to disable access to the stored content (Section 184 of the Finnish Information Society Code). In these situations the hosting provider must notify the content provider of the action taken. The notification must state the reason for removal (or blocking) and information on the right of the content provider to bring the matter for court hearing.[1820]

B. FRANCE

LEGISLATION – In France, the removal of unlawful content on websites is governed by various laws and regulations depending on the type of content.[1821] For example, the Intellectual Property Code contains provisions allowing the courts to order the removal of copyrights infringing content, while the French Data Protection Agency (CNIL) has the authority to order cessation of data processing activities which violate the Law on Information Technology, Data Files and Individual Liberties. The main legislation addressing removal (and blocking) of content is enshrined in Law No. 2004–575 of 21 June 2004 on ensuring confidence in the digital economy (hereinafter the "LCEN").[1822] The provisions of this law were amended by Law No. 2011–267 of 14 March 2011 on domestic security guidance and planning, called LOPPSI 2, and supplemented

---

1817 See *Ibid.*

1818 *Copyright Management Services Ltd.*, MAO:333/17. A. Teivainen, Market Court's ruling expected to stem flow of copyright letters, 5 July 2017, www.helsinkitimes.fi/finland/finland-news/domestic/14870-market-court-s-ruling-expected-to-stem-flow-of-piracy-letters.html. See also, S. Melart, BREAKING NEWS: Finnish Market Court ruling refers to Tele2 decision and throws a massive wrench into the works of copyright trolls, 17 June 2017, https://copy21.com/2017/06/breaking-news-finnish-market-court-ruling-refers-to-tele2-decision-and-throws-a-massive-wrench-into-the-works-of-copyright-trolls/.

1819 Market Court's ruling expected to stem flow of copyright letters, *o.c.*

1820 Swiss Institute of Comparative Law, Comparative Study on Filtering, blocking and take-down of illegal content on the Internet – Finland country report, *o.c.*, p. 222.

1821 See The Center for Internet and Society, World Intermediary Liability Map: France, http://cyberlaw.stanford.edu/page/wilmap-france.

1822 Loi n° 2004–575 du 21 juin 2004 pour la confiance dans l'économie numérique, www.wipo.int/wipolex/en/text.jsp?file_id=276258.

by Law No. 2014–1353 of 13 November 2014 on scaling up counter-terrorism provisions.[1823] Apart from the court and administrative removals, LCEN also provides an optional notification procedure in Article 6-I-5. Together with Article 6-I-2 providing conditions for civil liability exemptions for the hosts, and Article 6-I-3 providing similar conditions for criminal liability exemption, the three articles of LCEN constitute the French notice and take down procedure.[1824]

The French law on the liability of Internet intermediaries is essentially the implementation of the E-Commerce Directive.[1825] Interpretation of the rules, especially on the immunity for hosting service providers, has led to a rich although often controversial jurisprudence.[1826] The *'principal preoccupation'* of the French courts was a distinction between two special liability regimes, for hosts (*hébergeur*) and for publishers (*éditeur*).[1827] The French courts initially were reluctant to apply the safe harbour protection to hosting service providers.[1828] For example, in *Lafesse v. MySpace*, the Court did not allow MySpace the protection of Article 6-I-5 LCEN.[1829] The Court admitted that MySpace offered a technical hosting service, but its activities were not limited to those services. By providing a pre-designed page set-up for users' personal accounts, in combination with displaying the revenue-generating ads, MySpace earned a qualification not as a host (*hébergeur*), but as a publisher of content (*éditeur*).[1830] As a result, the Court declared that MySpace must take on the responsibilities of a publisher and ordered the deletion of a video under threat of a daily fine of 1000 EUR in case of delay, as well as imposition of damages.[1831] A series of similar decisions followed across the country.[1832]

1823 See Swiss Institute of Comparative Law, Comparative Study on Filtering, blocking and take-down of illegal content on the Internet – France country report, *o.c.*, p. 236 – 237.

1824 N. van Eijk, C. Jasserand, C. Wiersma and T. M. van Engers, "Moving towards Balance: A Study into Duties of Care on the Internet" (2010) Institute for Information Law & Leibniz Center for Law, University of Amsterdam, p. 100.

1825 S. Nérisson, "Intellectual Property Liability of Consumers, Facilitators and Intermediaries: the Position in France", in A. Kamperman Sanders and C. Heath, *Intellectual Property Liability of Consumers, Facilitators and Intermediaries*, Kluwer Law International 2012, p. 77.

1826 C. Angelopoulos, *European intermediary liability in copyright: A tort-based analysis*, *o.c.*, p. 121.

1827 L. Thoumyre, "Etude 464 – La responsabilité pénale et extra-contractuelle des acteurs de l'Internet" (Novembre 2009) Lamy droit des médias et de la communication, as referenced by C. Angelopoulos, *European intermediary liability in copyright: A tort-based analysis*, *o.c.*, p. 121.

1828 See M. Dhenne, "Hébergeurs et contrefaçons: de l'usage de la loyauté dans un régime de responsabilité limitée", 51 *RLDI* 58, 2009, as referenced by C. Angelopoulos, *European intermediary liability in copyright: A tort-based analysis*, *o.c.*, p. 122.

1829 *Jean Yves L. dit Lafesse c. Myspace*, Tribunal de Grande Instance de Paris, Ordonnance de référé 22 juin 2007.

1830 C. Angelopoulos, *European intermediary liability in copyright: A tort-based analysis*, *o.c.*, p. 122.

1831 *Ibid.*

1832 See: *Louis Vuitton Malletier c. Google*, Tribunal de Grande Instance de Paris, 4 February 2005 and Cour d'appel de Paris, 28 June 2006; *Gifam c. Google*, Tribunal de grande instance de

In some cases, distinguishing between the two regimes has led to interesting results. In *Tiscali v Lucky Comics*, the Paris Court of Appeal classified the internet website operator Tiscali as both a host and a publisher simultaneously.[1833] Tiscali, as a result, was held liable as a host, for failing to comply with the obligation imposed by Article 6-II LCEN, to keep data identifying its users; and as a publisher for uploaded content because the provided services were not merely technical.[1834] The case was later addressed by the *Cour de cassation*, which did not consider Tiscali a publisher of the objectionable content, but at the same time refused to apply the hosting immunity. The main reason to deny the exemption was that the provider offered its users the possibility of creating personal pages on the site and advertisers the possibility of buying advertising space on those pages, which the Court interpreted as exceeding the simple technical functions of storage.[1835] The Court applied the French law in force at the time, contained in Article 43-8 of the Law of 30 September 1989, which was later repealed in 2004.[1836] The judgement faced criticism because nothing in the old Freedom of Communication Act nor the LCEN indicated that merely deriving income from a service could in itself be sufficient to deny safe harbour protection.[1837]

Since this line of reasoning was rejected by the CJEU in *Google Adwords*[1838], the *Cour de cassation* switched course in July 2010. In four judgements, the Court annulled the lower courts' rulings rejecting immunity on the ground of Google's advertising activities and confirmed that immunity as a hosting service provider depends on the active or passive role played by the intermediary.[1839] The four decisions constitute a line dividing French jurisprudence into "avant Google"

Paris, 12 July 2006 and Cour d'appel de Paris, 1 February 2008; *Viaticum et Luteciel c. Google*, Tribunal de grande instance de Nanterre, 13 October 2003 and Cour d'appel de Versailles, 10 March 2005; *CNRRH, Pierre Alexis T. c. Google*, Tribunal de grande instance de Nanterre, 14 December 2004 and Cour d'appel de Versailles, 23 March 2006.

1833 *Tiscali Media c. Dargaud Lombard, Lucky Comics*, Cour d'appel de Paris, 7 June 2006.

1834 See S. Nérisson, "Intellectual Property Liability of Consumers, Facilitators and Intermediaries: the Position in France *o.c.*, p. 77.

1835 C. Angelopoulos, *European intermediary liability in copyright: A tort-based analysis*, *o.c.*, p. 122.

1836 *Loi n° 86-1067 du 30 septembre 1986 relative à la liberté de communication (Loi Léotard)* (Law No. 86-1067 of 30 September 1986 on freedom of communication) as amended by the *Loi no 2000-719 du 1er août 2000 modifiant la loi no 86-1067 du 30 septembre 1986 relative à la liberté de communication (Law No. 2000-719 of 1 August 2000 modifying the law No. 86-1067 of 30 September 1986 on freedom of communication)*.

1837 C. Angelopoulos, *European intermediary liability in copyright: A tort-based analysis*, *o.c.*, p. 123. See also R. Matulionyte and S. Nerisson, "The French Route to an ISP Safe Harbour, Compared to the German and US Ways", *International Review of Intellectual Property and Competition Law* (IIC), Vol. 42 Issue 1, 2011, p. 55.

1838 CJEU, joined cases C-236/08 and C-237/08, *Google France v Louis Vuitton et al*, 23 March 2010.

1839 *Google France c. Louis Vuitton Malletier* (06-20.230), *Google France c. GIFAM* (08-13944); *Google France c. CNRRH* (06-15136); *Google France c. SA Viaticum* (05-14331), Cour de cassation (Chambre commerciale, financière et économique), 13 July 2010.

and "après Google" stages.[1840] The shift became visible in 2012, when the *Cour de cassation* denied eBay protection under the hosting provision arguing that eBay played an active role when providing its services, which means it had knowledge and control over the hosted information.[1841] Specifically, the Court pointed out the fact that eBay provided facilities enabling sellers to optimise their sales and assisted in the definition and description of items for sale, including through the offer of the creation of a personalised marketplace or support by sales assistants. Moreover, eBay sent unsolicited emails to buyers encouraging them to purchase items on sale and inviting bidders to bid on similar items.

TYPES OF CONTENT –The French NTD procedure is of general application and can be applied to any type of content that violates national law.[1842] When interpreting Article 6-I-2 LCEN, the *Conseil Constitutionnel* declared that hosting providers are only under an obligation to remove notified content when it is: (a) manifestly unlawful; or when (b) its removal has been ordered by a court.[1843] If there is no court order (and the content is not manifestly unlawful) the hosting providers enjoy a certain margin of appreciation and can decide how to respond to a notification without risking their own liability.[1844]

The concept of "manifestly unlawful" has not been defined comprehensively. Article 6-I-7 LCEN did, however, introduce provisions for specific types of outrageous content (*contenus odieux*).[1845] Specifically, it introduced an obligation for host providers to take proactive measures to fight against such content as its suppression is in the general interest.[1846] This means that they have an obligation to set up an easily accessible signalling procedure (*procédure de signalement*), enabling anyone to report the presence of such content.[1847] Initially, the concept of

1840 See C. Castets-Renaud, "Le renouveau de la responsabilité délictuelle des intermédiaires de l'internet" (2012) Recueil Dalloz p. 827, as referenced by C. Angelopoulos, *European intermediary liability in copyright: A tort-based analysis*, *o.c.*, p. 123.

1841 *La société eBay Inc. c. la société Parfums Christian Dior* (11–10.508), Cour de cassation, 3 May 2012.

1842 See C. Rubin, Ministère de l'Economie, des Finances et de l'Industrie, Presentation of France concerning national legislative approach to notice and action, EC Expert group on electronic commerce (E01636), *o.c.*; see also Swiss Institute of Comparative Law, Comparative Study on Filtering, blocking and take-down of illegal content on the Internet – France country report, *o.c.*, p.243.

1843 Conseil Constitutionnel, Décision No 2004–496 DC du 10 juin 2004, Journal officiel du 22 juin 2004, p. 11182.

1844 See C. Jasserand, "Régime français de la responsabilité des intermédiaires techniques", *o.c.*, p. 1135, as referenced by C. Angelopoulos, *European intermediary liability in copyright: A tort-based analysis*, *o.c.*, p. 121.

1845 N. van Eijk, C. Jasserand, C. Wiersma and T. M. van Engers, "Moving towards Balance: A Study into Duties of Care on the Internet", *o.c.*, p. 105.

1846 C. Angelopoulos, *European intermediary liability in copyright: A tort-based analysis*, *o.c.*, p. 120.

1847 N. van Eijk, C. Jasserand, C. Wiersma and T. M. van Engers, "Moving towards Balance: A Study into Duties of Care on the Internet", *o.c.*, p. 105.

manifest unlawfulness was aimed solely at targeting child sexual abuse material, incitement to racial hatred or condoning crimes against humanity. The concept has been extended through jurisprudence to other categories, such as defamation, racist, anti-Semitic or revisionist content.[1848] Moreover, content constituting the criminal offence of inciting or condoning terrorism would most likely also be considered as manifestly unlawful.[1849] Interestingly, copyright infringements are not covered by the concept. The reason being that content which damages private interests is not considered as being "manifestly" unlawful.[1850]

THE PROCEDURE – According to the French legislation, hosting service providers do not have to remove content they host if they have no actual knowledge of the unlawful nature of the content (Article 6-I-2 LCEN). The LCEN lays down a rebuttable presumption of knowledge by the hosting service providers if they receive a notification containing information specified in the law. The notification must include information such as (1) the date, description and location of the facts; (2) the reasons why the content must be removed with a reference to the legal provisions and the factual justifications; (3) a copy of the correspondence sent to the author or editor of the information requesting the suspension, removal or modification of the content, or supporting evidence that it has been impossible to contact the author or editor (Article 6-I-5 LCEN).

Knowledge can be established through the notification, but it can also be proved by other means. However, the hosting service provider has a margin of appreciation and can decide whether or not they comply with the request for removal. Upon receiving a notification the hosting providers are free to remove such content and are only obliged to do so if the content is of manifestly unlawful nature.[1851] If this is not the case, the hosting provider can wait for a court order.[1852] According to Article 6-I-5 LCEN, after receiving a notification, the hosting provider is required to act 'expeditiously', similarly to the Directive. A French court

1848 See Swiss Institute of Comparative Law, Comparative Study on Filtering, blocking and take-down of illegal content on the Internet – France country report, *o.c.*, p. 243 and 244; and T. Verbiest, G. Spindler *et al.*, Study on the Liability of Internet Intermediaries, *o.c.*; P. Van Eecke, M Truyens, EU Study on the Legal Analysis of A Single Market for the Information Society – New Rules for a New Age?, *o.c.*, p. 39.

1849 See Swiss Institute of Comparative Law, Comparative Study on Filtering, blocking and take-down of illegal content on the Internet – France country report, *o.c.*, p. 243.

1850 R. Hardouin, "La jurisprudence, les textes, et la responsabilité des hébergeurs", *RLDI*, 39 (2008), p. 67; and R. Hardouin, "La connaissance de l'illicéité par les hébergeurs ou quand etre notifié ne signifie pas nécessairement devoir retirer" *Revue du droit des technologies de l'information, 47* (2012), p. 5, as referenced by C. Angelopoulos, *European intermediary liability in copyright: A tort-based analysis, o.c.*, p. 121. See also *Omar & Fred et autres c. Dailymotion*, Tribunal de grande instance de Paris (3ème chambre, 1ère section) jugement du 15 avril 2008; *Jean Yves Lafesse c. Dailymotion*, Tribunal de grande instance de Paris (3ème chambre, 1ère section) jugement du 15 avril 2008.

1851 See Paris Court of Appeal, 4 April 2013, Pole 1.

1852 See also *Conseil Constitutionnel*, Décision No 2004–496 DC du 10 juin 2004, Journal officiel du 22 juin 2004, p. 11182.

has interpreted this requirement in *S.A. Télévision Française 1 (TF1) c. Société YouTube LLC,* where it ruled that a 5-day delay is not expeditious enough.[1853]

It should also be pointed out that for manifestly illegal content, especially offences of child sexual abuse material or acts inciting or condoning terrorism, the LCEN also foresees a possibility of blocking via a mere administrative decision of the Central Office for Combating ICT-related Crime (OCLCTIC), which is part of the Directorate General of the National Police.[1854] The OCLCTIC can obtain information about manifestly illegal content, for example, through the signalling procedure installed by the hosting providers.[1855] The OCLCTIC can ask the hosting providers to remove the content from the Internet, while simultaneously informing the ISPs (Article 6–1.1 LCEN). If the removal is not completed within 24 hours, the OCLCTIC can request the ISP to block access to the concerned website.[1856] The OCLCTIC can also order the operators of search engines or directories of electronic addresses to stop the indexing of the sites in question.[1857]

Moreover, the French law provides the civil courts with a possibility to order hosting services or ISPs to take any appropriate measures to prevent or stop damage resulting from the content of an online public communication service. The courts, in such a case, first direct the order to the hosting service providers and if this is not possible, they direct the order to the ISPs (Article 6-I-8 LCEN).

C. GERMANY

LEGISLATION – In Germany, the E-Commerce Directive and its safe harbours were implemented into German law through the *Telemediengesetz* (TMG) of 26 February 2007.[1858] The transposition is almost verbatim with some exceptions for providers who work together with a recipient of the service to act illegally.[1859] Until recently, there were no specific legislations about blocking, filtering or taking down of content. The German system relied on general rules of law used to order hosting providers to take down and filter illegal content.[1860]

1853 *S.A. Télévision Française 1 (TF1) c. Société YouTube LLC, Tribunal de Grande Instance de Paris* (3ème chambre, 1ère section) jugement du 29 mai 2012. See also C. Angelopoulos, *European intermediary liability in copyright: A tort-based analysis*, *o.c.*, p. 121.

1854 Swiss Institute of Comparative Law, Comparative Study on Filtering, blocking and take-down of illegal content on the Internet – France country report, *o.c.*, p. 239.

1855 N. van Eijk, C. Jasserand, C. Wiersma and T. M. van Engers, "Moving towards Balance: A Study into Duties of Care on the Internet", *o.c.*, p. 105.

1856 Swiss Institute of Comparative Law, Comparative Study on Filtering, blocking and take-down of illegal content on the Internet – France country report, *o.c.*, p. 243.

1857 Swiss Institute of Comparative Law, Comparative Study on Filtering, blocking and take-down of illegal content on the Internet – France country report, *o.c.*, p. 243.

1858 *Telemediengesetz*, 26 February 2007, BGBl. I S. 179.

1859 C. Angelopoulos, *European intermediary liability in copyright: A tort-based analysis*, *o.c.*, p. 149.

1860 Swiss Institute of Comparative Law, Comparative Study on Filtering, blocking and take-down of illegal content on the Internet – Germany country report, *o.c.*, p. 261.

In 2017, a new law was introduced to help combat hate speech (and indirectly fake news) on social media. The Act to Improve Enforcement of the Law in Social Networks (Network Enforcement Act – Netzdurchführungsgesetz – NetzDG) entered into force on 1 October 2017.[1861] Since the law only recently came into force, there is not much information about the application, interpretation or effects it may lead to. Moreover, no case law is available at this point.

TYPES OF CONTENT – The new Act targets fake news and hate speech in general. Section 1(3) specifies precisely, by reference to the Criminal Code, what types of illegal content it is aimed at. The list includes, among others, communication offenses such as defamation, dissemination of propaganda material or use of symbols of unconstitutional organizations; encouragement of the commission of a serious violent offense endangering the State; commission of treasonous forgery; public incitement to crime; and incitement to hatred but also distribution of every kind of pornography.[1862]

THE PROCEDURE – The Act applies to social media networks that have two or more million registered users in Germany. Social media networks are defined as tele-media service providers that operate online platforms, for profit-making purposes, and which are designed to enable users to share content with other users or make that content publicly available (Section 1(1) NetzDG). The Act does not apply to email or messaging services.

Strictly speaking, the Act does not provide a procedure for removal of the targeted content but requires social media networks to develop and '*maintain an effective and transparent procedure for handling complaints about unlawful content*' (Section 3(1) NetzDG). The procedure must be easily recognisable, directly accessible and permanently available. It must, moreover, adhere to certain specifications. For example, the procedure must ensure that social media networks remove or block access to content that is manifestly unlawful within 24 hours of receiving the complaint (Section 3(2)2 NetzDG). However, the social network can reach an agreement with the competent law enforcement authority on a longer period for deleting or blocking any manifestly unlawful content. Content that is not manifestly unlawful must be removed or blocked '*immediately, this generally being within 7 days of receiving the complaint*' (Section 3(2)3 NetzDG). The 7-days

[1861] Gesetz zur Verbesserung der Rechtsdurchsetzung in sozialen Netzwerken [Netzdurchführungsgesetz – NetzDG], Drucksache 536/17, 30 June 2017. See German Federal Ministry of Justice and Consumer Protection, unofficial translation, https://www.bmjv.de/SharedDocs/Gesetzgebungsverfahren/Dokumente/NetzDG_engl.pdf.

[1862] Content 'which fulfils the requirements of the offences described in sections 86, 86a, 89a, 91, 100a, 111, 126, 129 to 129b, 130, 131, 140, 166, 184b in connection with 184d, 185 to 187, 241 or 269 of the Criminal Code and which is not justified'. See G. Spindler, "Internet Intermediary Liability Reloaded – The New German Act on Responsibility of Social Networks and its (In-) Compatibility with European Law", *o.c.*, p. 167.

limit may be exceeded if 1) the decision regarding the unlawfulness of the content depends '*on the falsity of a factual allegation or is clearly dependent on other factual circumstances*' (Section 3(2)3.a NetzDG); in such cases, the social network can give the user an opportunity to respond to the complaint before making the decision; 2) the social network refers the decision regarding unlawfulness to a recognised self-regulation institution (Section 3(2)3.b NetzDG). In case of removal, the social media network must retain the content as evidence and store it for a period of ten weeks (Section 3(2)4 NetzDG). Moreover, the social media network must immediately notify both the person submitting the complaint and the user about any decision, including reasons for the decision (Section 3(2)5 NetzDG).

The Act includes several provisions regarding accountability and transparency of the functioning of the removal process. For example, the Act provides that the handling of complaints shall be monitored via monthly checks by the social network's management. Any organisational deficiencies in dealing with incoming complaints shall be immediately rectified (Section 3(4) NetzDG). Moreover, the procedures may be monitored by an agency tasked to do so by the administrative authority (Section 3(5) NetzDG). Providers of social networks that receive more than 100 complaints per calendar year shall be obliged, additionally, to produce half-yearly German-language reports on the handling of complaints about unlawful content on their platforms. The reports must include specified information, such as, among others, (1) description of the mechanisms for submitting complaints and the criteria applied in deciding whether to delete or block unlawful content; (2) number of incoming complaints in the reporting period, broken down according to submission by complaints bodies or by users, and according to the reason for the complaint; (3) time between receiving complaints and deleting or blocking the unlawful content (Section 2(2) NetzDG). The social media networks are obliged to publish these reports in the Federal Gazette and on their own website.

The Act foresees also severe regulatory fines in case of non-compliance. Such a regulatory offence may be sanctioned with a regulatory fine of up to 500.000 Euros, and in some cases, up to 5 million Euros (Section 4(2) NetzDG). The regulatory offence may be sanctioned even if it is not committed in the Federal Republic of Germany (Section 4(3) NetzDG).

D. HUNGARY

LEGISLATION – In Hungary, the NTD procedure is regulated in Art. 13 of Act CVIII of 2001 on certain issues of electronic commerce services and information society services.[1863]

1863 Act CVIII of 2001 on certain issues of electronic commerce services and information society services, Promulgated: 24 December, 2001, available at: www.neuronit.com/documents/108_2001_el_comm_torv_20070502.pdf.

TYPES OF CONTENT – The provisions on NTD in the Hungarian Act apply to copyright infringements on any copyrighted work, performance, recording, audiovisual work or database, or of an exclusive right arising from trademark protection under the Act on the Protection of Trademarks and Geographical Indications of Origin (Article 13.1 of the Hungarian Act CVIII). In 2014, the mechanism has been extended to cover the personal rights of minors as well.[1864] The change was introduced as the government made it a priority to ensure the protection of personality rights of minors and to eliminate cyber bullying in particular.[1865] This measure is considered an "atypical" NTD mechanism (see more *infra*).[1866]

THE PROCEDURE – The Hungarian procedure is considered very similar to the US NTD procedure in the DMCA.[1867] However, there is one interesting distinction. The Hungarian NTD procedure actually foresees two procedures: (1) „hard" notice and takedown for IPR and trademark infringements; and (2) „soft" notice and action for infringements of personal rights of minors.[1868] "Hard" NTD requires content deletion without assessing whether the request is justifiable or not.[1869] "Soft" N&A allows the intermediary to examine the request and disregard those that he considers unjustified (which is why the government representative calls it N&A mechanism and not NTD).[1870]

Art. 13 of the Act on certain issues of electronic commerce services and information society services provides that rights holders may request the removal of information infringing their rights by sending a notice in the form of a private document with full probative force or a notarised deed to the service provider (Article 13.1 of the Hungarian Act CVIII). Further, the provision specifies that the notice should contain information on 1) the subject of the infringement and the facts that provide reasonable cause to believe that an infringement has taken place; 2) the data identifying the unlawful information; 3) the name, address of residence or head office, phone number and electronic mail address of the rights holder (Article 13.2 of the Hungarian Act CVIII). In case of a request concerning personality rights of minors, the procedure is essentially the same but some

1864 See Swiss Institute of Comparative Law, Comparative Study on Filtering, blocking and take-down of illegal content on the Internet – Hungary country report, *o.c.*, p. 310.

1865 See G. Csiszér, Ministry of National Development, Presentation of Hungary concerning national legislative approach to notice and action, EC Expert group on electronic commerce (E01636), *o.c.*

1866 *Ibid.*

1867 B. Rátai, et al. "Cyber Law in Hungary, in International Encyclopaedia of Laws", *Kluwer Law International*, The Netherlands, Suppl. 26, July 2010, p. 225. See also T. Verbiest, Spindler G, et al., Study on the liability of Internet Intermediaries – General trends in Europe, *o.c.*, p. 107.

1868 G. Csiszér, Ministry of National Development, Presentation of Hungary concerning national legislative approach to notice and action, *o.c.*

1869 *Ibid.*

1870 *Ibid.*

procedural deadlines are shorter. The request can be filed by the minor targeted by the infringement or his legal representative.[1871]

The procedure following the notification is described in detail. Within 12 hours of receiving the notice, the service provider shall arrange for disabling access to, or removal of, the information identified in the notice (Article 13.4 of the Hungarian Act CVIII). At the same time, within 3 working days the service provider should give written notice to the affected content provider (Article 13.4 of the Hungarian Act CVIII). The law specifies that the service provider shall refuse to remove the content pursuant to the notice, if it has already previously taken the requested measures in relation to the same content based on the notice of the same rights holder (or the proxy thereof), unless the removal was ordered by a court or authority (Article 13.5 of the Hungarian Act CVIII). This provision is meant to prevent repeated notices referring to the same content after the first notice has been resolved in a way that did not satisfy the rights holder (e.g. the content was put back).[1872] The Hungarian Act also foresees a possibility for the content provider to lodge an objection, within 8 working days of receiving the notice. The Act specifies that the counter-notice should contain, among others, a statement with a detailed explanation that the content provided does not infringe the right of the rights holder specified in the original notice (Article 13.6 of the Hungarian Act CVIII). Upon receiving the objection the service provider shall expeditiously make the relevant content accessible again and notify the rights holder by sending him the objection (Article 13.7 of the Hungarian Act CVIII). After the content is put back online, the rights holder can, within 10 working days, request an injunction for abandonment and prohibition, an order of payment, or file a criminal report with the police (Article 13.9 of the Hungarian Act CVIII). Within 12 hours of receiving the court decision ordering interim measures to that effect, the service provider shall once again remove the information identified in the notice (Article 13.9 of the Hungarian Act CVIII). Finally, the law specifies that the service provider shall not be liable for the successful removal of, or disabling access to the relevant information, when the service provider has acted in accordance with the prescribed provisions in good faith to ensure removal or disabling access thereto (Article 13.12 of the Hungarian Act CVIII).

The Hungarian procedure is widely accepted and considered to be well-functioning.[1873] In practice, hosting providers take notification seriously and remove content even in situations where the notice does not meet all the formal requirements.[1874] In 2007, the Spindler report did not report any court decisions

1871 *Ibid.*

1872 See B. Rátai, et al. Cyber Law in Hungary, in International Encyclopaedia of Laws, *o.c.*, p. 225.

1873 T. Verbiest, Spindler G, et al., Study on the liability of Internet Intermediaries – General trends in Europe, *o.c.*, p. 108.

1874 G. Csiszér, Ministry of National Development, Presentation of Hungary concerning national legislative approach to notice and action, *o.c.*

dealing with this specific provision.[1875] However, in 2010, Hungary witnessed a major case regarding liability of Internet intermediaries for users' comments, which went all the way to the European Court of Human Rights.[1876] The issue started when a self-regulatory body of Hungarian Internet content providers, MTE, published an opinion about two real estate management websites denouncing their business strategies and customer treatment.[1877] The opinion quickly attracted a number of vulgar and offensive comments. The same type of comments appeared when the opinion was reproduced by other portals. The company operating the real estate websites brought a civil action claiming infringement of its right to good reputation. After the referral the impugned comments were deleted from the portals. The regional Court and later also the Court of appeal found that the comments went beyond the acceptable limits of freedom of expression and rejected the argument that the applicants were passive intermediaries covered by the liability exemption in the E-Commerce Directive and in the Electronic Commercial Services Act. The Hungarian Supreme Court ('*Kuria*') shared the view that the applicants' liability consisted of having allowed the harmful publication. The two portals appealed to the ECtHR, arguing that the domestic courts unduly restricted their freedom of expression. In 2016, the ECtHR found that even though the applicants had not been recognized as intermediaries by the Hungarian courts, the interference was prescribed by law.[1878] The ECtHR concluded, however, that the interference violated the right to freedom of expression as the Hungarian domestic courts did not balance the interests of the involved parties, while the comments were offensive but did not constitute hate speech.[1879]

E. SOUTH KOREA

LEGISLATION – South Korea has taken a "vertical" approach to intermediaries' liability. Multiple laws, provisions and procedures regulate issues of copyright, telecommunications, protection of children and juveniles as well as matters related to election. The list includes: Copyright Act[1880], Telecommunications Business

1875 T. Verbiest, Spindler G, et al., Study on the liability of Internet Intermediaries – General trends in Europe, *o.c.*, p. 108.

1876 ECtHR, *Magyar Tartalomszolgáltatók Egyesülete and Index.hu Zrt v. Hungary (MTE and Index.hu)*, 2 February 2016.

1877 The analysis of this case is based on the blog post By P.J. Ombelet and A. Kuczerawy, Delfi revisited: the MTE & Index.hu v. Hungary case, 20 February 2016, https://www.law.kuleuven.be/citip/blog/delfi-revisited-the-mte-index-hu-v-hungary-case/.

1878 ECtHR, *Magyar Tartalomszolgáltatók Egyesülete and Index.hu Zrt v. Hungary (MTE and Index.hu)*, 2 February 2016, paras. 47.

1879 *Ibid.*, paras. 88 and 91.

1880 Copyright Act, Amended by Act No. 9625, Apr. 22, 2009; Act No. 10807, Jun. 30, 2011; Act No. 11110, 2 Dec. 2011, Act No. 14083, Mar. 22, 2016, Act No. 14634, Mar. 21, 2017. http://elaw.klri.re.kr/kor_service/lawView.do?hseq=25455&lang=ENG.

Act (TBA)[1881], Act on the Protection of Children and Juveniles against Sexual Abuse[1882], Act on Consumer Protection in Electronic Commerce[1883], Information and Communications Network Act (ICNA)[1884], the Public Official Election Act (POE Act)[1885] and Act on Establishment and Operation of Korean Communication Commission.[1886] NTD mechanisms can be found in the Copyright Act, and in the Information and Communications Network Act (ICNA).

TYPES OF CONTENT – The first type of NTD mechanism, based on the US DMCA, is provided by Article 103 of the Copyright Act.[1887] In 2009, the Copyright Act introduced the graduated response (three strikes) in Articles 133-2 and 133-3.

Another type of NTD mechanism is provided in Article 44-2 of the Information and Communications Network Act (ICNA).[1888] The procedure applies to content infringing privacy, defaming other persons, or otherwise violating rights of others. Apart from a procedure allowing individuals to request deletion of information, the ICNA provides an additional mechanism in Article 44-7, which empowers the Korea Communications Commission to issue orders to reject, suspend, or restrict handling of all types of infringing information.

THE PROCEDURE – The Korean intermediary liability regime foresees, effectively, two NTD procedures, for copyright infringements and for other types of content that infringes the rights of others (privacy infringements, defamation, and others). The latter procedure, provided in ICNA, also has two variations, where take-downs are requested either by the victims of the infringements or by the Korea Communications Commission.

1881 Telecommunications Business Act No.12035, Enforcement Date 14. Feb, 2014 13. Aug, 2013., Partial Amendment www.law.go.kr/lsInfoP.do?lsiSeq=142966&urlMode=engLsInfoR&viewCls=engLsInfoR#0000.

1882 Act on the Protection of Children and Juveniles Against Sexual Abuse, last amended by Act No. 11690, 23 March 2013 See: http://elaw.klri.re.kr/kor_service/lawView.do?hseq=28311&lang=ENG.

1883 Act on the Consumer Protection in Electronic Commerce, Etc., last amended by Act No. 11461, 1 June 2012 See: http://elaw.klri.re.kr/kor_service/lawView.do?hseq=25650&lang=ENG.

1884 Act on Promotion of Information and Communications Network Utilization and Information Protection, etc. (ICNA, Information and Communications Network Act), last amended by Act No. 11322, 17 February 2012. See: http://elaw.klri.re.kr/kor_service/lawView.do?hseq=25446&lang=ENG.

1885 Public Official Election Act, last amended by Act No. 11071, 7 November 2011 See: http://elaw.klri.re.kr/kor_service/lawView.do?hseq=25035&lang=ENG.

1886 Act on the Establishment and Operation of Korea Communications Commission, Amended by Act No. 11711, 23 March 2013 See: http://elaw.klri.re.kr/kor_service/lawView.do?hseq=28155&lang=ENG.

1887 See The Center for Internet and Society, World Intermediary Liability Map: South Korea, *o.c.*

1888 Act on Promotion of Information and Communications Network Utilization and Information Protection, etc. (ICNA), *o.c.*

A safe harbour for intermediaries shielding them from liability for third party copyright infringement is provided in Article 102 of the Copyright Act. The provision was amended in 2011 after the signing of free trade agreements between South Korea and the EU, and South Korea and the US.[1889] For this reason the structure of the safe harbour provision in Article 102 is similar to that of EU Directive 2000/31/EC and the DMCA.[1890] The provision sets out specific conditions necessary to qualify for the liability exemption for different types of Online Service Providers (OSPs): mere conduits, caching, hosting, and information location tools (Article 102 Copyright Act). Generally, the OSPs should not be held liable for a copyright infringement if they: (1) do not initiate the transmission of content, (2) do not select the content, (3) adopt measures to cancel accounts of repeated infringers and (4) do not interfere with standard technological measures used by copyright holders to identify and protect works (Article 102 (1)1Copyright Act). To benefit from the exemption, providers of the hosting services must additionally possess the authority and capability to control the infringement, and cannot obtain any monetary profit directly from such infringement; they must suspend reproduction or transmission of the content immediately upon obtaining actual knowledge or becoming aware of facts or circumstances from which the infringement is apparent; and they must designate a person to suspend reproduction or transmission and notify such a fact, according to the NTD procedure of Article 103 (Article 102 (1)3Copyright Act).

The NTD procedure for copyright infringement provides that any person who claims that their rights were infringed online may demand the online service provider to suspend the reproduction or transmission of the works (Article 103 (1) Copyright Act). The OSP should immediately comply and inform the claimant and the alleged infringer of such a suspension (Article 103 (1) Copyright Act).[1891] The reproducer or transmitter may request that content be restored by showing that the reproduction or transmission was lawful (Article 103 (3) Copyright Act). In such a case, the OSP has to promptly notify the rights holder about the objection and schedule a date for the restoration of the content (Article 103 (3) Copyright Act). However, the content shall not be restored if the copyright holder notifies the OSP, before the scheduled date, that they filed a lawsuit against the reproducer or transmitter (Article 103 (3) Copyright Act). The OSP will be exempted from liability arising from the claimed copyright infringement if it complies with the described procedure (Article 103 (5) Copyright Act).[1892] In other words, the Korean copyright law requires compliance with the take-down procedure before an OSP can be exempted from the liability. This is a significant difference between the EU and the US versions of the procedure, where not taking down content does

[1889] See The Center for Internet and Society, World Intermediary Liability Map: South Korea, *o.c.*
[1890] *Ibid.*
[1891] *Ibid.*
[1892] *Ibid.*

not automatically mean that the service provider become liable.[1893] Article 103 also provides that any person, who demands a take-down without legitimate grounds, shall make compensation for any incurred losses (Article 103 (6) Copyright Act).

Another NTD procedure is provided in Article 44-2 of the Information and Communications Network Act (ICNA).[1894] The ICNA procedure applies to content that intrudes on privacy, defames other persons, or otherwise violates the rights of others. According to Article 44-2 ICNA, upon presenting materials supporting the claim, a victim of such a violation may request the provider of information and communications services to delete the information or publish a rebuttal statement (Article 44-2 (1) ICNA). Upon receiving the request, the provider shall delete the information, take a temporary blocking measure, or any other necessary measure, and shall notify the applicant and the publisher of the information immediately (Article 44-2 (2) ICNA). According to the wording of the provision, the liability '*may be reduced or exempted*', which means the exemption is not mandatory.[1895] For this reason the service providers in Korea interpret Article 44-2 not as an exemption but rather, as an obligation that they cannot deviate from.[1896] If it is difficult to judge whether the information violates any right or it is anticipated that there will be a dispute between interested parties, the provider may take a temporary measure to block access to the information, irrespective of a request for deletion (Article 44-2 (4) ICNA). The period of time for the temporary measure shall not exceed 30 days (Article 44-2 (4) ICNA). In 2012, the Constitutional Court ruled that these provisions mean that the takedown obligation arises not just when the information is infringing another's rights but whenever there is a request for takedown with certification to that effect.[1897] Despite the fact that the provision requires service providers to react to all take down requests and, as a result, also affects lawful information, the Constitutional Court found there to be no infringement of freedom of expression as the public interest in taking down unlawful information prevails.[1898]

Article 44-2 also provides that every provider of information and communications services shall clearly state the details, procedure, and other matters concerning the take-down requests in their terms and conditions in advance (Article 44-2 (5) ICNA). It should be highlighted that the ICNA NTD described here foresees no procedure to request restoration of deleted or blocked information.[1899]

1893 *Ibid.*

1894 Act on Promotion of Information and Communications Network Utilization and Information Protection, etc. (ICNA), *o.c.*

1895 K. S. Park, Intermediary Liability: Not just Backwards but Going Back, NoC Online Intermediaries Case Studies Series – South Korea, *o.c.*

1896 *Ibid.*

1897 24-1(B) KCCR 578, 2010Hun-Ma88, 31 May 2012, as referenced by The Center for Internet and Society, World Intermediary Liability Map: South Korea, *o.c.*

1898 *Ibid.*

1899 The Center for Internet and Society, World Intermediary Liability Map: South Korea, *o.c.*

In 2009, the Korean Supreme Court issued a ruling concerning intermediary liability for third party infringing content.[1900] The Court held web portal sites Naver, Daum, SK Communications, and Yahoo Korea liable for the defamation of the plaintiff. The Court ruled that:

> 'Barring special circumstances, the intermediary shall be liable for illegal content to the same extent as a news agency and therefore shall be liable when (1) the illegality of the content is clear; (2) the provider was aware of the content; and (3) it is technically and financially possible to control the contents. On top of the duty to take down such content immediately, the intermediary has a duty to block similar postings later on.[1901]

Moreover, the Court specified that the provider could gain the awareness listed under 2) above:

> a) When the victim has requested specifically and individually for the takedown of the content; b) When, even without such request, the provider was concretely aware of how and why the content was posted OR c) When, even without request, it was apparently clear that the provider could have been aware of that content'.[1902]

The ruling did not concern the application of Article 44-2 ICNA because the victim of defamatory statements did not make take-down requests. Nevertheless, the ruling provides additional insight into the Korean approach to intermediary liability.

Finally, the ICNA contains another procedure for removal of content. Article 44-7 empowers the Korea Communication Commission (KCC) to order service providers to reject, suspend, or restrict processing of various types of illegal content, ranging from obscene or defamatory information to information aiding or abetting any crime.[1903] The KCC should provide intermediaries and users with an opportunity to submit their opinion on the matter. The KCC may forego this element of the procedure if 1) it is necessary to make a disposition urgently for public safety and welfare; 2) there is a ground specified by Presidential Decree to believe that it is obviously difficult or evidently unnecessary to hear an opinion; or 3) a person concerned clearly manifests their intent to give up the opportunity to present the opinion (Article 44-7 (4) ICNA). Article 73 (5) supplements the procedure with a penal provision, stating that any person who fails to comply with an order issued by the KCC shall be punished by imprisonment with prison labour for not more than two years or a fine not

1900 Supreme Court en banc Decision 2008Da53812, April 16, 2009.

1901 Translation by K. S. Park, "Intermediary Liability: Not just Backwards but Going Back", *o.c.*

1902 *Ibid.*

1903 For the full list of content see: Article 44-7 (1) Act on Promotion of Information and Communications Network Utilization and Information Protection (ICNA), *o.c.* See also The Center for Internet and Society, World Intermediary Liability Map: South Korea, *o.c.*

exceeding 10 million KRW (Article 73.5 ICNA). The two articles together give the KCC the power to censor almost any information on the Internet.[1904] The KCC is an administrative agency and the procedure described in Article 44-7 ICNA is, therefore, strictly speaking not a NTD mechanism. It is mentioned here to provide a clearer picture of the multiple paths to take down content in South Korea.

F. UNITED KINGDOM

LEGISLATION – In the UK, the issue of removal, blocking or filtering of infringing online content is addressed mainly through private regulation, such as Terms and Conditions of ISPs, their voluntary cooperation with police, copyright owners and other authorities, or partnerships between ISPs and domain name hosts and privately-run industry regulatory bodies, such as the IWF (see *infra*).[1905]

The general liability exemptions for Internet intermediaries are included in the Electronic Commerce Regulations 2002, which transposed the E-Commerce Directive into the UK law.[1906] There is no legislation specifically regulating the removal, blocking or filtering of infringing online content. However, some specific provisions addressing content removal have been included in Acts of Parliament and secondary legislation addressing copyright, defamation and terrorist activities.[1907] Two separate statutory NTD procedures targeting specific types of content exist: offences under the Terrorism Act 2006[1908] and offences under the Defamation Act 2013.[1909]

The Defamation Act 2013 reformed the libel laws (in England and Wales) and complemented the old Defamation Act 1996.[1910] The reform was considered necessary as the previous regulation, which was very claimant friendly and allowed for "libel tourism", gave the High Court of London the

1904 The Center for Internet and Society, World Intermediary Liability Map: South Korea, *o.c.*

1905 Swiss Institute of Comparative Law, Comparative Study on Filtering, blocking and take-down of illegal content on the Internet – United Kingdom country report, *o.c.*, p. 753.

1906 Electronic Commerce (EC Directive) Regulations 2002 (Statutory Instrument 2013/2002), available at www.legislation.gov.uk/uksi/2002/2013/contents/made

1907 Swiss Institute of Comparative Law, Comparative Study on Filtering, blocking and take-down of illegal content on the Internet – United Kingdom country report, *o.c.*, p. 753.

1908 Terrorism Act 2006, available at www.legislation.gov.uk/ukpga/2006/11/contents.

1909 Defamation Act 2013, available at www.legislation.gov.uk/ukpga/2013/26/contents/enacted.

1910 See A. S. Y. Cheung, "Liability of Internet Host Providers in Defamation Actions: From Gatekeepers to Identifiers", *University of Hong Kong Faculty of Law Research Paper No. 2014/013*, p. 28; see also Out-law.com, UK defamation law reforms take effect from start of 2014, 21 November 2013, https://www.theregister.co.uk/2013/11/21/uk_defamation_law_reforms_take_effect_from_start_of_2014/; and M. Harris, Defamation Act 2013: a step in the right direction, https://inforrm.org/2014/01/09/defamation-act-2013-a-step-in-the-right-direction-mike-harris/.

reputation of '*the libel capital of the world*'.[1911] Moreover, communication technologies have advanced to the level that it was questioned whether the legislation could cope with the new environment.[1912] Before the reform, there had been a number of relevant cases, which focused more on the liability of ISP hosts for defamatory third-party content, rather than the obligations to remove the material.[1913] In *Godfrey v Demon Internet Service,* it was found that an ISP could be liable for the content of sites which it hosts.[1914] In *Bunt v Tilley,* Judge Eady J stated that '*there must be knowing involvement in the process of publication of the relevant words*'.[1915] The High Court ruled, therefore, that an ISP which performs no more than a passive role (i.e. no editorial function) in facilitating postings on the internet cannot be considered a publisher at common law.[1916] A similar reasoning was applied in *Metropolitan International Schools Ltd v Designtechnica Corpn*, which concerned defamatory comments that appeared as a "snippet" of information in Google.[1917] Here, a distinction was made between removing offensive content by a search engine and by someone hosting a website. As a result, the Court ruled that Google cannot be held liable on the basis of authorisation, approval or acquiescence.[1918] In *Tamiz v Google Inc*, the Court of Appeal held that Google, could not be regarded as a publisher, but could be held liable for defamatory user-generated content appearing in blogs hosted by Google after being notified of the content's defamatory nature.[1919]

The changes introduced by the Defamation Act 2013, however, have limited the value of the earlier case law.[1920] According to the new Act, courts no longer have jurisdiction to hear and determine defamation actions brought against a person '*who was not the author, editor or publisher of the statement complained of, unless the court is satisfied that it was not reasonably practicable for an action to be brought against the author, editor or publisher*'.[1921] This means that courts may only consider defamation actions against an ISP where it was the direct

---

1911 I. Lloyd, "Cyber Law in the UK, in International Encyclopaedia of Laws", *Kluwer Law International*, The Netherlands, Suppl. 64 (2017), p. 243.

1912 See for example *McAlpine v. Bercow*, [2013] EWHC 1342 (QB), and the commentary by I. Lloyd, "Cyber Law in the UK", *o.c.*, p. 246.

1913 Swiss Institute of Comparative Law, Comparative Study on Filtering, blocking and take-down of illegal content on the Internet – United Kingdom country report, *o.c.*, p. 765.

1914 *Godfrey v Demon* [1999] Entertainment and Media Law Reports 542.

1915 *Bunt v Tilley* [2006] EWHC 407 (QB).

1916 P. Valcke, M. Lenaerts, A. Kuczerawy, "Who's Author, Editor and Publisher in User-Generated Content?", *o.c.*

1917 *Metropolitan International Schools Ltd v Designtechnica Corpn* [2011] 1 WLR 1743.

1918 P. Valcke, M. Lenaerts, A. Kuczerawy, "Who's Author, Editor and Publisher in User-Generated Content?", *o.c.*

1919 *Ibid.*

1920 Swiss Institute of Comparative Law, Comparative Study on Filtering, blocking and take-down of illegal content on the Internet – United Kingdom country report, *o.c.*, p. 765.

1921 See Defamation Act 2013, *o.c.*, section 10.

author, editor or publisher of the allegedly defamatory statement or where it was not possible to sue the actual author, editor or publisher.[1922] Even though there are no other statutory provisions for content removal in criminal or civil law, many hosts remove content upon complaint, regardless of its legitimacy, to avoid any risk of liability.[1923] Such removals are based on the application of Terms and Conditions or Community Guidelines.[1924]

Additionally, in the UK a special arrangement targeted at child abuse content exists. It is administered through a partnership between the ISPs and an industry regulatory body known as the Internet Watch Foundation (IWF).[1925] The IWF is a regulatory body with broad membership from the Internet Industry, including ISPs, mobile operators, search engines, content providers, and filtering companies.[1926] It was founded in 1996 by the Internet industry in cooperation with the Home Office and the police under a direct threat of government regulatory action if the Internet industry did not regulate itself.[1927] The IWF is a registered charity funded by the annual fees of its members[1928] as well as the EU.[1929] The members' fees are calculated based on the industry sector and company size.[1930] According to its website, the IWF was established to fulfil an independent role in receiving, assessing and tracing public complaints about child sexual abuse content on the Internet and to support the development of website rating systems.[1931] The IWF is praised by the government and other regulatory bodies and it is presented as a model for similar initiatives abroad.[1932]

1922 Swiss Institute of Comparative Law, Comparative Study on Filtering, blocking and take-down of illegal content on the Internet – United Kingdom country report, *o.c.*, p. 765.

1923 See for example, E. B. Laidlaw, "The responsibilities of free speech regulators: an analysis of the Internet Watch Foundation", *o.c.*, p. 320.

1924 Swiss Institute of Comparative Law, Comparative Study on Filtering, blocking and take-down of illegal content on the Internet – United Kingdom country report *o.c.*, p. 762.

1925 See Internet Watch Foundation, https://www.iwf.org.uk/. See also Swiss Institute of Comparative Law, Comparative Study on Filtering, blocking and take-down of illegal content on the Internet – United Kingdom country report, *o.c.*, p. 754.

1926 See IWF, https://www.iwf.org.uk/what-we-do/why-we-exist/our-history; and E. B. Laidlaw, "The responsibilities of free speech regulators: an analysis of the Internet Watch Foundation", *o.c.*, p. 315.

1927 E. B. Laidlaw, "The responsibilities of free speech regulators: an analysis of the Internet Watch Foundation, International Journal of Law and Information Technology", *o.c.*, p. 317.

1928 See IWF, https://www.iwf.org.uk/become-a-member/join-us/membership-fee.

1929 10% of the funding comes from the European Union's EU Safer Internet Programme as part of the UK Safer Internet Centre. See https://www.iwf.org.uk/what-we-do/how-we-assess-and-remove-content/eu-co-funding.

1930 See IWF, https://www.iwf.org.uk/become-a-member/join-us/membership-fee.

1931 See IWF, https://www.iwf.org.uk/what-we-do/why-we-exist/our-history.

1932 E. B. Laidlaw, "The responsibilities of free speech regulators: an analysis of the Internet Watch Foundation", *o.c.*, p. 315. See Ofcom, Identifying Appropriate Regulatory Solutions: Principles for Analysing Self- and Co-Regulation, http://stakeholders.ofcom.org.uk/binaries/consultations/coregulation/statement/statement.pdf.

The IWF operates on the basis of a memorandum of understanding between the Association of Chief Police Officers and the Crown Prosecution Service.[1933] Other than that, its operations are not described in any law, but they are defined in their Code of Practice for notice and takedown.[1934] Members of the IWF cannot opt-out of the Code.

The IWF's remit is to remove or block child sexual abuse content. To achieve the goal, the organization works together with industry and government.[1935] Specifically, the IWF operates an anonymous hotline to securely report child sexual abuse imagery and a notice and take down regime for potentially criminal content within its remit. Additionally, the IWF actively searches for child sexual abuse images and videos on the public Internet.[1936] Any reported or found abusive content is manually assessed by trained analysts following legal guidelines.[1937] If the content is hosted in the UK, the IWF sends takedown notices to the hosting providers, as well as to the non-members.[1938] Compliance with the IWF Code of Practice for Notice and Takedown is mandatory for its members and voluntary for non-members.[1939] Finally, the organization maintains a dynamic blacklist of URLs to be filtered and blocked by its members.[1940] However, any Internet service provider that wants to offer services to UK government departments or to be accredited as 'Friendly Wifi'[1941] needs to block access to the blacklisted webpages.[1942] The IWF does not require a specific filtering technology to be used by the members but most of them use the Cleanfeed system.[1943] It is not known what other filtering systems are employed.[1944] The blacklist is not made public so as not to point anyone to the illegal content.[1945] It is made available to national and international law enforcement agencies, and INHOPE hotlines (International Association of Internet Hotlines).[1946]

1933 Memorandum of Understanding Between Crown Prosecution Service (CPS) and the Association of Chief Police Officers (ACPO) concerning Section 46 Sexual Offences Act 2003, *o.c.*

1934 IWF, Code of Practice, https://www.iwf.org.uk/members/member-policies/funding-council/code-of-practice#F1.

1935 E. B. Laidlaw, "The responsibilities of free speech regulators: an analysis of the Internet Watch Foundation", *o.c.*, p. 316.

1936 See IWF, https://www.iwf.org.uk/what-we-do/why-we-exist/our-remit-and-vision.

1937 See IWF, https://www.iwf.org.uk/what-we-do/how-we-assess-and-remove-content/laws-and-assessment-levels.

1938 See IWF, https://www.iwf.org.uk/our-services/takedown-notices.

1939 IWF, Code of Practice, *o.c.*

1940 See IWF, https://www.iwf.org.uk/become-a-member/services-for-members/url-list.

1941 Friendly WiFi is a UK government-initiated safe certification standard for public WiFi. The Friendly WiFi symbol informs the users where the service meets minimum filtering standards – particularly in areas where children are present. See https://www.friendlywifi.com/.

1942 See IWF, https://www.iwf.org.uk/become-a-member/services-for-members/url-list.

1943 E. B. Laidlaw, "The responsibilities of free speech regulators: an analysis of the Internet Watch Foundation", *o.c.*, p. 318.

1944 *Ibid.*

1945 L. Edwards, "From Child Porn to China, in one Cleanfeed", *o.c.*

1946 E. B. Laidlaw, "The responsibilities of free speech regulators: an analysis of the Internet Watch Foundation", *o.c.*, p. 316.

TYPES OF CONTENT – The specific (statutory) rules foreseeing a NTD procedure are aimed at two types of content. First, a procedure exists for content constituting offence under the Terrorism Act 2006, that is, content supportive of terrorism.[1947] Second, in the fairly recent Defamation Act 2013 addressing defamatory content, there are provisions aimed at the operators of websites.[1948] The scheme operated by IWF targets sexual abuse content, specifically for 1) child sexual abuse content hosted anywhere in the world, 2) criminally obscene adult content hosted in the UK, and 3) non-photographic child sexual abuse images hosted in the UK.[1949]

THE PROCEDURE – There are three different procedures that are worthy of attention. As is shown below, none of them actually fits strictly the provided definition of notice and take down, as the notifications to the hosting service providers are issued by State authorities (police or court) or non-State regulatory bodies, as opposed to being issued by the rights holders themselves.

First, there is the NTD procedure for content supportive of terrorism, described in Part 1 Section 3 of the Terrorism Act 2006.[1950] According to these provisions, the police has the power to issue a notice requiring removal from public availability of content (statement, article or record) on the Internet deemed to be encouraging or inciting terrorists. The notice is issued by a constable. The notice should (1) declare that, in the opinion of the constable, the statement or the article or record is unlawfully terrorism-related; (2) require the relevant person to secure that the content (so far as it is so related) is not available to the public or is modified so as no longer to be related to terrorist activity; (3) warn the relevant person that a failure to comply with the notice within 2 working days will result in the content being regarded as having his endorsement; and (4) explain how he may become liable by virtue of the notice if the content becomes available to the public after he has complied with the notice (Part I Section 3 (3) Terrorism Act). If the content is removed after the notification, but is subsequently reposted (repeated statement), the requirements for a valid notice are considered as satisfied through the initial notification (Part I Section 3 (4) Terrorism Act). The requirements, however, are not satisfied with regard to repeated statement, if the person to whom the notice is addressed has taken every step he reasonably could to prevent the statement from becoming available to the public and is not aware of the publication of the repeated statement (Part I Section 3 (5) and (6) Terrorism Act).

1947 Terrorism Act 2006, Part I Section 3, available at www.legislation.gov.uk/ukpga/2006/11/section/3.

1948 Defamation Act 2013, section 13, available at www.legislation.gov.uk/ukpga/2013/26/contents/enacted.

1949 See more: IWF, The laws and assessment levels, https://www.iwf.org.uk/what-we-do/how-we-assess-and-remove-content/laws-and-assessment-levels.

1950 Terrorism Act 2006, Part I Section 3, *o.c.*

In the 2015 report for the Council of Europe, it was reported that 'all removal of unlawful terrorist content is achieved through informal contact between the police and ISPs and that it has never been necessary to use formal powers under the Terrorism Act 2006'.[1951]

Second, there is the NTD procedure for defamatory content, described in Section 13 of the Defamation Act 2013.[1952] According to this provision, where a court has found statements by the author to be defamatory, the court may order the operator of a website on which the defamatory statement is posted to remove the statement (Section 13 (1) Defamation Act). The order can be issued also in cases where the statement was not posted by the operator, and the operator was not a defendant in the action.[1953] In the words of the Act, the order can be issued *'to any person who was not the author, editor or publisher of the defamatory statement to stop distributing, selling or exhibiting material containing the statement'*.[1954]

As regards legal actions for defamation brought against the operator of a website, the Defamation Act 2013 allows a defence where the operator can show that it was not the operator who posted the statement on the website (Section 5 (1) and (2) Defamation Act). The defence can be defeated, however, if the claimant shows that it was not possible for him to identify the person who posted the statement, and where the claimant gave the operator a notice of complaint in relation to the statement, and the operator failed to respond in accordance with any provision contained in regulations (Section 5 (3) Defamation Act). The accompanying secondary legislation, the Defamation (Operators of Websites) Regulations 2013, specifies further details of the procedure. Websites operators have 48 hours to act in response to the order, to be afforded the protection of the statutory provision against any future court action for defamation.[1955] According to the Defamation Act 2013, a notice of complaint should specify 1) the complainant's name, 2) set out the statement concerned and explain why it is defamatory of the complainant, and 3) specify the location of the statement on the website (Section 5 (6) Defamation Act). The Regulations list the additional requirements for the notice of complaint. Such a notice must (1) specify the electronic mail address at which the complainant can be contacted; (2) set out the meaning which the complainant attributes to the statement referred to in the notice, (3) set out the aspects of the statement which the complainant believes

---

1951 Swiss Institute of Comparative Law, Comparative Study on Filtering, blocking and take-down of illegal content on the Internet – United Kingdom country report, *o.c.*, p. 756, in reference to House of Lords question to Government, Response of Lord Taylor of Holbeach, Hansard citation: House of Lords Debate, 23 September 2013, c421, see They Work For You website, www.theyworkforyou.com/wrans/?id=2013-09-23a.421.3.

1952 Defamation Act 2013, *o.c.*

1953 Swiss Institute of Comparative Law, Comparative Study on Filtering, blocking and take-down of illegal content on the Internet – United Kingdom country report, *o.c.*, p. 764.

1954 See Defamation Act 2013, Section 13 (1), *o.c.*

1955 The Defamation (Operators of Websites) Regulations 2013, Regulation 1.

are factually inaccurate or opinions not supported by fact; (4) confirm that the complainant does not have sufficient information about the poster to bring proceedings against that person, and (5) confirm whether the complainant consents to the operator providing the poster with his name and email address.[1956]

The third NTD procedure refers to the special scheme operated by the IWF to combat sexual abuse content. The procedure is not described in any law but rather in the IWF Code of Practice for Notice and Takedown.[1957] The Code defines the takedown procedure by which service providers remove or disable access to potentially illegal online content. It is directed at the service providers who are IWF members, but the IWF can send notices to non-members if they host content in the UK. The difference is that members cannot opt-out of the Code. Anyone can report illegal content on the IWF website anonymously. Following such a report, the IWF assesses the content and decides whether or not to proceed. The IWF is expected to conduct the assessment '*to a rigorous standard, against appropriate legislation and consistent with training received*'.[1958] Notices to the service providers are issued only '*where the IWF believes the material would be capable of sustaining a criminal prosecution if it were to be put before a jury*'.[1959] The IWF issues notices alerting hosting service providers that certain content hosted on their servers in the UK has been assessed as potentially illegal. Upon receipt of a Notice from the IWF, a hosting service provider must act expeditiously to remove or disable access to the notified content, or notify the IWF if the notice appears to be improperly issued, incomplete or not applicable.[1960] Disregarding the notice by the IWF members results in a breach of the Code. The Code also contains an adjudication process for the breaches during which the Chief Executive of the IWF investigates the breach and examines whether the notice was in fact issued incorrectly.[1961]

1956 The Defamation (Operators of Websites) Regulations 2013, Regulation 2.

1957 IWF, Code of Practice, *o.c.*

1958 *Ibid.*, Section 1 – Introduction, *o.c.*

1959 *Ibid.*

1960 *Ibid.*, Section 5 – Member obligation, *o.c.*

1961 The breach is first investigated through an initial inquiry, to inform about *the nature of the suspected breach, the salient facts and any mitigating circumstances*. On the basis of the findings it is decided whether the matter can be fully and satisfactorily resolved without further action. If this is not possible, a full inquiry is initiated and completed within 15 days. The inquiry examines any mitigating actions taken by the member in relation to the breach and reasons why the member did not act on the notice in question. At this point, if the matter is not resolved through an agreement, it can be referred to the relevant law enforcement agency or to another instance of an internal breach investigation (the Breach Sub-Committee). The Breach Sub-Committee may impose sanctions, for example file a report to a law enforcement authority, but their decision may still be appealed. IWF, Code of Practice, Section 8 – Adjudication process, *o.c.*

G. UNITED STATES

LEGISLATION – In the U.S. Section 202 of the Digital Millennium Copyright Act (codified at 17 U.S.C. §512) (hereafter: 'DMCA') provides a NTD procedure.[1962]

TYPES OF CONTENT – The NTD procedure in the DMCA is aimed solely at copyright infringing content.[1963]

THE PROCEDURE – In the DMCA, the procedure for removal of copyright infringing information is described in detail. Section 512(c) DMCA describes the conditions for liability exemption for "information residing on systems or networks at direction of users", which can benefit the providers of hosting services. Section 512(c)(3)(A) lists the elements of a notification, which requires (1) a physical or electronic signature of a person authorized to act on behalf of the owner of an exclusive right that is allegedly infringed; (2) identification of the copyrighted work claimed to have been infringed, or, a list of such works; (3) identification of the material that is claimed to be infringing or to be the subject of infringing activity, and that is to be removed and information reasonably sufficient to permit the service provider to locate the material; (4) information reasonably sufficient to permit the service provider to contact the complaining party, such as an address, telephone number, email address; (5) a statement that the complaining party has a good faith belief that use of the material in the manner complained of is not authorized by the copyright owner, its agent, or the law; (6) a statement that the information in the notification is accurate, and under penalty of perjury, that the complaining party is authorized to act on behalf of the owner of an exclusive right that is allegedly infringed. The same elements are required for a notification to the provider of information location tools (Section 512(d) DMCA).

Upon receiving a notification, the service provider should respond expeditiously to remove, or disable access to the impugned content (Section 512(c)(1)(C) DMCA). The DMCA also defines a procedure for restoring removed or disabled content. First, the service provider should take reasonable steps to promptly notify the content provider that it has removed or disabled access to content (Section 512(g)(2)(A) DMCA). The content provider then has a possibility to file a counter-notification. To be effective, a counter-notification must be a written communication provided to the service provider's designated agent that includes, among others, a statement under penalty of perjury that the subscriber has a good faith belief that the material was removed or disabled as a result of a mistake or misidentification of the material to be removed or disabled

1962 Section 202 of the Digital Millennium Copyright Act (codified at 17 U.S.C. §512), *o.c.*
1963 Section 202 of the Digital Millennium Copyright Act, *o.c.*

(Section 512(g)(3)(C) DMCA). This means that both the notification and counter-notification must contain a statement that it is not misrepresenting the facts. The penalty of perjury, however, refers to different elements of the statement (see more *infra*). Penalties for misrepresentations are further addressed in Section 512(f), although they apply only when the misrepresentation is material and knowing.[1964]

Upon receiving a counter notification, the provider should promptly provide the entity filing the original notification with a copy of the counter notification, and inform them that it will restore the removed material or cease disabling access to it within 10 business days (Section 512(g)(2)(B) DMCA). After that, the provider should replace the removed content not earlier than in 10, but not later than in 14 business days following receipt of the counter notice (Section 512(g)(2)(C) DMCA).[1965] The latter does not apply, however, if the provider first receives notice from the person who submitted the original notification that such person has filed an action seeking a court order to restrain the subscriber from engaging in infringing activity relating to the material on the service provider's system or network (Section 512(g)(2)(C) DMCA).

2. NOTICE AND STAY DOWN

A. FRANCE

LEGISLATION – The French law LCEN does not contain a specific provision which explicitly requires the introduction of a notice and stay down mechanism. The safe harbour for the hosting providers in Article 6-I-2 LCEN has at one point, however, been interpreted by lower courts in a way that led to de-facto introduction of such a mechanism through jurisprudence.[1966]

In 2007, the producer, director and distributor of the film "*Joyeux Noël*" initiated a lawsuit against the video-sharing platform Dailymotion for copyright infringement.[1967] While Dailymotion did qualify as a hosting service provider, the Court stated that the hosting immunity does not provide an exemption from liability, but only a limitation. Dailymotion, which put in place the architecture and technical means enabling illicit activities by its users, was

---

1964 See A. Holland et al., "Online Intermediaries Case Studies Series: Intermediary Liability in the United States", *o.c.*, p. 13.

1965 *Ibid.*

1966 See C. Jasserand, France -YouTube guilty but not liable? some more precisions on the status of hosting providers, stating that 'French Courts have a tendency to impose such an obligation on hosting providers shifting from a notice and take down rule to a notice and stay down rule', *o.c.*

1967 *Christian C., Nord Ouest Production c. Dailymotion, UGC Images*, Tribunal de Grande Instance de Paris, 13 July 2007.

considered ineligible for the safe harbour provision. The Court explained that intermediaries that provide users with means for infringing copyright have a duty to carry out prior control to prevent such behaviour. Since this was not the case, the Court found Dailymotion liable for copyright infringement and ordered it to pay damages. The Court's imposition of a new duty to prior monitoring was criticized but it soon evolved even further.[1968] Later that same year, the TGI of Paris held Google Video liable for copyright infringement for hosting a number of unauthorised copies of the documentary "*Les enfants perdus de Tranquility Bay*" on its website.[1969] Google Video qualified for the hosting safe harbour and disabled access to the infringing copies of the film expeditiously upon notification by the rights holders. Each removal, however, was followed by quick re-postings of the same content. The Court considered that once Google Video had been notified about the infringing copies, it was also under the obligation to implement any means necessary to avoid future dissemination. As a result, Google Video was exonerated from liability for the first instance of the infringement, which was addressed after the notification, but it was held liable for every subsequent re-posting of the same content.[1970] Such an interpretation of the LCEN converted the standard notice and take down provision into a judge-made notice and stay down regime.[1971]

Similar reasoning was applied by French courts on other occasions, sometimes with additional twists. In *YouTube v Omar et Fred,* the Court ruled that rights holders must also play an active role in the stay-down process.[1972] In that particular case, such an involvement required the rights holders to provide a copy of the original content for which protection was claimed as well as the authorisation to create a fingerprint.[1973] Other rulings took a stricter approach and rejected any requirement of rights holder cooperation.[1974] In *TF1 v YouTube,* however, the TGI of Paris did not find YouTube liable for content posted by users in violation of the broadcaster's rights.[1975] The decision was a result of YouTube

---

1968 See N. Jondet, The Silver Lining in Dailymotion's Copyright Cloud, Juriscom.net, 19 April 2008, p. 7–12.

1969 *SARL Zadig Productions, Jean-Robert Viallet et Mathieu Verboud c. Sté Google Inc. et AFA,* Tribunal de Grande Instance de Paris, 19 October 2007.

1970 See F. J. Cabrera Blázquez, "User-Generated Content Services and Copyright", *IRIS plus, Legal Observations of the European Audiovisual Observatory,* Issue 2008–5, p. 5.

1971 C. Angelopoulos, *European intermediary liability in copyright: A tort-based analysis, o.c.,* p. 125.

1972 *ADAMI, Omar S., Fred T. et a. c/ Sté YouTube,* Tribunal de Grande Instance de Paris, 22 September 2009.

1973 *Ibid.*

1974 P. Sirinelli, "Chronique de Jurisprudence – Mise à la disposition illicite d'oeuvres par l'intermédiaire des réseaux numériques", *Revue Internationale du Droit d'Auteur,* (2011) 228, p. 287, as referenced by C. Angelopoulos, *European intermediary liability in copyright: A tort-based analysis, o.c.,* p. 126.

1975 *S.A. Télévision Française 1 (TF1) c. Société YouTube LLC,* Tribunal de Grande Instance de Paris, 29 May 2012.

offering its 'Content ID' filtering system, which allows the identification of protected content to prevent future re-postings. The Court considered that by providing such means, YouTube ensured the real protection of the content and therefore fulfilled its obligations stemming from LCEN.[1976]

In 2011 the Paris Court of Appeal confirmed the notice and stay down approach in four judgements handed down on the same day.[1977] In each of the judgements, the Court held Google Video liable for copyright infringements by its users. In the previous instance, the *Tribunal de Commerce* had recognized Google's eligibility for the safe harbour protection but had issued an injunctive order for Google to refrain from future reproduction or communication to the public of the films in question, as well as from referencing any link allowing them to be viewed or downloaded.[1978] In the appeal, the Court ruled that the hosting service provider should not limit itself to the removal of the notified content, but also implement every possible technical measure to prevent future access to the disputed content through its search engine.[1979] In the Court's opinion, when the protected status of the video is notified to the provider, each new upload by the same or different users does not require a separate notification.[1980] Interestingly, at that time the CJEU was deliberating on the *SABAM v. Netlog* case[1981], but the French Court refused to delay the proceedings.

Finally, the *Cour de cassation* followed the line set by the CJEU in the two *Sabam* judgements and ended the stay-down regime. In three judgements issued in 2012, the Court declared that the stay-down obligation cannot be fulfilled by online providers without conducting general monitoring of content.[1982] The stay-down obligation would force Google to '*seek out illicit uploads*', and implement a '*blocking mechanism with no limitation in time*'. Such a result would be disproportionate to the pursued aim, therefore, Google should have benefited from the safe harbour provision in LCEN. Moreover, copyright holders must monitor the websites themselves and notify intermediaries of each new

---

1976 See C. Jasserand, France -YouTube guilty but not liable? some more precisions on the status of hosting providers, *o.c.*

1977 *Google Inc. c. Compagnie des phares et balises*, Cour d'appel de Paris, 14 January 2011; *Google Inc. c. Bac Films, The Factory*, Cour d'appel de Paris, 14 January 2011; *Google Inc. c. Bac Films, The Factory*, Cour d'appel de Paris, 14 January 2011; *Google Inc. c. Les Films de la Croisade, Goatworks Films*, Cour d'appel de Paris, 14 January 2011.

1978 C. Angelopoulos, *European intermediary liability in copyright: A tort-based analysis*, *o.c.*, p. 126.

1979 See C. Jasserand, Recent decisions of the Paris Court of Appeal: towards an extra duty of surveillance for hosting providers? *o.c.*

1980 The Court repeated this reasoning in *Google France et Google Inc., Auféminin.com v. H&K SARL, André Rau*, Cour d'appel, 4 February 2011.

1981 CJEU, *Belgische Vereniging van Auteurs, Componisten en Uitgevers CVBA (SABAM) v. Netlog NV*, Case C 360/10, 16 February 2012.

1982 *La société Google France c. la société Bach films (L'affaire Clearstream)* (11–13.669), Cour de cassation, 12 July 2012; *La société Google France c. La société Bac films (Les dissimulateurs)* (11–13666), Cour de cassation, 12 July 2012; *La société Google France c. André Rau* (Auféminin) (11–15.165; 11–15.188) Cour de cassation, 12 July 2012.

infringement linked to the same material. To remove or block re-uploaded content, a new notification is necessary to establish actual knowledge, without which no action can be taken.[1983] These decisions brought an end to the judge-made notice and stay down mechanism in France.[1984]

TYPES OF CONTENT – The stay-down regime in France was never codified and emerged only from an expansive interpretation of the hosting provider immunity in LCEN by the French courts. The aforementioned case-law indicates that the regime was mainly targeted at copyright infringing content.

THE PROCEDURE – The procedure of the judge-made notice and stay down mechanism was essentially the same as the notice and take down mechanism provided by LCEN. The main difference was that in order to benefit from the immunity, the hosting service providers had to hunt out every remaining or reposted unauthorised copy of the impugned content.[1985] As interpreted by the French courts, the obligation applied even if the content was re-posted by a different user. In order to do that efficiently the providers would have to use some form of automatic filtering technology, for example fingerprinting.[1986] Such techniques operate by screening all content that passes through the servers in order to detect any reposting of notified content. The French courts considered such monitoring not general but 'targeted and temporary', and as such, permitted by Article 6-I-7 para. 2 LCEN. The *Cour de cassation* finally admitted that the obligation is impossible to realize without conducting general monitoring.[1987]

B. GERMANY

LEGISLATION – Until recently, no specific legislation existed in Germany about blocking, filtering or taking down of content. Instead, Germany relied on the implementation of the E-Commerce Directive – the *Telemediengesetz* (TMG)[1988] and general rules of law in the areas of copyright, trademark and unfair

---

1983 C. Coslin, C. Gateau, No 'Stay Down' Obligation for Hosting Providers in France, https://www.scl.org/articles/2844-no-stay-down-obligation-for-hosting-providers-in-france.

1984 See C. Jasserand, France: The Court of Cassation puts an end to the Notice and Stay Down Rule, 14 August 2012, http://copyrightblog.kluweriplaw.com/2012/08/14/france-the-court-of-cassation-puts-an-end-to-the-notice-and-stay-down-rule/.

1985 C. Angelopoulos, *European intermediary liability in copyright: A tort-based analysis*, *o.c.*, p. 125.

1986 C. Angelopoulos, "Filtering the Internet for Copyrighted Content in Europe", *o.c.*, p. 2, 4, 9. See also F. J. Cabrera Blázquez, "User-Generated Content Services and Copyright", *o.c.*, p. 7.

1987 *La société Google France* c. *la société Bach films (L'affaire Clearstream)* (11–13.669), Cour de cassation, 12 July 2012; *La société Google France c. La société Bac films (Les dissimulateurs)* (11–13666), Cour de cassation, 12 July 2012; *La société Google France c. André Rau* (Auféminin) (11–15.165; 11–15.188) Cour de cassation, 12 July 2012.

1988 *Telemediengesetz*, 26 February 2007, BGBl. I S. 179.

competition, which allow granting general injunctive relief.[1989] In 2017, the new law to help combat fake news and hate speech on social media was introduced. Additionally, German courts created a special notion of "disturbance liability" (*Störerhaftung*) which is applied in the online context to hold the hosting providers liable for third party illegal content.[1990]

The *Störerhaftung* doctrine is applied in Germany to deal with intermediary contribution to infringements by others.[1991] The doctrine allows the issuance of cease and desist orders not only to the immediate wrongdoer and any participant in the wrongdoing but also the "disturbers" (*Störer*).[1992] Such disturbers are the parties that deliberately, adequately and causally contribute to an infringement by others. "Deliberately" refers to an intention to perform the action which creates or maintains the infringement, rather than an intention to contribute to an infringement.[1993] This is because good faith on behalf of the disturber is not relevant.[1994] The disturber must, however, have either the legal or the factual possibility to terminate the infringement by a third party.[1995]

Störerhaftung is a form of strict liability that is limited to injunctive relief.[1996] It is a tool to extend liability to third parties who have not themselves committed an infringement, but who are in a position to provide relief.[1997] It is not possible

1989 Swiss Institute of Comparative Law, Comparative Study on Filtering, blocking and take-down of illegal content on the Internet – Germany country report *o.c.*, p. 261.

1990 *Ibid.*

1991 See more in C. Busch, "Secondary Liability for Open Wireless Networks in Germany: Balancing Regulation and Innovation in the Digital Economy", in G. B. Dinwoodie, *Secondary Liability of Internet Service Providers*, Ius Comparatum – Global Studies in Comparative Law, Springer, 2018, p. 363.

1992 *Störerhaftung* originates from the jurisprudence. In Germany injunctive relief is not explicitly provided by the tort provisions of the *Bürgerliches Gesetzbuch* (BGB), yet it has been made available by analogy to the law of property. The theory of *Störerhaftung* was therefore developed through case law in the area of unfair competition law, as well as for the protection of absolute rights, i.e. rights which are enforceable against everyone, including copyright, trademark and patent law. *Störerhaftung* finds its roots outside tort liability in the property defence claims laid out in Articles 862 and 1004 BGB of Book 3 of the BGB, which enable injunctive relief essentially against cases of nuisance. See C. Angelopoulos, *European intermediary liability in copyright: A tort-based analysis*, *o.c.*, p. 150; CJEU, Opinion of Advocate General Jääskinen, case C-324/09, *L'Oréal v eBay International*, 9 December 2010, para. 56. See also J. Bornkamm, "E-Commerce Directive vs. IP Rights Enforcement – Legal Balance Achieved?" *o.c*; T. Hoeren, "German Law on Internet Liability of Intermediaries", *o.c.*

1993 J. Becher, "Copyright and User-Generated Content: Legal Challenges for Community-Based Businesses in Germany and the USA", Master's Thesis, Bucerius Law School/WHU Otto Beisheim School of Management 2010.

1994 BGH, *Constanze II*, 6 July 1954, I ZR 38/532.

1995 See T. Hoeren, "German Law on Internet Liability of Intermediaries", *o.c.*, p. 3. See also, K.-N. Peifer, "Platform Economy and Liability Questions – Desperately in Search of Concepts Lost in the Virtual World or "Störerhaftung" Resurrected?", IIC (2017) 48, p. 625.

1996 J. B. Nordemann, YouTube is a hosting provider, but one with extensive duties of care, say two German Courts, 6 November 2015, http://copyrightblog.kluweriplaw.com/2015/11/06/youtube-is-a-hosting-provider-but-one-with-extensive-duties-of-care-say-two-german-courts/.

1997 See T. Hoeren, "German Law on Internet Liability of Intermediaries", *o.c.*, p. 3.

to claim for damages against a defendant unless they were acting in fault.[1998] Breach of an injunction, however, constitutes contempt of court resulting in a disciplinary fine.[1999]

To hold the disturber liable, the disturbing circumstances must be readily apparent. Liability shall be imposed, however, if the disturber ignored their duty to review (*Prüfungspflicht*).[2000] The disturber's duty to review is a relatively recent addition to the doctrine of *Störerhaftung*. It was introduced as a restriction to the scope of application of *Störerhaftung*[2001], which had been criticized as an "almost limitless" overexpansion of disturber liability.[2002] In *Paperboy*, the Court ruled that there is no room for *Störerhaftung*, if the risk of unlawful conduct is not qualitatively altered by the alleged disturber's behaviour.[2003] Similarly, in *Schöner Wetten* the Court held that the scope of the duty to review should be assessed in light of the overall context of the disturber's actions, such as their knowledge of circumstances that indicate unlawful activity and the possibilities to reasonably recognise the unlawfulness of the act.[2004]

The duty to review is examined in each case to establish whether it is reasonable.[2005] One of the criteria for reasonability is that the duty cannot compromise the business model of the alleged disturber.[2006] For example, in what is referred to as *Internetversteigerung* trademark trilogy[2007], the German Federal Supreme Court (*Bundesgerichtshof* – BGH) concluded that an online auction platform does not have to examine each and every listing for a trademark infringement before allowing its publication, as such an obligation would put the site's entire business model at risk.[2008] Business models, however, even if legitimate, do not enjoy absolute protection. Occasionally, the BGH has demanded that service providers amend their business model to counter infringing third party conduct.[2009]

[1998] A. Wandtke, *Urheberrecht*, De Gruyter Recht 2009, 286–290 as referenced by C. Angelopoulos, *European intermediary liability in copyright: A tort-based analysis*, *o.c.*, p. 149.

[1999] G. Spindler, "Country Report – Germany" for "Study on the Liability of Internet Intermediaries", *o.c.*

[2000] BGH, *Architektenwettbewerb*, 10 October 1997, I ZR 129/96.

[2001] G. Spindler and M. Leistner, "Secondary Copyright Infringement – New Perspectives from Germany and Europe", *International Review of Intellectual Property and Competition Law* (IIC), (2006) 37(7), p. 788.

[2002] J. Wimmers, "Who Interferes? Liability for Third Party Content on the Internet in Germany", *o.c.*, p. 32.

[2003] BGH, *Paperboy*, 17 July 2003, I ZR 259/00.

[2004] BGH, *Schöner Wetten*, 1 April 2004, I ZR 317/01.

[2005] T. Hoeren, "German Law on Internet Liability of Intermediaries", *o.c.*, p. 3.

[2006] See M. Husovec, BGH on Liability of Rapidshare, 13 July 2012, www.husovec.eu/2012/07/bgh-on-liability-of-rapidshare.html.

[2007] BGH, *Internetversteigerung I*, 11 March 2004, I ZR 304/01; BGH, *Internetversteigerung II*, 19 April 2007, I ZR 35/04; BGH, *Internetversteigerung III*, 30 April 2008, I ZR 73/05.

[2008] See T. Hoeren, "German Law on Internet Liability of Intermediaries", *o.c.*, p. 8, 31.

[2009] J. B. Nordemann, "Liability for Copyright Infringements on the Internet: Host Providers (Content Providers) – The German Approach", *o.c.*, p. 37.

In *Internetversteigerung I,* the Court ruled that after receiving a proper notification leading to his knowledge, the operator of online marketplace has a duty to take down the specific infringing content but also to prevent further similar violations.[2010] It further explained that specific monitoring obligations as a reaction to notification were acceptable, as long as they were technically feasible. As a result, the duty to review was recognized as an obligation, triggered by a clear notice, to check whether the infringement has taken place elsewhere ("inquiry notice").[2011] The ruling established that the duty to monitor and take down any future infringements exists continuously from the moment of receipt of notification.[2012]

Interestingly, the duty to review does not apply only to identical copies of the content, or to copies uploaded by the same users.[2013] To the contrary, the duty extends to all following infringing acts of a similar nature that are easily recognisable.[2014] In short, the infringements must be '*similar in their core*' (the "*Kerntheorie*").[2015] According to Angelopoulos, the doctrine essentially achieves the same, or even a slightly broader effect, as the French judge-made "notice and stay down" regime.[2016]

The lasting effect of the obligation to monitor content was confirmed in the so-called *Rapidshare* saga.[2017] Rapidshare was a Swiss-based online hosting service for the storage of copyright-infringing files uploaded by users. The site took down the infringing content promptly upon receiving notices, but contested the duty to prevent future infringements.[2018]

First, the Düsseldorf Court ruled that Rapidshare had no obligation to take proactive manual action to supervise the content exchanged by users or to install automatic filters against unlawful content.[2019] The Court specifically cited the risk of over-blocking to justify its opinion. Moreover,

2010 BGH, *Internetversteigerung I (Rolex),* 11 March 2004, I ZR 304/01. In *Internetversteigerung II the court* confirmed the applicability of the previous findings under *Telemediengesetz.*

2011 A. Dietz, "Germany" in L Bently, P Geller & M Nimmer, *International Copyright Law and Practice,* Matthew Bender/LexisNexis, 2013, §8[1][c][i].

2012 *Ibid.*

2013 J Bornkamm, "E-Commerce Directive vs. IP Rights Enforcement – Legal Balance Achieved?", *o.c.*

2014 See *Ibid.*

2015 M. Leistner, "Störerhaftung und mittelbare Schutzrechtsverletzung", GRUR-Beil 1, 2010, as referenced by C. Angelopoulos, *European intermediary liability in copyright: A tort-based analysis, o.c.*, p. 154.

2016 C. Angelopoulos, *European intermediary liability in copyright: A tort-based analysis, o.c.*, p. 154.

2017 OLG Düsseldorf, *Rapidshare I,* 27 April 2010, I-20 U 166/09; OLG Hamburg, *Rapidshare II,* 14 March 2012, 5 U 87/09; OLG Düsseldorf, *Rapidshare III,* 21 December 2010, I-20 U 59/10; BGH, *Rapidshare I,* 12 July 2012, I ZR 18/11; BGH, *Rapidshare III,* 15 August 2013, I ZR 80/12.

2018 L. Essers, German, French Courts Disagree on Responsibility of ISPs for Illegal Content, 16 July 2012, https://www.pcworld.com/article/259294/germany_french_courts_disagree_on_responsibility_of_isps_for_illegal_content.html.

2019 OLG Düsseldorf, *Rapidshare I,* 27 April 2010, I-20 U 166/09.

the preventive measures, such as notice and take-down, taken by Rapidshare to avoid infringement, were considered reasonable and adequate. The same Court confirmed in *Atari v Rapidshare (Alone in the Dark)*[2020] that a duty to automatically filter content posted by its users would be "arbitrary" because keywords are not compelling evidence of an infringement.[2021] The Court highlighted that Rapidshare was used for legal purposes, and its business model did not depend on infringements, even though some users had committed them.[2022] In the next stage of the case, the BGH Court found Rapidshare to be a "disturber" (*Störer*).[2023] As a result, Rapidshare did not have an obligation to conduct proactive monitoring but could be held liable if it ignored a reasonable duty to review (*Prüfungspflicht*). The duty was in place from the moment Rapidshare was informed about an infringement through a notification. Once the notification was filed, the provider was expected to conduct searches for future infringements and take all reasonable measures to ensure users could not proceed with future infringement, providing that these measures did not threaten Rapidshare's business model.[2024]

In the meantime, the Hamburg Court, faced a similar case. In *Rapidshare II*[2025], the Hamburg Court concluded that mere removal of links after notification by rights holders was not sufficient and that Rapidshare was also obliged to actively monitor for any notified content to identify and delete future links to the infringing content. As an argument, the Court stated that many users associate the service with illegal content as Rapidshare had previously offered financial rewards for uploading popular files.[2026]

In *Rapidshare III (GEMA v Rapidshare,* also known as *The Reader)*[2027], the BGH agreed that Rapidshare's business model deserved protection. Nevertheless, the Court considered Rapidshare to have provided incentives to third parties to illegally share copyrighted content.[2028] For example, Rapidshare's revenues were

2020 OLG Düsseldorf, *Rapidshare III,* 21 December 2010, I-20 U 59/10.

2021 C. Angelopoulos, *European intermediary liability in copyright: A tort-based analysis, o.c.*, p. 156.

2022 See T. Engelhardt, German Federal Supreme Court on file hoster responsibility for third party content – "Rapidshare", 13 July 2012, http://germanitlaw.com/german-federal-supreme-court-on-file-hoster-responsibility-for-third-party-content-rapidshare/; see also M. Horten, File-hosting liability: are German courts alone in the dark?, 28 September 2012, www.iptegrity.com/index.php/internet-trials/793-file-hosting-liability-are-german-courts-alone-in-the-dark.

2023 BGH, *Rapidshare I,* 12 July 2012, I ZR 18/11.

2024 See M. Husovec, BGH on Liability of Rapidshare, *o.c.*

2025 OLG Hamburg, *Rapidshare II,* 14 March 2012, 5 U 87/09.

2026 The same argument also appeared in *Sharehoster II, see* OLG Hamburg, *Sharehoster II,* 30 September 2009, 5 U 111/08.

2027 BGH, *Rapidshare III,* 15 August 2013, I ZR 80/12.

2028 A. Harguth, File hosting in Germany carries increased copyright policing duties, 31 October 2013, https://www.lexology.com/library/detail.aspx?g=ef2396cc-39e8-493b-a893-bec38f9ef368.

generated through premium accounts which enhance massive data downloads.[2029] Moreover, the service could be used anonymously, which apparently encouraged illegal activities.[2030] Rapidshare, therefore, was obliged to take preventive measures (that could be technically and commercially expected), in addition to expeditious removal. Such preventive measures constitute *'a duty of care to be expected of [the website] according to reasonable judgement and set down in national legal regulations in order to discover and prevent specific types of illegal activity'*.[2031]

This approach has since been followed by the local courts. For example in *GEMA v YouTube*, the local Hamburg Court concluded that YouTube was under an obligation to undertake automated filtering by its ContentID software to identify any future infringement of previously notified content.[2032] Since ContentID would only spot identical videos, YouTube was also obliged to use a word-based filter to examine the title and the artist of the video.[2033]

TYPES OF CONTENT – The disturber liability in Germany involves the duty to review (monitor) content to prevent future infringements. The approach was developed through jurisprudence of the German courts by analogy to the regulation on infringements of corporeal property (§1004 German Civil Code).[2034] It is based on responsibility for nuisance, and not on responsibility for unlawful acts.[2035] The disturbance liability is generally used for private law issues, as the main element of the approach is that someone's property (also intellectual) is being disturbed. Most of the cases, therefore, deal with unfair competition disputes, as well as copyright, and trademark law.[2036]

In the area of unfair competition and protection of minors, disturber liability was used, for example, in *Jugendgefährdende Medien bei eBay*.[2037] In this case the BGH considered that the scope of the duty to review depends on the importance of the protected right (in this case protection of minors from content glorifying violence and Nazi-type propaganda) and the possibilities of the intermediary to acquire knowledge. Moreover, an intermediary might be required to prevent

2029 *Ibid.*
2030 *Ibid.*
2031 Translation from Case comment, "The Federal Supreme Court (Bundesgerichtshof): 'Rapidshare III'" (2014) International Review of Intellectual Property and Competition Law (IIC) 716, as referenced by C. Angelopoulos, *European intermediary liability in copyright: A tort-based analysis*, *o.c.*, p. 158.
2032 LG Hamburg, 20 April 2012, 310 O 461/10.
2033 See B. Clark, GEMA vs YouTube – what the Hamburg court really said…, 21 April 2012, http://ipkitten.blogspot.be/2012/04/gema-vs-youtube-what-hamburg-court.html.
2034 J. B. Nordemann, "Liability for Copyright Infringements on the Internet: Host Providers (Content Providers) – The German Approach", *o.c.*, p. 39.
2035 Swiss Institute of Comparative Law, Comparative Study on Filtering, blocking and take-down of illegal content on the Internet – Germany country report, *o.c.*, p. 266.
2036 See M. Leistner, "Structural aspects of secondary (provider) liability in Europe", *o.c.*, p. 82.
2037 BGH, *Jugendgefährdende Medien bei eBay*, 12 July 2007, I ZR 18/04.

other violations from the same user (repeated offenders).[2038] The disturber liability was also found in cases involving defamation and libel law, for example *Katzenfreund*.[2039] The most common application of the disturber liability, however, is for copyright and trademark disputes.[2040]

THE PROCEDURE – The German version of the notice and stay down is not described in any legal provision but instead comes from the courts' interpretation of the liability exemption for hosting providers. For this reason, the procedure cannot be found in any legislation and has to be extracted from the case-law.

The obligation to review content does not only refer to the same infringing content.[2041] The duty applies to all easily recognisable future infringements that are similar in their core. This means that after receiving a notification, the host provider is expected to block and remove obvious re-postings without waiting for a new notification.[2042] Obvious (or clear) infringements are considered to be of the same type in case it constitutes[2043]:

1) the same work and the same copy (in another file) or another but equally infringing copy[2044];
2) other works of the same category, provided they originate from the same perpetrator ("repeat offenders") and do not require a new legal assessment[2045];

2038 See J. B. Nordemann, "Liability for Copyright Infringements on the Internet: Host Providers (Content Providers) – The German Approach", *o.c.*, p. 42. See also The Center for Internet and Society, World Intermediary Liability Map: Germany, http://cyberlaw.stanford.edu/page/wilmap-germany.

2039 BGH, *Katzenfreund*, July 23, 2007, VI ZR 101/06. See The Center for Internet and Society, World Intermediary Liability Map: Germany, *o.c.*

2040 See the examples above such as the *Rapidshare* saga: OLG Düsseldorf, *Rapidshare I*, 27 April 2010, I-20 U 166/09; OLG Hamburg, *Rapidshare II*, 14 March 2012, 5 U 87/09; OLG Düsseldorf, *Rapidshare III*, 21 December 2010, I-20 U 59/10; BGH, *Rapidshare I*, 12 July 2012, I ZR 18/11; BGH, *Rapidshare III*, 15 August 2013, I ZR 80/12. For copyright, the disturber liability approach is complemented by Article 97(1) of the German copyright act (Gesetz über Urheberrecht und verwandte Schutzrechte – UrhG), which provides that: 'Any person who infringes copyright or any other right protected under this Act may be required by the injured party to eliminate the infringement or, where there is a risk of repeated infringement, may be required by the injured party to cease and desist. Entitlement to prohibit the infringer from future infringement shall also exist where the risk of infringement exists for the first time.' Translation from the official English text provided by the *Bundesministerium der Justiz und für Verbraucherschutz*, available at: www.gesetze-im-internet.de/englisch_urhg/englisch_urhg.html.

2041 J. B. Nordemann, "Liability for Copyright Infringements on the Internet: Host Providers (Content Providers) – The German Approach", *o.c.*, p. 43.

2042 A. Bayer, "Liability 2.0 – Does the Internet Environment Require New Standards for Secondary Liability? An Overview of the Current Legal Situation in Germany" in M. J. Adelmann *et al.*, *Patents and Technological Progress in a Globalized World*, Springer 2009, p. 365.

2043 J. B. Nordemann, "Liability for Copyright Infringements on the Internet: Host Providers (Content Providers) – The German Approach", *o.c.*, p. 42–43.

2044 See BGH, *Internetversteigerung II*, 19 April 2007, I ZR 35/04.

2045 See BGH, *Jugendgefährdende Medien bei eBay*, 12 July 2007, I ZR 18/04.

3) other works of other categories which were not contained in the original notification and do not originate with the initial infringer, if the hosting service is especially susceptible to infringements and the hosting provider is aware of that fact.[2046]

Unclear infringements are those which require expert legal advice to recognize them.[2047] So far it is not certain if a duty to review arises where the provider is notified of unclear infringements.[2048]

The host is required to take action only if the notice he received was specific and enabled him to identify the infringement without excessive difficulty.[2049] The Court seems to accept a certain degree of subsidiarity. *Blog-Eintrag* provided some clues with regard to the chain of events:

> 'As a rule, the affected person's objection is first to be communicated to the person responsible for the blog for comment. If a comment is not provided within a reasonable deadline in the circumstances, it is to be assumed that the objection is justified and the contested entry is to be deleted. If the person responsible for the blog denies, with substantiation, that the objection is justified, and if as a result there are legitimate doubts, the provider is as a matter of principle required to notify such to the party affected and if appropriate request evidence that shows the alleged infringement of the rights. If the person affected fails to comment or fails to submit any evidence required, there is no occasion for any further investigation'.[2050]

Moreover, the disturber is also subject to a secondary burden of proof.[2051] Despite his position as a defendant, the disturber is the only one with relevant knowledge of its technical infrastructure to state which measures are possible and which cannot reasonably be expected.[2052] If a defendant has taken all reasonable measures to prevent infringements, for example the prior examination process (e.g. automatic filtering) which did not identify the infringement, he cannot be held liable as no fault can be attributed to his actions.[2053]

2046 See OLG Hamburg, *Long Island Ice Tea*, 4 February 2009, 5 U 180/07; and OLG Zweibrücken, 14 May 2009, 4 U 139/08.

2047 J. B. Nordemann, "Liability for Copyright Infringements on the Internet: Host Providers (Content Providers) – The German Approach", *o.c.*, p. 43.

2048 *Ibid.* p. 37; J. B. Nordemann, "Intellectual Property Liability of Consumers, Facilitators and Intermediaries: the Position in Germany" in A. Kamperman Sanders & C. Heath, *Intellectual Property Liability of Consumers, Facilitators and Intermediaries*, Kluwer Law International, 2012, p. 37.

2049 BGH, *Blog-Eintrag*, 25 October 2011, I ZR 93/10.

2050 Translation from case comment, "Federal Supreme Court, 25 October 2011 – Case No. VI ZR 93/10: GERMANY – 'Blog Entry'*" (2012) 8 International Review of Intellectual Property and Competition Law (IIC) 982. See also: BGH, *Stiftparfüm*, 17 August 2011, I ZR 57/09.

2051 J. B. Nordemann, "Liability for Copyright Infringements on the Internet: Host Providers (Content Providers) – The German Approach *o.c.*, p. 40.

2052 *Ibid.*

2053 BGH, *Internetversteigerung I*, 11 March 2004, I ZR 304/01.

3. NOTICE AND NOTICE

A. CANADA

LEGISLATION – The Canadian intermediary liability regime has been shaped strongly by case law. The backbone of the regime can be found in *SOCAN v CAIP*, also called the "Tariff 22" case.[2054] In 1995, the Society of Composers, Authors and Music Publishers of Canada (SOCAN) applied to the Copyright Board of Canada for the approval of a new royalty ("Tariff 22") that would cover a broad range of copyrighted music transmitted over the Internet. SOCAN claimed that all parties involved in the transmission of music online, including Internet service providers, should be paying an appropriate royalty. The Supreme Court of Canada interpreted Section 2.4(1)(b) of the 1985 Copyright Act[2055] known as the "Common Carrier Exemption" to deny claimants royalties for copyrighted material transferred over the Internet.[2056] According to the ruling, ISPs are not liable as long as they are content neutral and act as "conduit" for information. If this is the case, they are considered not to have communicated the content at all.[2057] Under this interpretation intermediaries are also immune from defamation liability.[2058]

The Canadian notice and notice mechanism is a relatively new development.[2059] It was introduced in the Copyright Modernization Act SC 2012 (CMA), but the final provisions only took effect in January 2015.[2060] Section 31.1 of the CMA is actually a codification of the holding in *SOCAN v CAIP*, which requires neutrality as a condition for immunity.[2061] Section 41.25 of the CMA enacts the notice and notice procedure while the following sections specify the details related to notice. Interestingly, notice and notice has been effectively in place between ISPs and the music and cable industry since 2000 as a voluntary standard adopted to deal with copyright infringement.[2062]

2054 Supreme Court of Canada, Society of Composers, Authors and Music Publishers of Canada (SOCAN) v Canadian Assn. of Internet Providers (CAIP), 2004 SCC 45, June 30, 2004. See: http://scc-csc.lexum.com/scccsc/scc-csc/en/item/2159/index.do.

2055 Copyright Act, (R.S.C., 1985, c. C-42), http://laws-lois.justice.gc.ca/eng/acts/C-42/index.html.

2056 J. Panday *et al.*, Comparative Study Of Intermediary Liability Regimes Chile, Canada, India, South Korea, UK and USA in support of the Manila Principles On Intermediary Liability, *o.c.*, p. 26.

2057 Supreme Court of Canada, Society of Composers, Authors and Music Publishers of Canada (SOCAN) v Canadian Assn. of Internet Providers (CAIP), 2004 SCC 45, June 30, 2004, para. 111.

2058 *Ibid.*, para. 89.

2059 For the summary of the regime before the CMA see D. Seng, Comparative Analysis of National Approaches of the Liability of the Internet Intermediaries – Part I, WIPO, 2010, www.wipo.int/publications/en/details.jsp?id=4144&plang=EN.

2060 Copyright Modernization Act (S.C. 2012, c. 20), http://laws-lois.justice.gc.ca/eng/annualstatutes/2012_20/page-1.html.

2061 See J. Panday *et al.*, Comparative Study Of Intermediary Liability Regimes Chile, Canada, India, South Korea, UK and USA in support of the Manila Principles On Intermediary Liability, *o.c.*, p. 26.

2062 *Ibid.*, p. 27.

TYPES OF CONTENT – The notice and notice mechanism in Canada applies to copyright infringing content and activities, as defined in the Copyright Modernization Act of 2012.

THE PROCEDURE – The notice and notice procedure provides that a copyright owner may send a notice of claimed infringement to ISPs, including hosting service providers and information location tools (but in case of the latter the only remedy is injunction) (Article 41.25 CMA). A notice should be in writing in the form prescribed by regulation and should contain the following elements: (1) the claimant's name and address and any other particulars prescribed by regulation; (2) identification of the work or other subject-matter to which the claimed infringement relates; (3) the claimant's interest or right to the work; (4) the location of the data; (5) the infringement that is claimed; (6) the date and time of the commission of the claimed infringement; and (7) any other information that may be prescribed by regulation (Article 41.25(2) CMA). The ISP must forward the notice electronically, as soon as possible, and inform the claimant of the forwarding (Article 41.26(1) CMA). Other than the forwarding, the intermediary is not obliged to take down the content brought to its attention.[2063] Instead, the spotlight is shifted to the primary wrongdoer, who must choose whether to remove the content themselves or respond to the notification within a limited period of time.[2064] If the forwarding was not possible, the ISP has to inform the claimant of the reason why. Moreover, the ISP has to retain records that will allow evidence of the infringement to be presented in court and uncover the infringer's identity. The retain period is six months, or one year, if the claimant commences proceedings in court (Article 41.26(1) CMA). Proceedings for disclosure of subscriber information are known as "Norwich orders".[2065] The CMA provides that the costs of fulfilling the obligations of disclosure can be billed to rights holders for reimbursement (Article 41.26(2) CMA).[2066] The provision of the CMA was recently clarified by the Federal Court of Appeal in *Voltage Pictures, LLC v Joe Doe #1*.[2067] The Court stated that ISPs are expected to retain and verify subscriber information without payment of any fees.[2068] The ISPs may only charge their costs for disclosing this information. However, according to the Court,

---

2063 C. Angelopoulos, S. Smet, "Notice-and-fair-balance: how to reach a compromise between fundamental rights in European intermediary liability", *o.c.*, p. 295.

2064 *Ibid.*

2065 B. Sookman, Norwich orders: who pays under the notice and notice regime? Voltage v Doe, 10 May 2017, www.barrysookman.com/2017/05/10/who-pays-for-recording-and-verifying-subscriber-info-under-the-notice-and-notice-regime-voltage-v-doe/.

2066 See also F. Martin-Bariteau, "Internet Intermediaries Liability A North American Perspective /or/ Perspectives from the United States and Canada", in C. A. Pereira de Souza, M. Viola, R. Lemos (eds.), *Understanding Brazil's Internet Bill of Rights*, Rio de Janeiro: ITS Rio, 2015, p. 63.

2067 Federal Court of Appeal, *Voltage Pictures, LLC v Joe Doe* #1 2017 FCA 97, 9 May 2017.

2068 B. Sookman, Norwich orders: who pays under the notice and notice regime? *o.c.*

'[t]he actual, reasonable and necessary costs of delivery or electronic transmission of the records by the internet service provider are likely to be negligible. Similarly, the costs associated with a motion for a disclosure order are likely to be minimal.'[2069]

Failure to comply with the specified obligations by the ISP will not result in falling outside Section 31.1's safe harbour, but could lead to a fine by the court for a minimum amount of $5,000 and not more than $10,000 in statutory damages.[2070]

B. CHILE

LEGISLATION – In Chile, a regime limiting liability of intermediary service providers for copyright infringements of their users is provided in Law No. 20.435, amending Intellectual Property Law enacted on 4 May 2010 (Ley de Propiedad Intelectual, hereafter 'LPI').[2071] The regime was introduced following the entry into force of the Chile-US Free Trade Agreement (FTA).[2072]

TYPES OF CONTENT – The scope of the Law No. 20.435 LPI is limited to copyright infringements.[2073] The regime comes predominantly from the Intellectual Property Chapter of the Chile-US FTA.[2074] For this reason, the regime strongly follows the DMCA model, with one notable exception.[2075]

THE PROCEDURE – The main feature of the regime in Chile is that the decisions regarding content and content providers are taken by the courts. Service providers must comply with court injunctions, adopted before or during a judicial procedure.[2076] They can neither take down content nor disconnect a user on their own initiative or at rights holders' request.[2077]

2069 Federal Court of Appeal, *Voltage Pictures, LLC v Joe Doe* #1 2017 FCA 97, 9 May 2017, paras. 63 and 64.

2070 Article 41.26(3) of the Copyright Modernization Act (S.C. 2012, c. 20). See also F. Martin-Bariteau, "Internet Intermediaries Liability A North American Perspective /or/ Perspectives from the United States and Canada", *o.c.*, p. 63.

2071 Ley no. 20.435, modifica la Ley no. 17.336 sobre propiedad intelectual, https://www.leychile.cl/Navegar?idNorma=1012827&idParte=&idVersion=2010-05-04.

2072 Chile-USA Free Trade Agreement (FTA), 1 January 2004, https://ustr.gov/trade-agreements/free-trade-agreements/chile-fta/final-text.

2073 See more on the Law 20.435 in D. Alvarez Valenzuela, "The Quest for a Normative Balance: The Recent Reforms to Chile's Copyright Law", *o.c.*

2074 Chapter 17 of the Chile-USA FTA, *o.c.*

2075 J. Panday et al., Comparative Study Of Intermediary Liability Regimes Chile, Canada, India, South Korea, UK and USA in support of the Manila Principles On Intermediary Liability, *o.c.*, p. 29.

2076 A. Cerda Silva, Cyber Law in Chile, in International Encyclopaedia of Laws, *o.c.*, p. 126.

2077 *Ibid.*

Common obligations for all of the service providers[2078] to benefit from the liability exemption include, among others, a requirement that they '*adopt general and public conditions under which it may terminate contracts with content providers who have been found guilty of repeat copyright infringements*'.[2079]

Liability exemption for the providers of the hosting services requires that the provider (a) does not have actual knowledge of the illegality, (b) does not receive any economic benefit directly attributable to the infringing activity, (c) designates a representative for receiving notice of court orders, and (d) removes or expeditiously disables access to the stored material after receiving a court order (Article 85 Ñ, LPI).[2080]

Every service provider has a basic and general obligation to communicate to its users any received notice about alleged copyright infringement (Article 85 U, LPI). The original notice must comply with the following conditions: (1) it must be issued by the copyright holder or its representative and received electronically or in another written form; (2) the copyright holder or its representative must have a domicile or residency in Chile; (3) the notice must indicate the rights allegedly infringed, its owner, and the way infringement took place; (4) the notice must identify the infringing material and its location by URL or equivalent manner; and (5) the notice must contain sufficient data to identify the alleged infringing user (Article 85 U, LPI).[2081] If the notice fulfils these requirements, the service provider must communicate it to the concerned user, within five working days. Moreover, the service provider must attach the records provided by the copyright holder with the notice.[2082] At the request of the right holder, a court can order the Internet service provider to deliver the information necessary to identify the infringer (Article 85 S, LPI). This requirement refers only to the providers of the hosting services.[2083] The LPI does not specify to whom the Internet service provider must deliver the data allowing identification of the infringer. According to Cerda Silva, it should be provided to the court, which would permit the judge to evaluate whether or not to release the data to the copyright holder.[2084]

In order to actually remove an infringement, a copyright holder or its representative must request the court to order the taking down of infringing content and the disconnection of alleged infringers (Article 85 Q, LPI). A court could order these measures either during trial or prior to trial, as a preliminary

2078 The law distinguishes four categories of service providers: a) providers of transmission data, routing and connection, b) providers of temporal storage of data, c) providers of hosting services, and d) providers of search, linking ore referencing services.

2079 Article 85 O, LPI.

2080 See A. Cerda Silva, Cyber Law in Chile, in International Encyclopaedia of Laws *o.c.*, p. 128.

2081 See *Ibid.*, p. 129.

2082 *Ibid.*

2083 See *Ibid.*, p. 129 and 130.

2084 *Ibid.*, p. 130.

measure (Article 85 Q, LPI). In the latter case, if there are serious reasons justifying it, it can be ruled without presence of the content provider (Article 85 Q, LPI). The request must (1) identify the plaintiff and the defendant; (2) indicate the allegedly infringed rights, their owner, and the way the infraction took place; and (3) point out the infringing material and its location (Article 85 Q, LPI).[2085] If those conditions are satisfied, the court must issue an order for taking down or blocking the infringing content and notify the service provider (Article 85 Q, LPI). The affected content provider can request the court to nullify the decision, without prejudice to other rights.[2086] The request of the content provider must comply with the same basic conditions as the original request and should attach any supporting evidence (Article 85 Q, LPI). Submission of such a counter-request implies accepting the court's jurisdiction for resolving the case, which will be processed expeditiously (Article 85 Q, LPI).[2087]

In cases concerning the providers of hosting services, a court can only order removing or disabling access to the infringing content and terminating the accounts of the repeated offenders clearly identified as those who have committed copyright infringement.[2088] The law also contains a provision which aims to prevent false notifications. Anyone who knowingly provides false information about an alleged copyright infringement must compensate for (actual) damages any affected person for harms resulting from the Internet service providers' actions adopted because of that information (Article 85 T, LPI).[2089] The provision also includes a reference to the Criminal Code which sanctions an abuse of procedures with imprisonment of up to five years and monetary fines.[2090]

The detailed procedure provided by the LPI is, however, rarely used.[2091] In practice, copyright holders rely heavily on private notices sent in advance to alleged infringers, who usually take down content voluntarily.[2092] There have been several cases in Chile, but they concerned defamatory content posted online rather than copyright infringement. Generally, the Chilean courts are of the opinion that only the provider of defamatory content may be held liable.[2093] In 2012 in *Abbott v. Google*, the plaintiff sought an injunction and relief against a number of Chilean websites as well as Google, claiming that the websites, along with blogs hosted by Google, were making defamatory statement

2085 See *Ibid.*

2086 *Ibid.*, p. 131.

2087 See *Ibid.*, p. 130.

2088 *Ibid.*, p. 131.

2089 *Ibid.*, p. 133.

2090 Criminal Code, Art. 197. See A. Cerda Silva, Cyber Law in Chile, in International Encyclopaedia of Laws, *o.c.*, p. 134.

2091 See The Center for Internet and Society, World Intermediary Liability Map: Chile, *o.c.*

2092 A. Cerda Silva, Cyber Law in Chile, in International Encyclopaedia of Laws, *o.c.*, p. 134.

2093 See Court of Appeals of Concepción, *Fuentes vs Entel I*, Causa Rol No 243-99, 6 December 1999 and Court of Appeals of Concepción, *Fuentes vs Entel II*, Causa Rol No 1223-2003, 21 December 2007.

about him.[2094] The Court agreed and ordered the websites to remove the offensive content. In addition, the Court ordered Google to establish a filtering mechanism that automatically prevents the publication of "unequivocally" slanderous content.[2095]

C. FRANCE

LEGISLATION – Apart from the LCEN, France has adopted a separate law to combat copyright infringements online: Law No. 2009–669 of June 12, 2009, Promoting The Dissemination and Protection Of Creative Works on The Internet (HADOPI law).[2096] The law created a new administrative authority – HADOPI (*Haute Autorité pour la Diffusion des Oeuvres et la Protection des Droits sur Internet*), in charge of enforcing copyright protection. Novel in its approach, the law introduced a policy of "graduated response", also known as "three strikes and you're out".[2097] The graduated response is described as "*"notice and notice" with the "stick"*" and is aimed at Internet access providers (ISPs).[2098] The approach requires that after a specified number of warnings ("strikes") have been administered by the HADOPI agency, ISPs must apply certain sanctions to punish repeated misconducts by their users.[2099]

TYPES OF CONTENT – The law has been introduced specifically to promote dissemination and protection of creative works on the Internet. Its scope is limited to copyright infringements online as well as breaches of users' "duty of surveillance".[2100] The latter refers to the end-users' obligation to secure their Internet connection and monitor its use to prevent copyright infringements, laid down in the French Code of Intellectual Property.[2101] The law provides injunctive measures against any person likely to remedy the situation.[2102]

2094 Court of Appeals of Valparaíso, *Abbott v. Google*, Causa no 228/2012. Resolución no 50461, 30 July 2012. See The Center for Internet and Society, World Intermediary Liability Map: Chile, *o.c.*; and Abogado Pablo, Sentencia, responsabilidad de los administradores de las páginas webs, 9 September 2013, www.derecho-chile.cl/sentencia-responsabilidad-de-los-administradores-de-las-paginas-webs/.

2095 The Center for Internet and Society, World Intermediary Liability Map: Chile, *o.c.*

2096 Loi n° 2009–669 du 12 juin 2009 favorisant la diffusion et la protection de la création sur internet, www.wipo.int/wipolex/en/text.jsp?file_id=179252.

2097 L. Edwards, Report to World Intellectual Property Organisation (WIPO) on The Role and Responsibilities of Online Intermediaries in the Field of Copyright and Related Works, *o.c.*, p. 30.

2098 *Ibid.*

2099 See *Ibid.*

2100 C. Angelopoulos, *European intermediary liability in copyright: A tort-based analysis*, *o.c.*, p. 148.

2101 N. van Eijk, C. Jasserand, C. Wiersma and T. M. van Engers, "Moving towards Balance: A Study into Duties of Care on the Internet", *o.c.*, p. 26 and 112.

2102 The Center for Internet and Society, World Intermediary Liability Map: France, *o.c.*

THE PROCEDURE – The law created a new government agency (HADOPI) and empowered it to receive complaints from copyright holders.[2103] The agency would forward them to French ISPs who are obligated to assist the agency and the courts in handling copyright infringement, as well as breaches of users' duty of surveillance. Moreover, Internet service providers must propose to their subscribers efficient technical measures suitable to secure the Internet connection (listed by the HADOPI authority) and provide information about the possible sanctions in case of non-compliance.[2104] Under Article L.331–25 of the *Code de la propriété intellectuelle* (CPI), the HADOPI agency can request access providers to send warning emails to subscribers who do not comply with their duty of surveillance.[2105]

The procedure consists of two preliminary operations and one final repressive action which involves fines and potential suspension of Internet access.[2106] First warning is sent via email to the subscriber of the ISP, after having been identified as the source of the alleged infringement. The warning informs the subscriber of the alleged infringement and reminds them of the obligation to secure their Internet connection. The warning must inform the subscriber about his right to request further clarification regarding the charges and provide an overview of the possible penalties (Articles L. 335–7 and L. 335–7–1 of the HADOPI law).[2107] A second warning is sent if, within six months after the first one, the same subscriber is identified as a source of another infringement. The second email is accompanied by a certified acknowledgment of receipt (or other means to prove the actual receipt) and contains similar information to the first one. The subscriber can respond to the second warning within 15 days and provide a justification of the repeated misconduct.[2108] The third step is initiated if, within one year of the second warning, the same subscriber is again identified as a source of infringement. The HADOPI agency can start a procedure which can lead to a fine and also a temporary suspension of the Internet connection. The latter form of penalty comes with prohibition to subscribe to any other ISP for a period of the punishment, which can range from three months to one year.[2109] The access provider must cooperate and terminate the subscriber's Internet access or risk a fine.[2110] In the last phase, the subscriber can challenge the decision in front of a judge, by demonstrating that they were not responsible for the alleged infringement and that they took the necessary measures to secure the Internet connection. The subscriber, alternatively, can admit to committing the infringing act, which allows them to negotiate for a reduced suspension period.

2103 Loi n° 2009-669 du 12 juin 2009, *o.c.*

2104 N. van Eijk, C. Jasserand, C. Wiersma and T. M. van Engers, "Moving towards Balance: A Study into Duties of Care on the Internet", *o.c.*, p. 27.

2105 C. Angelopoulos, *European intermediary liability in copyright: A tort-based analysis*, *o.c.*, p. 148.

2106 P. de Filippi and D. Bourcier, "Three-Strikes Response to Copyright Infringement: The Case of HADOPI", *o.c.*, p. 134.

2107 *Ibid.*

2108 *Ibid.*, p. 134.

2109 *Ibid.*

2110 See N. van Eijk, C. Jasserand, C. Wiersma and T. M. van Engers, "Moving towards Balance: A Study into Duties of Care on the Internet", *o.c.*, p. 27.

At first, suspending access to the Internet was to be ordered directly by the HADOPI agency. Such an approach was quickly challenged on the grounds of its constitutionality. On 10 June 2009, the *Conseil Constitutionnel* rejected such a possibility (see more *infra*).[2111] Even though disconnection was declared possible, such a decision required a judicial procedure and therefore could not be taken by an administrative body.[2112] As a consequence, the law had to be supplemented with a new "HADOPI 2" Act[2113], according to which an actual suspension of the Internet connection could only be ruled by the criminal court.[2114]

On 19 October 2011, the *Conseil d'Etat* rejected the applications against the two HADOPI Acts accusing them of violating the right to a fair trial under Article 6 of the ECHR.[2115] The *Conseil d'Etat* argued that the measures foreseen by the procedure did not play a role of sanctions, but were merely intended to inform users of their legal obligations.[2116] In July 2013, the French Ministry of Culture issued a decree lifting the penalty of Internet access suspension for those who failed to secure their access to the network.[2117] Supposedly, the graduated response approach had failed to confer the estimated benefit.[2118] It was decided that in future, only fines may be issued for Internet users in fault of gross negligence in securing their Internet connection. Internet suspension, however, may still be imposed on anyone found guilty of an actual infringement.[2119] It should be mentioned that since the introduction of the HADOPI law in 2009 its effectiveness is rather moderate. By 2013, only one individual has been convicted for a copyright infringement and sentenced for suspension of the Internet access for 15 days and a fine of 600 euros.[2120] In the same year, the penalty of suspension was abolished.[2121] By 2017, the law led to 189 criminal convictions.[2122]

2111 Conseil Constitutionnel, Décision n° 2009-580 DC du 10 juin 2009, Journal officiel du 13 juin 2009, page 9675, texte n° 3. As referenced by C. Angelopoulos, *European intermediary liability in copyright: A tort-based analysis*, *o.c.*, p. 148.

2112 See P. de Filippi and D. Bourcier, "Three-Strikes Response to Copyright Infringement: The Case of HADOPI", *o.c.*, p. 135.

2113 *Loi n° 2009-1311 du 28 octobre 2009,* HADOPI 2, *o.c.*

2114 See P. de Filippi and D. Bourcier, "Three-Strikes Response to Copyright Infringement: The Case of HADOPI", *o.c.*, p. 141.

2115 Conseil d'Etat, *Société Apple Inc et Société I-Tunes Sarl*, 19 October 2011, n° 339154 and *French Data Network*, 19 October, 2011, n°339279 and n° 342405.

2116 See C. Angelopoulos, *European intermediary liability in copyright: A tort-based analysis*, *o.c.*, p. 148.

2117 *Décret n° 2013-596 du 8 juillet 2013, o.c.* The decree also followed the recommendations of the Lescure report, see more: P. Lescure, "Mission 'Acte II de l'exception culturelle' – Contribution aux politiques culturelles à l'ère numérique", May 2013.

2118 See C. Angelopoulos, *European intermediary liability in copyright: A tort-based analysis*, *o.c.*, p. 148.

2119 *Ibid.*

2120 See S. Columbus, France to disconnect first Internet users under three strikes regime, *o.c.*

2121 HADOPI, Rapport d' activité 2016-2017, https://www.hadopi.fr/sites/default/rapportannuel/HADOPI-Rapport-d-activite-2016-2017.pdf, p. 34, ft. 28.

2122 Seven Years of Hadopi: Nine Million Piracy Warnings, 189 Convictions, 1 December 2017, https://torrentfreak.com/seven-years-of-hadopi-nine-million-piracy-warnings-189-convictions-171201/.

D. SOUTH KOREA

LEGISLATION – South Korea presents a complex liability regime with a "vertical" approach to the problem, depending on the type of infringement.[2123] A graduated response is provided by the South Korean Copyright Act.[2124] The Copyright Act was amended in 2009 in order to introduce the graduated response, which was one of the requirements for entering into the US-Korea Free Trade Agreement.[2125] Since then the Act has been amended in 2016 and 2017 but the graduated response has not been eliminated (despite an intense campaign and a proposal by Mr. Jae-Cheon Choi and other members of the Korean National Assembly in 2013).[2126]

TYPES OF CONTENT – In 2009, South Korea introduced the graduated response (three strikes) in Articles 133-2 and 133-3 of the Copyright Act. The mechanism functions in addition to the NTD procedures for copyright and other types of infringing content.[2127]

THE PROCEDURE – Article 133-2 of the Copyright Act states that the Minister of Culture, Sports and Tourism (MCST) may order service providers to issue warnings to infringers or to websites hosting infringing content ('*reproducers and interactive transmitters*') ordering them to cease transmission or to delete infringing material.[2128] If the infringement continues despite three warnings, the Minister (after consultation with the Deliberation Committee) may order the service provider to suspend an account of the infringer or a website for up to six months (Article 133-2(2) of the Copyright Act). The suspension does not include e-mail accounts but includes other accounts given by the relevant online service provider (Article 133-2(2) of the Copyright Act). There is also a similar possibility to suspend online bulletin boards (Article 133-2(4) of the Copyright Act). The service provider who received such an order should notify

---

2123 See Annex 1E.

2124 Copyright Act, Amended by Act No. 9625, Apr. 22, 2009; Act No. 10807, Jun. 30, 2011; Act No. 11110, 2 Dec. 2011, Act No. 14083, Mar. 22, 2016, Act No. 14634, Mar. 21, 2017, http://elaw.klri.re.kr/kor_service/lawView.do?hseq=42726&lang=ENG.

2125 C. Doctorow, South Korea's US-led copyright policy leads to 65,000 acts of extrajudicial censorship/ disconnection/ threats by govt bureaucrats, *o.c.*

2126 See Copyright Reform – Abolishing Three-Strikes-Out Rule from Copyright Law, https://opennet.or.kr/copyright-reform; Bill to Amend the Copyright Act (Bill No. 3349), https://opennet.or.kr/copyright-reform/bill-to-amend-copyright-act; J. Y. Kim, South Korean Politician Moves to Repeal Biased Copyright Law, 28 March 2013, https://advox.globalvoices.org/2013/03/28/south-korean-politician-moves-to-repeal-biased-copyright-law/.

2127 See Annex 1.E.

2128 Article 133-2 (Orders, etc. for Deletion of Illegal Reproductions, etc. through Information and Communications Network) of the Copyright Act, http://elaw.klri.re.kr/kor_service/lawView.do?hseq=42726&lang=ENG. See also OECD, The Role of Internet Intermediaries in Advancing Public Policy Objectives – Forging partnerships for advancing policy objectives for the Internet economy, *o.c.*, p. 63.

the affected party seven days before the suspension takes effect (Article 133-2(3) of the Copyright Act). The online service provider shall notify the MCST of the result of the measures taken within a specified period of time (different for each action) from the receipt date of orders (Article 133-2(6) of the Copyright Act). The service provider, the infringer, and the host provider (who each have a direct stake in the orders) can have an opportunity to present their opinion in advance of fulfilling the order (Article 133-2(7) of the Copyright Act). Failure to comply with an MCST order by an OSP can lead to a fine of up to KRW 10 million.[2129] The MCST stopped issuing all types of orders in 2012.[2130]

The Copyright Act foresees another path to achieve the same result. According to Article 133-3, the procedure can be initiated by the Korea Copyright Protection Agency (KCPA) as a result of an investigation by the KCPA.[2131] The KCPA does not have the power to issue binding orders but it can recommend the same corrective measures as the MCST. Specifically, the KCPA can recommend that Online Service Providers (OSPs) issue warnings, delete material, stop transmission of material or suspend accounts (Article 133-3(1) of the Copyright Act). The OSPs must notify the KCPA about the actions taken in response to an issued recommendation within ten days (Article 133-3(3) of the Copyright Act). They are not required to implement the KCPA's recommendations, in such a case, however, the Agency may request the MCST to issue a binding order (Article 133-3(3) of the Copyright Act). The KCC has been far more active than the MCST in terms of its recommendations, and unlike MCST, it did not stop issuing recommendations in 2012.[2132]

4. FULL IMMUNITY

A. UNITED STATES

LEGISLATION – Full immunity in the US law is provided in Section 230(c) of the Communications Decency Act (CDA).[2133] Section 230 was initially a part of a greater law (addressing the transmission of offensive and obscene content to minors), which was struck down by the Supreme Court for its overbroad limitations on protected speech.[2134]

2129 Centre for Law and Democracy, Analysis of the Korean Copyright Act, *o.c.*, p. 5.
2130 *Ibid.*; and Copyright Reform – https://opennet.or.kr/copyright-reform.
2131 In the former version of the Copyright Act the function was entrusted to the Korean Copyright Commission (KCC). See old version of the document (Act No. 11110, Dec. 2, 2011), Article 133-3 of the Copyright Act, http://elaw.klri.re.kr/kor_service/lawView.do?hseq=25455&lang=ENG.
2132 Centre for Law and Democracy, Analysis of the Korean Copyright Act, *o.c.*, p. 5.
2133 47 U.S. Code §230 – Protection for private blocking and screening of offensive material.
2134 See *Reno v. ACLU*, 521 U.S. 844 (1997). See also P. Ehrlich, "Communications Decency Act 230", *o.c.*, p. 401. See more on Section 230 CDA in Part I Chapter 4.3.

TYPES OF CONTENT – Section 230 CDA addresses claims of defamation, invasion of privacy, tortious interference, civil liability for criminal law violations, and general negligence claims based on third-party content.[2135] It expressly excludes federal criminal law, intellectual property law (addressed in the DMCA), and the federal Electronic Communications Privacy Act or any state analogues.[2136]

NO PROCEDURE – Section 230 provides that Internet intermediaries ("interactive computer services") are not liable for the infringing or illegal content by third parties. They are not obliged to remove this type of content, even upon obtaining knowledge about the illegality. There is, therefore, no procedure for removal of content in Section 230 CDA. The law, nevertheless, is submitted to the same analysis under the positive assessment framework as the other mechanisms to examine whether and how such legislative approach satisfies the developed criteria.

2135 D. Ardia, "Free Speech Savior or Shield for Scoundrels: an Empirical Study of Intermediary Immunity Under Section 230 of the Communications Decency Act", *o.c.*, p. 452.

2136 47 U.S.C §230(e)(1)–(4).

BIBLIOGRAPHY

BOOKS AND THESES

Akandji-Kombe J.-F., Human rights handbooks, No. 7. *Positive Obligations under the European Convention on Human Rights. A guide to the implementation of the European Convention of Human Rights*, Council of Europe, 2007.

Angelopoulos C., *European intermediary liability in copyright: A tort-based analysis*, Doctoral book, University of Amsterdam, 2016.

Bailey S., Jones B. and Mowbray A.R., *Cases and Materials on Administrative Law*, 3rd edn., London, Sweet & Maxwell, 1997.

Barak A., *Proportionality. Constitutional Rights and their Limitations*, Cambridge Univerity Press, 2012.

Barendt E., *Freedom of speech*, Oxford University Press, 2005.

Benkler Y., *The Wealth of Networks: How Social Production Transforms Markets and Freedom*, Yale University Press, 2006.

Christoffersen J., *Fair Balance: Proportionality, Subsidiarity and Primarity in the European Convention on Human Rights*, 2009.

Clayton R., Tomlinson H., *Fair Trial Rights*, 2nd Edition, Oxford University Press, 2010.

Council of Europe, *Freedom of expression in Europe: case-law concerning article 10 of the European Convention on Human Rights*, Strasbourg, Council of Europe Publishing, 2007.

Dicey V., & Wade E. C. S., *Introduction to the study of the law of the constitution*, 10e ed., London: Macmillan, 1985.

Dinwoodie G. B. (ed.), *Secondary Liability of Internet Service Providers*, Ius Comparatum - Global Studies in Comparative Law, Springer, 2018.

Feldman D., *Civil Liberties and Human Rights in England and Wales*, 2nd edition, Oxford, OUP, 2002.

Garner B. A. (ed.), *Black's Law Dictionary*, Third Pocket Edition, 2001

Horten M., *The Copyright Enforcement Enigma - Internet Politics and the 'Telecoms Package'*, Palgrave Macmillan, 2011.

Husovec M., *Injunctions Against Intermediaries in the European Union - Accountable But Not Liable?*, Cambridge University Press 2017.

Kreiken F., *Large-scale copyright enforcement and human rights safeguards in online markets*, Doctoral book, TU Delft, 2017.

Laidlaw E. B., *Internet Gatekeepers, Human Rights and Corporate Social Responsibilities*, Doctoral book, London School of Economics and Political Science, 2012.

Leanza P., Pridal O., *The right to a fair trial: Article 6 of the European Convention on Human Rights*, Alphen aan den Rijn: Kluwer law international, 2014.

Lievens E., *Protecting Children in the Digital Era – the Use of Alternative Regulatory Instruments*, Martinus Nijhoff Publishers, International Studies in Human Rights, Leiden, 2010.

Luhmann N., *Law as a social system*, Translated by Ziegert K. A., *Oxford Socio-Legal Studies*, Oxford University Press, 2009.

Macnamara J., *The 21st Century Media (r)evolution: Emergent Communication Practices*, Peter Lang Publishing, 2010.

Macovei M., *Freedom of expression – A guide to the implementation of Article 10 of the European Convention of Human Rights*, Human rights handbooks, No. 2, Strasbourg, Council of Europe, 2004.

McGonagle T., *Freedom of expression and defamation: A study of the case law of the European Court of Human Rights*, Council of Europe Publishing, 2016.

Merrills G., *The Development of International Law by the European Court of Human Rights*, Manchester, MUP, 1993.

Meyer P., *The Vanishing Newspaper*, Columbia: University of Missouri Press, 2004.

Mole N. and Harby C., *The right to a fair trial: a guide to the implementation of Article 6 of the European Convention on Human Rights* (Human rights handbooks, No. 3), Strasbourg, Council of Europe, 2006.

Mowbray A.R., *The Development of Positive Obligations under the European Convention on Human Rights by the European Court of Human Rights*, Hart Publishing, Oxford – Portland Oregon, 2004.

Mowbray A.R., *Cases & Materials on the European Convention on Human Rights, London*, Butterworths, 2001.

Nowak J. E., R. D. Rotunda, *Principles of Constitutional Law*, 4th Edition, Concise Hornbooks, 2010.

Ovey C., R. White, Jacobs and White, *The European Convention on Human Rights*, Oxford, Oxford University Press, 2006.

Pariser E., *The Filter Bubble: How the New Personalized Web Is Changing What We Read and How We Think*, Penguin Books, 2012.

Park R. E., *The Immigrant Press and Its Control*, Harper & Brothers, New York, 1922.

Rawls J., *A theory of Justice*, Cambridge, Massachusetts: The Belknap Press of Harvard University Press, 1999.

Riordan J., *The Liability of Internet Intermediaries*, Oxford University Press, 2016.

Shapiro A. L., *The Control Revolution: How the Internet is Putting Individuals in Charge and Changing the World We Know*, PublicAffairs, 2000.

Shoemaker P., Vos T., *Gatekeeping Theory*, Routledge, 2009.

Smet S., *Resolving Conflicts between Human Rights: a legal theoretical analysis in the context of the ECHR*, Ghent University, 2013–2014.

Sottiaux S., *Terrorism and the Limitations of Rights. The European Convention on Human Rights and the United States Constitution*, Hart Publ., Oxford – Portland, Oregon, 2007.

Stone G. R. et al., *Constitutional Law*, 5th Edition, Aspen Publishers, 2005.

Tamanaha B. Z., *On the Rule of Law*, Cambridge University Press, 2004.

Thibaut J., Walker L., *Procedural Justice: A Psychological Analysis*, 1975.

Tridimas T., *The General Principles of EU Law*, 2nd ed., Oxford EC Law Library, 2007.

Tusikov N., *Chokepoints – Global Private Regulation on the Internet*, University of California Press, November 2016.

Tyler T. R., *Why People Obey the Law*, Princeton University Press, 2006.
van Dijk P., van Hoof F., van Rijn A., Zwaak L. (eds), *Theory and practice of the European Convention on Human Rights*, Antwerpen, Intersentia, 2006.
van Drooghenbroeck S., *La proportionnalité dans le droit de la Convention européenne des droits de l'homme: prendre l'idée simple au sérieux*, [Proportionality in the Law of the European Convention on Human Rights], Publications Fac St Louis 2001.
van Hoboken J., *Search Engine Freedom: On the Implications of the Right to Freedom of Expression for the Legal Governance of Web Search Engines*, Kluwer Law International, 2012.
Van Malleghem P. A., *Proportionality and the Erosion of Formalism*, Doctoral book, KU Leuven, 2016.
Vitkauskas D., Dikov G., *Protecting the right to a fair trial under the European Convention on Human Rights*, Council of Europe human rights handbooks, Council of Europe Strasbourg, 2012.
Voorhoof D. et al and McGonagle T. (Ed. Sup.), *Freedom of Expression, the Media and Journalists: Case-law of the European Court of Human Rights*, IRIS Themes, Vol. III, 4th edition, European Audiovisual Observatory, Strasbourg, 2017.
Voorhoof D., *Critical perspectives on the scope and interpretation of Article 10 of the European Convention on Human Rights (Mass media files No. 10)*, Strasbourg, Council of Europe Press, 1995.
Wakefield A., J. Fleming, *SAGE Dictionary of Policing*, SAGE Publications Ltd., 2009.
Wandtke A., *Urheberrecht*, De Gruyter Recht 2009.

ARTICLES, BOOK CHAPTERS AND EDITED WORKS

Ahlert C., Marsden C. and Yung C., "How Liberty Disappeared from Cyberspace: the Mystery Shopper Tests Internet Content Self-Regulation" http://pcmlp.socleg.ox.ac.uk/wp-content/uploads/2014/12/liberty.pdf.
Alvarez Valenzuela D., "The Quest for a Normative Balance: The Recent Reforms to Chile's Copyright Law", POLICY BRIEF 12. December 2011, https://www.ictsd.org/sites/default/files/research/2012/03/the-quest-for-a-normative-balance-the-recent-reforms-to-chilee28099s-copyright-law.pdf.
Andreescu M., "Principle of Proportionality, Criterion of Legitimacy in the Public Law", *Challenges of the Knowledge Society*, Vol.1, April 2011, pp.524–530.
Angelopoulos C., "Filtering for Copyrighted Content in Europe", *IRIS plus* Vol. 4, 2009.
Angelopoulos C., Smet S., "Notice-and-fair-balance: how to reach a compromise between fundamental rights in European intermediary liability", *Journal of Media Law*, Vol. 8, Issue 2, 2016, pp. 266–301.
Ardia D., "Free Speech Savior or Shield for Scoundrels: an Empirical Study of Intermediary Immunity
Under Section 230 of the Communications Decency Act", *Loyola of Los Angeles Law Review*, Vol. 43, No. 2, 2010, pp. 373 – 506.
Arnold M. A., et al., "Graduated Response Policy and the Behavior of Digital Pirates: Evidence from the French Three-Strike (Hadopi) Law", 2014. Available at: https://ssrn.com/abstract=2380522 or http://dx.doi.org/10.2139/ssrn.2380522.

Balkin J. M., "Media Access: A Question of Design", *George Washington Law Review*, Vol. 76, No. 4, 2008, pp. 101–118, p. 114–116.

Balkin J. M., "Old School/New School Speech Regulation", *Harvard Law Review*, Vol 127, 20 June 2014.

Bambauer D. E., "Orwell's Armchair", *University of Chicago Law Review*, Vol. 79, 2012, p. 863.

Barceló R. J., "Liability for on-line intermediaries: a European perspective", *European Intellectual Property Review*, Vol. 20, 1998.

Barceló R. J., "On-line intermediary liability issues: comparing EU and US legal frameworks", E.I.P.R. 2000.

Barceló R. J. and Koelman K., "Intermediary Liability In The E-Commerce Directive: So Far So Good, But It's Not Enough", *Computer Law & Security Report* 2000, vol. 4, pp. 231–239.

Barzilai-Nahon K., "Toward a Theory of Network Gatekeeping: A Framework for Exploring Information Control", *Journal of the American Society for Information Science and Technology*, Vol. 59, Issue 9, 2008, pp.1493–1512.

Bayer A., "Liability 2.0 – Does the Internet Environment Require New Standards for Secondary Liability? An Overview of the Current Legal Situation in Germany" in M. J. Adelmann *et al., Patents and Technological Progress in a Globalized World*, Springer 2009.

Becher J., "Copyright and User-Generated Content: Legal Challenges for Community-Based Businesses in Germany and the USA", Master's Book, Bucerius Law School/ WHU Otto Beisheim School of Management 2010.

Belli L. and Sappa C., "The Intermediary Conundrum: Cyber-Regulators, Cyber-Police or Both?", *JIPITEC* Vol. 8, 2017.

Benkler Y., "A Free Irresponsible Press: Wikileaks and the Battle over the Soul of the Networked Fourth Estate", *Harvard Civil Rights-Civil Liberties Law Review*, Vol. 46, 2011.

Birnhack M. D., Elkin-Koren N., "The invisible handshake: the re-emergence of the state in the digital environment", *Virginia Journal of Law and Technology, Vol. 8, Summer* 2003.

Black J., "Decentring Regulation: Understanding the Role of Regulation and Self-Regulation in a 'Post-Regulatory' World", *Current Legal Problems*, Vol. 54, Issue 1, January 2001, pp. 103–146.

Blackstock J., "The EU Charter of Fundamental Rights: scope and competence", *Justice Journal*, 2012, pp. 19–31.

Bornkamm J., "E-Commerce Directive vs. IP Rights Enforcement – Legal Balance Achieved?", *GRUR Int*, 2007.

Bridy A., Keller D., "U.S. Copyright Office Section 512 Study: Comments in Response to Notice of Inquiry", 31 March 2016.

Breed W., "Social control in the newsroom: A functional analysis", *Social Forces* Vol.33, Issue 4, May 1955, pp. 326–335.

Brems E., Lavrysen L., "Procedural Justice in Human Rights Adjudication: The European Court of Human Rights", *Human Rights Quarterly*, Vol. 35, 2013, pp. 176–200.

Brogi E., Parcu P. L., "The Evolving Regulation of the Media in Europe as an Instrument for Freedom and Pluralism", *EUI Working Paper RSCAS* 2014/09, 2014.

Busch C., "Secondary Liability for Open Wireless Networks in Germany: Balancing Regulation and Innovation in the Digital Economy", in G. B. Dinwoodie, *Secondary Liability of Internet Service Providers*, Ius Comparatum – Global Studies in Comparative Law, Springer, 2018.

Cabrera Blázquez F. J., "User-Generated Content Services and Copyright", *IRIS plus, Legal Observations of the European Audiovisual Observatory*, Issue 2008–5.

Cerda Silva A., "Cyber Law in Chile, in International Encyclopaedia of Laws", *Kluwer Law International*, The Netherlands, Suppl. 63, 2017.

Chemerinsky E., "The First Amendment: When the Government Must Make Content-Based Choices", *Cleveland State Law Review*, Vol. 42 1994, pp. 199–214.

Cheung A. S. Y., "Liability of Internet Host Providers in Defamation Actions: From Gatekeepers to Identifiers", *University of Hong Kong Faculty of Law Research Paper No. 2014/013.*

Clapham A.,"The 'Drittwirkung' of the Convention", in R.S.J. Macdonald, F. Matscher and H. Petzold, *The European system for the protection of human rights*, Dordrecht, Martinus Nijhoff Publishers, 1993.

Clapham A., *Human Rights in the Private Sphere*, Oxford, Clarendon Press, 1993.

Cooke L., "Controlling the Net: European approaches to content and access regulation", *Journal of Information Science*, Vol. 33 Issue 3, 2007, pp. 360–376.

Cotter T.F., "Some Observations on the Law and Economics of Intermediaries", *Michigan State Law Review*, Vol. 67, 2006, pp. 68–71.

Coudert F., Werkers E., "In The Aftermath of the Promusicae Case: How to Strike the Balance?", *International Journal of Law and Information Technology*, Vol. 18, Issue 1, 2010, pp. 50–71.

Cremona J.J., "The Proportionality Principle in the Jurisprudence of the European Court of Human Rights", in Beyerlin, Bothe, Hofmann and Petersmann (eds.), *Recht zwischen Umbrauch und Bewahrung – Festschrijft fur Rudolf Bernhardt*, 1995.

Dhenne M., "Hébergeurs et contrefaçons: de l'usage de la loyauté dans un régime de responsabilité limitée", 51 *RLDI* 58, 2009.

Dietz A., "Germany" in L. Bently, P. Geller & M. Nimmer, *International Copyright Law and Practice*, Matthew

Bender/LexisNexis, 2013, §8[1][c][i].

Dinwoodie G. B., "A Comparative Analysis of the Secondary Liability of Online Service Providers", in G. B. Dinwoodie, *Secondary Liability of Internet Service Providers*, Ius Comparatum – Global Studies in Comparative Law, Springer, 2018.

De Smet B., Lathouwers J., et al., "Artikel 6: recht op eerlijk proces" ["Article 6: right to fair trial"], in: J. Vande Lanotte, Y. Haeck, Handboek EVRM: Deel II: Artikelsgewijze commentaar (Volume I) [ECHR: Part II: Commentary on the articles], Antwerpen, Intersentia, 2004, 386.

Doda P., "Distinguishing Common Carriers from Common Thieves: Requiring Notice and Stay down for Structurally Infringing Host Sites That Discourage Legitimate Electronic Storage, Incentivize Copyright Infringement, and Exploit the DMCA 512 (c) Safe Harbor", *Journal of the Copyright Society of the USA*, Vol. 63, Issue 3, Summer 2016, pp. 515–534.

Ehrlich P., "Communications Decency Act 230", *Berkeley Technology Law Journal*, Vol. 17 Issue 1, 2002.

Fathaigh R. Ó., "Article 10 and the chilling effect principle", *European Human Rights Law Review*, Issue 3, 2013, pp. 304–313.

de Filippi P. and Bourcier D., "Three-Strikes Response to Copyright Infringement: The Case of HADOPI", in F. Musiani, D. L. Cogburn, L. DeNardis, N.S. Levinson, (eds.), *The Turn to Infrastructure in Internet Governance*, Palgrave-Macmillan, 2016.

Flaxman S., Goel S., Rao J.M., "Filter Bubbles, Echo Chambers, ad Online News Consumption", *Public Opinion Quarterly*, Vol. 80, Special Issue, 2016, pp. 298–320.

Franklin Z., "Justice for Revenge Porn Victims: Legal Theories to Overcome Claims of Civil Immunity by Operators of Revenge Porn Websites", *California Law Review*, Vol. 102, 2014.

Frantziou E., "The Horizontal Effect of the Charter of Fundamental Rights of the EU: Rediscovering the Reasons for Horizontality", *European Law Journal*, Vol. 21, No. 5, September 2015, pp. 657–679.

Freeman J., "Private Parties, Public Functions and the New Administrative Law", in D. Dyzenhaus (ed.), *Recrafting the Rule of Law*, Oxford: Hart Publishing, 1999, pp. 331–335.

Friedman L. W., Friedman H. H., "The New Media Technologies: Overview and Research Framework", April 2008, https://ssrn.com/abstract=1116771.

Frosio G., "Why Keep a Dog and Bark Yourself? From Intermediary Liability to Responsibility", *International Journal of Law and Information Technology*, Vol. 26, Issue 1, 1 March 2018, Pages 1–33.

Frosio G., "The Death of 'No Monitoring Obligations': A Story of Untameable Monsters", *Journal of Intellectual Property, Information Technology and E-Commerce Law (JIPITEC* – special Intermediary Liability & Human Rights Issue), Vol. 8 2017.

Frydman B., Rorive I., "Regulating Internet Content through Intermediaries in Europe and the USA", *Zeitschrift für Rechtssoziologie*, Vol. 23, No. 1, pp. 41–59, 2002.

Gellman R., "Disintermediation and the Internet", *Government Information Quarterly*, Vol. 13, Issue 1, 1996, pp. 1–8.

Gerards J., "How to improve the necessity test of the European Court of Human Rights", *International Journal of Constitutional Law*, Vol. 11 No. 2, 2013, pp. 466–490.

Gielow Jacobs L., "Clarifying the Content-Based/Content Neutral and Content/Viewpoint Determinations", *McGeorge Law Review*, Vol. 34, 2003.

Goldman E., "The Ten Most Important Section 230 Rulings", *Tulane Journal of Technology & Intellectual Property*, Vol. 20, 2017.

Hardouin R., "La jurisprudence, les textes, et la responsabilité des hébergeurs", *RLDI*, 39, 2008.

Hardouin R., "La connaissance de l'illicéité par les hébergeurs ou quand etre notifié ne signifie pas nécessairement devoir retirer" *Revue du droit des technologies de l'information, 47,* 2012.

Haynes Stuart A., "Google Search Results: Buried if not Forgotten", *North Carolina Journal of Law & Technology*, Vol. 15, Issue 3, Spring 2014.

Harris D.J., O'Boyle M., Bates E.P. & Buckley C., *Law of the European Convention on Human Rights*, 3rd ed., Oxford, Oxford University Press, 2014.

Helberger N., et al., "Legal Aspects of User Created Content" in IDATE, TNO, IViR, User-Created Content: Supporting a Participative Information Society, Study for the European Commission (DG INFSO), December 2008, available at: www.ivir.nl/publications/helberger/User_created_content.pdf.

Hempel F., “The right of reply under the European Convention on Human Rights: an analysis of Eker v Turkey App no 24016/05 (ECtHR, 24 October 2017)”, *Journal of Media Law*, 4 April 2018, p.1–20.

Hoeren T. and Yankova S., “The Liability of Internet Intermediaries – The German Perspective”, *International Review of Intellectual Property and Competition Law*, IIC 2012.

Hoeren T., “German Law on Internet Liability of Intermediaries”, LIDC Congress, Oxford 2011.

Hofmann H. CH., “Art. 47 – Right to Effective Remedy“ in S. Peers et al. (eds.), *The EU Charter of Fundamental Rights – A Commentary*, Hart Publishing, Oxford and Portland, Oregon, 2014.

Holland A. et al., “Online Intermediaries Case Studies Series: Intermediary Liability in the United States”, The Global Network of Internet & Society Research Centers, 2015.

Hui Kyong Chun W., “Did Somebody Say New Media?”, in W. Hui Kyong Chun and T. Keenan (eds.), *New Media, Old Media: A History and Theory Reader*, Routledge Taylor & Francis Group, 2006.

Husovec M., “Holey Cap! CJEU Drills (Yet) Another Hole in the E-Commerce Directive’s Safe Harbors”, *Journal of Intellectual Property Law & Practice*, Vol. 12, Issue 2, 1 February 2017, pp. 115–125.

Husovec M., “Intellectual Property Rights and Integration by Conflict: The Past, Present and Future”, *Cambridge Yearbook of European Legal Studies*, Vol. 18, 2016, pp. 239–269.

Husovec M., “Accountable, Not Liable: Injunctions Against Intermediaries”, *TILEC Discussion Paper No. 2016-012*, 2 May 2016, https://papers.ssrn.com/sol3/papers.cfm?abstract_id=2773768

Jacobs F.G., “Recent developments in the principle of Proportionality in European Community Law”, in E. Ellis (ed.), *The Principle of Proportionality in the Laws of Europe*, Hart Publishing, Oxford, 1999.

Jakobsen S.S., “Mobile Commerce and ISP Liability in the EU”, *International Journal of Law and Information Technology*, Vol. 19 no. 1, 2010.

Jakubowicz K., “Do we know a medium when we see one? New media ecology”, in M. E. Price, S. G. Verhulst, L. Morgan (eds.), *Routledge Handbook of Media Law*, Routledge, 2013, p. 454.

Jasserand C., “Régime français de la responsabilité des intermédiaires techniques”, *Les Cahiers de la propriété intellectuelle*, Vol. 25, Issue 3, 2013.

Johnson M. J., Wilcox P. W., “The World of Connected Things”, *The Journal of Government Financial Management*, Vol. 56, Issue 4, Winter 2007, pp. 48 – 53.

Jondet N., The Silver Lining in Dailymotion’s Copyright Cloud, Juriscom.net, 19 April 2008

Kagan E., “Private Speech, Public Purpose: The Role of Governmental Motive in First Amendment Doctrine”, *University of Chicago Law Review*, vol. 63, 1996.

Keats Citron D. and Wittes B., “The Internet Will Not Break: Denying Bad Samaritans Section 230 Immunity”, University of Maryland Francis King Carey School of Law, Legal Studies Research Paper No. 2017-22.

Keats Citron D., “Cyber Civil Rights”, *Boston University Law Review*, Vol. 89, Issue 61, 2009.

Keats Citron D., "Addressing Cyber Harassment: An Overview of Hate Crimes in Cyberspace", *Journal of Law, Technology & the Internet*, Vol. 6, 2015.

Keats Citron D., Franks M.A., "Criminalizing Revenge Porn", *Wake Forest Law Review*, Vol. 49, 2014, pp. 345–391.

Kestemont L., "Methods For traditional legal research", *Reader 'Methods of Legal Research'*, Research Master In Law, KU Leuven University Of Tilburg, 2014–2015.

Kleis Nielsen R., Ganter S. A., "Dealing with digital intermediaries: A case study of the relations between publishers and platforms", *New Media & Society*, 17 April 2017, pp. 1–18.

Koelman K.J., "Online Intermediary Liability", in P.B. Hugenholtz (ed.), *Copyright and Electronic Commerce. Legal Aspects of Electronic Copyright Management*, Information Law Series -8, Kluwer Law International, 2000, pp. 7–58.

Kosseff J., "Twenty Year of Intermediary Immunity: the US Experience", *Scripted*, Vol. 14, Issue 1, June 2017.

Kosseff J., "The Gradual Erosion of the Law that Shaped the Internet; Section 230's Evolution over two Decades", *Columbia Science and Technology Law Review*, Vol. 18, Issue 1.

Kraakman H.R., "Gatekeepers: The Anatomy of a Third-Party Enforcement Strategy", *Journal of Law, Economics, and Organization*, Vol. 2, No. 1, 1986, pp. 53–105.

Kreimer S. F., "Censorship by Proxy: The First Amendment, Internet Intermediaries, and the Problem of the Weakest Link", *Faculty Scholarship*, Paper 127, 2006.

Kuczerawy A., "The Power of Positive Thinking: Intermediary Liability and the Effective Enjoyment of the Right to Freedom of Expression", *JIPITEC* Vol. 8 2017, p. 226.

Kuczerawy A., "Intermediary Liability & Freedom of Expression: Recent Developments in the EU Notice & Action Initiative", *Computer Law and Security Review*, Vol. 31. Issue 1 2015, pages 46–56.

Kuczerawy A., Ausloos J., "NoC Online Intermediaries Case Studies Series: European Union and Google Spain", 2015, http://papers.ssrn.com/sol3/papers.cfm?abstract_id=2567183

Kuczerawy A., Ausloos J., "From Notice-and-Takedown to Notice-and-Delist: Implementing Google Spain", *Colorado Technology Law Journal*, Vol. 14, Issue 2, 2016, pp. 219–258.

Laidlaw E. B., "A framework for identifying Internet information gatekeepers", *International Review of Law, Computers & Technology*, Vol. 24, Issue 3, 2010, pp. 263–276.

Laidlaw E. B., "The responsibilities of free speech regulators: an analysis of the Internet Watch Foundation", *International Journal of Law and Information Technology*, Vol. 20, No. 4, 2012, pp. 312 – 345.

Laidlaw E. B., "Private Power, Public Interest: An Examination of Search Engine Accountability", *International Journal of Law and Information Technology*, Vol. 17 No. 1, 2008.

Leerssen P., "Cut Out By The Middle Man The Free Speech Implications Of Social Network Blocking and Banning In The EU", JIPITEC Vol. 6, 2015.

Leistner M.," Structural aspects of secondary (provider) liability in Europe", *Journal of Intellectual Property Law & Practice*, Vol. 9, No. 1, 2014.

Leistner M., "Störerhaftung und mittelbare Schutzrechtsverletzung", GRUR-Beil 1,2010.

Lenaerts K., "Exploring the Limits of the EU Charter of Fundamental Rights", *European Constitutional Law Review*, Vol. 8, 2012, p. 377.

Leczykiewicz D., "Horizontal application of the Charter of Fundamental Rights", *European Law Review*, Vol. 38, 2013, p. 479.

Levandowski A., "Using Copyright to Combat Revenge Porn", *NYU Journal of Intellectual Property & Entertainment Law*, Vol. 3, 2014.

Lewin K., "Frontiers in group dynamics. II. Channels of group life; social planning and action research". *Human Relations*, Vol.1, Nr 2, 1947, pp. 143–153.

Lindroos K., "Intermediary Liability for IP Infringement in Finland: CopyRight vs. CopyLeft - A Series of Legislative Proposals and Decade of Debates", in G. B. Dinwoodie, *Secondary Liability of Internet Service Providers,* Ius Comparatum – Global Studies in Comparative Law, Springer, 2018.

Lloyd I., "Cyber Law in the UK, in International Encyclopaedia of Laws", *Kluwer Law International*, The Netherlands, Suppl. 64, 2017.

Lodder A., "Directive 2000/31 on certain legal aspects of information society services, in particular electronic commerce, in the Internal Market", in A. Lodder A. and H. Kasspersen (eds.*), eDirectives: Guide to European Union Law on E-commerce – Article by Article Comments*, Kluwer Law international, 2002.

Kaspersen H. and Lodder A. (eds.), E-directive: guide to European Union law on e-commerce: commentary on the directives on distance selling, electronics signatures, electronic commerce, copyright in the information society, and data protection, Den Haag, Kluwer, 2002

Mann R. J., Belzley S. R., "The Promise of Internet Intermediary Liability", *William & Mary Law Review*, Vol.47, Issue 1, 2005.

Martin-Bariteau F., "Internet Intermediaries Liability A North American Perspective / or/ Perspectives from the United States and Canada", in C. A. Pereira de Souza, M. Viola, R. Lemos (eds.), *Understanding Brazil's Internet Bill of Rights*, Rio de Janeiro: ITS Rio, 2015

Maxeiner J. R., "Legal Certainty: A European Alternative to American Legal Indeterminacy?" *Tulane Journal of International & Comparative Law*, Vol. 15, No. 2, 2007.

McGonagle T., "The Council of Europe's standards on access to the media for minorities: A tale of near misses and staggered successes", in M. Amos, J. Harrison, & L. Woods, (eds.), *Freedom of Expression and the Media,* Leiden/Boston, Martinus Nijhoff Publishers, 2012, pp. 111–140.

McGonagle T., "The State and beyond: activating (non-)media voices", in H. Sousa et al. (ed.), *Media Policy and Regulation: Activating Voices, Illuminating Silences*, Conference contribution, Braga: University of Minho - Communication and Society Research Centre (CECS), 2013, pp. 187–198

McGonagle T., "The Council of Europe against online hate speech: Conundrums and challenges, Expert paper", doc.no. MCM 2013(005), the Council of Europe Conference of Ministers responsible for Media and Information Society, 'Freedom of Expression and Democracy in the Digital Age: Opportunities, Rights, Responsibilities', Belgrade, 7–8 November 2013.

McGonagle T., "Positive obligations concerning freedom of expression: mere potential or real power?" in O. Andreotti (ed.), *Journalism at risk: Threats, challenges and perspective*, Council of Europe, 2015, pp. 9–37.

McIntyre T.J. and Scott C., "Internet Filtering: Rhetoric, Legitimacy, Accountability and Responsibility'" in R. Brownsword and K. Yeung (eds), *Regulating Technologies: Legal Future, Regulatory Frames and Technological Fixes*, Hart Publishing 2008, pp. 109 – 124.

McNamee J., "The slide from "self-regulation" to corporate censorship", European Digital Rights Initiative, 2011, https://www.edri.org/files/EDRI_selfreg_final_20110124.pdf.

Meyer T. & Van Audenhove L., "Surveillance and regulating code: an analysis of graduated response in France", *Surveillance & Society*, Vol. 4, Issue 9, pp. 365–377.

Meyer T., "Graduated Response In France: The Clash of Copyright and the Internet", *Journal of Information Policy*, Vol. 2, 2012, pp. 107–127.

Moon S.-Y. and Kim D., "The 'Three Strikes' Policy in Korean Copyright Act 2009: Safe or Out?", *Washington Journal of Law, Technology & Arts*, Vol. 6, 2011.

Montero E., "La responsibilite des prestataires intermediaries sur les reseaux", in E. Montero (ed.), *Le commerce electronique europeen sur les rails?*, Cahiers du CRID, Brussel, Bruylant, 2001, 289–290.

Montero E. and Van Enis Q., "Enabling freedom of expression in light of filtering measures imposed on Internet intermediaries: Squaring the circle", *Computer Law & Security Review*, Vol. 27, 2011, pp. 21–35.

Montéro E., "Les responsabilités liées au web 2.0", *Revue du Droit des Technologies de l'Information* n° 32, 2008

Moore T. and Clayton R., "The Impact of Incentives on Notice and Takedown", Proc. of Seventh Workshop on the Economics of Information Security (WEIS 2008), 22 June 2008, www.cl.cam.ac.uk/~rncl/takedown.pdf.

Matulionyte R. and Nérisson S., "The French Route to an ISP Safe Harbour, Compared to the German and US Ways", *International Review of Intellectual Property and Competition Law* (IIC), Vol. 42 Issue 1, 2011.

Nérisson S., "Intellectual Property Liability of Consumers, Facilitators and Intermediaries: the Position in France", in A. Kamperman Sanders and C. Heath, *Intellectual Property Liability of Consumers, Facilitators and Intermediaries*, Kluwer Law International 2012.

Nordemann J. B., "Liability for Copyright Infringements on the Internet: Host Providers (Content Providers) – The German Approach", *Journal of Intellectual Property, Information Technology and Electronic Commerce Law (JIPITEC)*, Vol. 2, Issue 1, 2011.

Nordemann J. B., "Internet Copyright Infringement: Remedies against Internet Intermediaries – the European Perspective on Host and Access Providers", *Journal of the Copyright Society of the USA, Vol.* 59, Issue 4, 2012, p. 773.

Nordemann J. B., "Intellectual Property Liability of Consumers, Facilitators and Intermediaries: the Position in Germany" in A. Kamperman Sanders & C. Heath, *Intellectual Property Liability of Consumers, Facilitators and Intermediaries*, Kluwer Law International, 2012

Odermatt J., "A Giant Step Backwards? Opinion 2/13 on the EU's Accession to the European Convention on Human Rights", Leuven Centre for Global Governance Studies, Working Paper No. 150 – February 2015.

Ombelet P.J., Kuczerawy A., Valcke P., "Supervising Automated Journalists in the Newsroom: Liability for Algorithmically Produced News Stories", *Revue du droit des technologies de l'information*, Vol. 61 2016, pp. 5–19.

Pasquale F., "Restoring Transparency to Automated Authority", *Journal on Telecommunications and High Technology Law*, Vol. 9, No. 235, 2011.

Pech L., "Article 47(2)", in S. Peers et al. (eds.), *The EU Charter of Fundamental Rights – A Commentary*, Hart Publishing, Oxford and Portland, Oregon, 2014.

Peifer K.-N., "Platform Economy and Liability Questions – Desperately in Search of Concepts Lost in the Virtual World or "Sto¨rerhaftung" Resurrected?", IIC, 48, 2017.

Price M. and Verhulst S., "In search of the self: charting the course of self-regulation on the Internet in a global environment", in C. Marsden, *Regulating the global information society*, London, Routledge, 2000.

Randazza M. J., "Lenz v. Universal: A Call to Reform Section 512(f) of the DMCA and to Strengthen Fair Use", *Vanderbilt Journal of Entertainment & Technology Law*, Vol. 18, No. 3, 2016.

Rátai B., et al. "Cyber Law in Hungary, in International Encyclopaedia of Laws", *Kluwer Law International*, The Netherlands, Suppl. 26, July 2010.

Reese S. D., and Ballinger J., "The roots of a sociology of news: Remembering Mr. Gates and social control in the newsroom", *Journalism and Mass Communication Quarterly*, Vol. 78, Issue 4, December 2000, pp. 641–658.

Roberts C., "Gatekeeping theory: An evolution", Presented at Communication Theory and Methodology Division Association for Education in Journalism and Mass Communication, San Antonio, Texas, August 2005, www.reelaccurate.com/about/gatekeeping.pdf.

Schauer F., "Fear, risk and the First Amendment: Unravelling the chilling effect", *Boston University Law Review* 1978, Vol. 58, Issue 5, 685–732.

Schauer F., "The Exceptional First Amendment", KSG Working Paper No. RWP05-021, February 2005.

Schauer F., "Freedom of Expression Adjudication in Europe and America: A Case Study in Comparative Constitutional Architecture", KSG Working Paper No. RWP05-019, February 2005.

Shoemaker P., et al., "Individual and Routine Forces in Gatekeeping", *Journalism and Mass Communication Quarterly*, Vol. 78, Issue 2, June 2001, pp. 233–246.

De Schutter O., Tulkens F., "The European Court of Human Rights as a Pragmatic Institution", in E. Brems (ed.), *Conflicts Between Fundamental Rights*, Intersentia, Antwerp-Oxford- Portland, 2008

Seltzer W., "The Politics of Internet Control and Delegated Censorship", *The American Society of International Law*, April 10, 2008.

Seltzer W., "Free Speech Unmoored in Copyright's Safe Harbor: Chilling Effects of the DMCA on the First Amendment", *Harvard Journal of Law & Technology*, Vol. 24, Number 1 Fall 2010.

Sevanian A. M., "Section 230 of the Communications Decency Act: A 'Good Samaritan' Law Without the

Requirement of Acting as a 'Good Samaritan'", *UCLA Entertainment Law Review*, Vol. 21, Issue 1, 2014, p. 122–146.

Schabas P., Fischer I., DiMatteo C., "Canada's Copyright Modernization Act: A Delicate Rebalancing of Interests", *MLRC Bulletin*, Issue 2, 2013, www.medialaw.org/component/k2/item/1820-canada%E2%80%99s-copyright-modernization-act-a-delicate-rebalancing-of-interests.

Siddique H., "Facebook Removes Mexican Beheading Video", *The Guardian*, 23 October 2013, www.theguardian.com/technology/2013/oct/23/facebook-removes-beheading-video.

Singer J.B., "Stepping back from the gate: Online newspaper editors and the co-production of content in Campaign 2004", *Journalism and Mass Communication Quarterly*, Vol. 83, Issue 2, 2006, pp. 265–280.

Sirinelli P., "Chronique de Jurisprudence – Mise à la disposition illicite d'oeuvres par l'intermédiaire des réseaux numériques", *Revue Internationale du Droit d'Auteur*, (2011) 228.

Spindler G., "Internet Intermediary Liability Reloaded – The New German Act on Responsibility of Social Networks and its (In-) Compatibility with European Law", *JIPITEC*, Vol. 8, 2017.

Spindler G. and Leistner M., "Secondary Copyright Infringement – New Perspectives from Germany and Europe", *International Review of Intellectual Property and Competition Law* (IIC), (2006) 37(7).

Spirchez G.-B., "Current Aspects of the European Union Accession to the European Convention of Human Rights", *Euromentor*, Vol. 6 Issue 2, p. 123–129.

Stalla-Bourdillon S., "Chilling ISPs… when private regulators act without adequate public framework", *Computer Law & Security Review*, Vol. 26, 2010, pp. 290–297.

Stalla-Bourdillon S., "Internet intermediaries as responsible actors? Why it is time to rethink the e-Commerce Directive as well…", in L. Floridi and M. Taddeo, *The Responsibilities of Online Service Providers*, Springer, 2016.

Stalla-Bourdillon S., "Sometimes one is not enough! Securing freedom of expression, encouraging private regulation, or subsidizing Internet intermediaries or all three at the same time: the dilemma of Internet intermediaries' liability", *Journal of International Commercial Law and Technology* Vol. 7, Issue 2, 2012.

Starmer K., "Positive Obligations Under the Convention" in J. Jowell and J. Cooper (eds) *Understanding Human Rights Principles*, Oxford, Hart Publishing, 2001.

Stone G. R., "Content Regulation and the First Amendment", *William & Mary Law Review*, Vol. 25.

Urban J. and Quilter L., "Efficient Process or 'Chilling Effects'? Take-down Notices Under Section 512 of the Digital Millennium Copyright Act: Summary Report", http://mylaw.usc.edu/documents/512Rep-ExecSum_out.pdf.

Urban J., Karaganis J., and Schofield B. L., "Notice and Takedown in Everyday Practice", UC Berkeley Public Law Research Paper No. 2755628.

Tamanaha B. Z., "The Rule of Law for Everyone?", *St. John's Legal Studies Research Paper*, 2003, https://papers.ssrn.com/sol3/papers.cfm?abstract_id=312622.

Tambini D., Leonardi D., and Marsden C., "The privatisation of censorship: self regulation and freedom of expression", in D. Tambini, D. Leonardi, and C. Marsden, *Codifying cyberspace: communications self-regulation in the age of internet convergence*, Routledge / UCL Press, Abingdon, UK, 2008.

Thompson M., "Beyond Gatekeeping: The Normative Responsibility of Internet Intermediaries", *Vanderbilt Journal of Entertainment & Technology Law*, Vol. 18, No. 4, 2016, University of Hong Kong Faculty of Law Research Paper No. 2015/045.

Turner M. (ed.) & Llevat J., "The Spanish Supreme Court clarifies the concept of actual knowledge in connection with ISP's liability", *Computer Law & Security Review*, Volume 26, Issue 4, 2010.

Tushnet M., "The issue of state action/horizontal effect in comparative constitutional law", *International Journal of Constitutional Law*, Vol. 1, Number 1, 2003, pp. 79–98.

Valcke P., Stevens D., Werkers E., and Lievens E., "Audiovisual Media Services in the EU: Next Generation Approach or Old Wine in New Barrels?" *Communications & Strategies*, No. 71, 3rd Quarter 2008.

Valcke P., Lenaerts M. and Kuczerawy A., "Who's Author, Editor and Publisher in User-Generated Content?" in P. Lambert (ed.), *User Generated Content, in Social Networking: Law, Rights and Policy*, 2014, pp. 83–99.

Valcke P., Kuczerawy A., Ombelet P.J., "Did the Romans Get it Right? What Delfi, Google, eBay, and UPC TeleKabel Wien Have in Common", in L. Floridi and M. Taddeo (eds.), *The Responsibilities of Online Service Providers*, Springer, 2016.

Van Eecke P., "Online Service Providers and Liability: a Plea for a Balanced Approach", *Common Market Law Review*, Vol. 48, Issue 5, 2011, pp. 1455–1502.

Van Eecke P., Ooms B., "ISP liability and the e-commerce directive: a growing trend toward greater responsibility for ISPs", *Journal of Internet Law*, Vol. 11, Issue 3, 2007.

Voithofer R., "Designing new media education research: the materiality of data, representation and dissemination", *Educational Researcher*, Vol. 34, Issue 9, 2005, pp. 3–14.

Voorhoof D., "Freedom of Expression under the European Human Rights System. From Sunday Times (n° 1) v. U.K. (1979) to Hachette Filipacchi Associés ("Ici Paris") v. France (2009)", *Inter-American and European Human Rights Journal*, Vol. 2 Issue 1–2, 2010, pp. 3–49.

Walden I., Cool Y., Montero E., "Directive 2000/31/EC –Directive on electronic commerce" in A. Bullesbach, Y. Poullet, C. Prins (eds), *Concise European IT Law*, Kluwer Law International Alphen aan den Rijn, 2005.

Walker Echenique E., "Implementing the IP Chapter of the FTA between Chile and the USA: Criticism and Realities from a Developing Country Perspective", *SCRIPTED*, Volume 9, Issue 2, August 2012, pp. 233–257.

Wilson G., "Comparative Legal Scholarship" in M. McConville and W.H. Chui, (eds.), *Research Methods of Law*, Edinburgh, Edinburgh University Press, 2007, p. 87–103.

Wimmers J., "Who Interferes? Liability for Third Party Content on the Internet in Germany", *Intellectual Property Today*, August 2007.

Wong C., Dempsey J.X., "Mapping Digital Media: The Media and Liability for Content on the Internet", *Open Society Foundation, Reference Series*, No.12, 2011.

Woods L., "Freedom of expression in the European Union", *European Public Law*, Vol. 12, Issue 3, September 2006.

Woods L., "Article 11", in S. Peers et al. (eds.), *The EU Charter of Fundamental Rights – A Commentary*, Hart Publishing, Oxford and Portland, Oregon, 2014.

Wright R. G., "Content-Neutral and Content-Based Regulations of Speech: A Distinction That is No Longer Worth the Fuss", *Florida Law Review*, Vol. 67, 2016.

Yu P., The Graduated Response, *62 Florida Law Review*, 2010, pp. 1373 – 1430.

Zittrain J., "A History of Online Gatekeeping", *Harvard Journal of Law and Technology*, Vol. 19, No. 2, 2006.

BLOG POSTS

Abogado Pablo, Sentencia, responsabilidad de los administradores de las páginas webs, 9 September 2013, www.derecho-chile.cl/sentencia-responsabilidad-de-los-administradores-de-las-paginas-webs/.

Anderson D., Finnish law firms are using intimidation to profit from internet piracy, 4 May 2017, www.helsinkitimes.fi/finland/finland-news/domestic/14734-finnish-law-firms-are-using-intimidation-to-profit-from-internet-piracy.html.

Angelopoulos C., EU Copyright Reform: Outside the Safe Harbours, Intermediary Liability Capsizes into Incoherence, 6 October 2016,

http://kluwercopyrightblog.com/2016/10/06/eu-copyright-reform-outside-safe-harbours-intermediary-liability-capsizes-incoherence/.

El-Barmawy M. M., Your Filter Bubble is Destroying Democracy, 18 November 2016, https://www.wired.com/2016/11/filter-bubble-destroying-democracy/.

Brüß M., Austria refers Facebook 'Hate-Speech' case to the CJEU, 30 January 2018, http://ipkitten.blogspot.fr/2018/01/austria-refers-facebook-hate-speech.html.

Cadwalladr C., British courts may unlock secrets of how Trump campaign profiled US voters, The Guardian, 1 October 2017, https://www.theguardian.com/technology/2017/oct/01/cambridge-analytica-big-data-facebook-trump-voters.

Cadwalladr C. and Graham-Harrison E., Facebook and Cambridge Analytica face mounting pressure over data scandal, 19 March 2018, https://www.theguardian.com/news/2018/mar/18/cambridge-analytica-and-facebook-accused-of-misleading-mps-over-data-breach.

Canada's Approach to Intermediary Liability for Copyright Infringement: the Notice and Notice Procedure, Berkley Technology Law Journal, 2 March 2014, http://btlj.org/2014/03/canadas-approach-to-intermediary-liability-for-copyright-infringement-the-notice-and-notice-procedure/.

CDT, Cases Wrestle with Role of Online Intermediaries in Fighting Copyright Infringement, 26 June 2012, https://cdt.org/insight/cases-wrestle-with-role-of-online-intermediaries-in-fighting-copyright-infringement/.

CDT, Tackling 'Illegal' Content Online: The EC Continues Push for Privatised Law Enforcement, 3 October 2017, https://cdt.org/blog/tackling-illegal-content-online-the-ec-continues-push-for-privatised-law-enforcement/.

Champeau G., Hadopi: la négligence caractérisée est enfin définie… de manière très floue, 26 June 2010, www.numerama.com/magazine/16087-hadopi-la-negligence-caracterisee-est-enfin-definie-de-maniere-tres-floue.html.

Cheng J., Craigslist "brothel business" under fire again, 4 May 2010, https://arstechnica.com/tech-policy/2010/05/craigslist-brothel-business-under-fire-again/.

Clark B., GEMA vs YouTube – what the Hamburg court really said…, 21 April 2012, http://ipkitten.blogspot.be/2012/04/gema-vs-youtube-what-hamburg-court.html.

Cohn C., One Injunction to Censor Them All: Doe Injunctions Threaten Speech Online, 1 June 2016, https://www.knightfoundation.org/articles/one-injunction-censor-them-all-doe-injunctions-threaten-speech-online.

S. Columbus, France to disconnect first Internet users under three strikes regime, 27 July 2017, https://opennet.net/blog/2011/07/france-disconnect-first-internet-users-under-three-strikes-regime.

Copyright Reform – Abolishing Three-Strikes-Out Rule from Copyright Law, https://opennet.or.kr/copyright-reform.

C. Coslin, C. Gateau, No 'Stay Down' Obligation for Hosting Providers in France, https://www.scl.org/articles/2844-no-stay-down-obligation-for-hosting-providers-in-france.

Doctorow C., South Korea's US-led copyright policy leads to 65,000 acts of extrajudicial censorship/ disconnection/ threats by govt bureaucrats, 26 October 2010, https://boingboing.net/2010/10/26/south-koreas-us-led.html.

Donahue P., "Merkel Confronts Facebook's Zuckerberg Over Policing Hate Posts", *Bloomberg*, 26 September 2015, available at: www.bloomberg.com/news/articles/2015-09-26/merkel-confronts-facebook-s-zuckerberg-over-policing-hate-posts.

EDRi and Access Now withdraw from the EU Commission IT Forum discussions, 31 May 2016, https://edri.org/edri-access-now-withdraw-eu-commission-forum-discussions/.

EDRi, Guide to the Code of Conduct on Hate Speech, 3 June 2016, https://edri.org/guide-code-conduct-hate-speech/.

EDRi, Commission's position on tackling illegal content online is contradictory and dangerous for free speech, 28 September, 2017, https://edri.org/commissions-position-tackling-illegal-content-online-contradictory-dangerous-free-speech/.

Emerson S., Here's Twitter's Response to the Racist Harassment of Leslie Jones, Motherboard, 19 July 2016, https://motherboard.vice.com/en_us/article/pgkz37/heres-twitters-response-to-the-racist-harassment-of-leslie-jones.

Engelhardt T., German Federal Supreme Court on file hoster responsibility for third party content – "Rapidshare", 13 July 2012, http://germanitlaw.com/german-federal-supreme-court-on-file-hoster-responsibility-for-third-party-content-rapidshare/.

Essers L., German, French Courts Disagree on Responsibility of ISPs for Illegal Content, 16 July 2012, https://www.pcworld.com/article/259294/germany_french_courts_disagree_on_responsibility_of_isps_for_illegal_content.html.

Fernández Pérez M., VMSD: European Parliament set to vote whether it's allowed to vote, 17 May 2017, https://edri.org/avmsd-european-parliament-set-to-vote-whether-its-allowed-to-vote/.

Fernández Pérez M., Audiovisual Media Services Directive reform: Document pool, 15 May 2017, https://edri.org/avmsd-reform-document-pool/.

Fernández Pérez M., Commission Report on child protection online lacks facts and evidence, 12 July 2017, https://edri.org/commission-report-on-child-protection-online-lacks-facts-and-evidence/.

Fiedler K., Launch of the EU Internet Forum – behind closed doors and without civil society, 5 August 2015, https://edri.org/launch-of-the-eu-internet-forum-behind-closed-doors-and-without-civil-society/.

Geigner T., Google Report: 99.95 Percent Of DMCA Takedown Notices Are Bot-Generated Bullshit Buckshot, 23 February 2017, https://www.techdirt.com/articles/20170223/06160336772/google-report-9995-percent-dmca-takedown-notices-are-bot-generated-bullshit-buckshot.shtml.

Geist M., Misuse of Canada's Copyright Notice System Continues: U.S. Firm Sending Thousands of Notices With Settlement Demands, 5 March 2015, www.michaelgeist.

ca/2015/03/misuse-canadas-copyright-notice-system-continues-u-s-firm-sending-thousands-notices-settlement-demands/.

Goldman E., Blog Host Can't Be Bound by TRO for User Posts (Blockowicz redux)–Bobolas v. Does, 12 October 2010, http://blog.ericgoldman.org/2010/10/blog_host_cant/.

Goldman E., What Should We Do About Revenge Porn Sites Like Texxxan?, 9 February 2013, http://blog.ericgoldman.org/archives/2013/02/what_should_we.htm.

Goldman E., Yelp Forced To Remove Defamatory Reviews–Hassell v. Bird, 8 June 2016, http://blog.ericgoldman.org/archives/2016/06/yelp-forced-to-remove-defamatory-reviews-hassell-v-bird.htm.

Goldman E., The "Allow States and Victims to Fight Online Sex Trafficking Act of 2017" Bill Would Be Bad News for Section 230, 10 April 2017, http://blog.ericgoldman.org/archives/2017/04/the-allow-states-and-victims-to-fight-online-sex-trafficking-act-of-2017-bill-would-be-bad-news-for-section-230.htm.

Goldman E., Dozen Amicus Briefs Oppose the Worst Section 230 Ruling of 2016 (and One Supports It)–Hassell v. Bird, 20 April 2017, http://blog.ericgoldman.org/2017/04/dozen-amicus-briefs-oppose-the-worst-section-230-ruling-of-2016-and-one-supports-it-hassell-v-bird/.

Goldman E., Senate's "Stop Enabling Sex Traffickers Act of 2017"–and Section 230's Imminent Evisceration, 31 July 2017, http://blog.ericgoldman.org/archives/2017/07/senates-stop-enabling-sex-traffickers-act-of-2017-and-section-230s-imminent-evisceration.htm.

Goldman E., Section 512(f) Complaint Survives Motion to Dismiss–Johnson v. New Destiny Church, 30 August 2017, http://blog.ericgoldman.org/archives/2017/08/section-512f-complaint-survives-motion-to-dismiss-johnson-v-new-destiny-church.htm.

Goldman E., Section 512(f) Complaint Survives Motion to Dismiss–Johnson v. New Destiny Church, 30 August 2017, http://blog.ericgoldman.org/archives/2017/08/section-512f-complaint-survives-motion-to-dismiss-johnson-v-new-destiny-church.htm.

Goldman E., 'Worst of Both Worlds' FOSTA Signed Into Law, Completing Section 230's Evisceration, 11 April 2018, https://blog.ericgoldman.org/archives/2018/04/worst-of-both-worlds-fosta-signed-into-law-completing-section-230s-evisceration.htm.

Gotev G., Court of Justice rejects draft agreement of EU accession to ECHR, 14 January 2015, https://www.euractiv.com/section/justice-home-affairs/news/court-of-justice-rejects-draft-agreement-of-eu-accession-to-echr/.

Harguth A., File hosting in Germany carries increased copyright policing duties, 31 October 2013, https://www.lexology.com/library/detail.aspx?g=ef2396cc-39e8–493b-a893-bec38f9ef368.

Harmon E., "Notice-and-Stay-Down" Is Really "Filter-Everything", 21 January 2016, https://www.eff.org/deeplinks/2016/01/notice-and-stay-down-really-filter-everything.

Harris M., Defamation Act 2013: a step in the right direction, https://inforrm.org/2014/01/09/defamation-act-2013-a-step-in-the-right-direction-mike-harris/.

Harris S., 'Feels like blackmail': Canada needs to take a hard look at its piracy notice system, 2 November 2016, www.cbc.ca/news/business/copyright-infringement-notice-canada-piracy-1.3831492.

Harris S., U.S. cancels internet piracy notices while Canadians still get notices demanding settlement fees, 1 February 2017, www.cbc.ca/news/business/notice-system-piracy-copyright-internet-1.3960462.

Heesob's IP Blog, Facts and Figures on Copyright Three-Strike Rule in Korea, 24 October 2010, http://hurips.blogspot.be/2010/10/facts-and-figures-on-copyright-three.html.

Heesob's IP Blog, National Human Rights Body Recommends Abolishing Three-Strike-Out Rule, 27 March 2013, http://hurips.blogspot.be/2013/03/national-human-rights-body-recommends.html.

Hersher R., Backpage Shuts Down Adult Ads In The U.S., Citing Government Pressure, 10 January 2017, https://www.npr.org/sections/thetwo-way/2017/01/10/509127110/backpage-shuts-down-adult-ads-citing-government-pressure.

Horten M., File-hosting liability: are German courts alone in the dark?, 28 September 2012, www.iptegrity.com/index.php/internet-trials/793-file-hosting-liability-are-german-courts-alone-in-the-dark.

Horten M., Notice and action directive to be blocked as EU backs down, 28 July 2013, www.iptegrity.com/index.php/ipred/893-notice-and-action-directive-to-be-blocked-as-eu-backs-down.

Horten M., Notice of Action! Barnier to resurrect take-down directive, 6 February 2014, www.iptegrity.com/index.php/ipred/945-notice-of-action-eu-commission-to-revive-take-down-directive.

Hruska J., Six Strikes' programs from ISPs & MPAA ignites in nine days: Here's what you need to know, Extreme Tech, 19 November 2012, www.extremetech.com/internet/140774-six-strikesprograms-from-isps-mpaa-ignites-in-nine-days-heres-what-you-need-to-know.

Hurd I., The Princeton Encyclopedia of Self-Determination, https://pesd.princeton.edu/?q=node/255.

Husovec M., BGH on Liability of Rapidshare, 13 July 2012, www.husovec.eu/2012/07/bgh-on-liability-of-rapidshare.html.

Ingram M., First they came for the mugshot, but I said nothing…, GIGAOM, 7 October 2013, http://gigaom.com/2013/10/07/first-they-came-for-the-mugshot-websites-but-i-said-nothing/.

The IPKat, Commission unveils new copyright package, 14 September 2016, http://ipkitten.blogspot.be/2016/09/breaking-commission-unveils-new.html.

Jasserand C., Recent decisions of the Paris Court of Appeal: towards an extra duty of surveillance for hosting providers? 29 March 2011, http://copyrightblog.kluweriplaw.com/2011/03/29/recent-decisions-of-the-paris-court-of-appeal-towards-an-extra-duty-of-surveillance-for-hosting-providers/.

Jasserand C., France -Youtube guilty but not liable? some more precisions on the status of hosting providers, stating that 'French Courts have a tendency to impose such an obligation on hosting providers shifting from a notice and take down rule to a notice and stay down rule'. 18 June 2012, http://copyrightblog.kluweriplaw.com/2012/06/18/france-youtube-guilty-but-not-liable-some-more-precisions-on-the-status-of-hosting-providers/.

Jasserand C., France: The Court of Cassation puts an end to the Notice and Stay Down Rule, 14 August 2012, http://copyrightblog.kluweriplaw.com/2012/08/14/france-the-court-of-cassation-puts-an-end-to-the-notice-and-stay-down-rule/.

Jeong S., The History of Twitter's Rules, Motherboard, 14 January 2016, https://motherboard.vice.com/en_us/article/z43xw3/the-history-of-twitters-rules

Kilpatrick S. and Black R., Internet Intermediaries and Copyright Owners Take Notice: Canada's Notice-and-Notice Regime Comes into Force, January 2015, Intellectual Property Bulletin, http://mcmillan.ca/Internet-Intermediaries-and-Copyright-Owners-Take-Notice-Canadas-Notice-and-Notice-Regime-Comes-into-Force.

Kim J. Y., South Korean Politician Moves to Repeal Biased Copyright Law, 28 March 2013, https://advox.globalvoices.org/2013/03/28/south-korean-politician-moves-to-repeal-biased-copyright-law/.

Kopytoff V., Craigslist gets heat for prostitution ads, 27 March 2008, http://blog.sfgate.com/techchron/2008/03/27/craigslist-gets-heat-for-prostitution-ads/.

Kuczerawy A., The Code of Conduct on Online Hate Speech: an example of state interference by proxy? 20 July 2016, https://www.law.kuleuven.be/citip/blog/the-code-of-conduct-on-online-hate-speech-an-example-of-state-interference-by-proxy/.

Lambrecht I., The Filter Bubble: to burst or to blow over?, 29 November 2016, https://www.law.kuleuven.be/citip/blog/the-filter-bubble-to-burst-or-to-blow-over/.

Levin S., Carrie Wong J., Harding L., Facebook backs down from 'napalm girl' censorship and reinstates photo, 9 September 2016, https://www.theguardian.com/technology/2016/sep/09/facebook-reinstates-napalm-girl-photo.

Masnik M., A Look At How Many People Have Been Kicked Offline In Korea On Accusations (Not Convictions) Of Infringement, 26 October 2010, https://www.techdirt.com/articles/20101025/18093711583/a-look-at-how-many-people-have-been-kicked-offline-in-korea-on-accusations-not-convictions-of-infringement.shtml.

Masnick M., Court Rightly Finds That GoDaddy Isn't Liable For Revenge Porn Site, 17 April 2014, https://www.techdirt.com/articles/20140416/11585926935/court-rightly-finds-that-godaddy-isnt-liable-revenge-porn-site.shtml.

McMaster H., 5 May 2009, www.dmlp.org/sites/citmedialaw.org/files/2009-05-05-South%20Carolina%20AG%20Letter.pdf.

McNamee J., German Social Media law – sharp criticism from leading legal expert, 19 April 2017, https://edri.org/german-social-media-law-sharp-criticism-from-leading-legal-expert/.

McNamee J., Commission's position on tackling illegal content online is contradictory and dangerous for free speech, 28 September 2017, https://edri.org/commissions-position-tackling-illegal-content-online-contradictory-dangerous-free-speech/.

Melart S., BREAKING NEWS: Finnish Market Court ruling refers to Tele2 decision and throws a massive wrench into the works of copyright trolls, 17 June 2017, https://copy21.com/2017/06/breaking-news-finnish-market-court-ruling-refers-to-tele2-decision-and-throws-a-massive-wrench-into-the-works-of-copyright-trolls/.

Meyer D., Court tells Facebook: Stop deleting 'offensive' comment, 13 April 2018, https://www.zdnet.com/article/court-tells-facebook-stop-deleting-offensive-comment/.

Modern Poland Foundation, Commission claims that general monitoring is not general monitoring, 10 January 2018, https://edri.org/commission-claims-that-general-monitoring-is-not-general-monitoring/.

Morgan C., Why 'Popping' the Social Media Filter Bubble Misses the Point, 16 November 2016, https://motherboard.vice.com/en_us/article/pgkxng/why-popping-the-social-media-filter-bubble-misses-the-point.

Mullin J., Supreme Court turns down EFF's "Dancing Baby" fair use case, 20 June 2017, https://arstechnica.com/tech-policy/2017/06/supreme-court-wont-hear-dancing-baby-copyright-case/.

Nielsen N., Commission: 120 minutes to remove illegal online content, 9 January 2018, https://euobserver.com/justice/140482.

Nix J., Backpage.com sues state to halt law aimed at online child sex ads, 29 June2012, http://nashvillecitypaper.com/content/city-news/backpagecom-sues-state-halt-law-aimed-online-child-sex-ads.

Nocera J., Stuck in Google's Doghouse, New York Times, 12 September 2008, www.nytimes.com/2008/09/13/technology/13nocera.html.

Nordemann J. B., YouTube is a hosting provider, but one with extensive duties of care, say two German Courts, 6 November 2015, http://copyrightblog.kluweriplaw.com/2015/11/06/youtube-is-a-hosting-provider-but-one-with-extensive-duties-of-care-say-two-german-courts/.

O'Brien D., M. Sutton, Korean Lawmakers and Human Rights Experts Challenge Three Strikes Law, Electronic Frontiers Foundation, 29 March 2013, https://www.eff.org/deeplinks/2013/03/korea-stands-against-three-strikes.

Ombelet P.J. and Kuczerawy A., Delfi revisited: the MTE & Index.hu v. Hungary case, 20 February 2016, https://www.law.kuleuven.be/citip/blog/delfi-revisited-the-mte-index-hu-v-hungary-case/.

Out-law.com, UK defamation law reforms take effect from start of 2014, 21 November 2013, https://www.theregister.co.uk/2013/11/21/uk_defamation_law_reforms_take_effect_from_start_of_2014/

Peers S., The CJEU and the EU's accession to the ECHR: a clear and present danger to human rights protection, 18 December 2014, http://eulawanalysis.blogspot.be/2014/12/the-cjeu-and-eus-accession-to-echr.html.

Phys.org, Facebook apologises for censoring prehistoric Venus statue, 1 March 2018, https://phys.org/news/2018-03-facebook-apologises-censoring-prehistoric-venus.html.

Post D., A bit of Internet history, or how two members of Congress helped create a trillion or so dollars of value, 27 August 2015, https://www.washingtonpost.com/news/volokh-conspiracy/wp/2015/08/27/a-bit-of-internet-history-or-how-two-members-of-congress-helped-create-a-trillion-or-so-dollars-of-value/.

Rees M., Suspension: les 10 premiers internautes convoqués par l'Hadopi, 1 July 2011, https://www.nextinpact.com/archive/64415-hadopi-tmg-abonnes-convoques-suspension.htm.

Resnikoff P., Three Strikes: A Complete & Total Failure In South Korea…, 1 April 2013, https://www.digitalmusicnews.com/2013/04/01/effkorea/.

Rinehart W., The Election of 2016 and the Filter Bubble Book in 2017, 15 September 2016, https://medium.com/@willrinehart/the-election-of-2016-and-the-filter-bubble-book-in-2017-51cd7520ed7.

Romano A., A new law intended to curb sex trafficking threatens the future of the internet as we know it, 18 April 2018, https://www.vox.com/culture/2018/4/13/17172762/fosta-sesta-backpage-230-internet-freedom.

Saada Saar M., Craigslist's shame: Child sex ads, 10 August 2010, http://edition.cnn.com/2010/OPINION/08/02/saar.craigslist.child.trafficking/index.html.

Schmid J., Bouderbala S., Facebook denies 'censoring' 19th-century vagina painting, 1 February 2018, https://phys.org/news/2018-02-facebook-denies-censoring-19th-century-vagina.html.

Schmid M., Final Copyright "compromise": Upload filters for everyone but Google & Co, 23 February 2018, https://edri.org/final-copyright-compromise-upload-filters-everyone-google-co/.

Seven Years of Hadopi: Nine Million Piracy Warnings, 189 Convictions, 1 December 2017, https://torrentfreak.com/seven-years-of-hadopi-nine-million-piracy-warnings-189-convictions-171201/.

Sheffner B., Court: 'no recourse' for victims of defamatory postings under Section 230, 22 December 2009, http://copyrightsandcampaigns.blogspot.be/2009/12/court-no-recourse-for-victims-of.html.

Smith G., Towards a filtered internet: the European Commission's automated prior restraint machine, 25 October 2017, www.cyberleagle.com/2017/10/towards-filtered-internet-european.html.

Sookman B., Norwich orders: who pays under the notice and notice regime? Voltage v Doe, 10 May 2017, www.barrysookman.com/2017/05/10/who-pays-for-recording-and-verifying-subscriber-info-under-the-notice-and-notice-regime-voltage-v-doe/.

South Korea sees fewer crackdowns on copyright infringement: report, 13 August 2011, http://english.yonhapnews.co.kr/national/2011/08/13/43/0302000000AEN201108130 01100315F.HTML.

Stafford K., Michigan woman gets $500K in revenge-porn case, 26 August 2016, https://www.usatoday.com/story/news/nation-now/2016/08/26/michigan-revenge-porn-verdict/89393884/.

Stalla-Bourdillon S., The EU approach to content regulation online: tackling (il)legal content online with upload and re-upload filters! 11 October 2017, https://peepbeep.wordpress.com/2017/10/11/the-eu-approach-to-content-regulation-online-tackling-illegal-content-online-with-upload-and-re-upload-filters/.

Stone B., Craigslist Agrees to Curb Sex Ads, 6 November 2008, www.nytimes.com/2008/11/07/technology/internet/07craigslist.html.

Stur B., Brussels calls for faster removal of illegal content online, 9 January 2018, https://www.neweurope.eu/article/brussels-calls-faster-removal-illegal-content-online/.

Teivainen A., Market Court's ruling expected to stem flow of copyright letters, 5 July 2017, www.helsinkitimes.fi/finland/finland-news/domestic/14870-market-court-s-ruling-expected-to-stem-flow-of-piracy-letters.html.

Teivainen A., Finnish authorities receive complaints about "piracy letters", 25 July 2017, www.helsinkitimes.fi/finland/finland-news/domestic/14917-finnish-authorities-receive-complaints-about-piracy-letters.html.

Thompson D., Backpage.com, CEO plead guilty to state, US charges, 13 April 2018, https://apnews.com/42a8140a1b3c49a8a2f454bf79283474/Backpage.com,-CEO-plead-guilty-to-state,-US-charges.

Village Voice Founder's Son Criticizes Company for Advertisements That Others Can Use for Sex Trafficking of Minors, Joins Groundswell Campaign, 12 January 2012, https://www.prnewswire.com/news-releases/village-voice-founders-son-criticizes-company-for-advertisements-that-others-can-use-for-sex-trafficking-of-minors-joins-groundswell-campaign-137170558.html.

Vincent J., EU sends controversial internet copyright reforms back to the drawing board, 5 July 2018, https://www.theverge.com/2018/7/5/17535874/eu-copyright-law-article-11-13-rejected-first-vote.

Vincent J., EU takes first step in passing controversial copyright law that could 'censor the internet', 20 June 2018, https://www.theverge.com/2018/6/20/17482554/eu-european-union-copyright-filter-article-11-13-passes-juri-vote.

Rep. Ann Wagner introduced H.R. 4225, the "Stop Advertising Victims of Exploitation (SAVE) Act of 2014" in the U.S. House of Representatives, 13 March 2014, https://wagner.house.gov/notforsale.

Yun Che F., EU urges U.S. tech giants to act faster against hate speech, 4 December 2016, www.reuters.com/article/us-eu-hate-speech-idUSKBN13T0XI.

Zittrain J., Facebook Could Decide an Election Without Anyone Ever Finding Out, 2 June 2014, https://newrepublic.com/article/117878/information-fiduciary-solution-facebook-digital-gerrymandering.

POLICY DOCUMENTS

COUNCIL OF EUROPE

Committee of Ministers

Committee of Ministers, The Declaration of Freedom of Expression and Information Adopted by the Committee of Ministers on 29 April 1982 at its 70th Session, www.right2info.org/resources/publications/instruments-and-standards/coe_decl-on-foe-and-foi_1982.

Committee of Ministers, Declaration on freedom of communications on the Internet, Adopted by the Committee of Ministers on 28 May 2003 at the 840th meeting of the Ministers' Deputies, available at https://search.coe.int/cm/Pages/result_details.aspx?ObjectId=09000016805dfbd5.

Committee of Ministers, Recommendation CM/Rec(2007)11 on promoting freedom of expression and information in the new information and communications environment, Adopted by the Committee of Ministers on 26 September 2007 at the 1005th meeting of the Ministers' Deputies, available at https://search.coe.int/cm/Pages/result_details.aspx?ObjectId=09000016805d4d0e.

Committee of Ministers, Recommendation CM/Rec(2007)16 of the Committee of Ministers to member states on measures to promote the public service value of the Internet, Adopted by the Committee of Ministers on 7 November 2007 at the 1010th meeting of the Ministers' Deputies, available at https://search.coe.int/cm/Pages/result_details.aspx?ObjectId=09000016805d4a39.

Committee of Ministers, Recommendation CM/Rec(2011)7 of the Committee of Ministers to member states on a new notion of media, Adopted by the Committee of Ministers on 21 September 2011 at the 1121st meeting of the Ministers' Deputies, available at https://search.coe.int/cm/Pages/result_details.aspx?ObjectID=09000016805cc2c0.

Committee of Ministers, Recommendation CM/Rec(2014)6 of the Committee of Ministers to member States on a Guide to human rights for Internet users, Adopted by the Committee of Ministers on 16 April 2014 at the 1197th meeting of the Ministers' Deputies, available at https://rm.coe.int/CoERMPublicCommonSearchServices/DisplayDCTMContent?documentId=09000016804d5b31.

Committee of Ministers, Recommendation CM/Rec(2016)1 of the Committee of Ministers to member States on protecting and promoting the right to freedom of expression and the right to private life with regard to network neutrality, Adopted by the Committee of Ministers on 13 January 2016, at the 1244th meeting of the Ministers' Deputies, available at https://search.coe.int/cm/Pages/result_details.aspx?ObjectID=09000016805c1e59.

Committee of Ministers, Recommendation CM/Rec(2018)2 of the Committee of Ministers to member States on the roles and responsibilities of internet intermediaries, Adopted by the Committee of Ministers on 7 March 2018 at the 1309th meeting of the Ministers' Deputies, available at https://rm.coe.int/1680790e14.

Other

Standing Committee on Transfrontier Television, Statement (2002) 1 on human dignity and the fundamental rights of others, Adopted by the Committee on Transfrontier Television at its 31st meeting (12–13 September 2002).

Council of Europe Secretariat, Democracy, human rights and the rule of law in the Information Society, Contribution by the Council of Europe to the 2nd Preparatory Committee for the World Summit on the Information Society, 07 December 2002, available at https://www.coe.int/t/dgap/democracy/Activities/GGIS/Public_participation_internet_governance/IP1(2002)27_en.asp

Directorate General of Human Rights and Legal Affairs, Converging media – convergent regulators? The future of broadcasting regulatory authorities in South-Eastern Europe, Conference organised by the Council of Europe and the OSCE Mission to Skopje, 1–2 October 2007, Skopje, available at https://rm.coe.int/1680483b31.

Directorate General of Human Rights and Legal Affairs, Human rights guidelines for Internet Service Providers – Developed by the Council of Europe in co-operation with the European Internet Service Providers Association (EuroISPA), July 2008, available at https://rm.coe.int/16805a39d5.

EUROPEAN UNION

European Commission

European Commission, Green Paper on the convergence of the telecommunications, media and information technology sectors, and the implications for regulation, COM (1997) 623 final, 03 December 1997.

European Commission, First Report on the Application of Directive 2000/31/EC of the European Parliament and of the Council of 8 June 2000 on the Directive on Electronic Commerce, COM(2003) 702 final, Brussels, 21 November 2003.

European Commission, Public consultation on the future of electronic commerce in the internal market and the implementation of the Directive on electronic commerce (2000/31/EC), ended on 5 November 2010, http://ec.europa.eu/internal_market/consultations/2010/e-commerce_en.htm.

European Commission, Summary of the results of the Public Consultation on the future of electronic commerce in the Internal Market and the Implementation of the Directive on electronic commerce (2000/31/EC)

http://ec.europa.eu/internal_market/consultations/docs/2010/e-commerce/summary_report_en.pdf.

European Commission, Communication from the Commission to the European Parliament, the Council, the European Economic and Social Committee and the Committee of the Regions, A Single Market for Intellectual Property RightsBoosting creativity and innovation to provide economic growth, high quality jobs and first class products and services in Europe, COM(2011) 287 24 May 2011, http://ec.europa.eu/internal_market/copyright/docs/ipr_strategy/COM_2011_287_en.pdf.

European Commission, Online Services, Including E-commerce in Single Market, Commission Staff Working Paper, Accompanying the document: Communication from the Commission to the European Parliament, the Council The European Economic and Social Committee and the Committee of the Regions, A Coherent framework to boost confidence in the Digital Single Market of e-commerce and other online services, COM(2011) 942, 11 January 2012, {SEC(2011) 1641 final, available at http://ec.europa.eu/internal_market/e-commerce/docs/communication2012/SEC2011_1640_en.pdf.

European Commission, Commission Staff Working Document Online services, including e-commerce, in the Single Market, Brussels, 11 January 2012, SEC(2011) 1641 final, available at http://ec.europa.eu/internal_market/e-commerce/docs/communication2012/SEC2011_1641_en.pdf.

European Commission, Communication to the European Parliament, The Council, The Economic and Social Committee and The Committee of Regions, A coherent framework for building trust in the Digital Single Market for e-commerce and online services {SEC(2011) 1640 final}, 11 January 2012, available at http://eurlex.europa.eu/LexUriServ/LexUriServ.do?uri=COM:2011:0942:FIN:EN:PDF.

European Commission, Green Paper, Preparing for a Fully Converged Audiovisual World: Growth, Creation and Values, COM (2013) 231 final, Brussels, 24 April 2013.

European Commission, Report from the Commission to the European Parliament and the Council on the functioning of the Memorandum of Understanding on the Sale of Counterfeit Goods via the Internet, COM/2013/0209 final, http://eur-lex.europa.eu/legal-content/EN/TXT/?uri=CELEX%3A52013DC0209.

European Commission, Commission Communication to the European Parliament, The Council, The Economic and Social Committee and The Committee of Regions, Online Platforms and the Digital Single Market Opportunities and Challenges for Europe, Brussels, 25 May 2016 COM(2016) 288 final, http://eurlex.europa.eu/legalcontent/EN/TXT/HTML/?uri=CELEX:52016DC0288&from=EN.

European Commission, Full report on the results of the public consultation on the Regulatory environment for Platforms, Online Intermediaries and the Collaborative Economy: Online Platforms Public Consultation Synopsis Report, 25 May 2016, https://ec.europa.eu/digital-single-market/en/news/full-report-results-public-consultation-regulatory-environment-platforms-online-intermediaries.

European Commission, Proposal for a Directive amending AVMS Directive 2010/13/EU on the coordination of certain provisions laid down by law, regulation or administrative action in Member States concerning the provision of audiovisual media services in view of changing market realities, Brussels, 25 May 2016, COM/2016/0287 final – 2016/0151 (COD), http://eur-lex.europa.eu/legal-content/EN/TXT/?qid=1464618463840&uri=COM:2016:287:FIN.

European Commission, The Code of Conduct on Countering Illegal Hate Speech Online, May 2016, available at http://ec.europa.eu/newsroom/just/item-detail.cfm?item_id=54300.

European Commission, Proposal for a Directive of the European Parliament and of the Council on copyright in the Digital Single Market, Brussels, 14 September 2016, COM(2016) 593 final – 2016/0280 (COD), http://eur-lex.europa.eu/legalcontent/EN/TXT/?uri=CELEX:52016PC0593.

European Commission, Fighting illegal online hate speech: first assessment of the new code of conduct, 6 December 2016, http://ec.europa.eu/newsroom/just/item-detail.cfm?item_id=50840.

European Commission, Report from the Commission to the European Parliament and the Council assessing the extent to which the Member States have taken the necessary measures in order to comply with Directive 2011/93/EU of 13 December 2011 on combating the sexual abuse and sexual exploitation of children and child pornography, Brussels, 16 December 2016, COM(2016) 871 final, http://eur-lex.europa.eu/legal-content/EN/TXT/PDF/?uri=CELEX:52016DC0871&from=EN.

European Commission, Report from the Commission to the European Parliament and the Council assessing the implementation of the measures referred to in Article 25 of Directive 2011/93/EU of 13 December 2011 on combating the sexual abuse and sexual exploitation of children and child pornography, Brussels, 16 December 2016, COM(2016) 872 final, http://eur-lex.europa.eu/legalcontent/EN/TXT/PDF/?uri=CELEX:52016DC0872&from=EN.

European Commission, Code of Conduct on countering online hate speech – results of evaluation show important progress, 1 June 2017, http://ec.europa.eu/newsroom/just/item-detail.cfm?item_id=71674.

European Commission, Code of Conduct on countering illegal hate speech online: One year after – Fact Sheet, June 2017, http://ec.europa.eu/newsroom/just/item-detail.cfm?item_id=71674.

European Commission, Commission Communication to the European Parliament, The Council, The Economic and Social Committee and The Committee of Regions, Tackling Illegal Content Online – Towards an enhanced responsibility of online platforms, Brussels, 28 September 2017, COM(2017) 555 final, https://ec.europa.eu/digital-single-market/en/news/communication-tackling-illegal-content-online-towards-enhanced-responsibility-online-platforms.

European Commission, Communication from the Commission to the European Parliament, the Council, the European Economic and Social Committee, Guidance on certain aspects of Directive 2004/48/EC of the European Parliament and of the Council on the enforcement of intellectual property rights {SWD(2017) 431 final} – {SWD(2017) 432 final}, Brussels, 29.11.2017, COM(2017) 708 final.

European Commission, Results of Commission's last round of monitoring of the Code of Conduct against online hate speech, 19 January 2018, http://ec.europa.eu/newsroom/just/item-detail.cfm?item_id=612086.

European Commission, Communication from the Commission to the European Parliament and the Council Stronger protection, new opportunities – Commission guidance on the direct application of the General Data Protection Regulation as of 25 May 2018, Brussels, 24 January 2018, COM(2018) 43 final, http://eur-lex.europa.eu/legal-content/EN/TXT/PDF/?uri=CELEX:52018DC0043&from=EN.

European Commission, Recommendation on Measures to Effectively Tackle Illegal Content Online, Brussels, 1 March 2018, C(2018) 1177 final.

European Commission, Public consultation on measures to further improve the effectiveness of the fight against illegal content online, April 2018, https://ec.europa.eu/eusurvey/runner/illegal_content_onlin e.

European Commission, Proposal for a Regulation on promoting fairness and transparency for business users of online intermediation services, 26 April, https://ec.europa.eu/digital-single-market/en/news/regulation-promoting-fairness-and-transparency-business-users-online-intermediation-services.

European Commission, Impact assessment of the Proposal for a Regulation of the European Parliament and of the Council on promoting fairness and transparency for business users of online intermediation services, 26 April 2018, https://ec.europa.eu/digital-single-market/en/news/impact-assessment-proposal--promoting-fairness-transparency-online-platforms.

European Parliament

European Parliament, Directorate-General for Internal Policies, Policy Department C: Citizens' Rights And Constitutional Affairs, The European legal framework on hate speech, blasphemy and its interaction with freedom of expression, LIBE, 2015, www.europarl.europa.eu/thinktank/en/document.html?reference=IPOL_STU(2015)536460.

European Parliament resolution of 14 December 2017 on the implementation of Directive 2011/93/EU of the European Parliament and of the Council of 13 December 2011 on combating the sexual abuse and sexual exploitation of children and child pornography (2015/2129(INI)), 14 December 2017.

X, Proposal for a Directive on Copyright in the Digital Single Market, Draft compromise amendments on Article 13 and corresponding recitals, Version 1, 21 February 2018, https://juliareda.eu/wp-content/uploads/2018/02/20180221-Draft-CA-on-Article-13_v1.pdf.

Council of the European Union

Council of the European Union, EU Counter-terrorism Coordinator input for the preparation of the informal meeting of Justice and Home Affairs Ministers in Riga on 29 January 2015, DS 1035/15, 17 January 2015, see: www.statewatch.org/news/2015/jan/eu-council-ct-ds-1035–15.pdf.

Proposal for a Directive of the European Parliament and of the Council on copyright in the Digital Single Market – Consolidated Presidency Compromise Proposal. Interinstitutional File: 2016/0280 (COD), Brussels, 23 March 2018. http://data.consilium.europa.eu/doc/document/ST-7450–2018-INIT/en/pdf.

OECD

OECD, The Economic and Social Role of Internet Intermediaries, April 2010.

OECD, Directorate for Science, Technology and Industry, Committee for Information, Computer and Communication Policy, *The Role of Internet Intermediaries In Advancing Public Policy Objectives, Forging partnerships for advancing public policy objectives for the Internet economy*, Part II, 22 June 2011.

UNITED NATIONS

Human Rights Council, Guiding Principles on Business and Human Rights: Implementing the United Nations 'Protect, Respect and Remedy' Framework, 16 June 2011, www.ohchr.org/Documents/Publications/GuidingPrinciplesBusinessHR_EN.pdf.

United Nations, Report of the Special Rapporteur David Kaye on the promotion and protection of the right to freedom of opinion and expression, A/HRC/38/35, 6 April 2018, https://documents-dds-ny.un.org/doc/UNDOC/GEN/G18/096/72/PDF/G1809672.pdf?OpenElement.

NATIONAL POLICY DOCUMENTS

House of Representatives Report 104–458 (1996), at p. 194, https://www.congress.gov/104/crpt/hrpt458/CRPT-104hrpt458.pdf.

House of Commons Debates, 41st Parl, 1st Sess, No 31 (18 October 2011) at 1050 (Hon James Moore, Conservative Party of Canada).

Memorandum of Understanding Between Crown Prosecution Service (CPS) and the Association of Chief Police Officers (ACPO) concerning Section 46 Sexual Offences Act 2003, https://www.iwf.org.uk/sites/default/files/inline-files/CPS%20ACPO%20S46%20MoU%202014%202.pdf.

LEGISLATION

EUROPEAN LEGISLATION

Charter of Fundamental Rights of the European Union, 2000/C 364/1, 18 December 2000, www.europarl.europa.eu/charter/pdf/text_en.pdf.

Chile-USA Free Trade Agreement (FTA), 1 January 2004, https://ustr.gov/trade-agreements/free-trade-agreements/chile-fta/final-text.
Council of Europe, Convention for the Protection of Human Rights and Fundamental Freedoms, CETS No. 005, 04 November 1950, Rome, http://conventions.coe.int/Treaty/en/Treaties/Html/005.htm.
Directive 2000/31/EC of 8 June 2000 on certain legal aspects of information society services, in particular electronic commerce, in the Internal Market (Directive on electronic commerce), O.J. L 178, 17 July 2000.
Directive 2011/92/EU of the European Parliament and of the Council of 13 December 2011 on combating the sexual abuse and sexual exploitation of children and child pornography, and replacing Council Framework Decision 2004/68/JHA, OJ L 335, 17 December 2011.
Directive 2010/13/EU of the European Parliament and of the Council of 10 March 2010 on the coordination of certain provisions laid down by law, regulation or administrative action in Member States concerning the provision of audiovisual media services (Audiovisual Media Services Directive), OJ L 95/1 2010.
Directive on the harmonisation of certain aspects of copyright and related rights in the information society ("InfoSoc Directive"), 22 May 2001.
Directive on rental right and lending right and on certain rights related to copyright in the field of intellectual property ("Rental and Lending Directive"), 12 December 2006.
Directive on the resale right for the benefit of the author of an original work of art ("Resale Right Directive"), 27 September 2001.
Directive on the coordination of certain rules concerning copyright and rights related to copyright applicable to satellite broadcasting and cable retransmission ("Satellite and Cable Directive"), 27 September 1993.
Directive on the legal protection of computer programs ("Software Directive"), 23 April 2009.
Directive on the enforcement of intellectual property right ("IPRED"), 29 April 2004.
Corrigendum to Directive 2004/48/EC of the European Parliament and of the Council of 29 April 2004 on the enforcement of intellectual property rights, OJ L 157, 30 April 2004.
Directive on the legal protection of databases ("Database Directive"), 11 March 1996.
Directive on the term of protection of copyright and certain related rights amending the previous 2006 Directive ("Term Directive"), 27 September 2011.
Directive on certain permitted uses of orphan works ("Orphan Works Directive"), 25 October 2012.
Directive on collective management of copyright and related rights and multi-territorial licensing of rights in musical works for online use in the internal market ("CRM Directive"), 26 February 2014;
Directive on certain permitted uses of certain works and other subject matter protected by copyright and related rights for the benefit of persons who are blind, visually impaired or otherwise print-disabled (Directive implementing the Marrakech Treaty in the EU), 13 September 2017.
Regulation (EU) 2016/679 of the European Parliament and of the Council of 27 April 2016 on the protection of natural persons with regard to the processing of personal

data and on the free movement of such data, and repealing Directive 95/46/EC (General Data Protection Regulation), Official Journal of the European Union L 119/1, 4 May 2016.

Treaty on European Union, Consolidated Version, Official Journal of the European Union C 326/15, 26 October 2012.

NATIONAL LEGISLATION

Canada

Copyright Act, (R.S.C., 1985, c. C-42), http://laws-lois.justice.gc.ca/eng/acts/C-42/index.html

Copyright Modernization Act (S.C. 2012, c. 20), http://lawslois.justice.gc.ca/eng/annualstatutes/2012_20/page-1.html.

Chile

Ley no. 20.435, modifica la Ley no. 17.336 sobre propiedad intelectual, https://www.leychile.cl/Navegar?idNorma=1012827&idParte=&idVersion=2010-05-04

Finland

The Finnish Information Society Code (2014/917), which entered into force on 1 January 2015, Tietoyhteiskuntakaari, 7.11.2014/917, available: www.finlex.fi/en/laki/kaannokset/2014/en20140917.pdf.

Act on provision of information society services (458/2002), 5 June 2002, www.finlex.fi/fi/laki/kaannokset/2002/en20020458.pdf.

France

Loi n° 2004-575 du 21 juin 2004 pour la confiance dans l'économie numérique, www.wipo.int/wipolex/en/text.jsp?file_id=276258.

Loi n° 2009-669 du 12 juin 2009 favorisant la diffusion et la protection de la création sur internet, www.wipo.int/wipolex/en/text.jsp?file_id=179252.

Loi n° 2009-1311 du 28 octobre 2009 relative à la protection pénale de la propriété littéraire et artistique, Journal officiel du 29 octobre 2009, known as HADOPI 2.

Loi n° 86-1067 du 30 septembre 1986 relative à la liberté de communication (Loi Léotard) (Law No. 86-1067 of 30 September 1986 on freedom of communication) as amended by the *Loi no 2000-719 du 1er août 2000 modifiant la loi no 86-1067 du 30 septembre 1986 relative à la liberté de communication (Law No. 2000-719 of 1 August 2000 modifying the law No. 86-1067 of 30 September 1986 on freedom of communication).*

Décret n° 2013-596 du 8 juillet 2013 supprimant la peine contraventionnelle complémentaire de suspension de l'accès à un service de communication au public en ligne et relatif aux modalités de transmission des informations prévue à l'Article L.

331-21 du code de la propriété intellectuelle, Journal officiel n°0157 du 9 juillet 2013, page 11428, texte n° 60.
Conseil Constitutionnel, Décision No 2004-496 DC du 10 juin 2004, Journal officiel du 22 juin 2004, p. 11182.

Germany

Telemediengesetz, 26 February 2007, BGBl. I S. 179.
Gesetz zur Verbesserung der Rechtsdurchsetzung in sozialen Netzwerken [Netzdurchführungsgesetz - NetzDG], Drucksache 536/17, 30 June 2017. See German Federal Ministry of Justice and Consumer Protection, unofficial translation, https://www.bmjv.de/SharedDocs/Gesetzgebungsverfahren/Dokumente/NetzDG_engl.pdf.
Gesetz über Urheberrecht und verwandte Schutzrechte - UrhG (German copyright act), translation available at the *Bundesministerium der Justiz und für Verbraucherschutz*, available at: www.gesetze-im-internet.de/englisch_urhg/englisch_urhg.html.

Hungary

Act. XIX of 1998 on Criminal Proceedings Act (hereinafter: CPA) 158/B-158/D and 596/A.
Act C of 2012 on Criminal Code (CC).
Act CVIII of 2001 on certain issues of electronic commerce services and information society services, Promulgated: 24 December, 2001, www.neuronit.com/documents/108_2001_el_comm_torv_20070502.pdf

South Korea

Copyright Act, Amended by Act No. 9625, Apr. 22, 2009; Act No. 10807, Jun. 30, 2011; Act No. 11110,
2 Dec. 2011, Act No. 14083, Mar. 22, 2016, Act No. 14634, Mar. 21, 2017. http://elaw.klri.re.kr/kor_service/lawView.do?hseq=25455&lang=ENG.
Old version of the Copyright Act (Act No. 11110, Dec. 2, 2011), http://elaw.klri.re.kr/kor_service/lawView.do?hseq=25455&lang=ENG.
Act on Promotion of Information and Communications Network Utilization and Information Protection, etc.
(ICNA, Information and Communications Network Act), last amended by Act No. 11322, February 17, 2012.
See: http://elaw.klri.re.kr/kor_service/lawView.do?hseq=25446&lang=ENG.
Telecommunications Business Act No.12035, Enforcement Date 14. Feb, 2014 13. Aug, 2013., Partial
Amendment www.law.go.kr/lsInfoP.do?lsiSeq=142966&urlMode=engLsInfoR&viewCls=engLsInfoR#0000
Act on the Protection of Children and Juveniles Against Sexual Abuse, last amended by Act No. 11690,
23 March 2013 See: http://elaw.klri.re.kr/kor_service/lawView.do?hseq=28311&lang=ENG.

Act on the Consumer Protection in Electronic Commerce, Etc., last amended by Act No. 11461, 1 June 2012
See: http://elaw.klri.re.kr/kor_service/lawView.do?hseq=25650&lang=ENG.
Public Official Election Act, last amended by Act No. 11071, 7 November 2011 See:
http://elaw.klri.re.kr/kor_service/lawView.do?hseq=25035&lang=ENG.
Act on the Establishment and Operation of Korea Communications Commission, Amended by Act No. 11711, 23 March 2013 See: http://elaw.klri.re.kr/kor_service/lawView.do?hseq=28155&lang=ENG.

United Kingdom

UK Human Rights Act 1998, www.legislation.gov.uk/ukpga/1998/42/schedule/1.
Terrorism Act 2006, www.legislation.gov.uk/ukpga/2006/11/contents,
Defamation Act 2013, www.legislation.gov.uk/ukpga/2013/26/contents/enacted
Electronic Commerce (EC Directive) Regulations 2002 (Statutory Instrument 2013/2002), www.legislation.gov.uk/uksi/2002/2013/contents/made
The Defamation (Operators of Websites) Regulations 2013, https://www.legislation.gov.uk/ukdsi/2013/9780111104620

United States of America

United States Constitution, Bill of Rights, Adopted 1791.
Section 202 of the Digital Millennium Copyright Act (codified at 17 U.S.C. §512), available: https://www.law.cornell.edu/uscode/text/17/512
47 U.S. Code §230 – Protection for private blocking and screening of offensive material
State of Washington Senate Bill 6251, 7 June 2012, http://apps.leg.wa.gov/documents/billdocs/2011-12/Pdf/Bills/Session%20Laws/Senate/6251-S.SL.pdf;
State of Tennessee Public Chapter No. 1075, 1 May 2012, www.dmlp.org/sites/dmlp.org/files/pc1075.pdf.
Senate's "Stop Enabling Sex Traffickers Act of 2017" bill, S. 1693, https://www.portman.senate.gov/public/index.cfm/files/serve?File_id=1DA519D4-4B37-4C5E-B8B9-4A205C5E488F.
Rep. Ann Wagner's the "Allow States and Victims to Fight Online Sex Trafficking Act of 2017" bill, H.R. 1865, https://www.congress.gov/115/bills/hr1865/BILLS-115hr1865ih.pdf.
U.S. Congress, Allow States and Victims to Fight Online Sex Trafficking Act of 2017 115th Congress (2017–2018) – H.R.1865, https://www.congress.gov/bill/115th-congress/house-bill/1865/text.

OTHER REPORTS & STUDIES

Annual Report 2009 Korea APAA Copyright Committee, Major Amendments to Korean Copyright Act – April, 2009, www.apaaonline.org/pdf/APAA_56th_&_57th_council_meeting/copyright/2-Korea%20Copyright%20Cttee%20Country%20Report%202009.pdf.

Article 19, 'Promoting Free Expression and Access to Information: 2010 Implementation Report', www.article19.org/data/files/annual_reports_and_accounts/2010-annual-report.pdf.

Art. 19 Response to the Consultation on electronic commerce, November 2010, www.article19.org/data/files/pdfs/submissions/responseto-eu-consultation.pdf.

Article 19, EU: European Commission's Code of conduct for Countering Illegal Hate Speech Online and the Framework Decision – legal analysis, June 2016, https://www.article19.org/data/files/medialibrary/38430/EU-Code-of-conduct-analysis-FINAL.pdf.

Article 19, Germany: Act to Improve Enforcement of the Law on Social Networks – Legal Analysis, August 2017, https://www.article19.org/data/files/medialibrary/38860/170901-Legal-Analysis-German-NetzDG-Act.pdf

Angelopoulos C. et al., "Study of fundamental rights limitations for online enforcement through self-regulation", Institute for Information Law (IViR), 2016.

CDT, Chile's Notice-and-Takedown System for Copyright Protection: an Alternative Approach, August 2012, https://cdt.org/files/pdfs/Chile-notice-takedown.pdf.

Bojarski L., Schindlauer D., Wladasch K., The European Charter of Fundamental Rights as a Living Instrument – Manual, publication produced within the project "Making the CFREU a Living Instrument" (JUST/2012/FRAC/AG/2705), co-funded by the European Commission, 2014.

Centre for Law and Democracy, Analysis of the Korean Copyright Act, June 2013, www.law-democracy.org/live/wp-content/uploads/2013/06/Korea.Copyright.pdf.

Csiszér G., Ministry of National Development, Presentation of Hungary concerning national legislative approach to notice and action, EC Expert group on electronic commerce (E01636), 27 April 2017, http://ec.europa.eu/transparency/regexpert/index.cfm?do=groupDetail.groupDetail&groupID=1636.

CDT, Shielding the Messengers: Protecting Platforms for Expression and Innovation, Version 2, updated December 2012, https://cdt.org/insight/shielding-the-messengers-protecting-platforms-for-expression-and-innovation/.

Directorate of the Jurisconsult of the Council of Europe, Guide on Article 6 of the European Convention on Human Rights, Right to a fair trial (civil limb), Updated to 31 December 2017, available at https://www.echr.coe.int/Documents/Guide_Art_6_ENG.pdf.

EDRi, A letter to the Digital Economy Commissioner Mariya Gabriel, 20 October 2017, https://edri.org/files/letter_coherent_rightsbasedapproach_illegalcontent_20171020.pdf.

EDRi, Deconstructing the Article 13 of the Copyright proposal of the European Commission, Revision 2, https://edri.org/files/copyright/copyright_proposal_article13.pdf.

EDRi on IT-Forum, 16 December 2015, https://edri.org/files/IT-Forum_EDRi_Position.pdf.

EDRI, Recommendations on the German bill "Improving Law Enforcement on Social Networks" (NetzDG), 20 June 2017, https://edri.org/files/consultations/tris_netzdg_edricontribution_20170620.pdf.

EDRi's letter to the Commission on the blocking aspect of the Child Exploitation Directive, 2 November 2012,

https://edri.org/files/blocking_20121102.pdf.
European Commission's response to EDRi's letter on the blocking aspect of the Child Exploitation Directive, 26 November 2012, https://edri.org/files/priebe_response.pdf.
Edwards L., Report to World Intellectual Property Organisation (WIPO) on The Role and Responsibilities of Online Intermediaries in the Field of Copyright and Related Works, Geneva, June 2011.
European Parliament, Press Freedom in the EU: Legal Framework and Challenges, Briefing, April 2015, www.europarl.europa.eu/EPRS/EPRS-Briefing-554214-Press-freedom-in-the-EU-FINAL.pdf.
European Parliament speaks out against online homo- and transphobic hate speech, 29 April 2016, www.lgbt-ep.eu/press-releases/european-parliament-speaks-out-against-online-homo-and-transphobic-hate-speech/.
EU Internet Forum against Terrorism: Bringing together governments, Europol and technology companies to counter terrorist content and hate speech online, Brussels, 3 December 2015, http://europa.eu/rapid/press-release_IP-15-6243_en.htm.
Code of Conduct on illegal online hate speech announced by the European Commission and IT Companies, European Commission – Press release, Brussels, 31 May 2016, http://europa.eu/rapid/press-release_IP-16-1937_en.htm.
"Federal Supreme Court (Bundesgerichtshof): GERMANY", *International Review of Intellectual Property and Competition Law* (IIC) 2005, 573.
Galetta D.-U., Hofmann H. C. H., Mir Puigpelat O., and others, "The General Principles of EU Administrative Procedural Law, In-depth Analysis", Study commissioned by the European Parliament, Directorate-General for Internal Policies, Policy Department C – Citizen's Rights and Constitutional Affairs, the JURI Committee on Legal and Parliamentary Affairs, PE 519.224, June 2015.
GNI, Comments on the Public Consultation on Procedures for Notifying and Acting on Illegal Content Hosted by Online Intermediaries, 5 September 2012, http://globalnetworkinitiative.org/sites/default/files/GNI%20Comments%20on%20EC%20Notice%20and%20Action%20c onsult.pdf.
HADOPI, Rapport d' activité 2016–2017, https://www.hadopi.fr/sites/default/rapportannuel/HADOPI-Rapport-d-activite-2016-2017.pdf.
Hans-Bredow Institut, Regulated Self-Regulation as a Form of Modern Government: Study commissioned by the German Federal Commissioner for Cultural and Media Affairs (Interim Report, October 2001).
Hans-Bredow-Institut for Media Research, University of Hamburg, *Study on Co-Regulation Measures in the Media Sector*, Final Report, Study for the European Commission, Directorate Information Society and Media, 2006.
Hofmann H.C.H., Schneider J.-P., Ziller J., Administrative Procedures and the Implementation of EU Law and Policies, Contribution by the Research Network on EU Administrative Law (ReNEUAL) project on administrative procedure to the EU Commission's 'Assises de la Justice' conference in Brussels 21–22 November 2013 to the topic of EU ADMINISTRATIVE LAW, Law Working Paper Series, Paper number 2014-09.
Internet and Jurisdiction Policy Network, Cross-border Content Restrictions, Input Document for Workstream II of the second Global Internet and Jurisdiction Conference, November 2017.

Jakubowicz K., A Notion of new Media, Keynote speech prepared for delivery during the 1st Council of Europe Conference of Ministers Responsible for Media and New Communication Services, Reykjavik, May 28–29, 2009.

Joint Statement by Craigslist, the Attorneys General, and the National Center for Missing and Exploited Children ("NCMEC"), www.dmlp.org/sites/citmedialaw.org/files/2008-11-00-Craigslist%20AG%20Agreement.pdf.

Kastberg Nielsen C. *et al.*, Study on The Economic Impact of the Electronic Commerce Directive, Final Report, Part II, DG Internal Market and Services, European Commission, September 2007.

Korff D., The rule of law on the Internet and in the wider digital world, Issue paper published by the Commissioner for Human Rights, Strasbourg, 2014, available at https://rm.coe.int/16806da51c.

La Rue F., Report of the Special Rapporteur on the promotion and protection of the right to freedom of opinion and expression, United Nations. General Assembly. A/HRC/17/27.

Le Borgne-Bachschmidt F., et al., User-Created-Content: Supporting a participative Information Society Final Report, Understanding the Digital World, SMART 2007/2008.

Lescure P., Mission 'Acte II de l'exception culturelle' – Contribution aux politiques culturelles à l'ère numérique, May 2013.

Lenaerts K., Effective judicial protection in the EU, Intervention at the Conference 'Assises de la Justice – What role for Justice in the European Union?' hosted by the European Commission on 21–22 November 2013 in Brussels.

Lithwick D., Thibodeau M.-O., Bill C-11: An Act to amend the Copyright Act, Library of Parliament Legislative Summary, Publication No. 41-1-C11-E, 14 October 2011, Revised 20 April 2012.

Mandelkern Group on Better Regulation Final Report, 13 November 2001.

The Manila Principles on Intermediary Liability Background Paper, Version 1.0, 30 May 2015, https://www.eff.org/files/2015/07/08/manila_principles_background_paper.pdf.

Manila Principles on Intermediary Liability, Best Practices Guidelines for Limiting Intermediary Liability for Content to Promote Freedom of Expression and Innovation, A Global Civil Society Initiative, Version 1.0, March 24, 2015, https://www.eff.org/files/2015/10/31/manila_principles_1.0.pdf.

Nordemann J. B., Liability of Online Service Providers for Copyrighted Content – Regulatory Action Needed? In-depth analysis for Policy Department A upon request of the European Parliament's Committee on the Internal Market and Consumer Protection, IP/A/IMCO/2017-08 PE 614.207, January 2018.

Notification to the European Commission, Number 2017/0127/D – SERV60, Act improving law enforcement on social networks [NetzDG], http://ec.europa.eu/growth/tools-databases/tris/en/search/?trisaction=search.detail&year=2017&num=127.

Ofcom, Identifying Appropriate Regulatory Solutions: Principles for Analysing Self- and Co-Regulation, http://stakeholders.ofcom.org.uk/binaries/consultations/coregulation/statement/statement.pdf.

Ombelet P.J., Kuczerawy A., Valcke P., Legal / regulatory requirements analysis – Media law and Freedom of expression, Deliverable D1.2c, REVEAL project, 30 April 2016.

Open Letter to Commissioner Barnier, https://ameliaandersdotter.eu/sites/default/files/letter_commissioner_barnier_notice_and_takedown.pdf..

Open Letter by the National Association of Attorneys General, 23 July 2013, https://www.eff.org/sites/default/files/cda-ag-letter.pdf.

Opinion of Advocate General Trstenjak, delivered on 8 September 2011 in Case C-282/10, *Dominguez v. Centre Informatique Du Centre Ouest Atlantique*, judgment of 24 January 2012.

OSCE, Organisation for Security and Co-operation in Europe, The Office of the Representative on Freedom of the Media, REPORT Freedom of Expression on the internet, Study of legal provisions and practices related to freedom of expression, the free flow of information and media pluralism on the internet in OSCE participating states, 15 December 2011.

OSCE and Reporters Sans Frontiers, Joint declaration on guaranteeing media freedom on the Internet, 18 June 2005, available at: www.osce.org/fom/15657.

Panday J. et al., Comparative Study Of Intermediary Liability Regimes Chile, Canada, India, South Korea, UK and USA in support of the Manila Principles On Intermediary Liability, 1 July 2015.

Park K. S., Intermediary Liability: Not just Backwards but Going Back, NoC Online Intermediaries Case Studies Series – South Korea, https://publixphere.net/i/noc/page/OI_Case_Study_Intermediary_liability__Not_Just_Backward_but_Going_Back..

Praesidium of the Convention, Explanations relating to the Charter of Fundamental Rights, (2007/C 303/02) 14 December 2007.

Public Relations Unit of the European Court of Human Rights: The ECHR in 50 questions, 2014, https://www.echr.coe.int/Documents/50Questions_ENG.pdf.

Rubin C., Ministère de l'Economie, des Finances et de l'Industrie, Presentation of France concerning national legislative approach to notice and action, EC Expert group on electronic commerce (E01636), 27 April 2017, http://ec.europa.eu/transparency/regexpert/index.cfm?do=groupDetail.groupDetail&groupID=1636.

Rzeplinski A., Restrictions on the expression of opinions or disclosure of information on domestic or foreign policy of the State, Document prepared by the Secretary General's monitoring unit, Compliance with commitments entered into by Member States: Information concerning the Committee of Ministers' monitoring procedure, Freedom of expression and restrictions included in the penal code and other legal texts: seminars held in Budapest and in Strasbourg, Monitor/Inf (97) 3, Council of Europe.

Schaake M. et al., Open letter sent to Commissioner Ansip – MEPs want notice and action directive, 10 May 2107, https://marietjeschaake.eu/en/meps-want-notice-and-action-directive.

Seng D., Comparative Analysis of National Approaches of the Liability of the Internet Intermediaries – Part I, WIPO, 2010, www.wipo.int/publications/en/details.jsp?id=4144&plang=EN.

Spindler G., "Country Report – Germany" for "Study on the Liability of Internet Intermediaries", 2006, http://ec.europa.eu/internal_market/e-commerce/directive_en.htm.

Schaake M., et al., Letter to the commission on notice and action procedures, 5 December 2017, https://www.politico.eu/wp-content/uploads/2017/12/Notice-and-action-letter-MEPs-05122017.pdf

Stalla-Bourdillon S. et al., Open Letter to the European Commission – On the Importance of Preserving the Consistency and Integrity of the EU Acquis Relating to Content Monitoring within the Information Society, 19 October 2016, https://papers.ssrn.com/sol3/papers.cfm?abstract_id=2850483.

Stalla-Bourdillon S. et al., A Brief Exegesis of the Proposed Copyright Directive, 30 November 2016, https://papers.ssrn.com/sol3/papers.cfm?abstract_id=2875296.

Swiss Institute of Comparative Law, Comparative Study on Filtering, blocking and take-down of illegal content on the Internet, Report commissioned by the Council of Europe, 20 December 2015, www.coe.int/en/web/freedom-expression/study-filtering-blocking-and-take-down-of-illegal-content-on-the-internet.

United States Trade Representative. 2013 Special 301 Report, https://ustr.gov/about-us/policy-offices/press-office/reports-and-publications/2013/2013-special-301-report.

EU Network of Independent Experts on Fundamental Rights, Commentary of the Charter of Fundamental Rights of the European Union, June 2006.

Van Eecke P., Truyens M., EU Study on the Legal Analysis of A Single Market for the Information Society – New Rules for a New Age? A study commissioned by the European Commission's Information Society and Media Directorate-General, November 2009.

van Eijk N., Jasserand C., Wiersma C. and van Engers T. M., Moving towards Balance: A Study into Duties of Care on the Internet, Institute for Information Law & Leibniz Center for Law, University of Amsterdam.

Verbiest T., Spindler G., et al. Study on the liability of Internet Intermediaries, Markt/2006/09/E, 12 November 2007.

Voorhoof D., Co-regulation and European basic rights, Presentation at the Expert Conference on Media Policy *More trust in content – The potential of self- and co-regulation in digital media*, Leipzig, 9–11 May 2007.

CASE LAW

EUROPEAN CASE LAW

European Court of Human Rights

ECtHR, *Belgian Linguistic case*, 23 July 1968.
ECtHR, *Delcourt v. Belgium*, 17 January 1970.
ECtHR, *Klass and Others v. Germany*, 6 September 1978.
ECtHR, *Handyside v. the United Kingdom*, 7 December 1976.
ECtHR, *Sunday Times v. the United Kingdom*, 26 April 1979.
ECtHR, *Airey v Ireland*, 9 October, 1979.
ECtHR, *Young, James and Webster v. the United Kingdom*, 13 August 1981.
ECtHR, *X v. the United Kingdom*, 5 November 1981.
ECtHR, *Piersack v. Belgium*, 1 October 1982.
ECtHR, *Van der Mussele v. Belgium*, 23 November 1983, Series A no. 70.
ECtHR, *Silver and Others v United Kingdom*, 25 March 1983.
ECtHR, *Campbell and Fell v. the United Kingdom*, 28 June 1984

ECtHR, *Malone v. the United Kingdom*, 1984.
ECtHR, *Sramek v. Austria*, 22 October 1984.
ECtHR, *Barthold v. Germany*, 25 March 1985.
ECtHR, *X. and Y. v Netherlands*, 26 March 1985.
ECtHR, *Ashingdane v. the United Kingdom*, 28 May 1985.
ECtHR, *Rees v. the United Kingdom*, 17 October 1986.
ECtHR, *Leander v. Sweden*, 26 March 1987.
ECtHR, *B v. the United Kingdom*, 26 May 1987.
ECtHR, *W. v. The United Kingdom*, 8 July 1987.
ECtHR, *Boyle and Rice v United Kingdom*, 24 March 1988.
European Commission of Human Rights, *Kühnen v. Germany*, 12 May 1988.
ECtHR, *Plattform "Arzte fur das Leben" v Austria*, 21 June 1988.
ECtHR, *Muller v. Switzerland*, 1988.
ECtHR, *Barfod v. Germany*, 1989.
ECtHR, *Ediciones Tiempo SA v. Spain*, 12 July 1989.
ECtHR, *Kaya v. Turkey*, 19 February 1998.
ECtHR, *Soering v. UK*, 07 July 1989.
ECtHR, *Powell and Rayner*, 21 February 1990.
ECtHR, *Groppera Radio AG and others v. Switzerland*, 28 March 1990.
ECtHR, *Autronic AG v. Switzerland*, 22 May 1990.
ECtHR, *Sunday Times (2) v. the United Kingdom*, 1991.
ECtHR, *Observer and Guardian v. the United Kingdom*, 26 November 1991.
ECtHR, *Open Door and Dublin Well Woman v. Ireland*, 29 October 1992.
ECtHR, *Salesi v. Italy*, 26 February 1993.
ECtHR, *Costello-Roberts v. the United Kingdom*, 25 March 1993.
ECtHR, *Stanford v. The United Kingdom*, 23 February 1994.
ECtHR, *Hokkanen v. Finland*, 24 August 1994.
ECtHR, *Katte Klitsche de la Grange v. Italy*, 27 October 1994.
ECtHR, *López Ostra*, 09 December 1994.
ECtHR, *Goodwin v. the United Kingdom*, 1996.
ECtHR, *Vermeulen v. Belgium*, 20 February 1996.
ECtHR, *Buckley v. the United Kingdom*, 29 September 1996.
ECtHR, *Gul v Switzerland* 1996-I 165.
ECtHR, *Ankerl v. Switzerland*, 23 October, 1996.
ECtHR, *Chahal v United Kingdom*, 15 November 1996.
ECtHR, *Wingrove v. the United Kingdom*, 25 November 1996.
ECtHR, *Findlay v. the United Kingdom*, 25 February 1997.
ECtHR, *Kaya v. Turkey*, 19 February 1998.
ECtHR, *Ceylan v. Turkey* [GC], 8 July 1999.
ECtHR, *Chassagnou and Others v. France, [GC]*, 29 April 1999.
ECtHR, *Bladet Tromsø and Stensaas v. Norway*, 20 May 1999.
ECtHR, *Çakıcı v. Turkey [GC]*, 8 July 1999.
ECtHR, *Buscemi v. Italy*, 16 September 1999.
ECtHR, *Rowe and Davis v. the United Kingdom*, 16 February 2000.
ECtHR, *Ignoccolo-Zenide v. Romania*, 25 January 2000.
ECtHR, *Gast and Popp v. Germany*, 25 February 2000.
ECtHR, *Fuentes Bobo v. Spain*, 29 February 2000.

ECtHR, *Coëme and Ohters v. Belgium*, 22 June 2000.
ECtHR, *Frydlender v. France*, 27 June 2000.
ECtHR, *Kudla v Poland*, 26 October 2000.
ECtHR, *Chapman v. The United Kingdom*, 18 January 2001.
ECtHR, *Association Ekin v. France*, para. 58, ECHR 2001-VIII.
ECtHR, *Fogarty v United Kingdom*, para. 33, ECHR 2001-XI.
ECtHR, *Keenan v United Kingdom*, 3 April 2001.
ECtHR, *VGT Verein v. Tierfabriken*, 28 June 2001.
ECtHR, *Kutzner v. Germany*, 26 February 2002.
ECtHR, *Perna v. Italy*, 06 May 2003.
ECtHR, *Appleby and others v. the United Kingdom*, 06 May 2003.
ECtHR, *Garaudy v. France*, 24 June 2003.
ECtHR, *Hatton and Others v. the United Kingdom*, [GC] 8 July 2003
ECtHR, *Steur v. the Netherlands*, 28 October 2003;
ECtHR, *Gündüz v. Turkey*, 04 December 2003.
ECtHR, *Peck v. the United Kingdom*, no. 44647/98, ECHR 2003-I
ECtHR, *Suominen v. Finland*, 1 July 2003.
ECtHR, *Murphy v. Ireland*, 10 July 2003.
ECtHR, *Maestri v. Italy* [GC], no. 39748/98, para. 30, ECHR 2004-I.
ECtHR, *Editions Plon v. France*, ECHR 2004-IV.
ECtHR, *Perez v. France*, 12 February 2004.
ECtHR, *Maestri v. Italy*, 17 February 2004.
ECtHR, *Assanidzé v. Georgia*, 8 April 2004.
ECtHR, *Von Hannover v. Germany*, 26 April 2004.
ECtHR, *Öneryıldız v. Turkey*, 30 November 2004.
ECtHR, *Steel and Morris v. the United Kingdom*, 15 February 2005.
ECtHR, *Isayeva and Others v. Russia*, 24 February 2005.
ECtHR, *Melnychuk v. Ukraine*, Decision of inadmissibility of the European Court of Human Rights (Second Section) of 5 July 2005.
ECtHR, *Tanis and others v. Turkey*, 2 August 2005.
ECtHR, *Leyla Şahin v. Turkey*, 10 November 2005.
ECtHR, *Donadze v. Georgia*, 7 March 2006.
ECtHR, *Scordino (No. 1), Riccardi Pizzati, Musci, Giuseppe Mostacciuolo (Nos. 1 and 2), Cocchiarella, Apicella, Ernestina Zullo, Giuseppina and Orestina Procaccini v. Italy*, 29 March 2006.
ECtHR, *Korchuganova v. Russia*, No. 75039/01, 8 June 2006.
ECtHR, *Korchuganova v. Russia*, 8 June 2006.
ECtHR, *White v. Sweden*, 19 September 2006.
ECtHR, *Österreichischer Rundfunk v. Austria*,7 December 2006.
ECtHR, *Radio Twist a.s. v. Slovakia*, 19 December 2006.
ECtHR, *Veraart v. the Netherlands*, 30 November 2006.
ECtHR, *Associated Society of Locomotive Engineers & Firemen (ASLEF) v. the United Kingdom*, 27 February 2007.
ECtHR, *Vilho Eskelinen and Others v. Finland*, 19 April 2007.
ECtHR, *Gebremedhin [Gaberamadhien] v. France*, 26 April 2007.
ECtHR, *Glas Nadezhda and Elenkov v. Bulgaria*, 11 October 2007.

ECtHR, *Stoll v. Switzerland*, [GC], 10 December 2007.
ECtHR, *Guja v. Moldova* 12 February 2008.
ECtHR, *Khurshid Mustafa & Tarzibachi v. Sweden*, 16 December 2008.
ECtHR, *Standard Verlags GmbH (n° 2) v. Austria*, 4 June 2009.
ECtHR, *Meltex Ltd and Mesrop Movsesyan v. Armenia*, 17 June 2008.
ECtHR, *Verein gegen Tierfabriken Schweiz (VgT) v. Switzerland (No. 2)*, 30 June 2009.
ECtHR, *Féret v. Belgium*, 16 July 2009.
ECtHR, *Hachette Filipacchi Associés ("Ici Paris") v. France*, 23 July 2009.
ECtHR, *Ürper and Others v. Turkey*, 20 October 2009.
ECtHR, *Dink v. Turkey*, 14 September 2010.
ECtHR, *Mouvement Raëlien Suisse v. Switzerland*, 13 January 2011.
ECtHR, *M.S.S.* v. Belgium and Greece, 21 January 2011.
ECtHR, *Soltsyak v. Russia*, 10 February 2011.
ECtHR, *Aleksey Ovchinnikov v Russia*, 16 March 2011.
ECtHR, *RTBF v. Belgium*, 28 March 2011.
ECtHR, *Enukidze and Girgvliani v. Georgia*, 26 April 2011.
ECtHR, *Editorial Board of Pravoye Delo and Shtekel v. Ukraine*, 5 May 2011.
ECtHR, *Mosley v the United Kingdom*, 10 May 2011.
ECtHR, *Altuğ Taner Akçam v. Turkey*, 25 October 2011.
ECtHR, *Von Hannover v. Germany (no. 2)*, 7 February 2012.
ECtHR, *Axel Springer AG v. Germany*, 7 February 2012.
ECtHR, *Kaperzyński v. Poland*, 3 April 2012.
ECtHR, *Ahmet Yıldırım v. Turkey*, 18 March 2013.
ECtHR, *Węgrzynowski and Smolczewski v. Poland, Strasbourg*, 16 July 2013.
ECtHR, *Gladkiy v. Russia*, 6 March 2014.
ECtHR, *Delfi AS v.* Estonia, Grand Chamber, 16 June 2015.
ECtHR, *Perinçek v. Switzerland*, 15 October 2015.
ECtHR, *Couderc and Hachette Filipacchi Associés v. France*, 10 November 2015.
ECtHR, *Roman Zakharov v. Russia*, 4 December 2015.
ECtHR, *Magyar Tartalomszolgáltatók Egyesülete and Index.hu Zrt v. Hungary (MTE and Index.hu)*, 2 February 2016.
ECtHR, *Rolf Anders Daniel Pihl v. Sweden*, 7 February 2017.
ECtHR, *Marunic v. Croatia*, 28 March 2017.
ECtHR, *Eker v. Turkey App*, 24 October 2017.

Court of Justice of the European Union

CJEU, *Van Gend en Loos v. Nederlandse Administratie der Belastingen*, Case 26/62, 5 February 1963.
CJEU, Case 43/75, *Defrenne v. Sabena* (No 2), 8 April 1976.
CJEU, *Gondrand Frères*, C-169/80, 9 July 1981.
CJEU, *Les Verts v Parliament*, 294/83, 23 April 1986.
CJEU, *Johnston*, 222/84, 15 May 1986.
CJEU, *Heylens and Others*, 222/86, 15 October 1987.
CJEU, *Schräder v Hauptzollamt Gronau*, C-265/87, 11 July 1989.
CJEU, *Meridionale Industria Salumi and Others*, Joined cases 212 to 217/80, 12 November 1981.

CJEU, Joined Cases 205/82 to 215/82 *Deutsche Milchkontor and Others v Germany*, 21 September 1983.
CJEU, *Sabine von Colson and Elisabeth Kamann v Land Nordrhein-Westfalen*, C- 14/83, 10 April 1984.
CJEU, *Ireland v. Commission*, Case 325/85, 15 December 1987.
CJEU, *Commission of the European Communities v Italian Republic*, Case 257/86, 21 June 1988.
CJEU, *Commission v France and United Kingdom*, Joined Cases 92/87 and 93/87, 22 February 1989.
CJEU, *Commission v. France*, Case 30/89, 13 March 1990.
CJEU, *The Queen v Secretary of State for Transport, ex parte: Factortame Ltd and others*, C-213/89, 19 June 1990.
CJEU, *Commission v Germany*, Case 361/88, 30 May 1991.
CJEU, *Andrea Francovich and Danila Bonifaci and others v Italian Republic*, Joined cases C-6/90 and C-9/90, 19 November 1991.
CJEU, *Fisscher*, C-128/93, 28 September 1994.
CJEU, *Commission v. Luxembourg*, Case 220/94, 15 June 1995.
CJEU, *Jeroen van Schijndel and Johannes Nicolaas Cornelis van Veen v Stichting Pensioenfonds voor Fysiotherapeuten*, Joined cases C-430 and 431/93, 14 December 1995.
CJEU, *Peterbroeck, Van Campenhout & Cie SCS v Belgian State*, C-312/93, 14 December 1995.
CJEU, *Gebroeders van Es Douane Agenten vs Inspecteur der Invoerrechten en Accijnzen*, C-143/93, 13 February 1996.
CJEU, *Duff and Others*, C-63/93, 15 February 1996.
CJEU, *Palmisani*, C-261/95, 10 July 1997.
CJEU *Edilizia Industriale Siderurgica Srl (Edis) v Ministero delle Finanze*, C-231/96, 15 September 1998.
CJEU, *P Baustahlgewebe v Commission*, Case C-185/95, 17 December 1998.
CJEU, *Nunes et de Matos*, C-186/98, 8 July 1999.
CJEU, *Preston and Others*, C-78–98, 16 May 2000.
CJEU, *Abrahamsson and Anderson*, C-407/98, 6 July 2000.
CJEU, *Z v. Parliament*, C-270/99 P, 27 November 2001.
CJEU, *Netherlands* v *Council*, C301/97, 22 November 2001.
CJEU, *Unión de Pequeños Agricultores v Council*, Case C-50/00 P, 25 July 2002.
CJEU, *Eugen Schmidberger, Internationale Transporte und Planzüge v Republik Österreich*, C-112/00, 12 June 2003.
CJEU, *Commission v Jégo-Quéré*, C-263/02 P, 1 April 2004.
CJEU, *Spain* v *Commission*, Case C287/02, 9 June 2005.
CJEU, *Ireland v Commission*, C-199/03, 5 September 2005.
CJEU, *Halifax and Others*, C255/02, 21 February 2006.
CJEU, *Doktor and Others*, C-28/05, 15 June 2006.
CJEU, *Adeneler and Others*, C-212/04, 4 July 2006.
CJEU, *Laserdisken*, C-479/04, 12 September 2006.
CJEU, *Wilson v. Ordre des avocats du barreau de Luxembourg*, C-506/04, 19 September 2006.

CJEU, *ASML Netherlands BV v. Semiconductor Industry Services GmbH (SEMIS)*, C-283/05, 14 December 2006.
CJEU, *Unibet*, C-432/05, 13 March 2007.
CJEU, *The international Trasport Workers' Federation & The Finnish Seamen's Union v. Viking Line,* Case C-438/05, 1 December 2007.
CJEU, *Promusicae v. Telefonica de Espana*, C 275/06, 29 January 2008.
CJEU, *Marks & Spencer plc v Commissioners of Customs & Excise*, C-309/06, 10 April 2008.
CJEU, *Impact*, Case C-268/06, 15 April 2008.
CJEU, *Commission of the European Communities (Kadi I)*, Joined cases C-402/05 P and C-415/05 P, 3 September 2008.
CJEU, *UGT-Rioja and Others*, C-428/06 to C-434/06, 11 September 2008.
CJEU, *Yassin Abdullah Kadi and Al Barakaat International Foundation v Council of the European Union and Commission of the European Communities,* Joined cases C-402/05 P and C-415/05 P, 3 September 2008.
CJEU, *Tietosuojavaltuutettu v. Satakunnan Markkinapörssi Oy and Satamedia Oy*, C73/07, 16 December 2008.
CJEU, *Sopropé*, Case C-349/07, 18 December 2008.
CJEU, *Varec*, Case C-450/06, 4 June 2009.
CJEU, *Google France Inc.* v. *LouisVuitton Malletier e.a.* in Joined Cases C-236, 237 & 238/08, Opinion of Advocate General Poires Maduro, 22 September 2009.
CJEU, *Foshan Shunde Yongjian Housewares & Hardware* v *Council,* Case C141/08 P, 1 October 2009.
CJEU, *Commission* v *Ireland and Others,* Case C-89/08 P, 2 December 2009.
CJEU, *Transportes Urbanos y Servicios Generales*, Case C-118/08, 26 January 2010.
CJEU, *Alassini and Others*, Joined Cases C-317/08, C-318/08, C-319/08 and C-320/08, 18 March 2010.
CJEU, *Google France and Google v. Louis Vuitton Malletier a.o.*, Joined Cases C-236/08 to C-238/08, 23 March 2010.
CJEU, *Afton Chemical v Secretary of State for Transport,* C-343/09, 8 July 2010.
CJEU, *Sweden and Others* v *API and Commission*, Joined Cases C514/07 P, C528/07 P and C532/07 P, 21 September 2010.
CJEU, *DEB Deutsche Energiehandels- und Beratungsgesellschaft mbH v. Bundesrepublik Deutschland*, Case C-279/09, 22 December 2010.
CJEU, *Budějovický Budvar* I-08701, Case C-482/09, 22 September 2011, Opinion of AG.
CJEU, *L'Oréal v. eBay*, Case C-324/09, 12 July 2011.
CJEU, Brahim Samba Diouf v Ministre du Travail, de l'Emploi et de l'Immigration, C-69/10, 28 July 2011.
CJEU, *Evropaïki Dynamiki – Proigmena Systimata Tilepikoinonion Pliroforikis kai Tilematikis AE v European Investment Bank (BEI)*, T-461/08, 20 September 2011.
CJEU, *Scarlet v. SABAM*, C-70/10, 24 November 2011.
CJEU, *Chalkor AE Epexergasias Metallon*, Case C-386/10 P, 8 December 2011.
CJEU, *SABAM v. Netlog*, C-360/10, 16 February 2012.
CJEU, *TUI Travel and Others v Civil Aviation Authority*, C-629/10, Joined Cases C-581/10 and C-629/10, 23 October 2012.

CJEU, *Hristo Byankov v Glaven sekretar na Ministerstvo na vatreshnite raboti*, C-249/11, 4 October 2012.

CJEU, *Nelson and Others v Deutsche Lufthansa* AG, C-581/10, 23 October 2012.

CJEU, M. *M. v. Minister for Justice, Equality and Law Reform*, Ireland, Case C-277/11, 22 November 2012.

CJEU, *Banif Plus Bank*, Case C-472/11, 21 February 2013.

CJEU, *The Queen, on the application of David Edwards and Lilian Pallikaropoulos v Environment Agency and Others*, C-260/11, 11 April 2013.

CJEU, *ZZ v. Secretary of State for the Home Department*, C-300/11, 4 June 2013.

CJEU, *Inuit Tapiriit Kanatami and Others v Parliament and Council*, C-583/11 P, 3 October 2013.

CJEU, *Opinion 2/13 rejecting the draft agreement on the accession of the European Union to the ECHR*, 18 December 2014.

CJEU, *Case C-340/00P Commission v. Cwic, Opinion of the Advocate-General.*

CJEU, *UPC Telekabel Wien*, Case C 314/12, 27 March 2014.

CJEU, *Hernández and Others*, Case C-198/13, 10 July 2014.

CJEU, *Digital Rights Ireland Ltd and Seitlinger and others*, Joined Cases C 293/12 and C 594/12, 8 April 2014.

CJEU, *Coty Germany GmbH v Stadtsparkasse Magdeburg*, C-580/13, 16 July 2015.

CJEU, *Maximillian Schrems v. Data Protection Commissioner*, C-362/14, 6 October 2015.

CJEU, *Tobias Mc Fadden v. Sony Music Entertainment Germany GmbH*, Case C 484/14, 15 September 2016.

NATIONAL CASE-LAW

Austria

OGH, case number 6Ob116/17b, see https://www.ris.bka.gv.at/Dokumente/Justiz/JJT_20171025_OGH0002_0060OB00116_17B0000_000/JJT_20171025_OGH0002_0060OB00116_17B0000_000.pdf.

Belgium

Lancôme Parfums & Beauté & Cie v eBay International AG, eBay Europe SARL, eBay Belgium, Bruxelles, 7th chamber, n° A/07/06032, 31 July 2008.

Canada

Supreme Court of Canada, Society of Composers, Authors and Music Publishers of Canada (SOCAN) v

Canadian Assn. of Internet Providers (CAIP), 2004 SCC 45, June 30, 2004.

Federal Court of Appeal, *Voltage Pictures, LLC v Joe Doe* #1 2017 FCA 97, 9 May 2017.

Chile

Court of Appeals of Concepción, *Fuentes vs Entel I*, Causa Rol No 243-99, 6 December 1999
Court of Appeals of Concepción, *Fuentes vs Entel II*, Causa Rol No 1223-2003, 21 December 2007.
Court of Appeals of Valparaíso, *Abbott v. Google*, Causa no 228/2012. Resolución no 50461, 30 July 2012.

Finland

Supreme Court, *Finreactor*, KKO 2010:47, 30 June 2010.
Copyright Management Services Ltd., MAO:333/17, 12 June 2017.

France

Viaticum et Luteciel c. Google, Tribunal de grande instance de Nanterre, 13 October 2003 and Cour d'appel de Versailles, 10 March 2005.
Constitutional Council, No. 2004-496 DC, 10 June 2004.
CNRRH, Pierre Alexis T. c. Google, Tribunal de grande instance de Nanterre, 14 December 2004 and Cour d'appel de Versailles, 23 March 2006.
Tiscali Media c. Dargaud Lombard, Lucky Comics, Cour d'appel de Paris, 7 June 2006.
Louis Vuitton Malletier c. Google, Tribunal de Grande Instance de Paris, 4 February 2005 and Cour d'appel de Paris, 28 June 2006.
Jean Yves L. dit Lafesse c. Myspace, Tribunal de Grande Instance de Paris, Ordonnance de référé 22 June 2007.
Christian C., Nord Ouest Production c. Dailymotion, UGC Images, Tribunal de Grande Instance de Paris, 13 July 2007.
Gifam c. Google, Tribunal de grande instance de Paris, 12 July 2006 and Cour d'appel de Paris, 1 February 2008.
Omar & Fred et autres c. Dailymotion, Tribunal de grande instance de Paris (3ème chambre, 1ère section), 15 April 2008.
Jean Yves Lafesse c. Dailymotion, Tribunal de grande instance de Paris (3ème chambre, 1ère section), 15 April 2008.
SARL Zadig Productions, Jean-Robert Viallet et Mathieu Verboud c. Sté Google Inc. et AFA, Tribunal de Grande Instance de Paris, 19 October 2007.
Parfums Christian Dior and others v eBay Inc., eBay International AB AG, Paris, 1st chamber, B, 30 June 2008.
Conseil Constitutionnel, Décision n° 2009-580 DC, 10 June 2009.
Google Inc. c. Compagnie des phares et balises, Cour d'appel de Paris, 14 January 2011.
Google Inc. c. Bac Films, The Factory, Cour d'appel de Paris, 14 January 2011.
Google Inc. c. Bac Films, The Factory, Cour d'appel de Paris, 14 January 2011.
Google Inc. c. Les Films de la Croisade, Goatworks Films, Cour d'appel de Paris, 14 January 2011.
Google France et Google Inc., Auféminin.com v. H&K SARL, André Rau, Cour d'appel, 4 February 2011.
Conseil d'Etat, *Société Apple Inc et Société I-Tunes Sarl*, 19 October 2011, n° 339154.

French Data Network, 19 October 2011, n°339279 and n° 342405.

S.A. Télévision Française 1 (TF1) c. Société YouTube LLC, Tribunal de Grande Instance de Paris, 29 May 2012.

La société eBay Inc. c. la société Parfums Christian Dior (11–10.508), Cour de cassation, 3 May 2012.

La société Google France c. la société Bach films (L'affaire Clearstream) (11–13.669), Cour de cassation, 12 July 2012.

La société Google France c. La société Bac films (Les dissimulateurs) (11–13.666), Cour de cassation, 12 July 2012.

La société Google France c. André Rau (Auféminin) (11–15.165; 11–15.188) Cour de cassation, 12 July 2012.

Germany

BGH, *Constanze II*, 6 July 1954, I ZR 38/532.

BGH, 23 September 2003, VI ZR 335/02.

BGH, *Architektenwettbewerb*, 10 October 1997, I ZR 129/96.

BGH, *Paperboy*, 17 July 2003, I ZR 259/00.

BGH, *Internetversteigerung I*, 11 March 2004, I ZR 304/01.

BGH, *Schöner Wetten*, 1 April 2004, I ZR 317/01.

BGH, *Internetversteigerung II*, 19 April 2007, I ZR 35/04.

BGH, *Katzenfreund*, July 23, 2007, VI ZR 101/06.

BGH, *Jugendgefährdende Medien bei eBay*, 12 July 2007, I ZR 18/04.

BGH, *Katzenfreund*, July 23, 2007, VI ZR 101/06.

BGH, *Internetversteigerung III*, 30 April 2008, I ZR 73/05.

OLG Hamburg, *Sharehoster II*, 30 September 2009, 5 U 111/08.

OLG Hamburg, *Long Island Ice Tea*, 4 February 2009, 5 U 180/07.

OLG Zweibrücken, 14 May 2009, 4 U 139/08.

OLG Düsseldorf, *Rapidshare I*, 27 April 2010, I-20 U 166/09.

OLG Düsseldorf, *Rapidshare III*, 21 December 2010, I-20 U 59/10.

BGH, *Stiftparfüm*, 17 August 2011, I ZR 57/09.

BGH, *Blog-Eintrag*, 25 October 2011, I ZR 93/10.

OLG Hamburg, *Rapidshare II*, 14 March 2012, 5 U 87/09.

BGH, *Rapidshare I*, 12 July 2012, I ZR 18/11.

BGH, *Rapidshare III*, 15 August 2013, I ZR 80/12.

Netherlands

Dutch Supreme Court 25 November 2005, LJN Number AU4019, case number C04/234HR.

South Korea

Supreme Court en banc Decision 2008Da53812, April 16, 2009.

United Kingdom

McAlpine v. Bercow, [2013] EWHC 1342 (QB),
Godfrey v Demon [1999] Entertainment
Bunt v Tilley [2006] EWHC 407 (QB).
Metropolitan International Schools Ltd v Designtechnica Corpn [2011] 1 WLR 1743.

United States of America

Chaplinsky v. New Hampshire, 315 U.S. 568, 571 (1942).
Smith v. California, 361 U.S. 147 (1959).
New York Times Co. v. Sullivan, 376 U.S. 254 (1964).
Griswold v. Connecticut, 381 U.S. 479 (1965).
United States v. Reidel, 402 U.S. 351 (1971).
Sony Corp. of America v. Universal City Studios, Inc. 464 U.S. 417, 442 (1984).
Concurring opinion of Justice Antonin Scalia in United States Supreme Court, Bendix Autolite v. Midwesco Enterprises, 17 June 1988.
Cubby, Inc. v. CompuServe Inc., 776 F. Supp. 135 (S.D.N.Y. 1991).
Turner Broad. Sys., Inc. v. FCC, 512 U.S. 622, 642 (1994).
Stratton Oakmont v. Prodigy Servs. Co., 1995 WL 323710 (N.Y. Sup. Ct. May 24, 1995).
Zeran v. America Online, Inc., 129 F.3d 327 (4th Cir. 1997).
ACLU v. Reno, (1997) 521 U.S. 844.
Blumenthal v. Drudge, 992 F. Supp. 44 (D.D.C. 1998).
A&M Records, Inc. v. Napster, Inc., 239 F.3d 1004 (9th Cir. 2001)
Eldred v. Ashcroft, 537 U.S. 186 (2003).
Carafano v. Metrosplash.com, 339 F.3d 1119 (9th Cir. 2003).
Search King v. Google, No. CIV-02–1457-M, 2003 WL 21464568 (W.D. Okla. May 27, 2003).
Barrett v. Rosenthal, 114 Cal. App. 4th 1379, 1395 (2004).
Online Policy Group v. Diebold, Inc., 337 F. Supp. 2d 1195 (N.D. Cal. 2004).
*MCW, Inc. v. Badbusinessbureau.com, LLC, 2004 WL 833595, No. 3:02-CV-2727-G at *9 (N.D. Tex. April*
19, 2004).
Rossi v. Motion Picture Assoc. of Am., 391 F.3d 1000 (9th Cir. 2004)
Corbis Corporation v. Amazon.com, Inc., 351 F.Supp.2d 1090 (W.D. Wash. 2004).
Donato v. Moldow, 865 A.2d 711 (N.J. Super. Ct. 2005).
Metro-Goldwyn-Mayer Studios, Inc. v. Grokster, Ltd., 545 U.S. 913 (2005), 930 (2005).
Langdon v. Google, Inc., 474 F. Supp. 2d 631 (D. Del. 2007).
Perfect 10 v. Visa International, 494 F.3d 788 (9th Cir. 2007).
Fair Housing Council v. Roommates.com, LLC, 521 F.3d 1157, 1175 (9th Cir. 2008) (en banc).
Barnes v. Yahoo!, Inc, 570 F.3d 1096 (9th Cir. 2009).
Fed. Trade Comm'n v. Accusearch Inc., 570 F.3d 1187 (10th Cir. 2009).
Doe v. MySpace, Inc., 528 F. 3d 413 (5th Cir. 2008).
Global Royalties, Ltd. v. Xcentric Ventures, LLC, 544 F. Supp. 2d 929, 933 (D. Ariz. 2008).
Chicago Lawyers Comm. for Civil Rights v. Craigslist, 519 F.3d 666, 670 (7th Cir. 2008).
Barnes v. Yahoo!, Inc., 2009 WL 4823840 (D. Or. Dec. 11, 2009).
Dart v. Craigslist, Inc., 665 F. Supp.2d 961 (N.D. Ill. 2009).

Bobolas v. Does 1–100, 2010 WL 3923880 (D. Ariz. Oct. 1, 2010).
Viacom Int'l Inc. v. YouTube, Inc., 718 F. Supp. 2d 514, 524 (S.D.N.Y. 2010).
Blockowicz v. Williams, No. 10–1167 (7th Cir. Dec. 27, 2010).
Viacom International, Inc. v. YouTube, Inc., 676 F.3d 19 (2d Cir. 2012).
Nieman v. Versuslaw, No. 12–3104, 2012 WL 3201931 (C.D. Ill. Aug. 3, 2012).
Backpage.com v. Cooper, et al., 939 F.Supp.2d 805 (M.D. Tenn. 2013).
Universal Music Group v. Shelter Capital Partners, 718 F.3d 1006 (9th Cir. 2013).
Viacom International, Inc. v. YouTube, Inc., No. 07 Civ. 2103 (settled).
Columbia Pictures Indus. v. Gary Fung, 710 F.3d 1020, 21 March 2013.
GoDaddy.com, Inc. v. Toups, 2014 WL 1389776 (Tex. Ct. App. April 10, 2014).
Jones v. Dirty World Entertainment Recordings, LLC, 2014 WL 2694184 (6th Cir. 2014).
Lenz v. Universal Music Corp., 801 F.3d 1126 (2015), (9th Cir. 2015).
E-Ventures Worldwide, LLC v Google, [2016] Case No. 2:14-cv-646-FtM-29CM, 2016 U.S. Dist. LEXIS 62855 (M.D. Fla.).
Caraccioli v. Facebook, Inc., 2016 WL 859863 (N.D. Cal. March 7, 2016).
Amcol v Lemberg Law, LLC, [2016] No. 3:15–3422-CMC, 2016 U.S. Dist. LEXIS 18131 (D.S.C.).
Congoo v Revcontent, [2016] Civil Action No. 16–401 (MAS) (TJB), 2016 U.S. Dist. LEXIS 51051 (D.N.J.)
Hassell v. Bird, 2016 WL 3163296 (Cal. App. Ct. June 7, 2016).
Doe #14 v. Internet Brands, 824 F.3d 846 (9th Cir. 2016).
Jane Doe No. 1 v. Backpage.com, 817 F.3d 12 (1st Cir. 2016).
Cellular v ConsumerAffairs.com, [2016] 3:15-CV-1908-PK (D. Or.).
Diamond Ranch Academy v Filer, [2016] Case No. 2:14-CV-751-TC, 2016 U.S. Dist. LEXIS 18131 (D. Utah).
Doe v Internet Brands, Inc, [2016] Case No. 12–56638 (9th Cir.);
Diamond Ranch Academy v Filer, 2016 WL 633351 (D. Utah Feb. 17, 2016).
People v. Bollaert, 2016 WL 3536550 (Cal. App. Ct. June 28, 2016).
Fields v. Twitter, Inc., 2016 WL 6822065 (N.D. Cal. Nov. 18, 2016).
People v. Ferrer, Case No. 16FE019224 (Cal. Super. Ct. Dec. 9, 2016).
Cohen v. Facebook, Inc., 2017 WL 2192621 (E.D.N.Y. May 18, 2017);
Johnson v. New Destiny Christian Center Church, 2017 WL 3682357 (M.D. Fla. Aug. 25, 2017).
Gonzalez v. Google, Inc., 2017 WL 4773366 (N.D. Cal. Oct. 23, 2017).

WEBSITES

The Center for Internet and Society, World Intermediary Liability Map: Chile, https://cyberlaw.stanford.edu/page/wilmap-chile.
The Center for Internet and Society, World Intermediary Liability Map: Finland, https://cyberlaw.stanford.edu/page/wilmap-finland.
The Center for Internet and Society, World Intermediary Liability Map: France, http://cyberlaw.stanford.edu/page/wilmap-france.
The Center for Internet and Society, World Intermediary Liability Map: Germany, http://cyberlaw.stanford.edu/page/wilmap-germany.

The Center for Internet and Society, World Intermediary Liability Map: South Korea, http://cyberlaw.stanford.edu/page/wilmap-south-korea.

Council of Europe, Supervision of execution of judgments of the European Court of Human Rights, https://www.coe.int/en/web/cm/execution-judgments.

Digital Media Law Project, Immunity for Online Publishers Under the Communications Decency Act: Background on Publisher and Distributor Liability, www.dmlp.org/legal-guide/immunity-online-publishers-under-communications-decency-act.

Electronic Frontier Foundation, Takedown Hall of Shame, www.eff.org/takedowns.

European Commission, Consumer Conditions Scoreboard, Consumers at home in the single market http://ec.europa.eu/consumers/consumer_evidence/consumer_scoreboards/index_en.htm.

European Commission on Notice and Action Procedures, http://ec.europa.eu/internal_market/e-commerce/notice-andaction/index_en.htm.

European Commission, State of the Union 2016: Questions and answers on the modernisation of EU copyright rules for the digital age, Strasbourg, 14 September 2016, http://europa.eu/rapid/press-release_MEMO-16-3011_en.htm.

European Commission, Countering illegal hate speech online #NoPlace4Hate, 16 March 2018, http://ec.europa.eu/newsroom/just/item-detail.cfm?item_id=54300.

European Union, Regulations, Directives and other acts, https://europa.eu/european-union/eu-law/legal-acts_en.

Friendly WiFi, https://www.friendlywifi.com/.

Google Transparency Report, https://transparencyreport.google.com/.

Google, Remove information from Google, https://support.google.com/websearch/troubleshooter/3111061#ts=2889054%2C2889099.

Google Public Policy Blog, "Revenge porn" and search, 19 June 2015, https://publicpolicy.googleblog.com/2015/06/.

Human Rights and Internet Intermediary Regulation in Chile, Global Censorship Chokepoints, https://globalchokepoints.org/human-rights-and-internet-intermediary-regulation-chile.html.

ISPA, https://www.ispa.org.uk/about-us/ispa-code-of-practice/.

Internet Watch Foundation: https://www.iwf.org.uk/.

https://www.iwf.org.uk/what-we-do/why-we-exist/our-history

https://www.iwf.org.uk/what-we-do/how-we-assess-and-remove-content/eu-co-funding

https://www.iwf.org.uk/become-a-member/join-us/membership-fee.

https://www.iwf.org.uk/what-we-do/how-we-assess-and-remove-content/laws-and-assessment-levels.

https://www.iwf.org.uk/members/member-policies/funding-council/code-of-practice#F1.

https://www.iwf.org.uk/what-we-do/why-we-exist/our-remit-and-vision.

https://www.iwf.org.uk/our-services/takedown-notices.

https://www.iwf.org.uk/become-a-member/services-for-members/url-list.

IWF, A Human Rights Audit of the Internet Watch Foundation, by Lord MacDonald of River Glaven QC, 2014, https://www.iwf.org.uk/sites/default/files/inline-files/Human_Rights_Audit_web.pdf

Modernisation of the EU copyright rules, 14 September 2016, https://ec.europa.eu/digital-single-market/en/modernisation-eu-copyright-rules.

Open Rights Group web pages, Internet Watch Foundation, https://wiki.openrightsgroup.org/wiki/Internet_Watch_Foundation.

Onlinecensorship.org, https://onlinecensorship.org/.

Omegle, https://www.omegle.com/

Ripoff Report, About Us: Want to sue Ripoff Report?, 2011, www.ripoffreport.com/consumers-say-thank-you/want-to-sue-ripoff-report.

Roadmap – Initiative on a clean and open Internet: procedures for notifying and acting on illegal content hosted by online intermediaries, http://ec.europa.eu/governance/impact/planned_ia/docs/2012_markt_007_notice_and_takedown_procedures_en.pdf.

KU Leuven Centre for IT & IP Law

The KU Leuven Centre for IT & IP Law Series brings together the results of research activities of the Centre for IT & IP Law. The central research themes of the series concern the legal and ethical aspects of information technology, innovation and intellectual property.

Each book in the series focuses on the essential developments in the current legal framework, necessitated by the rapid evolution of technology in various fields, such as government, media, health care, informatics, digital economy, banking, transport and culture. The research is characterised by an interdisciplinary approach, constantly cross-fertilising legal, technical, economic, ethical and socio-cultural perspectives.

Books are published in English, Dutch and/or French.

Recently published in this series:
- Niels Vandezande, *Virtual Currencies*, 2018.
- Rán Trygvadóttir, *European Libraries and the Internet: Copyright and Extended Collective Licences*, 2018.

www.ingramcontent.com/pod-product-compliance
Ingram Content Group UK Ltd.
Pitfield, Milton Keynes, MK11 3LW, UK
UKHW051846100926
8556IPUK00005B/479

9 781780 687148